HISTORIANS AT WORK

Other Books by Peter Gay

The Bridge of Criticism: Dialogues on the Enlightenment (1970)

The Enlightenment: An Interpretation

Volume II, The Science of Freedom (1969)

Weimar Culture: The Outsider as Insider (1968)

A Loss of Mastery: Puritan Historians in Colonial America (1966)

The Enlightenment: An Interpretation

Volume I, The Rise of Modern Paganism (1966)

The Party of Humanity: Essays in the French Enlightenment (1964)

Voltaire's Politics: The Poet as Realist (1959)

The Dilemma of Democratic Socialism: Eduard Bernstein's Challenge to

Marx (1952)

Translations with Introductions:

Voltaire: Candide (1963)

Voltaire: Philosophical Dictionary, 2 vols. (1962)

Ernst Cassirer: The Question of Jean Jacques Rousseau (1954)

Anthologies:

Deism: An Anthology (1968)

John Locke on Education (1964)

NEW YORK, EVANSTON, SAN FRANCISCO, LONDON

Historians
at Work

VOLUME I

Edited by Peter Gay

and Gerald J. Cavanaugh

Harper & Row, Publishers

1817

FIRST EDITION

STANDARD BOOK NUMBER: 06-011473-8

LIBRARY OF CONGRESS CATALOG CARD NUMBER: 75-123930

Contents

General Introduction

A DEFINITION OF HISTORY

1.

History is easier to write than to define. In its long career as a discipline, history has offered many things to many men and its practitioners have made claims for their work that no amount of casuistry could reconcile. Even today, for all the wealth of the historical tradition, all its exposure to philosophical scrutiny, historians continue to disagree not merely on *how* to do what they are doing, but on *what* it is they are doing in the first place.

The unsettled state of the historical profession should surprise no one. The very length of the history of history, the very profusion of publications claiming to be history, have, far from settling, only exacerbated the debate. In our time the variety of history is dazzling, if not always for its quality, at least for its very variety. Technical and specialized monographs or ambitious global surveys, old-fashioned political biographies or psychoanalytical excursions, intellectual histories of intellectuals or intellectual histories of anti-intellectuals, economic, social, ethnic, medical, sexual histories coexist and often compete with one another.

This is the difficulty: they do not simply coexist. They are rivals, not simply for our attention, but often for our exclusive approval. The bewildering diversity of historical writing in our time is more than the product of the division of labor. It is more than a matter of specialists doing what they like, and can do best, and tolerantly observing the work of their fellow historians. The choice of one kind of history, or of one mode of doing history, often implies the rejection of other kinds, other modes. The perennial question, "What is history?" then, is all too often answered by the superb and straightforward reply: "My history."

This rivalry and this parochialism appear plainly in the definitions of history current in our time. Explicitly or implicitly, each of them is tendentious—at least it seems tendentious to those who reject it. True, professional historians have no difficulty agreeing on certain canons of procedure and certain ideals. They all think it essential to respect the worth of the past and to abstain, as much as lies within their conscious control, from imposing their preferences upon it; to search all available archives for relevant traces; to record with absolute fidelity all the sources they have tapped, all the ideas they have borrowed, all the words they have quoted, so that others—other historians and general readers—may inspect, criticize, and modify their conclusions. In addition, historians agree that it is appropriate to employ the resources of neighboring disciplines—geography, economics, psychology, political science—in their search for understanding. But beyond this range of agreement there are questions urgently demanding, yet far from approaching, resolution. Is history art or science? Should it be detached from, or engaged in, the social struggles of its own day? Should the historian cultivate or disdain the literary graces? Should he define history by what it has become in his time or by all the things it has been since the ancients? These are difficult questions; they go to the heart of the discipline. To evade them is to shirk the task of definition, to answer them is to take sides.

The last of these questions—does the history of history enter into its definition?—is of particular significance for this anthology. For we have compiled it not simply because the historians of earlier times remain interesting and amusing. They do, but this has not been our primary concern. We have gathered these long passages from Herodotus to writers of our day to show a certain continuity within the craft of history, to show that Herodotus and Burckhardt, Thucydides and Ranke, for all the distance that separates them, equally deserve the name of historian.

In one respect, such an enterprise is congenial to the historical thinking of our century. It has become almost obligatory to profess abhorrence of what is called "present-mindedness"—the habit of imposing on the past the standards of the present, and of moralizing over historical actions in disregard of the ethical and intellectual and cultural climate in which these actions were performed. The kind of history the Greeks wrote, we will be told, is as valid for its day as the kind of history we write is for ours.

But here modern historians reflecting upon the history of their discipline have found themselves in a curious dilemma. They have repudiated present-mindedness and practiced it. In fact, precisely those historians most vocally committed to impartial sympathy and empathetic concern for the past, the historicists, have shown the smallest empathy, for the historians who came before them.

The historicists deserve special attention here, for while they were at their peak in the late nineteenth century—Ranke was their greatest practitioner and became their saint—they have left their mark on historians down to this day. And that mark consists not simply of their practice but also of their preachments, and these include a comprehensive vision of their predecessors. "The core of historicism," as Friedrich Meinecke, the influential and sympathetic historian of the school put it in 1936, "consists in the supplanting of a generalizing view of historical-human forces by an individualizing view." This meant immersion in the archives to come as close as possible to the actors of the past, and a kind of principled indulgence with historical figures, a refusal to judge the past from some fancied higher position.

It was a great ideal, and the historicist school a great school: it is not our purpose here to denigrate historicists as they denigrated their own predecessors. But for R. G. Collingwood, as for Meinecke, earlier historians all the way from the Greeks down to and including the eighteenth-century philosophes, had suffered from an essentially "anti-historical mentality"; they had been, despite some brave attempts, really incapable of grasping "the profound transformations and the multiplicity of forms that the spiritual and intellectual life of individuals and communities experience." In happy contrast, the historicists alone, it seems, had the true sense of historical individuality and historical development: no historicism—the complacent verdict may be summarized—no history.

This judgment points to an important truth without being true. It is true enough that earlier historians moralized more freely than was good for them. Yet, in the first place, Ranke himself, in his magnificent histories of France, England, Prussia, and the German Reformation, failed to live up wholly to his own austere ideal. While his precursors took sides openly, celebrating heroes and castigating villains, Ranke's partisanship went underground. It was less evident, which was both a good thing (there was less of it) and a bad thing (it was hard to detect). Besides, Ranke's standards for good historical writing are not the only possible standards we can use. For to use them in that way would be to take the part for the whole, and compel us to discard Gibbon's *Decline and Fall of the Roman Empire,* Guicciardini's *History of Italy,* Tacitus' *Annales,* and Thucydides' *Peloponnesian War.* Yet these are books we still value and are right to value as histories. To discard them would be to do violence to our experience of these books, and no adequate definition should do violence to experience . What we propose to do, therefore, is to offer a wider definition than the partial definition of the historicists: true history, we hope to show in this anthology, is the product of historical thinking, and historical thinking is critical thinking about the past.

2.

This definition demands some explanation. The word *criticism* has acquired predominantly negative connotations; it denotes aggressive and normally destructive verbal disapproval. We criticize what we dislike, and criticism is the statement of our dislike. I use the term *critical thinking* in a more comprehensive and less polemical sense. Critical thinking is a habit of mind characteristic of some cultures—or, rather, of its dominant elites. It reflects a certain philosophical self-awareness and self-confidence; it is unattainable for the anxious visitor in a universe buffeted about by capricious fortune or omnipotent gods, or the impotent creature subjecting his reason to higher authorities—priests or witches, censors or Caesars. It is only when man begins to feel himself worthy of making judgments that he discovers and develops his natural curiosity and sets about satisfying his thirst for knowledge: the sense of dignity and the cultivation of curiosity go together. This is what Gibbon meant when he singled out the ancient Greeks for their concentration on man —"the philosophers of Greece deduced their morals from the nature of man rather than from that of God"—and derived from this way of thinking the Greeks' precious discovery of "the spirit of inquiry." That spirit was curiosity organized, methodized, systematized, open to criticism and hence to improvement. The critical spirit is the habit of asking questions, not in the random style of the child but in the orderly style of the adult. Its best-known offspring is science, its most marked effect is the pressure for change.

It would be a mistake to equate the critical spirit with the unmeasured ambition for omniscience. Both in the Classical Age and again in the Age of the Enlightenment, two ages in which the critical spirit was developed to its height, the prevailing philosophical mood was one of modesty. There were, to ancient Greek philosophers and modern Western philosophes, mysteries in the universe and in man that no amount of inquiry could ever resolve. The point was not to have all the answers, but to claim the right to ask all the questions. The critical spirit denied the very idea of a privileged sanctuary; neither politics, nor religion, nor the ruling dynasty—nor the past—was exempt from searching and impartial scrutiny. "Everything must be examined," Diderot wrote, "everything must be shaken up, without exception and without circumspection." And by everything Diderot meant everything. This is the voice of the critical spirit.

The bearing of this spirit on the writing of history is almost self-evident. A culture that confines its chroniclers to agreed-upon and aggrandizing tales, to recording without skeptical review the exploits of its kings, the miracles of its saints, the special benevolence of its gods, or the unique pre-eminence of its merchants, scientists, or athletes, is a culture without true history. The historian needs distance from his materials; he must question the authenticity of his documents, the correctness of his precursors, the validity of his information. If he does less, he is writing propaganda, or what Collingwood has curtly called, "theocratic history and myth"—pseudohistory masquerading as history.

3.

We said at the outset that all definitions take sides. Our definition of history as critical thinking about the past is no exception. It remains neutral among some of the debates that continue to divide the profession: it contributes nothing to the solution of the problem of historical knowledge, or the place of the historian in his culture. This neutrality has its virtues; it implies that historians on all sides of these questions may still write good history. But our definition is controversial elsewhere: it is more generous than the historicists' definition and less generous than the permissive view, which includes all possible statements about the past in the category of history. It finds room for the cloistered academician and the worldly man of letters, the statesman-historian and the monkish pedant, the patient monographer and the ambitious synthesizer. But it excludes the myth-ridden chroniclers of the ancient Near East. History, we assert with our definition, began with the Greeks.

Controversy begins at this point. What of the Pharaohs' victories that grateful or dutiful Egyptians carved on stone? What of the kings' exploits and prophets' warnings that the Hebrews reduced to writing? Is this claim for Greek primacy not itself a myth, imposed by snobbish classicists and parroted by docile pupils for generations? These objections are anything but frivolous and they deserve to be seriously met. In dividing modes of thinking into critical and mythical, we are offering two types of thought rarely found in all purity. Civilizations dominated by myth often developed highly sophisticated modes of reasoning; conversely, civilizations practicing criticism have often harbored elements of myth. In recent years, as our understanding of the ancient Near East has grown, historians of these civilizations have strenuously denied long-standing allegations that Babylon and Egypt were, by and large, hopelessly mired in superstition. They have been right to protest: it now seems clear, for instance, that the Babylonians could make complicated mathematical calculations and fairly advanced astronomical observations. But it is quite impermissible to leap from the assertion that these civilizations were civilized to the assertion that they therefore anticipated the Greeks in all things, including the conception and writing of true history. "It is generally believed that philosophical speculation began more or less with the Greeks and that the ancient peoples never troubled their minds with the why and how of things," Edward Chiera wrote over thirty years ago. "Why this should be, it is difficult to understand, especially in view of the high degree of civilization reached in both Mesopotamia and Egypt."

This defense misses its mark. These ancient civilizations were perfectly capable of producing thought—the very term "mythical thinking" asserts that some kind of thinking is going on—but the categories of this thought differed, in degree and in kind, from the critical thought of the Greeks. Categories of space and time, up and down, right and left, past and future, categories of cause and effect, true and false—these last two pairs of decisive import for historical thinking—were rudimentary, uncertain, or wholly absent. A god or a man or a temple could be many things at once; the same events could be solemnly recorded as happening at different times and to different individuals; again, events happening at different times and in different ways could be described as though they were one and the same. To the Babylonians and the Egyptians the world was a perpetual miracle, which is to say that it lacked the stability without which a truly historical report is impossible. "Even in the accounts of royal achievements which we should classify as historical texts"—to cite an example offered by the Egyptologist Henri Frankfort—"we find, to our exasperation, that everything that is singular and historical is treated as of little account. For example, we find that King Pepi II depicted his victory over the Libyans with such apparent care that he even had the names of captured Libyan chiefs written beside their images in the reliefs of his temple. But we happen to know that captured Libyan chiefs with precisely the same names figure in the reliefs of King Sahure, two hundred years earlier! In the same way Ramses III enumerated his conquests in Asia by name, but in so doing copied a list of Ramses II, who, in his turn, had utilized a list of Tuthmosis III." We have many other, similar documents, deceptively specific but actually wholly conventional; they do not report single events but symbolize enduring claims to greatness.

To moralize about such practices, to call them mendacity, is beside the point. Lacking all notions of individuality, natural causation, confirmation or denial, and self-criticism, the Egyptian found such repetitions not immoral but inescapable, not plagiarism but piety. Gods whose decrees were dark and whose characters changed mysteriously dominated the life of the ancient Egyptian, while his sense of the historical process remained static. "Throughout the 2,500 years of dynastic history," Ludlow Ball has written, "it does not seem to the writer that the Egyptians' view of history changed greatly."

Precisely like the Egyptians, the Mesopotamians had neither the word *history* nor the thing. With all their passion for the past, the peoples of Mesopotamia made it their main concern in life to appease divine powers; their so-called historical writings were in essence letters to the gods explaining away transgressions and begging for forgiveness. And here too, in the river valleys, very little changed: "The Mesopotamian view of history," as E. A. Speiser puts it bluntly, "once it had been formulated, remained substantially unchanged through the ages." The static quality of the Egyptian and the Babylonian mind is itself a symptom of their lack of historical consciousness; it is of the essence of historical thinking not merely to record change but to undergo it.

The ancient Hebrews are far more difficult to place; they prove, if such proof should be needed, that our two basic categories—critical and mythical thinking—rarely appear unmixed. The Hebrews' interest in history is too obvious to require documentation; their religion draws on and indeed depends on a series of events that happened only once and the contemplation of which supplies guidance to later generations. God created the world at a certain moment in time—it is no accident that later historians were bold enough to assign it a precise date; the children of Israel prospered or lived in bondage in particular moments at particular places, for a specified number of years; Moses recorded this history for the sake of his people for all time to come. Rituals and festivals were explicitly established to aid men's awareness of their history; when the Chosen People recalled its past, it lived in happiness, and when it forgot that past, it suffered as it deserved to suffer. Moses, charging the Jews with ingratitude, reproached them above all for their forgetfulness: "Remember the days of old, consider the years of many generations; ask your father, and he will show you; your elders, and they will tell you." For the first time, and in sharp contradistinction from neighboring cultures, the Jews drew sustenance from history rather than from the ever-recurrent rhythms of nature. Their religion was, in a sense, identical with history. "The Jewish religion," Salo Baron has said, "has been from the very beginning, and in progress of time has increasingly become, an *historical* religion, in permanent contrast to all *natural* religions." Religious rituals among the Jews acquired gravity, and religious laws authority, because they were historic, claiming a remote yet discernible ancestry in the early career of man on earth.

The Hebrews, too, were the first to subject historical views to drastic reformulation; the interpretation that the ancient Jews gave to their past evolved, slowly but significantly, from a great drama of human sin and divine response to an apocalyptic vision of the future—history, the Jews came to think, was moving inexorably toward its end. Under the pressure of the Babylonian exile and with the repeated postponement of redemption, Salo Baron has written, "the old promises of judgment on the ene-mies of God" were deferred "to a new, supernatural world to be created on the ruins of the old." And with this "went a new interpretation of past history;" the Jews viewed it "as a series of world empires decreed by God that would lead up to the final establishment of his own eternal empire."

The most sympathetic scholars concede that the historical writings of the ancient Hebrews display some glaring defects: normally the record is vague, events are often presented in two conflicting versions or, con-versely, two distinct events appear to be quite alike, the notion of causa-tion is exceedingly simple, numbers (like forty) reflect number magic rather than precise reporting, and folk tales or inspirational stories often invade and sometimes overwhelm the narrative. Yet are these not the failings of pioneers? The Jews' pious recourse to recorded, remembered, celebrated historical events, and the Jews' capacity for modifying the interpretation of these events has encouraged scholars to nominate the ancient Hebrews as the first to experience historical consciousness and the Old Testament as the first true history. "It is no accident," Salo Baron argues, "that among the oldest literary documents of the people are not only war songs, legends, and tales such as are found in other civilizations, but, primarily perhaps, laws and religious and moral teachings." Nor "is it an accident that this people was also the first to *write* great history," even greater than the Greeks after them: "Even the otherwise most dis-tinguished Greek historians, such as Herodotus and Thucydides, lacked something of the historic perspective of the Israelitic historians."

It should be obvious that this is a claim we find impossible to accept. A passion for the past is a necessary but not a sufficient precondition for historical thinking. On every page the historical portions of the Old Tes-tament reveal an incapacity to criticize the material; what many explain away as the defects of Hebrew "history" actually constitute its very char-acter. The coexistence of conflicting stories, the constant appeal to God's will as the sole efficient cause, the reliance on number magic and cre-ation legends are all characteristics of mythical thinking—transfigured perhaps by ethical fervor and ordered in unique sequence, but myth still. The road to true historical writing lay in a different direction.

4.

It remains true, of course, that while mythical thinking does not pro-duce history, myths may enshrine history. The Old Testament, it has been said, is an important "source book for ancient history." On this matter, the pendulum of learned opinion has oscillated widely and wildly: for devout Christian readers until quite recently, the Bible was not simply authentic history, but the most authentic history among all histories. Beginning late in the seventeenth century with the English Deists and continental skeptics, continuing with the anti-Christian propagandists of the eighteenth-century Enlightenment, and culminating with the nineteenth-century rationalists, the credibility of the Bible was put under severe doubt; some unbelievers went so far as to question the historicity of Jesus. Today, in response to the splendid work of discovery and decipherment done by archeologists specializing in the Near East, a more reasoned, more detached attitude has gained ground: there is widespread agreement that the writings of these ancient peoples, especially of the Hebrews but of the others as well, rest on factual foundations. Celebrated legends like the fall of Jericho or the universal flood have some basis, no matter how tenuous, in history. "It may be stated categorically," Nelson Glueck has argued, "that no archaeological discovery has ever controverted a biblical reference."

Yet reasonable doubts remain. Glueck's claim, it should be noted, is phrased negatively: it is not that archeology has confirmed the Bible, but that archeology has not disproved it. Yet even in this formulation the claim may be excessive, less in what it openly states than in what it covertly suggests. It seems that there is almost nothing we can ever know about such "events" as the fall of Jericho and other biblical reports, which seem at first reading firm and specific but which reveal themselves on closer study so general and elastic that they are compatible with many kinds of archeological discovery.

Yet even if the archeologists' claims turn out to be excessive, their discoveries remain of considerable interest to the historian, although the interest the discoveries have is not the interest the archeologists may think they have: they are a warning to the professional historian to use all evidence at his disposal, including the testimony of myth and legend, in his search for the authentic past. It is a sign of historical sophistication rather than naïveté to treat myths not as mere lies but as imaginative transformations of distant events, as clues—no more—to remote and almost inaccessible origins.

5.

The first modern critical historians were not willing to heed this warning or utilize these clues. When the intellectual attack on Christianity was first launched in all seriousness in the seventeenth and eighteenth centuries, the assailants, in the heat of battle, conveniently forgot to draw any distinction between myth and religion, or religion and superstition. All—myth, religion, superstition—were alike in this: they were untrue. Voltaire, a leader in the struggle for a secular view of the world, went so far as to insist that a Jesuit cannot write good history, and it became a commonplace in infidel circles in the eighteenth century to regard any kind of religious conviction as an insuperable obstacle to clear historical thinking or honest historical reporting. The most candid and most liberated of priests, the argument ran, was the victim of the institutions to which he must be loyal, and of the superstitions in which he must believe or, if he no longer believed them, must support in public. Even Gibbon, the most remarkable historian of the century, a scholar who knew the writings of pious investigators inside out and used them freely in the composition of his *Decline and Fall of the Roman Empire,* could muster no more than cold and grudging acknowledgments to his devout predecessors who had taught him far more than he would admit. Having reached the sixth century, Gibbon dismisses Tillemont, the *érudit* without whose histories of the early church Gibbon's own account would have been far poorer, with this farewell: "And here I must take leave forever of that incomparable guide—whose bigotry is overbalanced by the merits of erudition, diligence, veracity and scrupulous minuteness." If this is all that Gibbon could afford, his fellows in unbelief could afford even less.

It should be obvious that the philosophes' disdain for religious historians is unjustified. We have appealed to experience once before in this essay—we will do so again. Experience shows that just as skeptics and atheists can write bad history, religious men can write great history. Once again Ranke may stand as an example: for Ranke, his highly personal, thoroughly undoctrinaire Christianity was at once a divine command to serve in his vocation as a truthful historian and a divine clue to the process of history itself. God spoke to him and made him a historian; God governed the world and permitted the historian to discover the prescribed pattern. And Ranke is by no means the sole instance we could offer: there were, and are, many other historians whose religious convictions, far from preventing proper critical inquiry, created and confirmed a professional commitment to just such inquiry. If it is the historian's sublime task to discover and transmit the traces of God's hand in human affairs, he must discharge that task with diligence, accuracy, and, as Gibbon said of Tillemont, scrupulous minuteness. It follows that whether religion is a spur to historical thinking or an obstacle cannot be decided on principle or in advance; it depends upon the religion.

Religion, then, is not the only possible obstacle to historical thinking. A commitment to certain metaphysical or political positions, especially if it is an unconscious one, is bound to introduce biases, angles of vision, that are·not subject to correction because they are inaccessible to self-criticism. And if these commitments are shared by the culture as a whole, they remain inaccessible to that culture—as a whole. Bad history may be a treasured common possession. Similarly, a commitment to a certain literary genre or a historical school may introduce limitations on objectivity. All men are prisoners of the categories they use, especially of the categories they use so often that they no longer think about them. The rule is everywhere the same: whatever inhibits criticism distorts history.

We must add that while all historical thinking is critical, not all critical thinking is historical. As this anthology will demonstrate, the well-known charge that Enlightenment historians were not historians at all is not justified. Still, the Enlightenment's concern with anti-Christian polemics and its infatuation with theories of universal and uniform human nature directed the attention of eighteenth-century historians to what men had in common rather than what divided them and made them unique. And the Cartesian tradition, professedly critical to its very core, had little use for history. Criticism is indispensable but, by itself, not enough to make for good history.

It follows from all this that the notion of a perfectly objective history—of history as a science—is an ideal rather than a reality, an aim the historian seeks to approach rather than a possession he may calmly enjoy. But while it is an ideal, it is not a myth. It is often said that, after all, all cultures and all intellectual movements are equally ridden with myths; it is often said that just as the ancient Hebrews had their ruling myths, so did the fifteenth-century Humanists, and the eighteenth-century philosophes, and so do we. But this is lazy and fuzzy thinking. If all men share unexamined assumptions, the range and impermeability of such assumptions differ vastly from age to age and culture to culture. Cultures steeped in myth—this point is important enough to bear reiteration—have no instruments for rising above it; ages of criticism, for all their complacencies and unexpressed premises, have such instruments: publication, accessibility, documentation, examination, revision, and, in general and at its best, a kind of ruthless, impious fearlessness. Criticism exists to criticize everything, including its own work, and there is a decisive difference between an Egyptian creation myth which must simply be accepted and a modern political ideology which can be exposed and thus overcome. The distinction between mythical and critical thinking, with all the cautions we have introduced, remains valid and important for history.

To say this is not to say that all histories are much like one another. Happy families, as Tolstoy says, are all alike. As this anthology should make abundantly clear, good histories are happily very different from each other. In these four volumes we shall see many historians at work, across more than two millennia—some cold pessimists, others exuberant optimists; some patient chroniclers, others philosophical litterateurs; some Marxists, others Idealists. At the same time, different as they are in style and ideology and central concern, they belong together in this one characteristic: their passion for understanding and penetrating the past with all the intellectual resources at their command. It is on this point that they stand together, on this point that they all differ from Moses. For it was not Moses who was the first historian, but Herodotus.

Selected Bibliography

Salo Wittmayer Baron, *A Social and Religious History of the Jews,* vols. I and II, *Ancient Times* (2nd ed., 1952)

Ernst Cassirer, *The Philosophy of Symbolic Forms,* 3 vols. (tr. Ralph Manheim, 1953, 1955, 1957)

Edward Chiera, *They Wrote on Clay* (1938)

R. G. Collingwood, *The Idea of History* (1946)

Robert C. Dentan, ed., *The Idea of History in the Ancient Near East* (1955), especially Ludlow Bull, "Ancient Egypt," and E. A. Speiser, "Ancient Mesopotamia"

Henri Frankfort, *Ancient Egyptian Religion* (1948)

Henri Frankfort and others, *The Intellectual Adventure of Ancient Man* (1946)

Kurt von Fritz, *Die Griechische Geschichtsschreibung* (1967)

Peter Gay, *A Loss of Mastery: Puritan Historians in Colonial America* (1966)

Peter Gay, *The Enlightenment: An Interpretation,* vol. II, *The Science of Freedom* (1969)

John A. Wilson, *The Culture of Ancient Egypt* (ed. 1951)

HISTORIANS AT WORK

Herodotus

C. 490 B.C.—C. 430 B.C.

1

Of "the father of history" we know very little. Beyond what we can glean from his *History* and from references to him in other works of the Classical Age there is nothing of which we can be certain. He was born into an aristocratic family of Halicarnassus, in southwest Asia Minor, sometime between 490 and 480 B.C. After a factional struggle in his native city, in which his uncle (or cousin; the interpretations vary) was slain, Herodotus was banished (454 B.C.). He apparently visited Samos for a time before moving on to Athens where it is believed he made his home until 444 B.C. At that time he participated in the founding of the colony of Thurii, in Italy. In the years 465–444 he traveled extensively throughout Asia Minor, the Aegean islands, Egypt, and Thrace and as far as Babylon and the Scythian lands north of the Black Sea. He died, either in Thurii or in Athens, a few years after the outbreak of the Peloponnesian War (430 B.C.).

In his *History of the Persian Wars* Herodotus endeavored "to preserve from decay the remembrance of what men have done, and to prevent the great and wonderful actions of the Greeks and the Barbarians from losing their due meed of glory." But further, he sought "to put on record what were the grounds of their feud." Relying, as he tells us, on "his eyes, his judgment and his talent for enquiry," Herodotus succeeded in writing an eminently readable, and largely trustworthy account of the causes, course, and results of the Persian Wars. He had few written documents to assist him in his investigations of the Greek aspects of the war. In ancient Greece, history was transmitted orally and Herodotus himself must have read from his *History* to auditors in Athens and Thurii. In Persia, where there were written materials, he could not read the languages. He was therefore reduced to gathering oral testimony from survivors and descendents of survivors of an era whose events he was too young to have experienced.

To this endeavor he brought a penetrating intelligence, a healthy skeptical bent, and a wide and deep instruction in the works of the epic poets, the

1

historians, scientists, geographers, and philosophers of his culture. He weighed and carefully sifted the oral accounts of his witnesses, making clear to his audience which among them contained evidence that was indubitable, probable, possible, or impossible. He introduced empirically founded evidence concerning the ethnographic and geographic influences which had affected historical events and developments. Indeed, as Kurt von Fritz so persuasively argues, Herodotus was a geographer before he became a historian. Wherever he could, he substantiated oral reports by visiting and questioning people at the scene of the event. He included stories that were obviously mythic or epic in origin not because they were historically reliable but because they signified how people felt and thought and were thus historically relevant. He habitually engaged in digressions because they were artistically justified—all epics abounded in digressions—and functionally necessary. In the words of one of his admirers (quoted by J. B. Bury), "Herodotus knew that every narrative of great length wearies the ears of the hearer, if it dwell without a break on the same subject; but if pauses are introduced at intervals, it affects the mind agreeably. And so he desired to lend variety to his work and imitated Homer. If we take up his book, we admire it to the last syllable, and always want more." Similarly, drawing on the epic tradition, he provided the characters of his *History* with speeches, having them say what surely they ought to have said given their circumstances.

The *History of the Persian Wars* was written with purpose and passion. Although he was an Ionian Greek and may even be described as a "barbarophile," Herodotus yet believed that Athenian vigor, liberty, and democracy both explained Athens's instrumental role in the defeat of the Persians—"The Athenians were the saviors of Greece"—and later justified her domination of Greek affairs through her Empire. The Persian Wars lasted for almost a quarter of a century (500 B.C.–479 B.C.). Herodotus tells us among many other things of the rise of the Persian Empire under Cyrus, the humiliating defeat of proud Croesus and the two invasions of Greece by the Persians: the first under Darius turned back at Marathon (490 B.C.), the second under Xerxes slowed at Thermopylae and finally thrown back at Salamis (480 B.C.). With the destruction of the Persian fleet at Salamis, Greece was saved from subjection. Her Golden Age began. This was the story Herodotus wished to preserve for future generations to ponder. On a more philosophical level, however, he sought to enshrine the story of Greek, particularly Athenian, excellence and achievement and to preserve the moral lesson embodied in what he saw as the victory of Greek freedom over Persian autocracy. The Persian Wars offered him matter enough to construct his epic.

But, happily influenced as he was by the prevailing literary traditions, he nevertheless did not remain bound to them. He slipped away from the merely beautiful and imaginative and chose to look at the Persian Wars as something other than a worthy epic theme. He sought to understand what had happened and why it had happened and he explicitly recognized that it was not to the Greek myths or to Homer that one must look for such understanding. By combining an earnest inquirer's rigor and skepticism in the gathering and testing of available evidence with a poet's empathetic appreciation of the human condition, Herodotus broke through to "history" as we recognize it. He made a quiet but conscious rebellion against Homer and the mythopoeic mind, respectful of Calliope but vindicating Clio.

Selected Bibliography

J. B. Bury's *The Ancient Greek Historians* (1909) includes a good introduction to Herodotus, as does James T. Shotwell, *An Introduction to the History of History* (1936). Moses Finley, ed., *The Portable Greek Historians* (1960), and W. G. Forrest, ed., *Herodotus, History of the Greek and Persian War* (1963), offer perceptive analyses in the introductions to their editions. Both editors draw upon George Rawlinson's translation of *The Persian Wars*. Published from 1858 to 1861, it remains one of the best and is used in the Modern Library edition (1942), introduced by Francis R. B. Godolphin, from which we take our selections. "The Place of Herodotus in the History of Historiography" is the subject of an essay by Arnaldo Momigliano, first published in *History,* 43 (1958), 1–13. Momigliano concludes that Herodotus is indeed "the father of history," and for the most modern methodological reasons. The essay is included in Momigliano's *Studies in Historiography* (1966), a volume that contains many other insightful references to Herodotus. Kurt von Fritz, *Die Griechische Geschichtsschreibung* (1 vol. in 2, 1967), is a massive work; extraordinarily rich and comprehensive, it provides a point of departure for advanced students of both Herodotus and Thucydides. Von Fritz is especially enlightening in his discussions of the literary and historical traditions upon which Herodotus drew and in his analysis of the influence of geography and ethnography on Herodotus' historiography. J. L. Meyers, *Herodotus, Father of History* (1953), is an admirable and well argued interpretation of our historian. Michael Grant, *The Ancient Historians* (1970) is both erudite and stimulating on Herodotus and the other great classical historians. A very valuable collection of relatively recent studies of Herodotus has been edited by Walter Marg: *Herodot. Eine Auswahl aus der Neueren Forschung (Wege der Forschung,* vol. 26*),* 1962.

THE PERSIAN WARS

These are the researches of Herodotus of Halicarnassus, which he publishes, in the hope of thereby preserving from decay the remembrance of what men have done, and of preventing the great and wonderful actions of the Greeks and the Barbarians from losing their due meed of glory, and withal to put on record what were their grounds of feud.

According to the Persians best informed in history, the Phoenicians began the quarrel. This people, who had formerly dwelt on the shores of the Red Sea, having migrated to the Mediterranean and settled in the parts which they now inhabit, began at once, they say, to adventure on long voyages, freighting their vessels with the wares of Egypt and Assyria. They landed at many places on the coast, and among the rest at Argos, which was then pre-eminent above all the states included now under the common name of Hellas. Here they exposed their merchandise, and traded with the natives for five or six days; at the end of which time, when almost everything was sold, there came down to the beach a number of women, and among them the daughter of the king, who was, they say, agreeing in this with the Greeks, Io, the child of Inachus. The women were standing by the stern of the ship intent upon their purchases, when the Phoenicians, with a general shout, rushed upon them. The greater part made their escape, but some were seized and carried off. Io herself was among the captives. The Phoenicians put the women on board their vessel, and set sail for Egypt. Thus did Io pass into Egypt, according to the Persian story, which differs widely from the Phoenician: and thus commenced, according to their authors, the series of outrages.

At a later period, certain Greeks, with whose name they are unacquainted, but who would probably be Cretans, made a landing at Tyre, on the Phoenician coast, and bore off the king's daughter, Europe. In this they only retaliated; but afterwards the Greeks, they say, were guilty of a second violence. They manned a ship of war, and sailed to Aea, a city of Colchis, on the river Phasis; from whence, after despatching the rest of the business on which they had come, they carried off Medea, the daughter of the king of the land. The monarch sent a herald into Greece

From *The Persian Wars,* translated by George Rawlinson (New York: Random House, 1942). Pp. 3–6, 14–25, 27–29, 37–39, 72–78, 124–128, 407–408, 476–481, 493–502, 506–507, 510–512, 519–523, 546–549, 578–591, 621–634, 655–656.

to demand reparation of the wrong, and the restitution of his child; but the Greeks made answer, that having received no reparation of the wrong done them in the seizure of Io the Argive, they should give none in this instance.

In the next generation afterwards, according to the same authorities, Alexander the son of Priam, bearing these events in mind, resolved to procure himself a wife out of Greece by violence, fully persuaded, that as the Greeks had not given satisfaction for their outrages, so neither would he be forced to make any for his. Accordingly he made prize of Helen; upon which the Greeks decided that, before resorting to other measures, they would send envoys to reclaim the princess and require reparation of the wrong. Their demands were met by a reference to the violence which had been offered to Medea, and they were asked with what face they could now require satisfaction, when they had formerly rejected all demands for either reparation or restitution addressed to them.

Hitherto the injuries on either side had been mere acts of common violence; but in what followed the Persians consider that the Greeks were greatly to blame, since before any attack had been made on Europe, they led an army into Asia. Now as for the carrying off of women, it is the deed, they say, of a rogue; but to make a stir about such as are carried off, argues a man a fool. Men of sense care nothing for such women, since it is plain that without their own consent they would never be forced away. The Asiatics, when the Greeks ran off with their women, never troubled themselves about the matter; but the Greeks, for the sake of a single Lacedaemonian girl, collected a vast armament, invaded Asia, and destroyed the kingdom of Priam. Henceforth they ever looked upon the Greeks as their open enemies. For Asia, with all the various tribes of barbarians that inhabit it, is regarded by the Persians as their own; but Europe and the Greek race they look on as distinct and separate.

Such is the account which the Persians give of these matters. They trace to the attack upon Troy their ancient enmity towards the Greeks. The Phoenicians, however, as regards Io, vary from the Persian statements. They deny that they used any violence to remove her into Egypt; she herself, they say, having formed an intimacy with the captain, while his vessel lay at Argos, and suspecting herself to be with child, of her own free will accompanied the Phoenicians on their leaving the shore, to escape the shame of detection and the reproaches of her parents. Which of these two accounts is true I shall not trouble to decide. I shall proceed at once to point out the person who first within my own knowledge commenced aggressions on the Greeks, after which I shall go forward with my history, describing equally the greater and the lesser cities. For the cities which were formerly great, have most of them become insignificant; and such as are at present powerful, were weak in the olden time. I shall therefore discourse equally of both, convinced that human happiness never continues long in one stay.

Croesus, son of Alyattes, by birth a Lydian, was lord of all the nations to the west of the river Halys. This stream, which separates Syria from Paphlagonia, runs with a course from south to north, and finally falls into the Euxine. So far as our knowledge goes, he was the first of the barbarians who held relations with the Greeks, forcing some of them to become his tributaries, and entering into alliance with others. He conquered the Aeolians, Ionians, and Dorians of Asia, and made a treaty with the Lacedaemonians. Up to that time all Greeks had been free. For the Cimmerian attack upon Ionia, which was earlier than Croesus, was not a conquest of the cities, but only an inroad for plundering. . . .

On the death of Alyattes, Croesus, his son, who was in his thirty-fifth year, succeeded to the throne. Of the Greek cities, Ephesus was the first that he attacked. The Ephesians, when he laid siege to the place, made an offering of their city to Artemis, by stretching a rope from the town wall to the temple of the Goddess, which was distant from the ancient city, then besieged by Croesus, a space of about a mile. They were, as I said, the first Greeks whom he attacked. Afterwards, on some pretext or other, he made war in turn upon every Ionian and Aeolian state, bringing forward, where he could, a substantial ground of complaint; where such failed him, advancing some poor excuse.

In this way he made himself master of all the Greek cities in Asia, and forced them to become his tributaries; after which he began to think of building ships, and attacking the islanders. Everything had been got ready for this purpose, when Bias of Priene (or, as some say, Pittacus the Mytilenean) put a stop to the project. The king had made inquiry of this person, who was lately arrived at Sardis, if there were any news from Greece; to which he answered, "Yes, sire, the islanders are gathering 10,000 horse, designing an expedition against you and against your capital." Croesus, thinking he spoke seriously, broke out, "Ah, might the gods put such a thought into the minds as to attack the sons of the Lydians with cavalry!" "It seems, O king," rejoined the other, "that you desire earnestly to catch the islanders on horseback upon the mainland, you know well what would come of it. But what think you the islanders desire better, now that they hear you are about to build ships and sail against them, than to catch the Lydians at sea, and there revenge on them the wrongs of their brothers upon the mainland, whom you hold in slavery?" Croesus was charmed with the turn of the speech; and thinking there was reason in what was said, gave up his shipbuilding and concluded a league of amity with the Ionians of the isles.

Croesus afterwards, in the course of many years, brought under his sway almost all the nations to the west of the Halys. The Lycians and Cilicians alone continued free; all the other tribes he reduced and held in subjection. They were the following: the Lydians, Phrygians, Mysians, Mariandynians, Chalybians, Paphlagonians, Thynian and Bithynian Thracians, Carians, Ionians, Dorians, Aeolians and Pamphylians.

When all these conquests had been added to the Lydian empire, and the prosperity of Sardis was now at its height, there came thither, one after another, all the sages of Greece living at the time, and among them Solon, the Athenian. He was on his travels, having left Athens to be absent ten years, under the pretence of wishing to see the world, but really to avoid being forced to repeal any of the laws which, at the request of the Athenians, he had made for them. Without his sanction the Athenians could not repeal them, as they had bound themselves under a heavy curse to be governed for ten years by the laws which should be imposed on them by Solon.

On this account, as well as to see the world, Solon set out upon his travels, in the course of which he went to Egypt to the court of Amasis, and also came on a visit to Croesus at Sardis. Croesus received him as his guest, and lodged him in the royal palace. On the third or fourth day after, he bade his servants conduct Solon over his treasuries, and show him all their greatness and magnificence. When he had seen them all, and, so far as time allowed, inspected them, Croesus addressed this question to him, "Stranger of Athens, we have heard much of your wisdom and of your travels through many lands, from love of knowledge and a wish to see the world. I am curious therefore to inquire of you, whom, of all the men that you have seen, you consider the most happy?" This he asked because he thought himself the happiest of mortals: but Solon answered him without flattery, according to his true sentiments, "Tellus of Athens, sire." Full of astonishment at what he heard, Croesus demanded sharply, "And wherefore do you deem Tellus happiest?" To which the other replied, "First, because his country was flourishing in his days, and he himself had sons both beautiful and good, and he lived to see children born to each of them, and these children all grew up; and further because, after a life spent in what our people look upon as comfort, his end was surpassingly glorious. In a battle between the Athenians and their neighbours near Eleusis, he came to the assistance of his countrymen, routed the foe, and died upon the field most gallantly. The Athenians gave him a public funeral on the spot where he fell, and paid him the highest honours."

Thus did Solon admonish Croesus by the example of Tellus, enumerating the manifold particulars of his happiness. When he had ended, Croesus inquired a second time, who after Tellus seemed to him the happiest, expecting that, at any rate, he would be given the second place. "Cleobis and Bito," Solon answered, "they were of Argive race: their fortune was enough for their wants, and they were besides endowed with so much bodily strength that they had both gained prizes at the Games. Also this tale is told of them: There was a great festival in honour of the goddess Hera at Argos, to which their mother must needs be taken in a car. Now the oxen did not come home from the field in time: so the youths, fearful of being too late, put the yoke on their own necks, and themselves drew the car in which their mother rode. Five miles they drew her, and stopped before the temple. This deed of theirs was witnessed by the whole assembly of worshippers, and then their life closed in the best possible way. Herein, too, God showed forth most evidently, how much better a thing for man death is than life. For the Argive men stood thick around the car and extolled the vast strength of the youths; and the Argive women extolled the mother who was blessed with such a pair of sons; and the mother herself, overjoyed at the deed and at the praises it had won, standing straight before the image, besought the goddess to bestow on Cleobis and Bito, the sons who had so mightily honoured her, the highest blessing to which mortals can attain. Her prayer ended, they offered sacrifice, and partook of the holy banquet, after which the two youths fell asleep in the temple. They never woke more, but so passed from the earth. The Argives, looking on them as among the best of men, caused statues of them to be made, which they gave to the shrine at Delphi."

When Solon had thus assigned these youths the second place, Croesus broke in angrily, "What, stranger of Athens, is my happiness, then, valued so little by you, that you do not even put me on a level with private men?"

"Croesus," replied the other, "you asked a question concerning the condition of man, of one who knows that the power above us is full of jealousy, and fond of troubling our lot. A long life gives one to witness much, and experience much oneself, that one would not choose. Seventy years I regard as the limit of the life of man. In these seventy years are contained, without reckoning intercalary months, 25,200 days. Add an intercalary month to every other year, that the seasons may come round at the right time, and there will be, besides the seventy years, thirty-five such months, making an addition of 1,050 days. The whole number of the days contained in the seventy years will thus be 26,250, whereof not one but will produce events unlike the rest. Hence man is wholly accident. For yourself, Croesus, I see that you are wonderfully rich, and the lord of many nations; but with respect to your question, I have no answer to give, until I hear that you have closed your life happily. For assuredly he who possesses great store of riches is no nearer happiness than he who has what suffices for his daily needs, unless luck attend upon him, and so he continue in the enjoyment of all his good things to the end of life. For many of the wealthiest men have been unfavoured of fortune, and many whose means were moderate, have had excellent luck. Men of the former class excel those of the latter but in two respects; these last excel the former in many. The wealthy man is better able to content his desires, and to bear up against a sudden buffet of calamity. The other has less ability to withstand these evils (from which, however, his good luck keeps him clear), but he enjoys all these following blessings: he is whole of limb, a stranger to disease, free from misfortune, happy in his children, and comely to look upon. If, in addition to all this, he end his life well, he is of a truth the man of whom you are in search, the man who may rightly be termed happy. Call him, however, until he die, not happy but fortunate. Scarcely, indeed, can any man unite all these advantages: as there is no country which contains within it all that it needs, but each, while it possesses some things, lacks others, and the best country is that which contains the most; so no single human being is complete in every respect—something is always lacking. He who unites the greatest number of advantages, and retaining them to the day of his death, then dies peaceably, that man alone, sire, is, in my judgment, entitled to bear the name of 'happy.' But in every matter we must mark well the end; for oftentimes God gives men a gleam of happiness, and then plunges them into ruin."

Such was the speech which Solon addressed to Croesus, a speech which brought him neither largess nor honour. The king saw him depart with much indifference, since he thought that a man must be an arrant fool who made no account of present good, but bade men always wait and mark the end.

After Solon had gone away a dreadful vengeance, sent of God, came upon Croesus, to punish him, it is likely, for considering himself the happiest of men.

(Herodotus here interjects the story of how Croesus dreamed that his favorite son, Atys, was fated to die by the blow of an iron weapon. Despite all of Croesus' precautions the son does indeed suffer the predicted fate and Herodotus uses the story as a foreshadowing of the evils about to befall the father.)

At the end of this time the grief of Croesus was interrupted by intelligence from abroad. He learned that Cyrus, the son of Cambyses, had destroyed the empire of Astyages, the son of Cyaxares; and that the Persians were becoming daily more powerful. This led him to consider with himself whether it were possible to check the growing power of that people before it came to a head. With this design he resolved to make instant trial of the several oracles in Greece, and of the one in Libya. So he sent his messengers in different directions, some to Delphi, some to Abae in Phocis, and some to Dodona; others to the oracle of Amphiaraus; others to that of Trophonius; others, again, to Branchidae in Milesia. These were the Greek oracles which he consulted. To Libya he sent another embassy, to consult the oracle of Ammon. These messengers were sent to test the knowledge of the oracles, that, if they were found really to return true answers, he might send a second time, and inquire if he ought to attack the Persians.

The messengers who were despatched to make trial of the oracles were given the following instructions: they were to keep count of the days from the time of their leaving Sardis, and, reckoning from that date, on the hundredth day they were to consult the oracles, and to inquire of them what Croesus the son of Alyattes, king of Lydia, was doing at that moment. The answers given them were to be taken down in writing, and brought back to him. None of the replies remain on record except that of the oracle at Delphi. There, the moment that the Lydians entered the sanctuary, and before they put their questions, the priestess thus answered them in hexameter verse:

> I can count the sands, and I can measure the ocean;
> I have ears for the silent, and know what the dumb man meaneth;
> Lo! on my sense there striketh the smell of a shell-covered tortoise,
> Boiling now on a fire, with the flesh of a lamb, in a cauldron,
> Brass is the vessel below, and brass the cover above it.

These words the Lydians wrote down at the mouth of the priestess as she prophesied, and then set off on their return to Sardis. When all the messengers had come back with the answers which they had received, Croesus undid the rolls, and read what was written in each. Only one approved itself to him, that of the Delphic oracle. This he had no sooner heard than he instantly made an act of adoration, and accepted it as true, declaring that the Delphic was the only really oracular shrine, the only one that had discovered in what way he was in fact employed. For on the departure of his messengers he had set himself to think what was most impossible for any one to conceive of his doing, and then, waiting till the day agreed on came, he acted as he had determined. He took a tortoise and a lamb, and cutting them in pieces with his own hands, boiled them both together in a brazen cauldron, covered over with a lid which was also of brass.

Such then was the answer returned to Croesus from Delphi. What the answer was which the Lydians who went to the shrine of Amphiaraus and performed the customary rites, obtained of the oracle there, I have it not in my power to mention, for there is no record of it. All that is known is, that Croesus believed himself to have found there also an oracle which spoke the truth. . . .

The messengers who had the charge of conveying these treasures to the shrines, received instructions to ask the oracles whether Croesus should go to war with the Persians, and if so, whether he should strengthen himself by the forces of an ally. Accordingly, when they had reached their destinations and presented the gifts, they proceeded to consult the oracles in the following terms, "Croesus, king of Lydia and other countries, believing that these are the only real oracles in all the world, has sent you such presents as your discoveries deserved, and now inquires of you whether he shall go to war with the Persians, and if so, whether he shall strengthen himself by the forces of a confederate." Both the oracles agreed in the tenor of their reply, which was in each case a prophecy that if Croesus attacked the Persians, he would destroy a mighty empire, and a recommendation to him to look and see who were the most powerful of the Greeks, and to make alliance with them.

At the receipt of these oracular replies Croesus was overjoyed, and feeling sure now that he would destroy the empire of the Persians, he sent once more to Pytho, and presented to the Delphians, the number of whom had ascertained, two gold staters apiece. In return for this the Delphians granted to Croesus and the Lydians the privilege of precedency in consulting the oracle, exemption from all charges, the most honourable seat at the festivals, and the perpetual right of becoming at pleasure citizens of their town.

After sending these presents to the Delphians, Croesus a third time consulted the oracle, for having once proved its truthfulness, he wished to make constant use of it. The question whereto he now desired an answer was, "Whether his kingdom would be of long duration?" The following was the reply of the priestess:

> Wait till the time shall come when a mule is monarch of Media;
> Then, thou delicate Lydian, away to the pebbles of Hermus;
> Haste, oh! haste thee away, nor blush to behave like a coward.

Of all the answers that had reached him, this pleased him far the best, for it seemed incredible that a mule should ever come to be king of the Medes, and so he concluded that the sovereignty would never depart from himself or his seed after him. Afterwards he turned his thoughts to the alliance which he had been recommended to contract, and sought to ascertain by inquiry which was the most powerful of the Grecian states. His inquiries pointed out to him two states as pre-eminent above the rest. These were the Lacedaemonians and the Athenians, the former of Doric, the latter of Ionic blood. And indeed these two nations had held from very early times the most distinguished place in Greece, the one being a Pelasgic the other a Hellenic people, and the one having never quitted its original seats, while the other had been excessively migratory; for during the reign of Deucalion, Phthiotis was the country in which the Hellenes dwelt, but under Dorus, the son of Hellen, they moved to the tract at the base of Ossa and Olympus, which is called Histiaeotis; forced to retire from that region by the Cadmeians, they settled, under the name of Macedni, in the chain of Pindus. Hence they once more removed and came to Dryopis; and from Dryopis having entered the Peloponnese in this way, they became known as Dorians.

What the language of the Pelasgi was I cannot say with any certainty. If, however, we may form a conjecture from the tongue spoken by the Pelasgi of the present day, those, for instance, who live at Creston above the Tyrrhenians, who formerly dwelt in the district named Thessaliotis, and were neighbours of the people now called the Dorians, or those again who founded Placia and Scylace upon the Hellespont, who had previously dwelt for some time with the Athenians, or those, in short, of any of the cities which have dropped the name but are in fact Pelasgian; if, I say, we are to form a conjecture from any of these, we must pronounce that the Pelasgi spoke a barbarous language. If this were really so, and the entire Pelasgic race spoke the same tongue, the Athenians, who were certainly Pelasgi, must have changed their language at the same time that they passed into the Hellenic body; for it is a certain fact that the people of Creston speak a language unlike any of their neighbours, and the same is true of the Placianians, while the language spoken by these two people is the same; which shows that they both retain the idiom which they brought with them into the countries where they are now settled.

The Hellenic race has never, since its first origin, changed its speech. This at least seems evident to me. It was a branch of the Pelasgic, which separated from the main body, and at first was scanty in numbers and of little power; but it gradually spread and increased to a multitude of nations, chiefly by the voluntary entrance into its ranks of numerous tribes of barbarians. The Pelasgi, on the other hand, were, as I think, a barbarian race which never greatly multiplied.

On inquiring into the condition of these two nations, Croesus found that one, the Athenian, was in a state of grievous oppression and distraction under Pisistratus, the son of Hippocrates, who was at that time tyrant of Athens.

(Herodotus here expatiates on conditions in Athens, relating the events which culminated in the dictatorship of Pisistratus.)

Such was the condition of the Athenians when Croesus made inquiry concerning them. Proceeding to seek information concerning the Lacedaemonians, he learnt that, after passing through a period of great depression, they had lately been victorious in a war with the people of Tegea. . . .

Croesus, informed of all these circumstances, sent messengers to Sparta, with gifts in their hands, who were to ask the Spartans to enter into alliance with him. They received strict injunctions as to what they should say, and on their arrival at Sparta spoke as follows, "Croesus, king of the Lydians and of other nations, has sent us to speak thus to you, 'Lacedaemonians, the god has bidden me to make the Greek my friend; I therefore apply to you, in conformity with the oracle, knowing that you hold the first rank in Greece, and desire to become your friend and ally in all true faith and honesty.' "

Such was the message which Croesus sent by his heralds. The Lacedaemonians, who were aware beforehand of the reply given him by the oracle, were full of joy at the coming of the messengers, and at once took the oaths of friendship and alliance: this they did the more readily as they had previously contracted certain obligations towards him. They had sent to Sardis on one occasion to purchase some gold, intending to use it on a statue of Apollo—the statue, namely, which remains to this day at Thornax in Laconia, when Croesus, hearing of the matter, gave them as a gift the gold which they wanted.

This was one reason why the Lacedaemonians were so willing to make the alliance: another was, because Croesus had chosen them for his friends in preference to all the other Greeks. They therefore held themselves in readiness to come at his summons, and not content with so doing, they further had a huge vase made in bronze, covered with figures of animals all round the outside of the rim, and large enough to contain 2,700 gallons, which they sent to Croesus as a return for his presents to them. The vase, however, never reached Sardis. Its miscarriage is accounted for in two quite different ways. The Lacedaemonian story is, that when it reached Samos, on its way towards Sardis, the Samians having knowledge of it, put to sea in their ships of war and made it their prize. But the Samians declare, that the Lacedaemonians who had the vase in charge, happening to arrive too late, and learning that Sardis had fallen and that Croesus was a prisoner, sold it in their island, and the purchasers (who were, they say, private persons) made an offering of it at the shrine of Hera: the sellers were very likely on their return to Sparta to have said that they had been robbed of it by the Samians. Such, then, was the fate of the vase.

Meanwhile Croesus, taking the oracle in a wrong sense, led his forces into Cappadocia, fully expecting to defeat Cyrus and destroy the empire of the Persians. While he was still engaged in making preparations for his attack, a Lydian named Sandanis, who had always been looked upon as a wise man, but who after this obtained a very great name indeed among his countrymen, came forward and counselled the king in these words, "You are about, king, to make war against men who wear leathern trousers, and have all their other garments of leather; who feed not on what they like, but on what they can get from a soil that is sterile and unkindly; who do not indulge in wine, but drink water; who possess no figs nor anything else that is good to eat. If, then, you conquer them, what can you get from them, seeing that they have nothing at all? But if they conquer you, consider how much that is precious you will lose: if they once get a taste of our pleasant things, they will keep such hold of them that we shall never be able to make them loose their grasp. For my part, I am thankful to the gods, that they have not put it into the hearts of the Persians to invade Lydia."

Croesus was not persuaded by this speech, though it was true enough; for before the conquest of Lydia, the Persians possessed none of the luxuries or delights of life. . . .

There were two motives which led Croesus to attack Cappadocia: firstly, he coveted the land, which he wished to add to his own dominions; but the chief reason was, that he wanted to revenge on Cyrus the wrongs of Astyages, and was made confident by the oracle of being able so to do: for the Astyages, son of Cyaxares and king of the Medes, who had been dethroned by Cyrus, son of Cambyses, was Croesus' brother by marriage.

(In the following chapters, Herodotus describes the background to Croesus' decision to invade the Persian domain and the events which led to the destruction of the Kingdom of Lydia by the Persians under Cyrus.)

The Persians, who had long been impatient of the Median dominion, now that they had found a leader, were delighted to shake off the yoke. Meanwhile Astyages, informed of the doings of Cyrus, sent a messenger to summon him to his presence. Cyrus replied, "Tell Astyages that I shall appear in his presence sooner than he will like." Astyages, when he received this message, instantly armed all his subjects, and, as if God had deprived him of his senses, appointed Harpagus to be their general, forgetting how greatly he had injured him. So when the two armies met and engaged, only a few of the Medes, who were not in the secret, fought; others deserted openly to the Persians; while the great number counterfeited fear, and fled.

Astyages, on learning the shameful flight and dispersion of his army, broke out into threats against Cyrus, saying, "Cyrus shall nevertheless have no reason to rejoice"; and directly he seized the Magian interpreters, who had persuaded him to allow Cyrus to escape, and impaled them; after which, he armed all the Medes who had remained in the city, both young and old; and leading them against the Persians, fought a battle, in which he was utterly defeated, his army being destroyed, and he himself falling into the enemy's hands.

Harpagus then, seeing him a prisoner, came near, and exulted over him with many gibes and jeers. Among other cutting speeches which he made, he alluded to the supper where the flesh of his son was given him to eat, and asked Astyages to answer him now, how he enjoyed being a slave instead of a king? Astyages looked in his face, and asked him in return, why he claimed as his own the achievements of Cyrus? "Because," said Harpagus, "it was my letter which made him revolt, and so I am entitled to all the credit of the enterprise." Then Astyages declared, that "in that case he was at once the silliest and the most unjust of men: the silliest, if when it was in his power to put the crown on his own head, as it must assuredly have been, if the revolt was entirely his doing, he had placed it on the head of another; the most unjust, if on account of that supper he had brought slavery on the Medes. For, supposing that he was obliged to invest another with the kingly power, and not retain it himself, yet justice required that a Mede, rather than a Persian, should receive the dignity. Now, however, the Medes, who had been no parties to the wrong of which he complained, were made slaves instead of lords, and slaves moreover of those who till recently had been their subjects."

Thus after a reign of thirty-five years, Astyages lost his crown, and the Medes, in consequence of his cruelty, were brought under the rule of the Persians. Their empire over the parts of Asia beyond the Halys had lasted 128 years, except during the time when the Scythians had the dominion. Afterwards the Medes repented of their submission, and revolted from Darius, but were defeated in battle, and again reduced to subjection.

Now, however, in the time of Astyages, it was the Persians who under Cyrus revolted from the Medes, and became thenceforth the rulers of Asia. Cyrus kept Astyages at his court during the remainder of his life, without doing him any further injury. Such then were the circumstances of the birth and bringing up of Cyrus, and such were the steps by which he mounted the throne. It was at a later date that he was attacked by Croesus, and overthrew him, as I have related in an earlier portion of this history. The overthrow of Croesus made him master of the whole of Asia.

The customs which I know the Persians to observe are the following. They have no images of the gods, no temples nor altars, and consider the use of them a sign of folly. This comes, I think, from their not believing the gods to have the same nature with men, as the Greeks imagine. Their wont, however, is to ascend the summits of the loftiest mountains, and there to offer sacrifice to Zeus, which is the name they give to the whole circuit of the firmament. They likewise offer to the sun and moon, to the earth, to fire, to water, and to the winds. These are the only gods whose worship has come down to them from ancient times. At a later period they began the worship of Aphrodite, which they borrowed from the Arabians and Assyrians. Mylitta is the name by which the Assyrians know this goddess, whom the Arabians call Alitta, and the Persians Mitra.

To these gods the Persians offer sacrifice in the following manner: they raise no altar, light no fire, pour no libations, there is no sound of the flute, no putting on of chaplets, no consecrated barley-cake; but the man who wishes to sacrifice brings his victim to a spot of ground which is pure from pollution, and there calls upon the name of the god to whom he intends to offer. It is usual to have the turban encircled with a wreath, most commonly of myrtle. The sacrificer is not allowed to pray for blessings on himself alone, but he prays for the welfare of the king, and of the whole Persian people, among whom he is of necessity included. He cuts the victim in pieces, and having boiled the flesh, he lays it out upon the softest grass that he can find, trefoil especially. When all is ready, one of the Magi comes forward and chants a hymn, which they say recounts the origin of the gods. It is not lawful to offer sacrifice unless there is a Magus present. After waiting a short time the sacrificer carries the flesh of the victim away with him, and makes whatever use of it he pleases.

Of all the days in the year, the one which they celebrate most is their birthday. It is customary to have the board furnished on that day with an ampler supply than common. The richer Persians cause an ox, a horse, a camel, and an ass to be baked whole and so served up to them: the poorer classes use instead the smaller kinds of cattle. They eat little solid food but abundance of dessert, which is set on table a few dishes at a time; this it is which makes them say that "the Greeks, when they eat, leave off hungry, having nothing worth mention served up to them after the meats; whereas, if they had more put before them, they would not stop eating." They are very fond of wine, and drink it in large quantities. To vomit or obey natural calls in the presence of another, is forbidden among them. Such are their customs in these matters.

It is also their general practice to deliberate upon affairs of weight when they are drunk; and then on the morrow, when they are sober, the decision to which they came the night before is put before them by the master of the house in which it was made; and if it is then approved of, they act on it; if not, they set it aside. Sometimes, however, they are sober at their first deliberation, but in this case they always reconsider the matter under the influence of wine.

When they meet each other in the streets, you may know if the persons meeting are of equal rank by the following token; if they are, instead of speaking, they kiss each other on the lips. In the case where one is a little inferior to the other, the kiss is given on the cheek; where the difference of rank is great, the inferior prostrates himself upon the ground. Of nations, they honour most their nearest neighbours whom they esteem next to themselves; those who live beyond these they honour in the second degree; and so with the remainder, the further they are removed, the less the esteem in which they hold them. The reason is, that they look upon themselves as very greatly superior in all respects to the rest of mankind, regarding others as approaching to excellence in proportion as they dwell nearer to them; whence it comes to pass that those who are the farthest off must be the most degraded of mankind. Under the dominion of the Medes, the several nations of the empire exercised authority over each other in this order. The Medes were lords over all, and governed the nations upon their borders, who in their turn governed the states beyond, who likewise bore rule over the nations which adjoined on them. And this is the order which the Persians also follow in their distribution of honour; for that people, like the Medes, has a progressive scale of administration and government.

There is no nation which so readily adopts foreign customs as the Persians. Thus, they have taken the dress of the Medes, considering it superior to their own; and in war they wear the Egyptian breastplate. As soon as they hear of any luxury, they instantly make it their own: and hence, among other novelties, they have learned pederasty from the Greeks. Each of them has several wives, and a still larger number of concubines.

Next to prowess in arms, it is regarded as the greatest proof of manly excellence, to be the father of many sons. Every year the king sends rich gifts to the man who can show the largest number: for they hold that number is strength. Their sons are carefully instructed from their fifth to their twentieth year, in three things alone,—to ride, to draw the bow, and to speak the truth. Until their fifth year they are not allowed to come into the sight of their father, but pass their lives with the women. This is done that, if the child die young, the father may not be afflicted by its loss.

To my mind it is a wise rule, as also is the following—that the king shall not put any one to death for a single fault, and that none of the Persians shall visit a single fault in a slave with any extreme penalty; but in every case the services of the offender shall be set against his misdoings; and, if the latter be found to outweigh the former, the aggrieved party shall then proceed to punishment.

The Persians maintain that never yet did any one kill his own father or mother; but in all such cases they are quite sure that, if matters were sifted to the bottom, it would be found that the child was either a changeling or else the fruit of adultery; for it is not likely they say that the real father should perish by the hands of his child.

They hold it unlawful to talk of any thing which it is unlawful to do. The most disgraceful thing in the world, they think, is to tell a lie; the next worse, to owe a debt: because, among other reasons, the debtor is obliged to tell lies. If a Persian has the leprosy he is not allowed to enter into a city, or to have any dealings with the other Persians; he must, they say, have sinned against the sun. Foreigners attacked by this disorder, are forced to leave the country: even white pigeons are often driven away, as guilty of the same offence. They never defile a river with the secretions of their bodies, nor even wash their hands in one; nor will they allow others to do so, as they have a great reverence for rivers. There is another peculiarity, which the Persians themselves have never noticed, but which has not escaped my observation. Their names, which are expressive of some bodily or mental excellence, all end with the same letter— the letter which is called San by the Dorians, and Sigma by the Ionians. Any one who examines will find that the Persian names, one and all without exception, end with this letter.

Thus much I can declare of the Persians with entire certainty, from my own actual knowledge. There is another custom which is spoken of with reserve, and not openly, concerning their dead. It is said that the body of a male Persian is never buried, until it has been torn either by a dog or a bird of prey. That the Magi have this custom is beyond a doubt, for they practise it without any concealment. The dead bodies are covered with wax, and then buried in the ground.

The Magi are a very peculiar race, differing entirely from the Egyptian priests, and indeed from all other men whatsoever. The Egyptian priests make it a point of religion not to kill any live animals except those which they offer in sacrifice. The Magi, on the contrary, kill animals of all kinds with their own hands, excepting dogs and men. They even seem to take a delight in the employment, and kill, as readily as they do other animals, ants and snakes, and such like flying or creeping things. However, since this has always been their custom, let them keep to it. I return to my former narrative.

Immediately after the conquest of Lydia by the Persians, the Ionian and Aeolian Greeks sent ambassadors to Cyrus at Sardis, and prayed to become his lieges on the footing which they had occupied under Croesus. Cyrus listened attentively to their proposals, and answered them by a fable. "There was a certain piper," he said, "who was walking one day by the seaside, when he espied some fish; so he began to pipe to them, imagining they would come out to him upon the land. But as he found at last that his hope was vain, he took a net, and enclosing a great draught of fishes, drew them ashore. The fish then began to leap and dance; but the piper said, 'Cease your dancing now, as you did not choose to come and dance when I piped to you.'" Cyrus gave this answer to the Ionians and Aeolians, because, when he urged them by his messengers to revolt from Croesus, they refused; but now, when his work was done, they came to offer their allegiance. It was in anger, therefore, that he made them this reply. The Ionians, on hearing it, set to work to fortify their towns, and held meetings at the Panionium, which were attended by all excepting the Milesians, with whom Cyrus had concluded a separate treaty, by which he allowed them the terms they had formerly obtained from Croesus. The other Ionians resolved, with one accord, to send ambassadors to Sparta to implore assistance. . . .

On the death of Cyrus, Cambyses his son by Cassandane daughter of Pharnaspes took the kingdom. Cassandane had died in the lifetime of Cyrus, who had made a great mourning for her at her death, and had commanded all the subjects of his empire to observe the like. Cambyses, the son of this woman and of Cyrus, regarding the Ionian and Aeolian Greeks as vassals of his father, took them with him in his expedition against Egypt among the other nations which owned his sway.

Now the Egyptians, before the reign of their king Psammetichus, believed themselves to be the most ancient of mankind. Since Psammetichus, however, made an attempt to discover who were actually the primitive race, they have been of opinion that while they surpass all other nations, the Phrygians surpass them in antiquity. This king, finding it impossible to make out by dint of inquiry what men were the most ancient, contrived the following method of discovery: He took two children of the common sort, and gave them over to a herdsman to bring up at his folds, strictly charging him to let no one utter a word in their presence, but to keep them in a sequestered cottage, and from time to time introduce goats to their apartment, see that they got their fill of milk, and in all other respects look after them. His object herein was to know, after the indistinct babblings of infancy were over, what word they would first articulate. It happened as he had anticipated. The herdsman obeyed his orders for two years, and at the end of that time, on his one day opening the door of their room and going in, the children both ran up to him with outstretched arms, and distinctly said Becos. When this first happened the herdsman took no notice; but afterwards when he observed, on coming often to see after them, that the word was constantly in their mouths, he informed his lord, and by his command brought the children into his presence. Psammetichus then himself heard them say the word, upon which he proceeded to make inquiry what people there was who called anything becos, and hereupon he learnt that becos was the Phrygian name for bread. In consideration of this circumstance the Egyptians yielded their claims, and admitted the greater antiquity of the Phrygians.

That these were the real facts I learnt at Memphis from the priests of Hephaestus. The Greeks, among other foolish tales, relate that Psammetichus had the children brought up by women whose tongues he had previously cut out; but the priests said their bringing up was such as I have stated above. I got much other information also from conversation with these priests while I was at Memphis, and I even went to Heliopolis and to Thebes, expressly to try whether the priests of those places would agree in their accounts with the priests at Memphis. The Heliopolitans have the reputation of being the best skilled in history of all the Egyptians. What they told me concerning their religion it is not my intention to repeat, except the names of their deities, since I believe all men know equally little about the gods. If I relate anything else concerning these matters, it will only be when compelled to do so by the course of my narrative.

Now with regard to mere human matters, the accounts which they gave, and in which all agreed, were the following. The Egyptians, they said, were the first to discover the solar year, and to portion out its course into twelve parts. They obtained this knowledge from the stars. (To my mind they contrive their year much more cleverly than the Greeks, for these last every other year intercalate a whole month, but the Egyptians, dividing the year into twelve months of thirty days each, add every year a space of five days besides, whereby the circuit of the seasons is made to return with uniformity.) The Egyptians, they went on to affirm, first brought into use the names of the twelve gods, which the Greeks adopted from them; and first erected altars, images, and temples to the gods; and also first engraved upon stone the figures of animals. In most of these cases they proved to me that what they said was true. And they told me that the first man who ruled over Egypt was Min, and that in his time all Egypt, except the Thebaic nome, was a marsh, none of the land below lake Moeris then showing itself above the surface of the water. This is a distance of seven days' sail from the sea up the river.

What they said of their country seemed to me very reasonable. For any one who sees Egypt, without having heard a word about it before, must perceive, if he has only common powers of observation, that the Egypt to which the Greeks go in their ships is an acquired country, the gift of the river. The same is true of the land above the lake, to the distance of three days' voyage, concerning which the Egyptians say nothing, but which is exactly the same kind of country. . . .

Here I take my leave of the opinions of the Ionians, and proceed to deliver my own sentiments on these subjects. I consider Egypt to be the whole country inhabited by the Egyptians, just as Cilicia is the tract occupied by the Cilicians, and Assyria that possessed by the Assyrians. And I regard the only proper boundary-line between Libya and Asia to be that which is marked out by the Egyptian frontier. For if we take the boundary-line commonly received by the Greeks, we must regard Egypt as divided, along its whole length from Elephantine and the Cataracts to Cercasorus, into two parts, each belonging to a different portion of the world, one to Asia, the other to Libya; since the Nile divides Egypt in two from the Cataracts to the sea, running as far as the city of Cercasorus in a single stream, but at that point separating into three branches, whereof the one which bends eastward is called the Pelusiac mouth, and that which slants to the west, the Canobic. Meanwhile the straight course of the stream, which comes down from the upper country, and meets the apex of the Delta, continues on, dividing the Delta down the middle, and empties itself into the sea by a mouth, which is as celebrated, and carries as large a body of water, as most of the others, the mouth called the Sebennytic. Besides these there are two other mouths which run out of the Sebennytic called respectively the Saitic and the Mendesian. The Bolbitine mouth, and the Bucolic, are not natural branches, but channels made by excavation.

My judgment as to the extent of Egypt is confirmed by an oracle delivered at the shrine of Ammon, of which I had no knowledge at all until after I had formed my opinion. It happened that the people of the cities Marea and Apis, who live in the part of Egypt that borders on Libya, took a dislike to the religious usages of the country concerning sacrificial animals, and wished no longer to be restricted from eating the flesh of cows. So, as they believed themselves to be Libyans and not Egyptians, they sent to the shrine to say that, having nothing in common with the Egyptians, neither inhabiting the Delta nor using the Egyptian tongue, they claimed to be allowed to eat whatever they pleased. Their request, however, was refused by the god, who declared in reply that Egypt was the entire tract of country which the Nile overspreads and irrigates, and the Egyptians were the people who lived below Elephantine, and drank the waters of that river.

So said the oracle. Now the Nile, when it overflows, floods not only the Delta, but also the tracts of country on both sides of the stream which are thought to belong to Libya and Arabia, in some places reaching to the extent of two days' journey from its banks, in some even exceeding that distance, but in others falling short of it.

Concerning the nature of the river, I was not able to gain any information either from the priests or from others. I was particularly anxious to learn from them why the Nile, at the commencement of the summer solstice, begins to rise, and continues to increase for a hundred days—and why, as soon as that number is past, it forthwith retires and contracts its stream, continuing low during the whole of the winter until the summer solstice comes round again. On none of these points could I obtain any explanation from the inhabitants, though I made every inquiry, wishing to know what was commonly reported—they could neither tell me what special virtue the Nile has which makes it so opposite in its nature to all other streams, nor why, unlike every other river, it gives forth no breezes from its surface.

Some of the Greeks, however, wishing to get a reputation for cleverness, have offered explanations of the phenomena of the river, for which they have accounted in three different ways. Two of these I do not think it worth while to speak of, further than simply to mention what they are. One pretends that the Etesian winds cause the rise of the river by preventing the Nile water from running off into the sea. But in the first place it has often happened, when the Etesian winds did not blow, that the Nile has risen according to its usual wont; and further, if the Etesian winds produced the effect, the other rivers which flow in a direction opposite to those winds ought to present the same phenomena as the Nile, and the more so as they are all smaller streams, and have a weaker current. But these rivers, of which there are many both in Syria and Libya, are entirely unlike the Nile in this respect.

The second opinion is even more unscientific than the one just mentioned, and also, if I may so say, more marvellous. It is that the Nile acts so strangely, because it flows from the ocean, and that the ocean flows all round the earth.

The third explanation, which is very much more plausible than either of the others, is positively the furthest from the truth; for there is really nothing in what it says, any more than in the other theories. It is, that the inundation of the Nile is caused by the melting of snows. Now, as the Nile flows out of Libya, through Ethiopia, into Egypt, how is it possible that it can be formed of melted snow, running, as it does, from the hottest regions of the world into cooler countries? Many are the proofs whereby any one capable of reasoning on the subject may be convinced that it is most unlikely this should be the case. The first and strongest argument is furnished by the winds, which always blow hot from these regions. The second is, that rain and frost are unknown there. Now, whenever snow falls, it must of necessity rain within five days; so that, if there were snow, there must be rain also in those parts. Thirdly, it is certain that the natives of the country are black with the heat, that the kites and the swallows remain there the whole year, and that the cranes, when they fly from the rigours of a Scythian winter, flock thither to pass the cold season. If then, in the country whence the Nile has its source, or in that through which it flows, there fell ever so little snow, it is absolutely impossible that any of these circumstances could take place. . . .

Let us leave these things, however, to their natural course, to continue as they are and have been from the beginning. . . .

I must proceed with the matter whereof I was intending before to speak; to wit, the way in which the Athenians got quit of their tyrants.

(Herodotus proceeds to describe how the Athenians with the assistance of Sparta overthrew their tyrannical form of government.)

What they did and suffered worthy of note from the time when they gained their freedom until the revolt of Ionia from King Darius, and the coming of Aristagoras to Athens with a request that the Athenians would lend the Ionians aid, I shall now proceed to relate.

The power of Athens had been great before, but now that the tyrants were gone it became greater than ever. The chief authority was lodged with two persons, Cleisthenes, of the family of the Alcmaeonids, who is said to have been the persuader of the Pythian priestess, and Isagoras, the son of Tisander, who belonged to a noble house, but whose pedigree I am not able to trace further. Howbeit his kinsmen offer sacrifice to the Carian Zeus. These two men strove together for the mastery; and Cleisthenes, finding himself the weaker, called to his aid the common people. Hereupon, instead of the four tribes among which the Athenians had been divided hitherto, Cleisthenes made ten tribes, and parcelled out the Athenians among them. He likewise changed the names of the tribes; for whereas they had till now been called after Geleon, Aegicores, Argades, and Hoples, the four sons of Ion, Cleisthenes set these names aside, and

Athenians among them. He likewise changed the names of the tribes; for whereas they had till now been called after Geleon, Aegicores, Argades, and Hoples, the four sons of Ion, Cleisthenes set these names aside, and called his tribes after certain other heroes, all of whom were native, except Ajax. Ajax was associated because, although a foreigner, he was a neighbour and an ally of Athens. . . .

Thus did the Athenians increase in strength. And it is plain enough, not from this instance only, but from many everywhere, that freedom is an excellent thing; since even the Athenians, who, while they continued under the rule of tyrants, were not a whit more valiant than any of their neighbours, no sooner shook off the yoke than they became decidedly the first of all. These things show that, while undergoing oppression, they let themselves be beaten, since then they worked for a master; but so soon as they got their freedom, each man was eager to do the best he could for himself. So fared it now with the Athenians.

(In the following chapters Herodotus describes the intestine struggles in Greece and Ionia and the events leading up to the Persian decision to move against Athens.)

While Onesilus was engaged in the siege of Amathus, King Darius received tidings of the taking and burning of Sardis by the Athenians and Ionians; and at the same time he learnt that the author of the league, the man by whom the whole matter had been planned and contrived, was Aristagoras the Milesian. It is said he no sooner understood what had happened, than, laying aside all thought concerning the Ionians, who would, he was sure, pay dear for their rebellion, he asked who the Athenians were and, being informed, called for his bow, and placing an arrow on the string, shot upward into the sky, saying, as he let fly the shaft, "Grant me, Zeus, to revenge myself on the Athenians!" After this speech, he bade one of his servants every day, when his dinner was spread, three times repeat these words to him, "Master, remember the Athenians."

(After the conquest of Ionia the Persians conducted an expeditionary force across the Aegean Sea, landing near the city of Eretria on the island of Euboea, just across a narrow channel from Attica. After reducing that city the Persians turned toward the mainland and Athens.)

The barbarians were conducted to Marathon by Hippias, the son of Pisistratus, who the night before had seen a strange vision in his sleep. He seemed to have intercourse with his mother, and conjectured the dream to mean that he would be restored to Athens, recover the power which he had lost, and afterwards live to a good old age in his native country. Such was the sense in which he interpreted the vision. He now proceeded to act as guide to the Persians, and in the first place he landed the prisoners taken from Eretria upon the island that is called Aegileia, belonging to the Styreans, after which he brought the fleet to anchor off Marathon, and marshalled the bands of the barbarians as they disembarked. As he was thus employed it chanced that he sneezed and at the same time coughed with more violence than was his wont. Now as he was a man advanced in years, and the greater number of his teeth were loose, it so happened that one of them was driven out with the force of the cough, and fell down into the sand. Hippias took all the pains he could to find it, but the tooth was nowhere to be seen; whereupon he fetched a deep sigh, and said to the bystanders, "After all the land is not ours, and we shall never be able to bring it under. All my share in it is the portion of which my tooth has possession."

So Hippias believed that this fulfilled his dream.

The Athenians were drawn up in order of battle in a precinct belonging to Heracles, when they were joined by the Plataeans, who came in full force to their aid. Some time before, the Plataeans had put themselves under the rule of the Athenians, and these last had already undertaken many labours on their behalf. . . .

The Athenian generals were divided in their opinions; and some advised not to risk a battle, because they were too few to engage such a host as that of the Medes; while others were for fighting at once, and among these last was Miltiades. He therefore, seeing that opinions were thus divided, and that the less worthy counsel appeared likely to prevail, resolved to go to the Polemarch, and have a conference with him. For the man on whom the lot fell to be Polemarch, at Athens was entitled to give his vote with the ten generals, since anciently the Athenians allowed him an equal right of voting with them. The Polemarch at this juncture was Callimachus of Aphidnae; to him therefore Miltiades went, and said:

"With you it rests, Callimachus, either to bring Athens to slavery, or, by securing her freedom, to leave behind to all future generations a memory beyond even Harmodius and Aristogeiton. For never since the time that the Athenians became a people were they in so great a danger as now. If they bow their necks beneath the yoke of the Medes, the woes which they will have to suffer when given into the power of Hippias are already determined on; if, on the other hand, they fight and overcome, Athens may rise to be the very first city in Greece. How it comes to pass that these things are likely to happen, and how the determining of them in some sort rests with you, I will now proceed to make clear. We generals are ten in number, and our votes are divided; half of us wish to engage, half to avoid a combat. Now, if we do not fight, I look to see a great disturbance at Athens which will shake men's resolutions, and then I fear they will submit themselves; but if we fight the battle before any unsoundness shows itself among our citizens, let the gods but give us fair play, and we are well able to overcome the enemy. On you therefore we depend in this matter, which lies wholly in your own power. You have only to add your vote to my side and your country will be free, and not free only, but the first state in Greece. Or, if you prefer to give your vote to them who would decline the combat, then the reverse will follow."

Miltiades by these words gained Callimachus; and the addition of the Polemarch's vote caused the decision to be in favor of fighting. Hereupon all those generals who had been desirous of hazarding a battle, when their turn came to command the army, gave up their right to Miltiades. He however, though he accepted their offers, nevertheless waited, and would not fight, until his own day of command arrived in due course.

Then at length, when his own turn was come, the Athenian battle was set in array, and this was the order of it. Callimachus the Polemarch led the right wing, for it was at that time a rule with the Athenians to give the right wing to the Polemarch. After this followed the tribes, according as they were numbered, in an unbroken line; while last of all came the Plataeans, forming the left wing. And ever since that day it has been a custom with the Athenians, in the sacrifices and assemblies held each fifth year at Athens, for the Athenian herald to implore the blessing of the gods on the Plataeans conjointly with the Athenians. Now as they marshalled the host upon the field of Marathon, in order that the Athenian front might be of equal length with the Median, the ranks of the centre were diminished, and it became the weakest part of the line, while the wings were both made strong with a depth of many ranks.

So when the battle was set in array, and the victims showed themselves favourable, instantly the Athenians, so soon as they were let go, charged the barbarians at a run. Now the distance between the two armies was little short of a mile. The Persians, therefore, when they saw the Greeks coming on at speed, made ready to receive them, although it seemed to them that the Athenians were bereft of their senses, and bent upon their own destruction; for they saw a mere handful of men coming on at a run without either horsemen or archers. Such was the opinion of the barbarians; but the Athenians in close array fell upon them, and fought in a manner worthy of being recorded. They were the first of the Greeks, so far as I know, who introduced the custom of charging the enemy at a run, and they were likewise the first who dared to look upon the Median garb, and to face men clad in that fashion. Until this time the very name of the Medes had been a terror to the Greeks to hear.

The two armies fought together on the plain of Marathon for a length of time; and in the mid battle, where the Persians themselves and the Sacae had their place, the barbarians were victorious, and broke and pursued the Greeks into the inner country; but on the two wings the Athenians and the Plataeans defeated the enemy. Having so done, they suffered the routed barbarians to fly at their ease, and joining the two wings in one, fell upon those who had broken their own centre, and fought and conquered them. These likewise fled, and now the Athenians hung upon the runaways and cut them down, chasing them all the way to the shore, on reaching which they laid hold of the ships and called aloud for fire.

It was in the struggle here that Callimachus the Polemarch, after greatly distinguishing himself, lost his life; Stesilaus too, the son of Thrasilaus, one of the generals, was slain; and Cynaegirus, the son of Euphorion, having seized on a vessel of the enemy's by the ornament at the stern, had his hand cut off by the blow of an axe, and so perished; as likewise did many other Athenians of note and name.

Nevertheless the Athenians secured in this way seven of the vessels, while with the remainder the barbarians pushed off, and taking aboard their Eretrian prisoners from the island where they had left them, doubled Cape Sunium, hoping to reach Athens before the return of the Athenians. The Alcmaeonidae were accused by their countrymen of suggesting this course to them; they had, it was said, an understanding with the Persians, and made a signal to them, by raising a shield, after they were embarked in their ships.

The Persians accordingly sailed round Sunium. But the Athenians with all possible speed marched away to the defence of their city, and succeeded in reaching Athens before the appearance of the barbarians; and as their camp at Marathon had been pitched in a precinct of Heracles, so now they encamped in another precinct of the same god at Cynosarges. The barbarian fleet arrived, and lay to off Phalerum, which was at that time the haven of Athens; but after resting awhile upon their oars, they departed and sailed away to Asia. . . .

Now when tidings of the battle that had been fought at Marathon reached the ears of King Darius, the son of Hystaspes, his anger against the Athenians, which had been already roused by their attack upon Sardis, waxed still fiercer, and he became more than ever eager to lead an army against Greece. Instantly he sent off messengers to make proclamation through the several states, that fresh levies were to be raised, and these at an increased rate; while ships, horses, provisions, and transports were likewise to be furnished. So the men published his commands; and now all Asia was in commotion for three years, while everywhere, as Greece was to be attacked, the best and bravest were enrolled for the service, and had to make their preparations accordingly. . . .

Darius, when he had thus appointed Xerxes his heir, was minded to lead forth his armies; but he was prevented by death while his preparations were still proceeding. He died in the year following the revolt of Egypt, and the matters here related, after having reigned in all six and thirty years, leaving the revolted Egyptians and the Athenians alike unpunished. At his death the kingdom passed to his son, Xerxes.

Now Xerxes, on first mounting the throne, was coldly disposed towards the Grecian war, and made it his business to collect an army against Egypt. But Mardonius, the son of Gobryas, who was at the court, and had more influence with him than any of the other Persians, being his own cousin, the child of a sister of Darius, plied him with discourses like the following:

"Master, it is not fitting that they of Athens escape scot-free, after doing the Persians such great injury. Complete the work which you have in hand, and then, when the pride of Egypt is brought down, lead an army against Athens. So shall you have good report among men, and others shall fear hereafter to attack your country."

Thus far it was of vengeance that he spoke, but sometimes he would vary the theme, and observe by the way that Europe was a beautiful region, rich in all kinds of cultivated trees, and the soil excellent: no one, save the king, was worthy to own such a land.

All this he said, because he longed for adventures, and hoped to become Satrap of Greece under the king; and after a while he had his way, and persuaded Xerxes to do according to his desires. Other things, however, occurring about the same time, helped his persuasions. For, in the first place, it chanced that messengers arrived from Thessaly, sent by the Aleuadae, Thessalian kings, to invite Xerxes into Greece, and to promise him all the assistance which it was in their power to give. And further, the Pisistratidae, who had come up to Susa, used the same language as the Aleuadae, and worked upon him even more than they, by means of Onomacritus of Athens, an oracle-monger, and the same who set forth the prophecies of Musaeus in their order. The Pisistratidae had previously been at enmity with this man, but made up the quarrel before they removed to Susa. He was banished from Athens by Hipparchus, the son of Pisistratus, because he foisted into the writings of Musaeus a prophecy that the islands which lie off Lemnos would one day disappear in the sea. Lasus of Hermione caught him in the act of so doing. For this cause Hipparchus banished him, though till then they had been the closest of friends. Now, however, he went up to Susa with the sons of Pisistratus, and they talked very grandly of him to the king; while he, for his part, whenever he was in the king's company, repeated to him certain of the oracles; and while he took care to pass over all that spoke of disaster to the barbarians, brought forward the passages which promised them the greatest success. "It was fated," he told Xerxes, "that a Persian should bridge the Hellespont, and march an army from Asia into Greece." While Onomacritus thus plied Xerxes with his oracles, the Pisistratidae and Aleuadae did not cease to press on him their advice, till at last the king yielded, and agreed to lead forth an expedition.

First, however, in the year following the death of Darius, he marched against those who had revolted from him; and having reduced them, and laid all Egypt under a far harder yoke than ever his father had put upon it, he gave the government to Achaemenes, who was his own brother, and son to Darius. This Achaemenes was afterwards slain in his government by Tnaros, the son of Psammetichus, a Libyan.

After Egypt was subdued, Xerxes, being about to take in hand the expedition against Athens, called together an assembly of the noblest Persians, to learn their opinions, and to lay before them his own designs. So, when the men were met, the king spoke thus to them:

"Persians, I shall not be the first to bring in among you a new custom —I shall but follow one which has come down to us from our forefathers. Never yet, as our old men assure me, has our race reposed itself, since the time when Cyrus overcame Astyages, and so we Persians wrested the sceptre from the Medes. Now in all this God guides us, and we, obeying his guidance, prosper greatly. What need have I to tell you of the deeds of Cyrus and Cambyses, and my own father Darius, how many nations they conquered, and added to our dominions? You know right well what great things they achieved. But for myself, I will say, that from the day on which I mounted the throne, I have not ceased to consider by what means I may rival those who have preceded me in this post of honour, and increase the power of Persia as much as any of them. And truly I have pondered upon this, until at last I have found out a way whereby we may at once win glory, and likewise get possession of a land which is as large and as rich as our own—nay, which is even more varied in the fruits it bears—while at the same time we obtain satisfaction and re- venge. For this cause I have now called you together, that I may make known to you what I design to do. My intent is to throw a bridge over the Hellespont and march an army through Europe against Greece, that thereby I may obtain vengeance from the Athenians for the wrongs com- mitted by them against the Persians and against my father. Your own eyes saw the preparations of Darius against these men; but death came upon him, and balked his hopes of revenge. In his behalf, therefore, and in behalf of all the Persians, I undertake the war, and pledge myself not to rest till I have taken and burnt Athens, which has dared, unprovoked, to injure me and my father. Long since they came to Asia with Aristagoras of Miletus, who was one of our slaves, and entering Sardis, burnt its temples and its sacred groves; again, more lately, when we made a landing upon their coast under Datis and Artaphernes, how roughly they handled us you do not need to be told. For these reasons, therefore, I am bent upon this war; and I see likewise therewith united no few advantages. Once let us subdue this people, and those neighbours of theirs who hold the land of Pelops the Phrygian, and we shall extend the Persian territory as far as God's heaven reaches. The sun will then shine on no land beyond our borders; for I will pass through Europe from one end to the other, and with your aid make of all the lands which it contains one country. For thus, if what I hear be true, affairs stand: The nations whereof I have spoken, once swept away, there is no city, no country left in all the world, which will venture so much as to withstand us in arms. By this course then we shall bring all mankind under our yoke, alike those who are guilty and those who are innocent of doing us wrong. For yourselves, if you wish to please me, do as follows: When I announce the time for the army to meet together, hasten to the muster with a good will, every one of you; and know that to the man who brings with him the most gallant array I will give the gifts which our people consider the most honourable. This then is what you have to do. But to show that I am not self-willed in this matter I lay the business before you, and give you full leave to speak your minds upon it openly."

Xerxes, having so spoken, held his peace. . . .

The other Persians were silent, for all feared to raise their voice against the plan proposed to them. But Artabanus, the son of Hystaspes, and uncle of Xerxes, trusting to his relationship, was bold to speak:

"O king, it is impossible, if no more than one opinion is uttered, to make choice of the best: a man is forced then to follow whatever advice may have been given him; but if opposite speeches are delivered, then choice can be exercised. In like manner pure gold is not recognised by itself; but when we test it along with baser ore, we perceive which is the better. I counselled your father, Darius, who was my own brother, not to attack the Scyths, a race of people who had no town in their whole land. He thought however to subdue those wandering tribes, and would not listen to me, but marched an army against them, and before he returned home lost many of his bravest warriors. You are about, O king, to attack a people far superior to the Scyths, a people distinguished above others both by land and sea. It is fit therefore that I should tell you what danger you incur hereby. You say that you will bridge the Hellespont, and lead your troops through Europe against Greece. Now suppose some disaster befall you by land or sea, or by both. It may be even so, for the men are reputed valiant. Indeed one may measure their prowess from what they have already done; for when Datis and Artaphernes led their huge army against Attica, the Athenians singly defeated them. But grant they are not successful on both elements. Still, if they man their ships, and defeating us by sea, sail to the Hellespont, and there destroy our bridge, that, sire, were a fearful hazard. And here it is not by my own mother wit alone that I conjecture what will happen, but I remember how narrowly we escaped disaster once, when your father, after throwing bridges over the Thracian Bosporus and the Ister, marched against the Scythians, and they tried every sort of prayer to induce the Ionians, who had charge of the bridge over the Ister, to break the passage. On that day, if Histiaeus, the King of Miletus, had sided with the other princes, and not set himself to oppose their views, the empire of the Persians would have come to nought. Surely a dreadful thing is this even to hear said, that the king's fortunes depended wholly on one man.

"Think then no more of incurring so great a danger when no need presses, but follow the advice I tender. Break up this meeting, and when you have well considered the matter with yourself, and settled what you will do, declare to us your resolve. I know not of aught in the world that so profits a man as taking good counsel with himself; for even if things fall out against one's hopes, still one has counselled well, though fortune has made the counsel of no effect: whereas if a man counsels ill and luck follows, he has gotten a windfall, but his counsel is none the less silly. See how god with his lightning always smites the bigger animals, and will not suffer them to wax insolent, while those of a lesser bulk chafe him not. How likewise his bolts fall ever on the highest houses and the tallest trees? So plainly does he love to bring down everything that exalts itself. Thus often a mighty host is discomfited by a few men, when god in his jealousy sends fear or storm from heaven, and they perish in a way unworthy of them. For god allows no one to have high thoughts but himself. Again, hurry always brings about disasters, from which huge sufferings are wont to arise; but in delay lie many advantages, not apparent (it may be) at first sight, but such as in course of time are seen of all. Such then is my counsel, O king.

"And you, Mardonius, son of Gobryas, forbear to speak foolishly concerning the Greeks, who are men that ought not to be lightly esteemed by us. For while you revile the Greeks, you encourage the king to lead his own troops against them; and this, as it seems to me, is what you are specially striving to accomplish. Heaven grant you succeed not in your wish! For slander is of all evils the most terrible. In it two men do wrong, and one man has wrong done to him. The slanderer does wrong, for he abuses a man behind his back; and the hearer, for he believes what he has not searched into thoroughly. The man slandered in his absence suffers wrong at the hands of both; for one brings against him a false charge, and the other thinks him an evil-doer. If, however, it must needs be that we go to war with this people, at least allow the king to abide at home in Persia. Then let us both stake our children on the issue, and you choose out your men, and taking with you whatever number of troops you like, lead forth our armies to battle. If things go well for the king, as you say they will, let me and my children be put to death; but if they fall out as I prophesy, let your children suffer, and you too, if you come back alive. But should you refuse this wager, and still resolve to march an army against Greece, sure I am that some of those whom you leave behind you here will one day receive the sad tidings, that Mardonius has brought a great disaster upon the Persian people, and lies a prey to dogs and birds somewhere in the land of the Athenians, or else in that of the Lacedae-monians; unless indeed you have perished sooner by the way, experienc-ing in your own person the might of those men on whom you would induce the king to make war."

Thus Artabanus spoke. But Xerxes, full of wrath, replied to him:

"Artabanus, you are my father's brother—that shall save you from receiving the proper reward for your silly words. One shame however I will lay upon you, coward and faint-hearted as you are—you shall not come with me to fight these Greeks, but shall tarry here with the women. Without your aid I will accomplish all of which I spoke. For let me not be thought the child of Darius, the son of Hystaspes, the son of Arsames, the son of Ariaramnes, the son of Teispes, nor of Cyrus, the son of Cam-byses, the son of Teispes, the son of Achaemenes, if I take not vengeance on the Athenians. Full well I know that, were we to remain at rest, yet would not they, but would most certainly invade our country, if at least it be right to judge from what they have already done; for, remember, it was they who fired Sardis and attacked Asia. So now retreat is on both sides impossible, and the choice lies between doing and suffering injury; either our empire must pass under the dominion of the Greeks, or their land become the prey of the Persians; for there is no middle course left in this quarrel. It is right then that we, who have in times past received wrong, should now avenge it, and that I should thereby discover, what that great risk is, which I run in marching against these men—men whom Pelops the Phrygian, a vassal of my forefathers, subdued so ut-terly, that to this day both the land, and the people who dwell therein, alike bear the name of the conqueror." . . .

And so Xerxes gathered together his host, ransacking every corner of the continent.

Reckoning from the recovery of Egypt, Xerxes spent four full years in collecting his host, and making ready all things that were needful for his soldiers. It was not till the close of the fifth year that he set forth on his march, accompanied by a mighty multitude. For of all the armaments whereof any mention has reached us, this was by far the greatest; insomuch that no other expedition compared to this seems of any account, neither that which Darius undertook against the Scythians, nor the expedition of the Scythians (which the attack of Darius was designed to avenge), when they, being in pursuit of the Cimmerians, fell upon the Median territory, and subdued and held for a time almost the whole of Upper Asia; nor, again, that of the Atreidae against Troy, of which we hear in story; nor that of the Mysians and Teucrians, which was still earlier, wherein these nations crossed the Bosporus into Europe, and, after conquering all Thrace, pressed forward till they came to the Ionian sea, while southward they reached as far as the river Peneus.

All these expeditions, and others, if such there were, are as nothing compared with this. For was there a nation in all Asia which Xerxes did not bring with him against Greece? Or was there a river, except those of unusual size, which sufficed for his troops to drink? One nation furnished ships; another was arrayed among the foot-soldiers; a third had to supply horses; a fourth, transports for the horse and men likewise for the service; a fifth, ships of war towards the bridges; a sixth, ships and provisions.

And in the first place, because the former fleet had met with so great a disaster about Athos, preparations were made, for three years, in that quarter. . . .

Where it quits Phrygia and enters Lydia the road separates; the way on the left leads into Caria, while that on the right conducts to Sardis. If you follow this route, you must cross the Maeander, and then pass by the city Callatebus, where the men live who make honey out of wheat and the fruit of the tamarisk. Xerxes, who chose this way, found here a plane-tree so beautiful, that he presented it with golden ornaments, and put it under the care of one of his Immortals. The day after, he entered the Lydian capital.

Here his first care was to send off heralds into Greece, to demand earth and water, and to require that preparations should be made everywhere to feast the king. To Athens indeed and to Sparta he sent no such demand; but these cities excepted, his messengers went everywhere. Now the reason why he sent for earth and water to states which had already refused, was this: he thought that although they had refused when Darius made the demand, they would now be too frightened to venture to refuse. So he sent his heralds, wishing to know for certain how it would be.

Xerxes, after this, made preparations to advance to Abydos, where the bridge across the Hellespont from Asia to Europe was lately finished. Midway between Sestos and Madytus in the Hellespontine Chersonese, and right over against Abydos, there is a rocky tongue of land which runs out for some distance into the sea. This is the place where no long time afterwards the Greeks under Xanthippus, the son of Ariphron, took Artayctes the Persian, who was at that time governor of Sestos, and nailed him living to a plank. He was the Artayctes who brought women into the temple of Protesilaus at Elaeus, and there was guilty of most unholy deeds.

Towards this tongue of land then, the men to whom the business was assigned, carried out a double bridge from Abydos; and while the Phoenicians constructed one line with cables of white flax, the Egyptians in the other used ropes made of papyrus. Now it is about a mile across from Abydos to the opposite coast. When, therefore, the channel had been bridged successfully, it happened that a great storm arising broke the whole work to pieces, and destroyed all that had been done.

So when Xerxes heard of it, he was full of wrath, and straightway gave orders that the Hellespont should receive 300 lashes, and that a pair of fetters should be cast into it. Nay, I have even heard it said, that he bade the branders take their irons and therewith brand the Hellespont. It is certain that he commanded those who scourged the waters to utter, as they lashed them, these barbarian and wicked words: "Thou bitter water, thy lord lays on thee this punishment because thou hast wronged him without a cause, having suffered no evil at his hands. Verily King Xerxes will cross thee, whether thou wilt or no. Well dost thou deserve that no man should honour thee with sacrifice; for thou art of a truth a treacherous and unsavoury river." While the sea was thus punished by his orders, he likewise commanded that the overseers of the work should lose their heads.

Then they, whose business it was, executed the unpleasing task laid upon them. . . .

After Xerxes had thus spoken, and had sent Artabanus away to return to Susa, he summoned before him all the Persians of most repute, and when they appeared, addressed them in these words, "Persians, I have brought you together because I wished to exhort you to behave bravely, and not to sully with disgrace the former achievements of the Persian people, which are very great and famous. Rather let us, one and all, singly and jointly, exert ourselves to the uttermost; for the matter wherein we are engaged concerns the common weal. Strain every nerve, then, I beseech you, in this war. Brave warriors are the men we march against, if report says true; and such that, if we conquer them, there is not a people in all the world which will venture thereafter to withstand our arms. And now let us offer prayers to the gods who watch over the welfare of Persia, and then cross the channel."

All that day the preparations for the passage continued; and on the morrow they burned all kinds of spices upon the bridges, and strewed the way with myrtle-boughs, while they waited anxiously for the sun, which they hoped to see as he rose. And now the sun appeared; and Xerxes took a golden goblet and poured from it a libation into the sea, praying with his face turned to the sun that no misfortune might befall him such as to hinder his conquest of Europe, until he had penetrated to its uttermost boundaries. After he had prayed, he cast the golden cup into the Helles-pont, and with it a golden bowl, and a Persian sword of the kind which they call acinaces. I cannot say for certain whether it was as an offering to the sun-god that he threw these things into the deep, or whether he repented of having scourged the Hellespont, and thought by his gifts to make amends to the sea for what he had done.

When, however, his offerings were made, the army began to cross; and the foot-soldiers, with the horsemen, passed over by one of the bridges—that (namely) which lay towards the Euxine—while the beasts of burden and the camp-followers passed by the other, which looked on the Aegean. Foremost went the Ten Thousand Persians, all wearing garlands upon their heads; and after them a mixed multitude of many nations. These crossed upon the first day.

On the next day the horsemen began the passage; and with them went the soldiers who carried their spears with the point downwards, garlanded like the Ten Thousand; then came the sacred horses and the sacred chariot; next Xerxes with his lancers and the thousand horse; then the rest of the army. At the same time the ships sailed over to the opposite shore. According, however, to another account which I have heard, the king crossed the last.

As soon as Xerxes had reached the European side, he stood to con-template his army as they crossed under the lash. And the crossing continued during seven days and seven nights, without rest or pause. It is said that here, after Xerxes had made the passage, a Hellespon-tian exclaimed, "Why, O Zeus, do you, in the likeness of a Persian man, and with the name of Xerxes instead of your own, lead the whole race of mankind to the destruction of Greece? It would have been as easy for you to destroy it without their aid!" . . .

What the exact number of the troops of each nation was I cannot say with certainty—for it is not mentioned by any one—but the whole land army together was found to amount to 1,700,000 men. The man-ner in which the numbering took place was the following. A body of 10,000 men was brought to a certain place, and the men were made to stand as close together as possible; after which a circle was drawn around them, and the men were let go: then where the circle had been, a fence was built about the height of a man's middle; and the enclosure was filled continually with fresh troops, till the whole army had in this way been numbered. When the numbering was over, the troops were drawn up according to their several nations. . . .

King Xerxes had sent no heralds either to Athens or Sparta to ask earth and water, for a reason which I will now relate. When Darius some time before sent messengers for the same purpose, they were thrown, at Athens, into the pit of punishment, at Sparta into a well, and bidden to take therefrom earth and water for themselves, and carry it to their king. On this account Xerxes did not send to ask them. What calamity came upon the Athenians to punish them for their treatment of the heralds I cannot say, unless it were the laying waste of their city and territory; but that I believe was not on account of this crime.

On the Lacedaemonians, however, the wrath of Talthybius, Agamemnon's herald, fell with violence. Talthybius has a temple at Sparta, and his descendants, who are called Talthybiadae, still live there, and have the privilege of being the only persons who discharge the office of herald. When therefore the Spartans had done the deed of which we speak, the victims at their sacrifices failed to give good tokens; and this failure lasted for a very long time. Then the Spartans were troubled, and regarding what had befallen them as a grievous calamity, they held frequent assemblies of the people, and made proclamation through the town, "Was any Lacedaemonian willing to give his life for Sparta?" Upon this two Spartans, Sperthias, the son of Aneristus, and Bulis, the son of Nicolaus, both men of noble birth, and among the wealthiest in the place, came forward and freely offered themselves as an atonement to Xerxes for the heralds of Darius slain at Sparta. So the Spartans sent them away to the Medes to undergo death.

Nor is the courage which these men hereby displayed alone worthy of wonder, but so likewise are the following speeches which were made by them. On their road to Susa they presented themselves before Hydarnes. This Hydarnes was a Persian by birth, and had the command of all the nations that dwelt along the sea-coast of Asia. He accordingly showed them hospitality, and invited them to a banquet, where, as they feasted, he said to them, "Men of Lacedaemon, why will you not consent to be friends with the king? You have but to look at me and my fortune to see that the king knows well how to honour merit. In like manner you yourselves, were you to make your submission to him, would receive at his hands, seeing that he deems you men of merit, some government in Greece."

"Hydarnes," they answered, "you are a one-sided counsellor. You have experience of half the matter, but the other half is beyond your knowledge. A slave's life you understand, but never having tasted liberty, you cannot tell whether it be sweet or no. Had you known what freedom is, you would have bidden us fight for it, not with the spear only, but with the battle-axe."

So they answered Hydarnes.

And afterwards, when they came to Susa into the king's presence, and the guards ordered them to fall down and do obeisance, and went so far as to use force to compel them, they refused, and said they would never do any such thing, even were their heads thrust down to the ground, for it was not their custom to worship men, and they had not come to Persia for that purpose. So they fought off the ceremony; and having done so, addressed the king in words much like the following, "O King of the Medes, the Lacedaemonians have sent us hither, in the place of those heralds of yours who were slain in Sparta, to make atonement to you on their account."

Then Xerxes answered with true greatness of soul that he would not act like the Lacedaemonians, who, by killing the heralds, had broken the laws which all men hold in common. As he had blamed such conduct in them, he would never be guilty of it himself. And besides, he did not wish, by putting the two men to death, to free the Lacedaemonians from the stain of their former outrage.

This conduct on the part of the Spartans caused the anger of Talthybius to cease for a while, notwithstanding that Sperthias and Bulis returned home alive. But many years afterwards it awoke once more, as the Lacedaemonians themselves declare, during the war between the Peloponnesians and the Athenians. In my judgment this was a case wherein the hand of heaven was most plainly manifest. That the wrath of Talthybius should have fallen upon ambassadors, and not slacked till it had full vent, so much justice required; but that it should have come upon the sons of the very men who were sent up to the Persian king on its account—upon Nicolaus, the son of Bulis, and Aneristus, the son of Sperthias (the same who carried off fishermen from Tiryns, when cruising in a well-manned merchant-ship), this does seem to me to be plainly a supernatural circumstance. Yet certain it is that these two men, having been sent to Asia as ambassadors by the Lacedaemonians, were betrayed by Sitalces, the son of Tereus, king of Thrace, and Nymphodorus, the son of Pythes, a native of Abdera, and being made prisoners at Bisanthe, upon the Hellespont, were conveyed to Attica, and there put to death by the Athenians, at the same time as Aristeas, the son of Adeimantus, the Corinthian. All this happened, however, very many years after the expedition of Xerxes.

To return, however, to my main subject, the expedition of the Persian king, though it was in name directed against Athens, threatened really the whole of Greece. And of this the Greeks were aware some time before, but they did not all view the matter in the same light. Some of them had given the Persian earth and water, and were bold on this account, deeming themselves thereby secured against suffering hurt from the bar-

barian army; while others, who had refused compliance, were thrown
into extreme alarm. For whereas they considered all the ships in Greece
too few to engage the enemy, it was plain that the greater number of
states would take no part in the war, but warmly favoured the Medes.

And here I feel constrained to deliver an opinion, which most men, I
know, will dislike, but which, as it seems to me to be true, I am determined not to withhold. Had the Athenians, from fear of the approaching
danger, quitted their country, or had they without quitting it submitted
to the power of Xerxes, there would certainly have been no attempt to
resist the Persians by sea; in which case, the course of events by land
would have been the following. Though the Peloponnesians might have
carried ever so many breastworks across the Isthmus, yet their allies
would have fallen off from the Lacedaemonians, not by voluntary desertion, but because town after town must have been taken by the fleet of
the barbarians; and so the Lacedaemonians would at last have stood
alone, and, standing alone, would have displayed prodigies of valour, and
died nobly. Either they would have done thus, or else, before it came to
that extremity, seeing one Greek state after another embrace the cause
of the Medes, they would have come to terms with King Xerxes; and thus,
either way Greece would have been brought under Persia. For I cannot
understand of what possible use the walls across the Isthmus could have
been, if the king had had the mastery of the sea. If then a man should
now say that the Athenians were the saviours of Greece, he would not
exceed the truth. For they truly held the scales, and whichever side they
espoused must have carried the day. They too it was who, when they had
determined to maintain the freedom of Greece, roused up that portion of
the Greek nation which had not gone over to the Medes, and so, next to
the gods, they repulsed the invader. Even the terrible oracles which
reached them from Delphi, and struck fear into their hearts, failed to
persuade them to fly from Greece. They had the courage to remain faithful to their land, and await the coming of the foe. . . .

King Xerxes pitched his camp in the region of Malis called Trachinia,
while on their side the Greeks occupied the straits. These straits the
Greeks in general call Thermopylae (the Hot Gates); but the natives and
those who dwell in the neighbourhood, call them Pylae (the Gates). Here
then the two armies took their stand; the one master of all the region
lying north of Trachis, the other of the country extending southward of
that place to the verge of the continent.

The Greeks who at this spot awaited the coming of Xerxes were the
following: From Sparta, 300 men-at-arms; from Arcadia, 1,000 Tegeans
and Mantineans, 500 of each people; 120 Orchomenians, from the Ar-
cadian Orchomenus; and 1,000 from other cities: from Corinth, 400 men;
from Phlius, 200; and from Mycenae eighty. Such was the number from

the Peloponnese. There were also present, from Boeotia, 700 Thespians
and 400 Thebans.

Besides these troops, the Locrians of Opus and the Phocians had obeyed
the call of their countrymen, and sent, the former all the force they had,
the latter 1,000 men. For envoys had gone from the Greeks at Thermopylae among the Locrians and Phocians, to call on them for assistance, and to say, "They were themselves but the vanguard of the host,
sent to precede the main body, which might every day be expected to
follow them. The sea was in good keeping, watched by the Athenians, the
Aeginetans, and the rest of the fleet. There was no cause why they should
fear; for after all the invader was not a god but a man; and there never
had been, and never would be, a man who was not liable to misfortunes
from the very day of his birth, and those greater in proportion to his own
greatness. The assailant therefore, being only a mortal, must needs fall
from his glory." Thus urged, the Locrians and the Phocians had come
with their troops to Trachis.

The various nations had each captains of their own under whom they
served; but the one to whom all especially looked up, and who had the
command of the entire force, was the Lacedaemonian, Leonidas. . . .

The force with Leonidas was sent forward by the Spartans in advance
of their main body, that the sight of them might encourage the allies to
fight, and hinder them from going over to the Medes, as it was likely they
might have done had they seen Sparta backward. They intended presently, when they had celebrated the Carneian festival, which was what
now kept them at home, to leave a garrison in Sparta, and hasten in full
force to join the army. The rest of the allies also intended to act similarly;
for it happened that the Olympic festival fell exactly at this same period.
None of them looked to see the contest at Thermopylae decided so
speedily; wherefore they were content to send forward a mere advanced
guard. Such accordingly were the intentions of the allies.

The Greek forces at Thermopylae, when the Persian army drew near
to the entrance of the pass, were seized with fear, and a coucil was held
to consider about a retreat. It was the wish of the Peloponnesians generally that the army should fall back upon the Peloponnese, and there
guard the Isthmus. But Leonidas, who saw with what indignation the
Phocians and Locrians heard of this plan, gave his voice for remaining
where they were, while they sent envoys to the several cities to ask for
help, since they were too few to make a stand against an army like that
of the Medes.

While this debate was going on, Xerxes sent a mounted spy to observe
the Greeks, and note how many they were, and what they were doing. He
had heard, before he came out of Thessaly, that a few men were assembled at this place, and that at their head were certain Lacedaemonians,

under Leonidas, a descendant of Heracles. The horseman rode up to the camp, and looked about him, but did not see the whole army; for such as were on the further side of the wall (which had been rebuilt and was now carefully guarded) it was not possible for him to behold; but he observed those on the outside, who were emcamped in front of the rampart. It chanced that at this time the Lacedaemonians held the outer guard, and were seen by the spy, some of them engaged in gymnastic exercises, others combing their long hair. At this the spy greatly marvelled, but he counted their number, and when he had taken accurate note of everything, he rode back quietly; for no one pursued after him, or paid any heed to his visit. So he returned, and told Xerxes all that he had seen.

Upon this, Xerxes, who had no means of surmising the truth—namely, that the Spartans were preparing to do or die manfully—but thought it laughable that they should be engaged in such employments, sent and called to his presence Demaratus the son of Ariston, who still remained with the army. When he appeared, Xerxes told him all that he had heard, and questioned him concerning the news, since he was anxious to understand the meaning of such behavior on the part of the Spartans. Then Demaratus said, "I spoke to you, O King, concerning these men long since, when we had but just begun our march upon Greece; you, however, only laughed at my words, when I told you of all this, which I saw would come to pass. Earnestly do I struggle at all times to speak truth to you, sire; and now listen to it once more. These men have come to dispute the pass with us, and it is for this that they are now making ready. It is their custom, when they are about to hazard their lives, to adorn their heads with care. Be assured, however, that if you can subdue the men who are here and the Lacedaemonians who remain in Sparta, there is no other nation in all the world which will venture to lift a hand in their defence. You have now to deal with the first kingdom and town in Greece, and with the bravest men."

Then Xerxes, to whom what Demaratus said seemed altogether to surpass belief, asked further, "How is it possible for so small an army to contend with his?"

"O King," Demaratus answered, "let me be treated as a liar, if matters fall not out as I say."

But Xerxes was not persuaded any the more. Four whole days he suffered to go by, expecting that the Greeks would run away. When, however, he found on the fifth that they were not gone, thinking that their firm stand was mere impudence and recklessness, he grew wroth, and sent against them the Medes and Cissians, with orders to take them alive and bring them into his presence. Then the Medes rushed forward and charged the Greeks, but fell in vast numbers: others however took the places of the slain, and would not be beaten off, though they suffered terrible losses. In this way it became clear to all, and especially to the king, that though he had plenty of combatants, he had but very few warriors. The struggle, however, continued during the whole day.

Then the Medes, having met so rough a reception, withdrew from the fight; and their place was taken by the band of Persians under Hydarnes, whom the king called Immortals: they, it was thought, would soon finish the business. But when they joined battle with the Greeks, it was with no better success than the Median detachment—things went much as before —the two armies fighting in a narrow space, and the barbarians using shorter spears than the Greeks, and having no advantage from their numbers. The Lacedaemonians fought in a way worthy of note, and showed themselves far more skilful in fight than their adversaries, often turning their backs, and making as though they were all flying away, on which the barbarians would rush after them with much noise and shouting, when the Spartans at their approach would wheel round and face their pursuers, in this way destroying vast numbers of the enemy. Some Spartans likewise fell in these encounters, but only a very few. At last the Persians, finding that all their efforts to gain the pass availed nothing, and that whether they attacked by divisions or in any other way, it was to no purpose, withdrew to their own quarters.

During these assaults, it is said that Xerxes, who was watching the battle, thrice leaped from the throne on which he sat, in terror for his army.

Next day the combat was renewed, but with no better success on the part of the barbarians. The Greeks were so few that the barbarians hoped to find them disabled, by reason of their wounds, from offering any further resistance; and so they once more attacked them. But the Greeks were drawn up in detachments according to their cities, and bore the brunt of the battle in turns, all except the Phocians, who had been stationed on the mountain to guard the pathway. So when the Persians found no difference between that day and the preceding, they again retired to their quarters.

Now, as the king was at a loss, and knew not how he should deal with the emergency, Ephialtes, the son of Eurydemus, a man of Malis, came to him and was admitted to a conference. Stirred by the hope of receiving a rich reward at the king's hands, he had come to tell him of the pathway which led across the mountain to Thermopylae; by which disclosure he brought destruction on the band of Greeks who had there withstood the barbarians. . . . I leave his name on record as that of the man who did the deed.

Great was the joy of Xerxes on this occasion; and as he approved highly of the enterprise which Ephialtes undertook to accomplish, he forthwith sent upon the errand Hydarnes, and the Persians under him. The troops left the camp about the time of the lighting of the lamps. The pathway along which they went was first discovered by the Malians of these parts, who soon afterwards led the Thessalians by it to attack the Phocians, at the time when the Phocians fortified the pass with a wall, and so put themselves under covert from danger. And ever since, the path has always been put to an ill use by the Malians. . . .

The Persians took this path, and crossing the Asopus, continued their march through the whole of the night, having the mountains of Oeta on their right hand, and on their left those of Trachis. At dawn of day they found themselves close to the summit. Now the hill was guarded, as I have already said, by 1,000 Phocian men-at-arms, who were placed there to defend the pathway, and at the same time to secure their own country. They had been given the guard of the mountain path, while the other Greeks defended the pass below, because they had volunteered for the service, and had pledged themselves to Leonidas to maintain the post.

The ascent of the Persians became known to the Phocians in the following manner: During all the time that they were making their way up, the Greeks remained unconscious of it, inasmuch as the whole mountain was covered with groves of oak; but it happened that the air was very still, and the leaves which the Persians stirred with their feet made, as it was likely they would, a loud rustling, whereupon the Phocians jumped up and flew to seize their arms. In a moment the barbarians came in sight, and perceiving men arming themselves, were greatly amazed; for they had fallen in with an enemy when they expected no opposition. Hydarnes, alarmed at the sight, and fearing lest the Phocians might be Lacedaemonians, inquired of Ephialtes to what nation these troops belonged. Ephialtes told him the exact truth, whereupon he arrayed his Persians for battle. The Phocians, galled by the showers of arrows to which they were exposed, and imagining themselves the special object of the Persian attack, fled hastily to the crest of the mountain, and there made ready to meet death; but while their mistake continued, the Persians, with Ephialtes and Hydarnes, not thinking it worth their while to delay on account of Phocians, passed on and descended the mountain with all possible speed.

The Greeks at Thermopylae received the first warning of the destruction which the dawn would bring on them from the seer Megistias, who read their fate in the victims as he was sacrificing. After this deserters came in, and brought the news that the Persians were marching round by the hills: it was still night when these men arrived. Last of all, the scouts came running down from the heights, and brought in the same accounts, when the day was just beginning to break. Then the Greeks held a council to consider what they should do, and here opinions were divided: some were strong against quitting their post, while others contended to the contrary. So when the council had broken up, part of the troops departed and went their ways homeward to their several states; part however resolved to remain, and to stand by Leonidas to the last.

It is said that Leonidas himself sent away the troops who departed, because he tendered their safety, but thought it unseemly that either he or his Spartans should quit the post which they had been especially sent to guard. For my own part, I incline to think that Leonidas gave the order, because he perceived the allies to be out of heart and unwilling to encounter the danger to which his own mind was made up. He therefore commanded them to retreat, but said that he himself could not draw back with honour; knowing that, if he stayed, glory awaited him, and that Sparta in that case would not lose her prosperity. For when the Spartans, at the very beginning of the war, sent to consult the oracle concerning it, the answer which they received from the priestess was that either Sparta must be overthrown by the barbarians, or one of her kings must perish. The prophecy was delivered in hexameter verse, and ran thus:

> Oh! ye men who dwell in the streets of broad Lacedaemon,
> Either your glorious town shall be sacked by the children of Perseus,
> Or, in exchange, must all through the whole Laconian country
> Mourn for the loss of a king, descendant of great Heracles.
> He cannot be withstood by the courage of bulls or of lions,
> Strive as they may; he is mighty as Zeus; there is nought that shall stay him,
> Till he have got for his prey your king, or your glorious city.

The remembrance of this answer, I think, and the wish to secure the whole glory for the Spartans, caused Leonidas to send the allies away. This is more likely than that they quarrelled with him, and took their departure in such unruly fashion. . . .

So the allies, when Leonidas ordered them to retire, obeyed him and forthwith departed. Only the Thespians and the Thebans remained with the Spartans; and of these the Thebans were kept back by Leonidas as hostages, very much against their will. The Thespians, on the contrary, stayed entirely of their own accord, refusing to retreat, and declaring that they would not forsake Leonidas and his followers. So they abode with the Spartans, and died with them. Their leader was Demophilus, the son of Diadromes.

At sunrise Xerxes made libations, after which he waited until the time when the market-place is wont to fill, and then began his advance. Ephialtes had instructed him thus, as the descent of the mountain is much quicker, and the distance much shorter, than the way round the hills, and the ascent. So the barbarians under Xerxes began to draw nigh; and the Greeks under Leonidas, as they now went forth determined to die, advanced much further than on previous days, until they reached the more open portion of the pass. Hitherto they had held their station within the wall, and from this had gone forth to fight at the point where the pass was the narrowest. Now they joined battle beyond the defile, and carried slaughter among the barbarians, who fell in heaps. Behind them the captains of the squadrons, armed with whips, urged their men forward with continual blows. Many were thrust into the sea, and there perished; a still greater number were trampled to death by their own soldiers; no one heeded the dying. For the Greeks, reckless of their own safety and desperate, since they knew that, as the mountain had been crossed, their destruction was nigh at hand, exerted themselves with the most furious valour against the barbarians.

By this time the spears of the greater number were all shivered, and with their swords they hewed down the ranks of the Persians; and here, as they strove, Leonidas fell fighting bravely, together with many other famous Spartans, whose names I have taken care to learn on account of their great worthiness, as indeed I have those of all the 300. There fell too at the same time very many famous Persians: among them, two sons of Darius, Abrocomes and Hyperanthes, his children by Phratagune, the daughter of Artanes. Artanes was brother of King Darius, being a son of Hystaspes, the son of Arsames; and when he gave his daughter to the king, he made him heir likewise of all his substance; for she was his only child.

Thus two brothers of Xerxes here fought and fell. And now there arose a fierce struggle between the Persians and the Lacedaemonians over the body of Leonidas, in which the Greeks four times drove back the enemy, and at last by their great bravery succeeded in bearing off the body. This combat was scarcely ended when the Persians with Ephialtes approached; and the Greeks, informed that they drew nigh, made a change in the manner of their fighting. Drawing back into the narrowest part of the pass, and retreating even behind the cross wall, they posted themselves upon a hillock, where they stood all drawn up together in one close body, except only the Thebans. The hillock whereof I speak is at the entrance of the straits, where the stone lion stands which was set up in honour of Leonidas. Here they defended themselves to the last, such as still had swords using them, and the others resisting with their hands and teeth; till the barbarians, who in part had pulled down the wall and attacked them in front, in part had gone round and now encircled them upon every side, overwhelmed and buried the remnant left beneath showers of missile weapons.

Thus nobly did the whole body of Lacedaemonians and Thespians behave, but nevertheless one man is said to have distinguished himself above all the rest, to wit, Dieneces the Spartan. A speech which he made before the Greeks engaged the Medes, remains on record. One of the

Trachinians told him, "Such was the number of the barbarians, that when they shot forth their arrows the sun would be darkened by their multitude." Dieneces, not at all frightened at these words, but making light of the Median numbers, answered, "Our Trachinian friend brings us excellent tidings. If the Medes darken the sun, we shall have our fight in the shade." Other sayings too of a like nature are said to have been left on record by this same person. . . .

The slain were buried where they fell; and in their honour, nor less in honour of those who died before Leonidas sent the allies away, an inscription was set up, which said:

> Here did four thousand men from Pelops' land
> Against three hundred myriads bravely stand.

This was in honour of all. Another was for the Spartans alone:

> Go, stranger, and to Lacedaemon tell
> That here, obeying her behests, we fell.

This was for the Lacedaemonians. . . .

Another of the 300 is . . . said to have survived the battle, a man named Pantites, whom Leonidas had sent on an embassy into Thessaly. He, they say, on his return to Sparta, found himself in such disgrace that he hanged himself.

The Thebans under the command of Leontiades remained with the Greeks, and fought against the barbarians, only so long as necessity compelled them. No sooner did they see victory inclining to the Persians, and the Greeks under Leonidas hurrying with all speed towards the hillock, than they moved away from their companions, and with hands upraised advanced towards the barbarians, exclaiming, as was indeed most true, "They for their part wished well to the Medes, and had been among the first to give earth and water to the king; force alone had brought them to Thermopylae, and so they must not be blamed for the slaughter which had befallen the king's army." These words, the truth of which was attested by the Thessalians, sufficed to obtain the Thebans the grant of their lives. However, their good fortune was not without some drawback; for several of them were slain by the barbarians on their first approach; and the rest, who were the greater number, had the royal mark branded upon their bodies by the command of Xerxes, Leontiades, their captain, being the first to suffer. (This man's son, Eurymachus, was afterwards slain by the Plataeans, when he came with a band of 400 Thebans, and seized their city.)

Thus fought the Greeks at Thermopylae. . . .

Orders were now given to stand out to sea; and the ships proceeded towards Salamis, and took up the stations to which they were directed, without let or hindrance from the enemy. The day, however, was too far spent for them to begin the battle, since night already approached: so they prepared to engage upon the morrow. The Greeks, meanwhile, were in great distress and alarm, more especially those of the Peloponnese; who were troubled that they had been kept at Salamis to fight on behalf of the Athenian territory; and feared that, if they should suffer defeat, they would be pent up and besieged in an island, while their own country was left unprotected.

The same night the land army of the barbarians began its march towards the Peloponnese, where, however, all that was possible had been done to prevent the enemy from forcing an entry by land. As soon as ever news reached the Peloponnese, of the death of Leonidas and his companions at Thermopylae, the inhabitants flocked together from the various cities, and encamped at the Isthmus, under the command of Cleombrotus, son of Anaxandridas, and brother of Leonidas. Here their first care was to block up the Scironian way; after which it was determined in council to build a wall across the Isthmus. As the number assembled amounted to many tens of thousands, and there was not one who did not give himself to the work, it was soon finished. Stones, bricks, timber, baskets filled full of sand, were used in the building; and not a moment was lost by those who gave their aid, for they laboured without ceasing either by night or day. . . .

So the Greeks at the Isthmus toiled unceasingly as though in the greatest peril; since they never imagined that any great success would be gained by the fleet. The Greeks at Salamis, on the other hand, when they heard what the rest were about, felt greatly alarmed; but their fear was not so much for themselves, as for the Peloponnese. At first they conversed together in low tones, each man with his fellow, secretly, and marvelled at the folly shown by Eurybiades; but presently the smothered feeling broke out, and another assembly was held; whereat the old subjects provoked much talk from the speakers, one side maintaining that it was best to sail to the Peloponnese and risk battle for that, instead of abiding at Salamis and fighting for a land already taken by the enemy; while the other, which consisted of the Athenians, Aeginetans, and Megarians, was urgent to remain and have the battle fought where they were.

Then Themistocles, when he saw that the Peloponnesians would carry the vote against him, went out secretly from the council, and instructing a certain man what he should say, sent him on board a merchant ship to the fleet of the Medes. The man's name was Sicinnus; he was one of Themistocles' household slaves, and acted as tutor to his sons; in after times, when the Thespians were admitting persons to citizenship, Themistocles made him a Thespian, and a rich man to boot. The ship brought Sicinnus to the Persian fleet, and there he delivered his message to the leaders in these words:

"The Athenian commander has sent me to you without the knowledge of the other Greeks. He is a well-wisher to the king's cause, and would rather success should attend on you than on his countrymen; wherefore he bids me tell you, that fear has seized the Greeks and they are meditating a hasty flight. Now then it is open to you to achieve the best feat you ever accomplished, if only you hinder their escaping. They no longer agree among themselves, so that they will not now make any resistance —indeed you may see a fight already begun between such as favour and such as oppose your cause." The messenger, when he had thus expressed himself, departed and was seen no more.

Then the captains, believing all that the messenger had said, proceeded to land a large body of Persian troops on the islet of Psyttaleia, which lies between Salamis and the mainland; after which, about the hour of midnight, they advanced their western wing towards Salamis, so as to inclose the Greeks. At the same time the force stationed about Ceos and Cynosura moved forward, and filled the whole strait as far as Munychia with their ships. This advance was made to prevent the Greeks from escaping by flight, and to block them up in Salamis, where it was thought that vengeance might be taken upon them for the battles fought near Artemisium. The Persian troops were landed on the islet of Psyttaleia, because, as soon as the battle began, the men and wrecks were likely to be drifted thither, as the isle lay in the very path of the coming fight, and they would thus be able to save their own men and destroy those of the enemy. All these movements were made in silence, that the Greeks might have no knowledge of them; and they occupied the whole night, so that the men had no time to get their sleep.

I cannot say that there is no truth in prophecies, or feel inclined to call in question those which speak with clearness, when I think of the following:

> When they shall bridge with their ships to the sacred strand of Artemis
> Girt with the golden falchion, and eke to marine Cynosura,
> Mad hope swelling their hearts at the downfall of beautiful Athens—
> Then shall godlike Right extinguish haughty Presumption,
> Insult's furious offspring, who thinketh to overthrow all things.
> Brass with brass shall mingle, and Ares with blood shall empurple
> Ocean's waves. Then—then shall the day of Grecia's freedom
> Come from Victory fair, and Cronus' son all-seeing.

When I look to this, and perceive how clearly Bacis spoke, I neither venture myself to say anything against prophecies, nor do I approve of others impugning them.

Meanwhile, among the captains at Salamis, the strife of words grew fierce. As yet they did not know that they were encompassed, but imagined that the barbarians remained in the same places where they had seen them the day before.

In the midst of their contention, Aristides, the son of Lysimachus, who had crossed from Aegina, arrived in Salamis. He was an Athenian, and had been ostracised by the commonalty; yet I believe, from what I have heard concerning his character,that there was not in all Athens a man so worthy or so just as he. He now came to the council, and standing outside, called for Themistocles. Now Themistocles was not his friend, but his most determined enemy. However, under the pressure of the great dangers impending, Aristides forgot their feud, and called Themistocles out of the council, since he wished to confer with him. He had heard before his arrival of the impatience of the Peloponnesians to withdraw the fleet to the Isthmus. As soon therefore as Themistocles came forth, Aristides addressed him in these words, "Our rivalry at all times, and especially at the present season, ought to be a struggle, which of us shall most advantage our country. Let me then say to you, that so far as regards the departure of the Peloponnesians from this place, much talk and little will be found precisely alike. I have seen with my own eyes that which I now report; that, however much the Corinthians or Eurybiades himself may wish it, they cannot now retreat; for we are inclosed on every side by the enemy. Go in to them, and make this known."

"Your advice is excellent," answered the other, "and your tidings are also good. That which I earnestly desired to happen, your eyes have beheld accomplished. Know that what the Medes have now done was at my instance; for it was necessary, as our men would not fight here at their own free will, to make them fight whether they would or no. But come now, as you have brought the good news, go in and tell it. For if I speak to them, they will think it a feigned tale, and will not believe that the barbarians have inclosed us around. Therefore you go to them, and inform them how matters stand. If they believe you, it will be for the best; but if otherwise, it will not harm. For it is impossible that they should now flee away, if we are indeed shut in on all sides, as you say."

Then Aristides entered the assembly, and spoke to the captains: he had come, he told them, from Aegina, and had but barely escaped the blockading vessels—the Greek fleet was entirely inclosed by the ships of Xerxes—and he advised them to get themselves in readiness to resist the foe. Having said so much, he withdrew. And now another contest arose, for the greater part of the captains would not believe the tidings.

But while they still doubted, a Tenian trireme, commanded by Panaetius the son of Sosimenes, deserted from the Persians and joined the

Greeks, bringing full intelligence. For this reason the Tenians were inscribed upon the tripod at Delphi among those who overthrew the barbarians. With this ship, which deserted to their side at Salamis, and the
Lemnian vessel which came over before at Artemisium, the Greek fleet
was brought to the full number of 380 ships; otherwise it fell short by two
of that amount.

The Greeks now, not doubting what the Tenians told them, made ready
for the coming fight. At the dawn of day, all the men-at-arms were assembled together, and speeches were made to them, of which the best was
that of Themistocles; who throughout contrasted what was noble with
what was base, and bade them, in all that came within the range of man's
nature and constitution, always to make choice of the nobler part. Having
thus wound up his discourse, he told them to go at once on board their
ships, which they accordingly did; and about this time the trireme, that
had been sent to Aegina for the Aeacidae, returned; whereupon the
Greeks put to sea with all their fleet.

The fleet had scarce left the land when they were attacked by the
barbarians. At once most of the Greeks began to back water, and were
about touching the shore, when Ameinias of Pallene, one of the Athenian
captains, darted forth in front of the line, and charged a ship of the
enemy. The two vessels became entangled, and could not separate,
whereupon the rest of the fleet came up to help Ameinias, and engaged
with the Persians. Such is the account which the Athenians give of the
way in which the battle began; but the Aeginetans maintain that the
vessel which had been to Aegina for the Aeacidae, was the one that
brought on the fight. It is also reported, that a phantom in the form of
a woman appeared to the Greeks, and, in a voice that was heard from
end to end of the fleet, cheered them on to the fight; first, however, re-
buking them, and saying, "Strange men, how long are you going to back
water?" . . .

Far the greater number of the Persian ships engaged in this battle were
disabled—either by the Athenians or by the Aeginetans. For as the
Greeks fought in order and kept their line, while the barbarians were in
confusion and had no plan in anything that they did, the issue of the
battle could scarce be other than it was. Yet the Persians fought far more
bravely here than at Euboea, and indeed surpassed themselves; each did
his utmost through fear of Xerxes, for each thought that the king's eye
was upon himself.

What part the several nations, whether Greek or barbarian, took in the
combat, I am not able to say for certain; Artemisia, however, I know,
distinguished herself in such a way as raised her even higher than she
stood before in the esteem of the king. For after confusion had spread

throughout the whole of the king's fleet, and her ship was closely pursued by an Athenian trireme, she, having no way to fly, since in front of her were a number of friendly vessels, and she was nearest of all the Persians to the enemy, resolved on a measure which in fact proved her safety. Pressed by the Athenian pursuer, she bore straight against one of the ships of her own party, a Calyndian, which had Damasithymus, the Calyndian king, himself on board. I cannot say whether she had had any quarrel with the man while the fleet was at the Hellespont, or no— neither can I decide whether she of set purpose attacked his vessel, or whether it merely chanced that the Calyndian ship came in her way— but certain it is that she bore down upon his vessel and sank it, and that thereby she had the good fortune to procure herself a double advantage. For the commander of the Athenian trireme, when he saw her bear down on one of the enemy's fleet, thought immediately that her vessel was a Greek, or else had deserted from the Persians, and was now fighting on the Greek side; he therefore gave up the chase, and turned away to attack others.

Thus in the first place she saved her life by the action, and was enabled to get clear off from the battle; while further, it fell out that in the very act of doing the king an injury she raised herself to a greater height than ever in his esteem. For as Xerxes beheld the fight, he remarked (it is said) the destruction of the vessel, whereupon the bystanders observed to him, "Do you see, master, how well Artemisia fights, and how she has just sunk a ship of the enemy?" Then Xerxes asked if it were really Artemisia's doing; and they answered, "Certainly; for they knew her ensign": while all made sure that the sunken vessel belonged to the opposite side. Everything, it is said, conspired to prosper the queen—it was especially fortunate for her, that not one of those on board the Calyndian ship survived to become her accuser. Xerxes, they say, in reply to the remarks made to him, observed, "My men have behaved like women, and my women like men!" . . .

When the rout of the barbarians began, and they sought to make their escape to Phalerum, the Aeginetans, awaiting them in the channel, performed exploits worthy to be recorded. Through the whole of the confused struggle the Athenians employed themselves in destroying such ships as either made resistance or fled to shore, while the Aeginetans dealt with those which endeavoured to escape down the straits; so that the Persian vessels were no sooner clear of the Athenians than straightway they fell into the hands of the Aeginetan squadron. . . .

The Greeks who gained the greatest glory of all in the sea-fight of Salamis were the Aeginetans, and after them the Athenians. The individuals of most distinction were Polycritus the Aeginetan, and two Athenians, Eumenes of Anagyrus, and Ameinias of Pallene; the latter of

whom had pressed Artemisia so hard. And assuredly, if he had known
that the vessel carried Artemisia on board, he would never have given
over the chase till he had either succeeded in taking her, or else been
taken himself. For the Athenian captains had received special orders
touching the queen, and moreover a reward of 10,000 drachmas had been
proclaimed for any one who should make her prisoner; since there was
great indignation felt that a woman should appear in arms against
Athens. However, as I said before, she escaped; and so did some others
whose ships survived the engagement; and these were all now assembled
at the port of Phalerum. . . .

As soon as the sea-fight was ended, the Greeks drew together to Salamis
all the wrecks that were to be found in that quarter, and prepared themselves for another engagement, supposing that the king would renew the
fight with the vessels which still remained to him. Many of the wrecks
had been carried away by a westerly wind to the coast of Attica, where
they were thrown upon the strip of shore called Colias. Thus not only
were the prophecies of Bacis and Musaeus concerning this battle fulfilled
completely, but likewise, by the place to which the wrecks were drifted,
the prediction of Lysistratus, an Athenian soothsayer, uttered many
years before these events, and quite forgotten at the time by all the
Greeks, was fully accomplished. The words were:

> Then shall the sight of the oars fill Colian dames with amazement.

Now this must have happened as soon as the king was departed.

Xerxes, when he saw the extent of his loss, began to be afraid lest the
Greeks might be counselled by the Ionians, or without their advice might
determine, to sail straight to the Hellespont and break down the bridges
there; in which case he would be blocked up in Europe, and run great risk
of perishing. He therefore made up his mind to fly; but as he wished to
hide his purpose alike from the Greeks and from his own people, he set
to work to carry a mound across the channel to Salamis, and at the same
time began fastening a number of Phoenician merchant ships together,
to serve at once for a bridge and a wall. He likewise made many warlike
preparations, as if he were about to engage the Greeks once more at sea.
Now, when these things were seen, all grew fully persuaded that the king
was bent on remaining, and intended to push the war in good earnest.
Mardonius, however, was in no respect deceived; for long acquaintance
enabled him to read all the king's thoughts. Meanwhile, Xerxes, though
engaged in this way, sent off a messenger to carry intelligence of his
misfortune to Persia.

Nothing mortal travels so fast as these Persian messengers. The entire
plan is a Persian invention; and this is the method of it. Alone the whole
line of road there are men (they say) stationed with horses, in number

equal to the number of days which the journey takes, allowing a man and
horse to each day; and these men will not be hindered from accomplishing at their best speed the distance which they have to go, either by snow,
or rain, or heat, or by the darkness of night. The first rider delivers his
despatch to the second, and the second passes it to the third; and so it is
borne from hand to hand along the whole line, like the light in the
torch-race, which the Greeks celebrate to Hephaestus. The Persians give
the riding post in this manner, the name of angareion.

At Susa, on the arrival of the first message, which said that Xerxes was
the master of Athens, such was the delight of the Persians who had
remained behind, that they forthwith strewed all the streets with myrtle
boughs, and burnt incense, and fell to feasting and merriment. In like
manner, when the second message reached them, so sore was their dis-
may, that they all with one accord rent their garments, and cried aloud,
and wept and wailed without stint. They laid the blame of the disaster
on Mardonius; and their grief on the occasion was less on account of the
damage done to their ships, than owing to the alarm which they felt
about the safety of the king. Hence their trouble did not cease till Xerxes
himself, by his arrival, put an end to their fears.

(Herodotus next relates how Xerxes attempted to salvage at least some
prestige from his efforts, by "forgiving" the Athenians their trespasses and by
raising them to primacy in Greece in return for their subordination to him.)

As soon as Alexander had finished speaking, the ambassadors from
Sparta took the word and said, "We are sent here by the Lacedaemonians
to beg of you not to do a new thing in Greece, nor agree to the terms which
are offered you by the barbarian. Such conduct on the part of any of the
Greeks were alike unjust and dishonourable; but in you it would be worse
than in others, for divers reasons. It was by you that this war was kindled
at the first among us—our wishes were in no way considered; the contest
began for your territory—now the fate of Greece is involved in it. Besides,
it were surely an intolerable thing that the Athenians, who have always
hitherto been known as a nation to which many men owed their freedom,
should not become the means of bringing all other Greeks into slavery.
We feel, however, for the heavy calamities which press on you—the loss
of your harvest these two years, and the ruin in which your homes have
lain for so long a time. We offer you, therefore, on the part of the Lacedae-

monians and the allies, sustenance for your women and for the unwar-
like portion of your households, so long as the war endures. Do not be
seduced by Alexander the Macedonian, who softens down the rough
words of Mardonius. He does as is natural for him to do—a tyrant himself, he helps forward a tyrant's cause. But you, Athenians, should do
differently, at least if you be truly wise; for you should know that with
barbarians there is neither faith nor truth."

Thus the envoys spoke. After which the Athenians returned this answer to Alexander, "We know, as well as you do, that the power of the
Mede is many times greater than our own: we did not need to have that
cast in our teeth. Nevertheless we cling so to freedom that we shall offer
what resistance we may. Seek not to persuade us into making terms with
the barbarian—say what you will, you will never gain our assent. Return
rather at once, and tell Mardonius that our answer to him is this, 'So long
as the sun keeps his present course, we will never join alliance with
Xerxes. Nay, we shall oppose him unceasingly, trusting in the aid of
those gods and heroes whom he has lightly esteemed, whose houses and
whose images he has burnt with fire.' And come not again to us with
words like these; nor, thinking to do us a service, persuade us to unholy
actions. You are the guest and friend of our nation—we would not that
you should receive hurt at our hands."

Such was the answer which the Athenians gave to Alexander. To the
Spartan envoys they said, "It was natural no doubt that the Lacedaemonians should be afraid we might make terms with the barbarian; but nevertheless it was a base fear in men who knew so well of what temper and
spirit we are. Not all the gold that the whole earth contains—not the
fairest and most fertile of all lands—would bribe us to take part with the
Medes and help them to enslave our countrymen. Even could we have
brought ourselves to such a thing, there are many very powerful motives
which would now make it impossible. The first and chief of these is the
burning and destruction of our temples and the images of our gods,
which forces us to make no terms with their destroyer, but rather to
pursue him with our resentment to the uttermost. Again, there is our
common brotherhood with the Greeks: our common language, the altars
and the sacrifices of which we all partake, the common character which
we bear—did the Athenians betray all these, of a truth it would not be
well. Know then now, if you have not known it before, that while one
Athenian remains alive, we will never join alliance with Xerxes. We
thank you, however, for your forethought on our behalf, and for your
wish to give our families sustenance, now that ruin has fallen on us—the
kindness is complete on your part; but for ourselves, we will endure as
we may, and not be burdensome to you. Such then is our resolve. Be it

your care with all speed to lead out your troops; for if we surmise aright, the barbarian will not wait long before invading our territory, but will set out as soon as he learns our answer to be, that we will do none of those things which he requires of us. Now then is the time for us, before he enters Attica, to go ourselves into Boeotia, and give him battle."

When the Athenians had thus spoken, the ambassadors from Sparta departed, and returned to their own country. . . .

Thucydides

c. 456 B.C.—C. 404 B.C.

2

Thucydides has been called "the first truly critical historian of the world." It seems fitting as well as ironical that, as with "the father of history," we know very little of his life. An Athenian citizen, he was of the generation following that of Herodotus. By birth he was an aristocrat, descended from the noble Thracian family into which Miltiades, the hero of Marathon, had married. We may assume that he received a thorough education and that he was bred to serve in political and military affairs. When the Peloponnesian War broke out in 431 B.C. Thucydides was perhaps twenty-five years old. In 424 B.C. he was appointed as a general to command the Athenian forces in Thrace. The loss of Amphipolis to the enemy caused his dismissal and banishment. This forced retirement enabled him for the next twenty years to travel, to observe events and to devote himself to his *History*. He died soon after the fall of Athens in 404 B.C.

Thucydides wrote his *History of the Peloponnesian War,* as he put it, "beginning at the moment that it broke out, and believing that it would be a great war, and more worthy of relation than any that had preceded it." Although he made a distinction between the superficial and the profound causes of the war—the "real cause," he argued, was "the growth of the power of Athens, and the alarm which this inspired in Lacedaemon"—unlike Herodotus, he was not particularly concerned with them. Not causes but lessons were his object. He hoped that his *History* "will be judged useful by those inquirers who desire an exact knowledge of the past as an aid to the interpretation of the future, which in the course of human things must resemble if it does not reflect it." With this primary end in view Thucydides wrote a history utterly unlike that of Herodotus. Herodotus is expansive, Thucydides concentrates; Herodotus engages in digressions, Thucydides strictly limits his range of topics.

His subject is not nearly so much the Peloponnesian War—the epic struggle between democratic, imperial Athens and oligarchic, militaristic Sparta—

as the analysis of political power. Thucydides may thus be called "the father of *political* history." It was in the arena of politics that he saw the meaning of human effort. He believed that in understanding political events, and their social and military consequences, he could grasp the essential elements in human behavior, elements which accounted for what he saw as the cyclical movement of history. Thus he strove to focus on what was "esssential" and demonstrable: "The conclusions I have drawn from the proofs quoted may, I believe, safely be relied on." Consequently, he eschewed whenever possible descriptions of foreign lands, anecdotes about people, myths or religious practices, and any information not immediately relevant to his purpose.

Again departing from Herodotus' example, he concentrated on immediate events, on purely contemporary history. His conclusions, he wrote, "will not be disturbed either by the lays of a poet . . . or by the compositions of the chroniclers that are attractive at truth's expense; the subjects they treat of being out of the reach of evidence, and time having robbed most of them of historical value by enthroning them in the region of legend." Oral traditions, then, formed no part of his evidence. The defect in such traditions, he wrote, is that men "receive them all alike as they are delivered, without applying any critical test whatever." What Thucydides relied upon mainly was evidence supplied by eyewitnesses whom he could cross-examine and whose reports could be measured against the accounts of others. He treated his material critically and rationally, according to strict rules of admissible evidence. Indeed, part of his accomplishment as a historian lies in the rigorous standard of historical reliability he set up, an accomplishment facilitated by his purposeful attention to a narrow area of contemporary history: "And with reference to the narrative of events," he wrote, "far from permitting myself to derive it from the first source that came to hand, I did not even trust my own impressions, but it rests partly on what I saw myself, partly on what others saw for me, the accuracy of the report being always tried by the most severe and detailed tests possible."

Accuracy, relevance, and concentration on contemporary history, especially on political matters, were Thucydides' concerns and guides. Following them he wrote a *History* of his times that is characterized by critical analysis, rigorous pertinency, and a profound sense of the moral and spiritual elements that inform political affairs. He rejected as impossible any attempt at the historical investigation of events distant in time or foreign in place. In doing so he turned away from Herodotus but not from history. And we may agree with him that his historical work is "not an essay which is to win the applause of the moment, but a possession for all time."

Selected Bibliography

J. B. Bury, *The Ancient Greek Historians* (1909), names Thucydides "the first truly critical historian of the world." Bury's chapter on Thucydides is solid and

informative and may profitably be complemented by James T. Shotwell's more restrained appreciation of the historian's virtues *An Introduction to the History of History,* (1936). The claim that Thucydides was a "critical" or "scientific" historian has engendered a whole literature of its own. Among others, Francis Cornford (*Thucydides Mythistoricus,* 1907) has argued that Thucydides was on the one hand too "unscientific," in his inadequate grasp of the material or economic factors in history, and on the other much too influenced by Greek drama —the traditional tragic unfolding of events—to be upheld as one of the founders of "critical" historiography. John H. Finley, besides offering a fine introduction to the man and his *History,* convincingly answer such criticisms in his *Thucydides* (1942). Kurt von Fritz surveys and analyzes the whole "Thucydides question" in a magisterial inquiry, concluding with an encomium of Thucydides, historian (see *Die Griechische Geschichtsschreibung,* I:1, 823, 1967). Arnaldo Momigliano, *Studies in Historiography* (1966), is rich in suggestive references to Thucydides and his contribution to historiography. Of the many translations of Thucydides we have here selected from that of Richard Crawley, first published in 1874, reprinted in an Everyman's Library edition in 1910 and in a Modern Library college edition, with an introduction by John H. Finley, Jr., in 1951.

THE HISTORY OF
THE PELOPONNESIAN WAR

Thucydides, an Athenian, wrote the history of the war between the Peloponnesians and the Athenians, beginning at the moment that it broke out, and believing that it would be a great war, and more worthy of relation than any that had preceded it. This belief was not without its grounds. The preparations of both the combatants were in every department in the last state of perfection; and he could see the rest of the Hellenic race taking sides in the quarrel; those who delayed doing so at once having it in contemplation. Indeed this was the greatest movement yet known in history, not only of the Hellenes, but of a large part of the barbarian world—I had almost said of mankind. For though the events of remote antiquity, and even those that more immediately precede the war, could not from lapse of time be clearly ascertained, yet the evidences which an inquiry carried as far back as was practicable leads me to trust, all point to the conclusion that there was nothing on a great scale, either in war or in other matters.

For instance, it is evident that the country now called Hellas had in ancient times no settled population; on the contrary, migrations were of frequent occurrence, the several tribes readily abandoning their homes under the pressure of superior numbers. Without commerce, without freedom of communication either by land or sea, cultivating no more of their territory than the exigencies of life required, destitute of capital, never planting their land (for they could not tell when an invader might not come and take it all away, and when he did come they had no walls to stop him), thinking that the necessities of daily sustenance could be supplied at one place as well as another, they cared little for shifting their habitation, and consequently neither built large cities nor attained to any other form of greatness. The richest soils were always most subject to this change of masters; such as the district now called Thessaly, Boeotia, most of the Peloponnese, Arcadia excepted, and the most fertile

From *The History of the Peloponnesian War,* translated by Richard Crawley, translation revised by R. Feetham (London: J. M. Dent & Sons Ltd.). Reprinted by permission of J. M. Dent & Sons Ltd. and E. P. Dutton & Co., Inc. Pp. 3–15, 46–50, 78–83, 102–116, 118–121, 425–435, 437–453.

parts of the rest of Hellas. The goodness of the land favoured the aggrandisement of particular individuals, and thus created faction which
proved a fertile source of ruin. It also invited invasion. Accordingly Attica, from the poverty of its soil enjoying from a very remote period
freedom from faction, never changed its inhabitants. And here is no
inconsiderable exemplification of my assertion, that the migrations were
the cause of there being no correspondent growth in other parts. The
most powerful victims of war or faction from the rest of Hellas took
refuge with the Athenians as a safe retreat; and at an early period,
becoming naturalised, swelled the already large population of the city to
such a height that Attica became at last too small to hold them, and they
had to send out colonies to Ionia.

There is also another circumstance that contributes not a little to my
conviction of the weakness of ancient times. Before the Trojan war there
is no indication of any common action in Hellas, nor indeed of the universal prevalence of the name; on the contrary, before the time of Hellen,
son of Deucalion, no such appellation existed, but the country went by
the names of the different tribes, in particular of the Pelasgian. It was not
till Hellen and his sons grew strong in Phthiotis, and were invited as
allies into the other cities, that one by one they gradually acquired from
the connection the name of Hellenes; though a long time elapsed before
that name could fasten itself upon all. The best proof of this is furnished
by Homer. Born long after the Trojan war, he nowhere calls all of them
by that name, nor indeed any of them except the followers of Achilles
from Phthiotis, who were the original Hellenes: in his poems they are
called Danaans, Argives, and Achaeans. He does not even use the term
barbarian, probably because the Hellenes had not yet been marked off
from the rest of the world by one distinctive appellation. It appears therefore that the several Hellenic communities, comprising not only those
who first acquired the name, city by city, as they came to understand each
other, but also those who assumed it afterwards as the name of the whole
people, were before the Trojan war prevented by their want of strength
and the absence of mutual intercourse from displaying any collective
action.

Indeed, they could not unite for this expedition till they had gained
increased familiarity with the sea. And the first person known to us by
tradition as having established a navy is Minos. He made himself master
of what is now called the Hellenic sea, and ruled over the Cyclades, into
most of which he sent the first colonies, expelling the Carians and appointing his own sons governors; and thus did his best to put down piracy
in those waters, a necessary step to secure the revenues for his own use.

For in early times the Hellenes and the barbarians of the coast and
islands, as communication by sea became more common, were tempted

to turn pirates, under the conduct of their most powerful men; the motives being to serve their own cupidity and to support the needy. They
would fall upon a town unprotected by walls, and consisting of a mere
collection of villages, and would plunder it; indeed, this came to be the
main source of their livelihood, no disgrace being yet attached to such an
achievement, but even some glory. An illustration of this is furnished by
the honour with which some of the inhabitants of the continent still
regard a successful marauder, and by the question we find the old poets
everywhere representing the people as asking of voyagers—"Are they
pirates?"—as if those who are asked the question would have no idea of
disclaiming the imputation, or their interrogators of reproaching them
for it. The same rapine prevailed also by land.

And even at the present day many parts of Hellas still follow the old
fashion, the Ozolian Locrians, for instance, the Aetolians, the Acarnanians, and that region of the continent; and the custom of carrying arms
is still kept up among these continentals, from the old piratical habits.
The whole of Hellas used once to carry arms, their habitations being
unprotected, and their communication with each other unsafe; indeed,
to wear arms was as much a part of everyday life with them as with the
barbarians. And the fact that the people in these parts of Hellas are still
living in the old way points to a time when the same mode of life was
once equally common to all. The Athenians were the first to lay aside
their weapons, and to adopt an easier and more luxurious mode of life;
indeed, it is only lately that their rich old men left off the luxury of
wearing undergarments of linen, and fastening a knot of their hair with
a tie of golden grasshoppers, a fashion which spread to their Ionian
kindred, and long prevailed among the old men there. On the contrary
a modest style of dressing, more in conformity with modern ideas, was
first adopted by the Lacedaemonians, the rich doing their best to assimi-
late their way of life to that of the common people. They also set the
example of contending naked, publicly stripping and anointing themselves with oil in their gymnastic exercises. Formerly, even in the Olympic contests, the athletes who contended wore belts across their middles;
and it is but a few years since that the practice ceased. To this day among
some of the barbarians, especially in Asia, when prizes for boxing and
wrestling are offered, belts are worn by the combatants. And there are
many other points in which a likeness might be shown between the life
of the Hellenic world of old and the barbarian of to-day.

With respect to their towns, later on, at an era of increased facilities of
navigation and a greater supply of capital, we find the shores becoming
the site of walled towns, and the isthmuses being occupied for the purposes of commerce, and defence against a neighbour. But the old towns,
on account of the great prevalence of piracy, were built away from the

sea, whether on the islands or the continent, and still remain in their old sites. For the pirates used to plunder one another, and indeed all coast populations, whether seafaring or not.

The islanders, too, were great pirates. These islanders were Carians and Phoenicians, by whom most of the islands were colonised, as was proved by the following fact. During the purification of Delos by Athens in this war all the graves in the island were taken up, and it was found that above half their inmates were Carians: they were identified by the fashion of the arms buried with them, and by the method of interment, which was the same as the Carians still follow. But as soon as Minos had formed his navy, communication by sea became easier, as he colonised most of the islands, and thus expelled the malefactors. The coast populations now began to apply themselves more closely to the acquisition of wealth, and their life became more settled; some even began to build themselves walls on the strength of their newly-acquired riches. For the love of gain would reconcile the weaker to the dominion of the stronger, and the possession of capital enabled the more powerful to reduce the smaller towns to subjection. And it was at a somewhat later stage of this development that they went on the expedition against Troy.

What enabled Agamemnon to raise the armament was more, in my opinion, his superiority in strength, than the oaths of Tyndareus, which bound the Suitors to follow him. Indeed, the account given by those Peloponnesians who have been the recipients of the most credible tradition is this. First of all Pelops, arriving among a needy population from Asia with vast wealth, acquired such power that, stranger though he was, the country was called after him; and this power fortune saw fit materially to increase in the hands of his descendants. Eurystheus had been killed in Attica by the Heraclids. Atreus was his mother's brother; and to the hands of his relation, who had left his father on account of the death of Chrysippus, Eurystheus, when he set out on his expedition, had committed Mycenae and the government. As time went on and Eurystheus did not return, Atreus complied with the wishes of the Mycenaeans, who were influenced by fear of the Heraclids,—besides, his power seemed considerable, and he had not neglected to court the favour of the populace,—and assumed the sceptre of Mycenae and the rest of the dominions of Eurystheus. And so the power of the descendants of Pelops came to be greater than that of the descendants of Perseus. To all this Agamemnon succeeded. He had also a navy far stronger than his contemporaries, so that, in my opinion, fear was quite as strong an element as love in the formation of the confederate expedition. The strength of his navy is shown by the fact that his own was the largest contingent, and that of the Arcadians was furnished by him; this at least is what Homer says, if his testimony is deemed sufficient. Besides, in his account of the transmission of the sceptre, he calls him:

Of many an isle, and of all Argos king.

Now Agamemnon's was a continental power; and he could not have been master of any except the adjacent islands (and these would not be many) but through the possession of a fleet.

And from this expedition we may infer the character of earlier enterprises. Now Mycenae may have been a small place, and many of the towns of that age may appear comparatively insignificant, but no exact observer would therefore feel justified in rejecting the estimate given by the poets and by tradition of the magnitude of the armament. For I suppose if Lacedaemon were to become desolate, and the temples and the foundations of the public buildings were left, that as time went on there would be a strong disposition with posterity to refuse to accept her fame as a true exponent of her power. And yet they occupy two-fifths of Peloponnese and lead the whole, not to speak of their numerous allies without. Still, as the city is neither built in a compact form nor adorned with magnificent temples and public edifices, but composed of villages after the old fashion of Hellas, there would be an impression of inadequacy. Whereas, if Athens were to suffer the same misfortune, I suppose that any inference from the appearance presented to the eye would make her power to have been twice as great as it is. We have therefore no right to be sceptical, nor to content ourselves with an inspection of a town to the exclusion of a consideration of its power; but we may safely conclude that the armament in question surpassed all before it, as it fell short of modern efforts; if we can here also accept the testimony of Homer's poems, in which, without allowing for the exaggeration which a poet would feel himself licensed to employ, we can see that it was far from equalling ours. He has represented it as consisting of twelve hundred vessels; the Boeotian complement of each ship being a hundred and twenty men, that of the ships of Philoctetes fifty. By this, I conceive, he meant to convey the maximum and the minimum complement: at any rate he does not specify the amount of any others in his catalogue of the ships. That they were all rowers as well as warriors we see from his account of the ships of Philoctetes, in which all the men at the oar are bowmen. Now it is improbable that many supernumeraries sailed if we except the kings and high officers; especially as they had to cross the open sea with munitions of war, in ships, moreover, that had no decks, but were equipped in the old piratical fashion. So that if we strike the average of the largest and smallest ships, the number of those who sailed will appear inconsiderable, representing, as they did, the whole force of Hellas. And this was due not so much to scarcity of men as of money. Difficulty of subsistence made the invaders reduce the numbers of the army to a point at which it might live on the country during the prosecution of the war. Even after the victory they obtained on their arrival—and a victory there must have been, or the fortifications of the naval camp could never have been built —there is no indication of their whole force having been employed; on the contrary, they seem to have turned to cultivation of the Chersonese and to piracy from want of supplies. This was what really enabled the Trojans to keep the field for ten years against them; the dispersion of the enemy making them always a match for the detachment left behind. If they had brought plenty of supplies with them, and had perservered in the war without scattering for piracy and agriculture, they would have easily defeated the Trojans in the field; since they could hold their own against them with the division on service. In short, if they had stuck to the siege, the capture of Troy would have cost them less time and less trouble. But as want of money proved the weakness of earlier expeditions, so from the same cause even the one in question, more famous than its predecessors, may be pronounced on the evidence of what it effected to have been inferior to its renown and to the current opinion about it formed under the tuition of the poets.

Even after the Trojan war Hellas was still engaged in removing and settling, and thus could not attain to the quiet which must precede growth. The late return of the Hellenes from Ilium caused many revolutions, and factions ensued almost everywhere; and it was the citizens thus driven into exile who founded the cities. Sixty years after the capture of Ilium the modern Boeotians were driven out of Arne by the Thessalians, and settled in the present Boeotia, the former Cadmeis; though there was a division of them there before, some of whom joined the expedition to Ilium. Twenty years later the Dorians and the Heraclids became masters of Peloponnese; so that much had to be done and many years had to elapse before Hellas could attain to a durable tranquillity undisturbed by removals, and could begin to send out colonies, as Athens did to Ionia and most of the islands, and the Peloponnesians to most of Italy and Sicily and some places in the rest of Hellas. All these places were founded subsequently to the war with Troy.

But as the power of Hellas grew, and the acquisition of wealth became more an object, the revenues of the states increasing, tyrannies were by their means established almost everywhere,—the old form of government being hereditary monarchy with definite prerogatives,—and Hellas began to fit out fleets and apply herself more closely to the sea. It is said that the Corinthians were the first to approach the modern style of naval architecture, and that Corinth was the first place in Hellas where galleys were built; and we have Ameinocles, a Corinthian shipwright, making four ships for the Samians. Dating from the end of this war, it is nearly three hundred years ago that Ameinocles went to Samos. Again, the earliest sea-fight in history was between the Corinthians and Corcyrae-ans; this was about two hundred and sixty years ago, dating from the same time. Planted on an isthmus, Corinth had from time out of mind been a commercial emporium; as formerly almost all communication between the Hellenes within and without Peloponnese was carried on overland, and the Corinthian territory was the highway through which it travelled. She had consequently great money resources, as is shown by the epithet "wealthy" bestowed by the old poets on the place, and this enabled her, when traffic by sea became more common, to procure her navy and put down piracy; and as she could offer a mart for both branches of the trade, she acquired for herself all the power which a large revenue affords. Subsequently the Ionians attained to great naval strength in the reign of Cyrus, the first king of the Persians, and of his son Cambyses, and while they were at war with the former commanded for a while the Ionian sea. Polycrates also, the tyrant of Samos, had a powerful navy in the reign of Cambyses with which he reduced many of the islands, and among them Rhenea, which he consecrated to the Delian Apollo. About this time also the Phocaeans, while they were founding Marseilles, defeated the Carthaginians in a sea-fight. These were the most powerful navies. And even these, although so many generations had elapsed since the Trojan war, seem to have been principally composed of the old fifty-oars and long-boats, and to have counted few galleys among their ranks. Indeed it was only shortly before the Persian war and the death of Darius the successor of Cambyses, that the Sicilian tyrants and the Corcyraeans acquired any large number of galleys. For after these there were no navies of any account in Hellas till the expedition of Xerxes; Aegina, Athens, and others may have possessed a few vessels, but they were principally fifty-oars. It was quite at the end of this period that the war with Aegina and the prospect of the barbarian invasion enabled Themistocles to persuade the Athenians to build the fleet with which they fought at Salamis; and even these vessels had not complete decks.

The navies, then, of the Hellenes during the period we have traversed were what I have described. All their insignificance did not prevent their being an element of the greatest power to those who cultivated them, alike in revenue and in dominion. They were the means by which the islands were reached and reduced, those of the smallest area falling the easiest prey. Wars by land there were none, none at least by which power was acquired; we have the usual border contests, but of distant expeditions with conquest for object we hear nothing among the Hellenes. There was no union of subject cities round a great state, no spontaneous combination of equals for confederate expeditions; what fighting there was consisted merely of local warfare between rival neighbours. The nearest approach to a coalition took place in the old war between Chalcis and Eretria; this was a quarrel in which the rest of the Hellenic name did to some extent take sides.

Various, too, were the obstacles which the national growth encountered in various localities. The power of the Ionians was advancing with rapid strides, when it came into collision with Persia, under King Cyrus, who, after having dethroned Croesus and overrun everything between the Halys and the sea, stopped not till he had reduced the cities of the coast; the islands being only left to be subdued by Darius and the Phoenician navy. Again, wherever there were tyrants, their habit of providing simply for themselves, of looking solely to their personal comfort and family aggrandisement, made safety the great aim of their policy, and prevented anything great proceeding from them; though they would each have their affairs with their immediate neighbours. All this is only true of the mother country, for in Sicily they attained to very great power. Thus for a long time everywhere in Hellas do we find causes which make the states alike incapable of combination for great and national ends, or of any vigorous action of their own.

But at last a time came when the tyrants of Athens and the far older tyrannies of the rest of Hellas were, with the exception of those in Sicily, once and for all put down by Lacedaemon; for this city, though after the settlement of the Dorians, its present inhabitants, it suffered from factions for an unparalleled length of time, still at a very early period obtained good laws, and enjoyed a freedom from tyrants which was unbroken; it has possessed the same form of government for more than four hundred years, reckoning to the end of the late war, and has thus been in a position to arrange the affairs of the other states. Not many years after the deposition of the tyrants, the battle of Marathon was fought between the Medes and the Athenians. Ten years afterwards the barbarian returned with the armada for the subjugation of Hellas. In the face of this great danger the command of the confederate Hellenes was assumed by the Lacedaemonians in virtue of their superior power; and the Athenians having made up their minds to abandon their city, broke up their homes, threw themselves into their ships, and became a naval people. This coalition, after repulsing the barbarian, soon afterwards split into two sections, which included the Hellenes who had revolted from the king, as well as those who had aided him in the war. At the head of the one stood Athens, at the head of the other Lacedaemon, one the first naval, the other the first military power in Hellas. For a short time the league held together, till the Lacedaemonians and the Athenians quarrelled, and made war upon each other with their allies, a duel into which all the Hellenes sooner or later were drawn, though some might at first remain neutral. So that the whole period from the Median war to this, with some peaceful intervals, was spent by each power in war, either

with its rival, or with its own revolted allies, and consequently afforded
them constant practice in military matters, and that experience which
is learnt in the school of danger.

The policy of Lacedaemon was not to exact tribute from her allies, but
merely to secure their subservience to her interests by establishing oli-
garchies among them; Athens, on the contrary, had by degrees deprived
hers of their ships, and imposed instead contributions in money on all
except Chios and Lesbos. Both found their resources for this war separately to exceed the sum of their strength when the alliance flourished
intact.

Having now given the result of my inquiries into early times, I grant
that there will be a difficulty in believing every particular detail. The
way that most men deal with traditions, even traditions of their own
country, is to receive them all alike as they are delivered, without applying any critical test whatever. The general Athenian public fancy that
Hipparchus was tyrant when he fell by the hands of Harmodius and
Aristogiton; not knowing that Hippias, the eldest of the sons of Pisistratus, was really supreme, and that Hipparchus and Thessalus were his
brothers; and that Harmodius and Aristogiton suspecting, on the very
day, nay at the very moment fixed on for the deed, that information had
been conveyed to Hippias by their accomplices, concluded that he had
been warned, and did not attack him, yet, not liking to be apprehended
and risk their lives for nothing, fell upon Hipparchus near the temple of
the daughters of Leos, and slew him as he was arranging the Pana-
thenaic procession.

There are many other unfounded ideas current among the rest of the
Hellenes, even on matters of contemporary history which have not been
obscured by time. For instance, there is the notion that the Lacedaemonian kings have two votes each, the fact being that they have only one;
and that there is a company of Pitane, there being simply no such thing.
So little pains do the vulgar take in the investigation of truth, accepting
readily the first story that comes to hand. On the whole, however, the
conclusions I have drawn from the proofs quoted may, I believe, safely
be relied on. Assuredly they will not be disturbed either by the lays of a
poet displaying the exaggeration of his craft, or by the compositions of
the chroniclers that are attractive at truth's expense; the subjects they
treat of being out of the reach of evidence, and time having robbed most
of them of historical value by enthroning them in the region of legend.
Turning from these, we can rest satisfied with having proceeded upon
the clearest data, and having arrived at conclusions as exact as can be
expected in matters of such antiquity. To come to this war; despite the
known disposition of the actors in a struggle to overrate its importance,
and when it is over to return to their admiration of earlier events, yet an

examination of the facts will show that it was much greater than the wars which preceded it.

With reference to the speeches in this history, some were delivered before the war began, others while it was going on; some I heard myself, others I got from various quarters; it was in all cases difficult to carry them word for word in one's memory, so my habit has been to make the speakers say what was in my opinion demanded of them by the various occasions, of course adhering as closely as possible to the general sense of what they really said. And with reference to the narrative of events, far from permitting myself to derive it from the first source that came to hand, I did not even trust my own impressions, but it rests partly on what I saw myself, partly on what others saw for me, the accuracy of the report being always tried by the most severe and detailed tests possible. My conclusions have cost me some labour from the want of coincidence between accounts of the same occurrences by different eye-witnesses, arising sometimes from imperfect memory, sometimes from undue partiality for one side or the other. The absence of romance in my history will, I fear, detract somewhat from its interest; but if it be judged useful by those inquirers who desire an exact knowledge of the past as an aid to the interpretation of the future, which in the course of human things must resemble if it does not reflect it, I shall be content. In fine, I have written my work, not as an essay which is to win the applause of the moment, but as a possession for all time.

The Median war, the greatest achievement of past times, yet found a speedy decision in two actions by sea and two by land. The Peloponnesian war was prolonged to an immense length, and long as it was it was short without parallel for the misfortunes that it brought upon Hellas. Never had so many cities been taken and laid desolate, here by the barbarians, here by the parties contending (the old inhabitants being sometimes removed to make room for others); never was there so much banishing and blood-shedding, now on the field of battle, now in the strife of action. Old stories of occurrences handed down by tradition, but scantily confirmed by experience, suddenly ceased to be incredible; there were earthquakes of unparalleled extent and violence; eclipses of the sun occurred with a frequency unrecorded in previous history; there were great droughts in sundry places and consequent famines, and that most calamitous and awfully fatal visitation, the plague. All this came upon them with the late war, which was begun by the Athenians and Peloponnesians by the dissolution of the thirty years' truce made after the conquest of Euboea. To the question why they broke the treaty, I answer by placing first an account of their grounds of complaint and points of difference, that no one may ever have to ask the immediate cause which plunged the Hellenes into a war of such magnitude. The real cause I consider to be the one which was formally most kept out of sight. The growth of the power of Athens, and the alarm which this inspired in Lacedaemon, made war inevitable. Still it is well to give the grounds alleged by either side, which led to the dissolution of the treaty and the breaking out of war. . . .

After the Lacedaemonians had heard the complaints of the allies against the Athenians, and the observations of the latter, they made all withdraw, and consulted by themselves on the question before them. The opinions of the majority all led to the same conclusion; the Athenians were open aggressors, and war must be declared at once. But Archidamus, the Lacedaemonian king, came forward, who had the reputation of being at once a wise and a moderate man, and made the following speech:

"I have not lived so long, Lacedaemonians, without having had the experience of many wars, and I see those among you of the same age as myself, who will not fall into the common misfortune of longing for war from inexperience or from a belief in its advantage and its safety. This, the war on which you are now debating, would be one of the greatest magnitude, on a sober consideration of the matter. In a struggle with Peloponnesians and neighbours our strength is of the same character, and it is possible to move swiftly on the different points. But a struggle with a people who live in a distant land, who have also an extraordinary familiarity with the sea, and who are in the highest state of preparation in every other department; with wealth private and public, with ships, and horses, and heavy infantry, and a population such as no one other Hellenic place can equal, and lastly a number of tributary allies—what can justify us in rashly beginning such a struggle? Wherein is our trust that we should rush on it unprepared? Is it in our ships? There we are inferior; while if we are to practise and become a match for them, time must intervene. Is it in our money? There we have a far greater deficiency. We neither have it in our treasury, nor are we ready to contribute it from our private funds. Confidence might possibly be felt in our superiority in heavy infantry and population, which will enable us to invade and devastate their lands. But the Athenians have plenty of other land in their empire, and can import what they want by sea. Again, if we are to attempt an insurrection of their allies, these will have to be supported with a fleet, most of them being islanders. What then is to be our war? For unless we can either beat them at sea, or deprive them of the revenues which feed their navy, we shall meet with little but disaster. Meanwhile our honour will be pledged to keeping on, particularly if it be the opinion that we began the quarrel. For let us never be elated by the fatal hope of the war being quickly ended by the devastation of their lands. I fear rather that we may leave it as a legacy to our children; so improbable is it that the Athenian spirit will be the slave of their land, or Athenian experience be cowed by war.

"Not that I would bid you be so unfeeling as to suffer them to injure your allies, and to refrain from unmasking their intrigues; but I do bid you not to take up arms at once, but to send and remonstrate with them in a tone not too suggestive of war, nor again too suggestive of submission, and to employ the interval in perfecting our own preparations. The means will be, first, the acquisition of allies, Hellenic or barbarian it matters not, so long as they are an accession to our strength naval or pecuniary—I say Hellenic or barbarian, because the odium of such an accession to all who like us are the objects of the designs of the Athenians is taken away by the law of self-preservation—and secondly the development of our home resources. If they listen to our embassy, so much the better; but if not, after the lapse of two or three years our position will have become materially strengthened, and we can then attack them if we think proper. Perhaps by that time the sight of our preparations, backed by language equally significant, will have disposed them to submission, while their land is still untouched, and while their counsels may be directed to the retention of advantages as yet undestroyed. For the only light in which you can view their land is that of a hostage in your hands, a hostage the more valuable the better it is cultivated. This you ought to spare as long as possible, and not make them desperate, and so increase the difficulty of dealing with them. For if while still unprepared, hurried away by the complaints of our allies, we are induced to lay it waste, have a care that we do not bring deep disgrace and deep perplexity upon Peloponnese. Complaints, whether of communities or individuals, it is possible to adjust; but war undertaken by a coalition for sectional interests, whose progress there is no means of foreseeing, does not easily admit of creditable settlement.

"And none need think it cowardice for a number of confederates to pause before they attack a single city. The Athenians have allies as numerous as our own, and allies that pay tribute, and war is a matter not so much of arms as of money, which makes arms of use. And this is more than ever true in a struggle between a continental and a maritime power. First, then, let us provide money, and not allow ourselves to be carried away by the talk of our allies before we have done so: as we shall have the largest share of responsibility for the consequences be they good or bad, we have also a right to a tranquil inquiry respecting them.

"And the slowness and procrastination, the parts of our character that are most assailed by their criticism, need not make you blush. If we undertake the war without preparation, we should by hastening its commencement only delay its conclusion: further, a free and a famous city has through all time been ours. The quality which they condemn is really nothing but a wise moderation; thanks to its possession, we alone do not become insolent in success and give way less than others in misfortune; we are not carried away by the pleasure of hearing ourselves cheered on to risks which our judgment condemns; nor, if annoyed, are we any the more convinced by attempts to exasperate us by accusation. We are both warlike and wise, and it is our sense of order that makes us so. We are warlike, because self-control contains honour as a chief constituent, and honour bravery. And we are wise, because we are educated with too little learning to despise the laws, and with too severe a self-control to disobey them, and are brought up not to be too knowing in useless matters,—such as the knowledge which can give a specious criticism of an enemy's plans in theory, but fails to assail them with equal success in practice, —but are taught to consider that the schemes of our enemies are not dissimilar to our own, and that the freaks of chance are not determinable by calculation. In practice we always base our preparations against an enemy on the assumption that his plans are good; indeed, it is right to rest our hopes not on a belief in his blunders, but on the soundness of our provisions. Nor ought we to believe that there is much difference between man and man, but to think that the superiority lies with him who is reared in the severest school. These practices, then, which our ancestors have delivered to us, and by whose maintenance we have always profited, must not be given up. And we must not be hurried into deciding in a day's brief space a question which concerns many lives and fortunes and many cities, and in which honour is deeply involved,—but we must decide calmly. This our strength peculiarly enables us to do. As for the Athenians, send to them on the matter of Potidaea, send on the matter of the alleged wrongs of the allies, particularly as they are prepared with legal satisfaction; and to proceed against one who offers arbitration as against a wrongdoer, law forbids. Meanwhile do not omit preparation for war. This decision will be the best for yourselves, the most terrible to your opponents."

Such were the words of Archidamus. Last came forward Sthenelaidas, one of the Ephors for that year, and spoke to the Lacedaemonians as follows:

"The long speech of the Athenians I do not pretend to understand. They said a good deal in praise of themselves, but nowhere denied that they are injuring our allies and Peloponnese. And yet if they behaved well against the Mede then, but ill towards us now, they deserve double punishment for having ceased to be good and for having become bad. We meanwhile are the same then and now, and shall not, if we are wise, disregard the wrongs of our allies, or put off till tomorrow the duty of assisting those who must suffer to-day. Others have much money and ships and horses, but we have good allies whom we must not give up to the Athenians, nor by lawsuits and words decide the matter, as it is anything but in word that we are harmed, but render instant and powerful help. And let us not be told that it is fitting for us to deliberate under injustice; long deliberation is rather fitting for those who have injustice in contemplation. Vote therefore, Lacedaemonians, for war, as the honour of Sparta demands, and neither allow the further aggrandisement of Athens, nor betray our allies to ruin, but with the gods let us advance against the aggressors."

With these words he, as Ephor, himself put the question to the assembly of the Lacedaemonians. He said that he could not determine which was the loudest acclamation (their mode of decision is by acclamation not by voting); the fact being that he wished to make them declare their opinion openly and thus to increase their ardour for war. Accordingly he said, "All Lacedaemonians who are of opinion that the treaty has been broken, and that Athens is guilty, leave your seats and go there," pointing out a certain place; "all who are of the opposite opinion, there." They accordingly stood up and divided; and those who held that the treaty had been broken were in a decided majority. Summoning the allies, they told them that their opinion was that Athens had been guilty of injustice, but that they wished to convoke all the allies and put it to the vote; in order that they might make the war, if they decided to do so, on a common resolution. Having thus gained their point, the delegates returned home at once; the Athenian envoys a little later, when they had despatched the objects of their mission. This decision of the assembly judging that the treaty had been broken, was made in the fourteenth year of the thirty years' truce, which was entered into after the affair of Euboea.

The Lacedaemonians voted that the treaty had been broken, and that war must be declared, not so much because they were persuaded by the arguments of the allies, as because they feared the growth of the power of the Athenians, seeing most of Hellas already subject to them. . . .

To return to the Lacedaemonians. The history of their first embassy, the injunctions which it conveyed, and the rejoinder which it provoked, concerning the expulsion of the accursed persons, have been related already. It was followed by a second, which ordered Athens to raise the siege of Potidaea, and to respect the independence of Aegina. Above all, it gave her most distinctly to understand that war might be prevented by the revocation of the Megara decree, excluding the Megarians from the use of Athenian harbours and of the market of Athens. But Athens was not inclined either to revoke the decree, or to entertain their other proposals; she accused the Megarians of pushing their cultivation into the consecrated ground and the unenclosed land on the border, and of harbouring her runaway slaves. At last an embassy arrived with the Lacedaemonian ultimatum. The ambassadors were Ramphias, Melesippus, and Agesander. Not a word was said on any of the old subjects; there was simply this: "Lacedaemon wishes the peace to continue, and there is no reason why it should not, if you would leave the Hellenes independent." Upon this the Athenians held an assembly, and laid the matter before their consideration. It was resolved to deliberate once for all on all their demands, and to give them an answer. There were many speakers who came forward and gave their support to one side or the other, urging the necessity of war, or the revocation of the decree and the folly of allowing it to stand in the way of peace. Among them came forward Pericles, son of Xanthippus, the first man of his time at Athens, ablest alike in counsel and in action, and gave the following advice:

"There is one principle, Athenians, which I hold to through everything, and that is the principle of no concession to the Peloponnesians. I know that the spirit which inspires men while they are being persuaded to make war, is not always retained in action; that as circumstances change, resolutions change. Yet I see that now as before the same, almost literally the same, counsel is demanded of me; and I put it to those of you, who are allowing yourselves to be persuaded, to support the national resolves even in the case of reverses, or to forfeit all credit for their wisdom in the event of success. For sometimes the course of things is as arbitrary as the plans of man; indeed this is why we usually blame chance for whatever does not happen as we expected. Now it was clear before, that Lacedaemon entertained designs against us; it is still more clear now. The treaty provides that we shall mutually submit our differences to legal settlement, and that we shall meanwhile each keep what we have. Yet the Lacedaemonians never yet made us any such offer, never yet would accept from us any such offer; on the contrary, they wish complaints to be settled by war instead of by negotiation; and in the end we find them here dropping the tone of expostulation and adopting that of command. They order us to raise the siege of Potidaea, to let Aegina be independent, to revoke the Megara decree; and they conclude with an ultimatum warning us to leave the Hellenes independent. I hope that you will none of you think that we shall be going to war for a trifle if we refuse to revoke the Megara decree, which appears in front of their complaints, and the revocation of which is to save us from war, or let any feeling of self-reproach linger in your minds, as if you went to war for slight cause. Why, this trifle contains the whole seal and trial of your resolution. If you give way, you will instantly have to meet some greater demand, as having been frightened into obedience in the first instance; while a firm refusal will make them clearly understand that they must treat you more as equals. Make your decision therefore at once, either to submit before you are harmed, or if we are to go to war, as I for one think we ought, to do so without caring whether the ostensible cause be great or small, resolved against making concessions or consenting to a precarious tenure of our possessions. For all claims from an equal, urged upon a neighbour as commands, before any attempt at legal settlement, be they great or be they small, have only one meaning, and that is slavery.

"As to the war and the resources of either party, a detailed comparison will not show you the inferiority of Athens. Personally engaged in the cultivation of their land, without funds either private or public, the Peloponnesians are also without experience in long wars across sea, from the strict limit which poverty imposes on their attacks upon each other. Powers of this description are quite incapable of often manning a fleet or often sending out an army: they cannot afford the absence from their homes, the expenditure from their own funds; and besides, they have not command of the sea. Capital, it must be remembered, maintains a war more than forced contributions. Farmers are a class of men that are always more ready to serve in person than in purse. Confident that the former will survive the dangers, they are by no means so sure that the latter will not be prematurely exhausted, especially if the war last longer than they expect, which it very likely will. In a single battle the Peloponnesians and their allies may be able to defy all Hellas, but they are incapacitated from carrying on a war against a power different in character from their own, by the want of the single council-chamber requisite to prompt and vigorous action, and the substitution of a diet composed of various races, in which every state possesses an equal vote, and each presses its own ends, a condition of things which generally results in no action at all. The great wish of some is to avenge themselves on some particular enemy, the great wish of others to save their own pocket. Slow in assembling, they devote a very small fraction of the time to the consideration of any public object, most of it to the prosecution of their own objects. Meanwhile each fancies that no harm will come of his neglect, that it is the business of somebody else to look after this or that for him; and so, by the same notion being entertained by all separately, the common cause imperceptibly decays.

"But the principal point is the hindrance that they will experience from want of money. The slowness with which it comes in will cause delay; but the opportunities of war wait for no man. Again, we need not be alarmed either at the possibility of their raising fortifications in Attica, or at their navy. It would be difficult for any system of fortifications to establish a rival city, even in time of peace, much more, surely, in an enemy's country, with Athens just as much fortified against it, as it against Athens; while a mere post might be able to do some harm to the country by incursions and by the facilities which it would afford for desertion, but can never prevent our sailing into their country and raising fortifications there, and making reprisals with our powerful fleet. For our naval skill is of more use to us for service on land, than their military skill for service at sea. Familiarity with the sea they will not find an easy acquisition. If you who have been practising at it ever since the Median invasion have not yet brought it to perfection, is there any chance of anything considerable being effected by an agricultural, unseafaring population, who will besides be prevented from practising by the constant presence of strong squadrons of observation from Athens? With a small squadron they might hazard an engagement, encouraging their ignorance by numbers; but the restraint of a strong force will prevent their moving, and through want of practice they will grow more clumsy, and consequently more timid. It must be kept in mind that seamanship, just like anything else, is a matter of art, and will not admit of being taken up occasionally as an occupation for times of leisure; on the contrary, it is so exacting as to leave leisure for nothing else.

"Even if they were to touch the moneys at Olympia or Delphi, and try to seduce our foreign sailors by the temptation of higher pay, that would only be a serious danger if we could not still be a match for them, by embarking our own citizens and the aliens resident among us. But in fact by this means we are always a match for them; and, best of all, we have a larger and higher class of native coxswains and sailors among our own citizens than all the rest of Hellas. And to say nothing of the danger of such a step, none of our foreign sailors would consent to become an outlaw from his country, and to take service with them and their hopes, for the sake of a few days' high pay.

"This, I think, is a tolerably fair account of the position of the Peloponnesians; that of Athens is free from the defects that I have criticised in them, and has other advantages of its own, which they can show nothing to equal. If they march against our country we will sail against theirs, and it will then be found that the desolation of the whole of Attica is not the same as that of even a fraction of Peloponnese; for they will not be able to supply the deficiency except by a battle, while we have plenty of land both on the islands and the continent. The rule of the sea is indeed a great matter. Consider for a moment. Suppose that we were islanders: can you conceive a more impregnable position? Well, this in future should, as far as possible, be our conception of our position. Dismissing all thought of our land and houses, we must vigilantly guard the sea and the city. No irritation that we may feel for the former must provoke us to a battle with the numerical superiority of the Peloponnesians. A victory would only be succeeded by another battle against the same superiority: a reverse involves the loss of our allies, the source of our strength, who will not remain quiet a day after we become unable to march against them. We must cry not over the loss of houses and land but of men's lives; since houses and land do not gain men, but men them. And if I had thought that I could persuade you, I would have bid you go out and lay them waste with your own hands, and show the Peloponnesians that this at any rate will not make you submit.

"I have many other reasons to hope for a favourable issue, if you can consent not to combine schemes of fresh conquest with the conduct of the war, and will abstain from wilfully involving yourselves in other dangers; indeed, I am more afraid of our own blunders than of the enemy's devices. But these matters shall be explained in another speech, as events require; for the present dismiss these men with the answer that we will allow Megara the use of our market and harbours, when the Lacedaemonians suspend their alien acts in favour of us and our allies, there being nothing in the treaty to prevent either one or the other: that we will leave the cities independent, if independent we found them when we made the treaty, and when the Lacedaemonians grant to their cities an independence not involving subservience to Lacedaemonian interest, but such as each severally may desire: that we are willing to give the legal satisfaction which our agreements specify, and that we shall not commence hostilities, but shall resist those who do commence them. This is an answer agreeable at once to the rights and the dignity of Athens. It must be thoroughly understood that war is a necessity; but that the more readily we accept it, the less will be the ardour of our opponents, and that out of the greatest dangers communities and individuals acquire the greatest glory. Did not our fathers resist the Medes not only with resources far different from ours, but even when those resources had been abandoned; and more by wisdom than by fortune, more by daring than by strength, did not they beat off the barbarian and advance their affairs to their present height? We must not fall behind them, but must resist our enemies in any way and in every way, and attempt to hand down our power to our posterity unimpaired."

Such were the words of Pericles. The Athenians, persuaded of the wisdom of his advice, voted as he desired, and answered the Lacedaemonians as he recommended, both on the separate points and in the general; they would do nothing on dictation, but were ready to have the complaints settled in a fair and impartial manner by the legal method, which the terms of the truce prescribed. So the envoys departed home, and did not return again.

These were the charges and differences existing between the rival powers before the war, arising immediately from the affair at Epidamnus and Corcyra. Still intercourse continued in spite of them, and mutual communication. It was carried on without heralds, but not without suspicion, as events were occurring which were equivalent to a breach of the treaty and matter for war. . . .

In the . . . winter the Athenians gave a funeral at the public cost to those who had first fallen in this war. It was a custom of their ancestors, and the manner of it is as follows. Three days before the ceremony, the bones of the dead are laid out in a tent which has been erected; and their friends bring to their relatives such offerings as they please. In the funeral procession cypress coffins are borne in cars, one for each tribe; the bones of the deceased being placed in the coffin of their tribe. Among these is carried one empty bier decked for the missing, that is, for those whose bodies could not be recovered. Any citizen or stranger who pleases, joins in the procession: and the female relatives are there to wail at the burial. The dead are laid in the public sepulchre in the most beautiful suburb of the city, in which those who fall in war are always buried; with the exception of those slain at Marathon, who for their singular and extraordinary valour were interred on the spot where they fell. After the bodies have been laid in the earth, a man chosen by the state, of approved wisdom and eminent reputation, pronounces over them an appropriate panegyric; after which all retire. Such is the manner of the burying; and throughout the whole of the war, whenever the occasion arose, the established custom was observed. Meanwhile these were the first that had fallen, and Pericles, son of Xanthippus, was chosen to pronounce their eulogium. When the proper time arrived, he advanced from the sepulchre to an elevated platform in order to be heard by as many of the crowd as possible, and spoke as follows:

"Most of my predecessors in this place have commended him who made this speech part of the law, telling us that it is well that it should be delivered at the burial of those who fall in battle. For myself, I should have thought that the worth which had displayed itself in deeds, would be sufficiently rewarded by honours also shown by deeds; such as you now see in this funeral prepared at the people's cost. And I could have wished that the reputations of many brave men were not to be imperilled in the mouth of a single individual, to stand or fall according as he spoke well or ill. For it is hard to speak properly upon a subject where it is even difficult to convince your hearers that you are speaking the truth. On the one hand, the friend who is familiar with every fact of the story, may think that some point has not been set forth with that fulness which he wishes and knows it to deserve; on the other, he who is a stranger to the matter may be led by envy to suspect exaggeration if he hears anything above his own nature. For men can endure to hear others praised only so long as they can severally persuade themselves of their own ability to equal the actions recounted: when this point is passed, envy comes in and with it incredulity. However, since our ancestors have stamped this custom with their approval, it becomes my duty to obey the law and to try to satisfy your several wishes and opinions as best I may.

"I shall begin with our ancestors: it is both just and proper that they should have the honour of the first mention on an occasion like the present. They dwelt in the country without break in the succession from generation to generation, and handed it down free to the present time by their valour. And if our more remote ancestors deserve praise, much more do our own fathers, who added to their inheritance the empire which we now possess, and spared no pains to be able to leave their acquisitions to us of the present generation. Lastly, there are few parts of our dominions that have not been augmented by those of us here, who are still more or less in the vigour of life; while the mother country has been furnished by us with everything that can enable her to depend on her own resources whether for war or for peace. That part of our history which tells of the military achievements which gave us our several possessions, or of the ready valour with which either we or our fathers stemmed the tide of Hellenic or foreign aggression, is a theme too familiar to my hearers for me to dilate on, and I shall therefore pass it by. But what was the road by which we reached our position, what the form of government under which our greatness grew, what the national habits out of which it sprang; these are questions which I may try to solve before I proceed to my panegyric upon these men; since I think this to be a subject upon which on the present occasion a speaker may properly dwell, and to which the whole assemblage, whether citizens or foreigners, may listen with advantage.

"Our constitution does not copy the laws of neighbouring states; we are rather a pattern to others than imitators ourselves. Its administration favours the many instead of the few; this is why it is called a democracy. If we look to the laws, they afford equal justice to all in their private differences; if to social standing, advancement in public life falls to reputation for capacity, class considerations not being allowed to interfere with merit; nor again does poverty bar the way, if a man is able to serve the state, he is not hindered by the obscurity of his condition. The freedom which we enjoy in our government extends also to our ordinary life. There, far from exercising a jealous surveillance over each other, we do not feel called upon to be angry with our neighbour for doing what he likes, or even to indulge in those injurious looks which cannot fail to be offensive, although they inflict no positive penalty. But all this ease in our private relations does not make us lawless as citizens. Against this fear is our chief safeguard, teaching us to obey the magistrates and the laws, particularly such as regard the protection of the injured, whether they are actually on the statute book, or belong to that code which, although unwritten, yet cannot be broken without acknowledged disgrace.

"Further, we provide plenty of means for the mind to refresh itself from business. We celebrate games and sacrifices all the year round, and the elegance of our private establishments forms a daily source of pleasure and helps to banish the spleen; while the magnitude of our city draws the produce of the world into our harbour, so that to the Athenian the fruits of other countries are as familiar a luxury as those of his own.

"If we turn to our military policy, there also we differ from our antagonists. We throw open our city to the world, and never by alien acts exclude foreigners from any opportunity of learning or observing, although the eyes of an enemy may occasionally profit by our liberality; trusting less in system and policy than to the native spirit of our citizens; while in education, where our rivals from their very cradles by a painful discipline seek after manliness, at Athens we live exactly as we please, and yet are just as ready to encounter every legitimate danger. In proof of this it may be noticed that the Lacedaemonians do not invade our country alone, but bring with them all their confederates; while we Athenians advance unsupported into the territory of a neighbour, and fighting upon a foreign soil usually vanquish with ease men who are defending their homes. Our united force was never yet encountered by any enemy, because we have at once to attend to our marine and to despatch our citizens by land upon a hundred different services; so that, wherever they engage with some such fraction of our strength, a success against a detachment is magnified into a victory over the nation, and a defeat into a reverse suffered at the hands of our entire people. And yet if with habits not of labour but of ease, and courage not of art but of nature, we are still willing to encounter danger, we have the double advantage of escaping the experience of hardships in anticipation and of facing them in the hour of need as fearlessly as those who are never free from them.

"Nor are these the only points in which our city is worthy of admiration. We cultivate refinement without extravagance and knowledge without effeminacy; wealth we employ more for use than for show, and place the real disgrace of poverty not in owning to the fact but in declining the struggle against it. Our public men have, besides politics, their private affairs to attend to, and our ordinary citizens, though occupied with the pursuits of industry, are still fair judges of public matters; for, unlike any other nation, regarding him who takes no part in these duties not as unambitious but as useless, we Athenians are able to judge at all events if we cannot originate, and instead of looking on discussion as a stumbling-block in the way of action, we think it an indispensable preliminary to any wise action at all. Again, in our enterprises we present the singular spectacle of daring and deliberation, each carried to its highest point, and both united in the same persons; although usually decision is the fruit of ignorance, hesitation of reflexion. But the palm of courage will surely be adjudged most justly to those, who best know the difference between hardship and pleasure and yet are never tempted to shrink from danger. In generosity we are equally singular, acquiring our friends by conferring not by receiving favours. Yet, of course, the doer of the favour is the firmer friend of the two, in order by continued kindness to keep the recipient in his debt; while the debtor feels less keenly from the very consciousness that the return he makes will be a payment, not a free gift. And it is only the Athenians who, fearless of consequences, confer their benefits not from calculations of expediency, but in the confidence of liberality.

"In short, I say that as a city we are the school of Hellas; while I doubt if the world can produce a man, who where he has only himself to depend upon, is equal to so many emergencies, and graced by so happy a versatility as the Athenian. And that this is no mere boast thrown out for the occasion, but plain matter of fact, the power of the state acquired by these habits proves. For Athens alone of her contemporaries is found when tested to be greater than her reputation, and alone gives no occasion to her assailants to blush at the antagonist by whom they have been worsted, or to her subjects to question her title by merit to rule. Rather, the admiration of the present and succeeding ages will be ours, since we have not left our power without witness, but have shown it by mighty proofs; and far from needing a Homer for our panegyrist, or other of his craft whose verses might charm for the moment only for the impression which they gave to melt at the touch of fact, we have forced every sea and land to be the highway of our daring, and everywhere, whether for evil or for good, have left imperishable monuments behind us. Such is the Athens for which these men, in the assertion of their resolve not to lose her, nobly fought and died; and well may every one of their survivors be ready to suffer in her cause.

"Indeed if I have dwelt at some length upon the character of our country, it has been to show that our stake in the struggle is not the same as theirs who have no such blessings to lose, and also that the panegyric of the men over whom I am now speaking might be by definite proofs established. That panegyric is now in a great measure complete; for the Athens that I have celebrated is only what the heroism of these and their like have made her, men whose fame, unlike that of most Hellenes, will be found to be only commensurate with their deserts. And if a test of worth be wanted, it is to be found in their closing scene, and this not only in the cases in which it set the final seal upon their merit, but also in those in which it gave the first intimation of their having any. For there is justice in the claim that steadfastness in his country's battles should be as a cloak to cover a man's other imperfections; since the good action has blotted out the bad, and his merit as a citizen more than outweighed his demerits as an individual. But none of these allowed either wealth with its prospect of future enjoyment to unnerve his spirit, or poverty with its hope of a day of freedom and riches to tempt him to shrink from danger. No, holding that vengeance upon their enemies was more to be desired than any personal blessings, and reckoning this to be the most glorious of hazards, they joyfully determined to accept the risk, to make sure of their vengeance and to let their wishes wait; and while committing to hope the uncertainty of final success, in the business before them they thought fit to act boldly and trust in themselves. Thus choosing to die resisting, rather than to live submitting, they fled only from dishonour, but met danger face to face, and after one brief moment, while at the summit of their fortune, escaped, not from their fear, but from their glory.

"So died these men as became Athenians. You, their survivors, must determine to have as unaltering a resolution in the field, though you may pray that it may have a happier issue. And not contented with ideas derived only from words of the advantages which are bound up with the defence of your country, though these would furnish a valuable text to a speaker even before an audience so alive to them as the present, you must yourselves realise the power of Athens, and feed your eyes upon her from day to day, till love of her fills your hearts; and then when all her greatness shall break upon you, you must reflect that it was by courage, sense of duty, and a keen feeling of honour in action that men were enabled to win all this, and that no personal failure in an enterprise could make them consent to deprive their country of their valour, but they laid it at her feet as the most glorious contribution that they could offer. For this offering of their lives made in common by them all they each of them individually received that renown which never grows old, and for a sepulchre, not so much that in which their bones have been deposited, but that noblest of shrines wherein their glory is laid up to be eternally remembered upon every occasion on which deed or story shall fall for its commemoration. For heroes have the whole earth for their tomb; and in lands far from their own, where the column with its epitaph declares it, there is enshrined in every breast a record unwritten with no tablet to preserve it, except that of the heart. These take as your model, and judging happiness to be the fruit of freedom and freedom of valour, never decline the dangers of war. For it is not the miserable that would most justly be unsparing of their lives; these have nothing to hope for: it is rather they to whom continued life may bring reverses as yet unknown, and to whom a fall, if it came, would be most tremendous in its consequences. And surely, to a man of spirit, the degradation of cowardice must be immeasurably more grievous than the unfelt death which strikes him in the midst of his strength and patriotism!

"Comfort, therefore, not condolence, is what I have to offer to the parents of the dead who may be here. Numberless are the chances to which, as they know, the life of man is subject; but fortunate indeed are they who draw for their lot a death so glorious as that which has caused your mourning, and to whom life has been so exactly measured as to terminate in the happiness in which it has been passed. Still I know that this is a hard saying, especially when those are in question of whom you will constantly be reminded by seeing in the homes of others blessings of which once you also boasted: for grief is felt not so much for the want of what we have never known, as for the loss of that to which we have been long accustomed. Yet you who are still of an age to beget children must bear up in the hope of having others in their stead; not only will they help you to forget those whom you have lost, but will be to the state at once a reinforcement and a security; for never can a fair or just policy be expected of the citizen who does not, like his fellows, bring to the decision the interests and apprehensions of a father. While those of you who have passed your prime must congratulate yourselves with the thought that the best part of your life was fortunate, and that the brief span that remains will be cheered by the fame of the departed. For it is only the love of honour that never grows old; and honour it is, not gain, as some would have it, that rejoices the heart of age and helplessness.

"Turning to the sons or brothers of the dead, I see an arduous struggle before you. When a man is gone, all are wont to praise him, and should your merit be ever so transcendent, you will still find it difficult not merely to overtake, but even to approach their renown. The living have envy to contend with, while those who are no longer in our path are honoured with a goodwill into which rivalry does not enter. On the other hand, if I must say anything on the subject of female excellence to those of you who will now be in widowhood, it will be all comprised in this brief exhortation. Great will be your glory in not falling short of your natural character; and greatest will be hers who is least talked of among the men whether for good or for bad.

"My task is now finished. I have performed it to the best of my ability, and in words, at least, the requirements of the law are now satisfied. If deeds be in question, those who are here interred have received part of their honours already, and for the rest, their children will be brought up till manhood at the public expense: the state thus offers a valuable prize, as the garland of victory in this race of valour, for the reward both of those who have fallen and their survivors. And where the rewards for merit are greatest, there are found the best citizens.

"And now that you have brought to a close your lamentations for your relatives, you may depart."

Such was the funeral that took place during this winter, with which the first year of the war came to an end. In the first days of summer the Lacedaemonians and their allies, with two-thirds of their forces as before, invaded Attica, under the command of Archidamus, son of Zeuxidamus, king of Lacedaemon, and sat down and laid waste the country. Not many days after their arrival in Attica the plague first began to show itself among the Athenians. It was said that it had broken out in many places previously in the neighbourhood of Lemnos and elsewhere; but a pestilence of such extent and mortality was nowhere remembered. Neither were the physicians at first of any service, ignorant as they were of the proper way to treat it, but they died themselves the most thickly, as they visited the sick most often; nor did any human art succeed any better. Supplications in the temples, divinations, and so forth were found equally futile, till the overwhelming nature of the disaster at last put a stop to them altogether.

It first began, it is said, in the parts of Ethiopia above Egypt, and thence descended into Egypt and Libya and into most of the king's country. Suddenly falling upon Athens, it first attacked the population in Piraeus, —which was the occasion of their saying that the Peloponnesians had poisoned the reservoirs, there being as yet no wells there—and afterwards appeared in the upper city, when the deaths became much more frequent. All speculation as to its origin and its causes, if causes can be found adequate to produce so great a disturbance, I leave to other writers, whether lay or professional; for myself, I shall simply set down its nature, and explain the symptoms by which perhaps it may be recognised by the student, if it should ever break out again. This I can the better do, as I had the disease myself, and watched its operation in the case of others.

That year then is admitted to have been otherwise unprecedentedly free from sickness; and such few cases as occurred, all determined in this. As a rule, however, there was no ostensible cause; but people in good health were all of a sudden attacked by violent heats in the head, and redness and inflammation in the eyes, the inward parts, such as the throat or tongue, becoming bloody and emitting an unnatural and fetid breath. These symptoms were followed by sneezing and hoarseness, after which the pain soon reached the chest, and produced a hard cough. When it fixed in the stomach, it upset it; and discharges of bile of every kind named by physicians ensued, accompanied by very great distress. In most cases also an ineffectual retching followed, producing violent spasms, which in some cases ceased soon after, in others much later. Externally the body was not very hot to the touch, nor pale in its appearance, but reddish, livid, and breaking out into small pustules and ulcers. But internally it burned so that the patient could not bear to have on him clothing or linen even of the very lightest description; or indeed to be otherwise than stark naked. What they would have liked best would have been to throw themselves into cold water; as indeed was done by some of the neglected sick, who plunged into the rain-tanks in their agonies of unquenchable thirst; though it made no difference whether they drank little or much. Besides this, the miserable feeling of not being able to rest or sleep never ceased to torment them. The body meanwhile did not waste away so long as the distemper was at its height, but held out to a marvel against its ravages; so that when they succumbed, as in most cases, on the seventh or eighth day to the internal inflammation, they had still some strength in them. But if they passed this stage, and the disease descended further into the bowels, inducing a violent ulceration there accompanied by severe diarrhoea, this brought on a weakness which was generally fatal. For the disorder first settled in the head, ran its course from thence through the whole of the body, and even where it did not prove mortal, it still left its mark on the extremities; for it settled in the privy parts, the fingers and the toes, and many escaped with the loss of these, some too with that of their eyes. Others again were seized with an entire loss of memory on their first recovery, and did not know either themselves or their friends.

But while the nature of the distemper was such as to baffle all description, and its attacks almost too grievous for human nature to endure, it was still in the following circumstance that its difference from all ordinary disorders was most clearly shown. All the birds and beasts that prey upon human bodies, either abstained from touching them (though there were many lying unburied), or died after tasting them. In proof of this, it was noticed that birds of this kind actually disappeared; they were not about the bodies, or indeed to be seen at all. But of course the effects which I have mentioned could best be studied in a domestic animal like the dog.

Such then, if we pass over the varieties of particular cases, which were many and peculiar, were the general features of the distemper. Meanwhile the town enjoyed an immunity from all the ordinary disorders; or if any case occurred, it ended in this. Some died in neglect, others in the midst of every attention. No remedy was found that could be used as a specific; for what did good in one case, did harm in another. Strong and weak constitutions proved equally incapable of resistance, all alike being swept away, although dieted with the utmost precaution. By far the most terrible feature in the malady was the dejection which ensued when any one felt himself sickening, for the despair into which they instantly fell took away their power of resistence, and left them a much easier prey to the disorder; besides which, there was the awful spectacle of men dying like sheep, through having caught the infection in nursing each other. This caused the greatest mortality. On the one hand, if they were afraid to visit each other, they perished from neglect; indeed many houses were emptied of their inmates for want of a nurse: on the other, if they ventured to do so, death was the consequence. This was especially the case with such as made any pretensions to goodness: honour made them unsparing of themselves in their attendance in their friends' houses, where even the members of the family were at last worn out by the moans of the dying, and succumbed to the force of the disaster. Yet it was with those who had recovered from the disease that the sick and the dying found most compassion. These knew what it was from experience, and had now no fear for themselves; for the same man was never attacked twice—never at least fatally. And such persons not only received the congratulations of others, but themselves also, in the elation of the moment, half entertained the vain hope that they were for the future safe from any disease whatsoever.

An aggravation of the existing calamity was in the influx from the country into the city, and this was especially felt by the new arrivals. As there were no houses to receive them, they had to be lodged at the hot season of the year in stifling cabins, where the mortality raged without restraint. The bodies of dying men lay one upon another, and half-dead creatures reeled about the streets and gathered round all the fountains in their longing for water. The sacred places also in which they had quartered themselves were full of corpses of persons that had died there, just as they were; for as the disaster passed all bounds, men, not knowing what was to become of them, became utterly careless of everything, whether sacred or profane. All the burial rites before in use were entirely upset, and they buried the bodies as best they could. Many from want of the proper appliances, through so many of their friends having died already, had recourse to the most shameless sepultures: sometimes getting the start of those who had raised a pile, they threw their own dead body upon the stranger's pyre and ignited it; sometimes they tossed the corpse which they were carrying on the top of another that was burning, and so went off.

Now was this the only form of lawless extravagance which owed its origin to the plague. Men now coolly ventured on what they had formerly done in a corner, and not just as they pleased, seeing the rapid transitions produced by persons in prosperity suddenly dying and those who before had nothing succeeding to their property. So they resolved to spend quickly and enjoy themselves, regarding their lives and riches as alike things of a day. Perseverance in what men called honour was popular with none, it was so uncertain whether they would be spared to attain the object; but it was settled that present enjoyment, and all that contributed to it, was both honourable and useful. Fear of gods or law of man there was none to restrain them. As for the first, they judged it to be just the same whether they worshipped them or not, as they saw all alike perishing; and for the last, no one expected to live to be brought to trial for his offences, but each felt that a far severer sentence had been already passed upon them all and hung ever over their heads, and before this fell it was only reasonable to enjoy life a little.

Such was the nature of the calamity, and heavily did it weigh on the Athenians; death raging within the city and devastation without. Among other things which they remembered in their distress was, very naturally, the following verse which the old men said had long ago been uttered:

> A Dorian war shall come and with it death.

So a dispute arose as to whether dearth and not death had not been the word in the verse; but at the present juncture, it was of course decided in favour of the latter; for the people made their recollection fit in with their sufferings. I fancy, however, that if another Dorian war should ever afterwards come upon us, and a dearth should happen to accompany it, the verse will probably be read accordingly. The oracle also which had been given to the Lacedaemonians was now remembered by those who knew of it. When the God was asked whether they should go to war, he answered that if they put their might into it, victory would be theirs, and that he would himself be with them. With this oracle events were supposed to tally. For the plague broke out so soon as the Peloponnesians invaded Attica, and never entering Peloponnese (not at least to an extent worth noticing), committed its worst ravages at Athens, and next to Athens, at the most populous of the other towns. Such was the history of the plague. . . .

After the second invasion of the Peloponnesians a change came over the spirit of the Athenians. Their land had now been twice laid waste; and war and pestilence at once pressed heavy upon them. They began to find fault with Pericles, as the author of the war and the cause of all their misfortunes, and became eager to come to terms with Lacedaemon, and actually sent ambassadors thither, who did not however succeed in their mission. Their despair was now complete and all vented itself upon Pericles. When he saw them exasperated at the present turn of affairs and acting exactly as he had anticipated, he called an assembly, being (it must be remembered) still general, with the double object of restoring confidence and of leading them from these angry feelings to a calmer and more hopeful state of mind. He accordingly came forward and spoke as follows:

". . . You must not be seduced by citizens like these nor be angry with me—who, if I voted for war, only did as you did yourselves—in spite of the enemy having invaded your country and done what you could be certain that he would do, if you refused to comply with his demands; and although besides what we counted for, the plague has come upon us—the only point indeed at which our calculation has been at fault. It is this, I know, that has had a large share in making me more unpopular than I should otherwise have been,—quite undeservedly, unless you are also prepared to give me the credit of any success with which chance may present you. Besides, the hand of Heaven must be borne with resignation, that of the enemy with fortitude; this was the old way at Athens, and do not you prevent it being so still. Remember, too, that if your country has the greatest name in all the world, it is because she never bent before disaster; because she has expended more life and effort in war than any other city, and has won for herself a power greater than any hitherto known, the memory of which will descend to the latest posterity; even if now, in obedience to the general law of decay, we should ever be forced to yield, still it will be remembered that we held rule over more Hellenes than any other Hellenic state, that we sustained the greatest wars against their united or separate powers, and inhabited a city unrivalled by any other in resources or magnitude. These glories may incur the censure of the slow and unambitious; but in the breast of energy they will awake emulation, and in those who must remain without them an envious regret. Hatred and unpopularity at the moment have fallen to the lot of all who have aspired to rule others; but where odium must be incurred, true wisdom incurs it for the highest objects. Hatred also is short-lived; but that which makes the splendour of the present and the glory of the future remains for ever unforgotten. Make your decision, therefore, for glory then and honour now, and attain both objects by instant and zealous effort: do not send heralds to Lacedaemon, and do not betray any sign of being oppressed by your present sufferings, since they whose minds are least sensitive to calamity, and whose hands are most quick to meet it, are the greatest men and the greatest communities."

Such were the arguments by which Pericles tried to cure the Athenians of their anger against him and to divert their thoughts from their immediate afflictions. As a community he succeeded in convincing them; they not only gave up all idea of sending to Lacedaemon, but applied themselves with increased energy to the war; still as private individuals they could not help smarting under their sufferings, the common people having been deprived of the little that they ever possessed, while the higher orders had lost fine properties with costly establishments and buildings in the country, and, worst of all, had war instead of peace. In fact, the public feeling against him did not subside until he had been fined. Not long afterwards, however, according to the way of the multitude, they again elected him general and committed all their affairs to his hands, having now become less sensitive to their private and domestic afflictions, and understanding that he was the best man of all for the public necessities. For as long as he was at the head of the state during the peace, he pursued a moderate and conservative policy; and in his time its greatness was at its height. When the war broke out, here also he seems to have rightly gauged the power of his country. He outlived its commencement two years and six months, and the correctness of his previsions respecting it became better known by his death. He told them to wait quietly, to pay attention to their marine, to attempt no new conquests, and to expose the city to no hazards during the war, and doing this, promised them a favourable result. What they did was the very contrary, allowing private ambitions and private interests, in matters apparently quite foreign to the war, to lead them into projects unjust both to themselves and to their allies—projects whose success would only conduce to the honour and advantage of private persons, and whose failure entailed certain disaster on the country in the war. The causes of this are not far to seek. Pericles indeed, by his rank, ability, and known integrity, was enabled to exercise an independent control over the multitude—in short, to lead them instead of being led by them; for as he never sought power by improper means, he was never compelled to flatter them, but, on the contrary, enjoyed so high an estimation that he could afford to anger them by contradiction. Whenever he saw them unseasonably and insolently elated, he would with a word reduce them to alarm; on the other hand, if they fell victims to a panic, he could at once restore them to confidence. In short, what was nominally a democracy became in his hands government by the first citizen. With his successors it was different. More on a level with one another, and each grasping at supremacy, they ended by committing even the conduct of state affairs to the whims of the multitude. This, as might have been expected in a great and sovereign state, produced a host of blunders, and amongst them the Sicilian expedition; though this failed not so much through a miscalculation of the power of those against whom it was sent, as through a fault in the senders in not taking the best measures afterwards to assist those who had gone out, but choosing rather to occupy themselves with private cabals for the leadership of the commons, by which they not only paralysed operations in the field, but also first introduced civil discord at home. Yet after losing most of their fleet besides other forces in Sicily, and with faction already dominant in the city, they could still for three years make head against their original adversaries, joined not only by the Sicilians, but also by their own allies nearly all in revolt, and at last by the king's son, Cyrus, who furnished the funds for the Peloponnesian navy. Nor did they finally succumb till they fell the victims of their own intestine disorders. So superfluously abundant were the resources from which the genius of Pericles foresaw an easy triumph in the war over the unaided forces of the Peloponnesians.

(In Books III through VI, Thucydides describes the shifting fortunes of war and the political and military maneuvers of the protagonists. The struggle appears a stalemate until the Athenians in their ignorance and pride attempt to reduce Sicily with its Spartan allies to subjection. The tragic unfolding of that enterprise is related in Book VII, which we here open at Chapter 22 where Thucydides describes the "folly and obstinacy of Nicias," the Athenian commander.)

. . . The Athenians now fell into great disorder and perplexity, so that it was not easy to get from one side or the other any detailed account of the affair. By day certainly the combatants have a clearer notion, though even then by no means of all that takes place, no one knowing much of anything that does not go on in his own immediate neighbourhood; but in a night engagement (and this was the only one that occurred between great armies during the war) how could any one know anything for certain? Although there was a bright moon they saw each other only as men do by moonlight, that is to say, they could distinguish the form of the body, but could not tell for certain whether it was a friend or an enemy. Both had great numbers of heavy infantry moving about in a small space. Some of the Athenians were already defeated, while others were coming up yet unconquered for their first attack. A large part also of the rest of their forces either had only just got up, or were still ascending, so that they did not know which way to march. Owing to the rout that had taken place all in front was now in confusion, and the noise made it difficult to distinguish anything. The victorious Syracusans and allies were cheering each other on with loud cries, by night the only possible means of communication, and meanwhile receiving all who came against them; while the Athenians were seeking for one another, taking all in front of them for enemies, even although they might be some of their now flying friends; and by constantly asking for the watchword, which was their only means of recognition, not only caused great confusion among themselves by asking all at once, but also made it known to the enemy, whose own they did not so readily discover, as the Syracusans were victorious and not scattered, and thus less easily mistaken. The result was that if the Athenians fell in with a party of the enemy that was weaker than they, it escaped them through knowing their watchword; while if they themselves failed to answer they were put to the sword. But what hurt them as much, or indeed more than anything else, was the singing of the Paean, from the perplexity which it caused by being nearly the same on either side: the Argives and Corcyraeans and any other Dorian peoples in the army, struck terror into the Athenians whenever they raised their Paean, no less than did the enemy. Thus, after being once thrown into disorder, they ended by coming into collision with each other in many parts of the field, friends with friends, and citizens with citizens, and not only terrified one another, but even came to blows and could only be parted with difficulty. In the pursuit many perished by throwing themselves down the cliffs, the way down from Epipolae being narrow; and of those who got down safely into the plain, although many, especially those who belonged to the first armament, escaped through their better acquaintance with the locality, some of the newcomers lost their way and wandered over the country, and were cut off in the morning by the Syracusan cavalry and killed.

The next day the Syracusans set up two trophies, one upon Epipolae where the ascent had been made, and the other on the spot where the first check was given by the Boeotians; and the Athenians took back their dead under truce. A great many of the Athenians and allies were killed, although still more arms were taken than could be accounted for by the number of the dead, as some of those who were obliged to leap down from the cliffs without their shields escaped with their lives and did not perish like the rest.

After this the Syracusans, recovering their old confidence at such an unexpected stroke of good fortune, despatched Sicanus with fifteen ships to Agrigentum where there was a revolution, to induce if possible the city to join them; while Gylippus again went by land into the rest of Sicily to bring up reinforcements, being now in hope of taking the Athenian lines by storm, after the result of the affair on Epipolae.

In the meantime the Athenian generals consulted upon the disaster which had happened, and upon the general weakness of the army. They saw themselves unsuccessful in their enterprises, and the soldiers disgusted with their stay; disease being rife among them owing to its being the sickly season of the year, and to the marshy and unhealthy nature of the spot in which they were encamped; and the state of their affairs generally being thought desperate. Accordingly, Demosthenes was of opinion that they ought not to stay any longer; but agreeably to his original idea in risking the attempt upon Epipolae, now that this had failed, he gave his vote for going away without further loss of time, while the sea might yet be crossed, and their late reinforcement might give them the superiority at all events on that element. He also said that it would be more profitable for the state to carry on the war against those who were building fortifications in Attica, than against the Syracusans whom it was no longer easy to subdue; besides which it was not right to squander large sums of money to no purpose by going on with the siege.

This was the opinion of Demosthenes. Nicias, without denying the bad state of their affairs, was unwilling to avow their weakness, or to have it reported to the enemy that the Athenians in full council were openly voting for retreat; for in that case they would be much less likely to effect

it when they wanted without discovery. Moreover, his own particular
information still gave him reason to hope that the affairs of the enemy
would soon be in a worse state than their own, if the Athenians persevered in the siege; as they would wear out the Syracusans by want of
money, especially with the more extensive command of the sea now
given them by their present navy. Besides this, there was a party in
Syracuse who wished to betray the city to the Athenians, and kept sending him messages and telling him not to raise the siege. Accordingly,
knowing this and really waiting because he hesitated between the two
courses and wished to see his way more clearly, in his public speech on
this occasion he refused to lead off the army, saying he was sure the
Athenians would never approve of their returning without a vote of
theirs. Those who would vote upon their conduct, instead of judging the
facts as eye-witnesses like themselves and not from what they might
hear from hostile critics, would simply be guided by the calumnies of the
first clever speaker; while many, indeed most, of the soldiers on the spot,
who now so loudly proclaimed the danger of their position, when they
reached Athens would proclaim just as loudly the opposite, and would
say that their generals had been bribed to betray them and return. For
himself, therefore, who knew the Athenian temper, sooner than perish
under a dishonourable charge and by an unjust sentence at the hands of
the Athenians, he would rather take his chance and die, if die he must,
a soldier's death at the hand of the enemy. Besides, after all, the Syracusans were in a worse case than themselves. What with paying mercenaries, spending upon fortified posts, and now for a full year maintaining
a large navy, they were already at a loss and would soon be at a standstill:
they had already spent two thousand talents and incurred heavy debts
besides, and could not lose even ever so small a fraction of their present
force through not paying it, without ruin to their cause; depending as
they did more upon mercenaries than upon soldiers obliged to serve, like
their own. He therefore said that they ought to stay and carry on the siege,
and not depart defeated in point of money, in which they were much
superior.

Nicias spoke positively because he had exact information of the finan-
cial distress at Syracuse, and also because of the strength of the Athenian
party there which kept sending him messages not to raise the siege;
besides which he had more confidence than before in his fleet, and felt
sure at least of its success. Demosthenes, however, would not hear for a
moment of continuing the siege, but said that if they could not lead off
the army without a decree from Athens, and if they were obliged to stay
on, they ought to remove to Thapsus or Catana; where their land forces
would have a wide extent of country to overrun, and could live by plundering the enemy, and would thus do them damage; while the fleet would

have the open sea to fight in, that is to say, instead of a narrow space which was all in the enemy's favour, a wide sea-room where their science would be of use, and where they could retreat or advance without being confined or circumscribed either when they put out or put in. In any case he was altogether opposed to their staying on where they were, and insisted on removing at once, as quickly and with as little delay as possible; and in this judgment Eurymedon agreed. Nicias however still objecting, a certain diffidence and hesitation came over them, with a suspicion that Nicias might have some further information to make him so positive.

While the Athenians lingered on in this way without moving from where they were, Gylippus and Sicanus now arrived at Syracuse. Sicanus had failed to gain Agrigentum, the party friendly to the Syracusans having been driven out while he was still at Gela; but Gylippus was accompanied not only by a large number of troops raised in Sicily, but by the heavy infantry sent off in the spring from Peloponnese in the merchantmen, who had arrived at Selinus from Libya. They had been carried to Libya by a storm, and having obtained two galleys and pilots from the Cyrenians, on their voyage along shore had taken sides with the Euesperitae and had defeated the Libyans who were besieging them, and from thence coasting on to Neapolis, a Carthaginian mart, and the nearest point to Sicily, from which it is only two days' and a night's voyage, there crossed over and came to Selinus. Immediately upon their arrival the Syracusans prepared to attack the Athenians again by land and sea at once. The Athenian generals seeing a fresh army come to the aid of the enemy, and that their own circumstances, far from improving, were becoming daily worse, and above all distressed by the sickness of the soldiers, now began to repent of not having removed before; and Nicias no longer offering the same opposition, except by urging that there should be no open voting, they gave orders as secretly as possible for all to be prepared to sail out from the camp at a given signal. All was at last ready, and they were on the point of sailing away, when an eclipse of the moon, which was then at the full, took place. Most of the Athenians, deeply impressed by this occurrence, now urged the generals to wait; and Nicias, who was somewhat overaddicted to divination and practices of that kind, refused from that moment even to take the question of departure into consideration, until they had waited the thrice nine days prescribed by the soothsayers.

The besiegers were thus condemned to stay in the country; and the Syracusans getting wind of what had happened, became more eager than ever to press the Athenians, who had now themselves acknowledged that they were no longer their superiors either by sea or by land, as otherwise they would never have planned to sail away. Besides which the Syracusans did not wish them to settle in any other part of Sicily, where they would be more difficult to deal with, but desired to force them to fight at sea as quickly as possible, in a position favourable to themselves. Accordingly they manned their ships and practised for as many days as they thought sufficient. When the moment arrived they assaulted on the first day the Athenian lines, and upon a small force of heavy infantry and horse sallying out against them by certain gates, cut off some of the former and routed and pursued them to the lines, where, as the entrance was narrow, the Athenians lost seventy horses and some few of the heavy infantry.

Drawing off their troops for this day, on the next the Syracusans went out with a fleet of seventy-six sail, and at the same time advanced with their land forces against the lines. The Athenians put out to meet them with eighty-six ships, came to close quarters and engaged. The Syracusans and their allies first defeated the Athenian centre, and then caught Eurymedon, the commander of the right wing, who was sailing out from the line more towards the land in order to surround the enemy, in the hollow and recess of the harbour, and killed him and destroyed the ships accompanying him; after which they now chased the whole Athenian fleet before them and drove them ashore.

Gylippus seeing the enemy's fleet defeated and carried ashore beyond their stockades and camp, ran down to the breakwater with some of his troops, in order to cut off the men as they landed and make it easier for the Syracusans to tow off the vessels by the shore being friendly ground. The Tyrrhenians who guarded this point for the Athenians seeing them come on in disorder, advanced out against them and attacked and routed their van, hurling it into the marsh of Lysimeleia. Afterwards the Syracusan and allied troops arrived in greater numbers, and the Athenians fearing for their ships came up also to the rescue and engaged them, and defeated and pursued them to some distance and killed a few of their heavy infantry. They succeeded in rescuing most of their ships and brought them down by their camp; eighteen however were taken by the Syracusans and their allies, and all the men killed. The rest the enemy tried to burn by means of an old merchantman which they filled with faggots and pine-wood, set on fire and let drift down the wind which blew full on the Athenians. The Athenians, however, alarmed for their ships, contrived means for stopping it and putting it out, and checking the flames and the nearer approach of the merchantman, thus escaped the danger.

After this the Syracusans set up a trophy for the sea-fight and for the heavy infantry whom they had cut off up at the lines, where they took the horses; and the Athenians for the rout of the foot driven by the Tyrrhenians into the marsh, and for their own victory with the rest of the army.

The Syracusans had now gained a decisive victory at sea, where until now they had feared the reinforcement brought by Demosthenes, and deep, in consequence, was the despondency of the Athenians, and great their disappointment, and greater still their regret for having come on the expedition. These were the only cities that they had yet encountered, similar to their own in character, under democracies like themselves, which had ships and horses, and were of considerable magnitude. They had been unable to divide and bring them over by holding out the prospect of changes in their governments, or to crush them by their great superiority in force, but had failed in most of their attempts, and being already in perplexity, had now been defeated at sea, where defeat could never have been expected, and were thus plunged deeper in embarrassment than ever.

Meanwhile the Syracusans immediately began to sail freely along the harbour, and determined to close up its mouth, so that the Athenians might not be able to steal out in future, even if they wished. Indeed, the Syracusans no longer thought only of saving themselves, but also how to hinder the escape of the enemy; thinking, and thinking rightly, that they were now much the strongest, and that to conquer the Athenians and their allies by land and sea would win them great glory in Hellas. The rest of the Hellenes would thus immediately be either free or released from apprehension, as the remaining forces of Athens would be henceforth unable to sustain the war that would be waged against her; while they, the Syracusans, would be regarded as the authors of this deliverance, and would be held in high admiration, not only with all men now living but also with posterity. Nor were these the only considerations that gave dignity to the struggle. They would thus conquer not only the Athenians but also their numerous allies, and conquer not alone, but with their companions-in-arms, commanding side by side with the Corinthians and Lacedaemonians, having offered their city to stand in the van of danger, and having been in a great measure the pioneers of naval success.

Indeed, there were never so many peoples assembled before a single city, if we except the grand total gathered together in this war under Athens and Lacedaemon. . . .

Such were the auxiliaries brought together on either side, all of which had by this time joined, neither party experiencing any subsequent accession. It was no wonder, therefore, if the Syracusans and their allies thought that it would win them great glory if they could follow up their recent victory in the sea-fight by the capture of the whole Athenian armada, without letting it escape either by sea or by land. They began at once to close up the Great Harbour by means of boats, merchant vessels, and galleys moored broadside across its mouth, which is nearly a mile wide, and made all their other arrangements for the event of the Athenians again venturing to fight at sea. There was, in fact, nothing little either in their plans or their ideas.

The Athenians, seeing them closing up the harbour and informed of their further designs, called a council of war. The generals and colonels assembled and discussed the difficulties of the situation; the point which pressed most being that they no longer had provisions for immediate use (having sent on to Catana to tell them not to send any, in the belief that they were going away), and that they would not have any in future unless they could command the sea. They therefore determined to evacuate their upper lines, to enclose with a cross-wall and garrison a small space close to the ships, only just sufficient to hold their stores and sick, and manning all the ships, seaworthy or not, with every man that could be spared from the rest of their land forces, to fight it out at sea, and if victorious, to go to Catana, if not, to burn their vessels, form in close order, and retreat by land for the nearest friendly place they could reach, Hellenic or barbarian. This was no sooner settled than carried into effect: they descended gradually from the upper lines and manned all their vessels, compelling all to go on board who were of age to be in any way of use. They thus succeeded in manning about one hundred and ten ships in all, on board of which they embarked a number of archers and darters taken from the Acarnanians and from the other foreigners, making all other provisions allowed by the nature of their plan and by the necessities which imposed it. All was now nearly ready, and Nicias, seeing the soldiery disheartened by their unprecedented and decided defeat at sea, and by reason of the scarcity of provisions eager to fight it out as soon as possible, called them all together, and first addressed them, speaking as follows:

"Soldiers of the Athenians and of the allies, we have all an equal interest in the coming struggle, in which life and country are at stake for us quite as much as they can be for the enemy; since if our fleet wins the day, each can see his native city again, whever that city may be. You must not lose heart, or be like men without any experience, who fail in a first essay, and ever afterwards fearfully forebode a future as disastrous. But let the Athenians among you who have already had experience of many wars, and the allies who have joined us in so many expeditions, remember the surprises of war, and with the hope that fortune will not be always against us, prepare to fight again in a manner worthy of the number which you see yourselves to be.

"Now, whatever we thought would be of service against the crush of vessels in such a narrow harbour, and against the force upon the decks of the enemy, from which we suffered before, has all been considered with the helmsmen, and, as far as our means allowed, provided. A number of archers and darters will go on board, and a multitude that we should not have employed in an action in the open sea, where our science would be crippled by the weight of the vessels; but in the present land-fight that we are forced to make from shipboard all this will be useful. We have also discovered the changes in construction that we must make to meet theirs; and against the thickness of their cheeks, which did us the greatest mischief, we have provided grappling-irons, which will prevent an assailant backing water after charging, if the soldiers on deck here do their duty; since we are absolutely compelled to fight a land battle from the fleet, and it seems to be our interest neither to back water ourselves, nor to let the enemy do so, especially as the shore, except so much of it as may be held by our troops, is hostile ground.

"You must remember this and fight on as long as you can, and must not let yourselves be driven ashore, but once alongside must make up your minds not to part company until you have swept the heavy infantry from the enemy's deck. I say this more for the heavy infantry than for the seamen, as it is more the business of the men on deck; and our land forces are even now on the whole the strongest. The sailors I advise, and at the same time implore, not to be too much daunted by their misfortunes, now that we have our decks better armed and a greater number of vessels. Bear in mind how well worth preserving is the pleasure felt by those of you who through your knowledge of our language and imitation of our manners were always considered Athenians, even though not so in real-ity, and as such were honoured throughout Hellas, and had your full share of the advantages of our empire, and more than your share in the respect of our subjects and in protection from ill treatment. You, there-fore, with whom alone we freely share our empire, we now justly require not to betray that empire in its extremity, and in scorn of Corinthians, whom you have often conquered, and of Siceliots, none of whom so much as presumed to stand against us when our navy was in its prime, we ask you to repel them, and to show that even in sickness and disaster your skill is more than a match for the fortune and vigour of any other.

"For the Athenians among you I add once more this reflexion:—you left behind you no more such ships in your docks as these, no more heavy infantry in their flower; if you do aught but conquer, our enemies here will immediately sail thither, and those that are left of us at Athens will become unable to repel their home assailants, reinforced by these new allies. Here you will fall at once into the hands of the Syracusans—I need not remind you of the intentions with which you attacked them—and your countrymen at home will fall into those of the Lacedaemonians. Since the fate of both thus hangs upon this single battle—now, if ever, stand firm, and remember, each and all, that you who are now going on board are the army and navy of the Athenians, and all that is left of the state and the great name of Athens, in whose defence if any man has any advantage in skill or courage, now is the time for him to show it, and thus serve himself and save all."

After this address Nicias at once gave orders to man the ships. Meanwhile Gylippus and the Syracusans could perceive by the preparations which they saw going on that the Athenians meant to fight at sea. They had also notice of the grappling-irons, against which they specially provided by stretching hides over the prows and much of the upper part of their vessels, in order that the irons when thrown might slip off without taking hold. All being now ready, the generals and Gylippus addressed them in the following terms:

"Syracusans and allies, the glorious character of our past achievements and the no less glorious results at issue in the coming battle are, we think, understood by most of you, or you would never have thrown yourselves with such ardour into the struggle; and if there be any one not as fully aware of the facts as he ought to be, we will declare them to him. The Athenians came to this country first to effect the conquest of Sicily, and after that, if successful, of Peloponnese and the rest of Hellas, possessing already the greatest empire yet known, of present or former times, among the Hellenes. Here for the first time they found in you men who faced their navy which made them masters everywhere; you have already defeated them in the previous sea-fight, and will in all likelihood defeat them again now. When men are once checked in what they consider their special excellence, their whole opinion of themselves suffers more than if they had not at first believed in their superiority, the unexpected shock to their pride causing them to give way more than their real strength warrants; and this is probably now the case with the Athenians.

"With us it is different. The original estimate of ourselves which gave us courage in the days of our unskillfulness has been strengthened, while the convictions super-added to it that we must be the best seamen of the time, if we have conquered the best, has given a double measure of hope to every man among us; and, for the most part, where there is the greatest hope, there is also the greatest ardour for action. The means to combat us which they have tried to find in copying our armament are familiar to our warfare, and will be met by proper provisions; while they will never be able to have a number of heavy infantry on their decks, contrary to their custom, and a number of darters (born landsmen, one may say, Acarnanians and others, embarked afloat, who will not know how to discharge their weapons when they have to keep still), without hampering their vessels and falling all into confusion among themselves through fighting not according to their own tactics. For they will gain nothing by the number of their ships—I say this to those of you who may be alarmed by having to fight against odds—as a quantity of ships in a confined space will only be slower in executing the movements required, and most exposed to injury from our means of offence. Indeed, if you would know the plain truth, as we are credibly informed, the excess of their sufferings and the necessities of their present distress have made them desperate; they have no confidence in their force, but wish to try their fortune in the only way they can, and either to force their passage and sail out, or after this to retreat by land, it being impossible for them to be worse off than they are.

"The fortune of our greatest enemies having thus betrayed itself, and their disorder being what I have described, let us engage in anger, convinced that, as between adversaries, nothing is more legitimate than to claim to sate the whole wrath of one's soul in punishing the aggressor, and nothing more sweet, as the proverb has it, than the vengeance upon an enemy, which it will now be ours to take. That enemies they are and mortal enemies you all know, since they came here to enslave our country, and if successful had in reserve for our men all that is most dreadful, and for our children and wives all that is most dishonourable, and for the whole city the name which conveys the greatest reproach. None should therefore relent or think it gain if they go away without further danger to us. This they will do just the same, even if they get the victory; while if we succeed, as we may expect, in chastising them, and in handing down to all Sicily her ancient freedom strengthened and confirmed, we shall have achieved no mean triumph. And the rarest dangers are those in which failure brings little loss and success the greatest advantage."

After the above address to the soldiers on their side, the Syracusan generals and Gylippus now perceived that the Athenians were manning their ships, and immediately proceeded to man their own also. Meanwhile Nicias, appalled by the position of affairs, realising the greatness and the nearness of the danger now that they were on the point of putting out from shore, and thinking, as men are apt to think in great crises, that when all has been done they have still something left to do, and when all has been said that they have not yet said enough, again called on the captains one by one, addressing each by his father's name and by his own, and by that of his tribe, and adjured them not to belie their own personal renown, or to obscure the hereditary virtues for which their ancestors were illustrious; he reminded them of their country, the freest of the free, and of the unfettered discretion allowed in it to all to live as they pleased; and added other arguments such as men would use at such a crisis, and which, with little alteration, are made to serve on all occasions alike—appeals to wives, children, and national gods,—without caring whether they are thought commonplace, but loudly invoking them in the belief that they will be of use in the consternation of the moment. Having thus admonished them, not, he felt, as he would, but as he could,

Nicias withdrew and led the troops to the sea, and ranged them in as long
a line as he was able, in order to aid as far as possible in sustaining the
courage of the men afloat; while Demosthenes, Menander, and Eu-
thydemus, who took the command on board, put out from their own camp
and sailed straight to the barrier across the mouth of the harbour and to
the passage left open, to try to force their way out.

The Syracusans and their allies had already put out with about the
same number of ships as before, a part of which kept guard at the outlet,
and the remainder all round the rest of the harbour, in order to attack
the Athenians on all sides at once; while the land forces held themselves
in readiness at the points at which the vessels might put into the shore.
The Syracusan fleet was commanded by Sicanus and Agatharchus, who
had each a wing of the whole force, with Pythen and the Corinthians in
the centre. When the rest of the Athenians came up to the barrier, with
the first shock of their charge they overpowered the ships stationed there,
and tried to undo the fastenings; after this, as the Syracusans and allies
bore down upon them from all quarters, the action spread from the
barrier over the whole harbour, and was more obstinately disputed than
any of the preceding ones. On either side the rowers showed great zeal
in bringing up their vessels at the boatswains' orders, and the helmsmen
great skill in maneuvring, and great emulation one with another; while
the ships once alongside, the soldiers on board did their best not to let the
service on deck be outdone by the others; in short, every man strove to
prove himself the first in his particular department. And as many ships
were engaged in a small compass (for these were the largest fleets
fighting in the narrowest space ever known, being together little short of
two hundred), the regular attacks with the beak were few, there being no
opportunity of backing water or of breaking the line; while the collisions
caused by one ship chancing to run foul of another, either in flying from
or attacking a third, were more frequent. So long as a vessel was coming
up to the charge the men on the decks rained darts and arrows and stones
upon her; but once alongside, the heavy infantry tried to board each
other's vessel, fighting hand to hand. In many quarters also it happened,
by reason of the narrow room, that a vessel was charging an enemy on
one side and being charged herself on another, and that two, or sometimes more ships had perforce got entangled round one, obliging the
helmsmen to attend to defence here, offence there, not to one thing at
once, but to many on all sides; while the huge din caused by the number
of ships crashing together not only spread terror, but made the orders of
the boatswains inaudible. The boatswains on either side in the discharge
of their duty and in the heat of the conflict shouted incessantly orders and
appeals to their men; the Athenians they urged to force the passage out,
and now if ever to show their mettle and lay hold of a safe return to their

country; to the Syracusans and their allies they cried that it would be glorious to prevent the escape of the enemy, and conquering, to exalt the countries that were theirs. The generals, moreover, on either side, if they saw any in any part of the battle backing ashore without being forced to do so, called out to the captain by name and asked him—the Athenians, whether they were retreating because they thought the thrice hostile shore more their own than that sea which had cost them so much labour to win; the Syracusans, whether they were flying from the flying Athenians, whom they well knew to be eager to escape in whatever way they could.

Meanwhile the two armies on shore, while victory hung in the balance, were a prey to the most agonising and conflicting emotions; the natives thirsting for more glory than they had already won, while the invaders feared to find themselves in even worse plight than before. The all of the Athenians being set upon their fleet, their fear for the event was like nothing they had ever felt; while their view of the struggle was necessarily as chequered as the battle itself. Close to the scene of action and not all looking at the same point at once, some saw their friends victorious and took courage, and fell to calling upon heaven not to deprive them of salvation, while others who had their eyes turned upon the losers, wailed and cried aloud, and, although spectators, were more overcome than the actual combatants. Others, again, were gazing at some spot where the battle was evenly disputed; as the strife was protracted without decision, their swaying bodies reflected the agitation of their minds, and they suffered the worst agony of all, ever just within reach of safety or just on the point of destruction. In short, in that one Athenian army as long as the sea-fight remained doubtful there was every sound to be heard at once, shrieks, cheers, *"We win,"* *"We lose,"* and all the other manifold exclamations that a great host would necessarily utter in great peril; and with the men in the fleet it was nearly the same; until at last the Syracusans and their allies, after the battle had lasted a long while, put the Athenians to flight, and with much shouting and cheering chased them in open rout to the shore. The naval force, one one way, one another, as many as were not taken afloat, now ran ashore and rushed from on board their ships to their camp; while the army, no more divided, but carried away by one impulse, all with shrieks and groans deplored the event, and ran down, some to help the ships, others to guard what was left of their wall, while the remaining and most numerous part already began to consider how they should save themselves. Indeed, the panic of the present moment had never been surpassed. They now suffered very nearly what they had inflicted at Pylos; as then the Lacedaemonians with the loss of their fleet lost also the men who had crossed over to the island, so now the Athenians had no hope of escaping by land, without the help of some extraordinary accident.

The sea-fight having been a severe one, and many ships and lives having been lost on both sides, the victorious Syracusans and their allies now picked up their wrecks and dead, and sailed off to the city and set up a trophy. The Athenians, overwhelmed by their misfortune, never even thought of asking leave to take up their dead or wrecks, but wished to retreat that very night. Demosthenes, however, went to Nicias and gave it as his opinion that they should man the ships they had left and make another effort to force their passage out next morning; saying that they had still left more ships fit for service than the enemy, the Athenians having about sixty remaining as against less than fifty of their opponents. Nicias was quite of his mind; but when they wished to man the vessels, the sailors refused to go on board, being so utterly overcome by their defeat as no longer to believe in the possibility of success.

Accordingly they all now made up their minds to retreat by land. Meanwhile the Syracusan Hermocrates suspecting their intention, and impressed by the danger of allowing a force of that magnitude to retire by land, establish itself in some other part of Sicily, and from thence renew the war, went and stated his views to the authorities, and pointed out to them that they ought not to let the enemy get away by night, but that all the Syracusans and their allies should at once march out and block up the roads and seize and guard the passes. The authorities were entirely of his opinion, and thought that it ought to be done, but on the other hand felt sure that the people, who had given themselves over to rejoicing and were taking their ease after a great battle at sea, would not be easily brought to obey; besides, they were celebrating a festival, having on that day a sacrifice to Heracles, and most of them in their rapture at the victory had fallen to drinking at the festival, and would probably consent to anything sooner than to take up their arms and march out at that moment. For these reasons the thing appeared impracticable to the magistrates; and Hermocrates, finding himself unable to do anything further with them, had now recourse to the following stratagem of his own. What he feared was that the Athenians might quietly get the start of them by passing the most difficult places during the night; and he therefore sent, as soon as it was dusk, some friends of his own to the camp with some horsemen who rode up within earshot and called out to some of the men, as though they were well-wishers of the Athenians, and told them to tell Nicias (who had in fact some correspondence who informed him of what went on inside the town), not to lead off the army by night as the Syracusans were guarding the roads, but to make his preparations at his leisure and to retreat by day. After saying this they departed; and their hearers informed the Athenian generals, who put off going for that night on the strength of this message, not doubting its sincerity.

Since after all they had not set out at once, they now determined to stay also the following day to give time to the soldiers to pack up as well as they could the most useful articles, and, leaving everything else behind, to start only with what was strictly necessary for their personal subsistence. Meanwhile the Syracusans and Gylippus marched out and blocked up the roads through the country by which the Athenians were likely to pass, and kept guard at the fords of the streams and rivers, posting themselves so as to receive them and stop the army where they thought best; while their fleet sailed up to the beach and towed off the ships of the Athenians. Some few were burned by the Athenians themselves as they had intended; the rest the Syracusans lashed on to their own at their leisure as they had been thrown up on shore, without any one trying to stop them, and conveyed to the town.

After this, Nicias and Demosthenes now thinking that enough had been done in the way of preparation, the removal of the army took place upon the second day after the sea-fight. It was a lamentable scene, not merely from the single circumstance that they were retreating after having lost all their ships, their great hopes gone, and themselves and the state in peril; but also in leaving the camp there were things most grievous for every eye and heart to contemplate. The dead lay unburied, and each man as he recognised a friend among them shuddered with grief and horror; while the living whom they were leaving behind, wounded or sick, were to the living far more shocking than the dead, and more to be pitied than those who had perished. These fell to entreating and bewailing until their friends knew not what to do, begging them to take them and loudly calling to each individual comrade or relative whom they could see, hanging upon the necks of their tent-fellows in the act of departure, and following as far as they could, and when their bodily strength failed them, calling again and again upon heaven and shrieking aloud as they were left behind. So that the whole army being filled with tears and distracted after this fashion found it not easy to go, even from an enemy's land, where they had already suffered evils too great for tears and in the unknown future before them feared to suffer more. Dejection and self-condemnation were also rife among them. Indeed they could only be compared to a starved-out town, and that no small one, escaping; the whole multitude upon the march being not less than forty thousand men. All carried anything they could which might be of use, and the heavy infantry and troopers, contrary to their wont, while under arms carried their own victuals, in some cases for want of servants, in others through not trusting them; as they had long been deserting and now did so in greater numbers than ever. Yet even thus they did not carry enough,

as there was no longer food in the camp. Moreover their disgrace generally, and the universality of their sufferings, however to a certain extent
alleviated by being borne in company, were still felt at the moment a
heavy burden, especially when they contrasted the splendour and glory
of their setting out with the humiliation in which it had ended. For this
was by far the greatest reverse that ever befell an Hellenic army. They
had come to enslave others, and were departing in fear of being enslaved
themselves: they had sailed out with prayer and paeans, and now started
to go back with omens directly contrary; travelling by land instead of by
sea, and trusting not in their fleet but in their heavy infantry. Nevertheless the greatness of the danger still impending made all this appear
tolerable.

Nicias seeing the army dejected and greatly altered, passed along the
ranks and encouraged and comforted them as far as was possible under
the circumstances, raising his voice still higher and higher as he went
from one company to another in his earnestness, and in his anxiety that
the benefit of his words might reach as many as possible:

"Athenians and allies, even in our present position we must still hope
on, since men have ere now been saved from worse straits than this; and
you must not condemn yourselves too severely either because of your
disasters or because of your present unmerited sufferings. I myself who
am not superior to any of you in strength—indeed you see how I am in
my sickness—and who in the gifts of fortune am, I think, whether in
private life or otherwise, the equal of any, am now exposed to the same
danger as the meanest among you; and yet my life has been one of much
devotion towards the gods, and of much justice and without offence towards men. I have, therefore, still a strong hope for the future, and our
misfortunes do not terrify me as much as they might. Indeed we may
hope that they will be lightened: our enemies have had good fortune
enough; and if any of the gods was offended at our expedition, we have
been already amply punished. Others before us have attacked their
neighbours and have done what men will do without suffering more than
they could bear; and we may now justly expect to find the gods more kind,
for we have become fitter objects for their pity than their jealousy. And
then look at yourselves, mark the numbers and efficiency of the heavy
infantry marching in your ranks, and do not give way too much to despondency, but reflect that you are yourselves at once a city wherever you
sit down, and that there is no other in Sicily that could easily resist your
attack, or expel you when once established. The safety and order of the
march is for yourselves to look to; the one thought of each man being that
the spot on which he may be forced to fight must be conquered and held
as his country and stronghold. Meanwhile we shall hasten on our way
night and day alike, as our provisions are scanty; and if we can reach

some friendly place of the Sicels, whom fear of the Syracusans still keeps true to us, you may forthwith consider yourselves safe. A message has been sent on to them with directions to meet us with supplies of food. To sum up, be convinced, soldiers, that you must be brave, as there is no place near for your cowardice to take refuge in, and that if you now escape from the enemy, you may all see again what your hearts desire, while those of you who are Athenians will raise up again the great power of the state, fallen though it be. Men make the city and not walls or ships without men in them."

As he made this address, Nicias went along the ranks, and brought back to their place any of the troops that he saw straggling out of the line; while Demosthenes did as much for his part of the army, addressing them in words very similar. The army marched in a hollow square, the division under Nicias leading, and that of Demosthenes following, the heavy infantry being outside and the baggage-carriers and the bulk of the army in the middle. When they arrived at the ford of the river Anapus they there found drawn up a body of the Syracusans and allies, and routing these, made good their passage and pushed on, harassed by the charges of the Syracusan horse and by the missiles of their light troops. On that day they advanced about four miles and a half, halting for the night upon a certain hill. On the next they started early and got on about two miles further, and descended into a place in the plain and there encamped, in order to procure some eatables from the houses, as the place was inhabited, and to carry on with them water from thence, as for many furlongs in front, in the direction in which they were going, it was not plentiful. The Syracusans meanwhile went on and fortified the pass in front, where there was a steep hill with a rocky ravine on each side of it, called the Acraean cliff. The next day the Athenians advancing found themselves impeded by the missiles and charges of the horse and darters, both very numerous, of the Syracusans and allies; and after fighting for a long while, at length retired to the same camp, where they had no longer provisions as before, it being impossible to leave their position by reason of the cavalry.

Early next morning they started afresh and forced their way to the hill, which had been fortified, where they found before them the enemy's infantry drawn up many shields deep to defend the fortification, the pass being narrow. The Athenians assaulted the work, but were greeted by a storm of missiles from the hill, which told with the greater effect through its being a steep one, and unable to force the passage, retreated again and rested. Meanwhile occured some claps of thunder and rain, as often happens towards autumn, which still further disheartened the Athenians, who thought all these things to be omens of their approaching ruin. While they were resting Gylippus and the Syracusans sent a part of their army to throw up works in their rear on the way by which they had advanced; however, the Athenians immediately sent some of their men and prevented them; after which they retreated more towards the plain and halted for the night. When they advanced the next day the Syracusans surrounded and attacked them on every side, and disabled many of them, falling back if the Athenians advanced and coming on if they retired, and in particular assaulting their rear, in the hope of routing them in detail, and thus striking a panic into the whole army. For a long while the Athenians persevered in this fashion, but after advancing for four or five furlongs halted to rest in the plain, the Syracusans also withdrawing to their own camp.

During the night Nicias and Demosthenes, seeing the wretched condition of their troops, now in want of every kind of necessary, and numbers of them disabled in the numerous attacks of the enemy, determined to light as many fires as possible, and to lead off the army, no longer by the same route as they had intended, but towards the sea in the opposite direction to that guarded by the Syracusans. The whole of this route was leading the army not to Catana but to the other side of Sicily, towards Camarina, Gela, and the other Hellenic and barbarian towns in that quarter. They accordingly lit a number of fires and set out by night. Now all armies, and the greatest most of all, are liable to fears and alarms, especially when they are marching by night through an enemy's country and with the enemy near; and the Athenians falling into one of these panics, the leading division, that of Nicias, kept together and got on a good way in front, while that of Demosthenes, comprising rather more than half the army, got separated and marched on in some disorder. By morning, however, they reached the sea, and getting into the Helorine Road, pushed on in order to reach the river Cacyparis, and to follow the stream up through the interior, where they hoped to be met by the Sicels whom they had sent for. Arrived at the river, they found there also a Syracusan party engaged in barring the passage of the ford with a wall and a palisade, and forcing this guard, crossing the river and went on to another called the Erineus, according to the advice of their guides.

Meanwhile, when day came and the Syracusans and allies found that the Athenians were gone, most of them accused Gylippus of having let them escape on purpose, and hastily pursuing by the road which they had no difficulty in finding that they had taken, overtook them about dinner-time. They first came up with the troops under Demosthenes, who were behind and marching somewhat slowly and in disorder, owing to the night-panic above referred to, and at once attacked and engaged them, the Syracusan horse surrounding them with more ease now that they were separated from the rest, and hemming them in on one spot. The division of Nicias was five or six miles on in front, as he led them more rapidly, thinking that under the circumstances their safety lay not in staying and fighting, unless obliged, but in retreating as fast as possible, and only fighting when forced to do so. On the other hand, Demosthenese was, generally speaking, harassed more incessantly, as his post in the rear left him the first exposed to the attacks of the enemy; and now, finding that the Syracusans were in pursuit, he omitted to push on, in order to form his men for battle, and so lingered until he was surrounded by his pursuers and himself and the Athenians with him placed in the most distressing position, being huddled into an enclosure with a wall all round it, a road on this side and on that, and olive-trees in great number, where missiles were showered in upon them from every quarter. This mode of attack the Syracusans had with good reason adopted in preference to fighting at close quarters, as to risk a struggle with desperate men was now more for the advantage of the Athenians than for their own; besides, their success had now become so certain that they began to spare themselves a little in order not to be cut off in the moment of victory, thinking too that, as it was, they would be able in this way to subdue and capture the enemy.

In fact, after plying the Athenians and allies all day long from every side with missiles, they at length saw that they were worn out with their wounds and other sufferings; and Gylippus and the Syracusans and their allies made a proclamation, offering their liberty to any of the islanders who chose to come over to them; and some few cities went over. Afterwards a capitulation was agreed upon for all the rest with Demosthenes, to lay down their arms on condition that no one was to be put to death either by violence or imprisonment or want of the necessaries of life. Upon this they surrendered to the number of six thousand in all, laying down all the money in their possession, which filled the hollows of four shields, and were immediately conveyed by the Syracusans to the town.

Meanwhile Nicias with his division arrived that day at the river Erineus, crossed over and posted his army upon some high ground upon the other side. The next day the Syracusans overtook him and told him that the troops under Demosthenes had surrendered, and invited him to follow their example. Incredulous of the fact, Nicias asked for a truce to send a horseman to see, and upon the return of the messenger with the tidings that they had surrendered, sent a herald to Gylippus and the Syracusans, saying that he was ready to agree with them on behalf of the Athenians to repay whatever money the Syracusans had spent upon the war if they would let his army go; and offered until the money was paid to give Athenians as hostages, one for every talent. The Syracusans and Gylippus rejected this proposition, and attacked this division as they had the other, standing all round and plying them with missiles until the evening. Food and necessaries were as miserably wanting to the troops of Nicias as they had been to their comrades; nevertheless they watched for the quiet of the night to resume their march. But as they were taking up their arms the Syracusans perceived it and raised their paean, upon which the Athenians, finding that they were discovered, laid them down again, except about three hundred men who forced their way through the guards and went on during the night as they were able.

As soon as it was day Nicias put his army in motion, pressed, as before, by the Syracusans and their allies, pelted from every side by their missiles, and struck down by their javelins. The Athenians pushed on for the Assinarus, impelled by the attacks made upon them from every side by a numerous cavalry and the swarm of other arms, fancying that they should breathe more freely if once across the river, and driven on also by their exhaustion and craving for water. Once there they rushed in, and all order was at an end, each man wanting to cross first, and the attacks of the enemy making it difficult to cross at all; forced to huddle together, they fell against and trod down one another, some dying immediately upon the javelins, others getting entangled together and stumbling over the articles of baggage, without being able to rise again. Meanwhile the opposite bank, which was steep, was lined by the Syracusans, who showered missiles down upon the Athenians, most of them drinking greedily and heaped together in disorder in the hollow bed of the river. The Peloponnesians also came down and butchered them, especially those in the water, which was thus immediately spoiled, but which they went on drinking just the same, mud and all, bloody as it was, most even fighting to have it.

At last, when many dead now lay piled one upon another in the stream, and part of the army had been destroyed at the river, and the few that escaped from thence cut off by the cavalry, Nicias surrendered himself to Gylippus, whom he trusted more than he did the Syracusans, and told him and the Lacedaemonians to do what they liked with him, but to stop the slaughter of the soldiers. Gylippus, after this, immediately gave orders to make prisoners; upon which the rest were brought together alive, except a large number secreted by the soldiery, and a party was sent in pursuit of the three hundred who had got through the guard during the night, and who were now taken with the rest. The number of the enemy collected as public property was not considerable; but that secreted was very large, and all Sicily was filled with them, no convention having been made in their case as for those taken with Demosthenes. Besides this, a large portion were killed outright, the carnage being very great, and not exceeded by any in this Sicilian war. In the numerous other encounters upon the march, not a few also had fallen. Nevertheless many escaped, some at the moment, others served as slaves, and then ran away subsequently. These found refuge at Catana.

The Syracusans and their allies now mustered and took up the spoils and as many prisoners as they could, and went back to the city. The rest of their Athenian and allied captives were deposited in the quarries, this seeming the safest way of keeping them; but Nicias and Demosthenes were butchered, against the will of Gylippus, who thought that it would be the crown of his triumph if he could take the enemy's generals to Lacedaemon. One of them, as it happened, Demosthenes, was one of her greatest enemies, on account of the affair of the island and of Pylos; while the other, Nicias, was for the same reasons one of her greatest friends, owing to his exertions to procure the release of the prisoners by persuading the Athenians to make peace. For these reasons the Lacedaemonians felt kindly towards him; and it was in this that Nicias himself mainly confided when he surrendered to Gylippus. But some of the Syracusans who had been in correspondence with him were afraid, it was said, of his being put to the torture and troubling their success by his revelations; others, especially the Corinthians, of his escaping, as he was wealthy, by means of bribes, and living to do them further mischief; and these persuaded the allies and put him to death. This or the like was the cause of the death of a man who, of all the Hellenes in my time, least deserved such a fate, seeing that the whole course of his life had been regulated with strict attention to virtue.

The prisoners in the quarries were at first hardly treated by the Syracusans. Crowded in a narrow hole, without any roof to cover them, the heat of the sun and the stifling closeness of the air tormented them during the day, and then the nights, which came on autumnal and chilly, made them ill by the violence of the change; besides, as they had to do everything in the same place for want of room, and the bodies of those who died of their wounds or from the variation in the temperature, or from similar causes, were left heaped together one upon another, intolerable stenches arose; while hunger and thirst never ceased to afflict them, each man during eight months having only half a pint of water and a pint of corn given him daily. In short, no single suffering to be apprehended by men thrust into such a place was spared them. For some seventy days they thus lived all together, after which all, except the Athenians and any Siceliots or Italiots who had joined in the expedition, were sold. The total number of prisoners taken it would be difficult to state exactly, but it could not have been less than seven thousand.

This was the greatest Hellenic achievement of any in this war, or, in my opinion, in Hellenic history; at once more glorious to the victors, and most calamitous to the conquered. They were beaten at all points and altogether; all that they suffered was great; they were destroyed, as the saying is, with a total destruction, their fleet, their army—everything was destroyed, and few out of many returned home.

Polybius

c. 198 B.C.—C. 125 B.C.

3

Polybius was an Achaean Greek born c. 198 B.C. of a noble family during the period when the Hellenistic world was passing into the new Graeco-Roman system. While yet a young man he played an important role in the Achaean League (consisting mainly of city states in the northern Peloponnese) of which his father was a leading statesman. As a cavalry commander he participated in the Third Macedonian War against Rome and after the Roman victory of Pydna (168 B.C.), he was among the thousand Achaean hostages taken to Rome. There he entered into the household of Aemilius Paulus and quickly became an intimate friend of the young Scipio Aemilianus. For the next two decades he enjoyed the perquisites of the highest social circles in Rome and also found the opportunity to travel in Italy, Gaul, Spain, and northern Africa. He accompanied Scipio Africanus when the latter reduced Carthage in 146 B.C.

In his years at Rome he hit upon the idea of writing the history of, as he put it, the "means, and under what kind of polity, almost the whole inhabited world was conquered and brought under the dominion of the single city of Rome, and that too within a period of not quite fifty-three years." He brought to his task considerable talents and experience. He knew directly many of the political and military leaders in Greece and Rome. He had traveled through the lands which were the scenes of his *Histories*. He had read widely in the literature relevant to his study and he had access to official documents. Further, he had come to respect and even to love the Roman state which had vanquished his homeland.

In this work on the career of Rome from the Second Punic War to the conquest of Macedonia, Polybius constantly kept in mind the manner in which the Romans had controlled their vast dominions. "What kind of polity," he asked, was necessary in the performance of such a task? In his concentration on politics and on the statesmen entrusted with power as well as in his belief that "the study of history is . . . a training for political life,"

108

Polybius writes in the tradition of Thucydides and, indeed, he is chief among historians of the ancient world who consolidated that tradition. Thus Polybius concentrated on contemporary history and followed Thucydidean standards in discovering, evaluating, and utilizing evidence. Again like Thucydides, Polybius had recourse to literary sources, to archives and official documents, but he regarded eyewitness accounts as the best source for his history. He thus mastered and used the techniques of cross-examination and corroboration in his pursuit of the most reliable evidence.

Perhaps nowhere is his conceptual bias (and the influence of Thucydides) more apparent than in Book Six of his *Histories* where Polybius pauses in his narrative to survey political institutions in general and to analyze the Roman constitution in particular. For he held that "the feature of my work which was at once the best in itself, and the most instructive to students of it, was that it should enable them to know and fully realize in what manner, and under what kind of constitution" Rome succeeded to the mastery of the world. This was in keeping with his belief that "in every undertaking by a state we must regard as the most powerful agent for success or failure the form of its constitution." It is in Book Six, however, that Polybius allowed theory to overcome history. His discussion of the evolution of constitutional forms is based on the commonly held doctrine of a recurring cycle of political forms —monarchy, tyranny, aristocracy, oligarchy, democracy, anarchy, after which the cycle resumes. But his disquisition is speculative rather than historical and even his explanation of Rome's success as being founded on the rock of her "mixed constitution"—i.e., containing elements of monarchy, aristocracy, and democracy—is refuted by his admission that the constitution was essentially aristocratic when Rome reached her greatness during the Second Punic War.

Polybius thus manifests some of the strengths and weaknesses of ancient historiography, striving to be empirically based and pragmatic yet often enough slipping into the confines of an *a priori* or speculative approach. Nevertheless, even with his speculative lapses, Polybius remains a distinguished historian in his recognition of the obligation of historical accuracy and impartiality and in the soundness and appropriateness of his methodology. We may accept Macaulay's judgment, while demurring on his qualification, that in comparison with such historians as Plutarch, Polybius deserves our high praise.

Selected Bibliography

As with Herodotus and Thucydides, beginning students may consult with profit the works of both J. B. Bury, *The Ancient Greek Historians* (1909) and James T. Shotwell, *An Introduction to the History of History* (1936). Bury's positive but tempered judgment is set off nicely by Shotwell's frankly enthusiastic opinion of the historian's merit. The question of Polybius and the Roman constitution is addressed by Kurt von Fritz in *The Theory of the Mixed Constitution in Antiquity: A Critical Analysis of Polybius' Political Ideas* (1954). Von Fritz holds Polybius in high regard but concludes that "Polybius' cycle [of constitutions] is a gross simplification." Arnaldo Momigliano, *Studies in Historiography* (1966), is perceptive on Polybius' work. F. W. Walbank, *A Historical Commentary on Polybius* (1957–1967), in two volumes with at least one more to come, does justice to the serious theme and purpose of the historian. It contains an extensive bibliography. Walbank has also written the introduction to the Evelyn S. Shuckburgh translation (1889) of Polybius' *Histories* (2 vols., 1962), from which we take our selections.

THE HISTORIES

Had the praise of History been passed over by former Chroniclers it would perhaps have been incumbent upon me to urge the choice and special study of records of this sort, as the readiest means men can have of correcting their knowledge of the past. But my predecessors have not been sparing in this respect. They have all begun and ended, so to speak, by enlarging on this theme: asserting again and again that the study of History is in the truest sense an education, and a training for political life; and that the most instructive, or rather the only, method of learning to bear with dignity the vicissitudes of fortune is to recall the catastrophes of others. It is evident, therefore, that no one need think it his duty to repeat what has been said by many, and said well. Least of all myself: for the surprising nature of the events which I have undertaken to relate is in itself sufficient to challenge and stimulate the attention of every one, old or young, to the study of my work. Can any one be so indifferent or idle as not to care to know by what means, and under what kind of polity, almost the whole inhabited world was conquered and brought under the dominion of the single city of Rome, and that too within a period of not quite fifty-three years? Or who again can be so completely absorbed in other subjects of contemplation or study, as to think any of them superior in importance to the accurate understanding of an event for which the past affords no precedent?

We shall best show how marvellous and vast our subject is by comparing the most famous Empires which preceded, and which have been the favourite themes of historians, and measuring them with the superior greatness of Rome. There are but three that deserve even to be so compared and measured: and they are these. The Persians for a certain length of time were possessed of a great empire and dominion. But every time they ventured beyond the limits of Asia, they found not only their empire, but their own existence also in danger. The Lacedaemonians, after contending for supremacy in Greece for many generations, when they did get it, held it without dispute for barely twelve years. The

From *The Histories,* translated by Evelyn S. Shuckburgh (Bloomington, Indiana University Press, 1962). Reprinted by permission of the publisher. Vol. I, pp. 1–4, 458–474, 506–507; vol. II, pp. 2–5, 138–152.

Macedonians obtained dominion in Europe from the lands bordering on the Adriatic to the Danube,—which after all is but a small fraction of this continent,—and, by the destruction of the Persian Empire, they afterwards added to that the dominion of Asia. And yet, though they had the credit of having made themselves masters of a larger number of countries and states than any people had ever done, they still left the greater half of the inhabited world in the hands of others. They never so much as thought of attempting Sicily, Sardinia, or Libya: and as to Europe, to speak the plain truth, they never even knew of the most warlike tribes of the West. The Roman conquest, on the other hand, was not partial. Nearly the whole inhabited world was reduced by them to obedience: and they left behind them an empire not to be paralleled in the past or rivalled in the future. Students will gain from my narrative a clearer view of the whole story, and of the numerous and important advantages which such exact record of events offers. . . .

Now, had the states that were rivals for universal empire been familiarly known to us, no reference perhaps to their previous history would have been necessary, to show the purpose and the forces with which they approached an undertaking of this nature and magnitude. But the fact is that the majority of the Greeks have no knowledge of the previous constitution, power, or achievements either of Rome or Carthage. I therefore concluded that it was necessary to prefix this and the next book to my History. I was anxious that no one, when fairly embarked upon my actual narrative, should feel at a loss, and have to ask what were the designs entertained by the Romans, or the forces and means at their disposal, that they entered upon those undertakings, which did in fact lead to their becoming masters of land and sea everywhere in our part of the world. I wished, on the contrary, that these books of mine, and the prefatory sketch which they contained, might make it clear that the resources they started with justified their original idea, and sufficiently explained their final success in grasping universal empire and dominion.

There is this analogy between the plan of my History and the marvellous spirit of the age with which I have to deal. Just as Fortune made almost all the affairs of the world incline in one direction, and forced them to converge upon one and the same point; so it is my task as an historian to put before my readers a compendious view of the part played by Fortune in bringing about her general purpose. It was this peculiarity which originally challenged my attention, and determined me on undertaking this work. And combined with this was the fact that no writer of our time has undertaken a general history. Had any one done so my ambition in this direction would have been much diminished. But, in point of fact, I notice that by far the greater number of historians concern themselves with isolated wars and the incidents that accompany them: while as to a general and comprehensive scheme of events, their date, origin, and catastrophe, no one as far as I know has undertaken to examine it. I thought it, therefore, distinctly my duty neither to pass by myself, nor allow any one else to pass by, without full study, a characteristic specimen of the dealings of Fortune at once brilliant and instructive in the highest degree. For fruitful as Fortune is in change, and constantly as she is producing dramas in the life of men, yet never assuredly before this did she work such a marvel, or act such a drama, as that which we have witnessed. And of this we cannot obtain a comprehensive view from writers of mere episodes. It would be as absurd to expect to do so as for a man to imagine that he has learnt the shape of the whole world, its entire arrangement and order, because he has visited one after the other the most famous cities in it; or perhaps merely examined them in separate pictures. That would be indeed absurd: and it has always seemed to me that men, who are persuaded that they get a competent view of universal from episodical history, are very like persons who should see the limbs of some body, which had once been living and beautiful, scattered and remote; and should imagine that to be quite as good as actually beholding the activity and beauty of the living creature itself. But if some one could there and then reconstruct the animal once more, in the perfection of its beauty and the charm of its vitality, and could display it to the same people, they would beyond doubt confess that they had been far from conceiving the truth, and had been little better than dreamers. For indeed some idea of a whole may be got from a part, but an accurate knowledge and clear comprehension cannot. Wherefore we must conclude that episodical history contributes exceedingly little to the familiar knowledge and secure grasp of universal history. While it is only by the combination and comparison of the separate parts of the whole,—by observing their likeness and their difference,—that a man can attain his object: can obtain a view at once clear and complete; and thus secure both the profit and the delight of History.

I shall adopt as the starting-point of this book the first occasion on which the Romans crossed the sea from Italy. This is just where the History of Timaeus left off; and it falls in the 129th Olympiad. I shall accordingly have to describe what the state of their affairs in Italy was, how long that settlement had lasted, and on what resources they reckoned, and when they resolved to invade Sicily. For this was the first place outside Italy in which they set foot. The precise cause of their thus crossing I must state without comment; for if I let one cause lead me back to another, my point of departure will always elude my grasp, and I shall never arrive at the view of my subject which I wish to present. As to dates, then, I must fix on some era agreed upon and recognised by all: and as to events, one that admits of distinctly separate treatment; even though I may be obliged to go back some short way in point of time, and take a summary review of the intermediate transactions. For if the facts with which one starts are unknown, or even open to controversy, all that comes after will fail of approval and belief. But opinion being once formed on that point, and a general assent obtained, all the succeeding narrative becomes intelligible. . . .

I am aware that some will be at a loss to account for my interrupting the course of my narrative for the sake of entering upon the following disquisition on the Roman constitution. But I think that I have already in many passages made it fully evident that this particular branch of my work was one of the necessities imposed on me by the nature of my original design; and I pointed this out with special clearness in the preface which explained the scope of my history. I there stated that the feature of my work which was at once the best in itself, and the most instructive to the students of it, was that it would enable them to know and fully realise in what manner, and under what kind of constitution, it came about that nearly the whole world fell under the power of Rome in somewhat less than fifty-three years,—an event certainly without precedent. This being my settled purpose, I could see no more fitting period than the present for making a pause, and examining the truth of the remarks about to be made on this constitution. In private life if you wish to satisfy yourself as to the badness or goodness of particular persons, you would not, if you wish to get a genuine test, examine their conduct at a time of uneventful repose, but in the hour of brilliant success or conspicuous reverse. For the true test of a perfect man is the power of bearing with spirit and dignity violent changes of fortune. An examination of a constitution should be conducted in the same way: and therefore being unable to find in our day a more rapid or more signal change than that which has happened to Rome, I reserved my disquisition on its constitution for this place. . . .

What is really educational and beneficial to students of history is the clear view of the causes of events, and the consequent power of choosing the better policy in a particular case. Now in every practical undertaking by a state we must regard as the most powerful agent for success or failure the form of its constitution; for from this as from a fountain-head all conceptions and plans of action not only proceed, but attain their consummation. . . .

Of the Greek republics, which have again and again risen to greatness and fallen into insignificance, it is not difficult to speak, whether we recount their past history or venture an opinion on their future. For to report what is already known is an easy task, nor is it hard to guess what is to come from our knowledge of what has been. But in regard to the

Romans it is neither an easy matter to describe their present state, owing to the complexity of their constitution; nor to speak with confidence of their future, from our inadequate acquaintance with their peculiar institutions in the past whether affecting their public or their private life. It will require then no ordinary attention and study to get a clear and comprehensive conception of the distinctive features of this constitution.

Now, it is undoubtedly the case that most of those who profess to give us authoritative instruction on this subject distinguish three kinds of constitutions, which they designate *kingship, aristocracy, democracy.* But in my opinion the question might fairly be put to them, whether they name these as being the *only* ones, or as the *best.* In either case I think they are wrong. For it is plain that we must regard as the *best* constitution that which partakes of all these three elements. And this is no mere assertion, but has been proved by the example of Lycurgus, who was the first to construct a constitution—that of Sparta—on this principle. Nor can we admit that these are the *only* forms: for we have had before now examples of absolute and tyrannical forms of government, which, while differing as widely as possible from kingship, yet appear to have some points of resemblance to it; on which account all absolute rulers falsely assume and use, as far as they can, the title of king. Again there have been many instances of oligarchical governments having in appearance some analogy to aristocracies, which are, if I may say so, as different from them as it is possible to be. The same also holds good about democracy.

I will illustrate the truth of what I say. We cannot hold every absolute government to be a kingship, but only that which is accepted voluntarily, and is directed by an appeal to reason rather than to fear and force. Nor again is every oligarchy to be regarded as an aristocracy; the latter exists only where the power is wielded by the justest and wisest men selected on their merits. Similarly, it is not enough to constitute a democracy that the whole crowd of citizens should have the right to do whatever they wish or propose. But where reverence to the gods, succour of parents, respect to elders, obedience to laws, are traditional and habitual, in such communities, if the will of the majority prevail, we may speak of the form of government as a democracy. So then we enumerate six forms of government,—the three commonly spoken of which I have just mentioned, and three more allied forms, I mean *despotism, oligarchy* and *mob-rule.* The first of these arises without artificial aid and in the natural order of events. Next to this, and produced from it by the aid of art and adjustment, comes *kingship;* which degenerating into the evil form allied to it, by which I mean *tyranny,* both are once more destroyed and *aristocracy* produced. Again the latter being in the course of nature perverted to *oligarchy,* and the people passionately avenging the unjust acts of their rulers, *democracy* comes into existence; which again by its violence and contempt of law becomes sheer *mob-rule*. No clearer proof of the truth of what I say could be obtained than by a careful observation of the natural origin, genesis, and decadence of these several forms of government. For it is only by seeing distinctly how each of them is produced that a distinct view can also be obtained of its growth, zenith, and decadence, and the time, circumstance, and place in which each of these may be expected to recur. This method I have assumed to be especially applicable to the Roman constitution, because its origin and growth have from the first followed natural causes.

Now the natural laws which regulate the merging of one form of government into another are perhaps discussed with greater accuracy by Plato and some other philosophers. But their treatment, from its intricacy and exhaustiveness, is only within the capacity of a few. I will therefore endeavour to give a summary of the subject, just so far as I suppose it to fall within the scope of a practical history and the intelligence of ordinary people. For if my exposition appear in any way inadequate, owing to the general terms in which it is expressed, the details contained in what is immediately to follow will amply atone for what is left for the present unsolved.

What is the origin then of a constitution, and whence is it produced? Suppose that from floods, pestilences, failure of crops, or some such causes the race of man is reduced almost to extinction. Such things we are told have happened, and it is reasonable to think will happen again. Suppose accordingly all knowledge of social habits and arts to have been lost. Suppose that from the survivors, as from seeds, the race of man to have again multiplied. In that case I presume they would, like the animals, herd together; for it is but reasonable to suppose that bodily weakness would induce them to seek those of their own kind to herd with. And in that case too, as with the animals, he who was superior to the rest in strength of body or courage of soul would lead and rule them. For what we see happen in the case of animals that are without the faculty of reason, such as bulls, goats, and cocks,—among whom there can be no dispute that the strongest take the lead,—that we must regard as in the truest sense the teaching of nature. Originally then it is probable that the condition of life among men was this,—herding together like animals and following the strongest and bravest as leaders. The limit of this authority would be physical strength, and the name we should give it would be despotism. But as soon as the idea of family ties and social relation has arisen amongst such agglomerations of men, then is born also the idea of kingship, and then for the first time mankind conceives the notion of goodness and justice and their reverse.

The way in which such conceptions originate and come into existence is this. The intercourse of the sexes is an instinct of nature, and the result is the birth of children. Now, if any one of these children who have been brought up, when arrived at maturity, is ungrateful and makes no return to those by whom he was nurtured, but on the contrary presumes to injure them by word and deed, it is plain that he will probably offend and annoy such as are present, and have seen the care and trouble bestowed by the parents on the nurture and bringing up of their children. For seeing that men differ from the other animals in being the only creatures possessed of reasoning powers, it is clear that such a difference of conduct is not likely to escape their observation; but that they will remark it when it occurs, and express their displeasure on the spot: because they will have an eye to the future, and will reason on the likelihood of the same occurring to each of themselves. Again, if a man has been rescued or helped in an hour of danger, and, instead of showing gratitude to his preserver, seeks to do him harm, it is clearly probable that the rest will be displeased and offended with him, when they know it: sympathising with their neighbour and imagining themselves in his case. Hence arises a notion in every breast of the meaning and theory of duty, which is in fact the beginning and end of justice. Similarly, again, when any one man stands out as the champion of all in a time of danger, and braves with firm courage the onslaught of the most powerful wild beasts, it is probable that such a man would meet with marks of favour and preeminence from the common people; while he who acted in a contrary way would fall under their contempt and dislike. From this, once more, it is reasonable to suppose that there would arise in the minds of the multitude a theory of the disgraceful and the honourable, and of the difference between them; and that one should be sought and imitated for its advantages, the other shunned. When, therefore, the leading and most powerful man among his people ever encourages such persons in accordance with the popular sentiment, and thereby assumes in the eyes of his subject the appearance of being the distributor to each man according to his deserts, they no longer obey him and support his rule from fear of violence, but rather from conviction of its utility, however old he may be, rallying round him with one heart and soul, and fighting against all who form designs against his government. In this way he becomes a *king* instead of a *despot* by imperceptible degrees, reason having ousted brute courage and bodily strength from their supremacy.

This then is the natural process of formation among mankind of the notion of goodness and justice, and their opposites; and this is the origin and genesis of genuine kingship: for people do not only keep up the government of such men personally, but for their descendants also for many generations; from the conviction that those who are born from and educated by men of this kind will have principles also like theirs. But if they subsequently become displeased with their descendants, they do not any longer decide their choice of rulers and kinds by their physical strength or brute courage; but by the differences of their intellectual and reasoning faculties, from practical experience of the decisive importance of such a distinction. In old times, then, those who were once thus selected, and obtained this office, grew old in their royal functions, making magnificent strongholds and surrounding them with walls and extending their frontiers, partly for the security of their subjects, and partly to provide them with abundance of the necessaries of life; and while engaged in these works they were exempt from all vituperation or jealousy; because they did not make their distinctive dress, food, or drink, at all conspicuous, but lived very much like the rest, and joined in the everyday employments of the common people. But when their royal power became hereditary in their family, and they found every necessary for security ready to their hands, as well as more than was necessary for their personal support, then they gave the rein to their appetites; imagined that rulers must needs wear different clothes from those of subjects; have different and elaborate luxuries of the table; and must even seek sensual indulgence, however unlawful the source, without fear of denial. These things having given rise in the one case to jealousy and offence, in the other to outburst of hatred and passionate resentment, the kingship became a tyranny: the first step in disintegration was taken; and plots began to be formed against the government, which did not now proceed from the worst men but from the noblest, most high-minded, and most courageous, because these are the men who can least submit to the tyrannical acts of their rulers.

But as soon as the people got leaders, they co-operated with them against the dynasty for the reasons I have mentioned; and then *kingship* and *despotism* were alike entirely abolished, and *aristocracy* once more began to revive and start afresh. For in their immediate gratitude to those who had deposed the despots, the people employed them as leaders, and entrusted their interests to them; who, looking upon this charge at first as a great privilege, made the public advantage their chief concern, and conducted all kinds of business, public or private, with diligence and caution. But when the sons of these men received the same position of authority from their fathers,—having had no experience of misfortunes, and none at all of civil equality and freedom of speech, but having been bred up from the first under the shadow of their fathers' authority and lofty position,—some of them gave themselves up with passion to avarice and unscrupulous love of money, others to drinking and the boundless debaucheries which accompany it, and others to the violation of women or the forcible appropriation of boys; and so they turned an *aristocracy* into an *oligarchy*. But it was not long before they roused in the minds of the people the same feelings as before; and their fall therefore was very like the disaster which befel the tyrants.

For no sooner had the knowledge of the jealousy and hatred existing in the citizens against them emboldened some one to oppose the government by word or deed, than he was sure to find the whole people ready and prepared to take his side. Having then got rid of these rulers by assassination or exile, they do not venture to set up a king again, being still in terror of the injustice to which this led before; nor dare they intrust the common interests again to more than one, considering the recent example of their misconduct: and therefore, as the only sound hope left them is that which depends upon themselves, they are driven to take refuge in that; and so changed the constitution from an oligarchy to a *democracy,* and took upon themselves the superintendence and charge of the state. And as long as any survive who have had experience of oligarchical supremacy and domination, they regard their present constitution as a blessing, and hold equality and freedom as of the utmost value. But as soon as a new generation has arisen, and the democracy has descended to their children's children, long association weakens their value for equality and freedom, and some seek to become more powerful then the ordinary citizens; and the most liable to this temptation are the rich. So when they begin to be fond of office, and find themselves unable to obtain it by their own unassisted efforts and their own merits, they ruin their estates, while enticing and corrupting the common people in every possible way. By which means when, in their senseless mania for reputation, they have made the populace ready and greedy to receive bribes, the virtue of democracy is destroyed and it is transformed into a government of violence and the strong hand. For the mob, habituated to feed at the expense of others, and to have its hopes of a livelihood in the property of its neighbours, as soon as it has got a leader sufficiently ambitious and daring, being excluded by poverty from the sweets of civil honours, produces a reign of mere violence. Then come tumultuous assemblies, massacres, banishments, redivisions of land; until, after losing all trace of civilisation, it has once more found a master and a despot.

This is the regular cycle of constitutional revolutions, and the natural order in which constitutions change, are transformed, and return again to their original stage. If a man have a clear grasp of these principles he may perhaps make a mistake as to the dates at which this or that will happen to a particular constitution; but he will rarely be entirely mistaken as to the stage of growth or decay at which it has arrived, or as to the point at which it will undergo some revolutionary change. However, it is in the case of the Roman constitution that this method of inquiry will most fully teach us its formation, its growth, and zenith, as well as the changes awaiting it in the future; for this, if any constitution ever did, owed, as I said just now, its original foundation and growth to natural causes, and to natural causes will owe its decay. My subsequent narrative will be the best illustration of what I say. . . .

I have given an account of the constitution of Lycurgus, I will now endeavour to describe that of Rome at the period of their disastrous defeat at Cannae.

I am fully conscious that to those who actually live under this constitution I shall appear to give an inadequate account of it by the omission of certain details. Knowing accurately every portion of it from personal experience, and from having been bred up in its customs and laws from childhood, they will not be struck so much by the accuracy of the description, as annoyed by its omissions; nor will they believe that the historian has purposely omitted unimportant distinctions, but will attribute his silence upon the origin of existing institutions or other important facts to ignorance. What is told they depreciate as insignificant or beside the purpose; what is omitted they desiderate as vital to the question: their object being to appear to know more than the writers. But a good critic should not judge a writer by what he leaves unsaid, but from what he says: if he detects mis-statement in the latter, he may then feel certain that ignorance accounts for the former; but if what he says is accurate, his omissions ought to be attributed to deliberate judgment and not to ignorance. So much for those whose criticisms are prompted by personal ambition rather than by justice. . . .

Another requisite for obtaining a judicious approval for an historical disquisition, is that it should be germane to the matter in hand; if this is not observed, though its style may be excellent and its matter irreproachable, it will seem out of place, and disgust rather than please. . . .

As for the Roman constituton, it had three elements, each of them possessing sovereign powers: and their respective share of power in the whole state had been regulated with such a scrupulous regard to equality and equilibrium, that no one could say for certain, not even a native, whether the constitution as a whole were an aristocracy or democracy or despotism. And no wonder: for if we confine our observation to the power of the Consuls we should be inclined to regard it as despotic; if on that of the Senate, as aristocratic; and if finally one looks at the power possessed by the people it would seem a clear case of a democracy. What the exact powers of these several parts were, and still, with slight modifications, are, I will now state.

The Consuls, before leading out the legions, remain in Rome and are supreme masters of the administration. All other magistrates, except the Tribunes, are under them and take their orders. They introduce foreign ambassadors to the Senate; bring matters requiring deliberation before it; and see to the execution of its decrees. If, again, there are any matters of state which require the authorisation of the people, it is their business to see to them, to summon the popular meetings, to bring the proposals before them, and to carry out the decrees of the majority. In the preparations for war also, and in a word in the entire administration of a campaign, they have all but absolute power. It is competent to them to impose on the allies such levies as they think good, to appoint the Military Tribunes, to make up the roll for soldiers and select those that are suitable. Besides they have absolute power of inflicting punishment on all who are under their command while on active service: and they have authority to expend as much of the public money as they choose, being accompanied by a Quaestor who is entirely at their orders. A survey of these powers would in fact justify our describing the constitution as despotic, —a clear case of royal government. Now will it affect the truth of my description, if any of the institutions I have described are changed in our time, or in that of our posterity: and the same remarks apply to what follows.

The Senate has first of all the control of the treasury, and regulates the receipts and disbursements alike. For the Quaestors cannot issue any public money for the various departments of the state without a decree of the Senate, except for the service of the Consuls. The Senate controls also what is by far the largest and most important expenditure, that, namely, which is made by the censors every *lustrum* for the repair or construction of public buildings; this money cannot be obtained by the censors except by the grant of the Senate. Similarly all crimes committed in Italy requiring a public investigation, such as treason, conspiracy, poisoning, or wilful murder, are in the hands of the Senate. Besides, if any individual or state among the Italian allies requires a controversy to be settled, a penalty to be assessed, help or protection to be afforded,—all this is the province of the Senate. Or again, outside Italy, if it is necessary to send an embassy to reconcile warring communities, or to remind them of their duty, or sometimes to impose requisitions upon them, or to receive their submission, or finally to proclaim war against them,—this too is the business of the Senate. In like manner the reception to be given to foreign ambassadors in Rome, and the answers to be returned to them, are decided by the Senate. With such business the people have nothing to do. Consequently, if one were staying at Rome when the Consuls were not in town, one would imagine the constitution to be a complete aristocracy: and this has been the idea entertained by many Greeks, and by many kings as well, from the fact that nearly all the business they had with Rome was settled by the Senate.

After this one would naturally be inclined to ask what part is left for the people in the constituion, when the Senate has these various functions, especially the control of the receipts and expenditure of the exchequer; and when the Consuls, again, have absolute power over the details of military preparation, and an absolute authority in the field? There is, however, a part left the people, and it is a most important one. For the people is the sole fountain of honour and of punishment; and it is by these two things and these alone that dynasties and constitutions and, in a word, human society are held together: for where the distinction between them is not sharply drawn both in theory and practice, there no undertaking can be properly administered,—as indeed we might expect when good and bad are held in exactly the same honour. The people then are the only court to decide matters of life and death; and even in cases where the penalty is money, if the sum to be assessed is sufficiently serious, and especially when the accused have held the higher magistracies. And in regard to this arrangement there is one point deserving especial commendation and record. Men who are on trial for their lives at Rome, while sentence is in process of being voted,—if even only one of the tribes whose votes are needed to ratify the sentence has not voted, —have the privilege at Rome of openly departing and condemning themselves to a voluntary exile. Such men are safe at Naples or Praeneste or at Tibur, and at other towns with which this arrangement has been duly ratified on oath.

Again, it is the people who bestow offices on the deserving, which are the most honourable rewards of virtue. It has also the absolute power of passing or repealing laws; and, most important of all, it is the people who deliberate on the question of peace or war. And when provisional terms are made for alliance, suspension of hostilities, or treaties, it is the people who ratify them or the reverse.

These considerations again would lead one to say that the chief power in the state was the people's, and that the constitution was a democracy.

Such, then, is the distribution of power between the several parts of the state. I must now show how each of these several parts can, when they choose, oppose or support each other.

The Consul, then, when he has started on an expedition with the powers I have described, is to all appearance absolute in the administration of the business in hand; still he has need of the support both of people and Senate, and, without them, is quite unable to bring the matter to a successful conclusion. For it is plain that he must have supplies sent to his legions from time to time; but without a decree of the Senate they can be supplied neither with corn, nor clothes, nor pay, so that all the plans of a commander must be futile, if the Senate is resolved either to shrink from danger or hamper his plans. And again, whether a Consul shall bring any undertaking to a conclusion or no depends entirely upon the Senate: for it has absolute authority at the end of a year to send another Consul to supersede him, or to continue the existing one in his command.

Again, even to the successes of the generals the Senate has the power to add distinction and glory, and on the other hand to obscure their merits and lower their credit. For these high achievements are brought in tangible form before the eyes of the citizens by what are called "triumphs." But these triumphs the commanders cannot celebrate with proper pomp, or in some cases celebrate at all, unless the Senate concurs and grants the necessary money. As for the people, the Consuls are pre-eminently obliged to court their favour, however distant from home may be the field of their operations; for it is the people, as I have said before, that ratifies, or refuses to ratify, terms of peace and treaties; but most of all because when laying down their office they have to give an account of their administration before it. Therefore in no case is it safe for the Consuls to neglect either the Senate or the goodwill of the people.

As for the Senate, which possesses the immense power I have described, in the first place it is obliged in public affairs to take the multitude into account, and respect the wishes of the people; and it cannot put into execution the penalty for offences against the republic, which are punishable with death, unless the people first ratify its decrees. Similarly even in matters which directly affect the senators,—for instance, in the case of a law diminishing the Senate's traditional authority, or depriving senators of certain dignities and offices, or even actually cutting down their property,—even in such cases the people have the sole power of passing or rejecting the law. But most important of all is the fact that, if the Tribunes interpose their veto, the Senate not only are unable to pass a decree, but cannot even hold a meeting at all, whether formal or informal. Now, the Tribunes are always bound to carry out the decree of the people, and above all things to have regard to their wishes: therefore, for all these reasons the Senate stands in awe of the multitude, and cannot neglect the feelings of the people.

In like manner the people on its part is far from being independent of the Senate, and is bound to take its wishes into account both collectively and individually. For contracts, too numerous to count, are given out by the censors in all parts of Italy for the repairs or construction of public buildings; there is also the collection of revenue from many rivers, harbours, gardens, mines, and land—everything, in a word, that comes under the control of the Roman government: and in all these the people at large are engaged; so that there is scarcely a man, so to speak, who is not interested either as a contractor or as being employed in the works. For some purchase the contracts from the censors for themselves; and others go partners with them; while others again go security for these contractors, or actually pledge their property to the treasury for them. Now over all these transactions the Senate has absolute control. It can grant an extension of time; and in case of unforeseen accident can relieve the contractors from a portion of their obligation, or release them from it altogether, if they are absolutely unable to fulfil it. And there are many details in which the Senate can inflict great hardships, or, on the other hand, grant great indulgences to the contractors: for in every case the appeal is to it. But the most important point of all is that the judges are taken from its members in the majority of trials, whether public or private, in which the charges are heavy. Consequently, all citizens are much at its mercy; and being alarmed at the uncertainty as to when they may need its aid, are cautious about resisting or actively opposing its will. And for a similar reason men do not rashly resist the wishes of the Consuls, because one and all may become subject to their absolute authority on a campaign.

The result of this power of the several estates for mutual help or harm is a union sufficiently firm for all emergencies, and a constitution than which it is impossible to find a better. For whenever any danger from without compels them to unite and work together, the strength which is developed by the State is so extraordinary, that everything required is unfailingly carried out by the eager rivalry shown by all classes to devote their whole minds to the need of the hour, and to secure that any determination come to should not fail for want of promptitude; while each individual works, privately and publicly alike, for the accomplishment of the business in hand. Accordingly, the peculiar constitution of the State makes it irresistible, and certain of obtaining whatever it determines to attempt. Nay, even when these external alarms are past, and the people are enjoying their good fortune and the fruits of their victories, and, as usually happens, growing corrupted by flattery and idleness, show a tendency to violence and arrogance,—it is in these circumstances, more than ever, that the constitution is seen to possess within itself the power of correcting abuses. For when any one of the three classes becomes puffed up, and manifests an inclination to be contentious and unduly encroaching, the mutual interdependency of all the three, and the possibility of the pretensions of any one being checked and thwarted by the others, must plainly check this tendency: and so the proper equilibrium is maintained by the impulsiveness of the one part being checked by its fear of the other. . . .

That to all things, then, which exist there is ordained decay and change I think requires no further arguments to show: for the inexorable course of nature is sufficient to convince us of it.

But in all polities we observe two sources of decay existing from natural causes, the one external, the other internal and self-produced. The external admits of no certain or fixed definition, but the internal follows a definite order. What kind of polity, then, comes naturally first, and what second, I have already stated in such a way, that those who are capable of taking in the whole drift of my argument can henceforth draw their own conclusions as to the future of the Roman polity. For it is quite clear, in my opinion. When a commonwealth, after warding off many great dangers, has arrived at a high pitch of prosperity and undisputed power, it is evident that, by the lengthened continuance of great wealth within it, the manner of life of its citizens will become more extravagant; and that the rivalry for office, and in other spheres of activity, will become fiercer than it ought to be. And as this state of things goes on more and more, the desire of office and the shame of losing reputation, as well as the ostentation and extravagance of living, will prove the beginning of a deterioration. And of this change the people will be credited with being the authors, when they become convinced that they are being cheated by some from avarice, and are puffed up with flattery by others from love of office. For when that comes about, in their passionate resentment and acting under the dictates of anger, they will refuse to obey any longer, or to be content with having equal powers with their leaders, but will demand to have all or far the greatest themselves. And when that comes to pass the constitution will receive a new name, which sounds better than any other in the world, liberty or democracy; but, in fact, it will become that worst of all governments, mob-rule.

With this description of the formation, growth, zenith, and present state of the Roman polity, and having discussed also its difference, for better and worse, from other polities, I will now at length bring my essay on it to an end. . . .

Being about to narrate the exploits of Publius Scipio in Iberia, and in fact all the achievements in his life, I think it necessary to direct my readers' attention, to begin with, to his moral and mental qualities. For as he is perhaps the most illustrious man of any born before the present generation, everybody seeks to know what kind of man he was, and what advantages from natural ability or experience he enjoyed, to account for a career so crowded with brilliant achievement; and yet is compelled to remain in the dark, or to entertain false opinions, because those who write about him have not kept to the truth. The soundness of this assertion will be rendered evident in the course of my narrative to all who are capable of estimating the noblest and most gallant of his exploits. Now all other writers represent him as a man favoured by fortune, who succeeded in his undertakings contrary to rational expectation, and by the mere force of circumstances. They consider apparently such men to be, so to speak, more god-like and worthy of admiration, than those who act in every case by calculation. They do not seem to be aware of the distinction between credit for good fortune and credit for good conduct in the case of such men; and that the former may be assigned to any one however commonplace, while the latter belongs to those alone who act from

prudent calculation and clear intelligence: and it is these last whom we
should look upon as the most god-like and god-beloved.

Now it seems to me that in his character and views Publius was very
like Lycurgus the legislator of the Lacedaemonians. For we must not
suppose that it was from superstition that Lycurgus continually consulted the Pythian priestess in the establishment of the Lacedaemonian
constitution; nor that Publius depended on dreams and ominous words
for his success in securing empire for his country. But as both saw that
the majority of mankind cannot be got to accept contentedly what is new
and strange, nor to face dangers with courage, without some hope of
divine favour,—Lycurgus, by always supporting his own schemes by an
oracular response from the Pythia, secured better acceptation and credit
for his ideas; and Publius, by always in like manner instilling into the
minds of the vulgar an opinion of his acting on some divine suggestion
in the formation of his designs, caused those under his command to
confront dangerous services with greater courage and cheerfulness. But
that he invariably acted on calculation and with foresight, and that the
successful issue of his plans was always in harmony with rational expectation, will be evident by what I am about to relate.

For that he was beneficent and high-minded is acknowledged; but that
he was acute, sober-minded, and earnest in pursuit of his aims, no one
will admit, except those who have lived with him, and contemplated his
character, so to speak, in broad daylight. Of such Gaius Laelius was one.
He took part in everything he did or said from boyhood to the day of his
death; and he it was who convinced me of this truth: because what he
said appeared to me to be likely in itself, and in harmony with the
achievements of that great man. He told me that the first brilliant exploit
of Publius was when his father fought the cavalry engagement with
Hannibal near the Padus. He was then, as it seems, eighteen years old
and on his first campaign. His father had given him a squadron of picked
cavalry for his protection; but when in the course of the battle he saw his
father surrounded by the enemy, with only two or three horsemen near
him, and dangerously wounded, he first tried to cheer on his own squadron to go his father's assistance, but when he found them considerably
cowed by the numbers of the enemy surrounding them, he appears to
have plunged by himself with reckless courage into the midst of the
enemy: whereupon, his comrades being forced to charge also, the enemy
were overawed and divided their ranks to let them pass; and Publius the
elder, being thus unexpectedly saved, was the first to address his son as
his preserver in the hearing of the whole army. Having gained an acknowledged reputation for bravery by this exploit, he ever afterwards
freely exposed himself to every sort of personal danger, whenever his
country rested its hope of safety on him. And this is not the conduct of

a general who trusts to luck, but of one who has a clear head. . . .

The special province of history is, first, to ascertain what the actual words used were; and secondly, to learn why it was that a particular policy or argument failed or succeeded. For a bare statement of an occurrence is interesting indeed, but not instructive: but when this is supplemented by a statement of cause, the study of history becomes fruitful. For it is by applying analogies to our own circumstances that we get the means and basis for calculating the future; and for learning from the past when to act with caution, and when with greater boldness, in the present. The historian therefore who omits the words actually used, as well as all statement of the determining circumstances, and gives us instead conjectures and mere fancy compositions, destroys the special use of history. In this respect Timaeus is an eminent offender, for we all know that his books are full of such writing.

But perhaps some one may raise the question as to how it comes about that, being the sort of writer that I am showing him to be, he has obtained acceptance and credit among certain people. The reason is that his work abounds with hostile criticism and invective against others: and he has been judged, not by the positive merits of his own composition and his independent narrative, but by his skill in refuting his fellow historians; to which department he appears to me to have brought great diligence and an extraordinary natural aptitude. The case of the physicist Strato is almost precisely similar. As long as this man is endeavouring to discredit and refute the opinions of others, he is admirable: directly he brings forward anything of his own, or expounds any of his own doctrines, he at once seems to men of science to lose his faculties and become stupid and unintelligent. And for my part, I look upon this difference in writers as strictly analogous to the facts of everyday life. In this too it is easy to criticise our neighbours, but to be faultless ourselves is hard. One might almost say that those who are most ready at finding fault with others are most prone to errors in their own life. . . .

In the same way the science of genuine history is threefold: first, the dealing with written documents and the arrangement of the material thus obtained; second, topography, the appearance of cities and localities, the description of rivers and harbours, and, speaking generally, the peculiar features of seas and countries and their relative distances; thirdly, political affairs. Now, as in the case of medicine, it is the last branch that many attach themselves to, owing to their preconceived opinions on the subject. And the majority of writers bring to the undertaking no spirit of fairness at all: nothing but dishonesty, impudence and unscrupulousness. Like vendors of drugs, their aim is to catch popular credit and favour, and to seize every opportunity of enriching themselves. About such writers it is not worth while to say more.

But some of those who have the reputation of approaching history in a reasonable spirit are like the theoretical physicians. They spend all their time in libraries, and acquire generally all the learning which can be got from books, and then persuade themselves that they are adquately equipped for their task. . . . Yet in my opinion they are only partially qualified for the production of genuine history. To inspect ancient records indeed, with the view of ascertaining the notions entertained by the ancients of certain places, nations, polities and events, and of understanding the several circumstances and contingencies experienced in former times, is useful; for the history of the past directs our attention in a proper spirit to the future, if a writer can be found to give a statement of facts as they really occurred. But to persuade one's self, as Timaeus does, that such ability in research is sufficient to enable a man to describe subsequent transactions with success is quite foolish. It is as though a man were to imagine that an inspection of the works of the old masters would enable him to become a painter and a master of the art himself. . . .

It is in fact as impossible to write well on the operations in a war, if a man has had no experience of actual service, as it is to write well on politics without having been engaged in political transactions and vicissitudes. And when history is written by the book-learned, without technical knowledge, and without clearness of detail, the work loses all its value. For if you take from history its element of practical instruction, what is left of it has nothing to attract and nothing to teach. Again, in the topography of cities and localities, when such men attempt to go into details, being entirely without personal knowledge, they must in a similar manner necessarily pass over many points of importance; while they waste words on many that are not worth the trouble. . . .

And hence it is, that those who have gone through no such course of actual experience produce no genuine enthusiasm in the minds of their readers. Former historians showed their sense of the necessity of making professions to this effect in their writings. For when their subject was political, they were careful to state that the writer had of course been engaged in politics, and had had experience in matters of the sort; or if the subject was military, that he had served a campaign and been actually engaged; and again, when the matter was one of everyday life, that he had brought up children and had been married; and so on in every department of life, which we may expect to find adequately treated by those writers alone who have had personal experience, and have accordingly made that branch of history their own. It is difficult perhaps for a man to have been actually and literally engaged in everything: but in the most important actions and most frequently occurring he must have been so.

And that this is no impossibility, Homer is a convincing instance; for in him you may see this quality of personal knowledge frequently and conspicuously displayed. The upshot of all this is that the study of documents is only one of three elements in the preparation of an historian, and is only third in importance. And no clearer proof of this could be given than that furnished by the deliberative speeches, harangues of commanders, and orations of ambassadors as recorded by Timaeus. For the truth is, that the occasions are rare which admit of all possible arguments being set forth; as a rule, the circumstances of the case confine them to narrow limits. And of such speeches one sort are regarded with favour by men of our time, another by those of an earlier age; different styles again are popular with Aetolians, Peloponnesians, and Athenians. But to make digressions, in season and out of season, for the purpose of setting forth every possible speech that could be made, as Timaeus does by his trick of inventing words to suit every sort of occasion, is utterly misleading, pedantic, and worthy of a schoolboy essayist. And this practice has brought failure and discredit on many writers. Of course to select from time to time the proper and appropriate language is a necessary part of our art: but as there is no fixed rule to decide the quantity and quality of the words to be used on a particular occasion, great care and training is required if we are to instruct and not mislead our readers. The exact nature of the situation is difficult to communicate always; still it may be brought home to the mind by means of systematic demonstration, founded on personal and habitual experience. The best way of securing that this should be realised is for historians, first, to state clearly the position, the aims, and the circumstances of those deliberating; and then, recording the real speeches made, to explain to us the causes which contributed to the success or failure of the several speakers. Thus we should obtain a true conception of the situation, and by exercising our judgment upon it, and drawing analogies from it, should be able to form a thoroughly sound opinion upon the circumstances of the hour. But I suppose that tracing causes is difficult, while stringing words together in books is easy. Few again have the faculty of speaking briefly to the point, and getting the necessary training for doing so; while to produce a long and futile composition is within most people's capacity and is common enough.

(We take up Polybius' narrative at Book XV where the climactic struggle between Scipio and Hannibal is set forth.)

This was the signal for the recommencement of the war in a fiercer and more angry spirit than before. The Romans on their part, looking upon themselves as having been treated with perfidy, were possessed with a furious determination to conquer the Carthaginians; while the latter, conscious of the consequences of what they had done, were ready to go all lengths to avoid falling under the power of the enemy. With such feelings animating both sides, it was quite evident that the result would have to be decided on the field of battle. Consequently everybody, not only in Italy and Libya, but in Iberia, Sicily, and Sardinia, was in a state of excited expectation, watching with conflicting feelings to see what would happen. But meanwhile Hannibal, finding himself too weak in cavalry, sent to a certain Numidian named Tychaeus, who was a friend of Syphax, and was reputed to possess the most warlike cavalry in Libya, urging him "to lend his aid, and not let the present opportunity slip; as he must be well aware that, if the Carthaginians won the day, he would be able to maintain his rule; but if the Romans proved victorious, his very life would be in danger, owing to the ambition of Massanissa." This prince was convinced by these arguments, and joined Hannibal with two thousand horsemen. . . .

When the people of Carthage saw the cities in their territory being sacked, they sent a message to Hannibal begging him to act without delay, to come to close quarters with the enemy, and bring the matter to the decision of battle. He bade the messengers in answer "to confine their attention to other matters, and to leave such things to him, for he would choose the time for fighting himself." Some days afterwards he broke up his quarters at Adrumetum, and pitched his camp near Zama, a town about five days' march to the west of Carthage. From that place he sent spies to ascertain the place, nature, and strength of the Roman general's encampment. These spies were caught and brought to Scipio, who, so far from inflicting upon them the usual punishment of spies, appointed a tribune to show them everything in the camp thoroughly and without reserve; and when this had been done, he asked the men whether the appointed officer had been careful to point out everything to them. Upon their replying that he had, he gave them provisions and an escort, and despatched them with injunctions to be careful to tell Hannibal everything they had seen. On their return to his camp, Hannibal was so much struck with the magnanimity and high courage of Scipio, that he conceived a lively desire for a personal interview with him. With this purpose he sent a herald to say that he was desirous of a parley to discuss the matters at issue. When the herald had delivered his message, Scipio at once expressed his consent, and said that he would himself send him a message when it suited him to meet, naming the time and place. The herald returned to Hannibal with this answer. Next day Massanissa arrived with six thousand infantry and about four thousand cavalry. Scipio received him with cordiality, and congratulated him on having added to his sway all those who had previously been subject to Syphax. Thus reinforced, he removed his camp to Naragara: selecting it as a place which, among other advantages, enabled him to get water within a javelin's throw.

From this place he sent to the Carthaginian general, informing him that he was ready to meet him, and discuss matters with him. On hearing this, Hannibal moved his quarters to within thirty stades of Scipio, and pitched his camp on a hill, which seemed a favourable position for his present purpose, except that water had to be fetched from a considerable distance, which caused his soldiers great fatigue.

Next day both commanders advanced from their camps attended by a few horsemen. Presently they left these escorts and met in the intervening space by themselves, each accompanied by an interpreter. Hannibal was the first to speak, after the usual salutation. He said that "He wished that the Romans had never coveted any possession outside Italy, nor the Carthaginians outside Libya; for these were both noble empires, and were, so to speak, marked out by nature. But since," he continued, "our rival claims to Sicily first made us enemies, and then those for Iberia; and since, finally, unwarned by the lessons of misfortune, we have gone so far that the one nation has endangered the very soil of its native land, and the other is now actually doing so, all that there remains for us to do is to try our best to deprecate the wrath of the gods, and to put an end, as far as in us lies, to these feelings of obstinate hostility. I personally am ready to do this, because I have learnt by actual experience that Fortune is the most fickle thing in the world, and inclines with decisive favour now to one side and now to the other on the slightest pretext, treating mankind like young children.

"But it is about you that I am anxious, Scipio. For you are still a young man, and everything has succeeded to your wishes both in Iberia and Libya, and you have as yet never experienced the ebb tide of Fortune; I fear, therefore, that my words, true as they are, will not influence you. But do look at the facts in the light of one story, and that not connected with a former generation, but our own. Look at me! I am that Hannibal who, after the battle of Cannae, became master of nearly all Italy; and presently advancing to Rome itself, and pitching my camp within forty stades of it, deliberated as to what I should do with you and your country; but now I am in Libya debating with you, a Roman, as to the bare existence of myself and my countrymen. With such a reverse as that before your eyes, I beg you not to entertain high thoughts, but to deliberate with a due sense of human weakness on the situation; and the way to do that is among good things to choose the greatest, among evils the least. What man of sense, then, would deliberately choose to incur the risk which is now before you. If you conquer, you will add nothing of importance to your glory or to that of your country; while, if you are worsted, you will have been yourself the means of entirely cancelling all the honours and glories you have already won. What then is the point that I am seeking to establish by these arguments? It is that the Romans should retain all the countries for which we have hitherto contended—I mean Sicily, Sardinia, and Iberia; and that the Carthaginians should engage never to go to war with Rome for these; and also that all the islands lying between Italy and Libya should belong to Rome. For I am persuaded that such a treaty will be at once safest for the Carthaginians, and most glorious for you and the entire people of Rome."

In reply to this speech of Hannibal, Scipio said "That neither in the Sicilian nor Iberian war were the Romans the aggressors, but notoriously the Carthaginians, which no one knew better than Hannibal himself. That the gods themselves had confirmed this by giving the victory, not to those who struck the first and unprovoked blow, but to those who only acted in self-defence. That he was as ready as any one to keep before his eyes the uncertainty of Fortune, and tried his best to confine his efforts within the range of human infirmity. But if," he continued, "you had yourself quitted Italy before the Romans crossed to Libya with the offer of these terms in your hands I do not think that you would have been disappointed in your expectation. But now that your departure from Italy has been involuntary, and we have crossed into Libya and conquered the country, it is clear that matters stand on a very different footing. But above all, consider the point which affairs have reached now. Your countrymen have been beaten, and at their earnest prayer we arranged a written treaty, in which, besides the offer now made by you, it was provided that the Carthaginians should restore prisoners without ransom, should surrender all their decked vessels, pay five thousand talents, and give hostages for their performance of these articles. These were the terms which I and they mutually agreed upon; we both despatched envoys to our respective Senates and people,—we consenting to grant these terms, the Carthaginians begging to have them granted. The Senate agreed: the people ratified the treaty. But though they had got what they asked, the Carthaginians annulled the compact by an act of perfidy towards us. What course is left to me? Put yourself in my place and say. To withdraw the severest clauses of the treaty? Are we to do this, say you, not in order that by reaping the reward of treachery they may learn in future to outrage their benefactors, but in order that by getting what they ask for they may be grateful to us? Why, only the other day, after obtaining what they begged for as suppliants, because your presence gave them a slender hope of success, they at once treated us as hated foes and public enemies. In these circumstances, if a still severer clause were added to the conditions imposed, it might be possible to refer the treaty back to the people; but, if I were to withdraw any of these conditions, such a reference does not admit even of discussion. What then is the conclusion of my discourse? It is, that you must submit yourselves and your country to us unconditionally, or conquer us in the field."

After these speeches Hannibal and Scipio parted without coming to any terms; and next morning by daybreak both generals drew out their forces and engaged. To the Carthaginians it was a struggle for their own lives and the sovereignty of Libya; to the Romans for universal dominion and supremacy. And could any one who grasped the situation fail to be moved at the story? Armies more fitted for war than these, or generals who had been more successful or more thoroughly trained in all the operations of war, it would be impossible to find, or any other occasion on which the prizes proposed by destiny to the combatants were more momentous. For it was not merely of Libya or Europe that the victors in this battle were destined to become masters, but of all other parts of the world known to history,—a destiny which had not to wait long for its fulfilment. . . .

All arrangements for the battle being complete, and the two opposing forces of Numidian cavalry having been for some time engaged in skirmishing attacks upon each other, Hannibal gave the word to the men on the elephants to charge the enemy. But as they heard the horns and trumpets braying all round them, some of the elephants became unmanageable and rushed back upon the Numidian contingents of the Carthaginian army; and this enabled Massanissa with great speed to deprive the Carthaginian left wing of its cavalry support. The rest of the elephants charged the Roman velites in the spaces between the maniples of the line, and while inflicting much damage on the enemy suffered severely themselves; until, becoming frightened, some of them ran away down the vacant spaces, the Romans letting them pass harmlessly along, according to Scipio's orders, while others ran away to the right under a shower of darts from the cavalry, until they were finally driven clear off the field. It was just at the moment of this stampede of the elephants, that Laelius forced the Carthaginian cavalry into headlong flight, and along with Massanissa pressed them with a vigorous pursuit. While this was going on, the opposing lines of heavy infantry were advancing to meet others with deliberate step and proud confidence, except Hannibal's "army of Italy," which remained in its original position. When they came within distance the Roman soldiers charged the enemy, shouting as usual their war-cry, and clashing their swords against their shields:

while the Carthaginian mercenaries uttered a strange confusion of cries, the effect of which was indescribable, for, in the words of the poet, the "voice of all was not one"—

> nor one their cry:
> But manifold their speech as was their race.

The whole affair being now a trial of strength between man and man at close quarters, as the combatants used their swords and not their spears, the superiority was at first on the side of the dexterity and daring of the mercenaries, which enabled them to wound a considerable number of the Romans. The latter, however, trusting to the steadiness of their ranks and the excellence of their arms, still kept gaining ground, their rear ranks keeping close up with them and encouraging them to advance; while the Carthaginians did not keep up with their mercenaries nor support them, but showed a thoroughly cowardly spirit. The result was that the foreign soldiers gave way: and, believing that they had been shamelessly abandoned by their own side, fell upon the men on their rear as they were retreating, and began killing them; whereby many of the Carthaginians were compelled to meet a gallant death in spite of themselves. For as they were being cut down by their mercenaries they had, much against their inclination, to fight with their own men and the Romans at the same time; and as they now fought with desperation and fury they killed a good many both of their own men and of the enemy also. Thus it came about that their charge threw the maniples of the *hastati* into confusion; whereupon the officers of the *principes* caused their lines to advance to oppose them. However, the greater part of the mercenaries and Carthaginians had fallen either by mutual slaughter or by the sword of the *hastati*. Those who survived and fled Hannibal would not allow to enter the ranks of his army, but ordered his men to lower their spears and keep them back as they approached; and they were therefore compelled to take refuge on the wings or make for the open country.

The space between the two armies that still remained in position was full of blood, wounded men, and dead corpses; and thus the rout of the enemy proved an impediment of a perplexing nature to the Roman general. Everything was calculated to make an advance in order difficult,— the ground slippery with gore, the corpses lying piled up in bloody heaps, and with the corpses arms flung about in every direction. However Scipio caused the wounded to be carried to the rear, and the *hastati* to be recalled from the pursuit by the sound of a bugle, and drew them up where they were in advance of the ground on which the fighting had taken place, opposite the enemy's centre. He then ordered the *principes* and *triarii* to take close order, and, threading their way through the corpses, to deploy into line with the *hastati* on either flank. When they had surmounted the obstacles and got into line with the *hastati,* the two lines charged each other with the greatest fire and fury. Being nearly equal in numbers, spirit, courage, and arms, the battle was for a long time undecided, the men in their obstinate valour falling dead without giving way a step; until at last the divisions of Massanissa and Laelius, returning from the pursuit, arrived providentially in the very nick of time. Upon their charging Hannibal's rear, the greater part of his men were cut down in their ranks; while of those who attempted to fly very few escaped with their life, because the horsemen were close at their heels and the ground was quite level. On the Roman side there fell over fifteen hundred, on the Carthaginian over twenty thousand, while the prisoners taken were almost as numerous.

Such was the end of this battle, fought under these famous commanders: a battle on which everything depended, and which assigned universal dominion to Rome. . . .

Manifestations of emotion which go beyond what is customary among a particular people, if they are thought to be the result of genuine feeling evoked by extraordinary disasters, excite pity in the minds of those who see or hear them; and we are all in a manner moved by the novelty of the spectacle. But when such things appear to be assumed for the purpose of taking in the spectators and producing a dramatic effect, they do not provoke pity, but anger and dislike. And this was the case in regard to the Carthaginian envoys. Scipio deigned to give a very brief answer to their prayers, saying that "They, at any rate, deserved no kindness at the hands of the Romans, since they had themselves confessed that they were the aggressors in the war, by having, contrary to their treaty obligations, taken Saguntum and enslaved its inhabitants, and had recently been guilty of treachery and breaking the terms of a treaty to which they had subscribed and sworn. It was from a regard to their own dignity, to the vicissitudes of Fortune, and to the dictates of humanity that the Romans had determined to treat them with lenity and behave with magnanimity. And of this they would be convinced if they would take a right view of the case. For they ought not to consider it a hardship if they found themselves charged to submit to any punishment, to follow a particular line of conduct, or to give up this or that; they ought rather to regard it as an unexpected favour that any kindness was conceded to them at all; since Fortune, after depriving them of all right to pity and consideration, owing to their own unrighteous conduct, had put them in the power of their enemies." After this preamble he mentioned the concessions to be made to them, and the penalties to which they were to submit. . . .

This was the nature of Scipio's answer to the envoys, who hastened home and communicated its terms to their countrymen. It was then that the story goes that, upon a certain Senator intending to speak against accepting the terms and actually beginning to do so, Hannibal came forward and pulled the man down from the tribune; and when the other senators showed anger at this breach of custom, Hannibal rose again and "owned that he was ignorant of such things; but said that they must pardon him if he acted in any way contrary to their customs, remembering that he had left the country when he was but fourteen, and had only returned when now past forty-five. Therefore he begged them not to consider whether he had committed a breach of custom, but much rather whether he were genuinely feeling for his country's misfortunes; for that was the real reason for his having been guilty of his breach of manners. For it appeared to him to be astonishing, and, indeed, quite unaccountable, that any one calling himself a Carthaginian, and being fully aware of the policy which they had individually and collectively adopted against the Romans, should do otherwise than adore the kindness of Fortune for obtaining such favourable terms, when in their power, as a few days ago no one—considering the extraordinary provocation they had given—would have ventured to mention, if they had been asked what they expected would happen to their country, in case of the Romans proving victorious. Therefore he called upon them now not to debate, but unanimously to accept the terms offered, and with sacrifices to the gods to pray with one accord that the Roman people might confirm the treaty." His advice being regarded as both sensible and timely, they resolved to sign the treaty on the conditions specified; and the Senate at once despatched envoys to notify their consent.

Julius Caesar

4

Little need be said of the life and career of Caesar. "No other Roman," writes S. A. Handford,"—perhaps no man of any age or country—was at the same time so astute a politician, so resourceful an administrator, so successful a general, so brilliant an orator, and so gifted as an author." Born into a patrician family, receiving the education in history, philosophy, and rhetoric and the training in military science proper to his station, Caesar arrived at his maturity just as the strains imposed by Rome's imperial responsibilities were forcing a fundamental change in her republican constitution. The proposed agrarian reforms of the Gracchi (133–123 B.C.), designed to broaden the democratic base of Rome through a redistribution of landed property, had been blocked and overthrown, destroyed along with their authors by the opposition of aristocratic landowners. A century of political violence ensued. In 82 B.C., Sulla, a great soldier and an astute politician, at the head of a "dictatorship for the making of laws and the regulation of the common-wealth," attempted to revivify the Roman constitution and state. Through a policy of repression and concession he established internal peace. Among other reforms, he abolished the distinctions between Roman citizens and allies, between old citizens who had more rights and new citizens with fewer rights. In all of his reforms Sulla sought to maintain the old "Republican" forms and institutions insofar as possible. But, as Theodor Mommsen points out, Sulla was one of those great men "who swim against the current of the times." His reforms, like those of the Gracchi before him, failed. Caesar himself noted that the Republic had become a mere name without substance. During the 60's and 50's of the first century B.C., Caesar was involved in complicated political and military maneuvers the result of which brought him, in 45 B.C., to a position of uncontested power in Rome. Once he had secured the mastery of the state he set about to reform the constitution and to improve conditions throughout the Empire. Had he been given the time there is little doubt that his rule would have been beneficent and enlightened. An aristocratic clique, in defense of the ancient constitution and their own interests, assassinated him on the Ides of March, 44 B.C.

One of the factors that contributed to Caesar's rise to political supremacy was his successful campaign in Gaul. His victories there and the magnificent army he created, an army utterly devoted to him, provided him with both prestige and power, invaluable assets in the political struggles of the day. Caesar's *Commentaries on the Gallic War,* written in 52 B.C., were in part a conscious effort of what we would today call "image building": the original title seems to have been *Gaius Julius Caesar's Notes on his Achievements.* But the work was much more than propaganda designed to impress his contemporaries. Caesar wrote a true history of his campaigns in Gaul. The reliability of his account has often been impugned, but never successfully so; his descriptions of the Gauls and the Germans have been confirmed by anthropologists; his analysis of the various battles he waged has been found impeccable by military historians. His *Commentaries* are, then, fundamentally accurate, impartial, and much more than a narrative of his personal triumphs.

They are also marked by a lucidity and economy of style and by an absence of hyperbole that made reading them a delight to his contemporaries (and, even in translation, to us). Cicero wrote of them: "They deserve the highest praise; for they are bare, straightforward, and graceful. They are as free of all oratorical adornment as a naked body is free of clothing. . . . In historical writing there is nothing more agreeable than pure limpid brevity." Caesar himself referred to his *Commentaries* as providing materials for historians to work on but his contemporaries (Hirtius) concluded that his accomplishment had "deprived writers of a subject rather than provided them one." A maker of history, Caesar was also a writer of history.

Selected Bibliography

Ronald Syme, *The Roman Revolution* (1939, reprinted with corrections in 1952) and Theodor Mommsen, *The History of Rome,* translated by W. P. Dickson, edited by Dero A. Saunders and John H. Collins (1958), together constitute an admirable introduction to Caesar and his time. M. L. W. Laistner, *The Greater Roman Historians* (1947), has a judicious chapter on "Historical Writing in Rome to the Death of Caesar." It may be complemented by Michael Grant's informative survey in his *Roman Literature* (third edition, 1964), Chapter 2. Of the numerous recent translations of Caesar's *Gallic War,* those of Moses Hadas (1957) and S. A. Handford (1951, reprinted in 1967) deserve special mention particularly for their learned and balanced introductions. Detlaf Rasmussen has edited a rich and representative collection of essays, *Caesar,* in the *Wege der Forschung* series, vol.

43 (1967). See especially, Matthias Gelzer's article "Caesar als Historiker," pp. 438–473. T. Rice Holmes, Caesar's *Conquest of Gaul* (second edition, 1911), is an invaluable aid in the study of Caesar's work. The present selections are taken from F. P. Long's translation (1911).

THE CONQUEST OF GAUL

The country known collectively as Gaul presents in reality three distinct divisions, inhabited respectively by the Belgae, the Aquitani, and a race which, though commonly described by us as Gauls, is known in the vernacular as Celts. Between these three divisions there exist fundamental differences both of language, customs, and political organization. Geographically, the Gauls lie midway between the Aquitani and Belgae, the respective boundaries being the Garumna (Garonne) in the south, and the Matrona (Marne) and Sequana (Seine) in the north. Of the three the Belgae are conspicuously the bravest race, a fact doubtless derived from the peculiarity of their position, which not only keeps them strangers to the civilization and refinement so characteristic of the Province (Provence), and protects them against traders and all their attendant evils, but brings them also into closest contact with the Germans beyond the Rhine, between whom and themselves there exists perpetual war. The same cause, it may be noted in passing, produces in the Helvetii those striking martial qualities in which they so far excel all the other Gauls; there being scarcely a day that does not witness some border skirmish with their German neighbours, either in repelling a raid upon themselves, or in making reprisals across the frontier. The middle section of the country, inhabited, as already stated, by the Gauls, begins from the Rhone, and from there extends to the Garonne, the Outer Ocean, and the Belgae; whilst on its eastern border, at the territories of the Sequani and Helvetii, it marches with the Rhine. The general trend of the country is northwards. The Belgic division starts from the frontier of the Gauls, and from there stretches to the lower reaches of the Rhine, the country therefore facing north and east; whilst the Aquitani fill up all the region between the Garonne, the line of the Pyrenees, and the bend of the Bay of Biscay, fronting accordingly northwestwards.

Among the Helvetii at the time our narrative opens the most conspicuous figure, both as regards wealth and family descent, was a chieftain named Orgetorix. There years earlier, in the consulship of M. Messalla

---

From *Commentaries on the Gallic War*, translated by F. P. Long (1911). Pp. 1–6, 172–182, 184–198, 270–272.

and M. Pupius Piso, his restless craving for absolute power had led him
to inaugurate a secret movement among the ruling chiefs, by which he
persuaded the government to undertake a national migration from their
present homes, having as its object (what, according to him, would be an
easy result of their military supremacy), the ultimate domination of all
Gaul. Such a proposal won the more ready acceptance, from the natural
obstacles to expansion by which the Helvetii on all sides found themselves surrounded. Along their northern and eastern frontiers the Rhine
forms a barrier which by its formidable depth and width effectually bars
all outlet towards the Germans; westwards the lofty range of the Jura
blocks the way to the Sequani; southwards the lake of Geneva and the
Rhone cut off all access to the Province (Provence). The effect of these
obstacles was seriously to impede their freedom of movement, as well as
greatly to diminish the opportunities for border warfare; two restrictions
which, to a people of born fighters, were peculiarly distasteful. And further, there was the constant feeling amongst them that their present
limited area, embracing as it did no more than 240 miles in length and
180 in breadth, was neither adequate to their dense population, nor
worthy of their great military name and fame.

To these predisposing causes for action the appeal of Orgetorix added
the required occasion, and the Helvetian authorities at once decided to
make the necessary preparations for a general exodus. Sumpter beasts
and wagons were to be bought up wherever procurable, all the land
possible was to be laid down with corn, in order to guarantee supplies
upon the road, peace and friendship were to be secured with all neighbouring states. For these several measures two years were deemed to be
sufficient; the third, by a solemn resolution of the tribe, was fixed for the
departure. The general supervision of affairs was entrusted to Orgetorix,
and he accordingly undertook as his special duty the mission to foreign
states. The first to be visited were the Sequani; where, entering into
communication with a chief named Casticus, a son of that Cataman-
taloedis, who during his long reign over his people had been honoured
by the Senate with the coveted title of "Friend of Rome," he urged him
to seize upon the sceptre so lately wielded by his father. Proceeding next
to the Aedui, he made similar proposals to a prince called Dumnorix,
commending his suit by bestowing upon him the hand of his daughter
in marriage. He was to rise against his own brother Divitiacus, at that
time the acknowledged ruler of the Aeduan country and the trusted representative of the people. In the case of each, success was to be guaran-
teed by the approaching accession of himself to sovereign power at
home: and the military pre-eminence of the Helvetii being unquestioned
throughout Gaul, they were bidden to look to him for the acquisition of
their crown, through the civil and military resources that would then be

his. These allurements succeeded in their aim, and the three conspirators, having pledged one another to mutual loyalty, looked forward, when
once established on their thrones, to climbing, through a coalition of the
three most powerful and resolute tribes in the country, to the consolidated empire of a united Gaul.

But their secret was ill-kept: their plot was betrayed, and fully reported
to the Helvetian authorities. In accordance with tribal usage Orgetorix
was summoned to stand his trial in chains; conviction was to be followed
by being publicly burned at the stake. On the appointed day the accused
surrendered to his judges; but he came at the head of ten thousand serfs,
who had been specially drafted from his wide estates, and with countless
numbers of retainers and poor debtors also impressed for the occasion,
and, thus surrounded, successfully defied the court. Justly incensed at so
gross an outrage, the Helvetian authorities prepared to uphold the civil
arm by an appeal to the sword; and steps had already been taken to call
out the tribal levies, when suddenly Orgetorix died; nor is there wanting
the suspicion, strongly held by the Helvetii, that his death was self-
inflicted.

It was not, however, allowed to affect their decision as to migration.
When to the best of their judgment every arrangement had been perfected, under a strong impulse to take an irrevocable step that should
more easily reconcile them to whatever dangers fortune might have in
store, they deliberately burned down every one of their twelve fortified
towns, four hundred open villages, and every private residence throughout the land. At the same time all stocks of corn not destined to be carried
with them on the march were indiscriminately committed to the flames;
the only provisions permitted to remain being three months' supplies of
ground grain for each head of the population. Three of their nearest
neighbours, the Rauraci, Tulingi, and Latovici, were also induced to
follow their example of burning their towns and villages, and to throw
in their lot with the migratory movement; whilst another people, the
Boii, whose home had been formerly beyond the Rhine, but who had
since invaded Norican territory and there laid siege to Noreia (Neumarkt
in Styria), were invited to join them and received into close alliance.

Two routes, and two only, presented themselves as practicable for their
purpose. They might either pass through the country of the Sequani, by
a narrow and difficult defile running between Mount Jura and the Rhone;
—so narrow that even a single line of carts could hardly pass, and so
completely dominated by the frowning heights, that even a slender force
could easily bar it in their face—or they might go through the Roman
Province, a far easier and less complicated route, where, just across the
upper Rhone, which here forms the boundary, lay the friendly district of
the Allobroges. This people had been only lately reduced to obedience,

and numerous fords were also available in their country. The actual point of contact of the two tribes is the city of Geneva, which lies at the easternmost end of the Allobroges, and communicates by a bridge with the Helvetii on the opposite side. Either then, they argued, they would peacefully persuade the Allobroges, who hardly yet seemed reconciled to Roman rule, to grant them a passage through their borders, or else they would compel them by armed force. Everything being ready for the start, a date was fixed on which the entire nation was to assemble along the northern bank of the Rhone; this date being the twenty-eighth of March, in the consulship of Lucius Piso and Aulus Gabinius (58 B.C.).

The news that the Helvetii were contemplating a movement across the Province reached Caesar whilst still in Rome. Upon its receipt, he hastily quitted the capital, and travelling through post-haste to Further Gaul, quickly reached Geneva. Arrived here, he issued orders to raise the military forces of the Province to their utmost limit (the whole of Further Gaul, it should be mentioned, was at the time garrisoned by a single legion only), and to cut down the bridge at Geneva. His arrival had not escaped the notice of the Helvetian leaders, and a deputation of their chief notables, headed by the two chiefs Nammeius and Verucloetius, presently appeared to lay their case before the Roman governor. These informed him that their sole intention was to march through the Province without causing any disturbance of the peace, and only for the reason that no other route lay open to them, and that for this they humbly solicited his leave. In considering his answer, Caesar found it impossible to forget that these same Helvetii had not so many years before first routed a Roman army and afterwards forced it under the yoke, whilst causing the death also of its commander, the consul Lucius Cassius. This fact alone precluded a favourable reply; but apart altogether from this, it was difficult to believe that a people, who harboured no very friendly feelings towards Rome, would repress their natural instincts of plunder and pillage, if once allowed the chance of marching through the Province. On the other hand, it was essential to temporize till the concentration of the new levies was completed; and he therefore replied to the envoys that he should require to think over the matter, and that if they had anything further to urge they might return on April 13.

Meanwhile he proceeded to strengthen his own defences. . . .

At this point of our narrative it will not perhaps be thought inopportune if we pause to consider in some detail the national life of Gaul and Germany, and to show the more important aspects in which the two races differ from each other. To begin with the Gauls. The most remarkable feature about their political organization is the existence everywhere of two great antagonistic parties. Not merely do these parties divide each independent tribe, but the cleavage extends to every territorial division and subdivision, and may almost be said to permeate every individual household. In all cases the party leaders are appointed from those who are recognized by their constituents as the most prominent of their members, and to their judgment and decision every question of fact or policy is of necessity referred. In such a system would seem to lie the true explanation of a time-honoured custom throughout Gaul, which ensures of every poorer member of the community protection against more powerful neighbours; since every party leader is quick to resent and revenge any wrong or oppression that may be perpetrated on his clients, and indeed only holds his position of authority amongst them on condition of fulfilling this primary obligation. These characteristics of the internal state of each tribe obtain also in the country taken as a whole, and the same spirit of political partisanship splits it into two permanently hostile camps.

The respective heads of these two factions were, at the time of Caesar's arrival in the country, the Aedui and the Sequani. The former held an assured position of power by virtue alike of ancient prerogative and by their formidable list of subject communities; so that the Sequani, too weak to maintain the contest single-handed with the forces at their disposal, turned in the hour of their extremity to foreign alliance. At ruinous cost to themselves, both present and prospective, they induced Ariovistus and his Germans to cross the Rhine to their assistance; after which a succession of victories in the field, which swept away the whole of the Aeduan nobility, gave them such a predominating position over their rivals, that these for the time were virtually extinguished. Not only were considerable numbers of their supporters compelled to transfer their allegiance to the victorious party, and they themselves to give their chieftains' sons as hostages, but in their crippled state they had to swear to abstain in future from all unfriendly acts against the Sequani, to allow a strip of border territory to be forcibly occupied by their conquerors, and to see these firmly installed as a paramount power in Gaul. It was at this dark hour of his country's fortunes that Divitiacus undertook his mission to Rome in order to appeal to the Senate; but his effort was unavailing, and his return left matters where they were. The arrival of Caesar, however, caused a complete revolution in the conditions governing the contest. The Aeduan hostages were now given back to them, their ancient supporters renewed their former ties, and through the powerful influence exerted by Caesar, fresh states were induced to join the alliance (observing as they did that the members of the Aeduan confederacy enjoyed fairer terms and a juster rule than those elsewhere); whilst in every direction and by every means their authority and prestige was fostered and extended, until slowly but surely the premiership of the league passed from the hands of the Sequani. Their successors in the leadership were the Remi; and under this state, when once it was realized that Caesar's support was still bestowed as generously as before, many of those whose ancient feuds with the Aedui made a combination with that people intolerable, enrolled themselves as vassals to the Remi. Their new overlords, scrupulously upholding their rights as subjects, soon succeeded in building up for themselves an assured position of political power, that was as novel as it had been sudden in its growth. Thus at the period we have now reached, while the first place in public estimation belonged, without question, to the Aedui, the second was no less definitely conceded to the Remi.

That part of the Gallic population that is of any practical account may everywhere be divided into two heads: the position of the commons, who might form a third estate, may for our purposes be disregarded, since it is virtually that of slaves, powerless of themselves to initiate any political action, and wholly unrepresented in the councils of the nation. The majority, indeed, are so crushed down by debt and excessive taxation, or so much the victims of aggression by the rich, that they are glad to enter into voluntary servitude under some one or other of the great nobles, who then exercises over them all the rights of a master over slaves. The other two classes are those of the Druids and the Knights. Of the first the special province is religion in all its aspects. Every sacrifice, whether public or private, is conducted under their auspices, every manifestation of divine agency is brought to them for interpretation: they are the eagerly sought instructors of vast numbers of the nation's youth, and to the reverence accorded them there is hardly a limit. A dispute can scarcely arise, either between individuals or states, which is not referred to them for judgment. The graver criminal charges, such as murder, no less than such civil cases as those of inheritance or boundary disputes, are laid before the same tribunal; they it is who determine rewards and punishments, and to their decision should either party, whether a people or an individual, refuse obedience, it is excommunicated from all the religious life of the community. Than this dread penalty none is known among them more severe. Those on whom such sentence has been passed are regarded by their fellows as men polluted and accursed: their society is universally shunned; none will visit them, no one will speak to them, for to do either is to risk the fall of some dire calamity; the courts of law are closed to them, and from the public services they are rigorously excluded. At the head of all stands a single chief, the Archdruid, invested with supreme powers. Upon his death the succession either passes to the next in eminence, or, where there are several candidates of equal merit, the election is determined by vote of the Druids, and even occasionally by force of arms. Every year at a fixed date there is held a general assembly of the order at a sacred spot among the Carnutes, popularly believed to be the centre of Gaul; and to this grand assize all make their way who have outstanding quarrels, to abide by the decisions there given. The Druidical cult is generally supposed to have originated in Britain, and from thence to have been transplanted to Gaul; and to-day those who desire to learn the more esoteric side of the doctrine cross to that island in order to complete their studies.

As a class the Druids take no active part in war, and pay none of the ordinary taxes for that purpose: not only from direct military service but from other state burdens also they are uniformly exempt. Through the attractions held out by such a career no less than from private choice, large numbers join the ranks of the priesthood, and are sent by their parents and relatives to undergo the necessary training. In their schools they are said to learn by heart an extraordinary number of lines, and in consequence sometimes to remain under instruction for as many as twenty years. Although for most other purposes, in both their public and private accounts, they have adopted the Greek alphabet, yet they still retain a superstitious objection to committing the secrets of their doctrine to writing. In acting so they would seem to be guided by two main considerations. The first is their natural repugnance to the unrestricted publication of their tenets; the second is a fear lest their pupils, by too close a reliance on the written text, should relax the cultivation of their memory; experience generally showing that the constant presence of a manuscript serves only to weaken the natural powers of application and retention possessed by the mind. With regard to their actual course of studies, the main object of all education is, in their opinion, to imbue their scholars with a firm belief in the indestructibility of the human soul, which, according to their belief, merely passes at death from one tenement to another; for by such a doctrine alone, they say, which robs death of all its terrors, can the highest form of human courage be developed. Subsidiary to the teaching of this main principle, they hold various lectures and discussions on astronomy, on the extent and geographical distribution of the globe, on the different branches of natural philosophy, and on the many problems connected with religion.

The second great division is that of the Knights. These form the warrior class, and live exclusively by the sword: war makes their opportunity; and as, previous to Caesar's arrival, wars of provocation or retaliation were the normal state of things, they were in those days constantly engaged. Their order of precedence depends exclusively upon the number of followers and retainers they can lead into the field, and that in its turn depends upon the eminence of each either in descent or in worldly circumstances. Rank or title of any other kind is not recognized amongst them.

In the formal observances of religion, the Gauls are as a nation almost

excessively devout. This instinct leads them on such occasions as grievous bodily illness, impending battle, or similar dangers, to offer or to vow
a human sacrifice in place of animal victims, the Druids being called in
to officiate at the rites. Of this practice the underlying belief is that only
by the substitution of one human life for another can the inexorable
demands of heaven be satisfied; a principle that obtains in much of their
public ceremonial also. Others keep by them a grotesque and gigantic
image of some favourite god, into whose huge limbs of wicker-work those
destined for sacrifice are packed alive; fire is then placed beneath the
pile, and the souls of the victims pass away amid a torrent of roaring
flames. Though ready enough to admit that the gods are better pleased
when such punishment is inflicted on those convicted of theft or brigandage or other similar crime, yet, on the failure of this particular source of
supply, they do not hesitate to seek the instruments of atonement even
from the innocent.

Of all the gods, the one whose worship is most in vogue is Mercury.
Everywhere the most conspicuous by the number of his images, he is
commonly regarded as the revealer of all useful sciences, as the
trusty guide to wayfarers and travellers, and as the all-important
partner in trade and commerce. Next to him come Apollo, Jupiter,
and Minerva, and about them their ideas correspond fairly closely
with those current among the rest of mankind; viz. that Apollo expels
diseases, that Minerva teaches the principles of domestic arts and
crafts, that Jupiter wields the sceptre over heavenly beings, that Mars
holds in his hand the arbitrament of war. To the last-named god, on
the eve of a big battle, they not infrequently devote the spoils of the
campaign, and then whatever of the captured live stock remains on
the termination of the war is publicly slaughtered in his honour,
while all other kinds of booty are collected and heaped together in a
single place. Of such dedicated piles of loot standing in sacred enclo-
sures it is possible to see examples among many of the tribes; and
rare are the cases where contempt for sacrilege has led either to the
concealment at home of a piece of plunder, or to the theft of what has
once been offered. For such an offence the punishment is the most
terrible that torture can inflict.

Their supernatural descent from Father Dis is the unanimous tradition of all Gauls, based, as they declare, on the teaching of the Druids.
One curious result of this is that intervals of time are reckoned, not in
days, but in nights; and similarly birthdays or the first day of any new
month or year are observed in such a fashion as to make the preceding night always part of the festival day. Among other social customs,
perhaps the most noticeable is their seclusion of children. Boys are
never allowed to go and meet their sires, and for a boy of tender years

to be seen in public by the side of his father before he is capable of bearing arms is regarded as a great disgrace.

What money a husband receives in dowry from a wife is always doubled by an equal portion taken from his own estate, strict valuation being made on either side. Of this combined sum a common account is kept, and all profits from it set aside; whichever partner then outlives the other takes both shares, together with the interest accumulated during their married life. Over their wives, no less than over their children, husbands exercise the power of life and death; and whenever any member of their more distinguished families dies, if there be reason to suspect foul play, at the meeting of the male relatives which then takes place the wife is rigorously examined according to the process usually adopted with slaves, and if proved guilty, is put to death by burning and other refinements of cruelty. The obsequies of the Gauls are, in proportion to their standard of living, both costly and magnificent, and at them all objects believed to have been dear to the heart of the departed, including even animals, are flung upon the pyre: indeed, only a little while before the present account was written, at every properly conducted funeral slaves and retainers known to have been loved by the dead man were commonly burnt with their master.

Those of the tribes whose government passes for something more enlightened have a special enactment that any rumour or report on matter of vital interest, which may have been picked up across the frontier, shall be instantly carried to the authorities, and not divulged in other quarters; so frequently has it been found the case that this people of strong passions and weak judgment can be swept away by unreasoning panic, driven into the perpetration of crime, and hurried into a fatal course of public conduct, solely by their acceptance of some lying tale. When such information reaches them, the magistrates decide what they will guard as state secrets, and what they may with advantage issue to the public; and outside the council-chamber, it has to be remembered, no discussion of political questions is permitted.

Turning now to the Germans, we find among them a form of national life in sharp contrast to the one just described. Of anything like a religious caste, such as we see in the Druids, there is a complete absence, and a corresponding indifference to the multiplication of sacrifice. The only deities they recognize are those visible powers of nature whose kindly influence upon human labour is clearly manifest; viz. the Sun, Moon, and God of Fire; of the existence of any others they seem to be aware not even by hearsay. To them the business of life is summed up in hunting and the art of war, and their training in feats of hardship and endurance begins with earliest childhood. The postponement in a boy of the age of puberty is always a coveted distinction, and is believed to be a sign either of unusual height or of immense bodily strength. Sexual intercourse below the age of twenty is considered a disgrace to manhood; though, on the other hand, they are singularly free from all false modesty on this subject, and not only bathe together in their rivers, but even wear nothing more upon their bodies than a thin covering of deer or other skin, which necessarily leaves the greater portion bare.

The cultivation of the soil, in the strict meaning of the term, is little practised by them, and their diet consists for the main part of milk, cheese, and flesh. Neither the exclusive enjoyment nor the private ownership of land is permitted; but instead an annual distribution of it is made by the government officials and local chiefs, who determine both the extent and situation of the portion of land to be allotted to each class and family-association living together: every one of these groups being required to remove elsewhere a year afterwards. Of this practice the explanations given are various. It is said sometimes to owe its origin to a fear lest the charms of a fixed tenure should beget in the people a preference for the peaceful life of the farm over the more violent pleasures of war; to the covetousness inseparable from private ownership, which tempts the strong to oust the weaker from their holdings; to the desire of discouraging any elaborate form of building for protection against the natural vicissitudes of heat and cold; to the dread of arousing the latent love of money—that pernicious root of all discord and class hatred; or finally, to the conviction that their system alone reconciles the lower orders to their lot, when every man sees his own share of the national riches equal to that of the very highest in the land.

Among the tribes there is no more coveted distinction than to live in the centre of a vast wilderness, that has been carved out with their own swords along each and all of their frontiers. In their minds the true test of national greatness is the power of compelling all neighbours to retire before their face, and to keep at a respectful distance from their settlements; such devastation, moreover, acts as a form of security, since undoubtedly it relieves them from the constant fear of raids. Upon the outbreak of war, whether offensive or defensive, the conduct of hostilities is entrusted to a board of magistrates, specially elected, and wielding capital jurisdiction; in peace the place of a central government is taken by the local chiefs, who dispense justice and regulate disputes each in his own division or subdivision of the country. Open brigandage, provided its victims be not fellow tribesmen, carries with it no disgrace; rather it is held up to admiration as a natural outlet for the activities of youth, and a useful remedy against sloth. Whenever, therefore, any chief announces before the tribal council that he is ready to lead an expedition, and calls for volunteers to follow him, those who approve of both the man and his measure leap to their feet with offers of assistance, winning much

popularity by their action: should any of these then fail to make good
their promise, they will be branded as renegades and traitors, and confidence in their sincerity will be for ever afterwards shaken. Their observance of the ties of hospitality is invariably most strict, and any foreign
visitor, no matter what the object of his journey, may always rely on their
loyally protecting him against abuse, as though his person were inviola-
ble, and as long as he chooses to stay, the houses of all and the tables of
all are freely at his disposal.

There was a time when the German race was distinctly inferior in
martial qualities to the Gauls, and when the latter, habitually the agres-
sors, on account of their dense population and deficiency of land at home,
sent offshoots of their own to the other side of the Rhine. It was in this
way that some of the richest land in all Germany, lying round the great
Hercynian forest (or, to give it the name by which it is known to Eratos-
thenes and other Greeks, the "Orcynian"), passed into the hands of the
Tectosagan Volcae; and even to-day, thanks mainly to the double reputation they enjoy for fair dealing and hard hitting, that tribe is still maintaining itself in its adopted home, though sunk to the level of the surrounding population, and reproducing the well-known features of
German poverty, destitution, and general discomfort, with the same
rough style of living and of dress. The Gauls, on the other hand, have
steadily progressed, and owing to the nearness of the Roman provinces
and their introduction to articles of sea-borne commerce, the national
wealth has tended constantly to increase, and the standard of comfort
constantly to rise. Thus the growing sense of their own inferiority arising
from repeated overthrows in the field has resulted to-day even in their
own admission that in warlike qualities they are no longer a match for
their German foes. . . .

The calm that now lay over Gaul had enabled Caesar to fulfil his
original plan of visiting Northern Italy, and superintending in that part
of his government the civil administration of the courts. There he heard
of the murder of Clodius (Jan. 20), and acting upon the consequent resolution of the Senate which called on all the adult population of Italy to
take the oath of military service, he proceeded to order a levy throughout
the province. These unusual movements were of course at once reported
to the Gauls beyond the Alps, and their true significance being purposely
exaggerated and perverted by interested mischief-makers, Caesar was
represented as forcibly detained in Italy owing to the disturbances at
Rome, and as unable to rejoin his army through fear of an armed outbreak. So good an opportunity was eagerly embraced by those who had
long resented the yoke of foreign rule, and fresh throughts of war, on a
bolder and grander scale, now began to stir their minds. Secret councils
were convened in remote districts of the forest-lands, at which the na-

tional leaders, taking the death of Acco for their text, cunningly incited others to rebellion by the insinuation that his fate might very probably be theirs, and by generally lamenting the woes of their unhappy country. The great point was to discover some tribe to lead the way, and, induced by the sure prospect of generous reward from its fellows, though at the imminent risk of its own existence, to work out the common salvation of Gaul. The importance of severing Caesar from his army before their secret negotiations got abroad was fully recognized; but this feat was declared easy of accomplishment because, just as in the absence of their commander-in-chief, the legions would not think of stirring from their cantonments, so neither could he without an escort make his way to them. And come what might it was universally agreed that to fall fighting on the field of battle was infinitely better than to endure the loss of their ancient military renown, and of their sacred heritage of freedom as a people. . . .

These movements reached the ears of Caesar whilst he was still in Italy; and coming at a moment when, thanks to the vigorous measures adopted by Cn. Pompeius, affairs at the capital had been reduced to something approaching order, they made it possible for him to recross the Alps into the further Province. Arrived there, he was at once confronted by the exceedingly difficult problem of how best to reach his army. To summon the legions southwards into the Province would be to send them into action upon the road in his own absence; to make a dash northwards in order to join them was to entrust his person to the safe conduct of still nominally friendly tribes, and this at so critical a juncture would scarcely be advisable.

Meanwhile, however, circumstances had combined to solve the problem for him. The Cadurcan leader Lucterius had so far succeeded in his mission to the Ruteni as to win over that tribe to the national cause, passing thence to the Nitiobriges and Gabali, from each of whom he exacted hostages; and now, after strengthening himself by several fresh contingents, he was ready to descend upon the Roman Province with the object of striking at the town of Narbo (Narbonne). The news of this movement determined Caesar to relegate all other issues to secondary consideration, and to proceed at once to the threatened town. There he soon put fresh heart into the waverers, and then proceeded to erect a chain of forts along those sections of the Ruteni that lie on the Roman side of the frontier, the Arecomican Volcae, the district of Tolosa (Toulouse) and the environs of Narbo, all of which lay directly in the enemy's line of attack. At the same time a portion of the Provincial levies, as well as the new drafts lately come from Italy, were ordered to concentrate upon the Helvii, who are situated on the south-eastern flank of the Arverni (Auvergne).

These measures sufficiently checked the further advance of Lucterius, who, finding the ring of fortified posts too strong to pierce, presently beat a retreat, thus leaving Caesar free to go on to the Helvii. On the Cevennes, the mountain range that blocks the Helvii from the Arverni, midwinter had spread a pall of deep snow over the face of all the country, that sorely hindered progress: but, working with tireless energy at the task of clearing the drifts, that were often six feet high, the troops gradually laid bare thé roads, and soon the army was upon the frontiers of Auvergne.

Its inhabitants were overwhelmed by the extraordinary suddenness of the attack. The Cevennes had always been regarded as an impregnable barrier of defence, and never within the memory of man had the passes been open at this season even to a single wayfarer. Pressing his advantage, Caesar ordered his cavalry to scour the country to the utmost limits of their powers, and to overawe the enemy wherever found. The report that the Romans had taken the field was quickly communicated to Vercingetorix, and, as a first consequence, he was quickly surrounded by a crowd of terror-stricken Arverni, begging him to go to the rescue of their property before it was looted by the enemy, and reminding him that to him had been entrusted the sole conduct of the war. To these arguments he yielded a grudging recognition, and breaking up his camp among the Bituriges, began to move southwards towards the Avernian district.

Meanwhile Caesar, who had expected some such result in regard to Vercingetorix, after remaining two days in the neighbourhood, gave out that the need of obtaining fresh drafts of infantry and cavalry now summoned him away, and then quietly took his departure from camp. The command of the forces was left with one of the younger generals, D. Brutus, who had orders to continue the sweeping movements of the cavalry about the country during the commander-in-chief's absence, which would not, as he hoped, be extended beyond three days. These dispositions effected, without any suspicion even by his own attendants of the object of their journey, he travelled through with all haste to Vienna (Vienne), where, picking up a division of cavalry which had been sent on thither some days in advance, and was therefore now rested, and barely drawing rein either by day or night, he raced across the country of the Aedui towards the Lingones (Langres), where were two legions in winter quarters. In this way he trusted to his speed to frustrate any designs upon his own person that the Aeduan authorities might likewise be harbouring. Arrived at his destination, he at once sent word to the remaining legions, and before any inkling of his presence in these quarters had reached the Averni, the concentration of the Roman army was complete. At this unexpected news Vercingetorix once more fell back upon the Bituriges, from whence he moved to attack the town of Gorgobina, at this time inhabited by that section of the Boii which after the Helvetian war had been settled there by Caesar in political dependence upon the Aedui.

The enemy's new movement raised a serious difficulty for Caesar as to what course he should pursue. To keep the legions together for the rest of the winter while a city belonging to Aeduan subjects was openly carried by assault, was to confess before the Gallic world that the Romans were unable to defend their friends, and to risk, therefore, the universal defection of Gaul: on the other hand, to move from winter quarters earlier than usual, with transport a matter of much trouble, would probably lead to a breakdown in his supplies. Yet it seemed preferable to endure any degree of hardship than, by a tame acquiescence in such a humiliating ignominy, to alienate the sympathies of every Roman supporter: and therefore, after urging on the Aedui the importance of maintaining a regular succession of convoys, he sent word to the Boii that he himself was marching to their relief, bidding them at the same time stand firmly to their allegiance and present a bold front to the enemy. Then leaving two legions at Agedincum (Sens) along with the stores and baggage of the whole army, with the remaining forces he set out for the Boii.

The second day's march brought him to a town of the Bituriges named Vallaunodunum, and in order to leave no enemy in his rear who might afterwards threaten his communications, he prepared for its assault, and in two days had completed the necessary lines. On the third the enemy opening negotiations, they were allowed to surrender on condition they gave up all arms, brought out all draft animals, and handed over hostages to the number of six hundred. The carrying out of these terms was entrusted to C. Trebonius, a staff officer, and the army with the commander-in-chief then resumed its forward movement. Its next objective was Cenabum (Orleans), the capital of the Carnutes, for whose defence that tribe was only now preparing to introduce a garrison; since they had expected the siege of Vellaunodunum, of which they had just heard, to be an affair of some time. Two days' march brought the legions before the town; but, it being too late to deliver the assault that night, it was decided to defer it till the morning, and meanwhile the army camped outside the walls. The necessary preparations for attack having been carefully completed by the troops, as there was reason to fear that the enemy might, under cover of darkness, attempt to escape by the bridge connecting Cenabum with the further bank of the Liger (Loire), two legions were ordered to remain under arms throughout the night. This expectation was abundantly realized, and shortly before midnight the inhabitants quietly began the evacuation of the town by crossing the stream; but the movement being reported by his scouts to Caesar, the two legions, who by his orders were ready for any emergency, were at once directed to fire the gates and to enter the town. The victory was all but complete: along the bridge and narrow roads debouching upon it the crush had been so dense, that very few indeed of the enemy's masses had succeeded in making their escape. The town was first plundered and then burnt; and the troops having been rewarded with the spoil, the army now crossed the Liger and found itself in the country of the Bituriges.

The news of its approach caused a modification of plans on the part of Vercingetorix, and breaking off the siege then occupying him, he boldly advanced to throw down the gage of battle to Caesar himself. The latter meanwhile had interrupted his advance in order to attack the Biturigan town of Noviodunum, lying upon his line of march. A desire to negotiate had already been expressed by the garrison, and Caesar, anxious to complete his work with the same expedition which had hitherto proved so effective, had, in answer to their appeal for pardon and preservation, at once commanded the delivery of arms, animals, and hostages. Some of these had already been surrendered, and centurions with a file of soldiers had even entered the town for the purpose of completing the arrangements of collecting the arms and animals, when suddenly on the horizon the cavalry corps preceding the army of Vercingetorix was seen to be approaching. No sooner was the discovery made by the townspeople, than realizing that possible help was at hand, they raised a loud shout of defiance, and rushing to arms, shut all the gates and surged forward to man the walls. The centurions in the town, observing from the signals passing between the Gauls that some untoward circumstance had arisen, at once drew their swords, and having secured possession of the gates, ultimately withdrew every one of their men without loss.

Upon Caesar's orders the cavalry advanced from camp and at once engaged the enemy; but finding that they were being worsted he called up as reinforcements a body of some four hundred German troopers, which throughout these campaigns had been a permanent feature of his army. Before their charge the enemy broke and fled, and with heavy loss fell back upon their main column. Their overthrow revived to the full the alarms of the townsfolk, and, having arrested the suspected leaders in the recent renewal of resistance, they sent these out to Caesar under escort and again tendered their submission. This affair satisfactorily disposed of, the advance was continued towards Avaricum (Bourges), and as this town is the largest and strongest of all those belonging to the Bituriges, and forms the centre of an exceedingly rich and fertile district, there was good ground for believing that its recovery by the Romans would be followed by the surrender of the entire Biturigan people. . . .

From their position on the heights above the enemy had a wide prospect of all the rolling country at their feet, and recognizing the approach of the Roman commander-in-chief from the conspicuous colour of his uniform, usually worn by him in action, and the infantry battalions and cavalry squadrons following at his back, they lost no time in opening the engagement. As the two hostile lines advanced upon each other, both raised the shout of battle, a shout that was immediately taken up and echoed all down the line of ramparts even to the most distant point of the works. Discarding the use of the heavy javelin, the Romans trusted solely to their swords. The enemy maintained a stubborn fight till suddenly in their rear appeared the Roman cavalry; and fresh battalions coming up at the moment to swell the attack, the Gauls then turned and fled. The wave of fugitives broke itself upon the serried lines of horsemen waiting to receive them, and a fearful carnage ensued. Among the killed was Sedulius, the warrior chieftain of the Lemovices, while among those taken in the rout was the famous Arvernian leader Vercassivellaunus. Eighty-four regimental colours were brought as trophies to Caesar; and of the once majestic host that had marched to the relief of Alesia, only a tiny fraction struggled back to camp. The sight of this unresisting slaughter of their comrades crushed the last spark of hope from the spirits of the garrison, and a general retreat from the inner face of the lines now took place. This in turn reacted on those without, since immediately upon its news the entire Gallic encampment broke up in confusion and fled; and, but for the exhaustion of the troops caused by the repeated calls made upon their strength throughout an exceptionally trying day, the annihilation of the enemy must have followed. As it was, the cavalry a little after midnight was sent in pursuit, and catching up the rearguard, took heavy toll in killed and prisoners; the rest of the fugitives then scattered, and melted away to their homes.

On the morrow of this disastrous day Vercingetorix convened a meeting of his captains, and addressing them for the last time as their commander, told them that, as he had not entered on this war from motives of self-aggrandizement or pride, but solely as the champion of a downtrodden people, now that Fortune had proved ungracious, to her decision he meant to bow. But since such was to be the end, he was ready on his side, he continued, to submit himself absolutely to their decree; and they could either kill him, and so satisfy the just demands of the Romans, or they could deliver him alive into their hands. A message to this effect was sent out by the garrison to Caesar, who returned the answer that all arms must be surrendered, and every chief appear personally before him. Taking his seat at a point well within the fortified lines, a little distance from his own camp, the Roman governor then formally received their submission; the Gallic chiefs were brought out under escort, Vercingetorix was handed over as a prisoner, and all arms were thrown to the ground. The remaining Gauls, with the exception of the Aedui and Arverni, who were retained in the hope of bringing pressure to bear upon their governments, were then distributed as booty, one to every Roman soldier.

These measures satisfactorily disposed of, the Roman forces entered
Aeduan territory, and at once brought that people to its submission. A
little afterwards envoys arrived from the Arvernian authorities to announce on their behalf an unconditional surrender; and from them a
large number of hostages was demanded. The legions then went into
winter quarters. The Arvernian and Aeduan prisoners, some 20,000 in all,
were restored to their own people. The actual distribution of troops for
the winter months was as follows. Two legions and a force of cavalry
were sent under T. Labienus to the Sequani (Bescançom and district),
having M. Sempronius Rutilius attached: two under C. Fabius and L.
Minucius Basilus were stationed among the Remi (Rheims) to watch the
powerful Bellovaci (Beauvais); one marched with C. Antistius Reginus to
the Ambibareti (Upper Loire), another with T. Sextius to the Bituriges
(Bourges), and a third with C. Caninius Rebilus to the Ruteni (Rodez).
Two more were quartered on the Aedui along the Arar (Saône), with the
special duty of safeguarding and accelerating the supply of grain, the
first at Cabillonum (Chalons-sur-Saône) under Quintus Tullius Cicero,
the second under Publius Sulpicius at Matisco (Mâcon); whilst lastly, the
governor himself decided to make his head-quarters at the Aeduan capital of Bibracte. In recognition of the year's campaign, a general thanksgiving of twenty days was, on receipt of dispatches reporting the events,
accorded by the government in Rome. . . .

Titus Livius (Livy)

C. 59 B.C.—C. 17 A.D.

5

Titus Livius—Livy—was born at Padua c. 59 B.C. Of his family background we know nothing and of his own early life and education almost as little. What evidence we have indicates that Livy was educated in Padua, that he escaped military service, and that he traveled hardly at all before settling down in Rome while still a young man. He apparently enjoyed a quiet, studious life in Rome, sustained by the generous patronage of Caesar Augustus and others, and was devoted to his literary career. He died in Rome, famous as the great historian of that state, c. 17 A.D.

In his *History of Rome,* Livy set himself the task of "tracing the history of the Roman people, from the foundation of the city," a subject, as he wrote "both of immense labor, as being one which must be traced back for more than seven hundred years, and which, having set out from small beginnings, has increased to such a degree that it is now distressed by its own magnitude." In the Preface to his work, Livy manifests both his intellectual affinity for the study of the past and his philosophical restraint concerning his own time. In the tradition of Thucydides and Polybius he held that what "is particularly salutary and profitable in the study of history" are the political lessons applicable to present and future actions to be gotten from it. As for his own age, he judges it a time "when we can neither endure our vices, nor their remedies." Rome, just emerging from her prolonged period of civil war, offered much material to interest the historian, the political theorist and the moralist.

Nevertheless, Livy, comfortably ensconced in the increasingly tranquil "Republic" of Augustus, clearly exempted himself from the role of complainer. He was rather interested in his historical undertaking, to write of Rome, than which "there was never any state either greater, or more moral, or richer in good examples." His history was, in Ronald Syme's phrase, "patriotic, moral and hortatory." Livy was apparently sponsored by government agencies or at least patronized by government leaders and he seems not

157

to have minded a peaceful civic existence paid for in part by some restrictions on civic liberty. He was on terms of personal friendship with Augustus and having lived through the disorders which followed upon the murder of Caesar he had political and philosophical as well as personal reasons for countenancing the rigorous regime of the Principate. The question we may ask is to what extent this acceptance of Augustan rule colored his historical narrative. What seems immediately clear is that Livy was not simply a timeserver. Favorably disposed toward the new order of things, he nevertheless did not engage in excesses of partisanship in describing, for example, the actions and fate of Caesar's chief opponent, Pompey. In honoring Augustus, Livy did no dishonor to history.

Rather, he brought to his task a great devotion to history (but particularly to the history of Rome), a firm resolve to present the truth as he discerned it, and a noble (if often inadequate) respect for methodological exactness. He consulted the existing histories that were available to him, quoting his sources more often than most previous historians had done. He noted and questioned dubious evidence; he qualified generalizations that appeared to him too sweeping. Certainly, he had defects as a historian. At times he allowed anachronisms to enter his account; at other times his patriotism warped his judgment of Rome's enemies. His guilelessness and inexperience of the world often led him to misinterpret political leaders and to misconstrue their actions. Still, he was aware of and sought to overcome the difficulties involved in the recapturing of the past, particularly those connected with the lack of "written records which (he wrote) form the only trustworthy memorials of events." He was, in short, a working historian.

But he was also a brilliant and (necessarily, given the lacunae in his evidence) imaginative writer. His work is a history *and* an epic and it was to his qualities as a narrator that he owed the immediate and enormous success of his creation. Forced by the legendary nature of the sources of ancient Roman history to re-create almost intuitively those early times, Livy succeeded in writing chapters that have been described as "not scientifically but artistically and imaginatively true." His sources failed him but never his talents. Historian and artist combined in Livy to enable him to encompass eight centuries of Roman history with intellectual integrity and literary excellence.

Selected Bibliography

Ronald Syme's *The Roman Revolution* (1939, reprinted with corrections in 1952) and his *Tacitus* (2 vols., 1958) contain much valuable comment on Livy, particularly on his relationship to Augustus. See especially the chapter "History and Rome" in *Tacitus*, vol. I. M. L. W. Laistner offers, along with much helpful information, the finely argued (but minority) view that Livy was the greatest of the Roman historians, in *The Greater Roman Historians* (1947, third printing, 1966).

Michael Grant, *Roman Literature* (third edition, 1964), includes a helpful section on Livy and Erich Burck has edited an excellent collection of essays, *Wege zu Livius,* in the *Wege der Forschung* series, vol. 132 (1967). R. M. Ogilvie, *A Commentary on Livy,* Books 1–5 (1965), is an erudite and enlightening guide through some of the complexities of Livy's masterpiece. Of the many translations of Livy, that by D. Spillan and C. Edmunds (1892) provided the present selections.

THE HISTORY OF ROME

Whether in tracing the history of the Roman people, from the foundation of the city, I shall employ myself to a useful purpose, I am neither very certain, nor, if I were, dare I say: inasmuch as I observe, that it is both an old and hackneyed practice, later authors always supposing that they will either adduce something more authentic in the facts, or, that they will excel the less polished ancients in their style of writing. Be that as it may, it will, at all events, be a satisfaction to achievements of a people, the lords of the world; and if, amidst so great a number of historians, my reputation should remain in obscurity, I may console myself with the celebrity and lustre of those who shall stand in the way of my fame. Moreover, the subject is both of immense labour, as being one which must be traced back for more than seven hundred years, and which, having set out from small beginnings, has increased to such a degree that it is now distressed by its own magnitude. And, to most readers, I doubt not but that the first origin and the events immediately succeeding, will afford but little pleasure, while they will be hastening to these later times, in which the strength of this overgrown people has for a long period been working its own destruction. I, on the contrary, shall seek this, as a reward of my labour, viz. to withdraw myself from the view of the calamities, which our age has witnessed for so many years, so long as I am reviewing with my whole attention these ancient times, being free from every care that may distract a writer's mind, though it cannot warp it from the truth. The traditions which have come down to us of what happened before the building of the city, or before its building was contemplated, as being suitable rather to the fictions of poetry than to the genuine records of history, I have no intention either to affirm or refute. This indulgence is conceded to antiquity, that by blending things human with divine, it may make the origin of cities appear more venerable: and if any people might be allowed to consecrate their origin, and to ascribe it to the gods as its authors, such is the renown of the Roman people in war, that when they represent Mars, in particular, as their own parent

From *The History of Rome,* translated by D. Spillan and Cyrus Edmunds (London, G. Bell & Sons, Ltd.). Reprinted by permission of the publisher. Vol. I, pp. 2–5, 8–11, 14–20, 22–25; vol. II, pp. 582–584, 700–701, 765–767, 770–775, 811–821.

and that of their founder, the nations of the world may submit to this as patiently as they submit to their sovereignty. But in whatever way these and such like matters shall be attended to, or judged of, I shall not deem of great importance. I would have every man apply his mind seriously to consider these points, viz. what their life and what their manners were; through what men and by what measures, both in peace and in war, their empire was acquired and extended; then, as discipline gradually declined, let him follow in his thoughts their morals, at first as slightly giving way, anon how they sunk more and more, then began to fall headlong, until he reaches the present times, when we can neither endure our vices, nor their remedies. This it is which is particularly salutary and profitable in the study of history, that you behold instances of every variety of conduct displayed on a conspicuous monument; that from thence you may select for yourself and for your country that which you may imitate; thence note what is shameful in the undertaking, and shameful in the result, which you may avoid. But either a fond partiality for the task I have undertaken deceives me, or there never was any state either greater, or more moral, or richer in good examples, nor one into which luxury and avarice made their entrance so late and where poverty and frugality were so much and so long honoured; so that the less wealth there was, the less desire was there. Of late, riches have introduced avarice, and excessive pleasures a longing for them, amidst luxury and a passion for ruining ourselves and destroying every thing else. But let complaints, which will not be agreeable even then, when perhaps they will be also necessary, be kept aloof at least from the first stage of commencing so great a work. We should rather, if it was usual with us (historians) as it is with poets, begin with good omens, vows and prayers to the gods and goddesses to vouchsafe good success to our efforts in so arduous an undertaking.

Now first of all it is sufficiently established that, Troy having been taken, the utmost severity was shown to all the other Trojans; but that towards two, Aeneas and Antenor, the Greeks forbore all the rights of war, both in accordance with an ancient tie of hospitality, and because they had ever been the advisers of peace, and of the restoration of Helen —then that Antenor after various vicissitudes came into the innermost bay of the Adriatic Sea, with a body of the Heneti, who having been driven from Paphlagonia in consequence of a civil commotion, were in quest both of settlement and a leader, their king Pylaemenes having been lost at Troy; and that the Heneti and Trojans, having expelled the Euganei, who dwelt between the sea and the Alps, took possession of the country; and the place where they first landed is called Troy; from whence also the name of Trojan is given to the canton; but the nation in general is called Veneti: that Aeneas was driven from home by a similar calamity, but the fates leading him to the founding of a greater empire, he came first to Macedonia: that he sailed from thence to Sicily in quest of a settlement: that from Sicily he made for the Laurentine territory; this place also has the name of Troy. When the Trojans, having disembarked there, were driving plunder from the lands,—as being persons to whom, after their almost immeasurable wandering, nothing was left but their arms and ships,—Latinus the king, and the Aborigines, who then occupied those places, assembled in arms from the city and country to repel the violence of the new-comers. On this point the tradition is two-fold: some say, that Latinus, after being overcome in battle, made first a peace, and then an alliance with Aeneas: others, that when the armies were drawn out in battle-array, before the signals were sounded, Latinus advanced to the front of the troops and invited the leader of the adventurers to a conference. That he then inquired who they were, whence (they had come), or by what casualty they had left their home, and in quest of what they had landed on the Laurentine territory: after he heard that the host were Trojans, their chief Aeneas, the son of Anchises and Venus, and that, driven from their own country and their homes, which had been destroyed by fire, they were seeking a settlement and a place for building a town, struck with admiration of the noble origin of the nation and of the hero, and their spirit, alike prepared for peace or war, he confirmed the assurance of future friendship by giving his right hand: that upon this a compact was struck between the chiefs, and mutual greetings passed between the armies: that Aeneas was hospitably entertained by Latinus: that Latinus, in the presence of his household gods, added a family league to the public one, by giving Aeneas his daughter in marriage. This event confirms the Trojans in the hope of at length terminating their wanderings by a fixed and permanent settlement. They built a town. Aeneas calls it Lavinium, after the name of his wife. In a short time, too, a son was the issue of the new marriage, to whom his parents gave the name of Ascanius. . . .

But, in my opinion, the origin of so great a city, and the establishment of an empire next in power to that of the gods, was due to the Fates. The vestal Rhea, being deflowered by force, when she had brought forth twins, declares Mars to be the father of her illegitimate offspring, either because she believed it to be so, or because a god was a more creditable author of her offence. But neither gods nor men protect her or her children from the king's cruelty: the priestess is bound and thrown into prison; the children he commands to be thrown into the current of the river. By some interposition of providence, the Tiber having overflowed its banks in stagnant pools, did not admit of any access to the regular bed of the river; and the bearers supposed that the infants could be drowned in water however still; thus, as if they had effectually executed the king's orders, they exposed the boys in the nearest land-flood, where now stands the ficus Ruminalis (they say that it was called Romularis). The country thereabout was then a vast wilderness. The tradition is, that when the water, subsiding, had left the floating trough, in which the children had been exposed, on dry ground, a thirsty she-wolf, coming from the neighbouring mountains, directed her course to the cries of the infants, and that she held down her dugs to them with so much gentleness, that the keeper of the king's flock found her licking the boys with her tongue. It is said his name was Faustulus; and that they were carried by him to his homestead to be nursed by his wife Laurentia. Some are of opinion that she was called Lupa among the shepherds, from her being a common prostitute, and that this gave rise to the surprising story. The children thus born and thus brought up, when arrived at the years of manhood, did not loiter away their time in tending the folds or following the flocks, but roamed and hunted in the forests. Having by this exercise improved their strength and courage, they not only encountered wild beasts, but even attacked robbers laden with plunder, and afterwards divided the spoil among the shepherds. And in company with these, the number of their young associates daily increasing, they carried on their business and their sports.

They say, that the festival of the lupercal, as now celebrated, was even at that time solemnized on the Palatine hill, which, from Palanteum, a city of Arcadia, was first called Palatium, and afterwards Mount Palatine. There they say that Evander, who belonged to the tribe of Arcadians, that for many years before had possessed that country, appointed the observance of a feast, introduced from Arcadia, in such manner, that young men ran about naked in sport and wantonness, doing honour to Pan Lycaeus, whom the Romans afterwards called Inuus. That the robbers, through rage at the loss of their booty, having lain in wait for them whilst intent on this sport, as the festival was now well known, whilst Romulus vigorously defended himself, took Remus prisoner; that they delivered him up, when taken, to king Amulius, accusing him with the utmost effrontery. They principally alleged it as a charge against them, that they had made incursions upon Numitor's lands, and plundered them in a hostile manner, having assembled a band of young men for the purpose. Upon this Remus was delivered to Numitor to be punished. Now, from the very first, Faustulus had entertained hopes that the boys whom he was bringing up were of the blood royal; for he both knew that the childlren had been exposed by the king's orders, and that the time at which he had taken them up agreed exactly with that period: but he had been unwilling that the matter, as not being yet ripe for discovery, should be disclosed, till either a fit opportunity or necessity should arise. Necessity came first; accordingly, compelled by fear, he discovers the whole affair to Romulus. By accident also, whilst he had Remus in custody, and had heard that the brothers were twins, on comparing their age, and observing their turn of mind entirely free from servility, the recollection of his grandchildren struck Numitor; and on making inquiries he arrived at the same conclusion, so that he was well nigh recognising Remus. Thus a plot is concerted for the king on all sides. Romulus, not accompanied by a body of young men (for he was unequal to open force) but having commanded the shepherds to come to the palace by different roads at a fixed time, forces his way to the king; and Remus, with another party from Numitor's house, assists his brother, and so they kill the king.

Numitor, at the beginning of the fray, having given out that enemies had invaded the city, and assaulted the palace, after he had drawn off the Alban youth to secure the citadel with a garrison and arms, when he saw the young men, after they had killed the king, advancing to congratulate him, immediately called an assembly of the people, and represented to them the unnatural behaviour of his brother towards him, the extraction of his grandchildren, the manner of their birth and education, and how they came to be discovered; then he informed them of the king's death, and that he was killed by his orders. When the young princes, coming up with their band through the middle of the assembly, saluted their grandfather king, an approving shout, following from all the people present, ratified to him both that title and the sovereignty. Thus the government of Alba being committed to Numitor, a desire seized Romulus and Remus to build a city on the spot where they had been exposed and brought up. And there was an overflowing population of Albans and of Latins. The shepherds too had come into that design, and all these readily inspired hopes, that Alba and Lavinium would be but pretty places in comparison with the city which they intended to build. But ambition of the sovereignty, the bane of their grandfather, interrupted these designs, and thence arose a shameful quarrel from a beginning sufficiently amicable. For as they were twins, the respect due to seniority could not determine the point, they agreed to leave to the tutelary gods of the place to choose, by augury, which should give a name to the new city, which govern it when built.

Romulus chose the Palatine and Remus the Aventine hill as their stands to make their observations. It is said, that to Remus an omen came first, six vultures; and now, the omen having been declared, when double the number presented itself to Romulus, his own party saluted each king; the former claimed the kingdom on the ground of priority of time, the latter on account of the number of birds. Upon this, having met in an altercation, from the contest of angry feelings they turn to bloodshed; there Remus fell from a blow received in the crowd. A more common account is, that Remus, in derision of his brother, leaped over his new-built wall, and was, for that reason, slain by Romulus in a passion; who, after sharply chiding him, added words to this effect: "So shall every one fare, who shall dare to leap over my fortifications." Thus Romulus got the sovereignty to himself; the city, when built, was called after the name of its founder. . . .

And now the Roman state was become so powerful, that it was a match for any of the neighbouring nations in war, but, from the paucity of women, its greatness could only last for one age of man; for they had no hope of issue at home, nor had they any intermarriages with their neigh-bours. Therefore, by the advice of the Fathers, Romulus sent ambassa-dors to the neighbouring states to solicit an alliance and the privilege of intermarrage for his new subjects. "That cities, like every thing else, rose from very humble beginnings. That those which the gods and their own merit aided, gained great power and high renown. That he knew full well, both that the gods had aided the origin of Rome, and that merit would not be wanting. Wherefore that, as men, they should feel no reluc-tance to mix their blood and race with men." No where did the embassy obtain a favourable hearing: so much did they at the same time despise, and dread for themselves and their posterity, so great a power growing up in the midst of them. They were dismissed by the greater part with the repeated question, "Whether they had opened any asylum for women also, for that such a plan only could obtain them suitable matches?" The Roman youth resented this conduct bitterly, and the matter unquestiona-bly began to point towards violence. Romulus, in order that he might afford a favourable time and place for this, dissembling his resentment, purposely prepares games in honour of Neptunus Equestris; he calls them Consualia. He then orders the spectacle to be proclaimed among their neighbours; and they prepare for the celebration with all the mag-nificence they were then acquainted with, or were capable of doing, that they might render the matter famous, and an object of expectation. Great numbers assembled, from a desire also of seeing the new city; especially their nearest neighbours, the Caeninenses, Crustumini, and Antemnates. Moreover the whole multitude of the Sabines came, with their wives and children. Having been hospitably invited to the different houses, when they had seen the situation, and fortifications, and the city crowded with houses, they became astonished that the Roman power had increased so rapidly. When the time of the spectacle came on, and while their minds and eyes were intent upon it, according to concert a tumult began, and upon a signal given the Roman youth ran different ways to carry off the virgins by force. A great number were carried off at haphazard, accord-ing as they fell into their hands. Persons from the common people, who had been charged with the task, conveyed to their houses some women of surpassing beauty destined for the leading senators. They say that one, far distinguished beyond the others for stature and beauty, was carried off by the party of one Thalassius, and whilst many inquired to whom they were carrying her, they cried out every now and then, in order that no one might molest her, that she was being taken to Thalassius; that from this circumstance this term became a nuptial one. The festival being disturbed by this alarm, the parents of the young women retire in grief, appealing to the compact of violated hospitality, and invoking the god, to whose festival and games they had come, deceived by the pretence of religion and good faith. Neither had the ravished virgins better hopes of their condition, or less indignation. But Romulus in person went about and declared, "That what was done was owing to the pride of their fathers, who had refused to grant the privilege of marriage to their neighbours; but notwithstanding, they should be joined in lawful wedlock, participate in all their possessions and civil privileges, and, than which nothing can be dearer to the human heart, in their common children. He begged them only to assuage the fierceness of their anger, and cheerfully surrender their affections to those to whom fortune had consigned their persons." [He added,] "That from injuries love and friendship often arise; and that they should find them kinder husbands on this account, because each of them, besides the performance of his conjugal duty, would endeavour to the utmost of his power to make up for the want of their parents and native country." To this the caresses of the husbands were added, excusing what they had done on the plea of passion and love, arguments that work most successfully on women's hearts.

The minds of the ravished virgins were soon much soothed, but their parents by putting on mourning, and tears and complaints, roused the states. Nor did they confine their resentment to their own homes, but they flocked from all quarters to Titus Tatius, king of the Sabines; and because he bore the greatest character in these parts, embassies were sent to him. The Caeninenses, Crustumini, and Antemnates were people to whom a considerable portion of the outrage extended. To them Tatius and the Sabines seemed to proceed somewhat dilatorily. Nor even do the Crustumini and Antemnates bestir themselves with sufficient activity to suit the impatience and rage of the Caeninenses. Accordingly the state of the Caeninenses by itself makes an irruption into the Roman territory. But Romulus with his army met them ravaging the country in straggling parties, and by a slight engagement convinces them, that resentment without strength is of no avail. He defeats and routs their army, pursues it when routed, kills and despoils their king in battle, and having slain their general takes the city at the first assault. From thence having led back his victorious army, and being a man highly distinguished by his exploits, and one who could place them in the best light, went in state to the capitol, carrying before him, suspended on a frame curiously wrought for that purpose, the spoils of the enemy's general, whom he had slain, and there after he had laid them down at the foot of an oak held sacred by the shepherds, together with the offering, he marked out the bounds for a temple of Jupiter, and gave a surname to the god: "Jupiter Feretrius," he says, "I, king Romulus, upon my victory, present to thee these royal arms, and to thee I dedicate a temple within those regions which I have now marked out in my mind, as a receptacle for the grand spoils, which my successors, following my example, shall, upon their killing the kings or generals of the enemy, offer to thee." This is the origin of that temple, the first consecrated at Rome. It afterwards so pleased the gods both that the declaration of the founder of the temple should not be frustrated, by which he announced that his posterity should offer such spoils, and that the glory of that offering should not be depreciated by the great number of those who shared it. During so many years, and amid so many wars since that time, grand spoils have been only twice gained, so rare has been the successful attainment of that honour.

Whilst the Romans are achieving these exploits, the army of the Antemnates, taking advantage of their absence, makes an incursion into the Roman territories in a hostile manner. A Roman legion being marched out in haste against these also, surprise them whilst straggling through the fields. Accordingly the enemy were routed at the very first shout and charge: their town taken; and as Romulus was returning, exulting for this double victory, his consort, Hersilia, importuned by the entreaties of the captured women, beseeches him "to pardon their fathers, and to admit them to the privilege of citizens; that thus his power might be strengthened by a reconciliation." Her request was readily granted. After this he marched against the Crustumini, who were commencing hostilities; but as their spirits were sunk by the defeat of their neighbours, there was still less resistance there. Colonies were sent to both places but more were found to give in their names for Crustuminum, because of the fertility of the soil. Migrations in great numbers were also made from thence to Rome, chiefly by the parents and relatives of the ravished women. The last war broke out on the part of the Sabines, and proved by far the most formidable: for they did nothing through anger or cupidity; nor did they make a show of war, before they actually began it. To prudence stratagem also was added. Sp. Tarpeius commanded the Roman citadel; Tatius bribes his maiden daughter with gold, to admit armed soldiers into the citadel: she had gone by chance outside the walls to fetch water for the sacrifice. Those who were admitted crushed her to death by heaping their arms upon her; either that the citadel might seem rather to have been taken by storm, or for the purpose of establishing a precedent, that no faith should, under any circumstances, be kept with a traitor. A story is added, that the Sabines commonly wore on their left arm golden bracelets of great weight, and large rings set with precious stones, and that she bargained with them for what they had on their left hands; hence that their shields were thrown upon her instead of the golden presents. There are some who say that in pursuance of the compact to deliver up what was on their left hands, she expressly demanded their shields, and that appearing to act with treachery, she was killed by the reward of her own choosing.

The Sabines, however, kept possession of the citadel, and on the day after, when the Roman army, drawn up in order of battle, filled up all the ground lying between the Palatine and Capitoline hills, they did not descend from thence into the plain, till the Romans, fired with resentment, and with a desire of retaking the citadel, advanced to attack them. Two chiefs, one on each side, animated the battle, viz. Mettus Curtius on the part of the Sabines, Hostus Hostilius on that of the Romans. The latter, in the front ranks, supported the Roman cause by his courage and bravery, on disadvantageous ground. As soon as Hostus fell, the Roman line immediately gave way and was beaten to the old gate of the Palatium Romulus, himself too carried away with the general rout, raising his arms to heaven, says, "O Jupiter, commanded by thy birds, I here laid the first foundation of the city on the Palatine hill. The Sabines are in possession of the citadel, purchased by fraud. From thence they are now advancing hither, sword in hand, having already passed the middle of the valley. But do thou, father of gods and men, keep back the enemy at least from hence, dispel the terror of the Romans, and stop their shameful flight. Here I solemnly vow to build a temple to thee as Jupiter Stator, as a monument to posterity, that this city was saved by thy immediate aid." Having offered up this prayer, as if he had felt that his prayers were heard, he cries out, "At this spot, Romans, Jupiter, supremely good and great, commands you to halt, and renew the fight." The Romans halted as if they had been commanded by a voice from heaven; Romulus himself flies to the foremost ranks. Mettus Curtius, on the part of the Sabines, had rushed down at the head of his army from the citadel, and driven the Romans in disorder over the whole ground now occupied by the forum. He was already not far from the gate of the Palatium, crying out, "We have defeated these perfidious strangers, these dastardly enemies. They now feel that it is one thing to ravish virgins, another far different to fight with men." On him, thus vaunting, Romulus makes an attack with a band of the most courageous youths. It happened that Mettus was then fighting on horseback; he was on that account the more easily repulsed: the Romans pursue him when repulsed: and the rest of the Roman army, encouraged by the gallant behaviour of their king, routs the Sabines. Mettus, his horse taking fright at the din of his pursuers, threw himself into a lake; and this circumstance drew the attention of the Sabines at the risk of so important a person. He, however, his own party beckoning and calling to him, acquires new courage from the affection of his many friends, and makes his escape. The Romans and Sabines renew the battle in the valley between the hills; but Roman prowess had the advantage.

At this juncture the Sabine women, from the outrage on whom the war originated, with hair dishevelled and garments rent, the timidity of their sex being overcome by such dreadful scenes, had the courage to throw themselves amid the flying weapons, and making a rush across, to part the incensed armies, and assuage their fury; imploring their fathers on the one side, their husbands on the other, "that as fathers-in-law and sons-in-law they would not contaminate each other with impious blood, nor stain their offspring with parricide, the one their grandchildren, the other their children. If you are dissatisfied with the affinity between you, if with our marriages, turn your resentment against us; we are the cause of war, we of wounds and of bloodshed to our husbands and parents. It were better that we perish than live widowed or fatherless without one or other of you." The circumstance affects both the multitude and the leaders. Silence and a sudden suspension ensue. Upon this the leaders come forward in order to concert a treaty, and they not only conclude a peace, but form one state out of two. They associate the regal power, and transfer the entire sovereignty to Rome. The city being thus doubled, that some compliment might be paid to the Sabines, they were called Quirites, from Cures. As a memorial of this battle, they called the place where the horse, after getting out of the deep marsh, first set Curtius in shallow water, the Curtian Lake. This happy peace following suddenly a war so distressing, rendered the Sabine women still dearer to their husbands and parents, and above all to Romulus himself. Accordingly, when he divided the people into thirty curiae, he called the curiae by their names. Since, without doubt, the number of the Sabine women was considerably greater than this, it is not recorded whether those who were to give their names to the curiae were selected on account of their age, or their own or their husbands' rank, or by lot. At the same time three centuries of knights were enrolled, called Ramnenses, from Romulus; Tatienses, from Titus Tatius. The reason of the name and origin of the Luceres is uncertain. . . .

After performing these immortal achievements, while he was holding an assembly of the people for reviewing his army, in the plain near the lake of Capra, on a sudden a storm having arisen, with great thunder and lightning, enveloped the king in so dense a mist, that it took all sight of him from the assembly. Nor was Romulus after this seen on earth. The consternation being at length over, and fine clear weather succeeding so turbulent a day, when the Roman youth saw the royal seat empty, though they readily believed the fathers who had stood nearest him, that he was carried aloft by the storm, yet, struck with the dread as it were of orphanage, they preserved a sorrowful silence for a considerable time. Then, a commencement having been made by a few, the whole multitude salute Romulus a god, son of a god, the king and parent of the Roman city; they implore his favour with prayers, that he would be pleased always propitiously to preserve his own offspring. I believe that even then there were some, who silently surmised that the king had been torn in pieces by the hands of the fathers; for this rumour also spread, but was not credited; their admiration of the man, and the consternation felt at the moment, attached importance to the other report. By the contrivance also of one individual, additional credit is said to have been gained to the matter. For Proculus Julius, whilst the state was still troubled with regret for the king, and felt incensed against the senators, a person of weight, as we are told, in any matter however important, comes forward to the assembly, "Romans," he says, "Romulus, the father of this city, suddenly descending from heaven, appeared to me this day at daybreak. While I stood covered with awe, and filled with a religious dread, beseeching him to allow me to see him face to face, he said, Go tell the Romans, that the gods so will, that my Rome should become the capitol of the world. Therefore let them cultivate the art of war, and let them know and hand down to posterity, that no human power shall be able to withstand the Roman arms. Having said this, he ascended up to heaven." It is surprising what credit was given to the man on his making this announcement, and how much the regret of the common people and army, for the loss of Romulus, was assuaged upon the assurance of his immortality.

Meanwhile ambition and contention for the throne actuated the minds of the fathers; factions had not yet sprung up from the individuals, because, among a new people, no one person was eminently distinguished above the rest: the contest was carried on between the different orders. The descendants of the Sabines wished a king to be elected out of their body, lest, because there had been no king on their side since the death of Tatius, they might lose their claim to the crown according to the compact of equal participation. The old Romans spurned the idea of a foreign prince. Amid this diversity of views, however, all were anxious that there should be a king, they not having yet tasted the sweets of liberty. Fear then seized the senators, lest the minds of the surrounding states being incensed against them, some foreign power should attack the state, now without a government, and the army without a leader. It was therefore their wish that there should be some head, but no one could bring himself to give way to another. Thus the hundred senators divide the government among them, ten decuries being formed, and one selected from each decury, who was to have the chief direction of affairs.

Ten governed; one only was attended with the insignia of authority and the lictors: their power was limited to the space of five days, and it passed through all in rotation, and the interval between a kingly government lasted a year. From the circumstance it was called an Interregnum, a term which holds good even now. But the people began to murmur, that their slavery was multiplied, and that they had got a hundred sovereigns instead of one, and they seemed determined to bear no authority but that of a king, and that one of their own choosing. When the fathers perceived that such schemes were in agitation, thinking it advisable to offer them, of their own accord, what they were sure to lose; they thus conciliate the favour of the people by yielding to them the supreme power, yet in such a manner as to grant them no greater privilege than they reserved to themselves. For they decreed, that when the people should choose a king, the election should be valid, if the senate approved. And the same forms are observed at this day in passing laws and electing magistrates, though their efficacy has been taken away; for before the people begin to vote, the senators declare their approbation, whilst the result of the elections is still uncertain. Then the interrex, having called an assembly of the people, addressed them in this manner: "Do you, Romans, choose your-selves a king, and may it prove fortunate, happy, and auspicious to you; so the fathers have determined. Then, if you choose a prince worthy to succeed Romulus, the fathers will confirm your choice." This concession was so pleasing to the people, that, not to be outdone in generosity, they only voted, and required that the senate should determine who should be king of Rome. . . .

The transactions of the Romans, from the building of the city of Rome to the capture of the same city, first under kings, then under consuls, and dictators, and decemvirs, and consular tribunes, their wars abroad, their dissensions at home, I have exhibited in five books: matters obscure, as well by reason of their very great antiquity, like objects which from their great distance are scarcely perceptible, as also because in those times the use of letters, the only faithful guardian of the memory of events, was inconsiderable and rare: and, moreover, whatever was contained in the commentaries of the pontiffs, and other public and private records, were lost for the most part in the burning of the city. Henceforwards, from the second origin of the city, which sprung up again more healthfully and vigorously, as if from its root, its achievements at home and abroad shall be narrated with more clearness and authenticity. . . .

Nothing can be found farther from my intention, since the commence-ment of this history, than to disgress, more than necessity required, from the course of narration; and, by embellishing my work with variety, to

seek pleasing resting-places, as it were, for my readers, and relaxation
for my own mind: nevertheless, the mention of so great a king and commander, now calls forth to public view those silent reflections, with
which it has oftentimes occupied my mind; and disposes me to inquire,
what would have been the consequence, respecting the affairs of the
Romans, if they had happened to have been engaged in a war with
Alexander. The circumstances of greatest moment in war seem to be, the
number and bravery of the soldiers, the abilities of the commanders, and
fortune, which exerts a powerful sway over all human concerns, and
especially over those of war. Now these particulars, to one who considers
them both separately and collectively, must clearly convince an observer, that not only other kings and nations, but that even Alexander
himself, would have found the Roman empire invincible. And first to
begin with comparing the commanders. I do not, indeed, deny that Alexander was a captain of consummate merit; but still it renders him more
illustrious that he was single in command, and that he died young, while
his affairs were advancing in improvement, and while he had not yet
experienced a reverse of fortune. For, to pass by other illustrious kings
and leaders, who afford exemplary instances of the decline of human
greatness, what was it, but length of life, which subjected Cyrus (whom
the Greeks, in their panegyrics, exalt so far beyond all others) to the
caprice of fortune? And the same was, lately, the case of Pompey the
Great. I shall enumerate the Roman chiefs; not every one of every age,
but those very ones with whom, either as consuls or dictators, Alexander
might have been engaged: Marcus Valerius Corvus, Caius Marcius Ruti-
lus, Caius Sulpicius, Titus Manlius Torquatus, Quintus Publilius Philo,
Lucius Papirius Cursor, Quintus Fabius Maximus, the two Decii, Lucius
Volumnius, Manius Curius. Then follow a number of very extraordinary
men, had it so happened, that he had first engaged in war with Carthage,
and had come into Italy at a more advanced period of life. Every one of
these both possessed powers of mind and a capacity equal with Alexander; and also a regular system of military discipline had been transmitted from one to another, from the first rise of the city of Rome; a
system now reduced into the form of an art, completely digested in a train
of fixed and settled principles. According to these principles kings had
carried on wars; and afterwards, the expellers of those kings, the Junii
and Valerii; according to these the Fabii, the Quintii, the Cornelii, and
so too Furius Camillus, who was an old man in the earlier years of those
with whom Alexander must have fought. Manlius Torquatus had he met
him in the field, might, perhaps, have yielded to Alexander in discharg-
ing military duties in battle (for these also render him no less illustrious);
and so might Valerius Corvus; men who were distinguished soldiers,
before they became commanders. The same, too, might have been the

case with the Decii, who, after devoting their persons, rushed upon the enemy; or of Papirius Cursor, though possessed of such powers, both of body and mind. By the counsels of one youth, it is possible the wisdom of a whole senate, not to mention individuals, might have been baffled, [consisting of such members,] that he alone, who declared that "it consisted of kings," conceived a correct idea of a Roman senate. But then the danger was, that with more judgment than any one of those whom I have named he might choose ground for an encampment, provide supplies, guard against strategems, distinguish the season for fighting, form his line of battle, or strengthen it properly with reserves. He would have owned that he was not dealing with Darius, who drew after him a train of women and eunuchs; saw nothing about him but gold and purple; was encumbered with the trappings of his state, and should be called his prey, rather than his antagonist; whom therefore he vanquished without loss of blood, and had no other merit, on the occasion, than that of showing a proper spirit in despising empty show. The aspect of Italy would have appeared to him of a quite different nature from that of India, which he traversed in the guise of a reveller, at the head of a crew of drunkards, if he had seen the forests of Apulia, and the mountains of Lucania, with the vestiges of the disasters of his house, and where his uncle Alexander, king of Epirus, had been lately cut off.

We are now speaking of Alexander not yet intoxicated by prosperity, the seductions of which no man was less capable of withstanding. But, if he is to be judged from the tenor of his conduct in the new state of his fortune, and from the new disposition, as I may say, which he put on after his successes, he would have entered Italy more like Darius than Alexander; and would have brought thither an army who had forgotten Macedonia, and were degenerating into the manners of the Persians. It is painful, in speaking of so great a king, to recite his ostentatious change of dress; his requiring that people should address him with adulation, prostrating themselves on the ground, a practice insupportable to the Macedonians, had they even been conquered, much more so when they were victorious; the shocking cruelty of his punishments; his murdering his friends in the midst of feasting and wine; with the folly of the fiction respecting his birth. What must have been the consequence, if his love of wine had daily become more intense, of his fierce and uncontrollable anger? And as I mention not any one circumstance of which there is a doubt among writers, do we consider these as no disparagements to the qualifications of a commander? But then, as is frequently repeated by the silliest of the Greeks, who are fond of exalting of the reputation, even of the Parthians, at the expense of the Roman name, the danger was that the Roman people would not have had resolution to bear up against the splendour of Alexander's name, who, however, in my opinion, was not

known to them even by common fame; and while, in Athens, a state
reduced to weakness by the Macedonian arms, which at the very time
saw the ruin of Thebes smoking in its neighborhood, men had spirit
enough to declaim with freedom against him, as is manifest from the
copies of their speeches, which have been preserved; [we are to be told]
that out of such a number of Roman chiefs, no one would have freely
uttered his sentiments. How great soever our idea of this man's greatness
may be, still it is the greatness of an individual, constituted by the successes of a little more than ten years; and those who give it pre-eminence
on account that the Roman people have been defeated, though not in any
entire war, yet in several battles, whereas Alexander was never once
unsuccessful in a single fight, do not consider that they are comparing
the actions of one man, and that a young man, with the exploits of a
nation waging wars now eight hundred years. Can we wonder if, when
on the one side more ages are numbered than years on the other, fortune
varied more in so long a lapse of time than in the short term of thirteen
years? But why not compare the success of one general with that of
another? How many Roman commanders might I name who never lost
a battle? In the annals of the magistrates, and the records, we may run
over whole pages of consuls and dictators, with whose bravery, and successes also, the Roman people never once had reason to be dissatisfied.
And what renders them more deserving of admiration than Alexander,
or any king, is, that some of these acted in the office of dictator, which
lasted only ten, or it might be twenty days; none, in a charge of longer
duration than the consulship of a year; their levies obstructed by
plebeian tribunes; often late in taking the field; recalled, before the time,
on account of elections; amidst the very busiest efforts of the campaign,
their year of office expired; sometimes the rashness, sometimes the per-
verseness of a colleague, proving an impediment or detriment; and
finally succeeding to the unfortunate administration of a predecessor,
with an army of raw or ill-disciplined men. But, on the other hand, kings,
being not only free from every kind of impediment, but masters of circumstances and seasons, control all things in subserviency to their designs, themselves uncontrolled by any. So that Alexander, unconquered,
would have encountered unconquered commanders; and would have had
stakes of equal consequence pledged on the issue. Nay, the hazard had
been greater on his side; because the Macedonians would have had but
one Alexander, who was not only liable, but fond of exposing himself to
casualties; the Romans would have had many equal to Alexander, both
in renown, and in the greatness of their exploits; any one of whom might
live or die according to his destiny, without any material consequence to
the public. . . .

I may be permitted to premise at this division of my work, what most historians have professed at the beginning of their whole undertaking; that I am about to relate the most memorable of all wars that were ever waged: the war which the Carthaginians, under the conduct of Hannibal, maintained with the Roman people. For never did any states and nations more efficient in their resources engage in contest; nor had they themselves at any other period so great a degree of power and energy. They brought into action too no arts of war unknown to each other, but those which had been tried in the first Punic war; and so various was the fortune of the conflict, and so doubtful the victory, that they who conquered were more exposed to danger. The hatred with which they fought also was almost greater than their resources; the Romans being indignant that the conquered aggressively took up arms against their victors; the Carthaginians, because they considered that in their subjection it had been lorded over them with haughtiness and avarice. There is besides a story, that Hannibal, when about nine years old, while he boyishly coaxed his father Hamilcar that he might be taken to Spain, (at the time when the African war was completed, and he was employed in sacrificing previously to transporting his army thither) was conducted to the altar; and, having laid his hand on the offerings, was bound by an oath to prove himself, as soon as he could, an enemy to the Roman people. The loss of Sicily and Sardinia grieved the high spirit of Hamilcar: for he deemed that Sicily had been given up through a premature despair of their affairs; and that Sardinia, during the disturbances in Africa, had been treacherously taken by the Romans, while, in addition, the payment of a tribute had been imposed. . . .

Spring was now at hand, when Hannibal quitted his winter quarters, having both attempted in vain to cross the Apennines, from the intolerable cold, and having remained with great danger and alarm. The Gauls, whom the hope of plunder and spoil had collected, when, instead of being themselves engaged in carrying and driving away booty from the fields of others, they saw their own lands made the seat of war, and burdened by the wintering of the armies of both parties, turned their hatred back again from the Romans upon Hannibal: and though plots were frequently concerted against him by their chieftains, he was preserved by the treachery they manifested towards each other; disclosing their conspiracy with the same inconstancy with which they had conspired; and by changing sometimes his dress, at other times the fashion of his hair, he protected himself from treachery by deception. However, this fear was the cause of his more speedily quitting his winter quarters. Meanwhile Oneius Servilius, the consul, entered upon his office at Rome, on the ides of March. There, when he had consulted the senate on the state of the republic in general, the indignation against Flaminius was rekindled. They said "that they had created indeed two consuls, that they had but one; for what regular authority had the other, or what auspices? That their magistrates took these with them from home, from the tutelar deities of themselves and the state, after the celebration of the Latin holidays; the sacrifice upon the mountain being completed, and the vows duly offered up in the Capitol: that neither could an unofficial individual take the auspices, nor could one who had gone from home without them, take them new, and for the first time, in a foreign soil." Prodigies announced from many places at the same time, augmented the terror: in Sicily, that several darts belonging to the soldiers had taken fire; and in Sardinia, that the staff of a horseman, who was going his rounds upon a wall, took fire as he held it in his hand; that the shores had blazed with frequent fires; that two shields had sweated blood at Praeneste; that red-hot stones had fallen from the heavens at Arpi; that shields were seen in the heavens, and the sun fighting with the moon, at Capena; that two moons rose in the daytime; that the waters of Caere had flowed mixed with blood; and that even the fountain of Hercules had flowed sprinkled with spots of blood. . . .

It was decreed that those prodigies should be expiated, partly with full-grown, partly with sucking victims; and that a supplication should be made at every shrine for the space of three days; that the other things should be done accordingly as the gods should declare in their oracles to be agreeable to their will when the decemviri had examined the books. By the advice of the decemviri it was decreed, first, that a golden thunderbolt of fifty pounds' weight should be made as an offering to Juno and Minerva; that sacrifices of full-grown victims should be offered to Juno Regina on the Aventine; and to Juno Sospita at Lanuvium; that the matrons, contributing as much money as might be convenient to each, should carry it to the Aventine, as a present to Juno Regina; and that a lectisternium should be celebrated. Moreover, that the very freed-women should, according to their means, contribute money from which a present might be made to Feronia. When these things were done, the decemviri sacrificed with the larger victims in the forum at Ardea. Lastly, it being now the month of December, a sacrifice was made at the temple of Saturn at Rome, and a lectisternium ordered, in which senators prepared the couch and a public banquet. Proclamation was made through the city, that the Saturnalia should be kept for a day and a night; and the people were commanded to account that day as a holiday, and observe it for ever.

While the consul employs himself at Rome in appeasing the gods and holding the levy, Hannibal, setting out from his winter quarters, because it was reported that the consul Flaminius had now arrived at Arretium, although a longer but more commodious route was pointed out to him, takes the nearer road through a marsh where the Arno had, more than usual, overflowed its banks. . . .

Hannibal lays waste the country between the city Cortona and the lake Trasimenus, with all the devastation of war, the more to exasperate the enemy to revenge the injuries inflicted on his allies. They had now reached a place formed by nature for an ambuscade, where the Trasimenus comes nearest to the mountains of Cortona. A very narrow passage only intervenes, as though room enough just for that purpose had been left designedly; after that a somewhat wider plain opens itself, and then some hills rise up. On these he pitches his camp, in full view, where he himself with his Spaniards and Africans only might be posted. The Baliares and his other light troops he leads round the mountains; his cavalry he posts at the very entrance of the defile, some eminences conveniently concealing them; in order that when the Romans had entered, the cavalry advancing, every place might be enclosed by the lake and the mountains. Flaminius, passing the defiles before it was quite daylight, without reconnoitring, though he had arrived at the lake the preceding day at sunset, when the troops began to be spread into the wider plain, saw that part only of the enemy which was opposite to him; the ambuscade in his rear and overhead escaped his notice. And when the Carthaginian had his enemy enclosed by the lake and mountains, and surrounded by his troops, he gives the signal to all to make a simultaneous charge; and each running down the nearest way, the suddenness and unexpectedness of the event was increased to the Romans by a mist rising from the lake, which had settled thicker on the plain than on the mountains; and thus the troops of the enemy ran down from the various eminences, sufficiently well discerning each other, and therefore with the greater regularity. A shout being raised on all sides, the Roman found himself surrounded before he could well see the enemy; and the attack on the front and flank had commenced ere his line could be well formed, his arms prepared for action, or his swords unsheathed.

The consul, while all were panic-struck, himself sufficiently undaunted though in so perilous a case, marshals, as well as the time, and place permitted, the lines which were thrown into confusion by each man's turning himself towards the various shouts; and wherever he could approach or be heard, exhorts them, and bids them stand and fight: for that they could not escape thence by vows and prayers to the gods, but by exertion and valour; that a way was sometimes opened by the sword through the midst of marshalled armies, and that generally the less the fear the less the danger. However, from the noise and tumult, neither his advice nor command could be caught; and so far were the soldiers from knowing their own standards, and ranks, and position, that they had scarce sufficient courage to take up arms and make them ready for battle; and certain of them were surprised before they could prepare them, being burdened rather than protected by them; while in so great darkness there was more use of ears than of eyes. They turned their faces and eyes in every direction towards the groans of the wounded, the sounds of blows upon the body or arms, and the mingled clamours of the menacing and the affrighted. Some, as they were making their escape, were stopped, having encountered a body of men engaged in fight; and bands of fugitives returning to the battle, diverted others. After charges had been attempted unsuccessfully in every direction, and on their flanks the mountains and the lake, on the front and rear the lines of the enemy enclosed them, when it was evident that there was no hope of safety but in the right hand and the sword; then each man became to himself a leader, and encourager to action; and an entirely new contest arose, not a regular line, with principes, hastati, and triarii; nor of such a sort as that the vanguard should fight before the standards, and the rest of the troops behind them; nor such that each soldier should be in his own legion, cohort, or company: chance collects them into bands; and each man's own will assigned to him his post, whether to fight in front or rear; and so great was the ardour of the conflict, so intent were their minds upon the battle, that not one of the combatants felt an earthquake which threw down large portions of many of the cities of Italy, turned rivers from their rapid courses, carried the sea up into rivers, and levelled mountains with a tremendous crash.

The battle was continued near three hours, and in every quarter with fierceness; around the consul, however, it was still hotter and more determined. Both the strongest of the troops, and himself too, promptly brought assistance wherever he perceived his men hard pressed and distressed. But, distinguished by his armour, the enemy attacked him with the utmost vigour, while his countrymen defended him; until an Insubrian horseman, name Ducarius, knowing him also by his face, says to his countrymen, "Lo, this is the consul who slew our legions and laid waste our fields and city. Now will I offer this victim to the shades of my countrymen, miserably slain"; and putting spurs to his horse, he rushes through a very dense body of the enemy; and first slaying his armour-bearer, who had opposed himself to his attack as he approached, ran the consul through with his lance; the triarii, opposing their shields, kept him off when seeking to despoil him. Then first the flight of a great number began; and now neither the lake nor the mountains obstructed their hurried retreat; they run through all places, confined and precipitous, as though they were blind; and arms and men are tumbled one upon another. A great many, when there remained no more space to run, advancing into the water through the first shallows of the lake, plunge in, as far as they could stand above it with their heads and shoulders. Some there were whom inconsiderate fear induced to try to escape even by swimming; but as that attempt was inordinate and hopeless, they were either overwhelmed in the deep water, their courage failing, or wearied to no purpose, made their way back, with extreme difficulty, to the shallows; and there were cut up on all hands by the cavalry of the enemy, which had entered the water. Near upon six thousand of the foremost body having gallantly forced their way through the opposing enemy, entirely unacquainted with what was occurring in their rear, escaped from the defile; and having halted on a certain rising ground, and hearing only the shouting and clashing of arms, they could not know nor discern, by reason of the mist, what was the fortune of the battle. At length, the affair being decided, when the mist, dispelled by the increasing heat of the sun, had cleared the atmosphere, then, in the clear light, the mountains and plains showed their ruin, and the Roman army miserably destroyed; and thus, lest, being descried at a distance, the cavalry should be sent against them, hastily snatching up their standards, they hurried away with all possible expedition. On the following day, when, in addition to their extreme sufferings in other respects, famine also was at hand, Maharbal, who had followed them during the night with the whole body of cavalry, pledging his honour that he would let them depart with single garments, if they would deliver up their arms when they surrendered themselves; which promise was kept by Hannibal with Punic fidelity, and he threw them all into chains.

This is the celebrated battle at the Trasimenus, and recorded among the few disasters of the Roman people. Fifteen thousand Romans were slain in the battle. Ten thousand, who had been scattered in the flight through all Etruria, returned to the city by different roads. One thousand five hundred of the enemy perished in the battle; many on both sides died afterwards of their wounds. The carnage on both sides is related, by some authors, to have been many times greater. I, besides that I would relate nothing drawn from a worthless source, to which the minds of historians generally include too much, have as my chief authority Fabius, who was contemporary with the events of this war. Such of the captives as belonged to the Latin confederacy being dismissed without ransom, and the Romans thrown into chains, Hannibal ordered the bodies of his own men to be gathered from the heaps of the enemy, and buried: the body of Flaminius too, which was searched for with great diligence for burial, he could not find. On the first intelligence of this defeat at Rome, a concourse of the people, dismayed and terrified, took place in the forum. The matrons, wandering through the streets, ask all they meet, what sudden disaster was reported? What was the fate of the army? And when the multitude, like a full assembly, having directed their course to the

comitium and senate-house, were calling upon the magistrates, at
length, a little before sunset, Marcus Pomponius, the praetor, declares,
"We have been defeated in a great battle"; and though nothing more
definite was heard from him, yet, full of the rumours which they had
caught one from another, they carry back to their homes intelligence,
that the consul, with a great part of his troops, was slain; that a few only
survived, and these either widely dispersed in flight through Etruria, or
else captured by the enemy. As many as had been the calamities of the
vanquished army, into so many anxieties were the minds of those distracted whose relations had served under Flaminius, and who were unin-
formed of what had been the fate of their friends, nor does any one know
certainly what he should either hope or fear. During the next and several
successive days, a greater number of women almost than men stood at
the gates, waiting either for some one of their friends, or for intelligence
of them, surrounding and earnestly interrogating those they met: nor
could they be torn away from those they knew especially, until they had
regularly inquired into every thing. Then as they retired from the infor-
mants, you might discern their various expressions of countenance, according as intelligence, pleasing or sad, was announced to each; and
those who congratulated or condoled on their return home. The joy and
grief of the women were especially manifested. They report that one,
suddenly meeting her son, who had returned safe, expired at the very
door before his face—that another, who sat grieving at her house at the
falsely reported death of her son, became a corpse, from excessive joy, at
the first sight of him on his return. The praetors detained the senators in
the house for several days, from sunrise to sunset, deliberating under
whose conduct, and by what forces, the victorious Carthaginians could
be opposed.

Before their plans were sufficently determined another unexpected
defeat is reported: four thousand horse, sent under the conduct of C.
Centenius, propraetor, by Servilius to his colleague, were cut off by Hannibal in Umbria, to which place, on hearing of the battle at Trasimenus,
they had turned their course. The report of this event variously affected
the people. Some, having their minds preoccupied with heavier grief,
considered the recent loss of cavalry trifling, in comparison with their
former losses; others did not estimate what had occurred by itself, but
considered that, as in a body already labouring under disease, a slight
cause would be felt more violently than a more powerful one in a robust
constitution; so whatever adverse event befell the state in its then sickly
and impaired condition, ought to be estimated, not by the magnitude of
the event itself, but with reference to its exhausted strength, which could
endure nothing that could oppress it. The state therefore took refuge in
a remedy for a long time before neither wanted nor employed, the ap-

pointment of a dictator; and because the consul was absent, by whom alone it appeared he could be nominated; and because neither message nor letter could easily be sent to him through the country occupied by Punic troops; and because the people could not appoint a dictator, which had never been done to that day, the people created Quintus Fabius Maximus pro-dictator, and Marcus Minucius Rufus master of the horse. To them the senate assigned the task of strengthening the walls and towers of the city; of placing guards in such quarters as seemed good, and breaking down the bridges of the river, considering that they must now fight at home in defence of their city, since they were unable to protect Italy. . . .

When it was day, the outpost withdrawn first occasioned surprise, then, on a nearer approach, the unusual stillness. At length, the desertion being manifest, there is a general rush to the pavilions of the consuls, of those who announced the flight of the enemy so precipitate, that they left their camp, with their tents standing; and, that their flight might be the more secret, that numerous fires were left. Then a clamour arose that they should order the standards to be advanced, and lead them in pursuit of the enemy, and to the immediate plunder of the camp. The other consul too was as one of the common soldiers. Paulus again and again urged, that they should see their way before them, and use every precaution. Lastly, when he could no longer withstand the sedition and the leader of the sedition, he sends Marius Statilius, a prefect, with a Lucanian troop, to reconnoitre, who, when he had ridden up to the gates, ordered the rest to stay without the works, and entered the camp himself, attended by two horsemen. Having carefully examined every thing, he brings back word that it was manifestly a snare: that fires were left in that part of the camp which faced the enemy: that the tents were open, and that all their valuables were left exposed: that in some places he had seen silver carelessly thrown about the passages, as if laid there for plunder. This intelligence, which it was hoped would deter their minds from greediness, inflamed them; and the soldiers clamorously declaring, that unless the signal was given they would advance without their leaders, they by no means wanted one, for Varro instantly gave the signal for marching. Paulus, whom, unwilling from his own suggestions to move, the chickens had not encouraged by their auspices, ordered the unlucky omen to be reported to his colleague, when he was now leading the troops out of the gate. And though Varro bore it impatiently, yet the recent fate of Flaminius, and the recorded naval defeat of Claudius, the consul in the first Punic war, struck religious scruples into his mind. The gods themselves (it might almost be said) rather postponed than averted the calamity which hung over the Romans; for it fell out by mere accident, that when the soldiers did not obey the consul who ordered them to

return to the camp, two slaves, one belonging to a horseman of Formiae,
the other to one of Sidicinum, who had been cut off by the Numidians
among a party of foragers, when Servilius and Atilius were consuls, had
escaped on that day to their masters: and being brought into the presence
of the consuls, inform them that the whole army of Hannibal was lying
in ambush on the other side of the adjoining mountains. The seasonable
arrival of these men restored the consuls to their authority, when the
ambition of one of them had relaxed his influence with the soldiers, by
an undignified compliance.

Hannibal, perceiving that the Romans had been indiscretely prompted
rather than rashly carried to a conclusion, returned to his camp without
effecting any thing, as his stratagem was discovered. He could not remain there many days, in consequence of the scarcity of corn; and, moreover, not only among the soldiers, who were mixed up of the offscouring
of various nations, but even with the general himself, day by day new
designs arose: for first, when there had been murmuring of the soldiers,
and then an open and clamorous demand of their arrears of pay, and a
complaint first of the scarcity of provisions, and lastly of famine; and
there being a report that the mercenaries, particularly the Spanish, had
formed a plan of passing over to the enemy, it is affirmed that Hannibal
himself too sometimes entertained thoughts of flying into Gaul, so that,
having left all his infantry, he might hurry away with his cavalry. Such
being the plans in agitation, and such the state of feeling in the camp,
he resolved to depart thence into the regions of Apulia, which were
warmer, and therefore earlier in the harvest. Thinking also, that the
farther he retired from the enemy, the more difficult would desertion be
to the wavering. He set out by night, having, as before, kindled fires, and
leaving a few tents to produce an appearance; that a fear of an ambuscade, similar to the former, might keep the Romans in their places. But
when intelligence was brought by the same Lucanian Statilius, who had
reconnoitred every place on the other side the mountains, and beyond the
camp, that the enemy was seen marching at a distance, then plans began
to be deliberated on about pursuing him. The consuls persisted in the
same opinions they ever entertained; but nearly all acquiesced with
Varro, and none with Paulus except Servilius, the consul of the former
year. In compliance with the opinion of the majority, they set out, under
the impulse of destiny, to render Cannae celebrated by a Roman disaster.
Hannibal had pitched his camp near that village, with his back to the
wind Vulturnus, which, in those plains which are parched with drought,
carries with it clouds of dust. This circumstance was not only very
advantageous to the camp, but would be a great protection to them
when they formed their line; as they, with the wind blowing only on their
backs, would combat with an enemy blinded with the thickly blown
dust. . . .

Hannibal, who had kept his troops drawn up in order of battle till late in the day, when he had led the rest of them back into the camp, sends Numidians across the river to attack a watering party of the Romans from the lesser camp. Having routed this disorderly band by shouting and tumult before they had well reached the opposite bank, they advanced even to an outpost which was before the rampart, and near the very gates of the camp. It seemed so great an indignity, that now even the camp of the Romans should be terrified by a tumultuary band of auxiliaries, that this cause alone kept back the Romans from crossing the river forthwith, and forming their line, that the chief command was on that day held by Paulus. Accordingly Varro, on the following day, on which it was his turn to hold the command, without consulting his colleague, displayed the signal for battle, and forming his troops, led them across the river. Paulus followed, because he could better disapprove of the proceeding, than withhold his assistance. Having crossed the river, they add to their forces those which they had in the lesser camp; and thus forming their line, place the Roman cavalry in the right wing, which was next the river; and next them the infantry: at the extremity of the left wing the allied cavalry; within them the allied infantry, extending to the centre, and contiguous to the Roman legions. The darters, and the rest of the light-armed auxiliaries, formed the van. The consuls commanded the wings; Terentius the left, Aemilius the right. To Geminus Servilius was committed the charge of maintaining the battle in the centre.

Hannibal, at break of day, having sent before him the Baliares and other light-armed troops, crossed the river, and placed his troops in line of battle, as he had conveyed them across the river. The Gallic and Spanish cavalry he placed in the left wing, opposite the Roman cavalry: the right wing was assigned to the Numidian cavalry, the centre of the line being strongly formed by the infantry, so that both extremities of it were composed of Africans, between which Gauls and Spaniards were placed. One would suppose the Africans were for the most part Romans, they were so equipped with arms captured at the Trebia, and for the greater part at the Trasimenus. The shields of the Gauls and Spaniards were of the same shape; their swords unequal and dissimilar. The Gauls had very long ones, without points. The Spaniards, who were accustomed to stab more than to cut their enemy, had swords convenient from their shortness, and with points. The aspect of these nations in other respects was terrific, both as to the appearance they exhibited and the size of their persons. The Gauls were naked above the navel: the Spaniards stood arrayed in linen vests resplendent with surprising whiteness, and bordered with purple. The whole amount of infantry standing in battle-array was forty thousand, of cavalry ten. The generals who commanded the wings were, on the left Hasdrubal, on the right Maharbal: Hannibal himself, with his brother Mago, commanded the centre. The sum very conveniently shone obliquely upon both parties; the Romans facing the south, and the Carthaginians the north; either placed so designedly, or having stood thus by chance. The wind, which the inhabitants of the district call the Vulturnus, blowing violently in front of the Romans, prevented their seeing far by rolling clouds of dust into their faces.

The shout being raised, the auxiliaries charged, and the battle commenced in the first place with the light-armed troops: then the left wing, consisting of the Gallic and Spanish cavalry, engages with the Roman right wing, by no means in the manner of a cavalry battle; for they were obliged to engage front to front; for as on one side the river, on the other the line of infantry hemmed them in, there was no space left at their flanks for evolution, but both parties were compelled to press directly forward. At length the horses standing still, and being crowded together, man grappling with man, dragged him from his horse. The contest now came to be carried on principally on foot. The battle, however, was more violent than lasting; and the Roman cavalry being repulsed, turn their backs. About the conclusion of the contest between the cavalry, the battle between the infantry commenced. At first the Gauls and Spaniards preserved their ranks unbroken, not inferior in strength or courage: but at length the Romans, after long and repeated efforts, drove in with their even front and closely compacted line, that part of the enemy's line in the form of a wedge, which projected beyond the rest, which was too thin, and therefore deficient in strength. These men, thus driven back and hastily retreating, they closely pursued; and as they urged their course without interruption through this terrified band, as it fled with precipitation, were borne first upon the centre line of the enemy, and lastly, no one opposing them, they reached the African reserved troops. These were posted at the two extremities of the line, where it was depressed; while the centre, where the Gauls and Spaniards were placed, projected a little. When the wedge thus formed being driven in, at first rendered the true level, but afterwards, by the pressure, made a curvature in the centre, the Africans, who had now formed wings on each side of them, surrounded the Romans on both sides, who incautiously rushed into the intermediate space; and presently extending their wings, enclosed the enemy on the rear also. After this the Romans, who had in vain finished one battle, leaving the Gauls and Spaniards, whose rear they had slaughtered, in addition commence a fresh encounter with the Africans, not only disadvantageous, because being hemmed in they had to fight against troops who surrounded them, but also because, fatigued, they fought with those who were fresh and vigorous.

Now also in the left wing of the Romans, in which the allied cavalry were opposed to the Numidians, the battle was joined, which was at first languid, commencing with a stratagem on the part of the Carthaginians.

About five hundred Numidians, who, besides their usual arms, had swords concealed beneath their coats of mail, quitting their own party and riding up to the enemy under the semblance of deserters, with their bucklers behind them, suddenly leap down from their horses; and, throwing down their bucklers and javelins at the feet of their enemies, are received into their centre, and being conducted to the rear, ordered to remain there; and there they continued until the battle became general. But afterwards, when the thoughts and attention of all were occupied with the contest, snatching up the shields which lay scattered on all hands among the heaps of slain, they fell upon the rear of the Roman line, and striking their backs and wounding their hams, occasioned vast havoc, and still greater panic and confusion. While in one part terror and flight prevailed, in another the battle was obstinately persisted in, though with little hope. Hasdrubal, who was then commanding in that quarter, withdrawing the Numidians from the centre of the army, as the conflict with their opponents was slight, sends them in pursuit of the scattered fugitives, and joining the Africans, now almost weary with slaying rather than fighting the Spanish and Gallic infantry.

On the other side of the field, Paulus, though severely wounded from a sling in the very commencement of the battle, with a compact body of troops, frequently opposed himself to Hannibal, and in several quarters restored the battle, the Roman cavalry protecting him; who, at length when the consul had not strength enough even to manage his horse, dismounted from their horses. And when some one brought intelligence that the consul had ordered the cavalry to dismount, it is said that Hannibal observed, "How much rather would I that he delivered them to me in chains." The fight maintained by the dismounted cavalry was such as might be expected, when the victory was undoubtedly on the side of the enemy, the vanquished preferring death in their places to flight; and the conquerors, who were enraged at them for delaying the victory, butchering those whom they could not put to flight. They at length, however, drove the few who remained away, worn out with exertion and wounds. After that they were all dispersed, and such as could, sought to regain their horses for flight. Cenius Lentulus, a military tribune, seeing, as he rode by, the consul sitting upon a stone and covered with blood, said to him: "Lucius Aemilius! the only man whom the gods ought to regard as being guiltless of this day's disaster, take this horse, while you have any strength remaining, and I am with you to raise you up and protect you. Make not this battle more calamitous by the death of a consul. There is sufficient matter for tears and grief without this addition." In reply the consul said: "Do thou indeed go on and prosper, Cenius Servilius, in your career of virtue! But beware lest you waste in bootless commiseration the brief opportunity of escaping from the hands of the enemy. Go and tell

the fathers publicly, to fortify the city of Rome, and garrison it strongly
before the victorious enemy arrive: and tell Quintus Fabius individually,
that Lucius Aemilius lived, and now dies, mindful of his injunctions.
Allow me to expire amid these heaps of my slaughtered troops, that I may
not a second time be accused after my consulate, or stand forth as the
accuser of my colleague, in order to defend my own innocence by incrim-
inating another." While finishing these words, first a crowd of their flying
countrymen, after that the enemy, came upon them; they overwhelm the
consul with their weapons, not knowing who he was: in the confusion his
horse rescued Lentulus. After that they fly precipitately. Seven thousand
escaped to the lesser camp, ten to the greater, about two thousand to the
village itself of Cannae, who were immediately surrounded by Carthalo
and the cavalry, no fortifications protecting the village. The other consul,
whether by design or by chance, made good his escape to Venusia with
about seventy horse, without mingling with any party of the flying troops.
Forty thousand foot, two thousand seven hundred horse, there being an
equal number of citizens and allies, are said to have been slain. Among
these both the quaestors of the consuls, Lucius Atilius and Lucius Furius
Bibaculus; twenty-one military tribunes; several who had passed the
offices of consul, praetor, and aedile; among these they reckon Cenius
Servilius Germinus, and Marcus Minucius, who had been master of the
horse on a former year, and consul some years before: moreover eighty,
either senators, or who had borne those offices by which they might be
elected into the senate, and who had voluntarily enrolled themselves in
the legions. Three thousand infantry and three hundred cavalry are said
to have been captured in that battle.

Such is the battle of Cannae, equal in celebrity to the defeat at the Allia:
but as it was less important in respect to those things which happened
after it, because the enemy did not follow up the blow, so was it more
important and more horrible with respect to the slaughter of the army;
for with respect to the flight at the Allia, as it betrayed the city, so it
preserved the army. At Cannae, scarcely seventy accompanied the flying consul: almost the whole army shared the fate of the other who
died. . . .

When all others, surrounding the victorious Hannibal, congratulated
him, and advised that, having completed so great a battle, he should
himself take the remainder of the day and the ensuing night for rest, and
grant it to his exhausted troops; Maharbal, prefect of the cavalry, who
was of the opinion that no time should be lost, said to him, "Nay, rather,
that you may know what has been achieved by this battle, five days hence
you shall feast in triumph in the Capitol. Follow me: I will go first with
the cavalry, that they may know that I am arrived before they know of
me as approaching." To Hannibal this project appeared too full of joy,

and too great for his mind to embrace it and determine upon it at the instant. Accordingly, he replied to Maharbal, that "he applauded his zeal, but that time was necessary to ponder the proposal." Upon this Maharbal observed, "Of a truth the gods have not bestowed all things upon the same person. You know how to conquer, Hannibal; but you do not know how to make use of your victory." That day's delay is firmly believed to have been the preservation of the city and the empire. . . .

Flavius Josephus

6

Flavius Josephus was born A.D. 37 in Jerusalem into a prominent priest-ly-royal family. For our knowledge of the life of Josephus we are completely dependent upon his *Autobiography* and upon a few references to himself in *The Jewish War*. Josephus was undoubtedly well educated and he apparently studied for the priesthood. As a prominent young Pharisee (one of the major Judaic sects of the time) he was sent to Rome in 63–64 on a mission in behalf of some Jews who had been imprisoned, wrongfully it seems, by the Roman procurator of Judaea. His success in this mission initiated his long career as a diplomat, military leader, Jewish statesman, and man of letters. He participated in the "Jewish Rebellion," first as a reluctant leader of his people against Imperial Rome (67) then as a hostage-ally of the Romans in which role he counseled his compatriots to surrender. He was in the Roman camp when the final catastrophe enveloped Jerusalem in 70. His apostasy, as the majority of his co-religionists saw his behavior, was never forgiven.

Josephus, pro-Roman to begin with, had foreseen that a successful rebellion against Rome was an impossible undertaking and he had seized upon the opportunity to make a separate peace. He had flattered the Roman commander, Vespasian, predicting that he would return to Rome as Emperor. When the events of the year 69—that tumultuous year of which Tacitus writes so brilliantly—conspired to fulfill Josephus' prophecy, Vespasian saw to it that Josephus was well cared for. After the successful siege of Jerusalem, Josephus accompanied Vespasian's son Titus to Rome. For the next thirty years he lived very comfortably in Rome as a client of Vespasian's dynasty. During those years he wrote at least four works: *The Jewish War* (75–79); *Jewish Antiquities* (93–94), a history of the Jews from the Creation to the Jewish War (in which work he drew upon Herodotus, among other sources); his *Autobiography* (c. 94); and an essay, *Against Apion* (c. 97), in which he defends the Jews and Judaism against Greek polemicists. He lived on, in comparative ease and security, to the opening years of the second century.

One commentator has written of Josephus that, as a historian, he "had greatness thrust upon him": his account of The Jewish War is our unique source concerning those events and we must treasure it for that reason alone. In this history Josephus echoes the sentiments of Herodotus ("I thought it monstrous, therefore, to allow the truth in affairs of such moment to go astray") and the design of Thucydides ("My work is written for lovers of truth and not merely to gratify my readers"). As a work of historical art, however, it falls considerably below their accomplishment. Josephus wrote well but traditionally, with the digressions and interpolated speeches customarily found in ancient historiography. He tended to follow uncritically the various written and oral sources available to him. He had access to relevant documents and to officials and was himself an eyewitness of much he writes about yet his analysis of causation is weak and his interpretation of the meaning of events is too often colored by the defects (and strengths) of his own personality. Having previously concluded that Rome was invincible and revolt foolish, Josephus found it all too easy to show that what occurred was the working of ineluctable destiny. Or, as H. St. J. Thackeray has written, for Josephus, "Providence is visibly on the side of the great battalions."

Nevertheless, Josephus, who felt himself "driven by force and necessity to write history," managed to compile a work which, deficient as historiography in the modern sense of the term, remains a valid and valuable contribution to our understanding of the past and of the development of historiography itself. For Josephus' personal account of the Jewish War often enough rises to the level of history and introduces a novel element into the historical process: "The role of the providence of God in human affairs." In his life, his culture, and his histories, Josephus is a transitional figure between the Classical and Christian worlds.

Selected Bibliography

H. St. J. Thackeray, *Josephus the Man and Historian* (1929), remains the best study in English of our historian. Judicious and balanced throughout, it may be supplemented by Thackeray's introduction to his translation of Josephus in the Loeb Classical Library edition (begun in 1926), from which we take the present selections. Moses I. Finley has a valuable and very helpful introduction to his edition of *Josephus, The Jewish War and Other Selections* (1965). James T. Shotwell, *An Introduction to the History of History* (1936), includes a perceptive and enlightening chapter on Josephus and his work. Victor Tcherikover's work (translated by S. Applebaum), *Hellenistic Civilization and the Jews* (1961), splendidly sets the scene for Josephus in its inquiry into the Hellenistic period of Jewish history, down to 64 B.C.

THE WAR OF THE JEWS

The war of the Jews against the Romans—the greatest not only of the wars of our own time, but, so far as accounts have reached us, well nigh of all that ever broke out between cities or nations—has not lacked its historians. Of these, however, some, having taken no part in the action, have collected from hearsay casual and contradictory stories which they have then edited in a rhetorical style; while others, who witnessed the events, have, either from flattery of the Romans or from hatred of the Jews, misrepresented the facts, their writings exhibiting alternatively invective and encomium, but nowhere historical accuracy. In these circumstances, I—Josephus, son of Matthias, a Hebrew by race, a native of Jerusalem and a priest, who at the opening of the war myself fought against the Romans and in the sequel was perforce an onlooker—propose to provide the subjects of the Roman Empire with a narrative of the facts, by translating into Greek the account which I previously composed in my vernacular tongue and sent to the barbarians in the interior.

I spoke of this upheaval as one of the greatest magnitude. The Romans had their own internal disorders. The Jewish revolutionary party, whose numbers and fortunes were at their zenith, seized the occasion of the turbulence of these times for insurrection. As a result of these vast disturbances the whole of the Eastern Empire was in the balance; the insurgents were fired with hopes of its acquisition, their opponents feared its loss. For the Jews hoped that all their fellow-countrymen beyond the Euphrates would join with them in revolt; while the Romans, on their side, were occupied with their neighbours the Gauls, and the Celts were in motion. Nero's death, moreover, brought universal confusion; many were induced by this opportunity to aspire to the sovereignty, and a change which might make their fortune was after the heart of the soldiery.

I thought it monstrous, therefore, to allow the truth in affairs of such moment to go astray, and that, while Parthians and Babylonians and the

From *The War of the Jews,* translated by William Whiston (London, J. M. Dent & Sons Ltd., Everyman Library edition, 1959). Reprinted by permission of J. M. Dent & Sons Ltd. and E. P. Dutton & Co., Inc. Vol. II, pp. 3–11; vol. III, pp. 403–409, 433–469, 501–503.

most remote tribes of Arabia with our countrymen beyond the Euphrates and the inhabitants of Adiabene were, through my assiduity, accurately acquainted with the origin of the war, the various phases of calamity through which it passed and its conclusion, the Greeks and such Romans as were not engaged in the contest should remain in ignorance of these matters, with flattering or fictitious narratives as their only guide.

Though the writers in question presume to give their works the title of histories, yet throughout them, apart from the utter lack of sound information, they seem, in my opinion, to miss their own mark. They desire to represent the Romans as a great nation, and yet they continually depreciate and disparage the actions of the Jews. But I fail to see how the conquerors of a puny people deserve to be accounted great. Again, these writers have respect neither for the long duration of the war, nor for the vast numbers of the Roman army that it engaged, nor for the prestige of the generals, who, after such herculean labours under the walls of Jerusalem, are, I suppose, of no repute in these writers' eyes, if their achievement is to be underestimated.

I have no intention of rivalling those who extol the Roman power by exaggerating the deeds of my compatriots. I shall faithfully recount the actions of both combatants; but in my reflections on the events I cannot conceal my private sentiments, nor refuse to give my personal sympathies scope to bewail my country's misfortunes. For, that it owed its ruin to civil strife, and that it was the Jewish tyrants who drew down upon the holy temple the unwilling hands of the Romans and the conflagration, is attested by Titus Caesar himself, who sacked the city; throughout the war he commiserated the populace who were at the mercy of the revolutionaries, and often of his own accord deferred the capture of the city and by protracting the siege gave the culprits time for repentance. Should, however, any critic censure me for my strictures upon the tyrants or their bands of marauders or for my lamentations over my country's misfortunes, I ask his indulgence for a compassion which falls outside an historian's province. For of all the cities under Roman rule it was the lot of ours to attain to the highest felicity and to fall to the lowest depths of calamity. Indeed, in my opinion, the misfortunes of all nations since the world began fall short of those of the Jews; and, since the blame lay with no foreign nation, it was impossible to restrain one's grief. Should, however, any critic be too austere for pity, let him credit the history with the facts, the historian with the lamentations.

Yet I, on my side, might justly censure those erudite Greeks who, living in times of such stirring actions as by comparison reduce to insignificance the wars of antiquity, yet sit in judgment on these current events and revile those who make them their special study—authors whose principles they lack, even if they have the advantage of them in literary skill. For their own themes they take the Assyrian and Median empires, as if the narratives of the ancient historians were not fine enough. Yet, the truth is, these modern writers are their inferiors no less in literary power than in judgment. The ancient historians set themselves severally to write the history of their own times, a task in which their connection with the events added lucidity to their record; while mendacity brought an author into disgrace with readers who knew the facts. In fact, the work of committing to writing events which have not previously been recorded and of commending to posterity the history of one's own time is one which merits praise and acknowledgement. The industrious writer is not one who merely remodels the scheme and arrangement of another's work, but one who uses fresh materials and makes the framework of the history his own. For myself, at a vast expenditure of money and pains, I, a foreigner, present to Greeks and Romans this memorial of great achievements. As for the native Greeks, where personal profit or a lawsuit is concerned, their mouths are at once agape and their tongues loosed; but in the matter of history, where veracity and laborious collection of the facts are essential, they are mute, leaving to inferior and ill-informed writers the task of describing the exploits of their rulers. Let us at least hold historical truth in honour, since by the Greeks it is disregarded.

To narrate the ancient history of the Jews, the origin of the nation and the circumstances of their migration from Egypt, the countries which they traversed in their wanderings, the extent of the territory which they subsequently occupied, and the incidents which led to their deportation, would, I considered, be not only here out of place, but superfluous; seeing that many Jews before me have accurately recorded the history of our ancestors, and that these records have been translated by certain Greeks into their native tongue without serious error. I shall therefore begin my work at the point where the historians of these events and our prophets conclude. Of the subsequent history, I shall describe the incidents of the war through which I lived with all the detail and elaboration at my command; for the events preceding my lifetime I shall be content with a brief summary.

(We take up Josephus' narrative toward the climax of the siege of Jerusalem.)

Titus now ordered the troops that were with him to raze the foundations of Antonia and to prepare an easy ascent for the whole army. Then,
having learnt that on that day—it was the seventeenth of Panemus—the
so-called continual sacrifice had for lack of men ceased to be offered to
God and that the people were in consequence terribly despondent, he put
Josephus forward with instructions to repeat to John the same message
as before, namely "that if he was obsessed by a criminal passion for
battle, he was at liberty to come out with as many as he chose and fight,
without involving the city and the sanctuary in his own ruin; but that he
should no longer pollute the Holy Place nor sin against God; and that he
had his permission to perform the interrupted sacrifices with the help of
such Jews as he might select."

Josephus, standing so that his words might reach the ears not only of
John but also of the multitude, delivered Caesar's message in Hebrew,
with earnest appeals to them "to spare their country, to disperse the
flames that were already licking the sanctuary and to restore to God the
expiatory sacrifices." His words were received by the people in dejection
and silence; but the tyrant, after many invectives and imprecations upon
Josephus, ended by saying that he "could never fear capture, since the
city was God's."

At this Josephus cried aloud: "Pure indeed have you kept it for God! The
Holy Place too remains undefiled! Your looked-for Ally has suffered no
impiety from you and still receives His customary sacrifices! Most impious wretch, should anyone deprive you of your daily food, you would
consider him an enemy; and do you hope to have God, whom you have
bereft of His everlasting worship, for your Ally in this war? And do you
impute your sins to the Romans, who, to this day, are concerned for our
laws and are trying to force you to restore to God those sacrifices which
you have interrupted? Who would not bewail and lament for the city at
this amazing inversion, when aliens and enemies rectify your impiety,
while you, a Jew, nurtured in her laws, treat them more harshly even
than your foes?

"Yet, be sure, John, it is no disgrace to repent of misdeeds, even at the
last; and, if you desire to save your country, you have a noble example set
before you in Jeconiah, king of the Jews. He, when of old his conduct had
brought the Babylonian's army upon him, of his own free will left the city
before it was taken, and with his family endured voluntary captivity,
rather than deliver up these holy places to the enemy and see the house
of God in flames. Therefore is he celebrated in sacred story by all Jews,
and memory, in a stream that runs down the ages ever fresh, passes him
on to posterity immortal. A noble example, John, even were it dangerous
to follow; but I can warrant you even pardon from the Romans. Remember, too, that I who exhort you am your countryman, that I who make this

promise am a Jew; and it is right that you should consider who is your counsellor and whence he comes. For never may I live to become so abject a captive as to abjure my race or to forget the traditions of my forefathers!

"Once again are you indignant and shout your abuse at me; and indeed I deserve even harsher treatment for offering advice in fate's despite and for struggling to save those whom God has condemned. Who knows not the records of the ancient prophets and that oracle which threatens this poor city and is even now coming true? For they foretold that it would then be taken whensoever one should begin to slaughter his own countrymen. And is not the city, aye and the whole temple, filled with your corpses? God it is then, God Himself, who with the Romans is bringing the fire to purge His temple and exterminating a city so laden with pollutions."

At these words, spoken with lamentation and tears, Josephus's voice broke down with sobs. Even the Romans pitied him in his emotion and admired his resolution; but John and his followers were only the more exasperated against the Romans, being eager to get Josephus also into their power. . . .

Meanwhile, the victims perishing of famine throughout the city were dropping in countless numbers and enduring sufferings indescribable. In every house, the appearance anywhere of but a shadow of food was a signal for war, and the dearest of relatives fell to blows, snatching from each other the pitiful supports of life. The very dying were not credited as in want; nay, even those expiring were searched by the brigands, lest any should be concealing food beneath a fold of his garment and feigning death. Gaping with hunger, like mad dogs, these ruffians went staggering and reeling along, battering upon the doors in the manner of drunken men, and in their perplexity bursting into the same house twice or thrice within a single hour. Necessity drove the victims to gnaw anything, and objects which even the filthiest of brute beasts would reject they condescended to collect and eat: thus in the end they abstained not from belts and shoes and stripped off and chewed the very leather of their bucklers. Others devoured tufts of withered grass: indeed some collectors of stalks sold a trifling quantity for four Attic drachmas. But why tell of the shameless resort to inanimate articles of food induced by the famine, seeing that I am here about to describe an act unparalleled in the history whether of Greeks or barbarians, and as horrible to relate as it is incredible to hear? For my part, for fear that posterity might suspect me of monstrous fabrication, I would gladly have omitted this tragedy, had I not innumerable witnesses among my contemporaries. Moreover, it would be a poor compliment that I should pay my country in suppressing the narrative of the woes which she actually endured.

Among the residents of the region beyond Jordan was a woman named Mary, daughter of Eleazar, of the village of Bethezuba (the name means "House of Hyssop"), eminent by reason of her family and fortune, who had fled with the rest of the people to Jerusalem and there become involved in the siege. The bulk of her property, which she had packed up and brought with her from Peraea to the city, had been plundered by the tyrants; while the relics of her treasures, with whatever food she had contrived to procure, were being carried off by their satellites in their daily raids. With deep indignation in her heart, the poor woman constantly abused and cursed these extortioners and so incensed them against her. But when no one either out of exasperation or pity put her to death, weary of finding for others food, which indeed it was now impossible from any quarter to procure, while famine coursed through her intestines and marrow and the fire of rage was more consuming even than the famine, impelled by the promptings alike of fury and necessity, she proceeded to an act of outrage upon nature. Seizing her child, an infant at the breast, "Poor babe," she cried, "amidst war, famine, and sedition, to what end should I preserve thee? With the Romans slavery awaits us, should we live till they come; but famine is forestalling slavery, and more cruel than both are the rebels. Come, be thou food for me, to the rebels an avenging fury, and to the world a tale such as alone is wanting to the calamities of the Jews." With these words she slew her son, and then, having roasted the body and devoured half of it, she covered up and stored the remainder. At once the rebels were upon her and, scenting the unholy odour, threatened her with instant death unless she produced what she had prepared. Replying that she had reserved a goodly portion for them also, she disclosed the remnants of her child. Seized with instant horror and stupefaction, they stood paralysed by the sight. She, however, said, "This is my own child, and this my handiwork. Eat, for I too have eaten. Show not yourselves weaker than a woman, or more compassionate than a mother. But if you have pious scruples and shrink from my sacrifice, then let what I have eaten be your portion and the remainder also be left for me." At that they departed trembling, in this one instance cowards, though scarcely yielding even this food to the mother. The whole city instantly rang with the abomination, and each, picturing the horror of it, shuddered as though it had been perpetrated by himself. The starving folk longed for death, and felicitated those who had gone to their rest ere they had heard or beheld such evils.

The horrible news soon spread to the Romans. Of them some were incredulous, others were moved to pity, but the effect on the majority was to intensify their hatred of the nation. Caesar declared himself innocent in this matter also in the sight of God, protesting that *he* had offered the Jews peace, independence, and an amnesty for all past offences, while *they,* preferring sedition to concord, peace to war, famine to plenty and prosperity, and having been the first to set fire with their own hands to that temple which he and his army were preserving for them, were indeed deserving even of such food as this. He, however, would bury this abomination of infant-cannibalism beneath the ruins of their country, and would not leave upon the face of the earth, for the sun to behold, a city in which mothers were thus fed. Yet, he added, such food was less meet for mothers than for fathers, who even after such horrors still remained in arms. While expressing these sentiments, he had, moreover, in mind the desperation of these men, being convinced that they were past being brought to reason who had already endured all the miseries, to be spared the experience of which they might have been expected to relent.

Two of the legions having now completed their earthworks, on the eighth of the month Lous, Titus ordered the rams to be brought up opposite the western hall of the outer court of the temple. Before their arrival, the most redoubtable of all the siege-engines had for six days incessantly battered the wall without effect, the massiveness and nice adjustment of the stones being proof against it as against the rest. Another party endeavoured to undermine the foundations of the northern gate, and by great exertions succeeded in extricating the stones in front; but the gate, supported by the inner stones, stood firm. Finally, despairing of all attempts with engines and crowbars, the Romans applied ladders to the porticoes. The Jews made no haste to prevent this, but as soon as they mounted vigorously attacked them. Some they thrust back and hurled down headlong, others who encountered them they slew; many as they stepped off the ladders they cut down with their swords, before they could shield themselves with their bucklers; some ladders, again, laden with armed men, they tilted sideways from above and dashed to the ground; not, however, without suffering considerable slaughter themselves. The Romans who had brought up the standards fought fiercely around these, deeming their loss a dire disaster and disgrace; yet, eventually, these ensigns also were taken by the Jews, who destroyed all who had mounted. The remainder, intimidated by the fate of the fallen, then retired. Of the Romans, not one had not achieved something ere he fell; of the rebels, those who had gained distinction in previous engagements fought gallantly also in this, as did also Eleazar, nephew of the tyrant Simon. Titus, now that he saw that his endeavour to spare a foreign temple led only to the injury and slaughter of his troops, issued orders to set the gates on fire.

Meanwhile two deserters had joined him, Ananus of Emmaus, the most bloodthirsty of Simon's lieutenants, and Archelaus, son of Magaddatus, hoping for pardon because they were leaving the Jews at a mo-

ment of success. Titus, however, censured their action as a further knav-
ish trick; and, having heard of their cruelty in general to their countrymen, he was strongly minded to put them both to death, observing that
they had been driven by necessity, not led by inclination, to come over,
and that men who leapt from their native city only when enveloped in
the flames, for which they were themselves responsible, did not deserve
to live. Nevertheless, his good faith overcame his animosity, and he let
them go, though he did not put them on an equal footing with the rest.

The troops were by now setting fire to the gates, and the silver melting
all around quickly admitted the flames to the woodwork, whence they
spread in dense volumes and caught hold of the porticoes. The Jews,
seeing the fire encircling them, were deprived of all energy of body and
mind; in utter consternation none attempted to ward off or extinguish the
flames; paralysed they stood and looked on. Yet, though dismayed by the
ravage being wrought, they learnt no lesson with regard to what was left,
but, as if the very sanctuary were now ablaze, only whetted their fury
against the Romans. So throughout that day and the ensuing night the
fire prevailed; for they could only set light to portions of the porticoes, and
not to the whole range at once.

On the following day Titus, after giving orders to a division of his army
to extinguish the fire and make a road to the gates to facilitate the ascent
of the legions, called together his generals. Six of his chief staff-officers
were assembled, namely, Tiberius Alexander, the prefect of all the
forces, Sextus Cerealius, Larcius Lepidus, and Titus Phrygius, the respective commanders of the fifth, tenth, and fifteenth legions; Fronto
Haterius, prefect of the two legions from Alexandria, and Marcus Antonius Julianus, procurator of Judaea; and the procurators and tribunes
being next collected, Titus brought forward for debate the subject of the
temple. Some were of opinion that the law of war should be enforced,
since the Jews would never cease from rebellion while the temple remained as the focus for concourse from every quarter. Others advised
that if the Jews abandoned it and placed no weapons whatever upon it,
it should be saved, but that if they mounted it for purposes of warfare,
it should be burnt; as it would then be no longer a temple, but a fortress,
and thenceforward the impiety would be chargeable, not to the Romans
but to those who forced them to take such measures. Titus, however,
declared that, even were the Jews to mount it and fight therefrom, he
would not wreak vengeance on inanimate objects instead of men, nor
under any circumstances burn down so magnificent a work; for the loss
would affect the Romans, inasmuch as it would be an ornament to the
empire if it stood. Fortified by this pronouncement, Fronto, Alexander,
and Cerealius now came over to his view. He then dissolved the council,
and, directing the officers to allow the other troops an interval of repose,

that he might find them reinvigorated in action, he gave orders to the picked men from the cohorts to open a road through the ruins and extinguish the fire.

Throughout that day fatigue and consternation crushed the energies of the Jews; but, on the following day, with recruited strength and renewed courage, they sallied out through the eastern gate upon the guards of the outer court of the temple, at about the second hour. The Romans stubbornly met their charge and, forming a screen in front with their shields like a wall, closed up their ranks; it was evident, however, that they could not long hold together, being no match for the number and fury of their assailants. Caesar, who was watching the scene from Antonia, anticipating the breaking of the line, now brought up his picked cavalry to their assistance. The Jews could not withstand their onset: the fall of the foremost led to a general retreat. Yet whenever the Romans retired they returned to the attack, only to fall back once more when their opponents wheeled round; until, about the fifth hour of the day, the Jews were overpowered and shut up in the inner court of the temple.

Titus then withdrew to Antonia, determined on the following day, at dawn, to attack with his whole force, and invest the temple. That building, however, God, indeed long since, had sentenced to the flames; but now in the revolution of the years had arrived the fated day, the tenth of the month Lous, the day on which of old it had been burnt by the king of Babylon. The flames, however, owed their origin and cause to God's own people. For, on the withdrawal of Titus, the insurgents, after a brief respite, again attacked the Romans, and an engagement ensued between the guards of the sanctuary and the troops who were endeavouring to extinguish the fire in the inner court; the latter routing the Jews and pursuing them right up to the sanctuary. At this moment, one of the soldiers, awaiting no orders and with no horror of so dread a deed, but moved by some supernatural impulse, snatched a brand from the burning timber and, hoisted up by one of his comrades, flung the fiery missile through a low golden door, which gave access on the north side to the chambers surrounding the sanctuary. As the flame shot up, a cry, as poignant as the tragedy, arose from the Jews, who flocked to the rescue, lost to all thought of self-preservation, all husbanding of strength, now that the object of all their past vigilance was vanishing.

Titus was resting in his tent after the engagement, when a messenger rushed in with the tidings. Starting up just as he was, he ran to the temple to arrest the conflagration; behind him followed his whole staff of generals, while in their train came the excited legionaries, and there was all the hubbub and confusion attending the disorderly movement of so large a force. Caesar, both by voice and hand, signalled to the combatants to extinguish the fire; but they neither heard his shouts, drowned in the

louder din which filled their ears, nor heeded his beckoning hand, distracted as they were by the fight or their fury. The impetuosity of the
legionaries, when they joined the fray, neither exhortation nor threat
could restrain; passion was for all the only leader. Crushed together
about the entrances, many were trampled down by their companions;
many, stumbling on the still hot and smouldering ruins of the porticoes,
suffered the fate of the vanquished. As they drew nearer to the sanctuary
they pretended not even to hear Caesar's orders and shouted to those in
front of them to throw in the firebrands. The insurgents, for their part,
were now powerless to help; and on all sides was carnage and flight. Most
of the slain were civilians, weak and unarmed people, each butchered
where he was caught. Around the altar a pile of corpses was accumulat-
ing; down the steps of the sanctuary flowed a stream of blood, and the
bodies of the victims killed above went sliding to the bottom.

Caesar, finding himself unable to restrain the impetuosity of his fren-
zied soldiers and the fire gaining the mastery, passed with his generals
within the building and beheld the holy place of the sanctuary and all
that it contained—things far exceeding the reports current among foreigners and not inferior to their proud reputation among ourselves. As
the flames had nowhere yet penetrated to the interior, but were consuming the chambers surrounding the temple, Titus, correctly assuming that
the structure might still be saved, rushed out and by personal appeals
endeavoured to induce the soldiers to quench the fire; while he directed
Liberalius, a centurion of his bodyguard of lancers, to restrain, by resort
to clubs, any who disobeyed orders. But their respect for Caesar and their
fear of the officer who was endeavouring to check them were overpowered by their rage, their hatred of the Jews, and a lust for battle more
unruly still. Most of them were further stimulated by the hope of plunder,
believing that the interior was full of money and actually seeing that all
the surroundings were made of gold. However, the end was precipitated
by one of those who had entered the building, and who, when Caesar
rushed out to restrain the troops, thrust a firebrand, in the darkness, into
the hinges of the gate. At once a flame shot up from the interior, Caesar
and his generals withdrew, and there was none left to prevent those
outside from kindling a blaze. Thus, against Caesar's wishes, was the
temple set on fire.

Deeply as one must mourn for the most marvellous edifice which we
have ever seen or heard of, whether we consider its structure, its magnitude, the richness of its every detail, or the reputation of its Holy Places,
yet may we draw very great consolation from the thought that there is
no escape from Fate, for works of art and places any more than for living
beings. And one may well marvel at the exactness of the cycle of Destiny;
for, as I said, she waited until the very month and the very day on which

in bygone times the temple had been burnt by the Babylonians. From its first foundation by King Solomon up to its present destruction, which took place in the second year of Vespasian's reign, the total period amounts to one thousand one hundred and thirty years seven months and fifteen days; from its rebuilding by Haggai in the second year of the reign of Cyrus until its fall under Vespasian to six hundred and thirty-nine years and forty-five days. . . .

The Romans, thinking it useless, now that the temple was on fire, to spare the surrounding buildings, set them all alight, both the remnants of the porticoes and the gates, excepting two, one on the east and the other on the south; these also they subsequently razed to the ground. They further burnt the treasury-chambers, in which lay vast sums of money, vast piles of raiment, and other valuables; for this, in short, was the general repository of Jewish wealth, to which the rich had consigned the contents of their dismantled houses. They then proceeded to the one remaining portico of the outer court, on which the poor women and children of the populace and a mixed multitude had taken refuge, numbering six thousand. And before Caesar had come to any decision or given any orders to the officers concerning these people, the soldiers, carried away by rage, set fire to the portico from below; with the result that some were killed plunging out of the flames, others perished amidst them, and out of all that multitude not a soul escaped. They owed their destruction to a false prophet, who had on that day proclaimed to the people in the city that God commanded them to go up to the temple court, to receive there the tokens of their deliverance. Numerous prophets, indeed, were at this period suborned by the tyrants to delude the people, by bidding them await help from God, in order that desertions might be checked and that those who were above fear and precaution might be encouraged by hope. In adversity man is quickly persuaded; but when the deceiver actually pictures release from prevailing horrors, then the sufferer wholly abandons himself to expectation.

Thus it was that the wretched people were deluded at that time by charlatans and pretended messengers of the deity; while they neither heeded nor believed in the manifest portents that foretold the coming desolation, but, as if thunderstruck and bereft of eyes and mind, disregarded the plain warnings of God. So it was when a star, resembling a sword, stood over the city, and a comet which continued for a year. So again when, before the revolt and the commotion that led to war, at the time when the people were assembling for the feast of unleavened bread, on the eighth of the month Xanthicus, at the ninth hour of the night, so brilliant a light shone round the altar and the sanctuary that it seemed to be broad daylight; and this continued for half an hour. By the inexperienced this was regarded as a good omen, but by the sacred scribes it was at once interpreted in accordance with after events. At that same feast a cow that had been brought by some one for sacrifice gave birth to a lamb in the midst of the court of the temple; moreover, the eastern gate of the inner court—it was of brass and very massive, and, when closed towards evening, could scarcely be moved by twenty men; fastened with iron-bound bars, it had bolts which were sunk to a great depth into a threshold consisting of a solid block of stone—this gate was observed at the sixth hour of the night to have opened of its own accord. The watchmen of the temple ran and reported the matter to the captain, and he came up and with difficulty succeeded in shutting it. This again to the uninitiated seemed the best of omens, as they supposed that God had opened to them the gate of blessings; but the learned understood that the security of the temple was dissolving of its own accord and that the opening of the gate meant a present to the enemy, interpreting the portent in their own minds as indicative of coming desolation. Again, not many days after the festival, on the twenty-first of the month Artemisium, there appeared a miraculous phenomenon, passing belief. Indeed, what I am about to relate would, I imagine, have been deemed a fable, were it not for the narratives of eyewitnesses and for the subsequent calamities which deserved to be so signalized. For before sunset throughout all parts of the country chariots were seen in the air and armed battalions hurtling through the clouds and encompassing the cities. Moreover, at the feast which is called Pentecost, the priests on entering the inner court of the temple by night, as their custom was in the discharge of their ministrations, reported that they were conscious, first of a commotion and a din, and after that of a voice as of a host, "We are departing hence."

But a further portent was even more alarming. Four years before the war, when the city was enjoying profound peace and prosperity, there came to the feast at which it is the custom of all Jews to erect tabernacles to God, one Jesus, son of Ananias, a rude peasant, who, standing in the temple, suddenly began to cry out, "A voice from the east, a voice from the west, a voice from the four winds; a voice against Jerusalem and the sanctuary, a voice against the bridegroom and the bride, a voice against all the people." Day and night he went about all the alleys with this cry on his lips. Some of the leading citizens, incensed at these ill-omened words, arrested the fellow and severely chastised him. But he, without a word on his own behalf or for the private ear of those who smote him, only continued his cries as before. Thereupon, the magistrates, supposing, as was indeed the case, that the man was under some supernatural impulse, brought him before the Roman governor; there, although flayed to the bone with scourges, he neither sued for mercy nor shed a tear, but, merely introducing the most mournful of variations into his ejaculation, responded to each stroke with "Woe to Jerusalem!" When Albinus, the governor, asked him who and whence he was and why he uttered these cries, he answered him never a word, but unceasingly reiterated his dirge over the city, until Albinus pronounced him a maniac and let him go. During the whole period up to the outbreak of war he neither approached nor was seen talking to any of the citizens, but daily, like a prayer that he had conned, repeated his lament, "Woe to Jerusalem!" He neither cursed any of those who beat him from day to day, nor blessed those who offered him food: to all men that melancholy presage was his one reply. His cries were loudest at the festivals. So for seven years and five months he continued his wail, his voice never flagging nor his strength exhausted, until in the siege, having seen his presage verified, he found his rest. For, while going his round and shouting in piercing tones from the wall, "Woe once more to the city and to the people and to the temple," as he added a last word, "and woe to me also," a stone hurled from the ballista struck and killed him on the spot. So with those ominous words still upon his lips he passed away.

Reflecting on these things one will find that God has a care for men, and by all kinds of premonitory signs shows His people the way of salvation, while they owe their destruction to folly and calamities of their own choosing. Thus the Jews, after the demolition of Antonia, reduced the temple to a square, although they had it recorded in their oracles that the city and the sanctuary would be taken when the temple should become four-square. But what more than all else incited them to the war was an ambiguous oracle, likewise found in their sacred scriptures, to the effect that at that time one from their country would become ruler of the world. This they understood to mean someone of their own race, and many of their wise men went astray in their interpretation of it. The oracle, however, in reality signified the sovereignty of Vespasian, who was proclaimed Emperor on Jewish soil. For all that, it is impossible for men to escape their fate, even though they foresee it. Some of these portents, then, the Jews interpreted to please themselves, others they treated with contempt, until the ruin of their country and their own destruction convicted them of their folly. . . .

Thus was Jerusalem taken in the second year of the reign of Vespasian on the eighth of the month Gorpiaeus. Captured on five previous occasions, it was now for the second time devastated. Asochaeus, king of Egypt, and after him Antiochus, then Pompey, and subsequently Sossius in league with Herod took the city but preserved it. But before their days the king of Babylon had subdued it and laid it waste, fourteen hundred and sixty-eight years and six months after its foundation. Its original founder was a Canaanite chief, called in the native tongue "Righteous King"; for such indeed he was. In virtue thereof he was the first to officiate as priest of God and, being the first to build the temple, gave the city, previously called Solyma, the name of Jerusalem. The Canaanite population was expelled by David, the king of the Jews, who established his own people there; and four hundred and seventy-seven years and six months after his time it was razed to the ground by the Babylonians. The period from king David, its first Jewish sovereign, to its destruction by Titus was one thousand one hundred and seventy-nine years; and from its first foundation until its final overthrow, two thousand one hundred and seventy-seven. Howbeit, neither its antiquity, nor its ample wealth, nor its people spread over the whole habitable world, nor yet the great glory of its religious rites, could aught avail to avert its ruin. Thus ended the siege of Jerusalem.

Tacitus

7

Tacitus was the greatest of the Roman historians and his works have taught us much of what we know of Rome in the first Christian century. As usual with historians of the Classical Ages, however, we know little about his life. We are certain of nothing concerning his family, not even his place of birth. From various sources we can justifiably assume that he was born in A.D. 56 or 57, most probably into a provincial aristocratic family, and that he was educated for a life of military and, especially, of governmental service. He studied public speaking and moral philosophy and was thoroughly acquainted with both Virgilian epic and tragic drama. All of these arts were to assist him in the writing of his histories. But his work as a historian was facilitated as well by his active career in government. He served under three successive emperors as, variously, a praetor, a consul, and a proconsul. Like Thucydides and Polybius, he wrote of politics and politicians with insight gained from experience. He reached the culmination of his distinguished public career in 112–113 when he was proconsul in the province of Asia. It appears likely that he died some years after the accession of Hadrian (117).

Tacitus' earlier writings include a "Dialogue on Oratory" (c. 80), a laudatory biography of his father-in-law, Agricola (98), and the *Germania* (also 98), a study of "the origin, geography, institutions, and tribes of the Germans." His greatest works, from which we take our selections, the *Histories* and the *Annals,* appeared c. 105 and 116, respectively. Together, the two works cover the period in Roman history from 14 to 96. Of the original thirty books comprising the two histories only seventeen have come down to us. The extant version of the *Histories* covers the period from 69, the year of crisis when four different emperors held the throne, to the death of Domitian, in 96. What we have of the *Annals* includes the reign of Tiberius (14–37), the last seven years of Claudius (47–54), and the first twelve years of Nero (54–66).

Tacitus was clear as to his primary purpose in writing history: "This I regard as history's highest function, to let no worthy action be uncommemorated, and to hold out the reprobation of posterity as a terror to evil words and deeds." Tacitus, then, writes his histories with a moralist's eye, prepared to praise or condemn. But his judgments, he believes, are well-founded for his "purpose is to relate the facts . . . without bitterness or partiality [sine ira et studio], being far removed from any such motives." How well he restrained his anger and overcame his biases is a matter of debate. Regretting the Republic which, with its virtù and freedom, he knew was lost beyond recall, Tacitus did not always refrain from expressions of anger, contempt, and bitter irony in discussing the machinations of emperors, the sycophancy of aristocrats, and the servility of the masses. His narratives are in fact passionate accounts in which he displays, more or less openly, his sympathies and animosities. In commemorating "worthy actions" and in reprobating "evil words and deeds," his rhetoric and moral philosophy often enough impeded his critical faculties. To the extent that this occurred, his narratives are defective as histories. What is beyond dispute is his superb style, and his great descriptive power. He is, in Macaulay's phrase, "unrivalled among historians in the delineation of character"; Michael Grant has written that "he is the supreme artist and craftsman among ancient historians."

As an artist, then, Tacitus is unchallenged; as a historian, however, he has been subjected to criticism for arbitrary explanations of events, distorted portraits of some of the great personalities of the period, and the restricted scope of his histories. Nevertheless, his reputation as historian and the greatness of his achievement remains unshaken. He was diligent in his investigation of documents and other sources, and he was generally accurate in his assessment of men and events. His works reveal a mind that was alert, penetrating, and, perhaps most important, skeptical. As Ronald Syme notes: "The operations of an historian on the borderland of fact and fraud are the most exacting test of his powers. Several episodes establish the superior strategy of Cornelius Tacitus." Writing of the confused and tumultuous times from the Pricipate of Augustus through the tyranny of Domitian, Tacitus coped brilliantly and successfully with the complex political events which formed the substance of his histories. Equal to any of the great classical Roman historians in the method of history, he has no peer among them in the art of history.

Selected Bibliography

Ronald Syme's sympathetic but enormously learned and convincing *Tacitus* (2 vols., 1958) stands at the point of departure for all students of our historian. The work is readable, exciting, and an inducement to read Tacitus himself. See also, Syme's *The Roman Revolution* (1939, reprinted with corrections in 1952). M. W. L. Laistner, *The Greater Roman Historians* (1967), devotes two chapters to

Tacitus. Recognizing his literary excellence, Laistner yet judges Tacitus severely as a historian, noting what he deems his narrowness of view and his distortions of character. Laistner's opinion appears a minority one however, at least among more recent commentators. Bessie Walker, *The "Annals" of Tacitus* (Manchester, second edition, 1960), offers an intelligent guide to the unfolding of Tacitus' dramatic narrative. G. G. Ramsay includes a valuable introduction to his translation of *The Histories of Tacitus* (2 vols., 1915), a work which M. W. L. Laistner numbers among "the classic translations in English of an ancient author." Arnaldo Momigliano makes intelligent and pertinent reference to Tacitus throughout his *Studies in Historiography* (1966). Hugh Lloyd-Jones' introduction to his edition of the A. J. Church and W. J. Brodribb translation of *The Annals* and *The Histories* (1964) is erudite and informative. The same may be said of Moses Hadas' shorter introduction to the Modern Library edition of Church and Brodribb's translation of *The Complete Works of Tacitus* (1942), from which we take our selections.

THE ANNALS

Rome at the beginning was ruled by kings. Freedom and the consulship were established by Lucius Brutus. Dictatorships were held for a temporary crisis. The power of the decemvirs did not last beyond two years, nor was the consular jurisdiction of the military tribunes of long duration. The despotisms of Cinna and Sulla were brief; the rule of Pompeius and of Crassus soon yielded before Caesar; the arms of Lepidus and Antonius before Augustus; who, when the world was wearied by civil strife, subjected it to empire under the title of "Prince." But the successes and reverses of the old Roman people have been recorded by famous historians; and fine intellects were not wanting to describe the times of Augustus, till growing sycophancy scared them away. The histories of Tiberius, Caius, Claudius, and Nero, while they were in power, were falsified through terror, and after their death were written under the irritation of a recent hatred. Hence my purpose is to relate a few facts about Augustus —more particularly his last acts, then the reign of Tiberius, and all which follows, without either bitterness or partiality, from any motives to which I am far removed.

When after the destruction of Brutus and Cassius there was no longer any army of the Commonwealth, when Pompeius was crushed in Sicily, and when, with Lepidus pushed aside and Angonius slain, even the Julian faction had only Caesar left to lead it, then, dropping the title of triumvir, and giving out that he was a Consul, and was satisfied with a tribune's authority for the protection of the people, Augustus won over the soldiers with gifts, the populace with cheap corn, and all men with the sweets of repose, and so grew greater by degrees, while he concentrated in himself the functions of the Senate, the magistrates, and the laws. He was wholly unopposed, for the boldest spirits had fallen in battle, or in the proscription, while the remaining nobles, the readier they were to be slaves, were raised the higher by the wealth and promotion, so that, aggrandised by revolution, they preferred the safety of the

From *The Complete Works of Tacitus,* translated by A. J. Church and W. J. Brodribb (New York, Random House, 1942). Reprinted by permission of Random House, Inc., and Macmillan & Co. Ltd. Pp. 3–6, 11–14, 162–163, 320–326, 328–329, 347–356, 369–398, 657–666.

present to the dangerous past. Nor did the provinces dislike that condition of affairs, for they distrusted the government of the Senate and the people, because of the rivalries between the leading men and the rapacity of the officials, while the protection of the laws was unavailing, as they were continually deranged by violence, intrigue, and finally by corruption.

Augustus meanwhile, as supports to his despotism, raised to the pontificate and curile aedileship Claudius Marcellus, his sister's son, while a mere stripling, and Marcus Agrippa, of humble birth, a good soldier, and one who had shared his victory, to two consecutive consulships, and as Marcellus soon afterwards died, he also accepted him as his son-in-law. Tiberius Nero and Claudius Drusus, his stepsons, he honoured with imperial titles, although his own family was as yet undiminished. For he had admitted the children of Agrippa, Caius and Lucius, into the house of the Caesars; and before they had yet laid aside the dress of boyhood he had most fervently desired, with an outward show of reluctance, that they should be entitled "princes of the youth," and be consuls-elect. When Agrippa died, and Lucius Caesar as he was on his way to our armies in Spain, and Caius while returning from Armenia, still suffering from a wound, were prematurely cut off by destiny, or by their stepmother Livia's treachery, Drusus too having long been dead, Nero remained alone of the stepsons, and in him everything tended to centre. He was adopted as a son, as a colleague in empire and a partner in the tribunitian power, and paraded through all the armies, no longer through his mother's secret intrigues, but at her open suggestion. For she had gained such a hold on the aged Augustus that he drove out as an exile into the island of Planasia, his only grandson, Agrippa Postumus, who, though devoid of worthy qualities, and having only the brute courage of physical strength, had not been convicted of any gross offence. And yet Augustus had appointed Germanicus, Drusus's offspring, to the command of eight legions on the Rhine, and required Tiberius to adopt him, although Tiberius had a son, now a young man, in his house; but he did it that he might have several safeguards to rest on. He had no war at the time on his hands except against the Germans, which was rather to wipe out the disgrace of the loss of Quintilius Varus and his army than out of an ambition to extend the empire, or for any adequate recompense. At home all was tranquil, and there were magistrates with the same titles; there was a younger generation, sprung up since the victory of Actium, and even many of the older men had been born during the civil wars. How few were left who had seen the republic!

Thus the State had been revolutionised, and there was not a vestige left of the old sound morality. Stript of equality, all looked up to the commands of a sovereign without the least apprehension for the present, while Augustus in the vigour of life, could maintain his own position, that of his house, and the general tranquillity. When in advanced old age, he was worn out by a sickly frame, and the end was near and new prospects opened, a few people spoke in vain of the blessings of freedom, but most people dreaded and some longed for war. The popular gossip of the large majority fastened itself variously on their future masters. "Agrippa was savage, and had been exasperated by insult, and neither from age nor experience in affairs was equal to so great a burden. Tiberius Nero was of mature years, and had established his fame in war, but he had the old arrogance inbred in the Claudian family, and many symptoms of a cruel temper, though they were repressed, now and then broke out. He had also from earliest infancy been reared in an imperial house; consulships and triumphs had been heaped on him in his younger days; even in the years which, on the pretext of seclusion he spent in exile at Rhodes, he had no thoughts but of wrath, hypocrisy, and secret sensuality. There was his mother too with a woman's caprice. They must, it seemed, be subject to a female and to two striplings besides, who for a while would burden, and some day rend asunder the State."

While these and like topics were discussed, the infirmities of Augustus increased, and some suspected guilt on his wife's part. For a rumour had gone abroad that a few months before he had sailed to Planasia on a visit to Agrippa, with the knowledge of some chosen friends, and with the one companion, Fabius Maximus; that many tears were shed on both sides, with expressions of affection, and that thus there was a hope of the young man being restored to the home of his grandfather. This, it was said, Maximus had divulged to his wife Marcia, she again to Livia. All was known to Caesar, and when Maximus soon afterwards died, by a death some thought to be self-inflicted, there were heard at his funeral wailings from Marcia, in which she reproached herself for having been the cause of her husband's destruction. Whatever the fact was, Tiberius as he was just entering Illyria was summoned home by an urgent letter from his mother, and it has not been thoroughly ascertained whether at the city of Nola he found Augustus still breathing or quite lifeless. For Livia had surrounded the house and its approaches with a strict watch, and favourable bulletins were published from time to time, till, provision having been made for the demands of the crisis, one and the same report told men that Augustus was dead and that Tiberius Nero was master of the State. . . .

After this all prayers were addressed to Tiberius. He, on his part, urged various considerations, the greatness of the empire, his distrust of himself. "Only," he said, "the intellect of the Divine Augustus was equal to such a burden. Called as he had been by him to share his anxieties, he had learnt by experience how exposed to fortune's caprices was the task of universal rule. Consequently, in a state which had the support of so many great men, they should not put everything on one man, as many, by uniting their efforts would more easily discharge public functions." There was more grand sentiment than good faith in such words. Tiberius's language even in matters which he did not care to conceal, either from nature or habit, was always hesitating and obscure, and now that he was struggling to hide his feelings completely, it was all the more involved in uncertainty and doubt. The Senators, however, whose only fear was lest they might seem to understand him, burst into complaints, tears, and prayers. They raised their hands to the gods, to the statue of Augustus, and to the knees of Tiberius, when he ordered a document to be produced and read. This contained a description of the resources of the State, of the number of citizens and allies under arms, of the fleets, subject kingdoms, provinces, taxes, direct and indirect, necessary expenses and customary bounties. All these details Augustus had written with his own hand, and had added a counsel, that the empire should be confined to its present limits, either from fear or out of jealousy.

Meantime, while the Senate stooped to the most abject supplication, Tiberius happened to say that although he was not equal to the whole burden of the State, yet he would undertake the charge of whatever part of it might be intrusted to him. Thereupon Asinius Gallus said, "I ask you, Caesar, what part of the State you wish to have intrusted to you?" Confounded by the sudden inquiry he was silent for a few moments; then, recovering his presence of mind, he replied that it would by no means become his modesty to choose or to avoid in a case where he would prefer to be wholly excused. Then Gallus again, who had inferred anger from his looks, said that the question had not been asked with the intention of dividing what could not be separated, but to convince him by his own admission that the body of the State was one, and must be directed by a single mind. He further spoke in praise of Augustus, and reminded Tiberius himself of his victories, and of his admirable deeds for many years as a civilian. Still, he did not thereby soften the emperor's resentment, for he had long been detested from an impression that, as he had married Vipsania, daughter of Marcus Agrippa, who had once been the wife of Tiberius, he aspired to be more than a citizen, and kept up the arrogant tone of his father, Asinius Pollio.

Next, Lucius Arruntius, who differed but little from the speech of Gallus, gave like offence, though Tiberius had no old grudge against him, but simply mistrusted him, because he was rich and daring, had brilliant accomplishments, and corresponding popularity. . . .

Great too was the Senate's sycophancy to Augusta. Some would have her styled "parent"; others "mother of the country," and a majority proposed that to the name of Caesar should be added "son of Julia." The emperor repeatedly asserted that there must be a limit to the honours paid to women, and that he would observe similar moderation in those bestowed on himself, but annoyed at the invidious proposal, and indeed regarding a woman's elevation as a slight to himself, he would not allow so much as a lictor to be assigned her, and forbade the erection of an altar in memory of her adoption, and any like distinction. But for Germanicus Caesar he asked pro-consular powers, and envoys were despatched to confer them on him, and also to express sympathy with his grief at the death of Augustus. The same request was not made for Drusus, because he was consul elect and present at Rome. Twelve candidates were named for praetorship, the number which Augustus had handed down, and when the Senate urged Tiberius to increase it, he bound himself by an oath not to exceed it.

It was then for the first time that the elections were transferred from the Campus Martius to the Senate. For up to that day, though the most important rested with the emperor's choice, some were settled by the partialities of the tribes. Nor did the people complain of having the right taken from them, except in mere idle talk, and the Senate, being now released from the necessity of bribery and of degrading solicitations, gladly upheld the change, Tiberius confining himself to the recommendation of only four candidates who were to be nominated without rejection or canvass. Meanwhile the tribunes of the people asked leave to exhibit at their own expense games to be named after Augustus and added to the Calendar as the Augustales. Money was, however, voted from the exchequer, and though the use of the triumphal robe in the circus was prescribed, it was not allowed them to ride in a chariot. Soon the annual celebration was transferred to the praetor, to whose lot fell the administration of justice between citizens and foreigners.

This was the state of affairs at Rome when a mutiny broke out in the legions of Pannonia, which could be traced to no fresh cause except the change of emperors and the prospect it held out of license in tumult and of profit from a civil war. . . .

Much of what I have related and shall have to relate, may perhaps, I am aware, seem petty trifles to record. But no one must compare my annals with the writings of those who have described Rome in old days. They told of great wars, of the storming of cities, of the defeat and capture of kings, or whenever they turned by preference to home affairs, they related, with a free scope for digression, the strifes of consuls with tribunes, land and corn-laws, and the struggles between the commons and the aristocracy. My labours are circumscribed and inglorious; peace wholly unbroken or but slightly disturbed, dismal misery in the capital, an emperor careless about the enlargement of the empire, such is my theme. Still it will not be useless to study those at first sight trifling events out of which the movements of vast changes often take their rise.

All nations and cities are ruled by the people, the nobility, or by one man. A constitution, formed by selection out of these elements, it is easy to commend but not to produce; or, if it is produced, it cannot be lasting. Formerly, when the people had power or when the patricians were in the ascendant, the popular temper and the methods of controlling it, had to be studied, and those who knew most accurately the spirit of the Senate and aristocracy, had the credit of understanding the age and of being wise men. So now, after a revolution, when Rome is nothing but the realm of a single despot, there must be good in carefully noting and recording this period, for it is but few who have the foresight to distinguish right from wrong or what is sound from what is hurtful, while most men learn wisdom from the fortunes of others. Still, though this is instructive, it gives very little pleasure. Descriptions of countries, the various incidents of battles, glorious deaths of great generals, enchain and refresh a reader's mind. I have to present in succession the merciless biddings of a tyrant, incessant prosecutions, faithless friendships, the ruin of innocence, the same causes issuing in the same results, and I am everywhere confronted by a wearisome monotony in my subject matter. Then, again, an ancient historian has but few disparagers, and no one cares whether you praise more heartily the armies of Carthage or Rome. But of many who endured punishment or disgrace under Tiberius, the descendants yet survive; or even though the families themselves may be now extinct, you will find those who, from a resemblance of character, imagine that the evil deeds of others are a reproach to themselves. Again, even honour and virtue make enemies, condemning, as they do, their opposites by too close a contrast. But I return to my work. . . .

In the year of the consulship of Caius Vipstanus and Caius Fonteius, Nero deferred no more a long meditated crime. Length of power had matured his daring, and his passion for Poppaea daily grew more ardent. As the woman had no hope of marriage for herself or of Octavia's divorce while Agrippina lived, she would reproach the emperor with incessant vituperation and sometimes call him in a jest a mere ward who was under the rule of others, and was so far from having empire that he had not even his liberty. "Why," she asked, "was her marriage put off? Was it, forsooth, her beauty and her ancestors, with their triumphal honours, that failed to please, or her being a mother, and her sincere heart? No; the fear was that as a wife at least she would divulge the wrongs of the Senate, and the wrath of the people at the arrogance and rapacity of his mother. If the only daughter-in-law Agrippina could bear was one who wished evil to her son, let her be restored to her union with Otho. She would go anywhere in the world, where she might hear of the insults heaped on the emperor, rather than witness them, and be also involved in his perils."

These and the like complaints, rendered impressive by tears and by the cunning of an adulteress, no one checked, as all longed to see the mother's power broken, while not a person believed that the son's hatred would steel his heart to her murder.

Cluvius relates that Agrippina in her eagerness to retain her influence went so far that more than once at midday, when Nero, even at that hour, was flushed with wine and feasting, she presented herself attractively attired to her half-intoxicated son and offered him her person, and that when kinsfolk observed wanton kisses and caresses, portending infamy, it was Seneca who sought a female's aid against a woman's fascinations, and hurried in Acte, the freedgirl, who alarmed at her own peril and at Nero's disgrace, told him that the incest was notorious, as his mother boasted of it, and that the soldiers would never endure the rule of an impious sovereign. Fabius Rusticus tells us that it was not Agrippina, but Nero, who lusted for the crime, and that it was frustrated by the adroitness of that same freedgirl. Cluvius's account, however, is also that of all other authors, and popular belief inclines to it, whether it was that Agrippina really conceived such a monstrous wickedness in her heart, or perhaps because the thought of a strange passion seemed comparatively credible in a woman, who in her girlish years had allowed herself to be seduced by Lepidus in the hope of winning power, had stooped with a like ambition to the lust of Pallas, and had trained herself for every infamy by her marriage with her uncle.

Nero accordingly avoided secret interviews with her, and when she withdrew to her gardens or to her estates at Tusculum and Antium, he praised her for courting repose. At last, convinced that she would be too formidable, wherever she might dwell, he resolved to destroy her, merely deliberating whether it was to be accomplished by poison, or by the sword, or by any other violent means. Poison at first seemed best, but, were it to be administered at the imperial table, the result could not be referred to chance after the recent circumstances of the death of Britannicus. Again, to tamper with the servants of a woman who, from her familiarity with crime, was on her guard against treachery, appeared to be extremely difficult, and then, too, she had fortified her constitution by the use of antidotes. How again the dagger and its work were to be kept secret, no one could suggest, and it was feared too that whoever might be chosen to execute such a crime would spurn the order.

An ingenious suggestion was offered by Anicetus, a freedman, commander of the fleet at Misenum, who had been tutor to Nero in boyhood and had a hatred of Agrippina which she reciprocated. He explained that a vessel could be constructed, from which a part might by a contrivance be detached, when out at sea, so as to plunge her unawares into the water. "Nothing," he said, "allowed of accidents so much as the sea, and should she be overtaken by shipwreck, who would be so unfair as to impute to crime an offence committed by the winds and waves? The emperor would add the honour of a temple and of shrines to the deceased lady, with every other display of filial affection."

Nero liked the device, favoured as it also was by the particular time, for he was celebrating Minerva's five days' festival at Baiae. Thither he enticed his mother by repeated assurances that children ought to bear with the irritability of parents and to soothe their tempers, wishing thus to spread a rumour of reconciliation and to secure Agrippina's acceptance through the feminine credulity, which easily believes what gives joy. As she approached, he went to the shore to meet her (she was coming from Antium), welcomed her with outstretched hand and embrace, and conducted her to Bauli. This was the name of a country house, washed by a bay of the sea, between the promontory of Misenum and the lake of Baiae. Here was a vessel distinguished from others by its equipment, seemingly meant, among other things, to do honour to his mother; for she had been accustomed to sail in a trireme, with a crew of marines. And now she was invited to a banquet, that night might serve to conceal the crime. It was well known that somebody had been found to betray it, that Agrippina had heard of the plot, and in doubt whether she was to believe it, was conveyed to Baiae in her litter. There some soothing words allayed her fear; she was graciously received, and seated at table above the emperor. Nero prolonged the banquet with various conversation, passing from a youth's playful familiarity to an air of constraint, which seemed to indicate serious thought, and then, after protracted festivity, escorted her on her departure, clinging with kisses to her eyes and bosom, either to crown his hypocrisy or because the last sight of a mother on the eve of destruction caused a lingering even in that brutal heart.

A night of brilliant starlight with the calm of a tranquil sea was granted by heaven, seemingly, to convict the crime. The vessel had not gone far, Agrippina having with her two of her intimate attendants, one of whom, Crepereius Gallus, stood near the helm, while Acerronia, reclining at Agrippina's feet as she reposed herself, spoke joyfully of her son's repentance and of the recovery of the mother's influence, when at a given signal the ceiling of the place, which was loaded with a quantity of lead, fell in, and Crepereius was crushed and instantly killed. Agrippina and Acerronia were protected by the projecting sides of the couch, which happened to be too strong to yield under the weight. But this was not followed by the breaking up of the vessel; for all were bewildered, and those too, who were in the plot, were hindered by the unconscious majority. The crew then thought it best to throw the vessel on one side and so sink it, but they could not themselves promptly unite to face the emergency, and others, by counteracting the attempt, gave an opportunity of a gentler fall into the sea. Acerronia, however, thoughtlessly exclaiming that she was Agrippina, and imploring help for the emperor's mother, was despatched with poles and oars, and such naval implements as chance offered. Agrippina was silent and was thus the less recognized; still, she received a wound in her shoulder. She swam, then met with some small boats which conveyed her to the Lucrine lake, and so entered her house.

There she reflected how for this very purpose she had been invited by a lying letter and treated with conspicuous honour, how also it was near the shore, not from being driven by winds or dashed on rocks, that the vessel had in its upper part collapsed, like a mechanism anything but nautical. She pondered too the death of Acerronia; she looked at her own wound, and saw that her only safeguard against treachery was to ignore it. Then she sent her freedman Agerinus to tell her son how by heaven's favour and his good fortune she had escaped a terrible disaster; that she begged him, alarmed, as he might be, by his mother's peril, to put off the duty of a visit, as for the present she needed repose. Meanwhile, pretending that she felt secure, she applied remedies to her wound, and fomentations to her person. She then ordered search to be made for the will of Acerronia, and her property to be sealed, in this alone throwing off disguise.

Nero, meantime, as he waited for tidings of the consummation of the deed, received information that she had escaped with the injury of a slight wound, after having so far encountered the peril that there could be no question as to its author. Then, paralysed with terror and protesting that she would show herself the next moment eager for vengeance, either arming the slaves or stirring up the soldiery, or hastening to the Senate and the people, to charge him with the wreck, with her wound, and with the destruction of her friends, he asked what resource he had against all this, unless something could be at once devised by Burrus and Seneca. He had instantly summoned both of them, and possibly they were already in the secret. There was a long silence on their part; they feared they might remonstrate in vain, or believed the crisis to be such that Nero must perish, unless Agrippina were at once crushed. Thereupon Seneca was so far the more prompt as to glance back to Burrus, as if to ask him whether the bloody deed must be required of the soldiers. Burrus replied "that the praetorians were attached to the whole family of the Caesars, and remembering Germanicus would not dare a savage deed on his offspring. It was for Anicetus to accomplish his promise."

Anicetus, without a pause, claimed for himself the consummation of the crime. At those words, Nero declared that the day gave him empire, and that a freedman was the author of this mighty boon. "Go," he said, "with all speed and take with you the mean readiest to execute your orders." He himself, when he had heard of the arrival of Agrippina's messenger, Agerinus, contrived a theatrical mode of accusation, and, while the man was repeating his message, threw down a sword at his feet, then ordered him to be put in irons, as a detected criminal, so that he might invent a story how his mother had plotted the emperor's destruction and in the shame of discovered guilt had by her own choice sought death.

Meantime, Agrippina's peril being universally known and taken to be an accidental occurrence, everybody, the moment he heard of it, hurried down to the beach. Some climbed projecting piers; some the nearest vessels; others, as far as their stature allowed, went into the sea; some, again, stood with outstretched arms, while the whole shore rung with wailings, with prayers and cries, as different questions were asked and uncertain answers given. A vast multitude streamed to the spot with torches, and as soon as all knew that she was safe, they at once prepared to wish her joy, till the sight of an armed and threatening force scared them away. Anicetus then surrounded the house with the guard, and having burst open the gates, dragged off the slaves who met him, till he came to the door of her chamber, where a few still stood, after the rest had fled in terror at the attack. A small lamp was in the room, and one slave-girl with Agrippina, who grew more and more anxious, as no messenger came from her son, not even Agerinus, while the appearance of the shore was changed, a solitude one moment, then sudden bustle and tokens of the worst catastrophe. As the girl rose to depart, she exclaimed, "Do you too forsake me?" and looking around saw Anicetus, who had with him the captain of the trireme, Herculeius, and Obaritus, a centurion of marines. "If," said she, "you have come to see me, take back word that I have recovered, but if you are here to do a crime, I believe nothing about my son; he has ordered his mother's murder."

The assassins closed in round her couch, and the captain of the trireme first struck her head violently with a club. Then, as the centurion bared his sword for the fatal deed, presenting her person, she exclaimed, "Smite my womb," and with many wounds she was slain.

So far our accounts agree. That Nero gazed on his mother after her death and praised her beauty, some have related, while others deny it. Her body was burnt that same night on a dining couch, with a mean funeral; nor, as long as Nero was in power, was the earth raised into a mound, or even decently closed. Subsequently, she received from the solicitude of her domestics, a humble sepulchre on the road to Misenum, near the country house of Caesar the Dictator, which from a great height commands a view of the bay beneath. As soon as the funeral pile was lighted, one of her freedmen, surnamed Mnester, ran himself through with a sword, either from love of his mistress or from the fear of destruction.

Many years before Agrippina had anticipated this end for herself and had spurned the thought. For when she consulted the astrologers about Nero, they replied that he would be emperor and kill his mother. "Let him kill her," she said, "provided he is emperor."

But the emperor, when the crime was at last accomplished, realised its portentous guilt. The rest of the night, now silent and stupified, now and still oftener starting up in terror, bereft of reason, he awaited the dawn as if it would bring with it his doom. He was first encouraged to hope by the flattery addressed to him, at the prompting of Burrus, by the centurions and tribunes, who again and again pressed his hand and congratulated him on his having escaped an unforeseen danger and his mother's daring crime. Then his friends went to the temples, and, an example having once been set, the neighbouring towns of Campania testified their joy with sacrifices and deputations. He himself, with an opposite phase of hypocrisy, seemed sad, and almost angry at his own deliverance, and shed tears over his mother's death. But as the aspects of places change not, as do the looks of men, and as he had ever before his eyes the dreadful sight of that sea with its shores (some too believed that the notes of a funereal trumpet were heard from the surrounding heights, and wailings from the mother's grave), he retired to Neapolis and sent a letter to the Senate, the drift of which was that Agerinus, one of Agrippina's confidential freedmen, had been detected with the dagger of an assassin, and that in the consciousness of having planned the crime she had paid its penalty. . . .

Nero had long had a fancy for driving a four-horse chariot, and a no less degrading taste for singing to the harp, in a theatrical fashion, when he was at dinner. This he would remind people was a royal custom, and had been the practice of ancient chiefs; it was celebrated too in the praises of poets and was meant to show honour to the gods. Songs indeed, he said, were sacred to Apollo, and it was in the dress of a singer that that great and prophetic deity was seen in Roman temples as well as in Greek cities. He could no longer be restrained, when Seneca and Burrus thought it best to concede one point that he might not persist in both. A space was enclosed in the Vatican valley where he might manage his horses, without the spectacle being public. Soon he actually invited all the people of Rome, who extolled him in their praises, like a mob which craves for amusements and rejoices when a prince draws them the same way. However, the public exposure of his shame acted on him as an incentive instead of sickening him, as men expected. Imagining that he mitigated the scandal by disgracing many others, he brought on the stage descendants of noble families, who sold themselves because they were paupers. As they have ended their days, I think it due to their ancestors not to hand down their names. And indeed the infamy is his who gave them wealth to reward their degradation rather than to deter them from degrading themselves. He prevailed too on some well-known Roman knights, by immense presents, to offer their services in the amphitheatre; only pay from one who is able to command, carries with it the force of compulsion.

Still, not yet wishing to disgrace himself on a public stage, he instituted some games under the title of "juvenile sports," for which people of every class gave in their names. Neither rank nor age nor previous high promotion hindered any one from practising the art of a Greek or Latin actor and even stooping to gestures and songs unfit for a man. Noble ladies too actually played disgusting parts, and in the grove, with which Augustus had surrounded the lake for the naval fight, there were erected places for meeting and refreshment, and every incentive to excess was offered for sale. Money too was distributed, which the respectable had to spend under sheer compulsion and which the profligate gloried in squandering. Hence a rank growth of abominations and of all infamy. Never did a more filthy rabble add a worse licentiousness to our long corrupted morals. Even with virtuous training, purity is not easily upheld; far less amid rivalries in vice could modesty or propriety or any trace of good manners be preserved. Last of all, the emperor himself came on the stage, turning his lute with elaborate care and trying his voice with his attendants. There were also present, to complete the show, a guard of soldiers with centurions and tribunes, and Burrus, who grieved and yet applauded. Then it was that Roman knights were first enrolled under the title of Augustani, men in their prime and remarkable for their strength, some, from a natural frivolity, others from the hope of promotion. Day and night they kept up a thunder of applause, and applied to the emperor's person and voice the epithets of deities. Thus they lived in fame and honour, as if on the strength of their merits. . . .

But while the miseries of the State were daily growing worse, its supports were becoming weaker. Burrus died, whether from illness or from poison was a question. It was supposed to be illness from the fact that from the gradual swelling of his throat inwardly and the closing up of the passage he ceased to breathe. Many positively asserted that by Nero's order his throat was smeared with some poisonous drug under the pretence of the application of a remedy, and that Burrus, who saw through the crime, when the emperor paid him a visit, recoiled with horror from his gaze, and merely replied to his question, "I indeed am well." Rome felt for him a deep and lasting regret, because of the remembrance of his worth, because too of the merely passive virtue of one of his successors and the very flagrant iniquities of the other. For the emperor had appointed two men to the command of the praetorian cohorts, Faenius Rufus, for a vulgar popularity, which he owed to his administration of the corn-supplies without profit to himself; and Sofonius Tigellinus, whose inveterate shamelessness and infamy were an attraction to him. As might have been expected from their known characters, Tigellinus had the greater influence with the prince, and was the associate of his most secret profligacy, while Rufus enjoyed the favour of the people and of the soldiers, and this, he found, prejudiced him with Nero.

The death of Burrus was a blow to Seneca's power, for virtue had not the same strength when one of its companions, so to say, was removed, and Nero too began to lean on worse advisers. They assailed Seneca with various charges representing that he continued to increase a wealth which was already so vast as to be beyond the scale of a subject, and was drawing to himself the attachment of the citizens, while in the picturesqueness of his gardens and the magnificence of his country houses he almost surpassed the emperor. They further alleged against him that he claimed for himself alone the honours of eloquence, and composed poetry more assiduously, as soon as a passion for it had seized on Nero. "Openly inimical to the prince's amusements, he disparaged his ability in driving horses, and ridiculed his voice whenever he sang. When was there to be an end of nothing being publicly admired but what Seneca was thought to have originated? Surely Nero's boyhood was over, and he was all but in the prime of youthful manhood. He ought to shake off a tutor, furnished as he was with sufficiently noble instructors in his own ancestors."

Seneca, meanwhile, aware of these slanders, which were revealed to him by those who had some respect for merit, coupled with the fact that the emperor more and more shunned his intimacy, besought the opportunity of an interview. This was granted, and he spoke as follows:

"It is fourteen years ago, Caesar, that I was first associated with your prospects, and eight years since you have been emperor. In the interval, you have heaped on me such honours and riches that nothing is wanting to my happiness but a right use of it. I will refer to great examples taken not from my own but from your position. You great-grandfather Augustus granted to Marcus Agrippa the calm repose of Mitylene, to Caius Maecenas what was nearly equivalent to a foreign retreat in the capital itself. One of these men shared his wars; the other struggled with many laborious duties at Rome; both received awards which were indeed splendid, but only proportioned to their great merits. For myself, what other recompense had I for your munificence, than a culture nursed, so to speak, in the shade of retirement, and to which a glory attaches itself, because I thus seem to have helped on the early training of your youth, an ample reward for the service.

"You on the other hand have surrounded me with vast influence and boundless wealth, so that I often think within myself, Am I, who am but of an equestrian and provincial family, numbered among the chief men of Rome? Among nobles who can show a long succession of glories, has my new name become famous? Where is the mind once content with a humble lot? Is this the man who is building up his garden terraces, who paces grandly through these suburban parks, and revels in the affluence of such broad lands and such widely-spread investments? Only one apology occurs to me, that it would not have been right in me to have thwarted your bounty.

"And yet we have both filled up our respective measures, you in giving as much as a prince can bestow on a friend, and I in receiving as much as a friend can receive from a prince. All else only fosters envy, which, like all things human, sinks powerless beneath your greatness, though on me it weighs heavily. To me relief is a necessity. Just as I should implore support if exhausted by warfare or travel, so in this journey of life, old as I am and unequal even to the lightest cares, since I cannot any longer bear the burden of my wealth, I crave assistance. Order my property to be managed by your agents and to be included in your estate. Still I shall not sink myself into poverty, but having surrendered the splendours which dazzle me, I will henceforth again devote to my mind all the leisure and attention now reserved for my gardens and country houses. You have yet before you a vigorous prime, and that on which for so many years your eyes were fixed, supreme power. We, your older friends, can answer for our quiet behavior. It will likewise redound to your honour that you have raised to the highest places men who could also bear moderate fortune."

Nero's reply was substantially this: "My being able to meet your elaborate speech with an instant rejoinder is, I consider, primarily your gift, for you taught me how to express myself not only after reflection but at a moment's notice. My great-grandfather Augustus allowed Agrippa and Maeceans to enjoy rest after their labours, but he did it at an age carrying with it an authority sufficient to justify any boon, of any sort, he might have bestowed. But neither of them did he strip of the rewards he had given. It was by war and its perils they had earned them; for in these the youth of Augustus was spent. And if I had passed my years in arms, your sword and right hand would not have failed me. But, as my actual condition required, you watched over my boyhood, then over my youth, with wisdom, counsel, and advice. And indeed your gifts to me will, as long as life holds out, be lasting possessions; those which you owe to me, your parks, investments, your country houses, are liable to accidents. Though they seem much, many far inferior to you in merit have obtained more. I am ashamed to quote the names of freedmen who parade a greater wealth. Hence I actually blush to think that, standing as you do first in my affections, you do not as yet surpass all in fortune.

"Yours too is a still vigorous manhood, quite equal to the labours of business and to the fruit of those labours; and, as for myself, I am but treading the threshold of empire. But perhaps you count yourself inferior to Vitellius, thrice a consul, and me to Claudius. Such wealth as long thrift has procured for Volusius, my bounty, you think, cannot fully make up to you. Why not rather, if the frailty of my youth goes in any respect astray, call me back and guide yet more zealously with your help the manhood which you have instructed? It will not be your moderation, if you restore me your wealth, not your love of quiet, if you forsake your emperor, but my avarice, the fear of my cruelty, which will be in all men's mouths. Even if your self-control were praised to the utmost, still it would not be seemly in a wise man to get glory for himself in the very act of bringing disgrace on his friend."

To these words the emperor added embraces and kisses; for he was formed by nature and trained by habit to veil his hatred under delusive flattery. Seneca thanked him, the usual end of an interview with a despot. But he entirely altered the practices of his former greatness; he kept the crowds of his visitors at a distance, avoided trains of followers, seldom appeared in Rome, as though weak health or philosophical studies detained him at home.

When Seneca had fallen, it was easy to shake the position of Faenius Rufus by making Agrippina's friendship a charge against him. Tigellinus, who was daily becoming more powerful and who thought that the wicked schemings which alone gave him strength, would be better liked if he could secure the emperor's complicity in guilt, dived into Nero's most secret apprehensions, and, as soon as he had ascertained that Plautus and Sulla were the men he most dreaded, Plautus having been lately sent away to Asia, Sulla to Gallia Narbonensis, he spoke much of their noble rank and of their respective proximity to the armies of the East and of Germany. "I have no eye," he said, "like Burrus, to two conflicting aims, but only to Nero's safety, which is at least secured against treachery in Rome by my presence. As for distant commotions, how can they be checked? Gaul is roused at the name of the great dictator, and I distrust no less the nations of Asia, because of the renown of such a grandfather as Drusus. Sulla is poor, and hence comes his surpassing audacity; he shams apathy, while he is seeking an opening for his reckless ambition. Plautus again, with his great wealth, does not so much as affect a love of repose, but he flaunts before us his imitations of the old Romans, and assumes the self-consciousness of the Stoics along with a philosophy, which makes men restless, and eager for a busy life."

There was not a moment's delay. Sulla, six days afterwards, was murdered by assassins brought over to Massilia, while he was reclining at the dinner-table, before he feared or heard of his danger. The head was taken to Rome, and Nero scoffed at its premature grey hairs as if they were a disfigurement.

It was less of a secret that there was a design to murder Plautus, as his life was dear to many. The distance too by land and sea, and the interval of time, had given rise to rumours, and the popular story was that he had tampered with Corbulo, who was then at the head of great armies, and would be a special mark for danger, if illustrious and innocent men were to be destroyed. Again Asia, it was said, from its partiality for the young man, had taken up arms, and the soldiers sent to do the crime, not being sufficient in number or decided in purpose, and, finding themselves unable to execute their orders, had gone over to the new cause. These absurdities, like all popular gossip, gathered strength from the idle leisure of a credulous society.

As it was, one of Plautus's freedmen, thanks to swift winds, arrived before the centurion and brought him a message from his father-in-law, Lucius Antistius. "He was to avoid the obvious refuge of a coward's death, and in the pity felt for a noble name he would soon find good men to help him and daring spirits would rally round him. Meantime no resource was to be rejected. If he did but repel sixty soldiers (this was the number on the way), while tidings were being carried back to Nero, while another force was on its march, many events would follow which would ripen into war. Finally, by this plan he either secured safety, or he would suffer nothing worse by daring than by cowardice."

But all this had no effect on Plautus. Either he saw no resource before him, an unarmed exile as he was, or he was weary of an uncertain hope, or was swayed by his love of his wife and of his children, to whom he thought the emperor, if harassed by no anxiety, would be more merciful. Some say that another message came to him from his father-in-law, representing that no dreadful peril hung over him, and that two teachers of philosophy, Coeranus from Greece and Musonius from Etruria, advised him to await death with firmness rather than lead a precarious and anxious life. At all events, he was surprised at midday, when stripped for exercise. In that state the centurion slew him in the presence of Pelago, a eunuch, whom Nero had set over the centurion and his company, like a despot's minister over his satellites.

The head of the murdered man was brought to Rome. At its sight the emperor exclaimed (I give his very words), "Why would you have been a Nero?" Then casting off all fear he prepared to hurry on his marriage with Poppaea, hitherto deferred because of such alarms as I have described, and to divorce his wife Octavia, notwithstanding her virtuous life, because her father's name and the people's affection for her made her an offence to him. He wrote, however, a letter to the Senate, confessing nothing about the murders of Sulla and Plautus, but merely hinting that both had a restless temper, and that he gave the most anxious thought to the safety of the State. On this pretext a thanksgiving was decreed, and also the expulsion from the Senate of Sulla and Plautus, more grievous, however, as a farce than as an actual calamity.

Nero, on receiving this decree of the Senate and seeing that every piece of his wickedness was regarded as a conspicuous merit, drove Octavia from him, alleging that she was barren, and then married Poppaea. The woman who had long been Nero's mistress and ruled him first as a paramour, then as her husband, instigated one of Octavia's servants to accuse her of an intrigue with a slave. The man fixed on as the guilty lover was one by name Eucaerus, an Alexandrine by birth, skilled in singing to the flute. As a consequence, her slave-girls were examined under torture, and though some were forced by the intensity of agony into admitting falsehoods, most of them persisted in upholding the virtue of their mistress. One of them said, in answer to the furious menaces of Tigellinus, that Octavia's person was purer than his mouth. Octavia, however, was dismissed under the form of an ordinary divorce, and received possession of the house of Burrus and of the estates of Plautus, an ill-starred gift. She was soon afterwards banished to Campania under military surveillance. This led to incessant and outspoken remonstrances among the common people, who have less discretion and are exposed to few dangers than others from the insignificance of their position. Upon this Nero, though he did not repent of his outrage, restored to Octavia her position as wife.

Then people in their joy went up to the Capitol and, at last, gave thanks to the gods. They threw down the statues of Poppaea; they bore on their shoulders the images of Octavia, covering them with flowers, and setting them up in the forum and in the temples. There was even a burst of applause for the emperor, men hailing the recalled Octavia. And now they were pouring into the Palace in crowds, with loud shoutings, when some companies of soldiers rushed out and dispersed the tumultuous throng with blows, and at the point of the sword. Whatever changes had been made in the riot, were reversed, and Poppaea's honours restored. Ever relentless in her hatred, she was now enraged by the fear that either the violence of the mob would burst on her with yet fiercer fury, or that Nero would be swayed by the popular bias, and so, flinging herself at his knees, she exclaimed that she was not in the position of a rival fighting for marriage, though that was dearer to her than life, but that her very life was brought into jeopardy by the dependants and slaves of Octavia, who had assumed the name of the people, and dared in peace what could hardly happen in war. "Those arms," she said, "have been taken up against the emperor; a leader only is wanting, and he will easily be found in a commotion. Only let her whose mere beck, though she is far away, stirs up tumult, quit Campania, and make her way in person to Rome. And, again, what is my sin? What offence have I caused any one? Is it that I am about to give to the house of the Caesars a lawful heir? Do the people of Rome prefer that the offspring of an Egyptian flute-player should be raised to the imperial throne? In a word, if it be expedient, Nero should of his own choice rather than on compulsion send for her who ruled him, or else secure his safety by a righteous vengeance. The beginning of a commotion has often been quieted by slight precautions; but if people once despair of Octavia being Nero's wife, they will soon find her a husband."

Her various arguments, tending both to frighten and to enrage, at once alarmed and incensed her listener. But the suspicion about the slave was of little weight, and the torture of the slave-girls exposed its absurdity. Consequently it was decided to procure a confession from some one on whom could also be fastened a charge of revolutionary designs. Fittest for this seemed the perpetrator of the mother's murder, Anicetus, commander, as I have already mentioned, on the fleet at Misenum, who got but scant gratitude after that atrocious deed, and subsequently all the more vehement hatred, inasmuch as men look on their instruments in crime as a sort of standing reproach to them.

The emperor accordingly sent for Anicetus, and reminded him of his former service. "He alone," he said, "had come to the rescue of the prince's life against a plotting mother. Close at hand was a chance of winning no less gratitude by ridding him of a malignant wife. No violence or weapons were needed; only let him confess to an intrigue with Octavia." Nero then promised him a secret but ample immediate recompense, and some delightful retreat, while he threatened him with death in case of refusal. Anicetus, with the moral insensibility of his nature and a promptness inspired by previous atrocities, invented even more than was required of him, and confessed before friends whom the prince had called in, as a sort of judicial council. He was then banished to Sardinia, where he endured exile without poverty, and died a natural death.

Nero meanwhile declared by edict that the prefect had been corrupted into a design of gaining over the fleet, and added, in forgetfulness of his late charge of barrenness against Octavia, that, conscious of her profligacies, she had procured abortion, a fact he had himself ascertained. Then he confined her in the island of Pandataria. No exile ever filled the eyes of beholders with tears of greater compassion. Some still remembered Agrippina, banished by Tiberius, and the yet fresher memory of Julia, whom Claudius exiled, was present to men's thoughts. But they had life's prime for their stay; they had seen some happiness, and the horror of the

moment was alleviated by recollections of a better lot in the past. For
Octavia, from the first, her marriage-day was a kind of funeral, brought,
as she was, into a house where she had nothing but scenes of mourning,
her father and, an instant afterwards, her brother, having been snatched
from her by poison; then, a slave-girl raised above the mistress; Poppaea
married only to insure a wife's ruin, and, to end all, an accusation more
horrible than any death.

And now the girl, in her twentieth year, with centurions and soldiers
around her, already removed from among the living by the forecast of
doom, still could not reconcile herself to death. After an interval of a few
days, she received an order that she was to die, although she protested
that she was now a widow and only a sister, and appealed to their common ancestors, the Germanici, and finally to the name of Agrippina,
during whose life she had endured a marriage, which was miserable
enough indeed, but not fatal. She was then tightly bound with cords, and
the veins of every limb were opened; but as her blood was congealed by
terror and flowed too slowly, she was killed outright by the steam of an
intensely hot bath. To this was added the yet more appalling horror of
Poppaea beholding the severed head which was conveyed to Rome.

And for all this offerings were voted to the temples. I record the fact
with a special object. Whoever would study the calamities of that period
in my pages or those of other authors, is to take it for granted that as often
as the emperor directed banishments or executions, so often was there
a thanksgiving to the gods, and what formerly commemorated some
prosperous event, was then a token of public disaster. Still, if any decree
of the Senate was marked by some new flattery, or by the lowest servility,
I shall not pass it over in silence.

That same year Nero was believed to have destroyed by poison two of
his most powerful freedmen, Doryphorus, on the pretext of his having
opposed the marriage with Poppaea, Pallas for still keeping his boundless wealth by a prolonged old age. Romanus had accused Seneca in
stealthy calumnies, of having been an accomplice of Caisu Piso, but he
was himself crushed more effectually by Seneca on the same charge.
This alarmed Piso, and gave rise to a huge fabric of unsuccessful con-
spiracies against Nero. . . .

At Rome meanwhile trophies for the Parthian war, and arches were
erected in the centre of the Capitoline hill; these had been decreed by the
Senate, while the war was yet undecided, and even now they were not
given up, appearances being consulted, in disregard of known facts. And
to hide his anxious fears about foreign affairs, Nero threw the people's
corn, which was so old as to be spoilt, into the Tiber, with the view of
keeping up a sense of security about the supplies. There was no addition
to the price, although about two hundred ships were destroyed in the very

harbour by a violent storm, and one hundred more, which had sailed up the Tiber, by an accidental fire. Nero next appointed three ex-consuls, Lucius Piso, Ducennius Geminus, and Pompeius Paulinus, to the management of the public revenues, and inveighed at the same time against former emperors whose heavy expenditure had exceeded their legitimate income. He himself, he said, made the state an annual present of sixty million sesterces. . . .

During the consulship of Memmius Regulus and Verginius Rufus, Nero welcomed with something more than mortal joy the birth of a daughter by Poppaea, whom he called Augusta, the same title having also been given to Poppaea. The place of her confinement was the colony of Antium, where the emperor himself was born. Already had the Senate commended Poppaea's safety to the gods, and had made vows in the State's name, which were repeated again and again and duly discharged. To these was added a public thanksgiving, and a temple was decreed to the goddess of fecundity, as well as games and contests after the type of the ceremonies commemorative of Actium, and golden images of two Fortunes were to be set up on the throne of Jupiter of the Capitol. Shows too of the circus were to be exhibited in honour of the Claudian and Domitian families at Antium, like those at Bovillae in commemoration of Julii. Transient distinctions all of them, as within four months the infant died. Again there was an outburst of flattery, men voting the honours of deification, of a shrine, a temple, and a priest.

The emperor, too, was as excessive in his grief as he had been in his joy. It was observed that when all the Senate rushed out to Antium to honour the recent birth, Thrasea was forbidden to go, and received with fearless spirit an affront which foreboded his doom. Then followed, as rumour says, an expression from the emperor, in which he boasted to Seneca of his reconciliation with Thrasea, on which Seneca congratulated him. And now henceforth the glory and the peril of these illustrious men grew greater. . . .

That same year the emperor put into possession of the Latin franchise the tribes of the maritime Alps. To the Roman knights he assigned places in the circus in front of the seats of the people, for up to that time they used to enter in a promiscuous throng, as the Roscian law extended only to fourteen rows in the theatre. The same year witnessed shows of gladiators as magnificent as those of the past. Many ladies of distinction, however, and senators, disgraced themselves by appearing in the amphitheatre.

In the year of the consulship of Caius Laecanius and Marcus Licinius a yet keener impulse urged Nero to show himself frequently on the public stage. Hitherto he had sung in private houses or gardens, during the Juvenile games, but these he now despised, as being but little frequented,

and on too small a scale for so fine a voice. As, however, he did not venture
to make a beginning at Rome, he chose Neapolis, because it was a Greek
city. From this as his starting-point he might cross into Achaia, and
there, winning the well-known and sacred garlands of antiquity, evoke,
with increased fame, the enthusiasm of the citizens. Accordingly, a rabble of the townsfolk was brought together, with those whom the excitement of such an event had attracted from the neighbouring towns and
colonies, and such as followed in the emperor's train to pay him honour
or for various objects. All these, with some companies of soldiers, filled
the theatre at Neapolis.

There an incident occurred, which many thought unlucky, though to
the emperor it seemed due to the providence of auspicious deities. The
people who had been present, had quitted the theatre, and the empty
building then fell in without harm to anyone. Thereupon Nero in an
elaborate ode thanked the gods, celebrating the good luck which attended
the late downfall, and as he was on his way to cross the sea of Hadria,
he rested awhile at Beneventum, where a crowded gladiatorial show was
being exhibited by Vatinius. The man was one of the most conspicuously
infamous sights in the imperial court, bred, as he had been , in a shoe-
maker's shop, of a deformed person and vulgar wit, originally introduced
as a butt. After a time he grew so powerful by accusing all the best men,
that in influence, wealth, and ability to injure, he was pre-eminent even
in that bad company.

While Nero was frequently visiting the show, even amid his pleasures
there was no cessation to his crimes. For during the very same period
Torquatus Silanus was forced to die, because over and above his illustrious rank as one of the Junian family he claimed to be the great-grandson
of Augustus. Accusers were ordered to charge him with prodigality in
lavishing gifts, and with having no hope but in revolution. They said
further that he had nobles about him for his letters, books, and accounts,
titles all and rehearsals of supreme power. Then the most intimate of his
freedmen were put in chains and torn from him, till, knowing the doom
which impended, Torquatus divided the arteries in his arms. A speech
from Nero followed, as usual, which stated that though he was guilty and
with good reason distrusted his defence, he would yet have lived, had he
awaited the clemency of the judge.

Soon afterwards, giving up Achaia for the present (his reasons were
not certainly known), he returned to Rome, there dwelling in his secret
imaginations on the provinces of the east, especially Egypt. Then having
declared in a public proclamation that his absence would not be long and
that all things in the State would remain unchanged and prosperous, he
visited the temple of the Capitol for advice about his departure. There he
adored the gods; then he entered also the temple of Vesta, and there

feeling a sudden trembling thoughout his limbs, either from terror inspired by the deity or because, from the remembrance of his crimes, he was never free from fear, he relinquished his purpose, repeatedly saying that all his plans were of less account than his love of his country. "He had seen the sad countenances of the citizens, he heard their secret complainings at the prospect of his entering on so long a journey, when they could not bear so much as his brief excursions, accustomed as they were to cheer themselves under mischances by the sight of the emperor. Hence, as in private relationships the closest ties were the strongest, so the people of Rome had the most powerful claims and must be obeyed in their wish to retain him."

These and the like sentiments suited the people, who craved amusement, and feared, always their chief anxiety, scarcity of corn, should he be absent. The Senate and leading citizens were in doubt whether to regard him as more terrible at a distance or among them. After a while, as is the way with great terrors, they thought what happened the worst alternative.

Nero, to win credit for himself of enjoying nothing so much as the capital, prepared banquets in the public places, and used the whole city, so to say, as his private house. Of these entertainments the most famous for their notorious profligacy were those furnished by Tigellinus, which I will describe as an illustration, that I may not have again and again to narrate similar extravagance. He had a raft constructed on Agrippa's lake, put the guests on board and set it in motion by other vessels towing it. These vessels glittered with gold and ivory; the crews were arranged according to age and experience in vice. Birds and beasts had been procured from remote countries, and sea monsters from the ocean. On the margin of the lake were set up brothels crowded with noble ladies, and on the opposite bank were seen naked prostitutes with obscene gestures and movements. As darkness approached, all the adjacent grove and surrounding buildings resounded with song, and shone brilliantly with lights. Nero, who polluted himself by every lawful or lawless indulgence, had not omitted a single abomination which could heighten his depravity, till a few days afterwards he stooped to marry himself to one of that filthy herd, by name Pythagoras, with all the forms of regular wedlock. The bridal veil was put over the emperor; people saw the witnesses of the ceremony, the wedding dower, the couch and the nuptial torches; everything in a word was plainly visible, which, even when a woman weds darkness hides.

A disaster followed, whether accidental or treacherously contrived by the emperor, is uncertain, as authors have both accounts, worse, however, and more dreadful than any which have ever happened to this city by the violence of fire. It had its beginning in that part of the circus which adjoins the Palatine and Caelian hills, where, amid the shops containing inflammable wares, the conflagration both broke out and instantly became so fierce and so rapid from the wind that it seized in its grasp the entire length of the circus. For here there were no houses fenced in by solid masonry, or temples surrounded by walls, or any other obstacle to interpose delay. The blaze in its fury ran first through the level portions of the city, then rising to the hills, while it again devastated every place below them, it outstripped all preventive measures; so rapid was the mischief and so completely at its mercy the city, with those narrow winding passages and irregular streets, which characterised old Rome. Added to this were the wailings of terror-stricken women, and the feebleness of age, the helpless inexperience of childhood, the crowd who sought to save themselves or others, dragging out the infirm or waiting for them, and by their hurry in the one case, by their delay in the other, aggravating the confusion. Often, while they looked behind them, they were intercepted by flames on their side or in their face. Or if they reached a refuge close at hand, when this too was seized by the fire, they found that, even places, which they had imagined to be remote, were involved in the same calamity. At last, doubting what they should avoid or whither betake themselves, they crowded the streets or flung themselves down in the fields, while some who had lost their all, even their very daily bread, and others out of love for their kinsfolk, whom they had been unable to rescue, perished, though escape was open to them. And no one dared to stop the mischief, because of incessant menaces from a number of persons who forbade the extinguishing of the flames, because again others openly hurled brands, and kept shouting that there was one who gave them authority, either seeking to plunder more freely, or obeying orders.

Nero at this time was at Antium, and did not return to Rome until the fire approached his house, which he had built to connect the palace with the gardens of Maecenas. It could not, however, be stopped from devouring the palace, the house, everything around it. However, to relieve the people, driven out homeless as they were, he threw open to them the Campus Martius and the public buildings of Agrippa, and even his own gardens, and raised temporary structures to receive the destitute multitude. Supplies of food were brought up from Ostia and the neighbouring towns, and the price of corn was reduced to three sesterces a peck. These acts, though popular, produced no effect, since a rumour had gone forth everywhere that, at the very time when the city was in flames, the emperor appeared on a private stage and sang of the destruction of Troy, comparing present misfortunes with the calamities of antiquity.

At last, after five days, an end was put to the conflagration at the foot of the Esquiline hill, by the destruction of all buildings on a vast space, so that the violence of the fire was met by clear ground and an open sky. But before people had laid aside their fears, the flames returned, with no less fury this second time, and especially in the spacious districts of the city. Consequently, though there was less loss of life, the temples of the gods, and the porticoes which were devoted to enjoyment, fell in a yet more widespread ruin. And to this conflagration there attacked the greater infamy because it broke out on the Aemilian property of Tigellinus, and it seemed that Nero was aiming at the glory of founding a new city and calling it by his name. Rome, indeed, is divided into fourteen districts, four of which remained uninjured, three were levelled to the ground, while in the other seven were left only a few shattered, half-burnt relics of houses. . . .

Nero meanwhile availed himself of his country's desolation, and erected a mansion in which the jewels and gold, long familiar objects, quite vulgarised by our extravagance, were not so marvellous as the fields and lakes, with woods on one side to resemble a wilderness, and, on the other, open spaces and extensive views. The directors and contrivers of the work were Severus and Celer, who had the genius and the audacity to attempt by art even what nature had refused, and to fool away an emperor's resources. They had actually undertaken to sink a navigable canal from the lake Avernus to the mouths of the Tiber along a barren shore or through the face of hills, where one meets with no moisture which could supply water, except the Pomptine marshes. The rest of the country is broken rock and perfectly dry. Even if it could be cut through, the labour would be intolerable, and there would be no adequate result. Nero, however, with his love of the impossible, endeavoured to dig through the nearest hills to Avernus, and there still remain the traces of his disappointed hope.

Of Rome meanwhile, so much as was left unoccupied by his mansion, was not built up, as it had been after its burning by the Gauls, without any regularity or in any fashion, but with rows of streets according to measurement, with broad thoroughfares, with a restriction of the height of houses, with open spaces, and the further addition of colonnades, as a protection to the frontage of the blocks of tenements. These colonnades Nero promised to erect at his own expense, and to hand over the open spaces, when cleared of the debris, to the ground landlords. He also offered rewards proportioned to each person's position and property, and prescribed a period within which they were to obtain them on the completion of so many houses or blocks of building. He fixed on the marshes of Ostia for the reception of the rubbish, and arranged that the ships which had brought up corn by the Tiber, should sail down the river with cargoes of this rubbish. The buildings themselves, to a certain height, were to be solidly constructed, without wooden beams, of stone from

Gabii or Alba, that material being impervious to fire. And to provide that the water which individual license had illegally appropriated, might flow in greater abundance in several places for the public use, officers were appointed, and everyone was to have in the open court the means of stopping a fire. Every building, too, was to be enclosed by its own proper wall, not by one common to others. These changes which were liked for their utility, also added beauty to the new city. Some, however, thought that its old arrangement had been more conducive to health, inasmuch as the narrow streets with the elevation of the roofs were not equally penetrated by the sun's heat, while now the open space, unsheltered by any shade, was scorched by a fiercer glow.

Such indeed were the precautions of human wisdom. The next thing was to seek means of propitiating the gods, and recourse was had to the Sibylline books, by the direction of which prayers were offered to Vulcanus, Ceres, and Proserpina. Juno, too, was entreated by the matrons, first, in the Capitol, then on the nearest part of the coast, whence water was procured to sprinkle the fane and image of the goddess. And there were sacred banquets and nightly vigils celebrated by married women. But all human efforts, all the lavish gifts of the emperor, and the propitiations of the gods, did not banish the sinister belief that the conflagration was the result of an order. Consequently, to get rid of the report, Nero fastened the guilt and inflicted the most exquisite tortures on a class hated for their abominations, called Christians by the populace. Christus, from whom the name had its origin, suffered the extreme penalty during the reign of Tiberius at the hands of one of our procurators, Pontius Pilatus, and a most mischievous superstition, thus checked for the moment, again broke out not only in Judaea, the first source of the evil, but even in Rome, where all things hideous and shameful from every part of the world find their centre and become popular. Accordingly, an arrest was first made of all who pleaded guilty; then, upon their information, an immense multitude was convicted, not so much of the crime of firing the city, as of hatred against mankind. Mockery of every sort was added to their deaths. Covered with the skins of beasts, they were torn by dogs and perished, or were nailed to crosses, or were doomed to the flames and burnt, to serve as a nightly illumination, when daylight had expired.

Nero offered his gardens for the spectacle, and was exhibiting a show in the circus, while he mingled with the people in the dress of a charioteer or stood aloft on a car. Hence, even for criminals who deserved extreme and exemplary punishment, there arose a feeling of compassion; for it was not, as it seemed, for the public good, but to glut one man's cruelty, that they were being destroyed.

Meanwhile Italy was thoroughly exhausted by contributions of money, the provinces were ruined, as also the allied nations and the free states, as they were called. Even the gods fell victims to the plunder; for the temples in Rome were despoiled and the gold carried off, which, for a triumph or a vow, the Roman people in every age had consecrated in their prosperity or their alarm. Throughout Asia and Achaia not only votive gifts, but the images of deities were seized, Acratus and Secundus Carinas having been sent into those provinces. The first was a freedman ready for any wickedness; the latter, as far as speech went, was thoroughly trained in Greek learning, but he had not imbued his heart with sound principles. Seneca, it was said, to avert from himself the obloquy of sacrilege, begged for the seclusion of a remote rural retreat, and, when it was refused, feigning ill health, as though he had a nervous ailment, would not quit his chamber. According to some writers, poison was prepared for him at Nero's command by his own freedman, whose name was Cleonicus. This Seneca avoided through the freedman's disclosure, or his own apprehension, while he used to support life on the very simple diet of wild fruits, with water from a running stream when thirst prompted.

During the same time some gladiators in the town of Preaeneste, who attempted to break loose, were put down by a military guard stationed on the spot to watch them, and the people, ever desirous and yet fearful of change, began at once to talk of Spartacus, and of bygone calamities. Soon afterwards, tidings of a naval disaster was received, but not from war, for never had there been so profound a peace. Nero, however, had ordered the fleet to return to Campania on a fixed day, without making any allowance for the dangers of the sea. Consequently the pilots, in spite of the fury of the waves, started from Formiae, and while they were struggling to double the promontory of Misenum, they were dashed by a violent southwest wind on the shores of Cumae, and lost, in all directions, a number of their triremes with some smaller vessels.

At the close of the year people talked much about prodigies, presaging impending evils. Never were lightning flashes more frequent, and a comet too appeared, for which Nero always made propitiation with noble blood. Human and other births with two heads were exposed to public view, or were discovered in those sacrifices in which it is usual to immolate victims in a pregnant condition. And in the district of Placentia, close to the road, a calf was born with its head attached to its leg. Then followed an explanation of the diviners, that another head was preparing for the world, which however would be neither mighty nor hidden, as its growth had been checked in the womb, and it had been born by the wayside.

Silius Nerva and Atticus Vestinus then entered on the consulship, and now a conspiracy was planned, and at once became formidable, for which senators, knights, soldiers, even women, had given their names with eager rivalry, out of hatred of Nero as well as a liking for Caius Piso. A descendant of the Calpurnian house, and embracing in his connections through his father's noble rank many illustrious families, Piso had a splendid reputation with the people from his virtue or semblance of virtue. His eloquence he exercised in the defence of fellow-citizens, his generosity towards friends, while even for strangers he had a courteous address and demeanour. He had, too, the fortuitous advantages of tall stature and a handsome face. But solidity of character and moderation in pleasure were wholly alien to him. He indulged in laxity, in display, and occasionally in excess. This suited the taste of that numerous class who, when the attractions of vice are so powerful, do not wish for strictness or special severity on the throne.

The origin of the conspiracy was not in Piso's personal ambition. But I could not easily narrate who first planned it, or whose prompting inspired a scheme into which so many entered. That the leading spirits were Subrius Flavus, tribune of a praetorian cohort, and Sulpicius Asper, a centurion, was proved by the fearlessness of their death. Lucanus Annaeus, too, and Plautius Lateranus, imported into it an intensely keen resentment. Lucanus had the stimulus of personal motives, for Nero tried to disparage the fame of his poems and, with the foolish vanity of a rival, had forbidden him to publish them. As for Lateranus, a consul-elect, it was no wrong, but love of the State which linked him with the others. Flavius Scaevinus and Afranius Quintianus, on the other hand, both of senatorian rank, contrary to what was expected of them, undertook the beginning of this daring crime. Scaevinus, indeed, had enfeebled his mind by excess, and his life, accordingly, was one of sleepy languor. Quintianus, infamous for his effeminate vice, had been satirised by Nero in a lampoon, and was bent on avenging the insult.

So, while they dropped hints among themselves or among their friends about the emperor's crimes, the approaching end of empire, and the importance of choosing some one to rescue the State in its distress, they associated with them Tullius Senecio, Cervarius Proculus, Vulcatius Araricus, Julius Augurinus, Munatius Gratus, Antonius Natalis, and Marcius Festus, all Roman knights. Of these Senecio, one of those who was specially intimate with Nero, still kept up a show of friendship, and had consequently to struggle with all the more dangers. Natalis shared with Piso all his secret plans. The rest built their hopes on revolution. Besides Subrius and Sulpicius, whom I have already mentioned, they invited the aid of military strength, of Gavius Silvanus and Statius Proximus, tribunes of praetorian cohorts, and of two centurions, Maximus Scaurus and Venetus Paulus. But their mainstay, it was thought, was Faenius Rufus, the commander of the guard, a man of esteemed life and character, to whom Tigellinus with his brutality and shamelessness was superior in the emperor's regard. He harassed him with calumnies, and had often put him in terror by hinting that he had been Agrippina's paramour, and from sorrow at her loss was intent on vengeance. And so, when the conspirators were assured by his own repeated language that the commander of the praetorian guard had come over to their side, they once more eagerly discussed the time and place of the fatal deed. It was said that Subrius Flavus had formed a sudden resolution to attack Nero when singing on the stage, or when his house was in flames and he was running hither and thither, unattended, in the darkness. In the one case was the opportunity of solitude; in the other, the very crowd which would witness so glorious a deed, had roused a singularly noble soul; it was only the desire of escape, that foe to all great enterprises, which held him back.

Meanwhile, as they hesitated in prolonged suspense between hope and fear, a certain Epicharis (how she informed herself is uncertain, as she had never before had a thought of anything noble) began to stir and upbraid the conspirators. Wearied at last of their long delay, she endeavoured, when staying in Campania, to shake the loyalty of the officers of the fleet at Misenum, and to entangle them in a guilty complicity. She began thus. There was a captain in the fleet, Volusius Proculus, who had been one of Nero's instruments in his mother's murder, and had not, as he thought, been promoted in proportion to the greatness of his crime. Either, as an old acquaintance of the woman, or on the strength of a recent intimacy, he divulged to her his services to Nero and their barren result to himself, adding complaints, and his determination to have vengeance, should the chance arise. He thus inspired the hope that he could be persuaded, and could secure many others. No small help was to be found in the fleet, and there would be numerous opportunities, as Nero delighted in frequent enjoyment of the sea off Puteoli and Misenum.

Epicharis accordingly said more, and began the history of all the emperor's crimes. "The Senate," she affirmed, "had no power left it; yet means had been provided whereby he might pay the penalty of having destroyed the State. Only let Proculus gird himself to do his part and bring over to their side his bravest soldiers, and then look for an adequate recompense." The conspirators' names, however, she withheld. Consequently the information of Proculus was useless, even though he reported what he had heard to Nero. For Epicharis being summoned and confronted with the informer easily silenced him, unsupported as he was by a single witness. But she was herself detained in custody, for Nero suspected that even what was not proved to be true, was not wholly false.

The conspirators, however, alarmed by the fear of disclosure, resolved to hurry on the assassination at Baiae, in Piso's villa, whither the emperor, charmed by its loveliness, often went, and where, unguarded and without the cumbrous grandeur of his rank, he would enjoy the bath and the banquet. But Piso refused, alleging the odium of an act which would stain with an emperor's blood, however bad he might be, the sanctity of the hospitable board and the deities who preside over it. "Better," he said, "in the capital, in that hateful mansion which was piled up with the plunder of the citizens, or in public, to accomplish what on the State's behalf they had undertaken."

So he said openly, with however a secret apprehension that Lucius Silanus might, on the strength of his distinguished rank and the teachings of Caius Cassius, under whom he had been trained, aspire to any greatness and seize on empire, which would be promptly offered him by all who had no part in the conspiracy, and who would pity Nero as the victim of a crime. Many thought that Piso shunned also the enterprising spirit of Vestinus, the consul, who might, he feared, rise up in the cause of freedom, or, by choosing another emperor, make the State his own gift. Vestinus, indeed, had no share in the conspiracy, though Nero on that charge gratified an old resentment against an innocent man.

At last they decided to carry out their design on that day of the circus games, which is celebrated in honour of Ceres, as the emperor, who seldom went out, and shut himself up in his house or gardens, used to go to the entertainments of the circus, and access to him was the easier from his keen enjoyment of the spectacle. They had so arranged the order of the plot, that Lateranus was to throw himself at the prince's knees in earnest entreaty, apparently craving relief for his private necessities, and, being a man of strong nerve and huge frame, hurl him to the ground and hold him down. When he was prostrate and powerless, the tribunes and centurions and all the others who had sufficient daring were to rush up and do the murder, the first blow being claimed by Scaevinus, who had taken a dagger from the Temple of Safety, or, according to another account, from that of Fortune, in the town of Ferentum, and used to wear the weapon as though dedicated to some noble deed. Piso, meanwhile, was to wait in the sanctuary of Ceres, whence he was to be summoned by Faenius, the commander of the guard, and by the others, and then conveyed into the camp, accompanied by Antonia, the daughter of Claudius Caesar, with a view to evoke the people's enthusiasm. So it is related by Caius Pliny. Handed down from whatever source, I had no intention of suppressing it, however absurd it may seem, either that Antonia should have lent her name at her life's peril to a hopeless project, or that Piso, with his well-known affection for his wife, should have pledged himself to another marriage, but for the fact that the lust of dominion inflames the heart more than any other passion.

It was however wonderful how among people of different class, rank,

age, sex, among rich and poor, everything was kept in secrecy till be-
trayal began from the house of Scaevinus. The day before the treacherous attempt, after a long conversation with Antonius Natalis, Scaevinus
returned home, sealed his will, and, drawing from its sheath the dagger
of which I have already spoken, and complaining that it was blunted
from long disuse, he ordered it to be sharpened on a stone to a keen and
bright point. This task he assigned to his freedman Milichus. At the same
time he sat down to a more than usually sumptuous banquet, and gave
his favourite slaves their freedom, and money to others. He was himself
depressed, and evidently in profound thought, though he affected gaiety
in desultory conversation. Last of all, he directed ligatures for wounds
and the means of stanching blood to be prepared by the same Milichus,
who either knew of the conspiracy and was faithful up to this point, or
was in complete ignorance and then first caught suspicions, as most
authors have inferred from what followed. For when his servile imagina-
tion dwelt on the rewards of perfidy, and he saw before him at the same
moment boundless wealth and power, conscience and care for his patron's life, together with the remembrance of the freedom he had received, fled from him. From his wife, too, he had adopted a womanly and
yet baser suggestion; for she even held over him a dreadful thought, that
many had been present, both freedmen and slaves, who had seen what
he had; that one man's silence would be useless, whereas the rewards
would be for him alone who was first with the information.

Accordingly at daybreak Milichus went to the Servilian gardens, and,
finding the doors shut against him, said again and again that he was the
bearer of important and alarming news. Upon this he was conducted by
the gatekeepers to one of Nero's freedmen, Epaphroditus, and by him to
Nero, whom he informed of the urgent danger, of the formidable conspiracy, and of all else which he had heard or inferred. He showed him
too the weapon prepared for his destruction, and bade him summon the
accused.

Scaevinus on being arrested by the soldiers began his defence with the
reply that the dagger about which he was accused, had of old been regarded with a religious sentiment by his ancestors, that it had been kept
in his chamber, and been stolen by a trick of his freedman. He had often,
he said, signed his will without heeding the observance of particular
days, and had previously given presents of money as well as freedom to
some of his slaves, only on this occasion he gave more freely, because, as
his means were now impoverished and his creditors were pressing him,
he distrusted the validity of his will. Certainly his table had always been
profusely furnished, and his life luxurious, such as rigid censors would
hardly approve. As to the bandages for wounds, none had been prepared
at his order, but as all the man's other charges were absurd, he added an

accusation in which he might make himself alike informer and witness.

He backed up his words by an air of resolution. Turning on his accuser, he denounced him as an infamous and depraved wretch, with so fearless a voice and look that the information was beginning to collapse, when Milichus was reminded by his wife that Antonious Natalis had had a long secret conversation with Scaevinus, and that both were Piso's intimate friends.

Natalis was therefore summoned, and they were separately asked what the conversation was, and what was its subject. Then a suspicion arose because their answers did not agree, and they were both put in irons. They could not endure the sight and the threat of torture. Natalis however, taking the initiative, knowing as he did more of the whole conspiracy, and being also more practised in accusing, first confessed about Piso, next added the name of Annaeus Seneca, either as having been a messenger between him and Piso, or to win the favour of Nero, who hated Seneca and sought every means for his ruin. Then Scaevinus too, when he knew the disclosure of Natalis, with like pusillanimity, or under the impression that everything was now divulged, and that there could be no advantage in silence, revealed the other conspirators. Of these, Lucanus, Quintianus, and Senecio long persisted in denial; after a time, when bribed by the promise of impunity, anxious to excuse their reluctance, Lucanus named his mother Atilla, Quintianus and Senecio, their chief friends, respectively, Glitius Gallus and Annius Pollio.

Nero, meanwhile, remembering that Epicharis was in custody on the information of Volusius Proculus, and assuming that a woman's frame must be unequal to the agony, ordered her to be torn on the rack. But neither the scourge nor fire, nor the fury of the men as they increased the torture that they might not be a woman's scorn, overcame her positive denial of the charge. Thus the first day's inquiry was futile. On the morrow, as she was being dragged back on a chair to the same torments (for with her limbs all dislocated she could not stand), she tied a band, which she had stript off her bosom, in a sort of noose to the arched back of the chair, put her neck in it, and then straining with the whole weight of her body, wrung out of her frame its little remaining breath. All the nobler was the example set by a freedwoman at such a crisis in screening strangers and those whom she hardly knew, when freeborn men, Roman knights, and senators, yet unscathed by torture, betrayed, every one, his dearest kinsfolk. For even Lucanus and Senecio and Quintianus failed not to reveal their accomplices indiscriminately, and Nero was more and more alarmed, though he had fenced his person with a largely augmented guard.

Even Rome itself he put, so to say, under custody, garrisoning its walls with companies of soldiers and occupying with troops the coast and the river-banks. Incessantly were there flying through the public places, through private houses, country fields, and the neighbouring villages, horse and foot soldiers, mixed with Germans, whom the emperor trusted as being foreigners. In long succession, troops of prisoners in chains were dragged along and stood at the gates of his gardens. When they entered to plead their cause, a smile of joy on any of the conspirators, a casual conversation, a sudden meeting, or the fact of having entered a banquet or a public show in company, was construed into a crime, while to the savage questionings of Nero and Tigellinus were added the violent menaces of Faenius Rufus, who had not yet been named by the informers, but who, to get the credit of complete ignorance, frowned fiercely on his accomplices. When Subius Flavus at his side asked him by a sign whether he should draw his sword in the middle of the trial and perpetrate the fatal deed, Rufus refused, and checked the man's impulse as he was putting his hand to his sword-hilt.

Some there were who, as soon as the conspiracy was betrayed, urged Piso, while Milichus' story was being heard, and Scaevinus was hesitating, to go to the camp or mount the Rostra and test the feelings of the soldiers and of the people. "If," said they, "your accomplices join your enterprise, those also who are yet undecided, will follow, and great will be the fame of the movement once started, and this in any new scheme is all-powerful. Against it Nero has taken no precaution. Even brave men are dismayed by sudden perils; far less will that stage-player, with Tigellinus forsooth and his concubines in his train, raise arms against you. Many things are accomplished on trial which cowards think arduous. It is vain to expect secrecy and fidelity from the varying tempers and bodily constitutions of such a host of accomplices. Torture or reward can overcome everything. Men will soon come to put you also in chains and inflict on you an ignominious death. How much more gloriously will you die while you cling to the State and invoke aid for liberty. Rather let the soldiers fail, the people be traitors, provided that you, if prematurely robbed of life, justify your death to your ancestors and descendants."

Unmoved by these considerations, Piso showed himself a few moments in public, then sought the retirement of his house, and there fortified his spirit against the worst, till a troop of soldiers arrived, raw recruits, or men recently enlisted, whom Nero had selected, because he was afraid of the veterans, imbued, though they were, with a liking for him. Piso expired by having the veins in his arms severed. His will, full of loathsome flatteries of Nero, was a concession to his love of his wife, a base woman, with only a beautiful person to recommend her, whom he had taken away from her husband, one of his friends. Her name was Atria Galla; that of her former husband, Domitius Silus. The tame spirit of the man, the profligacy of the woman, blazoned Piso's infamy.

In quick succession Nero added the murder of Plautius Lateranus, consul-elect, so promptly that he did not allow him to embrace his children or to have the brief choice of his own death. He was dragged off to a place set apart for the execution of slaves, and butchered by the hand of the tribune Statius, maintaining a resolute silence, and not reproaching the tribune with complicity in the plot.

Then followed the destruction of Annaeus Seneca, a special joy to the emperor, not because he had convicted him of the conspiracy, but anxious to accomplish with sword what poison had failed to do. It was, in fact, Natalis alone who divulged Seneca's name, to this extent, that he had been sent to Seneca when ailing, to see him and remonstrate with him for excluding Piso from his presence, when it would have been better to have kept up their friendship by familiar intercourse; that Seneca's reply was that mutual conversations and frequent interviews were to the advantage of neither, but still that his own life depended on Piso's safety. Gavius Silvanus, tribune of a praetorian cohort, was ordered to report this to Seneca and to ask him whether he acknowledged what Natalis said and his own answer. Either by chance or purposely Seneca had returned on that day from Campania, and had stopped at a country-house four miles from Rome. Thither the tribune came next evening, surrounded the house with troops of soldiers, and then made known the emperor's message to Seneca as he was at dinner with his wife, Pompeia Paulina, and two friends.

Seneca replied that Natalis had been sent to him and had complained to him in Piso's name because of his refusal to see Piso, upon which he excused himself on the ground of failing health and the desire of rest. "He had no reason," he said, for "preferring the interest of any private citizen to his own safety, and he had no natural aptitude for flattery. No one knew this better than Nero, who had oftener experienced Seneca's freespokenness than his servility." When the tribune reported this answer in the presence of Poppaea and Tigellinus, the emperor's most confidential advisers in his moments of rage, he asked whether Seneca was meditating suicide. Upon this the tribune asserted that he saw no signs of fear, and perceived no sadness in his words or in his looks. He was accordingly ordered to go back and to announce sentence of death. Fabius Rusticus tells us that he did not return the way he came, but went out of his course to Faenius, the commander of the guard, and having explained to him the emperor's orders, and asked whether he was to obey them, was by him admonished to carry them out, for a fatal spell of cowardice was on them all. For this very Silvanus was one of the conspirators, and he was now abetting the crimes which he had united with them to avenge. But he spared himself the anguish of a word or of a look, and merely sent in to Seneca one of his centurions, who was to announce to him his last doom.

Seneca, quite unmoved, asked for tablets on which to inscribe his will, and, on the centurion's refusal, turned to his friends, protesting that as he was forbidden to requite to them, he bequeathed to them the only, but still the noblest possession yet remaining to him, the pattern of his life, which, if they remembered, they would win a name for moral worth and steadfast friendship. At the same time he called them back from their tears to manly resolution, now with friendly talk, and now with the sterner language of rebuke. "Where," he asked again and again, "are your maxims of philosophy, or the preparation of so many years' study against evils to come? Who knew not Nero's cruelty? After a mother's and a brother's murder, nothing remains but to add the destruction of a guardian and a tutor."

Having spoken these and like words, meant, so to say, for all, he embraced his wife; then softening awhile from the stern resolution of the hour, he begged and implored her to spare herself the burden of perpetual sorrow, and, in the contemplation of a life virtuously spent, to endure a husband's loss with honourable consolations. She declared, in answer, that she too had decided to die, and claimed for herself the blow of the executioner. Thereupon Seneca, not to thwart her noble ambition, from an affection too which would not leave behind him for insult one whom he dearly loved, replied: "I have shown you ways of smoothing life; you prefer the glory of dying. I will not grudge you such a noble example. Let the fortitude of so courageous an end be alike in both of us, but let there be more in your decease to win fame."

Then by one and the same stroke they sundered with a dagger the arteries of their arms. Seneca, as his aged frame, attenuated by frugal diet, allowed the blood to escape but slowly, severed also the veins of his legs and knees. Worn out by cruel anguish, afraid too that his sufferings might break his wife's spirit, and that, as he looked on her tortures, he might himself sink into irresolution, he persuaded her to retire into another chamber. Even at the last moment his eloquence failed him not; he summoned his secretaries, and dictated much to them which, as it has been published for all readers in his own words, I forbear to paraphrase.

Nero meanwhile, having no personal hatred against Paulina and not wishing to heighten the odium of his cruelty, forbade her death. At the soldiers' prompting, her slaves and freedmen bound up her arms, and stanched the bleeding, whether with her knowledge is doubtful. For as the vulgar are ever ready to think the worst, there were persons who believed that, as long as she dreaded Nero's relentlessness, she sought the glory of sharing her husband's death, but that after a time, when a more soothing prospect presented itself, she yielded to the charms of life. To this she added a few subsequent years, with a most praiseworthy remembrance of her husband, and with a countenance and frame white to a degree of pallor which denoted a loss of much vital energy.

Seneca meantime, as the tedious process of death still lingered on, begged Statius Annaeus, whom he had long esteemed for his faithful friendship and medical skill, to produce a poison with which he had some time before provided himself, the same drug which extinguished the life of those who were condemned by a public sentence of the people of Athens. It was brought to him and he drank it in vain, chilled as he was throughout his limbs, and his frame closed against the efficacy of the poison. At last he entered a pool of heated water, from which he sprinkled the nearest of his slaves, adding the exclamation, "I offer this liquid as a libation to Jupiter the Deliverer." He was then carried into a bath, with the steam of which he was suffocated, and he was burnt without any of the usual funeral rites. So he had directed in a codicil of his will, when even in the height of his wealth and power he was thinking of his life's close.

There was a rumour that Sabrius Flavus had held a secret consultation with the centurions, and had planned, not without Seneca's knowledge, that when Nero had been slain by Piso's instrumentality, Piso also was to be murdered, and the empire handed over to Seneca, as a man singled out for his splendid virtues by all persons of integrity. Even a saying of Flavus was popularly current, "that it mattered not as to the disgrace if a harp-player were removed and a tragic actor succeeded him." For as Nero used to sing to the harp, so did Piso in the dress of a tragedian.

The soldiers' part too in the conspiracy no longer escaped discovery, some in their rage becoming informers to betray Faenius Rufus, whom they could not endure to be both an accomplice and a judge. Accordingly Scaevinus, in answer to his browbeating and menaces, said with a smile that no one knew more than he did, and actually urged him to show gratitude to so good a prince. Faenius could not meet this with either speech or silence. Halting in his words and visibly terror-stricken, while the rest, especially Cervarius Proculus, a Roman knight, did their utmost to convict him, he was, at the emperor's bidding, seized and bound by Cassius, a soldier, who because of his well-known strength of limb was in attendance.

Shortly afterwards, the information of the same men proved fatal to Subrius Flavus. At first he grounded his defence on his moral contrast to the others, implying that an armed soldier, like himself, would never have shared such an attempt with unarmed and effeminate associates. Then, when he was pressed, he embraced the glory of a full confession. Questioned by Nero as to the motives which had led him on to forget his oath of allegiance, "I hated you," he replied, "yet not a soldier was more loyal to you while you deserved to be loved. I began to hate you when you became the murderer of your mother and your wife, a charioteer, an actor, and an incendiary." I have given the man's very words, because they were not, like those of Seneca, generally published, though the rough and vigorous sentiments of a soldier ought to be no less known.

Throughout the conspiracy nothing, it was certain, fell with more terror on the ears of Nero, who was as unused to be told of the crimes he perpetrated as he was eager in their perpetration. The punishment of Flavus was intrusted to Veianius Niger, a tribune. At his direction, a pit was dug in a neighbouring field. Flavus, on seeing it, censured it as too shallow and confined, saying to the soldiers around him, "Even this is not according to military rule." When bidden to offer his neck resolutely, "I wish," said he, "that your stroke may be as resolute." The tribune trembled greatly, and having only just severed his head at two blows, vaunted his brutality to Nero, saying that he had slain him with a blow and a half.

Sulpicius Asper, a centurion, exhibited the next example of fortitude. To Nero's question why he had conspired to murder him, he briefly replied that he could not have rendered a better service to his infamous career. He then underwent the prescribed penalty. Nor did the remaining centurions forget their courage in suffering their punishment. But Faenius Rufus had not equal spirit; he even put his laments into his will.

Nero waited in the hope that Vestinus also, the consul, whom he thought an impetuous and deeply disaffected man, would be involved in the charge. None however of the conspirators had shared their counsels with him, some from old feuds against him, most because they considered him a reckless and dangerous associate. Nero's hatred of him had had its origin in intimate companionship, Vestinus seeing through and despising the emperor's cowardice, while Nero feared the high spirit of his friend, who often bantered him with that rough humour which, when it draws largely on facts, leaves a bitter memory behind it. There was too a recent aggravation in the circumstance of Vestinus having married Statilia Messalina, without being ignorant that the emperor was one of her paramours.

As neither crime nor accuser appeared, Nero, being thus unable to assume the semblance of a judge, had recourse to the sheer might of despotism, and despatched Gerellanus, a tribune, with a cohort of soldiers, and with orders to forestall the designs of the consul, to seize what he might call his fortress, and crush his train of chosen youths. For Vestinus had a house towering over the Forum, and a host of handsome slaves of the same age. On that day he had performed all his duties as consul, and was entertaining some guests, fearless of danger, or perhaps by way of hiding his fears, when the soldiers entered and announced to him the tribune's summons. He rose without a moment's delay, and every preparation was at once made. He shut himself into his chamber; a physician was at his side; his veins were opened; with life still strong in him, he was carried into a bath, and plunged into warm water, without uttering a word of pity for himself. Meanwhile the guards surrounded those who had sat at his table, and it was only at a late hour of the night that they were dismissed, when Nero, having pictured to himself and laughed over their terror at the expectation of a fatal end to their banquet, said that they had suffered enough punishment for the consul's entertainment.

Next he ordered the destruction of Marcus Annaeus Lucanus. As the blood flowed freely from him, and he felt a chill creeping through his feet and hands, and the life gradually ebbing from his extremities, though the heart was still warm and he retained his mental power, Lucanus recalled some poetry he had composed in which he had told the story of a wounded soldier dying a similar kind of death, and he recited the very lines. These were his last words. After him, Senecio, Quintianus, and Scaevinus perished, not in the manner expected from the past effeminacy of their life, and then the remaining conspirators, without deed or word deserving record.

Rome all this time was thronged with funerals, the Capitol with sacrificial victims. One after another, on the destruction of a brother, a kinsman, or a friend, would return thanks to the gods, deck his house with laurels, prostrate himself at the knees of the emperor, and weary his hand with kisses. He, in the belief that this was rejoicing, rewarded with impunity the prompt informations of Antonius Natalis and Cervarius Proculus. Milichus was enriched with gifts and assumed in its Greek equivalent the name of Saviour. Of the tribunes, Gavius Silvanus, though acquitted, perished by his own hand; Statius Proximus threw away the benefit of the pardon he had accepted from the emperor by the folly of his end. Cornelius Martialis, Flavius Nepos, Statius Domitius were then deprived of the tribuneship, on the ground, not of actually hating the emperor, but of having the credit of it. Novius Priscus, as Seneca's friend, Glitius Gallus, and Annius Pollio, as men disgraced rather than convicted, escaped with sentences of banishment. Priscus and Gallus were accompanied respectively by their wives, Artoria Flaccilla and Egnatia Maximilla. The latter possessed at first a great fortune, still unimpaired, and was subsequently deprived of it, both which circumstances enhanced her fame.

Rufius Crispinus too was banished, on the opportune pretext of the conspiracy, but he was in fact hated by Nero, because he had once been Poppaea's husband. It was the splendour of their name which drove Verginius Flavus and Musonius Rufus into exile. Verginius encouraged the studies of our youth by his eloquence; Rufus by the teachings of philosophy. Cluvidienus Quietus, Julius Agrippa, Blitius Catulinus, Petronius Priscus, Julius Altinus, mere rank and file, so to say, had islands in the Aegean Sea assigned to them. Caedicia, the wife of Scaevinus, and Caesonius Maximus were forbidden to live in Italy, their penalty being the only proof they had of having been accused. Atilla, the mother of Annaeus Lucanus, without either acquittal or punishment, was simply ignored.

All this having been completed, Nero assembled the troops and distributed two thousand sesterces to every common soldier, with an addition of as much corn without payment, as they had previously the use of at the market price. Then, as if he was going to describe successes in war, he summoned the Senate, and awarded triumphal honours to Petronius Turpilianus, an ex-consul, to Cocceius Nerva, praetor-elect, and to Tigellinus, commander of the praetorians. Tigellinus and Nerva he so distinguished as to place busts of them in the palace in addition to triumphal statues in the Forum. He granted a consul's decorations to Nymphidius, on whose origin, as he now appears for the first time, I will briefly touch. For he too will be a part of Rome's calamities.

The son of a freedwoman, who had prostituted a handsome person among the slaves and freedmen of the emperors, he gave out that he was the offspring of Caius Caesar, for he happened to be of tall stature and to have a fierce look, or possibly Caius Caesar, who liked even harlots, had also amused himself with the man's mother.

Nero meanwhile summoned the Senate, addressed them in a speech, and further added a proclamation to the people, with the evidence which had been entered on records, and the confessions of the condemned. He was indeed perpetually under the lash of popular talk, which said that he had destroyed men perfectly innocent out of jealously or fear. However, that a conspiracy was begun, matured, and conclusively proved was not doubted at the time by those who took pains to ascertain the truth, and is admitted by those who after Nero's death returned to the capital. When every one in the Senate, those especially who had most cause to mourn, abased himself in flattery, Salienus Clemens denounced Junius Gallio, who was terror-stricken at his brother Seneca's death and was pleading for his life. He called him an enemy and traitor to the State, till the unanimous voice of the senators deterred him from perverting public miseries into an occasion for a personal resentment, and thus importing fresh bitterness into what by the prince's clemency had been hushed up or forgotten.

Then offerings and thanksgivings to the gods were decreed, with special honours to the Sun, who has an ancient temple in the circus where the crime was planned, as having revealed by his power the secrets of the conspiracy. The games too of Ceres in the circus were to be celebrated with more horse-races, and the month of April was to be called after the name of Nero. A temple also was to be erected to Safety, on the spot whence Scaevinus had taken his dagger. The emperor himself dedicated the weapon in the temple of the capital, and inscribed on it, "To Jupiter the Avenger." This passed without notice at the moment, but after the war of Julius Vindex it was construed as an omen and presage of impending vengeance. I find in the registers of the Senate that Cerialis Anicius, consul-elect, proposed a motion that a temple should as soon as possible be built at the public expense to the Divine Nero. He implied indeed by this proposal that the prince had transcended all mortal grandeur and deserved the adoration of mankind. Some however interpreted it as an omen of his death, seeing that divine honours are not paid to an emperor till he has ceased to live among men.

THE HISTORY

Early in this year Titus Caesar, who had been selected by his father to complete the subjugation of Judaea, and who had gained distinction as a soldier while both were still subjects, began to rise in power and reputation, as armies and provinces emulated each other in their attachment to him. The young man himself, anxious to be thought superior to his station, was ever displaying his gracefulness and his energy in war. By his courtesy and affability he called forth a willing obedience, and he often mixed with the common soldiers, while working or marching, without impairing his dignity as general. He found in Judaea three legions, the 5th, the 10th, and the 15th, all old troops of Vespasian's. To these he added the 12th from Syria, and some men belonging to the 18th and 3rd, whom he had withdrawn from Alexandria. This force was accompanied by twenty cohorts of allied troops and eight squadrons of cavalry, by the two kings Agrippa and Sohemus, by the auxiliary forces of king Antiochus, by a strong contingent of Arabs, who hated the Jews with the usual hatred of neighbours, and, lastly, by many persons brought from the capital and from Italy by private hopes of securing the yet unengaged affections of the Prince. With this force Titus entered the enemy's territory, preserving strict order on his march, reconnoitring every spot, and always ready to give battle. At last he encamped near Jerusalem.

As I am about to relate the last days of a famous city, it seems appropriate to throw some light on its origin.

Some say that the Jews were fugitives from the island of Crete, who settled on the nearest coast of Africa about the time when Saturn was driven from his throne by the power of Jupiter. Evidence of this is sought in the name. There is a famous mountain in Crete called Ida; the neighbouring tribe, the Idaei, came to be called Judaei by a barbarous lengthening of the national name. Others assert that in the reign of Isis the overflowing population of Egypt, led by Hierosolymus and Judas, discharged itself into the neighbouring countries. Many, again, say that they were a race of Ethiopian origin, who in the time of king Cepheus were driven by fear and hatred of their neighbours to seek a new dwelling-place. Others describe them as an Assyrian horde who, not having sufficient territory, took possession of part of Egypt, and founded cities of

246

their own in what is called the Hebrew country, lying on the borders of
Syria. Others, again, assign a very distinguished origin to the Jews, alleging that they were the Solymi, a nation celebrated in the poems of Homer,
who called the city which they founded Hierosolyma after their own
name.

Most writers, however, agree in stating that once a disease, which
horribly disfigured the body, broke out over Egypt; that king Bocchoris,
seeking a remedy, consulted the oracle of Hammon, and was bidden to
cleanse his realm, and to convey into some foreign land this race detested
by the gods. The people, who had been collected after diligent search,
finding themselves left in a desert, sat for the most part in a stupor of
grief, till one of the exiles, Moyses by name, warned them not to look for
any relief from God or man, forsaken as they were of both, but to trust
to themselves, taking for their heaven-sent leader that man who should
first help them to be quit of their present misery. They agreed, and in
utter ignorance began to advance at random. Nothing, however, distressed them so much as the scarcity of water, and they had sunk ready
to perish in all directions over the plain, when a herd of wild asses was
seen to retire from their pasture to a rock shaded by trees. Moyses followed them, and, guided by the appearance of a grassy spot, discovered
an abundant spring of water. This furnished relief. After a continuous
journey for six days, on the seventh they possessed themselves of a country, from which they expelled the inhabitants, and in which they
founded a city and a temple.

Moyses, wishing to secure for the future his authority over the nation,
gave them a novel form of worship, opposed to all that is practised by
other men. Things sacred with us, with them have no sanctity, while they
allow what with us is forbidden. In their holy place they have consecrated an image of the animal by whose guidance they found deliverance
from their long and thirsty wanderings. They slay the ram, seemingly in
derision of Hammon, and they sacrifice the ox, because the Egyptians
worship it as Apis. They abstain from swine's flesh, in consideration of
what they suffered when they were infected by the leprosy to which this
animal is liable. By their frequent fasts they still bear witness to the long
hunger of former days, and the Jewish bread, made without leaven, is
retained as a memorial of their hurried seizure of corn. We are told that
the rest of the seventh day was adopted, because this day brought with
it a termination of their toils; after a while the charm of indolence be-
guiled them into giving up the seventh year also to inaction. But others
say that it is an observance in honour of Saturn, either from the primitive
elements of their faith having been transmitted from the Idaei, who are
said to have shared the flight of that God, and to have founded the race,
or from the circumstance that of the seven stars which rule the destinies

of men Saturn moves in the highest orbit and with the mightiest power, and that many of the heavenly bodies complete their revolutions and courses in multiples of seven.

This worship, however introduced, is upheld by its antiquity; all their other customs, which are at once perverse and disgusting, owe their strength to their very badness. The most degraded out of other races, scorning their national beliefs, brought to them their contributions and presents. This augmented the wealth of the Jews, as also did the fact, that among themselves they are inflexibly honest and ever ready to show compassion, though they regard the rest of mankind with all the hatred of enemies. They sit apart at meals, they sleep apart, and though, as a nation, they are singularly prone to lust, they abstain from intercourse with foreign women; among themselves nothing is unlawful. Circumcision was adopted by them as a mark of difference from other men. Those who come over to their religion adopt the practice, and have this lesson first instilled into them, to despise all gods, to disown their country, and set at nought parents, children, and brethren. Still they provide for the increase of their numbers. It is a crime among them to kill any newly-born infant. They hold that the souls of all who perish in battle or by the hands of the executioner are immortal. Hence a passion for propagating their race and a contempt for death. They are wont to bury rather than to burn their dead, following in this the Egyptian custom; they bestow the same care on the dead, and they hold the same belief about the lower world. Quite different is their faith about things divine. The Egyptians worship many animals and images of monstrous form; the Jews have purely mental conceptions of Deity, as one in essence. They call those profane who make representations of God in human shape out of perishable materials. They believe that Being to be supreme and eternal, neither capable of representation, nor of decay. They therefore do not allow any images to stand in their cities, much less in their temples. This flattery is not paid to their kings, nor this honour to our Emperors. From the fact, however, that their priests used to chant to the music of flutes and cymbals, and to wear garlands of ivy, and that a golden vine was found in the temple, some have thought that they worshipped Father Liber, the conqueror of the East, though their institutions do not by any means harmonize with the theory; for Liber established a festive and cheerful worship, while the Jewish religion is tasteless and mean.

Eastward the country is bounded by Arabia; to the south lies Egypt; on the west are Phoenicia and the Mediterranean. Northward it commands an extensive prospect over Syria. The inhabitants are healthy and able to bear fatigue. Rain is uncommon, but the soil is fertile. Its products resemble our own. They have, besides, the balsam-tree and the palm. The palm-groves are tall and graceful. The balsam is a shrub; each branch, as it fills with sap, may be pierced with a fragment of stone or pottery. If steel is employed, the veins shrink up. The sap is used by physicians. Libanus is the principal mountain, and has, strange to say, amidst these burning heats, a summit shaded with trees and never deserted by its snows. The same range supplies and sends forth the stream of the Jordan. This river does not discharge itself into the sea, but flows entire through two lakes, and is lost in the third. This is a lake of vast circumference; it resembles the sea, but is more nauseous in taste; it breeds pestilence among those who live near by its noisome odour; it cannot be moved by the wind, and it affords no home either to fish or water-birds. These strange waters support what is thrown upon them, as on a solid surface, and all persons, whether they can swim or no, are equally buoyed up by the waves. At a certain season of the year the lake throws up bitumen, and the method of collecting it has been taught by that experience which teaches all other arts. It is naturally a fluid of dark colour; when vinegar is sprinkled upon it, it coagulates and floats upon the surface. Those whose business it is take it with the hand, and draw it on to the deck of the boat; it then continues of itself to flow in and lade the vessel till the stream is cut off. Nor can this be done by any instrument of brass or iron. It shrinks from blood or any cloth stained by the menstrua of women. Such is the account of old authors; but those who know the country say that the bitumen moves in heaving masses on the water, that it is drawn by hand to the shore, and that there, when dried by the evaporation of the earth and the power of the sun, it is cut into pieces with axes and wedges just as timber or stone would be.

Nor far from this lake lies a plain, once fertile, they say, and the site of great cities, but afterwards struck by lightning and consumed. Of this event, they declare, traces still remain, for the soil, which is scorched in appearance, has lost its productive power. Everything that grows spontaneously, as well as what is planted by hand, either when the leaf or flower have been developed, or after maturing in the usual form, becomes black and rotten, and crumbles into a kind of dust. I am ready to allow, on the one hand that cities, once famous, may have been consumed by fire from heaven, while, on the other, I imagine that the earth is infected by the exhalations of the lake, that the surrounding air is tainted, and that thus the growth of harvest and the fruits of autumn decay under the equally noxious influences of soil and climate. The river Belus also flows into the Jewish sea. About its mouth is a kind of sand which is collected, mixed with nitre, and fused into glass. This shore is of limited extent, but furnishes an inexhaustible supply to the exporter.

A great part of Judaea consists of scattered villages. They have also towns. Jerusalem is the capital. There stood a temple of immense wealth. First came the city with its fortifications, then the royal palace, then, within the innermost defences, the temple itself. Only the Jew might approach the gates; all but priests were forbidden to pass the threshold. While the East was under the sway of the Assyrians, the Medes, and the Persians, Jews were the most contemptible of the subject tribes. When the Macedonians became supreme, King Antiochus strove to destroy the national superstition, and to introduce Greek civilization, but was prevented by his war with the Parthians from at all improving this vilest of nations; for at this time the revolt of Arsaces had taken place. The Macedonian power was now weak, while the Parthian had not yet reached its full strength, and, as the Romans were still far off, the Jews chose kings for themselves. Expelled by the fickle populace, and regaining their throne by force of arms, these princes, while they ventured on the wholesale banishment of their subjects, on the destruction of cities, on the murder of brothers, wives, and parents, and the other usual atrocities of despots, fostered the national superstition by appropriating the dignity of the priesthood as the support of their political power.

Cneius Pompeius was the first of our countrymen to subdue the Jews. Availing himself of the right of conquest, he entered the temple. Thus it became commonly known that the place stood empty with no similitude of gods within, and that the shrine had nothing to reveal. The walls of Jerusalem were destroyed, the temple was left standing. After these provinces had fallen, in the course of our civil wars, into the hands of Marcus Antonius, Pacorus, king of the Parthians, seized Judaea. He was slain by Publius Ventidius, and the Parthians were driven back over the Euphrates. Caius Sosius reduced the Jews to subjection. The royal power, which had been bestowed by Antony on Herod, was augmented by the victorious Augustus. On Herod's death, one Simon, without waiting for the approbation of the Emperor, usurped the title of king. He was punished by Quintilius Varus then governor of Syria, and the nation, with its liberties curtailed, was divided into three provinces under the sons of Herod. Under Tiberius all was quiet. But when the Jews were ordered by Caligula to set up his statue in the temple, they preferred the alternative of war. The death of the Emperor put an end to the disturbance. The kings were either dead, or reduced to insignificance, when Claudius entrusted the province of Judaea to the Roman Knights or to his own freedmen, one of whom, Antonius Felix, indulging in every kind of barbarity and lust, exercised the power of a king in the spirit of a slave. He had married Drusilla, the granddaughter of Antony and Cleopatra, and so was the grandson-in-law, as Claudius was the grandson, of Antony.

Yet the endurance of the Jews lasted till Gessius Florus was procurator. In his time the war broke out. Cestius Gallus, legate of Syria, who attempted to crush it, had to fight several battles, generally with ill-success. Cestius dying, either in the course of nature, or from vexation, Vespasian was sent by Nero, and by help of his good fortune, his high reputation, and his excellent subordinates, succeeded within the space of two summers in occupying with his victorious army the whole of the level country and all the cities, except Jerusalem. The following year had been wholly taken up with civil strife, and had passed, as far as the Jews were concerned, in inaction. Peace having been established in Italy, foreign affairs were once more remembered. Our indignation was heightened by the circumstance that the Jews alone had not submitted. At the same time it was held to be more expedient, in reference to the possible results and contingencies of the new reign, that Titus should remain with the army.

Accordingly he pitched his camp, as I have related, before the walls of Jerusalem, and displayed his legions in order of battle.

The Jews formed their line close under their walls, whence, if successful, they might venture to advance, and where, if repulsed, they had a refuge at hand. The cavalry with some light infantry was sent to attack them, and fought without any decisive result. Shortly afterwards the enemy retreated. During the following days they fought a series of engagements in front of the gates, till they were driven within the walls by continual defeats. The Romans then began to prepare for an assault. It seemed beneath them to await the result of famine. The army demanded the more perilous alternative, some prompted by courage, many by sheer ferocity and greed of gain. Titus himself had Rome with all its wealth and pleasures before his eyes. Jerusalem must fall at once, or it would delay his enjoyment of them. But the commanding situation of the city had been strengthened by enormous works which would have been a thorough defence even for level ground. Two hills of great height were fenced in by walls which had been skilfully obliqued or bent inwards, in such a manner that the flank of an assailant was exposed to missiles. The rock terminated in a precipice; the towers were raised to a height of sixty feet, where the hill lent its aid to the fortifications, where the ground fell, to a height of one hundred and twenty. They had a marvellous appearance, and to a distant spectator seemed to be of uniform elevation. Within were other walls surrounding the palace, and, rising to a conspicuous height, the tower Antonia, so called by Herod, in honour of Marcus Antonius.

The temple resembled a citadel, and had its own walls, which were more laboriously constructed than the others. Even the colonnades with which it was surrounded formed an admirable outwork. It contained an inexhaustible spring; there were subterranean excavations in the hill, and tanks and cisterns for holding rain water. The founders of the state had foreseen that frequent wars would result from the singularity of its customs, and so had made every provision against the most protracted

siege. After the capture of their city by Pompey, experience and apprehension taught them much. Availing themselves of the sordid policy of
the Claudian era to purchase the right of fortification, they raised in time
of peace such walls as were suited for war. Their numbers were increased by a vast rabble collected from the overthrow of the other cities.
All the most obstinate rebels had escaped into the place, and perpetual
seditions were the consequence. There were three generals, and as many
armies. Simon held the outer and larger circuit of walls. John, also called
Bargioras, occupied the middle city. Eleazar had fortified the temple.
John and Simon were strong in numbers and equipment, Eleazar in
position. There were continual skirmishes, surprises, and incendiary
fires, and a vast quantity of corn was burnt. Before long John sent some
emissaries, who, under pretence of sacrificing, slaughtered Eleazar and
his partisans, and gained possession of the temple. The city was thus
divided between two factions, till, as the Romans approached, war with
the foreigner brought about a reconciliation.

Prodigies had occurred, which this nation, prone to superstition, but
hating all religious rites, did not deem it lawful to expiate by offering and
sacrifice. There had been seen hosts joining battle in the skies, the fiery
gleam of arms, the temple illuminated by a sudden radiance from the
clouds. The doors of the inner shrine were suddenly thrown open, and a
voice of more than mortal tone was heard to cry that the Gods were
departing. At the same instant there was a mighty stir as of departure.
Some few put a fearful meaning on these events, but in most there was
a firm persuasion, that in the ancient records of their priests was contained a prediction of how at this very time the East was to grow powerful, and rulers, coming from Judaea, were to acquire universal empire.
These mysterious prophecies had pointed to Vespasian and Titus, but the
common people, with the usual blindness of ambition, had interpreted
these mighty destinies of themselves, and could not be brought even by
disasters to believe the truth. I have heard that the total number of the
besieged, of every age and both sexes, amounted to six hundred thousand.
All who were able bore arms, and a number, more than proportionate to
the population, had the courage to do so. Men and women showed equal
resolution, and life seemed more terrible than death, if they were to be
forced to leave their country. Such was this city and nation; and Titus
Caesar, seeing that the position forbade an assault or any of the more
rapid operations of war, determined to proceed by earthworks and covered approaches. The legions had their respective duties assigned to
them, and there was a cessation from fighting, till all the inventions, used
in ancient warfare, or devised by modern ingenuity for the reduction of
cities, were constructed. . . .

Eusebius

8

Eusebius, "the father of ecclesiastical history," was born c. 260, probably in the city of Caesarea in Palestine. We know that as a young man he was prominent in the household of Pamphilus of Caesarea, a teacher and theologian who had assembled a large library upon which Eusebius was later to draw in writing his histories. Eusebius entered the priesthood and after some years of travel and imprisonment and threatened martyrdom during the decade of Diocletian's persecution of Christians (303–313) he was consecrated Bishop of Caesarea (314). In 325 he assisted at the Council of Nicaea where he played a most important role in moderating the violence of the theological controversies then racking the Church. At that time, too, he was apparently the ally and counselor of the great convert to Christianity, the Emperor Constantine, at whose side he sat during meetings of the Council and whose friendship he maintained until Constantine's death in 337. Eusebius himself died shortly after his friend and patron c. 339.

In the midst of his very active career Eusebius had managed an impressive literary achievement. He wrote numerous works against pagans and heretics, many theological treatises, and essays of Biblical exegesis, forty-six works in all, of which only a small number have come down to us. Among the books we have are two histories: the *Chronicle,* written in 303 but repeatedly revised down to 325, and *The History of the Church* (or *The Ecclesiastical History,* as it is variously called), written and re-edited betweed 311 and 325. The *Chronicle* is Eusebius' contribution to historical chronology for he correctly perceived that an accurate chronology is essential to historical studies. Eusebius drew upon classical and Christian historians and chronographers and assembled a composite chronology, arranged in parallel columns, of all the ancient kingdoms. The historical development which these columns appear to depict is one of gradual, ineluctable movement toward the Christian era. History, mathematics, geometry, all neatly compressed within this

253

Chronicle, reveal the Providence of God at work guaranteeing the triumph of Christianity.

Eusebius, in the *Chronicle,* sought to demonstrate the Christian goal of history not through appeals to received authority or pious hopes but rather through the presentation of historical facts. This attitude was carried over into his *History of the Church.* Eusebius was conscious of the fact that the Church in his time had undergone and survived intact a period of harsh persecution. He himself had suffered for his beliefs and had yet kept the faith. But the age of persecution, the testing time, had given way first to an age of toleration, then to one of official acceptance: from Church Persecuted to Church Triumphant. The historical record, Eusebius could legitimately maintain, surely indicated "the gracious and favoring interposition of God." Eusebius thus turned with confidence to secular history, locating the Christian Church within the context of the Roman Empire. In his *History of the Church,* he relies heavily on the Bible, particularly the New Testament, but he also utilizes such historians as Josephus, Tacitus, and Philo. The great library of Pamphilus served him in good stead and we know he used the church library in Jerusalem and of the royal archives at Edessa. Convinced that history was on his side, Eusebius approached his sources with a scholarly reserve and a respect for methodological correctnesss not otherwise to be expected from a high official of the Church writing of the institution whose mission was his life. He collected the important documents pertinent to his *History,* weaving many of them into his narrative; he exercised notable caution whenever his sources presented him improbable or contradictory accounts; he sought after and often enough attained accuracy in his own account. The *History of the Church* is an "Apology" but it is a critical apology, the work of a historian *engagé.* Eusebius could afford to be critical, for looking at history, he drew comfort from it. His church had weathered the storm, Christianity had been adopted by the Roman Emperors and honored by "the most populous of all nations, and most pious towards God, alike indestructible and invincible in that it ever finds help from God." In this hour of triumph, Eusebius composed The *History of the Church,* confidently placing Christianity securely within the traditional context of the "eternal" Roman Empire. Before the century was out, however, another great churchman and historian, Augustine, was to find it necessary to recast the history, and, more, the interpretation of Eusebius. But he was to build on the achievement of that "most important and reliable historian of the ancient Church."

Selected Bibliography

Arnaldo Momigliano has edited a collection of articles in *The Conflict Between Paganism and Christianity in the Fourth Century* (1963) which illuminates many of the problems that Eusebius addressed himself to. See especially Momigliano's essay, "Pagan and Christian Historiography in the Fourth Century A.D.," pp. 79–99. G. A. Williamson's introduction to his translation of Eusebius' *The History of the Church from Christ to Constantine* (1965) provides a good account of the man and his work. Williamson quotes with approval Guy Schofield's opinion of Eusebius as "the most important and reliable historian of the ancient church." Williamson's eulogistic approach may be complemented by Kirsopp Lake's introduction to his translation of *The Ecclesiastical History* (2 vols., 1926) and by the entry in Henry Wace and William Piercy, eds., *A Dictionary of Christian Biography and Literature* (1911). James T. Shotwell, *An Introduction to the History of History* (New York, 1936), has a perceptive and informative section on Eusebius. Heinrich Kraft has edited a German translation (by Philipp Haeuser [1932], revised by Hans Gartner), *Eusebius von Caesara, Kirchengeschichte* (1957), which includes a very good bibliography of the recent literature on Eusebius. The present selections are from the Kirsopp Lake, H. J. Lawlor, and J. E. L. Oulton translation (1894). Jean Sirenelli offers some valuable insights in his *Les vues historiques d'Eusèbe de Césarée durant la période prénicéene.* (1961; see the review in *History and Theory,* III, no. 3, 1963, pp. 318–323.)

THE ECCLESIASTICAL HISTORY

. . . , during the whole period of ten years of persecution there was no respite. . . . The seas were unnavigable, and none, no matter whence they sailed, could escape being subjected to all kinds of torments: stretched on the rack and having their sides torn, and being examined under all sorts of tortures in case they should possibly be coming from the enemy of the contrary part, and in the end subjected to crucifixion or punishment by fire. Moreover, every place was busy with the preparation of shields and armour, the getting ready of darts and spears and other warlike accoutrements, and of triremes and naval gear; and no one expected anything but an enemy attack all day long. And subsequently the famine and the pestilence broke out among them, about which we shall recount what is necessary at the proper time.

Such was the state of affairs that continued throughout the whole persecution; which came completely to an end, by the grace of God, in the tenth year, though indeed it began to abate after the eighth year. For when the divine and heavenly grace showed that it watched over us with kindly and propitious regard, then indeed our rulers also, those very persons who had long time committed acts of war against us, changed their mind in the most marvellous manner, and gave utterance to a recantation, quenching the fire of persecution that had blazed so furiously, by means of merciful edicts and the most humane ordinances. But this was not due to any human agency nor to the pity, as one might say, or humanity of the rulers. Far from it. For from the beginning up to the time they were daily plotting further and severer measures against us; from time to time they were inventing fresh assaults upon us by means of still more varied devices. But it was due to the manifestation of the Divine Providence itself, which, while it became reconciled to the people, attacked the perpetrator of these evils, and was wroth with him as the chief author of the wickedness of the persecution as a whole. For verily, though it was destined that these things should come to pass as a divine judgement, yet the Scripture says, "Woe, through whomsoever the

From *The Ecclesiastical History,* translated by Kirsopp Lake, H. J. Lawlor, and J. E. L. Oulton (New York, G. P. Putnam's Sons, 1926–1932). Reprinted by permission of the publisher. Vol. II, pp. 313–321, 329–351, 357–365, 371–375, 379–387.

offence cometh." A divinely-sent punishment, I say, executed vengeance upon him, beginning at his very flesh and proceeding to the soul. For all at once an abscess appeared in the midst of his privy parts, then a deeply-seated fistular ulcer; which could not be cured and ate their way into the very midst of his entrails. Hence there sprang an innumerable multitude of worms, and a deadly stench was given off, since the entire bulk of his members had, through gluttony, even before the disease, been changed into an excessive quantity of soft fat, which then became putrid and presented an intolerable and most fearful sight to those that came near it. As for the physicians, some of them were wholly unable to endure the exceeding and unearthly stench, and were butchered; others, who could not be of any assistance since the whole mass had swollen and reached a point where there was no hope of recovery, were put to death without mercy.

And wrestling with such terrible misfortunes he was conscience-stricken for the cruel deeds he had perpetrated against the godly. Collecting, therefore, his thoughts, he first openly confessed to the God of the universe; then he called those around him, and commanded them without delay to cause the persecution against Christians to cease, and by an imperial law and decree to urge them to build their churches and to perform their accustomed rites, offering prayers on the Emperor's behalf. Action immediately followed his word, and imperial ordinances were promulgated in each city, containing the recantation of the [persecution edicts] of our time, after this manner: "The Emperor Caesar Galerius Valerius Maximianus Invictus Augustus, Pontifex Maximus, Germanicus Maximus, Aegyptiacus Maximus, Thebaicus Maximus, Sarmaticus Maximus five times, Persicus Maximus twice, Carpicus Maximus six times, Armeniacus Maximus, Medicus Maximus, Adiabenicus Maximus, holding the Tribunician Power for the twentieth time, Emperor for the nineteenth time, Consul for the eighth, Father of his country, Proconsul: . . . And the Emperor Caesar Flavius Valerius Constantinus Pius Felix Invictus Augustus, Pontifex Maximus, holding the Tribunician Power, Emperor for the fifth time, Consul, Father of his country, Proconsul: [And the Emperor Caesar Valerius Licinianus Licinius Pius Felix Invictus Augustus, Pontifex Maximus, holding the Tribunician Power for the fourth time, Emperor for the third time, Consul, Father of his country, Proconsul: to the people of their provinces, greeting].

"Among the other measures that we frame for the use and profit of the state, it had been our own wish formerly that all things should be set to rights in accordance with the ancient laws and public order of the Romans; and to make provision for this, namely, that the Christians also, such as had abandoned the persuasion of their own ancestors, should return to a sound mind; seeing that through some reasoning they had been possessed of such self-will and seized with such folly that, instead of following the institutions of the ancients, which perchance their own forefathers had formerly established, they made for themselves, and were observing, laws merely in accordance with their own disposition and as each one wished, and were assembling various multitudes in divers places: Therefore when a command of ours soon followed to the intent that they should betake themselves to the institutions of the ancients, very many indeed were subjected to peril, while very many were harassed and endured all kinds of death; And since the majority held to the same folly, and we perceived that they were neither paying the worship due to the gods of heaven nor honouring the god of the Christians; having regard to our clemency and the invariable custom by which we are wont to accord pardon to all men, we thought it right in this case also to extend most willingly our indulgence: That Christians may exist again and build the houses in which they used to assemble, always provided that they do nothing contrary to order. In another letter we shall indicate to the judges how they should proceed. Wherefore, in accordance with this our indulgence, they will be bound to beseech their own god for our welfare, and that of the state, and their own; that in every way both the well being of the state may be secured, and they may be enabled to live free from care in their own homes."

Such is the character of this edict in the Latin tongue, translated into Greek as well as may be. Now it is time to consider carefully what happened subsequently.

The recantation of the imperial will set forth above was promulgated broadcast throughout Asia and in the neighbouring provinces. After this had thus been done, Maximin, the tyrant of the East, a monster of impiety if ever there was one, who had been the bitterest enemy of piety toward the God of the universe, was by no means pleased with what was written, and instead of making known the letter set forth above gave verbal commands to the rulers under him to relax the war against us. For since he might not otherwise gainsay the judgement of his superiors, he put in a corner the law set forth above; and, taking measures how it might never see the light of day in the districts under him, by an oral direction he commanded the rulers under him to relax the persecution against us. And they intimated to each other in writing the terms of the order. Sabinus, for instance, whom they had honoured with the rank of most excellent prefect, made known the Emperor's decision to the provincial governors in a Latin epistle. The translation of the same runs as follows:

"With a most earnest and devoted zeal the Divinity of our most divine masters, the Emperors, has for a long time determined to lead all men's thoughts into the holy and right path of life, so that those also who seemed to follow customs foreign to the Romans should perform the acts of worship due to the immortal gods. But the obstinacy and most unyielding determination of some was carried to such a length, that neither could they be turned back from their own purpose by just reasoning embodied in the order, nor did they fear the punishment that threatened. Since therefore it has come about that many by such conduct endanger themselves, in accordance with the noble piety that is theirs, the Divinity of our masters, the most mighty Emperors, deeming it foreign to their divine purpose that for such a reason they should so greatly endanger these men, gave commandment through my Devotedness to write to thy Intelligence, that if any of the Christians be found following the religion of his nation, thou shouldest set him free from molestation directed against him and from danger, nor shouldest thou deem anyone punishable on this charge, since so long a passage of time has proved that they can in no wise be persuaded to abandon such obstinate conduct. Let it be thy Solicitude's duty, therefore, to write to the curators and the duumvirs and the magistrates of the district of every city, that they may know that it is not beseeming for them to take any further notice of that letter."

Whereupon the rulers of the provinces, having concluded that the purport of what had been written to them was a genuine expression, made known by means of letters the imperial resolve to curators, duumvirs and rural magistrates. And not only did they further these measures by writing, but also much more so by action. With a view to carrying out the imperial will, as many as they kept shut up in prisons for their confession of the Deity they brought into the light of day and set free, releasing such of these same persons as were consigned to the mines for punishment. For this, in truth, they mistakenly conceived to be the Emperor's wish. And when these things had thus been carried into effect, as though some light shined forth all at once out of a gloomy night, one might see churches thronged in every city, and crowded assemblies, and the rites performed thereat in the customary manner. And every single one of the unbelieving heathen was in no small degree amazed at these happenings, marvelling at the miracle of so great a change, and extolling the Christians' God as alone great and true. Of our own people, those who had faithfully and bravely contended throughout the conflict of persecutions once more resumed their confident bearing in the sight of all; but those whose faith had been diseased and souls storm-tost eagerly strove for their own healing, beseeching and begging the strong for the right hand of safety, and supplicating God to be merciful to them. And then also the noble champions of godliness, freed from their evil plight in the mines, returned to their own homes. Proudly and joyously they went through every city, full of unspeakable mirth and a boldness that cannot even be expressed in words. Yea, thronging crowds of men went on their journey, praising God in the midst of thoroughfares and market-places with songs and psalms; and you might see those who shortly before had been prisoners undergoing the harshest punishment and driven from their native lands, now regaining with gay and joyful countenances their own hearths so that even those who formerly were thirsting for our blood, seeing the wondrous thing contrary to all expectation, rejoiced with us at what had happened.

This the tyrant could no longer endure, hater as he was of that which is good, and plotter against every virtuous man (he was the ruler, as we said, of the eastern parts); nor did he suffer matters thus to be carried on for six entire months. Numerous, therefore, were his devices to overturn the peace: at first he attempted on some pretext to shut us out from assembling in the cemeteries, then through the medium of certain evil men he sent embassies to himself against us, having urged the citizens of Antioch to ask that they might obtain from him, as a very great boon, that he should in no wise permit any of the Christians to inhabit their land, and to contrive that others should make the same suggestion. The originator of all this sprang up at Antioch itself in the person of Theotecnus, a clever cheat and an evil man, and quite unlike his name. He was accounted to hold the post of curator in the city.

This man, then, many times took the field against us; and, having been at pains by every method to hunt our people out of hiding-places as if they were unholy thieves, having employed every device to slander and accuse us, having been the cause even of death to countless numbers, he ended by erecting a statue of Zeus the Befriender with certain juggleries and sorceries, and having devised unhallowed rites for it and ill-omened initiations and abominable purifications, he exhibited his wonder-working by what oracles he pleased, even in the Emperor's presence. And moreover this fellow, in order to flatter and please him who was ruling, stirred up the demon against the Christians, and said that the god, forsooth, had given orders that the Christians should be driven away beyond the borders of the city and country round about, since they were his enemies.

This man was the first to act thus of set purpose, and all the other officials who lived in the cities under the same rule hastened to make a like decision, the provincial governors having seen at a glance that it was pleasing to the Emperor, and having suggested to their subjects to do the very same thing. And when the tyrant had given a most willing assent to their petitions by a rescript, once more the persecution against us was rekindled.

Maximin himself appointed as priests of the images in each city and, moreover, as high priests, those who were especially distinguished in the public services and had made their mark in the entire course thereof.

These persons brought great zeal to bear on the worship of the gods whom they served. Certainly, the outlandish superstition of the ruler was inducing, in a word, all under him, both governors and governed, to do everything against us in order to secure his favour; in return for the benefits which they thought to secure from him, they bestowed upon him this greatest of boons, namely, to thirst for our blood and to display some more novel tokens of malice toward us.

Having forged, to be sure, Memoirs of Pilate and our Saviour, full of every kind of blasphemy against Christ, with the approval of their chief they sent them round to every part of his dominions, with edicts that they should be exhibited openly for everyone to see in every place, both town and country, and that the primary teachers should give them to the children, instead of lessons, for study and committal to memory.

While this was thus being carried out, another person, a commander, whom the Romans style *dux,* caused certain infamous women to be abducted from the market-place at Damascus in Phoenicia, and, by continually threatening them with the infliction of tortures, compelled them to state in writing that they were once actually Christians, and privy to their unhallowed deeds, and that the Christians practised in the very churches lewdness and everything else that he wished these women to say in defamation of our faith. He also made a memorandum of their words and communicated it to the Emperor, and moreover at his command published this document also in every place and city.

But not long afterwards he, that is to say, the commander, died by his own hand, and thus paid the penalty for his wickedness.

But as for us, banishments and severe persecutions were again renewed, and the rulers in every province once more rose up cruelly against us, with the result that some of those eminent in the divine Word were taken, and received the sentence of death without mercy. . . .

At this point I think it necessary to insert this same document of Maximin that was set up on tablets, so as to make manifest at once the boastful, overweening arrogance of this hater of God, and the divine Justice that followed close upon his heels with its sleepless hatred of the evil in wicked men. It was this which smote him; and not long afterwards he reversed his policy with regard to us, and made a decree by laws in writing.

> *Copy of a Translation of the Rescript of Maximin in answer to the Petitions against us, taken from the Tablet at Tyre.*
> Now at length, the feeble boldness of the human mind has shaken off and dispersed all blinding mists of error, that error which hitherto was attacking the senses of men not so much wicked as wretched, and was wrapping them in the baneful darkness of ignorance; and it has been enabled to recognize that it is governed and established by the benevolent providence of the immortal gods.

It passes belief to say how grateful, how exceeding pleasant and agreeable, it has proved to us that you have given a very great proof of your godly disposition; since even before this none could be ignorant what regard and piety you were displaying towards the immortal gods, in whom is manifested a faith, not of bare and empty words, but constant and admirable in its noble deeds. Wherefore your city might worthily be called a temple and dwelling-place of the immortal gods. . . .

After other remarks he adds:

Let them behold in the broad plains the crops already ripe with waving ears of corn, the meadows, thanks to opportune rains, brilliant with plants and flowers, and the weather that has been granted us temperate and very mild; further, let all rejoice since through our piety, through the sacrifices and veneration we have rendered, the most powerful and intractable air has been propitiated, and let them take pleasure in that they therefore enjoy the most serene peace securely and in quiet. And let as many as have been wholly rescued from that blind folly and error and returned to a right and goodly frame of mind rejoice indeed the more, as if they were delivered from an unexpected hurricane or severe illness and were reaping life's sweet enjoyment for the future. But if they persist in their accursed folly, let them be separated and driven far away from your city and neighbourhood, even as you requested; that so, in accordance with your praiseworthy zeal in this respect, your city may be separated from all pollution and impiety, and, following its natural desire, may respond with due reverence to the worship of the immortal gods.

And that you may know how pleasing this your request has been to us, and how fully disposed to benevolence our soul is, of its own accord apart from petitions and entreaties: we permit your Devotedness to ask whatsoever bounty you wish, in return for this your godly intent. And now let it be your resolve so to do and receive. For you will obtain your bounty without delay, the granting of which to your city will furnish a testimony for evermore of our godly piety towards the immortal gods, and a proof to your sons and descendants that you have met with the due meed of reward from our benevolence on account of these your principles of conduct.

This was emblazoned against us in every province, excluding every ray of hope from our condition, at least as far as human help is concerned; so that, in accordance with the divine oracle itself, if possible even the elect themselves should be caused to stumble at these things. In truth, expectation was already almost failing in very many souls, when all at once, while those serving the writ set forth against us were on their way and had not yet finished their journey in some districts, the Champion of His own Church, even God, stopping, as it were, the proud boasting of the tyrant against us, displayed His heavenly aid on our behalf.

The customary rains, indeed, and showers of the then prevailing winter season were withholding their usual downpour upon the earth, and we were visited with an unexpected famine, and on top of this a plague and an outbreak of another kind of disease. This latter was an ulcer, which on account of its fiery character was called an anthrax. Spreading as it did over the entire body it used to endanger greatly its victims; but it was the eyes that it marked out for special attack, and so it was the means of blinding numbers of men as well as women and children.

In addition to this, the tyrant had the further trouble of the war against the Armenians, men who from ancient times had been friends and allies of the Romans; but as they were Christians and exceedingly earnest in their piety towards the Diety, this hater of God, by attempting to compel them to sacrifice to idols and demons, made of them foes instead of friends, and enemies instead of allies.

The fact that all these things came together all at once, at one and the same time, served to refute utterly the tyrant's insolent boasting against the Deity; . . .

Such were the wages received for the proud boasting of Maximin and for the petitions presented by the cities against us; while the proofs of the Christians' zeal and piety in every respect were manifest to all the heathen. For example, they alone in such an evil state of affairs gave practical evidence of their sympathy and humanity: all day long some of them would diligently persevere in performing the last offices for the dying and burying them (for there were countless numbers, and no one to look after them); while others would gather together in a single assemblage the multitude of those who all throughout the city were wasted with the famine, and distribute bread to them all, so that their action was on all men's lips, and they glorified the God of the Christians, and, convinced by the deeds themselves, acknowledged that they alone were truly pious and God-fearing.

After these things were thus accomplished, God, the great and heavenly Champion of the Christians, when He had displayed His threatening and wrath against all men by the aforesaid means, in return for their exceeding great attacks against us, once again restored to us the bright and kindly radiance of His providential care for us. Most marvellously, as in a thick darkness, He caused the light of peace to shine upon us from Himself, and made it manifest to all that God Himself had been watching over our affairs continually, at times scourging and in due season correcting His people by means of misfortunes, and again on the other hand after sufficient chastisement showing mercy and goodwill to those who fix their hopes on Him.

Thus in truth Constantine, who, as aforesaid, was Emperor and sprung from an Emperor, pious and sprung from a most pious and in every respect most prudent father, and Licinius, who ranked next to him—both honoured for their understanding and piety—were stirred up by the King of kings, God of the universe and Saviour, two men beloved of God,

against the two most impious tyrants; and when war was formally engaged, God proved their ally in the most wonderful manner, and Maxentius fell at Rome at the hands of Constantine; while he of the East did not
long survive him, for he too perished by a most disgraceful death at the
hands of Licinius, who had not yet become mad.

But to resume. Constantine, the superior of the Emperors in rank and
dignity, was the first to take pity on those subjected to tyranny at Rome;
and, calling in prayer upon God who is in heaven, and His Word, even
Jesus Christ the Saviour of all, as his ally, he advanced in full force,
seeking to secure for the Romans their ancestral liberty. Maxentius, to be
sure, put his trust rather in devices of magic than in the goodwill of his
subjects, and in truth did not dare to advance even beyond the city's gates,
but with an innumerable multitude of heavy-armed soldiers and countless bodies of legionaries secured every place and district and city that
had been reduced to slavery by him in the environs of Rome and in all
Italy. The Emperor, closely relying on the help that comes from God,
attacked the first, second and third of the tyrant's armies, and capturing
them all with ease advanced over a large part of Italy, actually coming
very near to Rome itself. Then, that he might not be compelled because
of the tyrant to fight against Romans, God Himself as if with chains
dragged the tyrant far away from the gates; and those things which were
inscribed long ago in the sacred books against wicked men—to which as
a myth very many gave no faith, yet were they worthy of faith to the
faithful—now by their very clearness found faith, in a word, with all,
faithful and faithless, who had the miracle before their eyes. As, for
example, in the days of Moses himself and the ancient and godly race of
the Hebrews, "Pharaoh's chariots and his host hath he cast into the sea,
his chosen horsemen, even captains, they were sunk in the Red Sea, the
deep covered them"; in the same way also Maxentius and the armed
soldiers and guards around him "went down into the depths like a stone,"
when he turned his back before the God-sent power that was with Constantine, and was crossing the river that lay in his path, which he himself
had bridged right well by joining of boats, and so formed into an engine
of destruction against himself. Wherefore one might say: "He hath made
a pit, and digged it, and shall fall into the ditch which he made. His work
shall return upon his own head, and his wickedness shall come down
upon his own pate."

Thus verily, through the breaking of the bridge over the river, the
passage across collapsed, and down went the boats all at once, men and
all, into the deep; and first of all he himself, that most wicked of men, and
then also the shield-bearers around him, as the divine oracles foretell,
sank as lead in the mighty waters. So that suitably, if not in words, at least
in deeds, like the followers of the great servant Moses, those who had won

the victory by the help of God might in some sort hymn the very same words which were uttered against the wicked tyrant of old, and say: "Let us sing unto the Lord, for gloriously hath he been glorified: the horse and his rider hath he thrown into the sea. The Lord is my strength and protector, he is become my salvation"; and "Who is like unto thee, O Lord, among the gods? who is like thee, glorified in saints, marvellous in praises, doing wonders?" These things, and such as are akin and similar to them, Constantine by his very deeds sang to God the Ruler of all and Author of the victory; then he entered Rome with hymns of triumph, and all the senators and other persons of great note, together with women and quite young children and all the Roman people, received him in a body with beaming countenances to their very heart as a ransomer, saviour and benefactor, with praises and insatiable joy. But he, as one possessed of natural piety towards God, was by no means stirred by their shouts nor uplifted by their praises, for well he knew that his help was from God; and straightway he gave orders that a memorial of the Saviour's Passion should be set up in the hand of his own statue; and indeed when they set him in the most public place in Rome holding the Saviour's sign in his right hand, he bade them engrave this very inscription in these words in the Latin tongue: "By this salutary sign, the true proof of bravery, I saved and delivered your city from the yoke of the tyrant; and moreover I freed and restored to their ancient fame and splendour both the senate and the people of the Romans."

And after this Constantine himself, and with him the emperor Licinius, whose mind was not yet deranged by the madness into which he afterwards fell, having propitiated God as the Author of all their good fortune, both with one will and purpose drew up a most perfect law in the fullest terms on behalf of the Christians; and to Maximin, who was still ruler of the provinces of the East and playing at being their friend, they sent on an account of the marvellous things that God had done for them, as well as of their victory over the tyrant, and the law itself. And he, tyrant that he was, was greatly troubled at the intelligence; but, not wishing to seem to yield to others, nor yet to suppress the command through fear of those who had enjoined it, as if of his own motion he penned perforce this first letter on behalf of the Christians to the governors under him; in which he belies himself, and feigns that he had done things he never had. . . .

Since he issued these commands under the compulsion of necessity and not of his own free will, no one any longer regarded him as truthful or even trustworthy, because after a similar concession he had already on a former occasion showed himself to be changeable and false of dispostion. None of our people therefore dared to convene an assembly or to present himself in public, because the letter did not allow him even this. This alone it laid down, that we should be kept from harsh treatment, but it gave no orders about holding meetings or erecting church-buildings or practising any of our customary acts. And yet the advocates of peace and piety, [Constantine and Licinius], had written to him to allow this, and had conceded it to all their subjects by means of edicts and laws. In truth, this monster of iniquity had resolved not to give in as regards this matter; until he was smitten by the divine Justice, and at the last against his will forced to do so. . . .

But when he joined battle, he found himself bereft of divine Providence, for, by the direction of Him who is the one and only God of all, the victory was given to Licinius who was then ruling. First of all, the armed soldiers in whom he had trusted were destroyed; and when his bodyguard had left him defenceless and wholly deserted, and had gone over to him who was ruling, the wretched man divested himself with all speed of the imperial insignia that ill became him, and in a cowardly, base and unmanly way quietly slipt into the crowd. Then he ran about here and there, hiding himself in the fields and villages; and for all his courting of safety he escaped with difficulty the hands of his enemies, his deeds themselves proclaiming how very trustworthy and true are the divine oracles, in which it has been said: "There is no king saved by much power, and a giant will not be saved by his great strength. A horse is a vain thing for safety, and will not be saved by his great power. Behold, the eyes of the Lord are upon them that fear him, upon them that hope in his mercy; to deliver their souls from death." Thus, then, did the tyrant, filled with shame, come to his own territory. And first in his mad fury he put to death many priests and prophets of those gods who had formerly been his admiration, and whose oracles had incited him to begin the war, on the ground that they were charlatans and deceivers and, above all, betrayers of his safety. Next, he gave glory to the Christians' God, and drew up a law on behalf of their liberty in the most complete and fullest manner. Then straightway, no respite being granted him, he ended his life by a miserable death. . . .

He who a short while previously looked upon us as impious and godless and the pests of society, so that we were not permitted to dwell in, I will not say, a city, but even a spot in the country or a desert—this same person drew up ordinances and legislation on behalf of the Christians; and those who shortly before were being destroyed by fire and sword and given to wild beasts and birds for food before his eyes, and were enduring every kind of chastisement and punishment and loss of life in the most pitiable manner, as if they were godless and wicked, these he now allows both to observe their form of worship and to build churches; and the tyrant himself confesses that they possess certain rights!

And when he had made these confessions, as if meeting with some kind of reward on this very account—that is, suffering less, to be sure, than it behoved him to suffer—he was smitten all at once by a stroke of God, and perished in the second encounter of the war. But the circumstances of his death were not such as fall to the lot of generals on a campaign, who time after time contend bravely on behalf of virtue and friends, and with a good courage meet a glorious end in battle; but he suffered his due punishment like an impious enemy of God, skulking at home while his army was still stationed in battle-array on the field. All at once he was smitten by a stroke of God over his whole body, with the result that he fell prone under the onslaught of terrible pains and agonies; he was wasted by hunger, and his flesh entirely consumed by an invisible, divinely-sent fire; the form which his body once possessed wasted away and vanished, and there remained only a form of dry bones, like some phantom shape long since reduced to a skeleton, so that those present could not but think that his body had become the tomb of his soul, which had been buried in what was now a corpse and completely wasted away. And as the heat consumed him still more fiercely in the very depths of his marrow, his eyes projected, and falling from their sockets left him blind. Yet he still breathed in this condition, making confession to the Lord invoked death. So with his last breath he acknowledged that he suffered thus justly because of his violence against Christ; and then gave up the ghost.

When Maximin was thus removed—he who was the only one left of the enemies of godliness, and showed himself the worst of all—by the grace of Almighty God the renewal of the churches from the foundation was set on foot, and the word of Christ received a due increase upon its former freedom, and was clearly heard to the glory of the God of the universe; while the impiety of the enemies of godliness was covered with the most abject shame and dishonour. For Maximin himself was the first to be proclaimed by the rulers as a common enemy of all, and posted in public edicts on tablets as a most impious, most hateful and God-hating tyrant. As to the portraits which were set up in every city to his honour and that of his children, some were hurled from a height to the ground and smashed to pieces, others had their faces blackened over with dark-coloured paint and so rendered useless; the statues likewise, as many as had been set up in his honour, were cast down and broken in the same manner, and lay as an object of merriment and sport to those who wished to insult or abuse them. . . .

So it was that Theotecnus also was summoned by Justice, who in no wise consigned to oblivion what he did against the Christians. For after he had set up the idol at Antioch, he seemed to be prospering, and had actually been deemed worthy of a governorship by Maximin; but when Licinius came to the city of the Antiochenes, he made a search for charlatans, and plied with tortures the prophets and priests of the new-made idol, to find out by what contrivance they were practising this deceit. And when the infliction of the tortures made concealment impossible for them, and they revealed that the whole mystery was a deceit manufactured by the art of Theotecnus, he inflicted a just punishment upon them all, putting to death, after a long series of tortures, first Theotecnus himself, and then also the partners in his charlatanry.

To all these were added the sons of Maximin, whom he had already caused to share the imperial dignity and to be set up in paintings and pictures. And those who formerly boasted kinship with the tyrant and were moved by pride to lord it over all men underwent the same sufferings, accompanied by the most abject disgrace, as those mentioned above; for they received not correction, nor did they know to understand the exhortation in the sacred books which says: "Put not your trust in princes, in the sons of men, in whom there is no help. His breath shall go forth and he shall return to his earth. In that day all his thoughts shall perish." Thus verily when the impious ones had been purged away, the kingdom that belonged to them was preserved stedfast and undisputed for Constantine and Licinius alone; who, when they had made it their very first action to purge the world of enmity against God, conscious of the good things that He had bestowed upon them, displayed their love of virtue and of God, their piety and gratitude towards the Deity, by their enactment on behalf of the Christians.

Augustine

9

Augustine was born in 354 A.D. in the Roman province of Numidia, North Africa. His father was a pagan but his mother, Monica, was a zealous Christian and instrumental in Augustine's late but total acceptance of the Christian faith. The family had some social standing but inadequate economic resources and Augustine completed his education only through the benefaction of a wealthy family friend. Augustine received a thoroughly literary education with a strong emphasis on the Latin masters: Cicero, Virgil, Terence, and Varro (whose *Antiquitatum Libri,* a systematic survey of Roman life from the founding of the city, is quoted repeatedly in *The City of God*). Augustine's education in philosophy was limited, primarily because he never mastered Greek and thus was dependent upon translated materials which were, in fact, popular renderings of the great Greek philosophers. At the age of twenty he began his professional career, first as a schoolteacher in his home town, then as a professor of rhetoric in Carthage. In 383 he moved to Rome and the following year to Milan, at that time one of the capital cities of the Empire.

During those years of teaching and study, Augustine, almost a convert to Manichaeism, was struggling with his ambivalent attitude toward Christian doctrine and his unequivocal attachment to what he later called "the sinfulness and vanity of life." In Milan he came under the influence of St. Ambrose, whose "spiritual" explanations of the Old Testament helped Augustine toward acceptance of Christian views, and of the Neoplatonist school of Christian theology. In 386, Augustine underwent a moving conversion experience and decided to enter the Church. His hope was to renounce the world and to live a life of retreat, prayer, and contemplation but in 391 the parishioners of the church of Hippo acclaimed him as their priest. Thus began his ecclesiastical career which was to last forty years, most of which he served as Bishop of the diocese of Hippo. In addition to his episcopal duties, which were onerous, Augustine engaged in a great literary production: his written

269

works would fill fifteen standard encyclopedia volumes. He wrote numerous theological works which formed a great part of the basis of patristic theology, and thus of medieval theology; he carried on long and passionate literary wars against heretics, writing polemics against Donatists, Pelagians, and Arians; his autobiographical *Confessions* (c. 390) is one of the classics of Western literature; and in *The City of God* (413–426) he wrote a magnificent philosophical history, expounding the meaning of history and of Christianity. He died in 430, while his beloved province was being overrun by the barbarian Vandals.

In *The City of God,* Augustine presented a powerful defense of the role of Christianity in the Roman Empire. His essay was occasioned by the anger of pagan Romans against Christianity after the sack of Rome by Alaric and his Goths in 410: the implication was that Rome had been immune from foreign invasions until she forsook her ancient gods and adopted Christianity as her official religion. In his defense of the Church, Augustine offered a new interpretation of the social, political, and spiritual history of mankind. He also offered a new view of history itself. He was not concerned with preserving the memory of great events, as was Herodotus. Nor did he see history as offering lessons for statesmen, as did Thucydides and Polybius. He did not seek to explain or to describe the greatness of Rome, as did Livy, or to recount her decline from republican virtue, as did Tacitus. Nor did he attempt a history of Christianity and the Church within the broad sweep of universal history, as did Eusebius. Rather, as a defender of the Christian Church, his thought permeated with the Platonic conception of the ideal city and with the Pauline interpretation of the divine commonwealth into which only the righteous may enter, Augustine postulated the existence of two historical worlds, that of the city of this world and that of the city of God. He established a dualism between the two cities, the one ephemeral and corruptible, where kings rule absolutely and subjects obey unquestioningly because "the powers that be are ordained of God"; the other eternal and incorruptible, where God rules and all true Christians live in spiritual allegiance. The history of the temporal city was relegated to a decidedly secondary, almost irrelevant position; that of the heavenly city gained primacy: what mattered to mankind was habitation in the eternal not sojourning in the transitory city. His history, then, was a discussion of the two cities' "origins," their "process or progress" and "their appointed ends." With Augustine history became a specifically Christian drama and all of the subjects historians had previously deemed significant —the Persian Wars, the founding and expansion of Rome—paled into insignificance beside the truly great events in the history of humanity—the fall of Adam, the Incarnation, the Resurrection, the promise of the Second Coming. Not content with refuting pagan assaults on Christianity, Augustine advanced a philosophy of history that both exonerated Christians and also sought to persuade pagans of the truth and justness of the Christian view. Thus, the first Book of his work opens with a discussion of "that most glorious society and

celestial city of God's faithful" and of "the adversaries of the name of Christ";
the last Book concludes triumphantly with "the eternal felicity of the City of
God." Human history took on a new theme, a new meaning and a new
direction with Augustine's *City of God,* a consummate achievement as a
philosophy of history.

And yet, Augustine was a poor historian. His approach to empirical data
was always by way of a preconceived theoretical bias: one must first believe
(he wrote) before one may understand. Whatever the force of other argument
or documentation, the Bible, properly interpreted, was always the source of
truth and accuracy. Indeed, without the Bible Augustine would not have been
capable of a historical approach for, as he wrote in his *Confessions:* "Man's
life on earth is short and he cannot, by his own perception, see the connexion
between the conditions of earlier times and of other nations, which he has
not experienced himself, and those of his own times, which are familiar to
him." The Bible, however, the inspired Word of God, gave Augustine the
form and content necessary for his historiographic purposes. Erudite as he
was, his enormous learning was put not to a critical inquiry into the process
of human history but rather into the expounding of a received and revered
doctrine. Not the activities of men but the unfolding of God's plan formed
the basis of history. In a real sense, then, Augustine's history is, to borrow
Gilbert Murray's phrase, a "failure of nerve," "a loss of self-confidence, of
hope in this life and of faith in normal human effort." What makes Augustine
enormously important in the development of historiography, therefore, is not
his critical apparatus or methodological approach. Rather, it is his overwhelming vision, expressed in beautiful and passionate language, of the historical process which became the accepted and undoubted interpretation of
history among Catholic Christians for more than a thousand years. And, along
with Augustine's magisterial philosophy of history, the Christian West
adopted and molded to its uses his views on the state and society, on human
sexuality, and on the relationship of the Christian to the earthly city.

The City of God reflects in many ways the conflict going on within Augustine himself and within his society at large between the values of the old
classical culture and those of the new Christian world view. In the end, the
Galilean conquered the Roman, at least for a time. For his own city and
province it has been said, Augustine had been "the last of the Romans." For
the Christian West, however, he was undoubtedly among the first and greatest of the Catholics, and it is in this latter role that he completed his monumental history of the City of God.

Selected Bibliography

Ernest Barker has provided a scholarly, informative introduction to the Everyman's Library edition of *The City of God* (2 vols., 1945). It is Barker's view that,

at least for his own city, St. Augustine may be considered "the last of the Romans." Étienne Gilson, *Introduction à l'étude de Saint Augustin* (third edition, 1949), performs an admirable and erudite service. (There is an English translation, *The Christian Philosophy of Saint Augustine,* 1960.) Arnaldo Momigliano's "Pagan and Christian Historiography in the Fourth Century A.D." is particularly pertinent on Augustine. Theodor E. Mommsen's article, "Saint Augustine and the Idea of Progress," *Journal of the History of Ideas,* XII (1951), 346–374 and his paper, "Orosius and Augustine," are both original and enlightening contributions. They are included in Eugene F. Rice, Jr., ed., *Theodor E. Mommsen, Medieval and Renaissance Studies* (1959; reissued in 1966). Mommsen has appended a short but valuable bibliography of works dealing with Augustine's historical ideas. See the essay "Saint Augustine and the Idea of Progress," note 12 or Eugene F. Rice, Jr., ed., *op. cit.,* p. 274, n. 12. George E. McCraken has provided a fine introduction and bibliography with his translation of *The City of God* (7 vols., 1957). Wilhelm Kamlah's *Christentum und Geschichtlichkeit* (second edition, 1951) is an enormously erudite inquiry into Augustine's contribution to historical thinking. Henri Marron, *Saint Augustine and His Influence Through the Ages* (English translation, 1957), is a good popular introduction. The present selections are from the Marcus Dods translation, the whole of which is available in the Modern Library edition (1950).

THE CITY OF GOD

Book First

The glorious city of God is my theme in this work, which you, my dearest
son Marcellinus, suggested, and which is due to you by my promise. I
have undertaken its defence against those who prefer their own gods to
the Founder of this city—a city surpassingly glorious, whether we view
it as it still lives by faith in this fleeting course of time, and sojourns as
a stranger in the midst of the ungodly, or as it shall dwell in the fixed
stability of its eternal seat, which it now with patience waits for, expecting until "righteousness shall return unto judgment," and it obtain, by
virtue of its excellence, final victory and perfect peace. A great work this,
and an arduous; but God is my helper. For I am aware what ability is
requisite to persuade the proud how great is the virtue of humility, which
raises us, not by a quite human arrogance, but by a divine grace, above
all earthly dignities that totter on this shifting scene. For the King and
Founder of this city of which we speak, has in Scripture uttered to His
people a dictum of the divine law in these words: "God resisteth the
proud, but giveth grace unto the humble." But this, which is God's
prerogative, the inflated ambition of a proud spirit also affects, and
dearly loves that this be numbered among its attributes, to

> Show pity to the humbled soul,
> And crush the sons of pride.

And therefore, as the plan of this work we have undertaken requires, and
as occasion offers, we must speak also of the earthly city, which, though
it be mistress of the nations, is itself ruled by its lust of rule.

For to this earthly city belong the enemies against whom I have to
defend the city of God. Many of them, indeed, being reclaimed from their
ungodly error, have become sufficiently creditable citizens of this city;
but many are so inflamed with hatred against it, and are so ungrateful
to its Redeemer for His signal benefits, as to forget that they would now
be unable to utter a single word to its prejudice, had they not found in

From *The City of God,* translated by Marcus Dods (London, T. & T. Clark).
Reprinted by permission of T. & T. Clark and Random House, Inc. Pp. 3–5, 38–42,
52–60, 62–65, 70–73, 441, 464–468, 477, 669–672, 675–678, 680–687, 690–699, 706–
709.

its sacred places, as they fled from the enemy's steel, that life in which they now boast themselves. Are not those very Romans, who were spared by the barbarians through their respect for Christ, become enemies to the name of Christ? The reliquaries of the martyrs and the churches of the apostles bear witness to this; for in the sack of the city they were open sanctuary for all who fled to them, whether Christian or Pagan. To their very threshold the bloodthirsty enemy raged; there his murderous fury owned a limit. Thither did such of the enemy as had any pity convey those to whom they had given quarter, lest any less mercifully disposed might fall upon them. And, indeed, when even those murderers who everywhere else showed themselves pitiless came to these spots where that was forbidden which the licence of war permitted in every other place, their furious rage for slaughter was bridled, and their eagerness to take prisoners was quenched. Thus escaped multitudes who now reproach the Christian religion, and impute to Christ the ills that have befallen their city; but the preservation of their own life—a boon which they owe to the respect entertained for Christ by the barbarians—they attribute not to our Christ, but to their own good luck. They ought rather, had they any right perceptions, to attribute the severities and hardships inflicted by their enemies, to that divine providence which is wont to reform the depraved manners of men by chastisement, and which exercises with similar afflictions the righteous and praiseworthy—either translating them, when they have passed through the trial, to a better world, or detaining them still on earth for ulterior purposes. And they ought to attribute it to the spirit of these Christian times, that, contrary to the custom of war, these bloodthirsty barbarians spared them, and spared them for Christ's sake, whether this mercy was actually shown in promiscuous places, or in those places specially dedicated to Christ's name, and of which the very largest were selected as sanctuaries, that full scope might thus be given to the expanisve compassion which desired that a large multitude might find shelter there. Therefore ought they to give God thanks, and with sincere confession flee for refuge to His name, that so they may escape the punishment of eternal fire—they who with lying lips took upon them this name, that they might escape the punishment of present destruction. For of those whom you see insolently and shamelessly insulting the servants of Christ, there are numbers who would not have escaped that destruction and slaughter had they not pretended that they themselves were Christ's servants. Yet now, in ungrateful pride and most impious madness, and at the risk of being punished in everlasting darkness, they perversely oppose that name under which they fraudulently protected themselves for the sake of enjoying the light of this brief life. . . .

But I have still some things to say in confutation of those who refer the disasters of the Roman republic to our religion, because it prohibits the offering of sacrifices to the gods. For this end I must recount all, or as many as may seem sufficient, of the disasters which befell that city and its subject provinces, before these sacrifices were prohibited; for all these disasters they would doubtless have attributed to us, if at that time our religion had shed its light upon them, and had prohibited their sacrifices. I must then go on to show what social well-being the true God, in whose hand are all kingdoms, vouchsafed to grant to them that their empire might increase. I must show why He did so, and how their false gods, instead of at all aiding them, greatly injured them by guile and deceit. And, lastly, I must meet those who, when on this point convinced and confuted by irrefragable proofs, endeavour to maintain that they worship the gods, not hoping for the present advantages of this life, but for those which are to be enjoyed after death. And this, if I am not mistaken, will be the most difficult part of my task, and will be worthy of the loftiest argument; for we must then enter the lists with the philosophers, not the mere common herd of philosophers, but the most renowned, who in many points agree with ourselves, as regarding the immortality of the soul, and that the true God created the world, and by His providence rules all He has created. But as they differ from us on other points, we must not shrink from the task of exposing their errors, that, having refuted the gainsaying of the wicked with such ability as God may vouchsafe, we may assert the city of God, and true piety, and the worship of God, to which alone the promise of true and everlasting felicity is attached. Here, then, let us conclude, that we may enter on these subjects in a fresh book.

Book Second

If the feeble mind of man did not presume to resist the clear evidence of truth, but yielded its infirmity to wholesome doctrines, as to a health-giving medicine, until it obtained from God, by its faith and piety, the grace needed to heal it, they who have just ideas, and express them in suitable language, would need to use no long discourse to refute the errors of empty conjecture. But this mental infirmity is now more prevalent and hurtful than ever, to such an extent that even after the truth has been as fully demonstrated as man can prove it to man, they hold for the very truth their own unreasonable fancies, either on account of their great blindness, which prevents them from seeing what is plainly set before them, or on account of their opinionative obstinacy, which prevents them from acknowledging the force of what they do see. There therefore frequently arises a necessity of speaking more fully on those points which are already clear, that we may, as it were, present them not to the eye, but even to the touch, so that they may be felt even by those who close their eyes against them. And yet to what end shall we ever bring our discussions, or what bounds can be set to our discourse, if we proceed on the principle that we must always reply to those who reply to us? For those who are either unable to understand our arguments, or are so hardened by the habit of contradiction, that though they understand they cannot yield to them, reply to us, and, as it is written, "speak hard things," and are incorrigibly vain. Now, if we were to propose to confute their objections as often as they with brazen face chose to disregard our arguments, and as often as they could by any means contradict our statements, you see how endless, and fruitless, and painful a task we should be undertaking. And therefore I do not wish my writings to be judged even by you, my son Marcellinus, nor by any of those others at whose service this work of mine is freely and in all Christian charity put, if at least you intend always to require a reply to every exception which you hear taken to what you read in it; for so you would become like those silly women of whom the apostle says that they are "always learning, and never able to come to the knowledge of the truth."

In the foregoing book, having begun to speak of the city of God, to which I have resolved, Heaven helping me, to consecrate the whole of this work, it was my first endeavour to reply to those who attribute the wars by which the world is being devastated, and specially the recent sack of Rome by the barbarians, to the religion of Christ, which prohibits the offering of abominable sacrifices to devils. I have shown that they ought rather to attribute it to Christ, that for His name's sake the barbarians, in contravention of all custom and law of war, threw open as sanctuaries the largest churches, and in many instances showed such reverence to Christ, that not only His genuine servants, but even those who in their terror feigned themselves to be so, were exempted from all those hardships which by the custom of war may lawfully be inflicted. Then out of this there arose the question, why wicked and ungrateful men were permitted to share in these benefits; and why, too, the hardships and calamities of war were inflicted on the godly as well as on the ungodly. And in giving a suitably full answer to this large question, I occupied some considerable space, partly that I might relieve the anxieties which disturb many when they observe that the blessings of God, and the common and daily human casualties, fall to the lot of bad men and good without distinction; but mainly that I might minister some consolation to those holy and chaste women who were outraged by the enemy, in such a way as to shock their modesty, though not to sully their purity, and that I might preserve them from being ashamed of life, though they have no guilt to be ashamed of. And then I briefly spoke against those who with a most shameless wantonness insult over those poor Christians who were subjected to those calamities, and especially over those brokenhearted and humiliated, though chaste and holy women; these fellows themselves being most depraved and unmanly profligates, quite degenerate from the genuine Romans whose famous deeds are abundantly recorded in history, and everywhere celebrated, but who have found in their descendants the greatest enemies of their glory. In truth, Rome, which was founded and increased by the labours of these ancient heroes, was more shamefully ruined by their descendants, while its walls were still standing, than it is now by the razing of them. For in this ruin there fell stones and timbers; but in the ruin those profligates effected, there fell, not the mural, but the moral bulwarks and ornaments of the city, and their hearts burned with passions more destructive than the flames which consumed their houses. Thus I brought my first book to a close. And now I go on to speak of those calamities which that city itself, or its subject provinces, have suffered since its foundation; all of which they would equally have attributed to the Christian religion, if at that early period the doctrine of the gospel against their false and deceiving gods had been as largely and freely proclaimed as now. . . .

We have still to inquire why the poets who write the plays, and who by the law of the twelve tables are prohibited from injuring the good name of the citizens, are reckoned more estimable than the actors, though they so shamefully asperse the character of the gods? Is it right that the actors of these poetical and God-dishonouring effusions be branded, while their authors are honoured? Must we not here award the palm to a Greek, Plato, who, in framing his ideal republic, conceived that poets should be banished from the city as enemies of the state? He could not brook that the gods be brought into disrepute, nor that the minds of the citizens be depraved and besotted, by the fictions of the poets. Compare now human nature as you see it in Plato, expelling poets from the city that the citizens be uninjured, with the divine nature as you see it in these gods exacting plays in their own honour. Plato strove, though unsuccessfully, to persuade the light-minded and lascivious Greeks to abstain from so much as writing such plays; the gods used their authority to extort the acting of the same from the dignified and sober-minded Romans. And not content with having them acted, they had them dedicated to themselves, consecrated to themselves, solemnly celebrated in their own honour. To which, then, would it be more becoming in a state to decree divine honours—to Plato, who prohibited these wicked and licentious plays, or to the demons who delighted in blinding men to the truth of what Plato unsuccessfully sought to inculcate?

This philosopher, Plato, has been elevated by Labeo to the rank of a demigod, and set thus upon a level with such as Hercules and Romulus. Labeo ranks demigods higher than heroes, but both he counts among the deities. But I have no doubt that he thinks this man whom he reckons a demigod worthy of greater respect not only than the heroes, but also than the gods themselves. The laws of the Romans and the speculations of Plato have this resemblance, that the latter pronounces a wholesale condemnation of poetical fictions, while the former restrain the licence of satire, at least so far as men are the objects of it. Plato will not suffer poets even to dwell in his city: the laws of Rome prohibit actors from being enrolled as citizens; and if they had not feared to offend the gods who had asked the services of the players, they would in all likelihood have banished them altogether. It is obvious, therefore, that the Romans could not receive, nor reasonably expect to receive, laws for the regulation of their conduct from their gods, since the laws they themselves enacted far surpassed and put to shame the morality of the gods. The gods demand stage-plays in their own honour; the Romans exclude the players from all civic honours: the former commanded that they should be celebrated by the scenic representation of their own disgrace; the latter commanded that no poet should dare to blemish the reputation of any citizen. But that demigod Plato resisted the lust of such gods as these, and showed the Romans what their genius had left incomplete; for he absolutely excluded poets from his ideal state, whether they composed fictions with no regard to truth, or set the worst possible examples before wretched men under the guise of divine actions. We for our part, indeed, reckon Plato neither a god nor a demigod; we would not even compare him to any of God's holy angels, nor to the truth-speaking prophets, nor to any of the apostles or martyrs of Christ, nay, not to any faithful Christian man. The reason of this opinion of ours we will, God prospering us, render in its own place. Nevertheless, since they wish him to be considered a demigod, we think he certainly is more entitled to that rank, and is every way superior, if not to Hercules and Romulus (though no historian could ever narrate nor any poet sing of him that he had killed his brother, or committed any crime), yet certainly to Priapus, or a Cynocephalus, or the Fever—divinities whom the Romans have partly received from foreigners, and partly consecrated by home-grown rites. How, then, could gods such as these be expected to promulgate good and wholesome laws, either for the prevention of moral and social evils, or for their eradication where they had already sprung up?—gods who used their influence even to sow and cherish profligacy, by appointing that deeds truly or falsely ascribed to them should be published to the people by means of theatrical exhibitions, and by thus gratuitously fanning the flame of human lust with the breath of a seemingly divine approbation. In vain does Cicero, speaking of poets, exclaim against this state of things in these words: "When the plaudits and acclamation of the people, who sit as infallible judges, are won by the poets, what darkness benights the mind, what fears invade, what passions inflame it!"

But is it not manifest that vanity rather than reason regulated the choice of some of their false gods? This Plato, whom they reckon a demi-god, and who used all his eloquence to preserve men from the most dangerous spiritual calamities, has yet not been counted worthy even of a little shrine; but Romulus, because they can call him their own, they have esteemed more highly than many gods, though their secret doctrine can allow him the rank only of a demigod. To him they allotted a flamen, that is to say, a priest of a class so highly esteemed in their religion (distinguished, too, by their conical mitres), that for only three of their gods were flamens appointed—the Flamen Dialis for Jupiter, Martialis for Mars, and Quirinalis for Romulus (for when the ardour of his fellow-citizens had given Romulus a seat among the gods, they gave him this new name Quirinus). And thus by this honour Romulus has been pre-ferred to Neptune and Pluto, Jupiter's brothers, and to Saturn himself, their father. They have assigned the same priesthood to serve him as to serve Jove; and in giving Mars (the reputed father of Romulus) the same honour, is this not rather for Romulus' sake than to honour Mars?

Moreover, if the Romans had been able to receive a rule of life from their gods, they would not have borrowed Solon's laws from the Atheni-ans, as they did some years after Rome was founded; and yet they did not keep them as they received them, but endeavoured to improve and amend them. Although Lycurgus pretended that he was authorized by Apollo to give laws to the Lacedemonians, the sensible Romans did not choose to believe this, and were not induced to borrow laws from Sparta. Numa Pompilius, who succeeded Romulus in the kingdom, is said to have framed some laws, which, however, were not sufficient for the regulation of civic affairs. Among these regulations were many pertain-ing to religious observances, and yet he is not reported to have received even these from the gods. With respect, then, to moral evils, evils of life and conduct—evils which are so mighty, that, according to the wisest pagans, by them states are ruined while their cities stand uninjured—their gods made not the smallest provision for preserving their worship-pers from these evils, but, on the contrary, took special pains to increase them, as we have previously endeavoured to prove. . . .

I will therefore pause, and adduce the testimony of Sallust himself, whose words in praise of the Romans (that "equity and virtue prevailed among them not more by force of laws than of nature") have given occasion to this discussion. He was referring to that period immediately after the expulsion of the kings, in which the city became great in an incredibly short space of time. And yet this same writer acknowledges in the first book of his history, in the very exordium of his work, that even at that time, when a very brief interval had elapsed after the government had passed from kings to consuls, the more powerful men began to act unjustly, and occasioned the defection of the people from the patricians, and other disorders in the city. For after Sallust had stated that the Romans enjoyed greater harmony and a purer state of society between the second and third Punic wars than at any other time, and that the cause of this was not their love of good order, but their fear lest the peace they had with Carthage might be broken (this also, as we mentioned, Nasica contemplated when he opposed the destruction of Carthage, for he supposed that fear would tend to repress wickedness, and to preserve wholesome ways of living), he then goes on to say: "Yet, after the destruction of Carthage, discord, avarice, ambition, and the other vices which are commonly generated by prosperity, more than ever increased." If they "increased," and that "more than ever," then already they had appeared, and had been increasing. And so Sallust adds this reason for what he said. "For," he says, "the oppressive measures of the powerful, and the consequent secessions of the plebs from the patricians, and other civil dissensions, had existed from the first, and affairs were administered with equity and well-tempered justice for no longer a period than the short time after the expulsion of the kings, while the city was occupied with the serious Tuscan war and Tarquin's vengeance." You see how, even in that brief period after the expulsion of the kings, fear, he acknowledges, was the cause of the interval of equity and good order. They were afraid, in fact, of the war which Tarquin waged against them, after he had been driven from the throne and the city, and had allied himself with the Tuscans. But observe what he adds: "After that, the patricians treated the people as their slaves, ordering them to be scourged or beheaded just as the kings had done, driving them from their holdings, and harshly tyrannizing over those who had no property to lose. The people, overwhelmed by these oppressive measures, and most of all by exorbitant usury, and obliged to contribute both money and personal service to the constant wars, at length took arms, and seceded to Mount Aventine and Mount Sacer, and thus obtained for themselves tribunes and protective laws. But it was only the second Punic war that put an end on both sides to discord and strife." You see what kind of men the Romans were, even so early as a few years after the expulsion of the kings; and it is of these men he says, that "equity and virtue prevailed among them not more by force of law than of nature."

Now, if these were the days in which the Roman republic shows fairest and best, what are we to say or think of the succeeding age, when, to use the words of the same historian, "changing little by little from the fair and virtuous city it was, it became utterly wicked and dissolute"? This was, as he mentions, after the destruction of Carthage. Sallust's brief sum and sketch of this period may be read in his own history, in which he shows how the profligate manners which were propagated by prosperity resulted at last even in civil wars. He says: "And from this time the primitive manners, instead of undergoing an insensible alteration as hitherto they had done, were swept away as by a torrent; the young men were so depraved by luxury and avarice, that it may justly be said that no father had a son who could either preserve his own patrimony, or keep his hands off other men's." Sallust adds a number of particulars about the vices of Sylla, and the debased condition of the republic in general; and other writers make similar observations though in much less striking language.

However, I suppose you now see, or at least any one who gives his attention has the means of seeing, in what a sink of iniquity that city was plunged before the advent of our heavenly King. For these things happened not only before Christ had begun to teach, but before He was even born of the Virgin. If, then, they dare not impute to their gods the grievous evils of those former times, more tolerable before the destruction of Carthage, but intolerable and dreadful after it, although it was the gods who by their malign craft instilled into the minds of men the conceptions from which such dreadful vices branched out on all sides, why do they impute these present calamities to Christ, who teaches life-giving truth, and forbids us to worship false and deceitful gods, and who, abominating and condemning with His divine authority those wicked and hurtful lusts of men, gradually withdraws His own people from a world that is corrupted by these vices, and is falling into ruins, to make of them an eternal city, whose glory rests not on the acclamations of vanity, but on the judgment of truth?

Here, then, is this Roman republic, "which has changed little by little from the fair and virtuous city it was, and has become utterly wicked and dissolute." It is not I who am the first to say this, but their own authors, from whom we learned it for a fee, and who wrote it long before the coming of Christ. You see how, before the coming of Christ, and after the destruction of Carthage, "the primitive manners, instead of undergoing insensible alteration, as hitherto they had done, were swept away as by a torrent; and how depraved by luxury and avarice the youth were." Let them now, on their part, read to us any laws given by their gods to the Roman people, and directed against luxury and avarice. And would that they had only been silent on the subjects of chastity and modesty, and had not demanded from the people indecent and shameful practices, to which they lent a pernicious patronage by their so-called divinity. Let them read our commandments in the Prophets, Gospels, Acts of the Apostles, or Epistles; let them peruse the large number of precepts against avarice and luxury which are everywhere read to the congregations that meet for this purpose, and which strike the ear, not with the uncertain sound of a philosophical discussion, but with the thunder of God's own oracle pealing from the clouds. And yet they do not impute to their gods the luxury and avarice, the cruel and dissolute manners, that had rendered the republic utterly wicked and corrupt, even before the coming of Christ; but whatever affliction their pride and effeminacy have exposed them to in these latter days, they furiously impute to our religion. If the kings of the earth and all their subjects, if all princes and judges of the earth, if young men and maidens, old and young, every age, and both sexes; if they whom the Baptist addressed, the publicans and the soldiers, were all together to harken to and observe the precepts of the Christian religion regarding a just and virtuous life, then should the republic adorn the whole earth with its own felicity, and attain in life everlasting to the pinnacle of kingly glory. But because this man listens, and that man scoffs, and most are enamoured of the blandishments of vice rather than the wholesome severity of virtue, the people of Christ, whatever be their condition—whether they be kings, princes, judges, soldiers, or provincials, rich or poor, bond or free, male or female—are enjoined to endure this earthly republic, wicked and dissolute as it is, that so they may by this endurance win for themselves an eminent place in that most holy and august assembly of angels and republic of heaven, in which the will of God is the law.

But the worshippers and admirers of these gods delight in imitating their scandalous iniquities, and are nowise concerned that the republic be less depraved and licentious. Only let it remain undefeated, they say, only let it flourish and abound in resources; let it be glorious by its victories, or still better, secure in peace; and what matters it to us? This is our concern, that every man be able to increase his wealth so as to supply his daily prodigalities, and so that the powerful may subject the weak for their own purposes. Let the poor court the rich for a living, and that under their protection they may enjoy a sluggish tranquillity; and let the rich abuse the poor as their dependants, to minister to their pride. Let the people applaud not those who protect their interests, but those who provide them with pleasure. Let no severe duty be commanded, no impurity forbidden. Let kings estimate their prosperity, not by the righteousness, but by the servility of their subjects. Let the provinces stand loyal to the kings, not as moral guides, but as lords of their possessions and purveyors of their pleasures; not with a hearty reverence, but a crooked and servile fear. Let the laws take cognizance rather of the injury done to another man's property, than of that done to one's own person. If a man be a nuisance to his neighbour, or injure his property, family, or person, let him be actionable; but in his own affairs let every one with impunity do what he will in company with his own family, and with those who willingly join him. Let there be a plentiful supply of public prostitutes for every one who wishes to use them, but specially for those who are too poor to keep one for their private use. Let there be erected houses of the largest and most ornate description: in these let there be provided the most sumptuous banquets, where every one who pleases may, by day or night, play, drink, vomit, dissipate. Let there be everywhere heard the rustling of dancers, the loud, immodest laughter of the theatre; let a succession of the most cruel and the most voluptuous pleasures maintain a perpetual excitement. If such happiness is distasteful to any, let him be branded as a public enemy; and if any attempt to modify or put an end to it, let him be silenced, banished, put an end to. Let these be reckoned the true gods, who procure for the people this condition of things, and preserve it when once possessed. Let them be worshipped as they wish; let them demand whatever games they please, from or with their own worshippers; only let them secure that such felicity be not imperilled by foe, plague, or disaster of any kind. What sane man would compare a republic such as this, I will not say to the Roman empire, but to the palace of Sardanapalus, the ancient king who was so abandoned to pleasures, that he caused it to be inscribed on his tomb, that now that he was dead, he possessed only those things which he had swallowed and consumed by his appetites while alive? If these men had such a king as this, who, while self-indulgent, should lay no severe restraint on them, they would more enthusiastically consecrate to him a temple and a flamen than the ancient Romans did to Romulus.

But if our adversaries do not care how foully and disgracefully the Roman republic be stained by corrupt practices, so long only as it holds together and continues in being, and if they therefore pooh-pooh the testimony of Sallust to its "utterly wicked and profligate" condition, what will they make of Cicero's statement, that even in his time it had become entirely extinct, and that there remained extant no Roman republic at all?

This is the confession of Cicero, long indeed after the death of Africanus, whom he introduced as an interlocutor in his work *De Republica,* but still before the coming of Christ. Yet, if the disasters he bewails had been lamented after the Christian religion had been diffused, and had begun to prevail, is there a man of our adversaries who would not have thought that they were to be imputed to the Christians? Why, then, did their gods not take steps then to prevent the decay and extinction of that republic, over the loss of which Cicero, long before Christ had come in the flesh, sings so lugubrious a dirge? Its admirers have need to inquire whether, even in the days of primitive men and morals, true justice flourished in it; or was it not perhaps even then, to use the casual expression of Cicero, rather a coloured painting than the living reality? But, if God will, we shall consider this elsewhere. For I mean in its own place to show that—according to the definitions in which Cicero himself, using Scipio as his mouthpiece, briefly propounded what a republic is, and what a people is, and according to many testimonies, both of his own lips and of those who took part in that same debate—Rome never was a republic, because true justice had never a place in it. But accepting the more feasible definitions of a republic, I grant there was a republic of a certain kind, and certainly much better administered by the more ancient Romans than by their modern representatives. But the fact is, true justice has no existence save in that republic whose founder and ruler is Christ, if at least any choose to call this a republic; and indeed we cannot deny that it is the people's weal. But if perchance this name, which has become familiar in other connections, be considered alien to our common parlance, we may at all events say that in this city is true justice; the city of which Holy Scripture says, "Glorious things are said of thee, O city of God."

But what is relevant to the present question is this, that however admirable our adversaries say the republic was or is, it is certain that by the testimony of their own most learned writers it had become, long before the coming of Christ, utterly wicked and dissolute, and indeed had no existence, but had been destroyed by profligacy. To prevent this, surely these guardian gods ought to have given precepts of morals and a rule of life to the people by whom they were worshipped in so many temples, with so great a variety of priests and sacrifices, with such numberless and diverse rites, so many festal solemnities, so many celebrations of magnificent games. But in all this the demons only looked after their own interest, and cared not at all how their worshippers lived, or rather were at pains to induce them to lead an abandoned life, so long as they paid these tributes to their honour, and regarded them with fear. If any one denies this, let him produce, let him point to, let him read the laws which the gods had given against sedition, and which the Gracchi transgressed when they threw everything into confusion; or those Marius, and Cinna, and Carbo broke when they involved their country in civil wars, most iniquitous and unjustifiable in their causes, cruelly conducted, and yet more cruelly terminated; or those which Sylla scorned, whose life, character, and deeds, as described by Sallust and other historians, are the abhorrence of all mankind. Who will deny that at that time the republic had become extinct? . . .

But, further, is it not obvious that the gods have abetted the fulfillment of men's desires, instead of authoritatively bridling them? For Marius, a low-born and self-made man, who ruthlessly provoked and conducted civil wars, was so effectually aided by them, that he was seven times consul, and died full of years in his seventh consulship, escaping the hands of Sylla, who immediately afterwards came into power. Why, then, did they not also aid him, so as to restrain him from so many enormities? For if it is said that the gods had no hand in his success, this is no trivial admission, that a man can attain the dearly coveted felicity of this life even though his own gods be not propitous; that men can be loaded with the gifts of fortune as Marius was, can enjoy health, power, wealth, honours, dignity, length of days, though the gods be hostile to him; and that, on the other hand, men can be tormented as Regulus was, with captivity, bondage, destitution, watchings, pain, and cruel death, though the gods be his friends. To concede this is to make a compendious confession that the gods are useless, and their worship superfluous. If the gods have taught the people rather what goes clean counter to the virtues of the soul, and that integrity of life which meets a reward after death; if even in respect of temporal and transitory blessings they neither hurt those whom they hate nor profit whom they love, why are they worshipped, why are they invoked with such eager homage? Why do men murmur in difficult and sad emergencies, as if the gods had retired in anger? and why, on their account, is the Christian religion injured by the most unworthy calumnies? If in temporal matters they have power either for good or for evil, why did they stand by Marius, the worst of Rome's citizens, and abandon Regulus, the best? Does this not prove themselves to be most unjust and wicked? And even if it be supposed that for this very reason they are the rather to be feared and worshipped, this is a mistake; for we do not read that Regulus worshipped them less assiduously than Marius. Neither is it apparent that a wicked life is to be chosen, on the ground that the gods are supposed to have favoured Marius more than Regulus. For Metellus, the most highly esteemed of all the Romans, who had five sons in the counselship, was prosperous even in this life; and Catiline, the worst of men, reduced to poverty and defeated in the war his own guilt had aroused, lived and perished miserably. Real and secure felicity is the peculiar possession of those who worship that God by whom alone it can be conferred.

It is thus apparent, that when the republic was being destroyed by profligate manners, its gods did nothing to hinder its destruction by the direction or correction of its manners, but rather accelerated its destruction by increasing the demoralization and corruption that already existed. They need not pretend that their goodness was shocked by the iniquity of the city, and that they withdrew in anger. For they were there, sure enough; they are detected, convicted: they were equally unable to break silence so as to guide others, and to keep silence so as to conceal themselves. I do not dwell on the fact that the inhabitants of Minturnae took pity on Marius, and commended him to the gooddess Marica in her grove, that she might give him success in all things, and that from the abyss of despair in which he then lay he forthwith returned unhurt to

Rome, and entered the city the ruthless leader of a ruthless army; and they who wish to know how bloody was his victory, how unlike a citizen, and how much more relentlessly than any foreign foe he acted, let them read the histories. But this, as I said, I do not dwell upon; nor do I attribute the bloody bliss of Marius to, I know not what Minturnian goddess [Marica], but rather to the secret providence of God, that the mouths of our adversaries might be shut, and that they who are not led by passion, but by prudent consideration of events, might be delivered from error. And even if the demons have any power in these matters, they have only that power which the secret decree of the Almighty allots to them, in order that we may not set too great store by earthly prosperity, seeing it is oftentimes vouchsafed even to wicked men like Marius; and that we may not, on the other hand, regard it as an evil, since we see that many good and pious worshippers of the one true God are, in spite of the demons, pre-eminently successful; and, finally, that we may not suppose that these unclean spirits are either to be propitiated or feared for the sake of earthly blessings or calamities: for as wicked men on earth cannot do all they would, so neither can these demons, but only in so far as they are permitted by the decree of Him whose judgments are fully comprehensible, justly reprehensible by none. . . .

Cicero, a weighty man, and a philosopher in his way, when about to be made edile, wished the citizens to understand that, among the other duties of his magistracy, he must propitiate Flora by the celebration of games. And these games are reckoned devout in proportion to their lewdness. In another place, and when he was now consul, and the state in great peril, he says that games had been celebrated for ten days together, and that nothing had been omitted which could pacify the gods: as if it had not been more satisfactory to irritate the gods by temperance, than to pacify them by debauchery; and to provoke their hate by honest living, than soothe it by such unseemly grossness. For no matter how cruel was the ferocity of those men who were threatening the state, and on whose account the gods were being propitiated: it could not have been more hurtful than the alliance of gods who were won with the foulest vices. To avert the danger which threatened men's bodies, the gods were conciliated in a fashion that drove virtue from their spirits; and the gods did not enroll themselves as defenders of the battlements against the besiegers, until they had first stormed and sacked the morality of the citizens. This propitiation of such divinities—a propitiation so wanton, so impure, so immodest, so wicked, so filthy, whose actors the innate and praiseworthy virtue of the Romans disabled from civic honours, erased from their tribe, recognised as polluted and made infamous;—this propitiation, I say, so foul, so detestable, and alien from every religious feeling, these fabulous and ensnaring accounts of the criminal actions of the gods, these scandalous actions which they either shamefully and wickedly committed, and more shamefully and wickedly feigned, all this the whole city learned in public both by the words and gestures of the actors. They saw that the gods delighted in the commission of these things, and therefore believed that they wished them not only to be exhibited to them, but to be imitated by themselves. But as for that good and honest instruction which they speak of, it was given in such secrecy, and to so few (if indeed given at all), that they seemed rather to fear it might be divulged, than that it might not be practised.

They, then, are but abandoned and ungrateful wretches, in deep and fast bondage to that malign spirit, who complain and murmur that men are rescued by the name of Christ from the hellish thraldom of these unclean spirits, and from a participation in their punishment, and are brought out of the night of pestilential ungodliness into the light of most healthful piety. Only such men could murmur that the masses flock to the churches and their chaste acts of worship, where a seemly separation of the sexes is observed; where they learn how they may so spend this earthly life, as to merit a blessed eternity hereafter; where Holy Scripture and instruction in righteousness are proclaimed from a raised platform in presence of all, that both they who do the word may hear to their salvation, and they who do it not may hear to judgment. And though some enter who scoff at such precepts, all their petulance is either quenched by a sudden change, or is restrained through fear or shame. For no filthy and wicked action is there set forth to be gazed at or to be imitated; but either the precepts of the true God are recommended, His miracles narrated, His gifts praised, or His benefits implored.

This, rather, is the religion worthy of your desires, O admirable Roman race—the progeny of your Scaevolas and Scipios, of Regulus, and of Fabricius. This rather covet, this distinguish from that foul vanity and crafty malice of the devils. If there is in your nature any eminent virtue, only by true piety is it purged and perfected, while by impiety it is wrecked and punished. Choose now what you will pursue, that your praise may be not in yourself, but in the true God, in whom is no error. For of popular glory you have had your share; but by the secret providence of God, the true religion was not offered to your choice. Awake, it is now day; as you have already awaked in the persons of some in whose perfect virtue and sufferings for the true faith we glory: for they, contending on all sides with hostile powers, and conquering them all by bravely dying, have purchased for us this country of ours with their blood; to which country we invite you, and exhort you to add yourselves to the number of the citizens of this city, which also has a sanctuary of its own in the true remission of sins. Do not listen to those degenerate sons of thine who slander Christ and Christians, and impute to them these disastrous times,

though they desire times in which they may enjoy rather impunity for
their wickedness than a peaceful life. Such has never been Rome's ambition even in regard to her earthly country. Lay hold now on the celestial
country, which is easily won, and in which you will reign truly and for
ever. For there shalt thou find no vestal fire, no Capitoline stone, but the
one true God

> No date, no goal will here ordain:
> But grant an endless, boundless reign.

No longer, then, follow after false and deceitful gods; abjure them
rather, and despise them, bursting forth into true liberty. Gods they are
not, but malignant spirits, to whom your eternal happiness will be a sore
punishment. Juno, from whom you deduce your origin according to the
flesh, did not so bitterly grudge Rome's citadels to the Trojans, as these
devils whom yet ye repute gods, grudge an everlasting seat to the race of
mankind. And thou thyself hast in no wavering voice passed judgment
on them, when thou didst pacify them with games, and yet didst account
as infamous the men by whom the plays were acted. Suffer us, then, to
assert thy freedom against the unclean spirits who had imposed on thy
neck the yoke of celebrating their own shame and filthiness. The actors
of these divine crimes thou hast removed from offices of honour; suppli-
cate the true God, that He may remove from thee those gods who delight
in their crimes—a most disgraceful thing if the crimes are really theirs,
and a most malicious invention if the crimes are feigned. Well done, in
that thou hast spontaneously banished from the number of your citizens
all actors and players. Awake more fully: the majesty of God cannot be
propitiated by that which defiles the dignity of man. How, then, can you
believe that gods who take pleasure in such lewd plays, belong to the
number of the holy powers of heaven, when the men by whom these
plays are acted are by yourselves refused admission into the number of
Roman citizens even of the lowest grade? Incomparably more glorious
than Rome, is that heavenly city in which for victory you have truth; for
dignity, holiness; for peace, felicity; for life, eternity. Much less does it
admit into its society such gods, if thou dost blush to admit into thine
such men. Wherefore, if thou wouldst attain to the blessed city, shun the
society of devils. They who are propitiated by deeds of shame, are unworthy of the worship of right-hearted men. Let these, then, be
obliterated from your worship by the cleansing of the Christian religion,
as those men were blotted from your citizenship by the censor's mark.

But, so far as regards carnal benefits, which are the only blessings the
wicked desire to enjoy, and carnal miseries, which alone they shrink
from enduring, we will show in the following book that the demons have
not the power they are supposed to have; and although they had it, we

ought rather on that account to despise these blessings, than for the sake of them to worship those gods, and by worshipping them to miss the attainment of these blessings they grudge us. But that they have not even this power which is ascribed to them by those who worship them for the sake of temporal advantages, this, I say, I will prove in the following book; so let us here close the present argument.

Book Fourteenth

We have already stated in the preceding books that God, desiring not only that the human race might be able by their similarity of nature to associate with one another, but also that they might be bound together in harmony and peace by the ties of relationship, was pleased to derive all men from one individual, and created man with such a nature that the members of the race should not have died, had not the two first (of whom the one was created out of nothing, and the other out of him) merited this by their disobedience; for by them so great a sin was committed, that by it the human nature was altered for the worse, and was transmitted also to their posterity, liable to sin and subject to death. And the kingdom of death so reigned over men, that the deserved penalty of sin would have hurled all headlong even into the second death, of which there is no end, had not the undeserved grace of God saved some therefrom. And thus it has come to pass, that though there are very many and great nations all over the earth, whose rites and customs, speech, arms, and dress, are distinguished by marked differences, yet there are no more than two kinds of human society, which we may justly call two cities, according to the language of our Scriptures. The one consists of those who wish to live after the flesh, the other of those who wish to live after the spirit; and when they severally achieve what they wish, they live in peace, each after their kind. . . .

Although, therefore, lust may have many objects, yet when no object is specified, the word lust usually suggests to the mind the lustful excitement of the organs of generation. And this lust not only takes possession of the whole body and outward members, but also makes itself felt within, and moves the whole man with a passion in which mental emotion is mingled with bodily appetite, so that the pleasure which results is the greatest of all bodily pleasures. So possessing indeed is this pleasure, that at the moment of time in which it is consummated, all mental activity is suspended. What friend of wisdom and holy joys, who, being married, but knowing, as the apostle says, "how to possess his vessel in santification and honour, not in the disease of desire, as the Gentiles who know not God," would not prefer, if this were possible, to beget children without this lust, so that in this function of begetting offspring the members created for this purpose should not be stimulated by the heat of lust, but should be actuated by his volition, in the same way as his other members serve him for their respective ends? But even those who delight in this pleasure are not moved to it at their own will, whether they confine themselves to lawful or transgress to unlawful pleasures; but sometimes this lust importunes them in spite of themselves, and sometimes fails them when they desire to feel it, so that though lust rages in the mind, it stirs not in the body. Thus, strangely enough, this emotion not only fails to obey the legitimate desire to beget offspring, but also refuses to serve lascivious lust; and though it often opposes its whole combined energy to the soul that resists it, sometimes also it is divided against itself, and while it moves the soul, leaves the body unmoved.

Justly is shame very specially connected with this lust; justly, too, these members themselves, being moved and restrained not at our will, but by a certain independent autocracy, so to speak, are called "shameful." Their condition was different before sin. For as it is written, "They were naked and were not ashamed"—not that their nakedness was unknown to them, but because nakedness was not yet shameful, because not yet did lust move those members without the will's consent; not yet did the flesh by its disobedience testify against the disobedience of man. For they were not created blind, as the unenlightened vulgar fancy; for Adam saw the animals to whom he gave names, and of Eve we read, "The woman saw that the tree was good for food, and that it was pleasant to the eyes." Their eyes, therefore, were open, but were not open to this, that is to say, were not observant so as to recognise what was conferred upon them by the garment of grace, for they had no consciousness of their members warring against their will. But when they were stripped of this grace, that their disobedience might be punished by fit retribution, there began in the movement of their bodily members a shameless novelty which made nakedness indecent: it at once made them observant and made them ashamed. And therefore, after they violated God's command by open transgression, it is written: "And the eyes of them both were opened, and they knew that they were naked; and they sewed fig leaves together, and made themselves aprons." "The eyes of them both were opened," not to see, for already they saw, but to discern between the good they had lost and the evil into which they had fallen. And therefore also the tree itself which they were forbidden to touch was called the tree of the knowledge of good and evil from this circumstance, that if they ate of it it would impart to them this knowledge. For the discomfort of sickness reveals the pleasure of health. "They knew," therefore, "that they were naked"— naked of that grace which prevented them from being ashamed of bodily nakedness while the law of sin offered no resistance to their mind. And thus they obtained a knowledge which they would have lived in blissful ignorance of, had they, in trustful obedience to God, declined to commit that offence which involved them in the experience of the hurtful effects of unfaithfulness and disobedience. And therefore, being ashamed of the disobedience of their own flesh, which witnessed to their disobedience while it punished it, "they sewed fig leaves together, and made themselves aprons," that is, cinctures for their privy parts; for some interpreters have rendered the word by *succinctoria. Campestria* is, indeed, a Latin word, but it is used of the drawers or aprons used for a similar purpose by the young men who stripped for exercise in the *campus;* hence those who were so girt were commonly called *campestrati.* Shame modestly covered that which lust disobediently moved in opposition to the will which was thus punished for its own disobedience. Consequently all nations, being propagated from that one stock, have so strong an instinct to cover the shameful parts, that some barbarians do not uncover them even in the bath, but wash with their drawers on. In the dark solitudes of India also, though some philosophers go naked, and are therefore called gymnosophists, yet they make an exception in the case of these members, and cover them.

Lust requires for its consummation darkness and secrecy; and this not only when lawful intercourse is desired, but even such fornication as the earthly city has legalized. Where there is no fear of punishment, these permitted pleasures still shrink from the public eye. Even where provision is made for this lust, secrecy also is provided; and while lust found it easy to remove the prohibitions of law, shamelessness found it impossible to lay aside the veil of retirement. For even shameless men call this shameful; and though they love the pleasure, dare not display it. What! does not even conjugal intercourse, sanctioned as it is by law for the propagation of children, legitimate and honourable though it be, does it not seek retirement from every eye? Before the bridegroom fondles his bride, does he not exclude the attendants, and even the paranymphs, and such friends as the closest ties had admitted to the bridal chamber? The greatest master of Roman eloquence says, that all right actions wish to be set in the light, i.e. desire to be known. This right action, however, has such a desire to be known, that yet it blushes to be seen. Who does not know what passes between husband and wife that children may be born? Is it not for this purpose that wives are married with such ceremony? And yet, when this well-understood act is gone about for the procreation of children, not even the children themselves, who may already have been born to them, are suffered to be witnesses. This right action seeks the light, in so far as it seeks to be known, but yet dreads being seen. And why so, if not because that which is by nature fitting and decent is so done as to be accompanied with a shame-begetting penalty of sin? . . .

Accordingly, two cities have been formed by two loves: the earthly by the love of self, even to the contempt of God; the heavenly by the love of God, even to the contempt of self. The former, in a word, glories in itself, the latter in the Lord. For the one seeks glory from men; but the greatest glory of the other is God, the witness of conscience. The one lifts up its head in its own glory; the other says to its God, "Thou art my glory, and the lifter up of mine head." In the one, the princes and the nations it subdues are ruled by the love of ruling; in the other, the princes and the subjects serve one another in love, the latter obeying, while the former take thought for all. The one delights in its own strength, represented in the persons of its rulers; the other says to its God, "I will love Thee, O Lord, my strength." And therefore the wise men of the one city, living according to man, have sought for profit to their own bodies or souls, or both, and those who have known God "glorified Him not as God, neither were thankful, but became vain in their imaginations, and their foolish heart was darkened; professing themselves to be wise"—that is, glorying in their own wisdom, and being possessed by pride—"they became fools, and changed the glory of the incorruptible God into an image made like to corruptible man, and to birds, and four-footed beasts, and creeping things." For they were either leaders or followers of the people in adoring images, "and worshipped and served the creature more than the Creator, who is blessed for ever." But in the other city there is no human wisdom, but only godliness, which offers due worship to the true God, and looks for its reward in the society of the saints, of holy angels as well as holy men, "that God may be all in all."

Book Nineteenth

As I see that I have still to discuss the fit destinies of the two cities, the earthly and the heavenly, must first explain, so far as the limits of this work allow me, the reasonings by which men have attempted to make for themselves a happiness in this unhappy life, in order that it may be evident, not only from divine authority, but also from such reasons as can be adduced to unbelievers, how the empty dreams of the philosophers differ from the hope which God gives to us, and from the substantial fulfilment of it which He will give us as our blessedness. Philosophers have expressed a great variety of diverse opinions regarding the ends of goods and of evils, and this question they have eagerly canvassed, that they might, if possible, discover what makes a man happy. For the end of our good is that for the sake of which other things are to be desired, while it is to be desired for its own sake; and the end of evil is that on account of which other things are to be shunned, while it is avoided on its own account. Thus, by the *end of good,* we at present mean, not that by which good is destroyed, so that it no longer exists, but that by which it is finished, so that it becomes complete; and by the *end of evil* we mean, not that which abolishes it, but that which completes its development. These two ends, therefore, are the supreme good and the supreme evil; and, as I have said, those who have in this vain life professed the study of wisdom have been at great pains to discover these ends, and to obtain the supreme good and avoid the supreme evil in this life. And although they erred in a variety of ways, yet natural insight has prevented them from wandering from the truth so far that they have not placed the supreme good and evil, some in the soul, some in the body, and some in both. From this tripartite distribution of the sects of philosophy, Marcus Varro, in his book *De Philosophia,* has drawn so large a variety of opinions, that, by a subtle and minute analysis of distinctions, he numbers without difficulty as many as 288 sects—not that these have actually existed, but sects which are possible.

To illustrate briefly what he means, I must begin with his own introductory statement in the above-mentioned book, that there are four things which men desire, as it were by nature without a master, without the help of any instruction, without industry or the art of living which is called virtue, and which is certainly learned: either pleasure, which is an agreeable stirring of the bodily sense; or repose, which excludes every bodily inconvenience; or both these, which Epicurus calls by the one name, pleasure; or the primary objects of nature, which comprehend the things already named and other things, either bodily, such as health, and safety, and integrity of the members, or spiritual, such as the greater and less mental gifts that are found in men. Now these four things—pleasure, repose, the two combined, and the primary objects of nature—exist in us in such sort that we must either desire virtue on their account, or them for the sake of virtue, or both for their own sake; and consequently there arise from this distinction twelve sects, for each is by this consideration tripled. I will illustrate this in one instance, and, having done so, it will not be difficult to understand the others. According, then, as bodily pleasure is subjected, preferred, or united to virtue, there are three sects. It is subjected to virtue when it is chosen as subservient to virtue. Thus it is a duty of virtue to live for one's country, and for its sake to beget children, neither of which can be done without bodily pleasure. For there is pleasure in eating and drinking, pleasure also in sexual intercourse. But when it is preferred to virtue, it is desired for its own sake, and virtue is chosen only for its sake, and to effect nothing else than the attainment or preservation of bodily pleasure. And this, indeed, is to make life hideous; for where virtue is the slave of pleasure it no longer deserves the name of virtue. Yet even this disgraceful distortion has found some philosophers to patronize and defend it. Then virtue is united to pleasure when neither is desired for the other's sake, but both for their own. And therefore, as pleasure, according as it is subjected, preferred, or united to virtue, makes three sects, so also do repose, pleasure and repose combined, and the prime natural blessings, make their three sects each. For as men's opinions vary, and these four things are sometimes subjected, sometimes preferred, and sometimes united to virtue, there are produced twelve sects. But this number again is doubled by the addition of one difference, viz. the social life; for whoever attaches himself to any of these sects does so either for his own sake alone, or for the sake of a companion, for whom he ought to wish what he desires for himself. And thus there will be twelve of those who think some one of these opinions should be held for their own sakes, and other twelve who decide that they ought to follow this or that philosophy not for their own sakes only, but also for the sake of others whose good they desire as their own. These twenty-four sects again are doubled, and become forty-eight by adding a difference taken from the New Academy. For each of these four and twenty sects can hold and defend their opinion as certain, as the Stoics defended the position that the supreme good of man consisted solely in virtue; or they can be held as probable, but not certain, as the New Academics did. There are, therefore, twenty-four who hold their philosophy as certainly true, other twenty-four who hold their opinions as probable, but not certain. Again, as each person who attaches himself to any of these sects may adopt the mode of life either of the Cynics or of the other philosophers, this distinction will double the number, and so make ninety-six sects. Then, lastly, as each of these sects may be adhered to either by men who love a life of ease, as those who have through choice or necessity addicted themselves to study, or by men who love a busy life, as those who, while philosophizing, have been much occupied with state affairs and public business, or by men who choose a mixed life, in imitation of those who have apportioned their time partly to erudite leisure, partly to necessary business: by these differences the number of the sects is tripled, and becomes 288.

I have thus, as briefly and lucidly as I could, given in my own words the opinions which Varro expresses in his book. But how he refutes all the rest of these sects, and chooses one, the Old Academy, instituted by Plato, and continuing to Polemo, the fourth teacher of that school of philosophy which held that their system was certain; and how on this ground he distinguishes it from the New Academy, which began with Polemo's successor Arcesilaus, and held that all things are uncertain; and how he seeks to establish that the Old Academy was as free from error as from doubt—all this, I say, were too long to enter upon in detail, and yet I must not altogether pass it by in silence. Varro then rejects, as a first step, all those differences which have multiplied the number of sects; and the ground on which he does so is that they are not differences about the supreme good. He maintains that in philosophy a sect is created only by its having an opinion of its own different from other schools on the point of the ends-in-chief. For man has no other reason for philosophizing than that he may be happy; but that which makes him happy is itself the supreme good. In other words, the supreme good is the reason of philosophizing; and therefore that cannot be called a sect of philosophy which pursues no way of its own towards the supreme good. Thus, when it is asked whether a wise man will adopt the social life, and desire and be interested in the supreme good of his friend as in his own, or will, on the contrary, do all that he does merely for his own sake, there is no question here about the supreme good, but only about the propriety of associating or not associating a friend in its participation: whether the wise man will do this not for his own sake, but for the sake of his friend in whose good he delights as in his own. So, too, when it is asked whether all things about which philosophy is concerned are to be considered uncertain, as by the New Academy, or certain, as the other philosophers maintain, the question here is not what end should be pursued, but whether or not we are to believe in the substantial existence of that end; or, to put it more plainly, whether he who pursues the supreme good must maintain that it is a true good, or only that it appears to him to be true, though possibly it may be delusive—both pursuing one and the same good. The distinction, too, which is founded on the dress and manners of the Cynics, does not touch the question of the chief good, but only the question whether he who pursues that good which seems to himself true should live as do the Cynics. There were, in fact, men who, though they pursued different things as the supreme good, some choosing pleasure, others virtue, yet adopted that mode of life which gave the Cynics their name. Thus, whatever it is which distinguishes the Cynics from other philosophers, this has no bearing on the choice and pursuit of that good which constitutes happiness. For if it had any such bearing, then the same habits of life would necessitate the pursuit of the same chief good, and diverse habits would necessitate the pursuit of different ends. . . .

They say that this happy life is also social, and loves the advantages of its friends as its own, and for their sake wishes for them what it desires for itself, whether these friends live in the same family, as a wife, children, domestics; or in the locality where one's home is, as the citizens of the same town; or in the world at large, as the nations bound in common human brotherhood; or in the universe itself, comprehended in the heavens and the earth, as those whom they call gods, and provide as friends for the wise man, and whom we more familiarly call angels. Moreover, they say that, regarding the supreme good and evil, there is no room for doubt, and that they therefore differ from the New Academy in this respect, and they are not concerned whether a philosopher pursues those ends which they think true in Cynic dress and manner of life or in some other. And, lastly, in regard to the three modes of life, the comtemplative, the active, and the composite, they declare in favour of the third. That these were the opinions and doctrines of the Old Academy, Varro asserts on the authority of Antiochus, Cicero's master and his own, though Cicero makes him out to have been more frequently in accordance with the Stoics than with the Old Academy. But of what importance is this to us, who ought to judge the matter on its own merits, rather than to understand accurately what different men have thought about it?

If, then, we be asked what the city of God has to say upon these points, and, in the first place, what its opinion regarding the supreme good and evil is, it will reply that life eternal is the supreme good, death eternal the supreme evil, and that to obtain the one and escape the other we must live rightly. And thus it is written, "The just lives by faith," for we do not as yet see our good, and must therefore live by faith; neither have we in ourselves power to live rightly, but can do so only if He who has given us faith to believe in His help do help us when we believe and pray. As for those who have supposed that the sovereign good and evil are to be found in this life, and have placed it either in the soul or the body, or in both, or, to speak more explicitly, either in pleasure or in virtue, or in both; in repose or in virtue, or in both; in pleasure and repose, or in virtue, or in all combined; in the primary objects of nature, or in virtue, or in both—all these have, with a marvellous shallowness, sought to find their blessedness in this life and in themselves. Contempt has been poured upon such ideas by the Truth, saying by the prophet, "The Lord knoweth the thoughts of men" (or, as the Apostle Paul cites the passage, "The Lord knoweth the thoughts of the *wise*") "that they are vain."

For what flood of eloquence can suffice to detail the miseries of this life? Cicero, in the *Consolation* on the death of his daughter, has spent all his ability in lamentation; but how inadequate was even his ability here? For when, where, how in this life can these primary objects of nature be possessed so that they may not be assailed by unforeseen accident? Is the body of the wise man exempt from any pain which may dispel pleasure, from any disquietude which may banish repose? The amputation or decay of the members of the body puts an end to its integrity, deformity blights its beauty, weakness its health, lassitude its vigour, sleepiness or sluggishness its activity—and which of these is it that may not assail the flesh of the wise man? Comely and fitting attitudes and movements of the body are numbered among the prime natural blessings; but what if some sickness makes the members tremble? What if a man suffers from curvature of the spine to such an extent that his hands reach the ground, and he goes upon all-fours like a quadruped? Does not this destroy all beauty and grace in the body, whether at rest or in motion? What shall I say of the fundamental blessings of the soul, sense and intellect, of which the one is given for the perception, and the other for the comprehension of truth? But what kind of sense is it that remains when a man becomes deaf and blind? Where are reason and intellect when disease makes a man delirious? We can scarcely, or not at all, refrain from tears, when we think of or see the actions and words of such frantic persons, and consider how different from and even opposed to their own sober judgment and ordinary conduct their present demeanour is. And what shall I say of those who suffer from demoniacal possession? Where is their own intelligence hidden and buried while the malignant spirit is using their body and soul according to his own will? And who is quite sure that no such thing can happen to the wise man in this life? Then, as to the perception of truth, what can we hope for even in this way while in the body, as we read in the true book of Wisdom, "The corruptible body weigheth down the soul, and the earthly tabernacle presseth down the mind that museth upon many things"? And eagerness, or desire of action, if this is the right meaning to put upon the Greek ὁρμή, is also reckoned among the primary advantages of nature; and yet is it not this which produces those pitiable movements of the insane, and those actions which we shudder to see, when sense is deceived and reason deranged?

In fine, virtue itself, which is not among the primary objects of nature, but succeeds to them as the result of learning, though it holds the highest place among human good things, what is its occupation save to wage perpetual war with vices—not those that are outside of us, but within; not other men's, but our own—a war which is waged especially by that virtue which the Greeks call σωφροσύνη, and we temperance, and which bridles carnal lusts, and prevents them from winning the consent of the spirit to wicked deeds? For we must not fancy that there is no vice in us, when, as the apostle says, "The flesh lusteth against the spirit;" for to this vice there is a contrary virtue, when, as the same writer says, "The spirit lusteth against the flesh." "For these two," he says, "are contrary one to the other, so that you cannot do the things which you would." But what is it we wish to do when we seek to attain the supreme good, unless that the flesh should cease to lust against the spirit, and that there be no vice in us against which the spirit may lust? And as we cannot attain to this in the present life, however ardently we desire it, let us by God's help accomplish at least this, to preserve the soul from succumbing and yielding to the flesh that lusts against it, and to refuse our consent to the perpetration of sin. Far be it from us, then, to fancy that while we are still engaged in this intestine war, we have already found the happiness which we seek to reach by victory. And who is there so wise that he has no conflict at all to maintain against his vices?

We give a much more unlimited approval to their idea that the life of
the wise man must be social. For how could the city of God (concerning
which we are already writing no less than the nineteenth book of this
work) either take a beginning or be developed, or attain its proper destiny, if the life of the saints were not a social life? But who can enumerate
all the great grievances with which human society abounds in the misery
of this mortal state? Who can weigh them? Hear how one of their comic
writers makes one of his characters express the common feelings of all
men in this matter: "I am married; this is one misery. Children are born
to me; they are additional cares." What shall I say of the miseries of love
which Terence also recounts—"slights, suspicions, quarrels, war to-day,
peace to-morrow"? Is not human life full of such things? Do they not
often occur even in honourable friendships? On all hands we experience
these slights, suspicions, quarrels, war, all of which are undoubted evils;
while, on the other hand, peace is a doubtful good, because we do not
know the heart of our friend, and though we did know it to-day, we should
be as ignorant of what it might be to-morrow. Who ought to be, or who
are more friendly than those who live in the same family? And yet who
can rely even upon this friendship, seeing that secret treachery has often
broken it up, and produced enmity as bitter as the amity was sweet, or
seemed sweet by the most perfect dissimulation? It is on this account that
the words of Cicero so move the heart of every one, and provoke a sigh:
"There are no snares more dangerous than those which lurk under the
guise of duty or the name of relationship. For the man who is your
declared foe you can easily baffle by precaution; but this hidden, intestine, and domestic danger not merely exists, but overwhelms you before
you can foresee and examine it." It is also to this that allusion is made
by the divine saying, "A man's foes are those of his own household"—
words which one cannot hear without pain; for though a man have sufficient fortitude to endure it with equanimity, and sufficient sagacity to
baffle the malice of a pretended friend, yet if he himself is a good man,
he cannot but be greatly pained at the discovery of the perfidy of wicked
men, whether they have always been wicked and merely feigned goodness, or have fallen from a better to a malicious disposition. If, then,
home, the natural refuge from the ills of life, is itself not safe, what shall
we say of the city, which, as it is larger, is so much the more filled with
lawsuits civil and criminal, and is never free from the fear, if sometimes
from the actual outbreak, of disturbing and bloody insurrections and
civil wars?

What shall I say of these judgments which men pronounce on men, and
which are necessary in communities, whatever outward peace they enjoy? Melancholy and lamentable judgments they are, since the judges
are men who cannot discern the consciences of those at their bar, and are

therefore frequently compelled to put innocent witnesses to the torture
to ascertain the truth regarding the crimes of other men. What shall I say
of torture applied to the accused himself? He is tortured to discover
whether he is guilty, so that, though innocent, he suffers must undoubted
punishment for crime that is still doubtful, not because it is proved that
he committed it, but because it is not ascertained that he did not commit
it. Thus the ignorance of the judge frequently involves an innocent person in suffering. And what is still more unendurable—a thing, indeed, to
be bewailed, and, if that were possible watered with fountains of tears
—is this, that when the judge puts the accused to the question, that he
may not unwittingly put an innocent man to death, the result of this
lamentable ignorance is that this very person, whom he tortured that he
might not condemn him if innocent, is condemned to death both tortured
and innocent. For if he has chosen, in obedience to the philosophical
instructions to the wise man, to quit this life rather than endure any
longer such tortures, he declares that he has committed the crime which
in fact he has not committed. And when he has been condemned and put
to death, the judge is still in ignorance whether he has put to death an
innocent or a guilty person, though he put the accused to the torture for
the very purpose of saving himself from condemning the innocent; and
consequently he has both tortured an innocent man to discover his innocence, and has put him to death without discovering it. If such darkness
shrouds social life, will a wise judge take his seat on the bench or no?
Beyond question he will. For human society, which he thinks it a wickedness to abandon, constrains him and compels him to this duty. And he
thinks it no wickedness that innocent witnesses are tortured regarding
the crimes of which other men are accused; or that the accused are put
to the torture, so that they are often overcome with anguish, and, though
innocent, make false confessions regarding themselves, and are punished; or that, though they be not condemned to die, they often die during,
or in consequence of, the torture; or that sometimes the accusers, who
perhaps have been prompted by a desire to benefit society by bringing
criminals to justice, are themselves condemned through the ignorance of
the judge, because they are unable to prove the truth of their accusations
though they are true, and because the witnesses lie, and the accused
endures the torture without being moved to confession. These numerous
and important evils he does not consider sins; for the wise judge does
these things, not with any intention of doing harm, but because his ignorance compels him, and because human society claims him as a judge.
But though we therefore acquit the judge of malice, we must none the
less condemn human life as miserable. And if he is compelled to torture
and punish the innocent because his office and his ignorance constrain
him, is he a happy as well as a guiltless man? Surely it were proof of more

profound considerateness and finer feeling were he to recognise the misery of these necessities, and shrink from his own implication in that misery; and had he any piety about him, he would cry to God, "From my necessities deliver Thou me."

After the state or city comes the world, the third circle of human society—the first being the house, and the second the city. And the world, as it is larger, so it is fuller of dangers, as the greater sea is the more dangerous. And here, in the first place, man is separated from man by the difference of languages. For if two men, each ignorant of the other's language, meet, and are not compelled to pass, but, on the contrary, to remain in company, dumb animals, though of different species, would more easily hold intercourse than they, human beings though they be. For their common nature is no help to friendliness when they are prevented by diversity of language from conveying their sentiments to one another; so that a man would more readily hold intercourse with his dog than with a foreigner. But the imperial city has endeavoured to impose on subject nations not only her yoke, but her language, as a bond of peace, so that interpreters, far from being scarce, are numberless. This is true; but how many great wars, how much slaughter and bloodshed, have provided this unity! And though these are past, the end of these miseries has not yet come. For though there have never been wanting, nor are yet wanting, hostile nations beyond the empire, against whom wars have been and are waged, yet, supposing there were no such nations, the very extent of the empire itself has produced wars of a more obnoxious description—social and civil wars—and with these the whole race has been agitated, either by the actual conflict or the fear of a renewed outbreak. If I attempted to give an adequate description of these manifold disasters, these stern and lasting necessities, though I am quite unequal to the task, what limit could I set? But, say they, the wise man will wage just wars. As if he would not all the rather lament the necessity of just wars if he remembers that he is a man; for if they were not just he would not wage them, and would therefore be delivered from all wars. For it is the wrongdoing of the opposing party which compels the wise man to wage just wars; and this wrong-doing, even though it gave rise to no war, would still be matter of grief to man because it is man's wrong-doing. Let every one, then, who thinks with pain on all these great evils, so horrible, so ruthless, acknowledge that this is misery. And if any one either endures or thinks of them without mental pain, this is a more miserable plight still, for he thinks himself happy because he has lost human feeling. . . .

The philosophers who wished us to have the gods for our friends rank the friendship of the holy angels in the fourth circle of society, advancing now from the three circles of society on earth to the universe, and embracing heaven itself. And in this friendship we have indeed no fear that the angels will grieve us by their death or deterioration. But as we cannot mingle with them as familiarly as with men (which itself is one of the grievances of this life), and as Satan, as we read, sometimes transforms himself into an angel of light, to tempt those whom it is necessary to discipline, or just to deceive, there is great need of God's mercy to preserve us from making friends of demons in disguise, while we fancy we have good angels for our friends; for the astuteness and deceitfulness of these wicked spirits is equalled by their hurtfulness. And is this not a great misery of human life, that we are involved in such ignorance as, but for God's mercy, makes us a prey to these demons? And it is very certain that the philosophers of the godless city, who have maintained that the gods were their friends, had fallen a prey to the malignant demons who rule that city, and whose eternal punishment is to be shared by it. For the nature of these beings is sufficiently evinced by the sacred or rather sacrilegious observances which form their worship, and by the filthy games in which their crimes are celebrated, and which they themselves originated and exacted from their worshippers as a fit propitiation.

But not even the saints and faithful worshippers of the one true and most high God are safe from the manifold temptations and deceits of the demons. For in this abode of weakness, and in these wicked days, this state of anxiety has also its use, stimulating us to seek with keener longing for that security where peace is complete and unassailable. There we shall enjoy the gifts of nature, that is to say, all that God the Creator of all natures has bestowed upon ours—gifts not only good, but eternal—not only of the spirit, healed now by wisdom, but also of the body renewed by the resurrection. There the virtues shall no longer be struggling against any vice or evil, but shall enjoy the reward of victory, the eternal peace which no adversary shall disturb. This is the final blessedness, this the ultimate consummation, the unending end. Here, indeed, we are said to be blessed when we have such peace as can be enjoyed in a good life; but such blessedness is mere misery compared to that final felicity. When we mortals possess such peace as this mortal life can afford, virtue, if we are living rightly, makes a right use of the advantages of this peaceful condition; and when we have it not, virtue makes a good use even of the evils a man suffers. But this is true virtue, when it refers all the advantages it makes a good use of, and all that it does in making good use of good and evil things, and itself also, to that end in which we shall enjoy the best and greatest peace possible.

And thus we may say of peace, as we have said of eternal life, that it is the end of our good; and the rather because the Psalmist says of the city of God, the subject of this laborious work, "Praise the Lord, O Jerusalem; praise thy God, O Zion: for He hath strengthened the bars of thy gates;

He hath blessed thy children within thee; who hath made thy borders peace." For when the bars of her gates shall be strengthened, none shall go in or come out from her; consequently we ought to understand the peace of her borders as that final peace we are wishing to declare. For even the mystical name of the city itself, that is, *Jerusalem,* means, as I have already said, "Vision of Peace." But as the word peace is employed in connection with things in this world in which certainly life eternal has no place, we have preferred to call the end or supreme good of this city life eternal rather than peace. Of this end the apostle says, "But now, being freed from sin, and become servants to God, ye have your fruit unto holiness, and the end life eternal." But, on the other hand, as those who are not familiar with Scripture may suppose that the life of the wicked is eternal life, either because of the immortality of the soul, which some of the philosophers even have recognised, or because of the endless punishment of the wicked, which forms a part of our faith, and which seems impossible unless the wicked live for ever, it may therefore be advisable, in order that every one may readily understand what we mean, to say that the end or supreme good of this city is either peace in eternal life, or eternal life in peace. For peace is a good so great, that even in this earthly and mortal life there is no word we hear with such pleasure, nothing we desire with such zest, or find to be more thoroughly gratifying. So that if we dwell for a little longer on this subject, we shall not, in my opinion, be wearisome to our readers, who will attend both for the sake of understanding what is the end of this city of which we speak, and for the sake of the sweetness of peace which is dear to all. . . .

The peace of the body then consists in the duly proportioned arrangement of its parts. The peace of the irrational soul is the harmonious repose of the appetites, and that of the rational soul the harmony of knowledge and action. The peace of body and soul is the well-ordered and harmonious life and health of the living creature. Peace between man and God is the well-ordered obedience of faith to eternal law. Peace between man and man is well-ordered concord. Domestic peace is the well-ordered concord between those of the family who rule and those who obey. Civil peace is a similar concord among the citizens. The peace of the celestial city is the perfectly ordered and harmonious enjoyment of God, and of one another in God. The peace of all things is the tranquillity of order. Order is the distribution which allots things equal and unequal, each to its own place. And hence, though the miserable, in so far as they are such, do certainly not enjoy peace, but are severed from that tranquillity of order in which there is no disturbance, nevertheless, inasmuch as they are deservedly and justly miserable, they are by their very misery connected with order. They are not, indeed, conjoined with the blessed, but they are disjoined from them by the law of order. And though they are disquieted, their circumstances are notwithstanding adjusted to them, and consequently they have some tranquillity of order, and therefore some peace. But they are wretched because, although not wholly miserable, they are not in that place where any mixture of misery is impossible. They would, however, be more wretched if they had not that peace which arises from being in harmony with the natural order of things. When they suffer, their peace is in so far disturbed; but their peace continues in so far as they do not suffer, and in so far as their nature continues to exist. As, then, there may be life without pain, while there cannot be pain without some kind of life, so there may be peace without war, but there cannot be war without some kind of peace, because war supposes the existence of some natures to wage it, and these natures cannot exist without peace of one kind or other.

And therefore there is a nature in which evil does not or even cannot exist; but there cannot be a nature in which there is no good. Hence not even the nature of the devil himself is evil, in so far as it is nature, but it was made evil by being perverted. Thus he did not abide in the truth, but could not escape the judgment of the Truth; he did not abide in the tranquillity of order, but did not therefore escape the power of the Ordainer. The good imparted by God to his nature did not screen him from the justice of God by which order was preserved in his punishment; neither did God punish the good which He had created, but the evil which the devil had committed. God did not take back all He had imparted to his nature, but something He took and something He left, that there might remain enough to be sensible of the loss of what was taken. And this very sensibility to pain is evidence of the good which has been taken away and the good which has been left. For, were nothing good left, there could be no pain on account of the good which had been lost. For he who sins is still worse if he rejoices in his loss of righteousness. But he who is in pain, if he derives no benefit from it, mourns at least the loss of health. And as righteousness and health are both good things, and as the loss of any good thing is matter of grief, not of joy—if, at least, there is no compensation, as spiritual righteousness may compensate for the loss of bodily health—certainly it is more suitable for a wicked man to grieve in punishment than to rejoice in his fault. As, then, the joy of a sinner who has abandoned what is good is evidence of a bad will, so his grief for the good he has lost when he is punished is evidence of a good nature. For he who laments the peace his nature has lost is stirred to do so by some relics of peace which make his nature friendly to itself. And it is very just that in the final punishment the wicked and godless should in anguish bewail the loss of the natural advantages they enjoyed, and should perceive that they were most justly taken from them by that God whose benign liberality they had despised. God, then, the most wise Crea-

tor and most just Ordainer of all natures, who placed the human race
upon earth as its greatest ornament, imparted to men some good things
adapted to this life, to wit, temporal peace, such as we can enjoy in this
life from health and safety and human fellowship, and all things needful
for the preservation and recovery of this peace, such as the objects which
are accommodated to our outward senses, light, night, the air, and waters
suitable for us, and everything the body requires to sustain, shelter, heal,
or beautify it: and all under this most equitable condition, that every man
who made a good use of these advantages suited to the peace of his mortal
condition, should receive ampler and better blessings, namely, the peace
of immortality, accompanied by glory and honour in an endless life made
fit for the enjoyment of God and of one another in God; but that he who
used the present blessings badly should both lose them and should not
receive the others.

The whole use, then, of things temporal has a reference to this result
of earthly peace in the earthly community, while in the city of God it is
connected with eternal peace. And therefore, if we were irrational animals, we should desire nothing beyond the proper arrangement of the
parts of the body and the satisfaction of the appetites—nothing, therefore, but bodily comfort and abundance of pleasures, that the peace of the
body might contribute to the peace of the soul. For if bodily peace be
awanting, a bar is put to the peace even of the irrational soul, since it
cannot obtain the gratification of its appetites. And these two together
help out the mutual peace of soul and body, the peace of harmonious life
and health. For as animals, by shunning pain, show that they love bodily
peace, and, by pursuing pleasure to gratify their appetites, show that they
love peace of soul, so their shrinking from death is a sufficient indication
of their intense love of that peace which binds soul and body in close
alliance. But, as man has a rational soul, he subordinates all this which
he has in common with the beasts to the peace of his rational soul, that
his intellect may have free play and may regulate his actions, and that
he may thus enjoy the well-ordered harmony of knowledge and action
which constitutes, as we have said, the peace of the rational soul. And for
this purpose he must desire to be neither molested by pain, nor disturbed
by desire, nor extinguished by death, that he may arrive at some useful
knowledge by which he may regulate his life and manners. But, owing
to the liability of the human mind to fall into mistakes, this very pursuit
of knowledge may be a snare to him unless he has a divine Master, whom
he may obey without misgiving, and who may at the same time give him
such help as to preserve his own freedom. And because, so long as he is
in this mortal body, he is a stranger to God, he walks by faith, not by sight;
and he therefore refers all peace, bodily or spiritual or both, to that peace
which mortal man has with the immortal God, so that he exhibits the

well-ordered obedience of faith to eternal law. But as this divine Master inculcates two precepts—the love of God and the love of our neighbour —and as in these precepts a man finds three things he has to love—God, himself, and his neighbour—and that he who loves God loves himself thereby, it follows that he must endeavour to get his neighbour to love God, since he is ordered to love his neighbour as himself. He ought to make this endeavour in behalf of his wife, his children, his household, all within his reach, even as he would wish his neighbour to do the same for him if he needed it; and consequently he will be at peace, or in well-ordered concord, with all men, as far as in him lies. And this is the order of this concord, that a man, in the first place, injure no one, and, in the second, do good to every one he can reach. Primarily, therefore, his own household are his care, for the law of nature and of society gives him readier access to them and greater opportunity of serving them. And hence the apostle says, "Now, if any provide not for his own, and especially for those of his own house, he hath denied the faith, and is worse than an infidel." This is the origin of domestic peace, or the well-ordered concord of those in the family who rule and those who obey. For they who care for the rest rule—the husband the wife, the parents the children, the masters the servants; and they who are cared for obey—the women their husbands, the children their parents, the servants their masters. But in the family of the just man who lives by faith and is as yet a pilgrim journeying on to the celestial city, even those who rule serve those whom they seem to command; for they rule not from a love of power, but from a sense of the duty they owe to others—not because they are proud of authority, but because they love mercy.

This is prescribed by the order of nature: it is thus that God has created man. For "let them," He says, "have dominion over the fish of the sea, and over the fowl of the air, and over every creeping thing which creepeth on the earth." He did not intend that His rational creature, who was made in His image, should have dominion over anything but the irrational creation—not man over man, but man over the beasts. And hence the righteous men in primitive times were made shepherds of cattle rather than kings of men, God intending thus to teach us what the relative position of the creatures is, and what the desert of sin is; for it is with justice, we believe, that the condition of slavery is the result of sin. And this is why we do not find the word "slave" in any part of Scripture until righteous Noah branded the sin of his son with this name. It is a name, therefore, introduced by sin and not by nature. The origin of the Latin word for slave is supposed to be found in the circumstance that those who by the law of war were liable to be killed were sometimes preserved by their victors, and were hence called servants. And these circumstances could never have arisen save through sin. For even when we wage a just war, our adversaries must be sinning; and every victory, even though gained by wicked men, is a result of the first judgment of God, who humbles the vanquished either for the sake of removing or of punishing their sins. Witness that man of God, Daniel, who, when he was in captivity, confessed to God his own sins and the sins of his people, and declares with pious grief that these were the cause of the captivity. The prime cause, then, of slavery is sin, which brings man under the dominion of his fellow—that which does not happen save by the judgment of God, with whom is no unrighteousness, and who knows how to award fit punishments to every variety of offence. But our Master in heaven says, "Every one who doeth sin is the servant of sin." And thus there are many wicked masters who have religious men as their slaves, and who are yet themselves in bondage; "for of whom a man is overcome, of the same is he brought in bondage." And beyond question it is a happier thing to be the slave of a man than of a lust; for even this very lust of ruling, to mention no others, lays waste men's hearts with the most ruthless dominion. Moreover, when men are subjected to one another in a peaceful order, the lowly position does as much good to the servant as the proud position does harm to the master. But by nature, as God first created us, no one is the slave either of man or of sin. This servitude is, however, penal, and is appointed by that law which enjoins the preservation of the natural order and forbids its disturbance; for if nothing had been done in violation of that law, there would have been nothing to restrain by penal servitude. And therefore the apostle admonishes slaves to be subject to their masters, and to serve them heartily and with good-will, so that, if they cannot be freed by their masters, they may themselves make their slavery in some sort free, by serving not in crafty fear, but in faithful love, until all unrighteousness pass away, and all principality and every human power be brought to nothing, and God be all in all.

And therefore, although our righteous fathers had slaves, and administered their domestic affairs so as to distinguish between the condition of slaves and the heirship of sons in regard to the blessings of this life, yet in regard to the worship of God, in whom we hope for eternal blessings, they took an equally loving oversight of all the members of their household. And this is so much in accordance with the natural order, that the head of the household was called *paterfamilias;* and this name has been so generally accepted, that even those whose rule is unrighteous are glad to apply it to themselves. But those who are true fathers of their households desire and endeavour that all the members of their household, equally with their own children, should worship and win God, and should come to that heavenly home in which the duty of ruling men is no longer necessary, because the duty of caring for their everlasting happiness has also ceased; but, until they reach that home, masters ought to feel their position of authority a greater burden than servants their service. And if any member of the family interrupts the domestic peace by disobedience, he is corrected either by word or blow, or some kind of just and legitimate punishment, such as society permits, that he may himself be the better for it, and be readjusted to the family harmony from which he had dislocated himself. For as it is not benevolent to give a man help at the expense of some greater benefit he might receive, so it is not innocent to spare a man at the risk of his falling into graver sin. To be innocent, we must not only do harm to no man, but also restrain him from sin or punish his sin, so that either the man himself who is punished may profit by his experience, or others be warned by his example. Since, then, the house ought to be the beginning or element of the city, and every beginning bears reference to some end of its own kind, and every element to the integrity of the whole of which it is an element, it follows plainly enough that domestic peace has a relation to civic peace —in other words, that the well-ordered concord of domestic obedience and domestic rule has a relation to the well-ordered concord of civic obedience and civic rule. And therefore it follows, further, that the father of the family ought to frame his domestic rule in accordance with the law of the city, so that the household may be in harmony with the civic order.

But the families which do not live by faith seek their peace in the earthly advantages of this life; while the families which live by faith look for those eternal blessings which are promised, and use as pilgrims such advantages of time and of earth as do not fascinate and divert them from God, but rather aid them to endure with greater ease, and to keep down the number of those burdens of the corruptible body which weigh upon the soul. Thus the things necessary for this mortal life are used by both kinds of men and families alike, but each has its own peculiar and widely different aim in using them. The earthly city, which does not live by faith, seeks an earthly peace, and the end it proposes, in the well-ordered concord of civic obedience and rule, is the combination of men's wills to attain the things which are helpful to this life. The heavenly city, or rather the part of it which sojourns on earth and lives by faith, makes use of this peace only because it must, until this mortal condition which necessitates it shall pass away. Consequently, so long as it lives like a captive and a stranger in the earthly city, though it has already received the promise of redemption, and the gift of the Spirit as the earnest of it, it makes no scruple to obey the laws of the earthly city, whereby the things necessary for the maintenance of this mortal life are administered; and thus, as this life is common to both cities, so there is a harmony between them in regard to what belongs to it. But, as the earthly city has had some philosophers whose doctrine is condemned by the divine teaching, and who, being deceived either by their own conjectures or by demons, supposed that many gods must be invited to take an interest in human affairs, and assigned to each a separate function and a separate department—to one the body, to another the soul; and in the body itself, to one the head, to another the neck, and each of the other members to one of the gods; and in like manner, in the soul, to one god the natural capacity was assigned, to another education, to another anger, to another lust; and so the various affairs of life were assigned—cattle to one, corn to another, wine to another, oil to another, the woods to another, money to another, navigation to another, wars and victories to another, marriages to another, births and fecundity to another, and other things to other gods: and as the celestial city, on the other hand, knew that one God only was to be worshipped, and that to Him alone was due that service which the Greeks call λατρεία, and which can be given only to a god, it has come to pass that the two cities could not have common laws of religion, and that the heavenly city has been compelled in this matter to dissent, and to become obnoxious to those who think differently, and to stand the brunt of their anger and hatred and persecutions, except in so far as the minds of their enemies have been alarmed by the multitude of the Christians and quelled by the manifest protection of God accorded to them. This heavenly city, then, while it sojourns on earth, calls citizens out of all nations, and gathers together a society of pilgrims of all languages, not scrupling about diversities in the manners, laws, and institutions whereby earthly peace is secured and maintained, but recognising that, however various these are, they all tend to one and the same end of earthly peace. It therefore is so far from rescinding and abolishing these diversities, that it even preserves and adapts them, so long only as no hindrance to the worship of the one supreme and true God is thus introduced. Even the heavenly city, therefore, while in its state of pilgrimage, avails itself of the peace of earth, and, so far as it can without injuring faith and godliness, desires and maintains a common agreement among men regarding the acquisition of the necessaries of life, and makes this earthly peace bear upon the peace of heaven; for this alone can be truly called and esteemed the peace of the reasonable creatures, consisting as it does in the perfectly ordered and harmonious enjoyment of God and of one another in God. When we shall have reached that peace, this mortal life shall give place to one that is eternal, and our body shall be no more this animal body which by its corruption weighs down the soul, but a spiritual body feeling no want, and in all its members subjected to the will. In its pilgrim state the heavenly city possesses this peace by faith; and by this faith it lives righteously when it refers to the attainment of that peace every good action towards God and man; for the life of the city is a social life.

As regards the uncertainty about everything which Varro alleges to be the differentiating characteristic of the New Academy, the city of God thoroughly detests such doubt as madness. Regarding matters which it apprehends by the mind and reason it has most absolute certainty, although its knowledge is limited because of the corruptible body pressing down the mind, for, as the apostle says, "We know in part." It believes also the evidence of the senses which the mind uses by aid of the body; for [if one who trusts his senses is sometimes deceived], he is more wretchedly deceived who fancies he should never trust them. It believes also the Holy Scriptures, old and new, which we call canonical, and which are the source of the faith by which the just lives, and by which we walk without doubting whilst we are absent from the Lord. So long as this faith remains inviolate and firm, we may without blame entertain doubts regarding some things which we have neither perceived by sense nor by reason, and which have not been revealed to us by the canonical Scriptures, nor come to our knowledge through witnesses whom it is absurd to disbelieve.

It is a matter of no moment in the city of God whether he who adopts the faith that brings men to God adopts it in one dress and manner of life or another, so long only as he lives in conformity with the commandments of God. And hence, when philosophers themselves become Christians, they are compelled, indeed, to abandon their erroneous doctrines, but not their dress and mode of living, which are no obstacle to religion. So that we make no account of that distinction of sects which Varro adduced in connection with the Cynic school, provided always nothing indecent or self-indulgent is retained. As to these three modes of life, the contemplative, the active, and the composite, although, so long as a man's faith is preserved, he may choose any of them without detriment to his eternal interests, yet he must never overlook the claims of truth and duty. No man has a right to lead such a life of contemplation as to forget in his own ease the service due to his neighbour; nor has any man a right to be so immersed in active life as to neglect the contemplation of God. The charm of leisure must not be indolent vacancy of mind, but the investigation or discovery of truth, that thus every man may make solid attainments without grudging that others do the same. And, in active life, it is not the honours or power of this life we should covet, since all things under the sun are vanity, but we should aim at using our position and influence, if these have been honourably attained, for the welfare of those who are under us, in the way we have already explained. It is to this the apostle refers when he says, "He that desireth the episcopate desireth a good work." He wished to show that the episcopate is the title of a work, not of an honour. It is a Greek word, and signifies that he who governs, superintends, or takes care of those whom he governs: for ἐπί means over, and σχοπεῖν, to see; therefore

ἐπισχοπεῖν means *to oversee*. So that he who loves to govern rather than
to do good is no bishop. Accordingly no one is prohibited from the search
after truth, for in this leisure may most laudably be spent; but it is unseemly to covet the high position requisite for governing the people, even
though that position be held and that government be administered in a
seemly manner. And therefore holy leisure is longed for by the love of
truth; but it is the necessity of love to undertake requisite business. If no
one imposes this burden upon us, we are free to sift and contemplate
truth; but if it be laid upon us, we are necessitated for love's sake to
undertake it. And yet not even in this case are we obliged wholly to
relinquish the sweets of contemplation; for were these to be withdrawn,
the burden might prove more than we could bear.

Since, then, the supreme good of the city of God is perfect and eternal
peace, not such as mortals pass into and out of by birth and death, but
the peace of freedom from all evil, in which the immortals ever abide,
who can deny that that future life is most blessed, or that, in comparison
with it, this life which now we live is most wretched, be it filled with all
blessings of body and soul and external things? And yet, if any man uses
this life with a reference to that other which he ardently loves and confidently hopes for, he may well be called even now blessed, though not in
reality so much as in hope. But the actual possession of the happiness of
this life, without the hope of what is beyond, is but a false happiness and
profound misery. For the true blessings of the soul are not now enjoyed;
for that is no true wisdom which does not direct all its prudent observations, manly actions, virtuous self-restraint, and just arrangements, to
that end in which God shall be all and all in a secure eternity and perfect
peace.

But it may be replied, Who is this God, or what proof is there that He
alone is worthy to receive sacrifice from the Romans? One must be very
blind to be still asking who this God is. He is the God whose prophets
predicted the things we see accomplished. He is the God from whom
Abraham received the assurance, "In thy seed shall all nations be
blessed." That this was fulfilled in Christ, who, according to the flesh
sprang from that seed, is recognised, whether they will or no, even by
those who have continued to be the enemies of this name. He is the God
whose divine Spirit spake by the men whose predictions I cited in the
preceding books, and which are fulfilled in the Church which has extended over all the world. This is the God whom Varro, the most learned
of the Romans, supposed to be Jupiter, though he knows not what he says;
yet I think it right to note the circumstance that a man of such learning
was unable to suppose that this God had no existence or was contemptible, but believed Him to be the same as the supreme God. In fine, He is

the God whom Porphyry, the most learned of the philosophers, though
the bitterest enemy of the Christians, confesses to be a great God, even
according to the oracles of those whom he esteems gods. . . .

But if we discard this definition of a people, and, assuming another, say
that a people is an assemblage of reasonable beings bound together by
a common agreement as to the objects of their love, then, in order to
discover the character of any people, we have only to observe what they
love. Yet whatever it loves, if only it is an assemblage of reasonable
beings and not of beasts, and is bound together by an agreement as to the
objects of love, it is reasonably called a people; and it will be a superior
people in proportion as it is bound together by higher interests, inferior
in proportion as it is bound together by lower. According to this definition
of ours, the Roman people is a people, and its weal is without doubt a
commonwealth or republic. But what its tastes were in its early and
subsequent days, and how it declined into sanguinary seditions and then
to social and civil wars, and so burst asunder or rotted off the bond of
concord in which the health of a people consists, history shows, and in
the preceding books I have related at large. And yet I would not on this
account say either that it was not a people, or that its administration was
not a republic, so long as there remains an assemblage of reasonable
beings bound together by a common agreement as to the objects of love.
But what I say of this people and of this republic I must be understood
to think and say of the Athenians or any Greek state, of the Egyptians,
of the early Assyrian Babylon, and of every other nation, great or small,
which had a public government. For, in general, the city of the ungodly,
which did not obey the command of God that it should offer no sacrifice
save to Him alone, and which, therefore, could not give to the soul its
proper command over the body, nor to the reason its just authority over
the vices, is void of true justice.

For though the soul may seem to rule the body admirably, and the
reason the vices, if the soul and reason do not themselves obey God, as
God has commanded them to serve Him, they have no proper authority
over the body and the vices. For what kind of mistress of the body and
the vices can that mind be which is ignorant of the true God, and which,
instead of being subject to His authority, is prostituted to the corrupting
influences of the most vicious demons? It is for this reason that the
virtues which it seems to itself to possess, and by which it restrains the
body and the vices that it may obtain and keep what it desires, are rather
vices than virtues so long as there is no reference to God in the matter.
For although some suppose that virtues which have a reference only to
themselves, and are desired only on their own account, are yet true and
genuine virtues, the fact is that even then they are inflated with pride,

and are therefore to be reckoned vices rather than virtues. For as that which gives life to the flesh is not derived from flesh, but is above it, so that which gives blessed life to man is not derived from man, but is something above him; and what I say of man is true of every celestial power and virtue whatsoever.

Wherefore, as the life of the flesh is the soul, so the blessed life of man is God, of whom the sacred writings of the Hebrews say, "Blessed is the people whose God is the Lord." Miserable, therefore, is the people which is alienated from God. Yet even this people has a peace of its own which is not to be lightly esteemed, though, indeed, it shall not in the end enjoy it, because it makes no good use of it before the end. But it is our interest that it enjoy this peace meanwhile in this life; for as long as the two cities are commingled, we also enjoy the peace of Babylon. For from Babylon the people of God is so freed that it meanwhile sojourns in its company. And therefore the apostle also admonished the Church to pray for kings and those in authority, assigning as the reason, "that we may live a quiet and tranquil life in all godliness and love." And the prophet Jeremiah, when predicting the captivity that was to befall the ancient people of God, and giving them the divine command to go obediently to Babylonia, and thus serve their God, counselled them also to pray for Babylonia, saying, "In the peace thereof shall ye have peace"—the temporal peace which the good and the wicked together enjoy.

But the peace which is peculiar to ourselves we enjoy now with God by faith, and shall hereafter enjoy eternally with Him by sight. But the peace which we enjoy in this life, whether common to all or peculiar to ourselves, is rather the solace of our misery than the positive enjoyment of felicity. Our very righteousness, too, though true in so far as it has respect to the true good, is yet in this life of such a kind that it consists rather in the remission of sins than in the perfecting of virtues. Witness the prayer of the whole city of God in its pilgrim state, for it cries to God by the mouth of all its members, "Forgive us our debts as we forgive our debtors." And this prayer is efficacious not for those whose faith is "without works and dead," but for those whose faith "worketh by love." For as reason, though subjected to God, is yet "pressed down by the corruptible body," so long as it is in this mortal condition, it has not perfect authority over vice, and therefore this prayer is needed by the righteous. For though it exercises authority, the vices do not submit without a struggle. For however well one maintains the conflict, and however thoroughly he has subdued these enemies, there steals in some evil thing, which, if it does not find ready expression in act, slips out by the lips, or insinuates itself into the thought; and therefore his peace is not full so long as he is at war with his vices. For it is a doubtful conflict he wages with those that resist, and his victory over those that are defeated is not secure, but full of anxiety and effort. Amidst these temptations, therefore, of all which it has been summarily said in the divine oracles, "Is not human life upon earth a temptation?" who but a proud man can presume that he so lives that he has no need to say to God, "Forgive us our debts"? And such a man is not great, but swollen and puffed up with vanity, and is justly resisted by Him who abundantly gives grace to the humble. Whence it is said, "God resisteth the proud, but giveth grace to the humble." In this, then, consists the righteousness of a man, that he submit himself to God, his body to his soul, and his vices, even when they rebel, to his reason, which either defeats or at least resists them; and also that he beg from God grace to do his duty, and the pardon of his sins, and that he render to God thanks for all the blessings he receives. But, in that final peace to which all our righteousness has reference, and for the sake of which it is maintained, as our nature shall enjoy a sound immortality and incorruption, and shall have no more vices, and as we shall experience no resistance either from ourselves or from others, it will not be necessary that reason should rule vices which no longer exist, but God shall rule the man, and the soul shall rule the body, with a sweetness and facility suitable to the felicity of a life which is done with bondage. And this condition shall there be eternal, and we shall be assured of its eternity; and thus the peace of this blessedness and the blessedness of this peace shall be the supreme good.

But, on the other hand, they who do not belong to this city of God shall inherit eternal misery, which is also called the second death, because the soul shall then be separated from God its life, and therefore cannot be said to live, and the body shall be subjected to eternal pains. And consequently this second death shall be the more severe, because no death shall terminate it. But war being contrary to peace, as misery to happiness, and life to death, it is not without reason asked what kind of war can be found in the end of the wicked answering to the peace which is declared to be the end of the righteous? The person who puts this question has only to observe what it is in war that is hurtful and destructive, and he shall see that it is nothing else than the mutual opposition and conflict of things. And can he conceive a more grievous and bitter war than that in which the will is so opposed to passion, and passion to the will, that their hostility can never be terminated by the victory of either, and in which the violence of pain so conflicts with the nature of the body, that neither yields to the other? For in this life, when this conflict has arisen, either pain conquers and death expels the feeling of it, or nature conquers and health expels the pain. But in the world to come the pain continues that it may torment, and the nature endures that it may be sensible of it; and neither ceases to exist, lest punishment also should cease. Now, as it is through the last judgment that men pass to these ends, the good to the supreme good, the evil to the supreme evil, I will treat of this judgment in the following book.

Orosius

c. 385—c. 420

10

Orosius was a younger contemporary of Saint Augustine, born c. 385 in the Roman Iberian provinces (whether in what is now Spain or Portugal is uncertain). We know little of his early life. He entered the Church as a young man after receiving what his writings indicate to have been a sound education in both classical and Christian culture. In 414, Orosius fled his homeland, which was then being overrun by barbarians, and took refuge in North Africa where he was welcomed by Augustine who found him "a man of quick understanding, ready speech, and burning zeal. . . ." He performed various embassies for Augustine, traveling to the Holy Land and engaging in the Pelagian controversy then raging furiously. Upon his return to Hippo, Orosius, at Augustine's request, began his great work, the *Seven Books of History Against the Pagans*. The treatise was completed in 418 and it is believed that Orosius died soon after.

The *Seven Books* forms the basis of Orosius' lasting reputation. The treatise is in fact a complement to Augustine's *City of God* and like that work it is an apology, a "reply to the empty chatter and perversity of those who . . . are called pagans." While Augustine concerned himself with the lofty philosophical implications of the Christian view of history, Orosius engaged in the mundane task of elaborating the empirical, historical basis of that philosophy and of demonstrating the falsity of the pagan view that the world had become a sorrier place since the advent of Christianity. As Orosius writes: "You bade me, therefore, discover from all the available data of histories and annals whatever instances past ages have afforded of the burdens of war, the ravages of disease, the horrors of famine, of terrible earthquakes, extraordinary floods, dreadful eruptions of fire, thunderbolts and hailstorms, and also instances of the cruel miseries caused by parricides and disgusting crimes."

In carrying out Augustine's mandate, Orosius availed himself of much classical scholarship, ransacking the pages of Livy, Tacitus, and Caesar, among many others, for material congenial to his purpose. He summarized

315

most existing historical work on the empires of Babylonia, Macedon, Carthage, and Rome and included in his narrative a concise description of the geography of the "world" as it was then conceived. Throughout his history, Orosius drew upon Christian authors—Eusebius and Augustine, for example —and upon the Bible to illustrate and to support his interpretations. He did this work zealously and uncritically and it is not surprising that he found what he was seeking: "I have discovered that the days of the past were not only as oppressive as those of the present but that they were the more terribly wretched the further they were removed from the consolation of true religion." Like Augustine, Orosius had no doubts concerning the meaning and movement of history. He believed that "the world and man are directed by a Divine Providence." His *Seven Books,* then, are not a historical inquiry into causes and developments but rather a marshalling of "facts" within a Christian chronology to demonstrate an assumed truth, that truth being the validity of the Christian world view.

Orosius is important in historiography neither for his approach to history, which was sadly deficient, nor for his additions to historical knowledge, which were few enough. Rather, again like Augustine, he is important for his contribution to the philosophy of history, a Christian philosophy which turned away from the classical conception of history and rooted itself firmly in Biblical and Patristic theology. There is a further, important point which must be stressed. Throughout the Middle Ages, the *Seven Books* was regarded as an authoritative work on ancient history. Expressly written to buttress Augustine's arguments against the pagans, given the imprimatur of the great Bishop of Hippo, and, moreover, more apt to be read than Augustine's massive work, the *Seven Books* provided medieval historians the materials for their philosophy of history, a philosophy which they took to be Augustinian. Yet, Orosius, consciously or not, departed from the Augustinian position on many vital points. Where Augustine saw constant misery as the lot of mankind in the earthly city, Orosius found evidence of material and spiritual "progress." Augustine discerned no historical evolution either of peoples or monarchies; Orosius elaborated the ancient theory of the four successive monarchies— Babylonian, Carthaginian, Macedonian, and Roman—culminating, under divine guidance, with the establishment of the universal monarchy under Augustus at the very time of the birth of the Universal Savior. These events, Orosius concluded, augured well for Christians. Orosius was thus much closer in outlook to Eusebius than to Augustine. He was, in Theodor E. Mommsen's phrase, a "Christian progressivist" and as such diverged from the stern Pauline philosophy of his master. There is indeed evidence that Augustine was aware of this divergence: in one of the later books of *The City of God* he takes specific objection to a few Orosian positions and elsewhere he indicates a decline in his appreciation of his pupil's merit. But medieval historians appear unaware of the divergence. They took Orosius as Augustinian and perpetuated a philosophy of history that was in actuality a combination of the ideas of Augustine, Orosius, and Eusebius. In any event, it is clear that Orosius' "apology" was of great weight in the shifting of the balance from the classical to the Christian world view.

Selected Bibliography

The relationship between Orosius and Augustine is finely analyzed by Theodor E. Mommsen in his essay "Orosius and Augustine," included in Eugene F. Rice, Jr., ed., *Theodor E. Mommsen, Medieval and Renaissance Studies* (1959; reissued in 1966). Irving Woodworth Raymond provides a helpful introduction to his translation of Orosius' *Seven Books of History Against the Pagans* (1936). The present selections are from Raymond's edition. Another translation of the work has recently appeared, by Roy J. Defarrari (1964). Henry Wace and William Piercy, eds., *A Dictionary of Christian Biography and Literature* (1911), include an informative entry on Orosius.

SEVEN BOOKS OF HISTORY
AGAINST THE PAGANS

I have obeyed your instructions, blessed Augustine, and may my achievement match my good intentions. I am not at all certain, however, that I have done the work well. You, indeed, have already assumed the burden of judging whether I was capable of doing what you requested, but I am content with the evidence of obedience alone, if I have really done justice to that obedience by my will and my effort. So on a great and spacious family estate many different animals are able to help in the work of the estate, yet the care of the dogs is a particular concern. For these animals alone are so endowed by nature that they are driven on instinctively to do the things in which they are trained; through some inborn spirit of obedience they are held in check only by their fear of certain punishment, until the time when they are given permission, by word or sign, to do as they please. Indeed they have qualities peculiarly their own, so superior to those of brutes that they approach those of human beings, that is, they distinguish, they love, and they serve. When they distinguish between masters and strangers they do not really hate the strangers whom they attack but rather are zealous for their masters whom they love; in their attachment to their master and home they keep watch, not because they are so disposed naturally, but because they are inspired by a love filled with anxiety. Hence, according to the mystic revelation in the Gospels, the woman of Canaan was not ashamed to mention, nor did our Lord disdain to hear, that little dogs were eating the crumbs under their master's table. Nor did the blessed Tobias, following the guidance of an angel, scorn to have a dog as his companion. Therefore since the love that all have for you is in my case united with a special love, I have willingly obeyed your wish. My humble self owes all that I have accomplished to your fatherly advice, and my entire work is yours, because it proceeds from you and returns to you, so that my only contribution must be that I did it gladly.

You bade me reply to the empty chatter and perversity of those who,

From *Seven Books of History Against the Pagans,* translated by Irving W. Raymond (New York, Columbia University Press, 1936). Reprinted by permission of the publisher. Pp. 29–34, 60–61, 69–73, 316–320, 323–329, 332–334, 336–339.

aliens to the City of God, are called "pagans" *(pagani)* because they come from the countryside *(ex pagis)* and the crossroads of the rural districts, or "heathen" *(gentiles)* because of their wisdom in earthly matters. Although these people do not seek out the future and moreover either forget or know nothing of the past, nevertheless they charge that the present times are unusually beset with calamities for the sole reason that men believe in Christ and worship God while idols are increasingly neglected. You bade me, therefore, discover from all the available data of histories and annals whatever instances past ages have afforded of the burdens of war, the ravages of disease, the horrors of famine, of terrible earthquakes, extraordinary floods, dreadful eruptions of fire, thunderbolts and hailstorms, and also instances of the cruel miseries caused by parricides and disgusting crimes. I was to set these forth systematically and briefly in the course of my book. It certainly is not right for your reverence to be bothered with so trifling a treatise as this while you are intent on completing the eleventh book of your work against these same pagans. When your ten previous books appeared, they, like a beacon from the watchtower of your high position in the Church, at once flashed their shining rays over all the world. Also your holy son, Julian of Carthage, a servant of God, strongly urged me to carry out his request in this matter in such a way that I might justify his confidence in asking me.

I started to work and at first went astray, for as I repeatedly turned over these matters in my mind the disasters of my own times seemed to have boiled over and exceeded all usual limits. But now I have discovered that the days of the past were not only as oppressive as those of the present but that they were the more terribly wretched the further they were removed from the consolation of true religion. My investigation has shown, as was proper it should, that death and a thirst for bloodshed prevailed during the time in which the religion that forbids bloodshed was unknown; that as the new faith dawned, the old grew faint; that while the old neared its end, the new was already victorious; that the old beliefs will be dead and gone when the new religion shall reign alone. We must, of course, make an exception of those last, remote days at the end of the world when Antichrist shall appear and when judgment shall be pronounced, for in these days there shall be distress such as there never was before, as the Lord Christ by His own testimony predicted in the Holy Scriptures. At that time, according to that very standard which now is and ever shall be—yes, by a clearer and more searching discrimination—the saints shall be rewarded for the unbearable sufferings of those days and the wicked shall be destroyed.

Nearly all writers of history (Greek as well as Latin) who have perpetuated in their various works the deeds of kings and peoples for the sake of forming an enduring record have commenced their histories with Ninus, the son of Belus and king of the Assyrians. Indeed, these historians with their very limited insight would have us believe that the origin of the world and the creation of man was without beginning. Yet they definitely state that kingdoms and wars began with Ninus, as if forsooth the human race had existed up to that time in the manner of beasts and then, as though shaken and aroused, it awoke for the first time to a wisdom previously unknown to it. For my part, however, I have determined to date the beginning of man's misery from the beginning of his sin, touching only a few points and these but briefly.

From Adam, the first man, to Ninus, whom they call "The Great" and in whose time Abraham was born, 3,184 years elapsed, a period that all historians have either disregarded or have not known. But from Ninus, or from Abraham, to Caesar Augustus, that is, to the birth of Christ, which took place in the forty-second year of Caesar's rule, when, on the conclusion of peace with the Parthians, the gates of Janus were closed and wars ceased over all the world, there were 2,015 years. During this later period, whether one considers the men of action or the historians, the labors of all of them, both literary and active, were lavishly expended. My subject, therefore, requires a brief mention of at least a few facts from those books which, in their account of the origin of the world, have gained credence by the accuracy with which their prophecies were later fulfilled. I used these books not because I propose to press their authority upon anyone, but because it is worth while to repeat the common opinions that we ourselves all share.

In the first place, we hold that if the world and man are directed by a Divine Providence that is as good as it is just, and if man is both weak and stubborn on account of the changeableness of his nature and his freedom of choice, then it is necessary for man to be guided in the spirit of filial affection when he has need of help; but when he abuses his freedom, he must be reproved in a spirit of strict justice. Everyone who sees mankind reflected through himself and in himself perceives that this world has been disciplined since the creation of man by alternating periods of good and bad times. Next we are taught that sin and its punishment began with the very first man. Furthermore, even our opponents, who begin with the middle period and make no mention of the ages preceding, have described nothing but wars and calamities. What else are these wars but evils which befall one side or the other? Those evils which existed then, as to a certain extent they exist now, were doubtless either palpable sins or the hidden punishments for sin. What, then, prevents us from unfolding the beginning of this story, the main body of which has been set forth by others, and from showing, if in briefest outline, that the earlier period, which, we have pointed out, covered far more centuries than the latter, underwent the same kind of miseries?

I shall, therefore, speak of the period from the creation of the world to the founding of the City, and then of the period extending to the principate of Caesar and the birth of Christ, from which time dominion over the world has remained in the hands of the City down to the present day. So far as I can recall them, viewing them as if from a watchtower, I shall present the conflicts of the human race and shall speak about the different parts of the world which, set on fire by the torch of greed, now blaze forth with evils. With this in mind, I believe I must describe first the world itself, which the human race inhabits, how it was divided by our ancestors into three parts, and what regions and provinces compose its divisions. In this way when the theaters of war and the ravages of diseases shall be described, whoever wishes to do so may the more easily obtain a knowledge not only of the events and their dates but of their geography as well. . . .

But I am forced to confess that in the interest of anticipating the end of my book, I have left out many details concerning the evil conditions of the age and have abbreviated everything, since in no way could I have ever passed through so thick a forest of evils unless I had hastened my journey by frequent leaps. Inasmuch as the Assyrian kingdom was governed by about fifty kings and was hardly ever at peace during the one thousand one hundred and sixty years that elapsed before the reign of Sardanapalus (offensive and defensive wars were always being waged) what purpose will be served if I attempt to recall these events by enumerating them, to say nothing of describing them? This is especially so since I must discuss the deeds of the Greeks, and above all I must survey those of the Romans. Neither is there any need for me to recount the disgraceful deeds of Tantalus and Pelops, which are even more disgraceful when told. You will recall how the Phrygian king Tantalus most scandalously seized Ganymedes, the son of Tros, king of the Dardanians, and how he took him into his disgusting embrace. The poet Phanocles confirms the story and also mentions the fact that a great war arose on this account. Perhaps Phanocles tells this story because he wished this same Tantalus to appear as the servant of the gods when he corrupted the stolen boy in his own home in order to prepare him for the lust of Jove. Tantalus, indeed, did not hesitate to employ at Jove's banquets even his own son Pelops. . . .

Thirty years before the founding of the City, the Peloponnesians and the Athenians waged a great war into which both peoples entered with their full strength and enthusiasm. Each side was finally forced by mutual destruction to withdraw from combat and to terminate the war, as if both had been defeated. At this time a tribe of Amazons, accompanied by the Cimmerians, made a sudden incursion into Asia and wrought severe, prolonged, and widespread devastation and carnage.

Twenty years before the founding of the City, the Lacedaemonians involved in ruin the entire resources of Greece by waging a war of untiring fury against the Messenians, because the latter had outraged their virgins during the offering of a solemn sacrifice. The Lacedaemonians had bound themselves by great curses and had pledged themselves by solemn vows never to return home until they had captured Messena. Nevertheless they were recalled home when they had become weary from the siege which, though lasting ten years, had brought them none of the fruits of victory. They were also moved by the complaints of their wives who drew attention to their long widowhood and the danger of their becoming sterile. After deliberating on the matter, they became fearful that with no possibility of begetting children their own perseverance would promote their ruin even more than the Messenian War. They therefore sent back to Sparta those selected soldiers who, after taking the oath of allegiance, had come to the army as reinforcements. These soldiers were allowed to have promiscuous relations with all the women, a license infamous enough and not of any real use. But the Lacedaemonians persevered in their plan, captured the Messenians by fraud, and reduced them to slavery. When they had suffered cruel domination, scourgings, and chains for a long while, the Messenians shook off the yoke, took up arms, and renewed hostilities.

The Lacedaemonians chose the Athenian poet Tyrtaeus to be their leader in this war. After being routed in three battles, they made good their losses by adding to their army a band of slaves who had been granted their freedom. Even then they thought that they ought to give up the struggle because of threatening danger, but they were again inflamed by a poem composed by their poet and leader Tyrtaeus. When he recited the poem before the assembly of the people, they at once rushed again into the struggle. Their feelings were so greatly stirred when they attacked that hardly ever has a bloodier battle raged. Although the Lacedaemonians finally won the victory, the Messenians renewed the struggle a third time. Neither did the Lacedaemonians delay. Each side brought many troops to supplement its own forces. The Athenians prepared to attack the Lacedaemonians in a new quarter while the latter were engaged elsewhere. But the Lacedaemonians did not remain passive. Though they themselves were embroiled with the Messenians, they dispatched Peloponnesian troops to engage the Athenians in battle. The Athenians, who had sent a small fleet to Egypt, could not match the enemy's strength and were easily defeated in a naval engagement. Later, when this fleet had returned and the Athenian forces had also been strengthened by the flower of their troops, they challenged the victors to battle.

Abandoning the campaign against the Messenians, the Lacedaemoni-

ans turned their arms against the Athenians. A long and severe war
followed in which there was a succession of victories and defeats, and it
was uncertain which side would be victorious; finally, while the issue
was still hanging in the balance, both withdrew from the fray. (It must
be most clearly understood that it was Sparta herself that was given the
title of the Lacedaemonian state and hence the Lacedaemonians are
called Spartans.) When the Lacedaemonians were later recalled to the
Messenian War, they made an agreement with the Thebans, in order that
the Athenians might not have any rest in the interim. They promised to
restore to the Thebans the rule over the Boeotians, which the latter had
lost in the days of the Persian War, on the condition that the Thebans
would undertake a way against the Athenians in their behalf. So great
a fury possessed the Spartans that, even though they were already engaged in two wars, they would not refuse to undertake a third, provided
they could obtain new allies against their enemies.

Alarmed by such a storm of wars, the Athenians chose two leaders:
Pericles, a man of proven courage, and Sophocles, a writer of tragedies.
Dividing their forces, the Athenians, ravaged far and wide the territories
of the Spartans and added many cities of Asia to the Athenian Empire.
From this beginning the struggles continued for fifty years on land and
sea with victory ever doubtful, until the Spartans, with their wealth
dissipated and their confidence completely shattered, were regarded as
disgraced even by their own allies.

But we think of little moment those afflictions which lay so heavily
upon Greece. What we at present find difficult to bear is any interference
whatsoever in our pleasures or any restraint placed upon our passions,
even for a moment. There is this difference, however, between men of
that age and of this: the men of that age endured with patience those
unbearable burdens because they were born and raised amid them and
knew no better times, whereas men of our age, accustomed to perpetual
peace in a life of tranquillity and pleasure, are disturbed by every little
cloud of anxiety that envelops them. If only they would pray to Him who
can end this period of unrest, trifling though it be, and to Whom they owe
this continued peace which was unknown to other ages!

Remembering that I promised (even though I limit the order of my
narrative by some sort of division) to tell the history of the world from
the creation to the foundation of the City, let me here bring to an end this
book, which has set forth the story from the foundation of the world. My
following book then may begin from the foundation of the City. It will
contain the account of the evils of those days, which became more closely
intertwined, forasmuch as men indeed grew more versed and skilled in
wickedness. . . .

There is no person living today, I think, who does not acknowledge that

God created man in this world. Hence, whenever man sins, the world also
becomes subject to censure, and owing to our failure to control the passions that we ought to restrain, this earth on which we live is punished
by having its animal life die out and its crops fail. It follows, too, that if
we are the creation of God, we are also properly the object of His concern.
For who loves us more than He who made us? Who orders our existence
better than He who has created and loves us? Who can order and control
our actions more wisely or more firmly than He who foresaw what must
be done and then brought to pass what He had foreseen? Hence those who
have not read, feel, and those who have read, recognize, that all power
and all government come from God. But if powers are the gift of God, all
the more so are the kingdoms from which all other powers proceed. If the
kingdoms, however, are rivals, it is better that some one kingdom be
supreme, to which all the other kingdoms are subject. Thus, for instance,
in the beginning there was the Babylonian kingdom, then the
Macedonian, later the African, and finally the Roman, which endures
even unto our own day. By the same inscrutable plan, four main kingdoms were pre-eminent in successive stages at the four cardinal points
of the world, to wit, the Babylonian kingdom in the East, the Carthaginian in the South, the Macedonian in the North, and the Roman in
the West. Between the first and the last, that is, between the Babylonian
and the Roman, bridging as it were the space of years between an aged
father and his little son, there intervened the brief period of supremacy
of the African and Macedonian empires, circumstances rather than the
law of inheritance determining their role as guardians and trustees. I
shall now try to explain as clearly as possible whether this is really the
truth. . . .

In the year of the City seven hundred and fifty-two, when all nations,
from the East to the West, from the North to the South, and throughout
the entire circuit of the Ocean, were united in the bonds of peace, Caesar
Augustus had the gates of Janus closed for the third time. From that time
onward they remained bolted in complete stillness for almost twelve
years. Rust even gathered upon them and it was not until Augustus was
a very old man that they were forced to be opened because of a revolt of
the Athenians and the commotion raised by the Dacians. During this
period when the gates of Janus were closed, the emperor strove by the
maintenance of peace to nourish and to enlarge the state which he had
acquired by war, establishing many laws to inculcate in men the habit
of discipline through a reverence that was willingly given. The title
"lord" he avoided on the ground that he was only a man. Once, indeed,
when he was attending a play, this line was spoken in the farce: "Oh,
what a just and gracious lord"; whereupon the entire audience sprang to
its feet and applauded violently, as if these words had been spoken of

him. He immediately checked their unseemly flattery with a look and a gesture, and on the following day rebuked them in a severely worded edict. Thereafter he would not permit even his own children or grand-children to call him lord either in jest or in earnest.

At that time, that is, in the year when Caesar, by God's ordination, established the firmest and truest peace, Christ was born, Whose coming that peace waited upon and at Whose birth the angels joyfully sang in the hearing of men, "Glory to God in the highest, and on earth peace to men of good will." It was at this time that he who had secured universal supremacy refused to be called Lord of men, or rather dared not, when the true Lord of all mankind was born among men. It was also in this year when God had deigned to assume the appearance and nature of man, that this same Caesar, whom God had predestined for this great mystery, for the first time ordered a census to be taken of each and every province and that all men should be enrolled. In these days, then, Christ was born and His name was entered in the Roman census list immediately after His birth. This is that earliest and most famous acknowledgment which designated Caesar first of all men and the Romans lords of the world; for in the census list all men were entered individually, and in it the very Maker of all men wished to be found and enrolled as a man among men. From the very foundation of the world and the beginning of the human race an honor of this kind had never been granted, not even to Babylon or to Macedonia, not to mention any kingdom of lesser rank. Neither is there any doubt that it is clear to everyone from his own knowledge, faith, and investigation, that it was by the will of our Lord Jesus Christ that this City prospered, was protected, and brought to such heights of power, since to her, in preference to all others, He chose to belong when He came, thereby making it certain that He was entitled to be called a Ro-man citizen according to the declaration made in the Roman census list.

Now that I have reached the epoch when the Lord Christ first enlight-ened this world by His coming and granted a very peaceful reign to Caesar, let me conclude this sixth book of mine. The seventh, provided God gives me the requisite strength, will embrace the budding years of Christianity, its growth amid efforts made to suppress it, and its present state of advancement which is so sharply criticized by those whose state-ments force us to reply in kind. Since I have from the beginning declared both that men are sinners and that they are punished for their sins, so now, apart from the proposition that all men in general are inclined to sin and individually are chastised for their sins, I shall set forth first the various persecutions of the Christians and the retributions that followed.

Sufficient evidence has now been gathered, I think, that these truths may be publicly submitted for the approval of my critics without my making use of any secret known only to a small number of the faithful.

The One and true God, whom the Christian religion preaches, made the world and its creatures when He so willed, setting His creation in order through many separate acts, though in many of these acts His agency was not recognized. He established it for one purpose, when He was revealed by one event, and at one time He manifested and proved His power and patience in various ways. In this regard, indeed, I have for some time noticed that people who are narrow-minded and pessimistic resent the fact that great patience is associated with great power. If, indeed, He had the power, they say, to create the world, to establish peace therein, and to make known to it the worship and the knowledge of Himself, what need was there of so great a patience, or, as they themselves regard it, so pernicious a patience, that in the end the sins, disasters, and sufferings of mankind finally brought about conditions which could just as well have been produced in the beginning through the might of the God whom you are preaching? To these persons, indeed, I might truly answer that the human race from the beginning was so created and fashioned that, living according to the precepts of religion, in peace, and without toil, it might gain eternal life as a reward for its obedience. But having abused the goodness of the Creator, who had given it freedom, it turned His gift of liberty into stubborn disobedience and passed from the contempt of God into forgetfulness of God. In view of this, the patience of God is just in either case; for even if He is held in contempt He does not wholly destroy anyone to whom He wishes to be merciful, but by virtue of His power, as long as it is His will, He permits the man who despises Him to suffer trials. Hence it follows that it is always just for Him to guide such people in their ignorance, as He will in time, upon their repentance, mercifully restore to them the riches of their former grace.

These arguments, though advanced with great force and truth, do require, after all, a devout and willing listener. My present audience, however, whether or not they may come to believe at some future time, are certainly unbelievers now. Therefore I shall bring forward rather quickly arguments which, though my opponents may not approve, they certainly cannot disprove. Now, within the limits of our human comprehension, we and our opponents both revere religion and acknowledge and worship a higher power. The difference lies only in the nature of our belief; whereas we acknowledge that all things are from one God and through one God, they think there are as many gods as there are things. If, they say, it was in the power of the God whom you preach to make the Roman Empire so large and exalted, why then did His patience prevent it from reaching that state earlier? I shall answer them in the same vein: If it was in the power of the gods whom you preach to make the Roman Empire so large and exalted, why then did the patience of their gods prevent it from reaching that state earlier? Was it because the gods themselves did not exist? Or because Rome herself did not exist? Were the gods not worshipped at that time? Or did Rome not yet seem ready for power? If the gods were not yet in existence, their argument fails; but why discuss the delay of the gods, when I have not even discovered their nature? If, on the other hand, the gods were in existence, either their power, as my opponents really believe, or their patience was at fault; that is, either they could have acted and failed to do so, or else they wished to act but had not the power to do so. Or, if it seems more plausible to say that there were indeed gods at that time who could have aided the progress of the Romans, but that there were as yet no Romans who could rightly be assisted, I reply that we are looking for a power capable of creating suitable material to work on, not for mere workmanlike skill in shaping material already there. Our concern is with those whom the heathen consider as great gods, not with base artisans whose skill is useless unless their material is at hand. If indeed it was always possible for these gods to foreknow and to ordain—their foreknowledge should rather be assumed, since, in the case of omnipotence, to foreknow and to will concerning its own works are the same—whatever was foreknown and ordained ought not to have been delayed but to have been put into effect. Especially is this so since the pagans say that their Jove was wont to amuse himself by turning anthills into tribes of men. Nor do I think that we need to consider further the performance of rites, inasmuch as in the midst of continual sacrifices there was no end or relief from incessant disasters, except when Christ, the Saviour of the world, appeared. Although I think that it has already been sufficiently shown that the peace of the Roman Empire was prearranged for His coming, nevertheless I will endeavor to add a few more arguments to the previous ones.

In the seven hundred and fifty-second year of the City, Christ was born and brought the religion that gives salvation to the world. He is in truth the rock placed in the center of things. Whosoever strikes against Him shall be dashed to pieces, and whosoever believeth in Him shall be saved. He is in truth the glowing fire which illumines those who follow Him and consumes those who assail Him. He is Christ Himself, the Head of the Christians, the Saviour of the good, the Punisher of the wicked, the Judge of all. He set a pattern in word and in deed for those who were to follow Him and, in order to teach them patience in the persecutions that they would undergo for the sake of eternal life, He began His own sufferings as soon as He was brought into the world by the Virgin's travail. For no sooner had Herod, king of Judea, learned of His birth than he resolved to slay Him and, while he was seeking out this one infant, had a great many infants put to death. Hence we see the wicked suffer a just punishment for their malicious attacks; and hence, when the course of the world is peaceful, it is so because of those who believe, and when the world is vexed and disturbed, it is due to the punishments of blasphemers. Faithful Christians, however, are safe in any event, since at least they have either the assurance of rest in the life to come or the advantage of peace in this life. I shall show this more clearly by the facts themselves, as I relate them in order.

After the Lord Jesus Christ, the Redeemer of the world, had come to earth and had been enrolled in Caesar's census as a Roman citizen, the gates of war were kept closed twelve years, as I have said, in the happy serenity of peace. In the meantime Caesar Augustus sent his grandson Gaius to govern the provinces of Egypt and Syria. As Gaius was passing by the borders of Palestine, on his way from Egypt, he disdained, as Suetonius Tranquillus tells us, to worship at Jerusalem in the Temple of God, which was at that time venerated and much frequented. When he told Augustus about his conduct, the latter had the poor judgment to praise it as wise. Then so dreadful a famine visited the Romans in the forty-eighth year of Caesar's rule that Caesar ordered the gladiatorial bands, all foreigners, and also great numbers of slaves to be expelled from the City. Physicians and teachers were excepted. Thus, when the princeps sinned against the Holy One of God and the people were seized by famine, the greatness of the offense was shown by the nature of the punishment. Let me next quote the words of Cornelius Tacitus: "Janus was opened in the old age of Augustus and remained so until the rule of Vespasian, while new tribes were sought at the ends of the earth, often with gain and sometimes with loss." So much for Cornelius.

After the capture and overthrow of Jerusalem, as the prophets had foretold, and after the total destruction of the Jewish nation, Titus, who had been appointed by the decree of God to avenge the blood of the Lord Jesus Christ, celebrated with his father Vespasian his victory by a triumph and closed the Temple of Janus. Now, although the Temple of Janus was opened in the last days of Caesar, nevertheless there were no alarms of war for long periods thereafter, even though the army was ready for battle. Our Lord Jesus Christ Himself also had these facts in mind in the Gospels; for, when the whole world in those days was enjoying great quiet and all nations were united under the shelter of peace, He was asked by His disciples about the end of the coming times and replied in part as follows: "And you shall hear of wars and rumors of wars: see that you be not troubled: for all these things must come to pass, but the end is not yet. For nation shall rise against nation, and kingdom against kingdom: and there shall be pestilences, famines, and earthquakes, in diverse places. All these are the beginning of sorrows. Then shall they deliver you up to be afflicted, and shall kill you: and you shall be hated of all nations for my name's sake."

Thus He taught in His divine foresight and not only strengthened the faithful by His warning but also confounded the unbelieving by His prediction.

In the seven hundred and sixty-seventh year of the City, after the death of Augustus Caesar, Tiberius Caesar assumed the sovereignty and held it for twenty-three years. He waged no wars in person nor did his commanders wage any important wars, except that uprisings of peoples in some localities were anticipated and quickly crushed. To be sure, in the fourth year of his reign, Germanicus, the son of Drusus and father of Caligula, celebrated a triumph over the Germans, against whom he had been sent by Augustus in the latter's old age. Tiberius himself, however, during the greater part of his reign administered the affairs of the state with so deep a sense of responsibility and so great moderation that he wrote to some governors who had advised an increase in the tribute levied upon the provinces to the effect that "it is the duty of a good shepherd to shear his flock and not to flay them."

When the Lord Christ had suffered and risen from the dead and had sent forth His disciples to preach, Pilate, the governor of the province of Palestine, made a report to the emperor Tiberius and to the Senate concerning the passion and resurrection of Christ, and also the subsequent miracles that had been publicly performed by Him or were being done by His disciples in His name. Pilate also stated that a rapidly increasing multitude believed Him to be a god. When Tiberius, amid great approval, proposed to the Senate that Christ should be considered a god, the Senate became indignant because the matter had not been referred to it earlier in accordance with the usual custom, so that it might be the first to pass upon the recognition of a new cult. The Senate therefore refused to deify Christ and issued an edict that the Christians should be banished from the City. There was also the special reason that Sejanus, the prefect of Tiberius, was inflexibly opposed to the recognition of this religion. Nevertheless in an edict Tiberius threatened denouncers of Christians with death.

Now it came about that the emperor little by little abandoned his most praiseworthy policy of moderation in order to take revenge upon the Senate for its opposition; for he took pleasure in doing whatever he wished and from the mildest of princes he became the most savage of wild beasts. He proscribed a great army of senators and drove them to death. Of the twenty noblemen whom he had selected as his counselors, he left scarcely two unharmed and destroyed the others on various pretexts. He put to death his prefect Sejanus who was trying to stir up a revolution. There were clear indications that he poisoned both Drusus, his son by birth, and Germanicus, his son by adoption. He also killed his grandchildren, the sons of Germanicus. To recite his deeds one by one would be too horrible and scandalous. Suffice it to say that his lust and cruel rage grew so violent that those who had scorned to be saved under the rule of Christ were punished under the rule of Caesar.

In the twelfth year of Tiberius, a strange and unbelievable disaster occurred at the city of Fidenae. While the people were watching a gladiatorial performance, the seats of the amphitheater collapsed and killed more than twenty thousand persons. In truth, the ages to come may well heed the lesson of this great catastrophe that befell those who had so eagerly assembled to witness the death of their fellow men. And this at the very time when God had been pleased to become man for the sake of securing man's salvation!

In the seventeenth year of this emperor, the Lord Jesus Christ of His own free will submitted to His passion. Nevertheless, it was through their own impiety that the Jews arrested Him and nailed Him to the cross. At that time a very severe earthquake shook the whole world. The rocks upon the mountains were rent, and many sections of the largest cities were overthrown by its unusual violence. On that day, too, at the sixth hour, the sun was also entirely obscured and a hideous darkness suddenly overshadowed the earth; in the words of the poet,

> a godless age feared eternal night.

It is, however, perfectly plain that the sun's light was not cut off either by the moon or by clouds. For we are told that the moon, being fourteen days old at the time, was in the opposite quarter of the heavens, farthest from the sun, and that the stars were shining throughout the entire sky at that hour of the daytime or rather in that awful night. These facts are attested not only by the authority of the Holy Gospels but also by several books of the Greeks.

From the time of the passion of our Lord to this day, the Jews, who had persecuted Him to the extent of their power, have complained incessantly of an unbroken succession of disasters, until finally their nation, drained of its lifeblood and scattered abroad, disappeared from history. For Tiberius dispatched the youth of the Jewish nation to provinces having an unhealthful climate, using their military obligation as a pretext. He also forced the remainder of the Jews, as well as those who practiced similar rites, to leave Rome, threatening to make them slaves for life if they failed to obey. When the earthquake mentioned above demolished many cities of Asia, he remitted their tribute and made a donation to them from his own purse as well. The circumstances of the death of Tiberius led to suspicions that he had been poisoned.

In the seven hundred and ninetieth year of the City, Gaius Caligula, the third emperor counting from Augustus, began his reign. He ruled barely four years. He was more wicked than all his predecessors and seemed well worthy to be an instrument of vengeance upon the blaspheming

Romans and the persecuting Jews. Let me show in a word the extent of his savagery by quoting the exclamation that is attributed to him: "Would that the Roman people had but a single neck!" Furthermore, he often complained bitterly about the state of his times because they had been marked by no public disasters.

O, blessed beginnings of Christianity! So great was your power over the affairs of men that even the cruelty of man could only wish for disaster without finding them. See how hungry savagery loudly complains of the general peace:

> Within, impious rage,
> Sitting on savage arms, his hands
> Bound behind his back with a hundred brazen knots,
> Will send forth horrible roars from bloody lips.

Up to this time mutinous slaves and runaway gladiators terrified Rome, overturned Italy, ruined Sicily, and were dreaded by mankind throughout almost the whole world. But in the days of salvation, that is, in Christian times, not even a hostile Caesar could break the peace. Caligula, after making almost incredible preparations, set out to find an enemy in order to give his idle troops an opportunity to fight. Traversing Germany and Gaul he stopped on the seacoast opposite Britain. There he received the submission of Minocynobelinus who had been banished by his father, the king of the Britons, and who was now wandering about accompanied by a few followers. Lacking a ground for war, Caligula returned to Rome.

At this time the Jews, already harassed by misfortunes everywhere as a retribution for Christ's passion, were crushed in a riot that had broken out in Alexandria. They were driven from the city. Thereupon they commissioned a certain Philo, unquestionably a scholar of the first rank, to go as their representative to the emperor and set forth their grievances. But Caligula, who hated mankind in general, particularly detested the Jews. He therefore treated Philo's mission with contempt and commanded that all the holy places of the Jews, and especially that famous ancient sanctuary in Jerusalem, should be profaned with heathen sacrifices and filled with statues and images. He also gave orders that he himself should be worshipped there as a god. When Pilate, the governor who had pronounced the death sentence upon Christ and who had been the instigator as well as the object of many riots in Jerusalem, received this order, he was so tormented that he stabbed himself with his own hand and so quickly put an end to his miseries.

In addition to his other acts of lust, Gaius Caligula committed the crime of violating his own sisters. He then condemned them to exile and later ordered their execution and that of all other exiles. He himself, however, was murdered by his bodyguard. Among his private papers there were found two notebooks. One of these he had entitled *The Dagger,* the other, *The Sword.* Each contained the names of the most distinguished men of the two orders, senatorial and equestrian, together with marks indicating those who were to be killed. A huge chest of various poisons was also found. Claudius Caesar soon afterward ordered these poisons to be thrown into the sea, whereupon the waters became polluted and killed great numbers of fish, whose dead bodies were cast up by the waves along all the neighboring shores.

A really strong evidence of God's mercy may be seen in his manifestation of grace toward a people of whom only part were destined to become believers, and from the tempering of His wrath against them at that time when they persisted in their unbelief. How great a multitude of human beings escaped the death that had been prepared for them may be surmised and was indeed clear to all from the numbers of fish that had been poisoned. What havoc so great an amount of poison might have caused in the unfortunate city, if it had been skillfully used, is evident, since even its careless disposal polluted the sea. . . .

In the eight hundred and eighth year of the City, Nero Caesar, the fifth in succession from Augustus, became princeps. He held the office for almost fourteen years. In every vice and crime he followed his uncle, Gaius Caligula, and indeed he even surpassed him. There was no form of wickedness that he did not practice—wantonness, lust, extravagance, avarice, and cruelty. In the first place, his wantonness led him to visit nearly all the theaters of Italy and Greece, where he disgraced himself by wearing motley attire. Indeed he often imagined that he carried away the palm symbolizing victory from heralds, musicians, actors, and charioteers. Then the violence of his lusts became so great that he is said to have respected neither his mother's nor his sister's honor nor any blood relationship. Also he took a man to wife and was himself received as a wife by a man. His extravagance was so unbridled that he fished with nets of gold, which were drawn up by cords of purple, and he bathed in hot and cold perfumed waters. It is even said that he never traveled with less than a thousand carriages. He caused Rome to be burned in order to enjoy the spectacle and for six days and seven nights feasted his eyes on the blazing city. The warehouses, built of square stone, and the huge tenements of a bygone day, which the spreading flames could not reach, were demolished by great machines originally designed for use in foreign wars, and these buildings were then set on fire. The unfortunate plebeians were driven for shelter to monuments and tombs. The emperor himself viewed the conflagration from the lofty Tower of Maecenas. And while enjoying the beauty of the flames, it is said that he declaimed the Iliad in a tragedian's costume. The avarice of Nero was likewise so uncontrolled that, after the burning of the City, which Augustus, according to his boast, had changed from brick into marble, he would not allow anyone to approach the remains of his own property, but himself seized everything that had by any chance escaped the flames. He also ordered the Senate to appropriate ten million sesterces a year for his expenses. He deprived a great many senators of their property without cause, and in one day wiped out the entire wealth of all the merchants and inflicted torture upon them as well. His insane cruelty made him so savage that he killed the greater part of the Senate and almost annihilated the equestrian order. He did not even refrain from murdering members of his own family and without scruple destroyed his mother, brother, sister, wife, and all the rest of his blood relations and kinsmen.

All this mass of crime was crowned by Nero's daring impiety toward God. He was the first emperor to torture and put to death Christians at Rome and he ordered them to be harassed by a like persecution throughout all the provinces. In his attempt to root out their very name, he put to death Peter and Paul, the most blessed apostles of Christ, one by the cross and the other by the sword. Soon wretched Rome was engulfed by disasters pressing in upon her from every side. The following autumn so great a plague visited the City that thirty thousand funerals were entered in the register of the goddess Libitina. Britain at once suffered a disaster. Two of the principal towns were sacked and a great number of Roman citizens and their allies were slaughtered and destroyed. In the East, moreover, the important Armenian provinces were lost. Roman legions were forced to pass beneath the Parthian yoke, and Syria was retained only with great difficulty. In Asia an earthquake destroyed three cities, Laodicia, Hierapolis, and Colossae. In the meantime, Nero learned that the army in Spain had proclaimed Galba emperor. His courage and his hope utterly collapsed. In the midst of his wicked and unbelievable attempts to ruin and even to destroy the state, the Senate declared him a public enemy. He ignominiously fled and killed himself four miles from the City. With Nero the entire family of the Caesars became extinct.

During the eight hundred and twenty-fifth year of the City, after the passing of violent but brief storms in the form of illegal attempts to seize the throne, peace and calm returned under the rule of Vespasian. To go back a little in my story, the Jews, who after Christ's passion first were utterly forsaken by the grave of God and then beset on all sides by every kind of misfortune, were led astray by certain oracular responses given on Mount Carmel. These foretold that leaders would come out of Judaea and seize control of the government. Applying this prediction to themselves, the Jews broke out in rebellion. They massacred the Roman garrisons, put to flight the governor of Syria when he came with reinforcements, captured his standard, and cut his forces to pieces.

Vespasian, whom Nero sent against them, took his elder son Titus with him as one of his lieutenants. He also brought with him to Syria a number of strong legions. After taking many of the towns, he blockaded the Jews in Jerusalem, where they had gathered in large numbers because it was a feast day. On learning of Nero's death, he declared himself emperor. He was strongly urged to take this step by numerous kings and generals but most of all by the words of Joseph, a leader of the Jews. This man, when made prisoner and put in chains, had most confidently declared, as Suetonius tells us, that he would be released directly by the same person who had imprisoned him, but that that person would be the emperor. Vespasian, leaving his son Titus in camp to manage the siege of Jerusalem, set out for Rome by way of Alexandria. But when he heard that Vitellius had been killed, he stopped at Alexandria for a short time.

Titus, on his part, wore down the Jews by a long close siege. He finally made a breach in the city walls by using engines and all kinds of military apparatus, though not without the loss of many of his men. But it took more strength and a much longer time to capture the inner fortification of the Temple. A number of the priests and chief men had shut themselves up there and were maintaining its defense. When Titus had finally gained control of it, the construction and antiquity of the Temple aroused his admiration. He was for some time undecided whether he should burn it since its survival would encourage the enemy or whether he should preserve it as a memorial of his victory. But now that the Church of God had already blossomed forth richly throughout the world, it was His will that this building should be removed as an empty shell that had outlasted its usefulness. Therefore, Titus, after being acclaimed imperator by the army, set on fire and destroyed the Temple of Jerusalem, which, from the day of its founding to its final overthrow, had endured for 1102 years. All the walls of the city were leveled to the ground. According to Cornelius and Suetonius, six hundred thousand Jews were killed in this war. But Joseph the Jew, who was in command of the war at that time and who later found pardon and favor with Vespasian by predicting his accession, writes that eleven hundred thousand perished by the sword and by famine and that the remainder of the Jews were driven off in various conditions of misfortune and scattered throughout the world. These are said to have numbered about ninety thousand.

The emperors Vespasian and Titus celebrated their victory over the Jews by a magnificent triumphal entry into Rome. Of all the three hundred and twenty triumphs that had been held from the founding of the City until that time, so fair and strange a sight had not been seen by man —father and son riding in the same triumphal chariot after their glorious victory over those who had offended the Father and the Son. Now that all wars and uprisings had been put down at home and abroad, these emperors without delay proclaimed universal peace and decreed that double-faced Janus should be confined by the barring of his gates. This was the sixth time that this had occurred since the founding of the City. It was indeed right that the same honor should be paid to the avenging of the Lord's Passion as had been bestowed upon His Nativity. The Roman state then made great progress without suffering any of the tumults of war. Achaia, Lycia, Rhodes, Byzantium, Samos, Thrace, Cilicia, and Commagene were for the first time reduced to provinces and obeyed the judges and the laws of Rome.

In the ninth year of this emperor's reign, an earthquake destroyed three cities of Cyprus and at Rome there was a great plague. Vespasian died of dysentery at his country place among the Sabines in the ninth year of his principate.

In the eight hundred and twenty-eighth year of the City, Titus, eighth in the succession from Augustus if we exclude Otho and Vitellius from the list of emperors, succeeded Vespasian. He reigned for two years. His reign was so quiet that it is said that he did not shed the blood of a single person during his administration of the government. At this time, however, a conflagration suddenly broke out at Rome and consumed a great number of public buildings. It is also related that the top of Mount Bebius blew off and poured forth masses of molten lava and that these torrents of fire destroyed the surrounding country with its cities and their inhabitants. Titus succumbed to disease in the same country estate where his father had died. He was deeply mourned by all.

Gregory of Tours 538—594

11

Gregory, Bishop of Tours from 573 until his death in 594, was born at Clermont, Auvergne, into a prominent Gallo-Roman family. He experienced a privileged upbringing and education and was directed while yet quite young toward an ecclesiastical career. He appears to have lived his entire life within the confines of western France, centering around Tours, with a few visits to such cities as Paris, Metz, and Coblenz. Through his powerful family connections and by virtue of his position as Bishop of Tours Gregory came in contact with the most important people within his large diocese and throughout Gaul. He was a witness to or a participant in many of the events he describes in the *History of the Franks.*

Gregory turned to history because he wished, as he put it, "to commemorate the past, in order that it may come to the knowledge of the future." More particularly, he wanted to preserve the memory of his patron saint, Martin of Tours, and to record the events and personalities he deemed significant in an age of political turmoil and cultural decay. Gregory drew upon such sources as Eusebius, Jerome, and Orosius and, in some parts of the *History,* he utilized oral accounts provided by his many relatives and fellow ecclesiastics. With some reason, then, he has been called a Christian Herodotus. It is evident that he was well read in Biblical and Patristic writings and that he had some knowledge of Virgil and Sallust among the classical authors. However, in that age which was witness to the catastrophe of the culture and the institutions of the Roman Empire in the west, he shared the general attitude of his contemporaries toward all pagan literature, regarding it as dangerous, possibly diabolical in inspiration, and liable to lead Christians away from Salvation. His *History,* then, is Christian historiography. Gregory begins with Genesis, touches briefly upon the vicissitudes of the Roman Empire and leads up to the reception of Christianity in Roman Gaul. He then moves on to an account of the Frankish invasion and occupation of Gaul, relating how the

336

Franks conquered and were in turn converted, under Clovis, to Christianity.

In all of these developments Gregory sees the hand of God. With the breakdown of the Roman Empire the Church alone maintained at least a part of the cultural legacy of the past. Only the Church, with its legal, educational, and administrative institutions, preserved a semblance of ordered government. In such an ecclesiastical society the emphasis fell on spiritual and supernatural workings. Gregory's *History* is replete with accounts of miracles and of instances of divine intervention in the natural order of things. The outcome of wars, the death of a king or the birth of an heir, a violent storm or an outbreak of plague—all of these are invested with more than human or natural meaning. In all of them Gregory seeks after portents, hints as to the will and work of God. Developments in western Europe had forced Christian historiography onto a plane far removed from the majestic philosophical outlook of Augustine.

Even with his religious (or rather, superstitious) bias, however, Gregory wrote a *History* and not a compilation of fables. Auguste Molinier describes him as "at once passionate and indifferent; passionate in everything that concerned the Church . . . ; indifferent in matters concerning the laity." But since practically all aspects of life at that time fell within the purview of the Church, we may conclude that Gregory's *History* is the record of an impassioned observer of events both ecclesiastic and secular. The original title of his work was, apparently, *The Ecclesiastical History of the Franks*. There was no other way to write history at that time. Admittedly poorly written, marked by credulity and superstition, biased and uncritical in assessing the respective roles of Church and State, the work nevertheless has valid claim to the status of historiography. The *History* is the sincere record of a thoughtful and concerned witness who strives to be honest in his assessments and authoritative in his accounts. Gregory's work points ahead to the chronicles that were to pass as historiography in the Middle Ages; it is enough of a history to have earned for the author the title of "Father of the History of France."

Selected Bibliography

Auguste Molinier, *Les sources de l'histoire de France* (5 vols., 1901–1905), includes an informative entry on Gregory, with a helpful bibliography. Molinier accepts the view of Gregory as "Father of the History of France." O. M. Dalton provides an erudite and extensive introduction to Gregory. It is the first volume of the two volume edition of his translation of Gregory's *The History of the Franks* (1927). Ernest Brehaut has published an intelligently and sensitively edited version, *Gregory of Tours, History of the Franks* (1916). It conveys the essential Gregory, losing little of the specific Gregorian flavor. The present selections are

from the Brehaut edition which also contains an informative and valuable introduction. The *Société de l'histoire de France* published a translation of Gregory's
Les livres des miracles (1857). The editors wisely included an interesting and still
pertinent introduction to Gregory's works, written in 1699 by Dom Ruinart, one of
the many Benedictine monks of the time who contributed much to the development of modern historiographic method.

HISTORY OF THE FRANKS

With liberal culture on the wane, or rather perishing in the Gallic cities, there were many deeds being done both good and evil: the heathen were raging fiercely; kings were growing more cruel; the church, attacked by heretics, was defended by Catholics; while the Christian faith was in general devoutly cherished, among some it was growing cold; the churches also were enriched by the faithful or plundered by traitors—and no grammarian skilled in the dialectic art could be found to describe these matters either in prose or verse; and many were lamenting and saying: "Woe to our day, since the pursuit of letters has perished from among us and no one can be found among the people who can set forth the deeds of the present on the written page." Hearing continually these complaints and others like them I [have undertaken] to commemorate the past, in order that it may come to the knowledge of the future; and although my speech is rude, I have been unable to be silent as to the struggles between the wicked and the upright; and I have been especially encouraged because, to my surprise, it has often been said by men of our day, that few understand the learned words of the rhetorician but many the rude language of the common people. I have decided also that for the reckoning of the years the first book shall begin with the very beginning of the world, and I have given its chapters below. . . .

In the fifteenth year of king Childebert our deacon returned from Rome with relics of the saints and related that in the ninth month of the previous year the river Tiber so flooded the city of Rome that ancient temples were destroyed and the store-houses of the church were overturned and several thousand measures of wheat in them were lost. A multitude of snakes, among them a great serpent like a big log, passed down into the sea by the channel of this river, but these creatures were smothered among the rough and salty waves of the sea and cast up on the shore. Immediately after came the plague which they call *inguinaria*. It came in the middle of the eleventh month and according to what is read in the prophet Ezekiel: "Begin at my sanctuary," it first of all smote the pope

From *History of the Franks*, translated by Ernest Brehaut (New York, Columbia University Press, 1916). Reprinted by permission of the publisher. Pp. 1, 227–228, 231–233, 235–239, 243–244.

Pelagius and soon killed him. Upon his death a great mortality among
the people followed from this disease. But since the church of God could
not be without a head all the people chose Gregory the deacon. He belonged to one of the first senatorial families and from his youth was
devoted to God and with his own means had established six monasteries
in Sicily and a seventh within the Roman walls; and giving to these such
an amount of land as would suffice to furnish their daily food, he sold the
rest and all the furniture of his house and distributed the money among
the poor; and he who had been used to appear in the city arrayed in silken
robes and glittering jewels was now clad in cheap garments, and he
devoted himself to the service of the Lord's altar and was assigned as
seventh levite to aid the pope. And such was his abstinence in food, his
sleeplessness in prayer, his determination in fasting that his stomach
was weakened and he could scarcely stand upright. His was so versed in
grammar, dialectic, and rhetoric that he was believed second to none in
the city. He strove earnestly to avoid this high office for fear that a certain
pride at attaining the honor might sweep him back into the worldly
vanities he had rejected. And so he sent a letter to the emperor Mauricius
whose son he had taken from the holy font, adjuring him and entreating
him with many prayers never to grant his consent to the people to raise
him to this place of honor. But Germanus, prefect of Rome, forestalled
the messenger and had him arrested and the letter destroyed, and himself sent to the emperor the choice which the people had made. And the
emperor on account of his friendship with the deacon thanked God that
he had found a place of honor and sent his command to appoint him.

[Because of the plague Gregory makes an address to the people of Rome
to meet it by prayer.]

When he spoke these words bands of clergy gathered and he bade them
sing psalms for three days and pray for God's mercy. Every three hours
choirs of singers came to the church crying through the streets of the city
"Kyrie eleison." Our deacon who was there said that in the space of one
hour while the people uttered cries of supplication to the Lord eighty fell
to the ground and died. But the bishop did not cease to urge the people
not to cease from prayer. It was from Gregory while he was still deacon
that our deacon received the relics of the saints as we have said.

And when Gregory was making ready to go to a hiding place he was
seized and brought by force to the church of the blessed apostle Peter and
there he was consecrated to the duties of bishop and made pope of the
city. Our deacon did not leave until Gregory returned from the port to
become bishop, and he saw his ordination with his own eyes. . . .

And Chedinus with thirteen dukes entered Italy on the left and took five
strongholds and exacted oaths of fealty. But dysentery affected his army
severely—because the air was new to his men and disagreed with them

—and many died of it. But when the wind rose and it rained and the air began to freshen a little it brought health in place of sickness. Why more? For about three months they wandered through Italy without accomplishing anything or being able to take vengeance on their enemies, since they were shut up in strongholds, or to capture the king and take vengeance on him, since he was shut up within the walls of Pavia, and then the army sickened as we have said because of the unhealthfulness of the air and grew weak from hunger and prepared to return home after exacting oaths of fidelity and subjecting to the king's rule the people of the country which his father had held before and from which they took captives and other booty. And returning thus they were so starved that they sold their armor and clothing to buy food before they came to their native place. . . .

Maurice caused the Carthaginians who had killed king Childebert's legates the previous year, to be bound and loaded with chains and sent them to Childebert's presence, twelve in number, under these conditions, that if he wished to put them to death he should have permission: or if he would allow them to be ransomed he should receive three hundred gold pieces for each and be content; and thus he was to choose whichever he wished, that the disagreement might be more readily forgotten and no further cause of enmity arise between them. But king Childebert refused to accept the bound men and said: "It is uncertain in my mind whether these men you bring are the homicides or others, perhaps slaves of somebody or other, whereas our men who were killed in your country were free born." Grippo in particular, who had been legate at the time with the men who were killed, was present and said: "The prefect of the city with two or three thousand men whom he had gathered made an attack on us and killed my comrades; and I would have perished with them if I hadn't been able to make a brave defence. I can go to the place and identify the men. It is these that your emperor ought to punish if, as you say, he proposes to keep peace with our master." And so the king decided to send to the emperor for the guilty men and he bade these depart.

In these days Chuppa, who had once been king Chilperic's constable, made an inroad into the territory of Tours and desired to take flocks and other property as if he were taking booty. But the inhabitants had warning and a multitude gathered and began to pursue him. He lost his plunder and two of his men were killed: he escaped with nothing and two other men were captured; they were sent in fetters to king Childebert. He ordered them to be thrown into prison and examined as to who it was by whose aid Chuppa escaped from being captured by his pursuers. They answered that it was through a stratagem of the vicar Animodus, who had the power of a judge in that district. At once the king sent a letter and ordered the count of the city to send him in chains to the king's presence;

and if he should attempt resistance he was to crush him by force and even kill him, if he wished to gain the king's favor. But Animodus made no resistance but gave sureties and went as he was told, and finding Flavian the court-official he pleaded together with his companion and was not found guilty; they were acquitted and ordered to return home. However he first gave presents to the court-official. Chuppa a second time roused some of his people and purposed to carry off the daughter of Badigysel, former bishop of Mans, to marry her. He made a night attack with a band of his companions on the village of Mareil to fulfil his purpose, but Magnatrude, the mother of the girl and head of the household, had warning of him and his treachery; she went out against him with her slaves and repelled him by force, killing many of his men; and he did not come off without disgrace. . . .

In the same city king Childebert most piously remitted all the tribute of the churches as well as of the monasteries and of the clergy who were attached to a church and of whoever were engaged in cultivating the church land. For the collectors of the tribute had suffered great losses, since in the course of long time and succeeding generations the estates had been divided into small parts and the tribute could be collected only with difficulty, and Childebert by inspiration of God directed that the trouble should be remedied and the amount which was due to the fisc from these should not be exacted from the collectors, and that arrearage should not deprive any tiller of church land of his benefice. . . .

In the fifteenth year of king Childebert which is the twenty-ninth of Gunthram, while king Gunthram was hunting in the Vosges forest he found traces of the killing of a buffalo. And when he harshly demanded of the keeper of the forest who had dared to do this in the king's forest, the keeper named Chundo the king's chamberlain. Upon this he ordered Chundo to be arrested and taken to Chalon loaded with chains. And when the two were confronted with each other in the king's presence and Chundo said that he had never presumed to do what he was charged with, the king ordered a trial by battle. Then the chamberlain offered his nephew to engage in the fight in his place and both appeared on the field; the youth hurled his lance at the keeper of the forest and pierced his foot; and he presently fell on his back. The youth then drew the sword which hung from his belt but while he sought to cut his fallen adversary's throat he himself received a dagger thrust in the belly. Both fell dead. Seeing this Chundo started to run to Saint Marcellus's church. But the king shouted to seize him before he touched the sacred threshold and he was caught and tied to a stake and stoned. After this the king was very penitent at having shown himself so headlong in anger as to kill hastily for a trifling guilt a man who was faithful and useful to him. . . .

The scandal which by the help of the devil had arisen in the monastery at Poitiers was growing worse every day and Chrodield was sitting all prepared for strife, having gathered to herself, as I have said above, murderers, sorcerers, adulterers, run-away slaves and men guilty of all other crimes. And so she gave orders to them to break into the monastery at night and drag the abbess from it. But the latter heard the uproar coming and asked to be carried to the chest containing the relics of the holy cross—for she was painfully troubled with gout—thinking that she would be kept safe by their aid. Accordingly when the men had entered and lit the candles and were hurrying with weapons ready here and there through the monastery looking for her, they went into the oratory and found her lying on the ground before the chest of the holy cross. There-upon one who was fiercer than the rest, having come on purpose to commit this crime, namely, to cleave the abbess in two with the sword, was given a knife stab by another, the divine providence aiding in this, I suppose. The blood gushed out and he fell to the ground without fulfill-ing the vow he had foolishly made. Meantime Justina, the prioress, and the other sisters had taken the cloth of the altar which was before the Lord's cross and covered the abbess with it, putting the lights out at the same time. But the men came with drawn swords and spears and tore the nuns' clothes and almost crushed their hands and seized the prioress instead of the abbess, since it was dark, and pulled her robes off and tore her hair down and dragged her out and carried her off to place her under guard at St. Hilary's Church; but, as the dawn was coming on, they per-ceived when near the church that it was not the abbess, and presently they told the woman to return to the monastery. They returned, too, and seized the abbess and dragged her away and confined her near St. Hila-ry's Church in a place where Basina lodged, setting guards at the door so that no one should give aid to the captive. At the next twilight they entered the monastery and when they found no candles to light they took a cask from the storehouse which had been pitched and left to dry and set fire to it, and there was a great light while it burned, and they made plunder of all the furniture of the monastery, leaving only what they were unable to carry off. This happened seven days before Easter. And as the bishop was distressed at all this and could not calm this strife of the devil, he sent to Chrodield, saying: "Let the abbess go, so that she shall not be kept in prison during these days; otherwise I will not celebrate the Lord's Easter festival nor shall any catechumen receive baptism in this city unless you order the abbess to be set free from the confinement in which she is held. And if you refuse to let her go, I will call the citizens together and rescue her." When he said this, Chrodield appointed assas-sins, saying: "If any one tries to carry her off by violence, give her a thrust with the sword at once." Now Flavian came in those days; he had lately been appointed *domesticus,* and by his aid the abbess entered St. Hilary's

Church and was free. Meantime murders were being committed at the holy Radegunda's tomb, and certain persons were hacked to death in a disturbance before the very chest that contained the relics of the holy cross. And since this madness increased daily because of Chrodield's pride, and continual murders and other deeds of violence, such as I have mentioned above, were being done by her faction, and she had become so swollen up with boastfulness that she looked down with lofty contempt upon her own cousin Basina, the latter began to repent and say: "I have done wrong in supporting haughty Chrodield. Behold I am an object of contempt to her and made to appear a rebel against my abbess." She changed her course and humbled herself before the abbess and asked for peace with her; and they were equally of one thought and purpose. Then when the outrages broke out again, the men who were with the abbess, while resisting an attack which Chrodield's followers had made, wounded one of Basina's men who fell dead. But the abbess' men took refuge behind the abbess in the church of the confessor, and on this account Basina left the abbess and departed. But the men fled a second time, and the abbess and Basina entered again into friendly relations as before. Afterward many feuds arose between these factions; and who could ever set forth in words such wounds, such killings, and such wrong-doings, where scarcely a day passed without a murder, or an hour without a quarrel, or a moment without tears. King Childebert heard of this, and sent an embassy to king Gunthram to propose that bishops of both kingdoms should meet and punish these actions in accordance with the canons. And king Childebert ordered my humble self to sit on this case, together with Eberegisel of Cologne and Maroveus himself, bishop of Poitiers; and king Gunthram sent Gundigisil of Bordeaux with his provincials, since he was the metropolitan of this city. But I began to object, saying: "I will not go to this place unless the rebellion which has arisen because of Chrodield, is forcibly put down by the judge." For this reason a command was sent to Macco, who was then count, in which he was ordered to put the rebellion down by force if they should resist. Chrodield heard of this and ordered her assassins to stand armed before the door of the oratory, thinking they would fight against the judge, and if he wished to use force, they would resist with equal force. So it was necessary for this count to go there with armed men and to beat some with clubs and pierce others with spears, and when they resisted fiercely he had to attack and overwhelm them with the sword. When Chrodield saw this, she took the Lord's cross, the miraculous power of which she had before despised, and came out to meet them saying: "Do no violence to me, I beg of you, for I am a queen, daughter of one king and cousin of another; don't do it, lest a time may come for me to take vengeance on you." But the throng paid little heed to what she said but rushed, as I have said, upon those who were resisting and bound them and dragged them from the monastery and tied them to stakes and beat them fiercely and cut off the hair of some, the hands of others, and in a good many cases the ears and nose, and the rebellion was crushed and there was peace. Then the bishops who were present sat on the tribunal of the church, and Chrodield appeared and gave vent to much abuse of the abbess and many charges, asserting that she had a man in the monastery who wore woman's clothes and was treated as a woman although he had been very clearly shown to be a man, and that he was in constant attendance on the abbess herself, and she pointed her finger at him and said: "There he is himself." And when this man had taken the stand before all in woman's clothes, as I have stated, he said that he was impotent and therefore had put these clothes on; but he did not know the abbess except by name and he asserted that he had never seen her or spoken with her, as he lived more than forty miles from the city of Poitiers. Then as she had not proved the abbess guilty of this crime, she added: "What holiness is there in this abbess who makes men eunuchs and orders them to live with her as if she were an empress." The abbess, being questioned, replied that she knew nothing of this matter. Meantime when Chrodield had given the name of the man who was a eunuch, Reoval, the chief physician, appeared and said: "This man when he was a child was diseased in the thigh and was so ill that his life was despaired of; his mother went to the holy Radegunda to request that he should have some attention. But she called me and bade me give what assistance I could. Then I castrated him in the way I had once seen physicians do in Constantinople, and restored the boy in good health to his sorrowing mother; I am sure the abbess knows nothing of this matter." Now when Chrodield had failed to prove the abbess guilty on this charge also, she began fiercely to make others. But I have decided that it is better to insert the charges and the rebuttals of each in my narrative just as they are contained in the decision which was given as regards these same persons. . . .

After this when the decision was made known and they were excommunicated and the abbess restored to the monastery, they went to king Childebert, adding crime to crime, naming forsooth certain persons to the king who not only lived in adultery with the abbess but also sent messengers daily to his enemy Fredegunda. On hearing this the king sent men to bring them in chains. But when they were examined and no wrongdoing was found, they were let go. . . .

In this year there was such a light shed over the earth in the night that one would think it mid-day; moreover balls of fire were frequently noticed at night speeding across the sky and lighting the world. There was doubt about Easter for the reason that Victor wrote in his cycle that Easter came on the fifteenth day of the moon. But to prevent Christians from celebrating this festival at the same time of the moon as the Jews, he added: "But the Latins [place it] on the twenty-second of the moon." For this reason many in Gaul celebrated on the fifteenth of the moon but we celebrated on the twenty-second. We made careful inquiry but the springs in Spain which are filled by a divine power were filled at our Easter.

There was a great earthquake on the eighteenth day before the Kalends of the fifth month, being the fourth day [of the week], early in the morning when dawn was coming. The sun was eclipsed in the middle of the eighth month and its light was so diminished that it scarcely gave as much light as the horns of the moon on the fifth day. There were heavy rains, loud thunders in the autumn and the streams were very full. The bubonic plague cruelly destroyed the people of Viviers and Avignon. . . .

I wrote ten books of Histories, seven of Miracles, one on the Lives of the Fathers; a commentary in one book on Psalms; one book also on the Services of the Church. And though I have written these books in a style somewhat rude, I nevertheless conjure you all, God's bishops who are destined to rule the lowly church of Tours after me, by the coming of our Lord Jesus Christ and the judgment day, feared by the guilty, if you will not be condemned with the devil and depart in confusion from the judgment, never cause these books to be destroyed or rewritten, selecting some passages and omitting others, but let them all continue in your time complete and undiminished as they were left by us. And bishop of God, whoever you may be, if our Martianus has trained you in the seven disciplines, that is, if he has taught you by means of grammar to read, by dialectic to apprehend the arguments in disputes, by rhetoric to recognize the different meters, by geometry to comprehend the measurement of the earth and of lines, by astrology to contemplate the paths of the heavenly bodies, by arithmetic to understand the parts of numbers, by harmony to fit the modulated voice to the sweet accents of the verse; if in all this you are practiced so that my style will seem rude, even so I beg of you do not efface what I have written. But if anything in these books pleases you I do not forbid your writing it in verse provided my work is left safe.

William of Malmesbury

12

We know very little of the life of William of Malmesbury. It is believed he was born c. 1095. He tells us that his parents (who were of Norman-English stock) encouraged his education and we know that he entered the monastery at Malmesbury (whence his name) while still a boy. He rose to the post of choir leader, was named librarian of the monastery, and was also considered for but not elected abbot. He was hardly a cloistered monk. His reputation for erudition and scholarship (both relatively impressive, given his time) carried his name beyond the monastery walls. He was sought after as a historian and biographer and he was also involved in some of the political affairs of his time. In the midst of this active career he died at Malmesbury c. 1145.

William confesses in one of his works that the "pleasure (of books) possessed me from childhood: this source of delight has grown with my years." It was thus no accident that led him to the librarianship of his monastery. All of his adult life he collected books for his library, visiting many other monasteries for the purpose of obtaining manuscripts and copies of works, both Christian and pagan, he deemed valuable. He seems to have read and assimilated every book he collected, whether in theology, literature, biography or history, and himself wrote numerous books of miracles, biographies, chronicles and histories. He was particularly interested in history which, he wrote, "by an agreeable recapitulation of past events, excites its readers, by example, to frame their lives to the pursuit of good, or to aversion from evil." This view of the use of history is everywhere evident in the work that established William's reputation as a historian, his *Chronicle of the Kings of England*.

In that work, written c. 1120 and revised several times thereafter, William traces the history of the English and their kings from the fifth century down to his own time. He does this in traditional true chronicle form, joining a Christian chronology to a periodization based on the reigns and genealogies of the kings of England. In content as well William is a chronicler; he includes in his history accounts of miracles, moral tales, reports of plagues and other natural calamities, long digressions, usually of a monitory nature, and always relates the human condition to divine influence.

But William does not remain at the level of mere chronicles. He makes a noble effort to encompass the historical events which had unfolded in England and particularly those related to the Norman conquest of his homeland. His interpretation all too often lapses into providential or moral views in which he dilates on the sinfulness of the English who, justly chastised by God, fall prey to the more virtuous Normans. His basic theme is that of God working out His plan through historical time. Yet in his love for truth, his diligence in gathering sources, his desire "to bring to light events lying concealed in the confused mass of antiquity," and especially in his skeptical and critical approach to his evidence, both written and oral, he consistently breaks through to history. Thus, he calls his reader's attention to the defects in the ancient chronicles he uses in writing on the earlier centuries of English history while noting his preference for what he himself had seen or had heard from "credible authority" for contemporary events. Or again, he observes how difficult it is for either an Englishman or a Norman to write of William I, the former too quick to blame, the latter too quick to praise or excuse. Aware of the difficulty of attaining reasonable objectivity he yet trusts that "as the blood of either people flows in my veins, I shall steer a middle course." And, as a historian must, he selects as well as compiles, not reproducing his authorities whole but rather taking from them what is essential and pertinent, weaving a narrative out of others' chronicles. "History," J. A. Giles has written, "was the darling pursuit of Malmesbury." He succeeded, as he had hoped, in writing a chronicle-history "useful to the present age, and pleasing to posterity."

Selected Bibliography

J. A. Giles' edition, *William of Malmesbury, Chronicle of the Kings of England* (1889), includes a preface which is informative and intelligent throughout. Giles conveniently lists all of Malmesbury's writings and his notes are pertinent and enlightening. D. J. A. Matthew, *The Norman Conquest* (1966), devotes some pages to an informed and persuasive critique of Malmesbury's interpretation of the causes of the Norman victory without attempting to deny Malmesbury's claim to our respect as a historian (see pp. 288–297). Matthew's critique is especially pertinent when read in conjunction with James Gairdner's interesting and very favorable appreciation of Malmesbury in *Early Chroniclers of Europe: England* (n.d.), pp. 76–88. David C. Douglas draws upon Malmesbury as a trustworthy source in his *William the Conquerer* (1964), a work that is much more than a biography, discussing as it does "the Norman impact upon England." For the background and traditions within which Malmesbury worked see Peter Hunter Blair, *The World of Bede* (1970) and Robert W. Hanning, *The Vision of History in Early Britain* (1966).

CHRONICLE OF THE KINGS
OF ENGLAND

The Author's Epistle to Robert, Earl of Gloucester, son of King Henry.

To my respected Lord, the renowned Earl Robert, son of the King, health, and, as far as he is able, his prayers, from William, Monk of Malmesbury.

The virtue of celebrated men holds forth as its greatest excellence, its tendency to excite the love of persons even far removed from it: hence the lower classes make the virtues of their superiors their own, by venerating those great actions, to the practice of which they cannot themselves aspire. Moreover, it redounds altogether to the glory of exalted characters, both that they do good, and that they gain the affection of their inferiors. To you, Princes, therefore, it is owing, that we act well; to you, indeed, that we compose anything worthy of remembrance; your exertions incite us to make you live for ever in our writings, in return for the dangers you undergo to secure our tranquillity. For this reason, I have deemed it proper to dedicate the History of the Kings of England, which I have lately published, more especially to you, my respected and truly amiable Lord. None, surely, can be a more suitable patron of the liberal arts than yourself, in whom are combined the magnanimity of your grandfather, the munificence of your uncle, the circumspection of your father; more especially as you add to the qualities of these men, whom you alike equal in industry and resemble in person, this peculiar characteristic, a devotion to learning. Nor is this all: you condescend to honour with your notice those literary characters who are kept in obscurity, either by the malevolence of fame, or the slenderness of their fortune. And as our nature inclines us, not to condemn in others what we approve in ourselves, therefore men of learning find in you manners congenial to their own; for, without the slightest indication of moroseness, you regard them with kindness, admit them with complacency, and dismiss them with regret. Indeed, the greatness of your fortune has made no difference in you, except that your beneficence can now almost keep pace with your inclination.

From *Chronicle of the Kings of England*, translated by J. Sharpe, edited by J. A. Giles (London, G. Bell & Sons, Ltd., 1889). Reprinted by permission of the publisher. Pp. 1–4, 40–42, 45–49, 53–55, 57–67, 72–77.

Accept, then, most illustrious Sir, a work in which you may contemplate yourself as in a glass, where your Highness's sagacity will discover that you have imitated the actions of the most exalted characters, even before you could have heard their names. The Preface to the first book declares the contents of this work; on deigning to peruse which, you will briefly collect the whole subject-matter. Thus much I must request from your Excellency, that no blame may attach to me because my narrative often wanders wide from the limits of our own country, since I design this as a compendium of many histories, although, with a view to the larger portion of it, I have entitled it a History of the Kings of England.

Preface

The history of the English, from their arrival in Britain to his own times, has been written by Bede, a man of singular learning and modesty, in a clear and captivating style. After him you will not, in my opinion, easily find any person who has attempted to compose in Latin the history of this people. Let others declare whether their researches in this respect have been, or are likely to be, more fortunate; my own labour, though diligent in the extreme, has, down to this period, been without its reward. There are, indeed, some notices of antiquity, written in the vernacular tongue after the manner of a chronicle, and arranged according to the years of our Lord. By means of these alone, the times succeeding this man have been rescued from oblivion: for of Elward, a noble and illustrious man, who attempted to arrange these chronicles in Latin, and whose intention I could applaud if his language did not disgust me, it is better to be silent. Nor has it escaped my knowledge, that there is also a work of my Lord Eadmer, written with a chastened elegance of style, in which, beginning from King Edgar, he has but hastily glanced at the times down to William the First: and thence, taking a freer range, gives a narrative, copious, and of great utility to the studious, until the death of Archbishop Ralph. Thus from the time of Bede there is a period of two hundred and twenty-three years left unnoticed in his history; so that the regular series of time, unsupported by a connected relation, halts in the middle. This circumstance has induced me, as well out of love to my country, as respect for the authority of those who have enjoined on me the undertaking, to fill up the chasm, and to season the crude materials with Roman art. And that the work may proceed with greater regularity, I shall cull somewhat from Bede, whom I must often quote, glancing at a few facts, but omitting more.

The First Book, therefore, contains a succinct account of the English, from the time of their descent on Britain, till that of King Egbert, who, after the different Princes had fallen by various ways, gained the monarchy of almost the whole island.

But as among the English arose four powerful kingdoms, that is to say, of Kent, of the West Saxons, of the Northumbrians, and of the Mercians, of which I purpose severally to treat if I have leisure; I shall begin with that which attained the earliest to maturity, and was also the first to decay. This I shall do more clearly, if I place the kingdoms of the East Angles, and of the East Saxons, after the others, as little meriting either my labours, or the regard of posterity.

The Second Book will contain the chronological series of the Kings to the coming of the Normans.

The three following Books will be employed upon the history of three successive kings, with the addition of whatever, in their times, happened elsewhere, which, from its celebrity, may demand a more particular notice. This, then, is what I purpose, if the Divine favour shall smile on my undertaking, and carry me safely by those rocks of rugged diction, on which Elward, in his search after sounding and farfetched phrases, so unhappily suffered shipwreck. "Should any one, however," to use the poet's expression, "peruse this work with sensible delight," I deem it necessary to acquaint him, that I vouch nothing for the truth of long past transactions, but the consonance of the time; the veracity of the relation must rest with its authors. Whatever I have recorded of later times, I have either myself seen, or heard from credible authority. However, in either part, I pay but little respect to the judgment of my contemporaries: trusting that I shall gain with posterity, when love and hatred shall be no more, if not a reputation for eloquence, at least credit for diligence. . . .

A long period has elapsed since, as well through the care of my parents as my own industry, I became familiar with books. This pleasure possessed me from my childhood: this source of delight has grown with my years. Indeed I was so instructed by my father, that, had I turned aside to other pursuits, I should have considered it as jeopardy to my soul and discredit to my character. Wherefore mindful of the adage "covet what is necessary," I constrained my early age to desire eagerly that which it was disgraceful not to possess. I gave, indeed, my attention to various branches of literature, but in different degrees. Logic, for instance, which gives arms to eloquence, I contented myself with barely hearing. Medicine, which ministers to the health of the body, I studied with somewhat more attention. But now, having scrupulously examined the several branches of Ethics, I bow down to its majesty, because it spontaneously unveils itself to those who study it, and directs their minds to moral practice; History more especially; which, by an agreeable recapitulation of past events, excites its readers, by example, to frame their lives to the pursuit of good, or to aversion from evil. When, therefore, at my own expense, I had procured some historians of foreign nations, I proceeded, during my domestic leisure, to inquire if any thing concerning our own country could be found worthy of handing down to posterity. Hence it arose, that, not content with the writings of ancient times, I began, myself, to compose; not indeed to display my learning, which is comparatively nothing, but to bring to light events lying concealed in the confused mass of antiquity. In consequence rejecting vague opinions, I have studiously sought for chronicles far and near, though I confess I have scarcely profited any thing by this industry. For perusing them all, I still remained poor in information; though I ceased not my researches as long as I could find any thing to read. However, what I have clearly ascertained concerning the four kingdoms, I have inserted in my first book, in which I hope truth will find no cause to blush, though perhaps a degree of doubt may sometimes arise. I shall now trace the monarchy of the West Saxon kingdom, through the line of successive princes, down to the coming of the Normans: which if any person will condescend to regard with complacency, let him in brotherly love observe the following rule: "If before, he knew only these things, let him not be disgusted because I have inserted them; if he shall know more, let him not be angry that I have not spoken of them"; but rather let him communicate his knowledge to me, while I yet live, that at least, those events may appear in the margin of my history, which do not occur in the text.

Chapter III
Of the kings of the Northumbrians [A.D. 450]

We have before related briefly, and now necessarily repeat, that Hengist, having settled his own government in Kent had sent his brother Otha, and his son Ebusa, men of activity and tried experience, to seize on the northern parts of Britain. Sedulous in executing the command, affairs succeeded to their wishes. For frequently coming into action with the inhabitants, and dispersing those who attempted resistance, they conciliated with uninterrupted quiet such as submitted. Thus, though through their own address and the good will of their followers, they had established a certain degree of power, yet never entertaining an idea of assuming the royal title, they left an example of similar moderation to their immediate posterity. For during the space of ninety-nine years, the Northumbrian leaders, contented with subordinate power, lived in subjection to the kings of Kent. Afterwards, however, this forbearance ceased; either because the human mind is ever prone to degeneracy, or because that race of people was naturally ambitious. In the year, therefore, of our Lord's incarnation, 547, the sixtieth after Hengist's death, the principality was converted into a kingdom. The most noble Ida, in the full vigour of life and of strength, first reigned there. But whether he himself seized the chief authority, or received it by the consent of others, I by no means venture to determine, because the truth is unrevealed. However, it is sufficiently evident, that, sprung from a great and ancient lineage, he reflected much splendour on his illustrious descent, by his pure and unsullied manners. Unconquerable abroad, at home he tempered his kingly power with peculiar affability. Of this man, and of others, in their respective places, I could lineally trace the descent, were it not that the very names, of uncouth sound, would be less agreeable to my readers than I wish. It may be proper though to remark, that Woden had three sons; Weldeg, Withleg, and Beldeg; from the first, the kings of Kent derived their origin; from the second, the kings of Mercia; and from the third, the kings of the West-Saxons and Northumbrians, with the exception of the two I am going to particularize. This Ida, then, the ninth from Beldeg, and the tenth from Woden, as I find positively declared, continued in the government fourteen years.

His successor Alla, originating from the same stock, but descending from Woden by a different branch, conducted the government, extended by his exertions considerably beyond its former bounds, for thirty years. In his time, youths from Northumbria were exposed for sale, after the common and almost native custom of this people; so that, even as our days have witnessed, they would make no scruple of separating the nearest ties of relationship through the temptation of the slightest advantage. Some of these youths then, carried from England for sale to Rome, became the means of salvation to all their countrymen. For exciting the attention of that city, by the beauty of their countenances and the elegance of their features, it happened that, among others, the blessed Gregory, at that time archdeacon of the apostolical see, was present. Admiring such an assemblage of grace in mortals, and, at the same time, pitying their abject condition, as captives, he asked the standers-by, "of what race are these? Whence come they?" They reply, "by birth they are Angles; by country are Deiri (Deira being a province of Northumbria); subjects of King Alla, and Pagans." Their concluding characteristic he accompanied with heartfelt sighs: the others he elegantly alluded, saying, "that these Angles, *angel*-like, should be delivered from *(de) ira,* and taught to sing *Alle-luia."* Obtaining permission without delay from pope Benedict, the industry of this excellent man was all alive to enter on the journey to convert them; and certainly his zeal would have completed this intended labour, had not the mutinous love of his fellow citizens recalled him, already on his progress. He was a man as celebrated for his virtues, as beloved by his countrymen; for by his matchless worth, he had even exceeded the expectations they had formed of him from his youth. His good intention, though frustrated at this time, received afterwards, during his pontificate, an honourable termination, as the reader will find in its proper place. I have made this insertion with pleasure, that my readers might not lose this notice of Alla, mention of whom is slightly made in the life of Pope Gregory, who, although he was the primary cause of introducing Christianity among the Angles, yet, either by the counsel of God, or some mischance, was never himself permitted to know it. The calling, indeed, descended to his son. . . .

In this manner, all his rivals being slain or banished, Edwin, trained by many adversities, ascended, not meanly qualified, the summit of power. When the haughtiness of the Northumbrians had bent to his dominion, his felicity was crowned by the timely death of Redwald, whose subjects, during Edwin's exile among them, having formerly experienced his ready courage and ardent disposition, now willingly swore obedience to him. Granting to the son of Redwald the empty title of king, himself managed all things as he thought fit. At this juncture, the hopes and the resources of the Angles centred totally in him; nor was there a single province of Britain which did not regard his will, and prepare to obey it, except Kent: for he had left the Kentish people free from his incursions, because he had long meditated a marriage with Ethelburga, sister of their king. When she was granted to him, after a courtship long protracted, to the intent that he should not despise that woman when possessed whom he so ardently desired when withheld, these two kingdoms became so united by the ties of kindred, that, there was no rivalry in their powers, no difference in their manners. Moreover, on this occasion, the faith of Christ our Lord, infused into those parts by the preaching of Paulinus, reached first the king himself, whom the queen, among other proofs of conjugal affection, was perpetually instructing; nor was the admonition of bishop Paulinus wanting in its place. For a long time, he was wavering and doubtful; but once received, he imbibed it altogether. Then he invited neighbouring kings to the faith; then he erected churches, and neglected nothing for its propagation. In the meanwhile, the merciful grace of God smiled on the devotion of the king; insomuch, that not only the nations of Britain, that is to say, the Angles, Scots, and Picts, but even the Orkney and Mevanian isles, which we now call Anglesey, that is, islands of the Angles, both feared his arms, and venerated his power. At that time, there was no public robber; no domestic thief; the tempter of conjugal fidelity was far distant; the plunderer of another man's inheritance was in exile: a state of things redounding to his praise, and worthy of celebration in our times. In short, such was the increase of his power, that justice and peace willingly met and kissed each other, imparting mutual acts of kindness. And now indeed would the government of the Angles have held a prosperous course, had not an untimely death, the stepmother of all earthly felicity, by a lamentable turn of fortune, snatched this man from his country. For in the forty-eighth year of his age, and the seventeenth of his reign, being killed, together with his son, by the princes whom he had formerly subjugated, Cadwalla of the Britons and Penda of the Mercians, rising up against him, he became a melancholy example of human vicissitude. He was inferior to none in prudence: for he would not embrace even the Christian faith till he had examined it most carefully; but when once adopted, he esteemed nothing worthy to be compared to it.

Edwin thus slain, the sons of Ethelfrid, who were also the nephews of Edwin, Oswald, and Oswy, now grown up, and in the budding prime of youth, re-sought their country, together with Eanfrid, their elder brother, whom I forgot before to mention. The kingdom, therefore, was now divided into two. Indeed, Northumbria, long since separated into two provinces, had elected Alla, king of the Deirans, and Ida, of the Bernicians. Wherefore Osric, the cousin of Edwin, succeeding to Deira, and Eanfrid, the son of Ethelfrid, to Bernicia, they exulted in the recovery of their hereditary right. They had both been baptized in Scotland, though they were scarcely settled in their authority, ere they renounced their faith: but shortly after they suffered the just penalty of their apostasy through the hostility of Cadwalla. The space of a year, passed in these transactions, improved Oswald, a young man of great hope, in the science of government. Armed rather by his faith, for he had been admitted to baptism while in exile with many nobles among the Scots, than by his military preparations, on the first onset he drove Cadwalla, a man elated with the recollection of his former deeds, and, as he used himself to say, "born for the extermination of the Angles," from his camp, and afterwards destroyed him with all his forces. For when he had collected the little army which he was able to muster, he excited them to the conflict, in which, laying aside all thought of flight, they must determine either to conquer or die, by suggesting, "that it must be a circumstance highly disgraceful for the Angles to meet the Britons on such unequal terms, as to fight against those persons for safety, whom they had been used voluntarily to attack for glory only; that therefore they should maintain their liberty with dauntless courage, and the most strenuous exertions; but, that of the impulse to flight no feeling whatever should be indulged." In consequence they met with such fury on both sides, that, it may be truly said, no day was ever more disastrous for the Britons, or more joyful for the Angles: so completely was one party routed with all its forces, as never to have hope of recovering again; so exceedingly powerful did the other become, through the effects of faith and the accompanying courage of the king. From this time, the worship of idols fell prostrate in the dust; and he governed the kingdom, extended beyond Edwin's boundaries, for eight years, peaceably and without the loss of any of his people. Bede, in his History, sets forth the praises of this king in a high style of panegyric, of which I shall extract such portions as may be necessary, by way of conclusion. With what fervent faith his breast was inspired, may easily be learned from this circumstance. If at any time Aidan the priest addressed his auditors on the subject of their duty, in the Scottish tongue, and no interpreter was present, the king himself would directly, though habited in the royal robe, glittering with gold, or glowing with Tyrian purple, graciously assume that office, and explain the foreign idiom in his native language. It is well known too, that frequently at entertainments, when the guests had whetted their appetites and bent their inclinations on the feast, he would forego his own gratification; procuring, by his abstinence, comfort for the poor. So that I think the truth of that heavenly sentence was fulfilled even on earth, where the celestial oracle hath said, "He that dispersed abroad, he hath given to the poor, his righteousness remaineth for ever." And moreover, what the hearer must wonder at, and cannot deny, that identical royal right hand, the dispenser of so many alms, remains to this day perfect, with the arm, the skin and nerves, though the remainder of the body, with the exception of the bones, mouldering into dust, has not escaped the common lot of mortality. It is true the corporeal remains of some of the saints are unconscious altogether of decay. Wherefore let others determine by what standard they will fix their judgment; I pronounce this still more gracious and divine on account of its singular manifestation; because things ever so precious degenerate by frequency, and whatever is more unusual, is celebrated more generally. I should indeed be thought prolix were I to relate how diligent he was to address his prayers on high, and to fill the heavens with vows. This virtue of Oswald is too well known to require the support of our narrative. For at what time would that man neglect his supplications, who in the insurrection excited by Penda king of the Mercians, his guards being put to flight and himself actually carrying a forest of darts in his breast, could not be prevented by the pain of his wounds or the approach of death, from praying for the souls of his faithful companions? In such manner this personage, of surpassing celebrity in this world, and highly in favour with God, ending a valuable life, transmitted his memory to posterity by a frequency of miracles; and indeed most deservedly. For it is not common, but even more rare than a white crow, for men to abound in riches, and not give indulgence to their vices.

When he was slain, his arms with the hands and his head were cut off by the insatiable rage of his conqueror, and fixed on a stake. The dead trunk indeed, as I have mentioned, being laid to rest in the calm bosom of the earth, turned to its native dust; but the arms and hands, through the power of God, remain, according to the testimony of an author of veracity, without corruption. These being placed by his brother Oswy in a shrine, at the city of Bebbanburg, so the Angles call it, and shown for a miracle, bear testimony to the fact. Whether they remain at that place at the present day, I venture not rashly to affirm, because I waver in my opinion. If other historians have precipitately recorded any matter, let them be accountable: I hold common report at a cheaper rate, and affirm nothing but what is deserving of entire credit. . . .

He had for successor his son, Osred, a boy of eight years old; who disgracing the throne for eleven years, and spending an ignominious life in the seduction of nuns, was ultimately taken off by the hostility of his relations. Yet he poured out to them a draught from the same cup; for Kenred after reigning two, and Osric eleven years, left only this to be recorded of them; that they expiated by a violent death, the blood of their master, whom they supposed they had rightfully slain. Osric indeed deserved a happier end, for, as a heathen says, he was more dignified than other shades, because, while yet living he had adopted Ceolwulf, Kenred's brother, as his successor. Then Ceolwulf ascended the giddy height of empire, seventh in descent from Ida: a man competent in other respects, and withal possessed of a depth of literature, acquired by good abilities and indefatigable attention. Bede vouches for the truth of my assertion, who, at the very juncture when Britain most abounded with scholars, offered his History of the Angles, for correction, to his prince more especially; making choice of his authority, to confirm by his high station what had been well written; and of his learning, to rectify by his talents what might be carelessly expressed.

In the fourth year of his reign, Bede, the historian, after having written many books for the holy church, entered the heavenly kingdom, for which he had so long languished, in the year of our Lord's incarnation 734; of his age the fifty-ninth. A man whom it is easier to admire than worthily to extol: who, though born in a remote corner of the world, was able to dazzle the whole earth with the brilliancy of his learning. For even Britain, which by some is called another world, since, surrounded by the ocean, it was not thoroughly known by many geographers, possesses, in its remotest region, bordering on Scotland, the place of his birth and education. This region, formerly exhaling the grateful odour of monasteries, or glittering with a multitude of cities built by the Romans, now desolate through the ancient devastations of the Danes, or those more recent of the Normans, presents but little to allure the mind. Here is the river Wear, of considerable breadth and rapid tide; which running into the sea, receives the vessels, borne by gentle gales, on the calm bosom of its haven. Both its banks have been made conspicuous by one Benedict, who there built churches and monasteries; one dedicated to Peter, and the other to Paul, united in the bond of brotherly love and of monastic rule. The industry and forbearance of this man, any one will admire who reads the book which Bede composed concerning his life and those of the succeeding abbats: his industry, in bringing over a multitude of books, and being the first person who introduced in England constructors of stone edifices, as well as makers of glass windows; in which pursuits he spent almost his whole life abroad: the love of his country and his taste for elegance beguiling his painful labours, in the earnest desire of conveying something to his countrymen out of the common way; for very rarely before the time of Benedict were buildings of stone seen in Britain, nor did the solar ray cast its light through the transparent glass. Again, his forbearance: for when in possession of the monastery of St. Augustine at Canterbury, he cheerfully resigned it to Adrian, when he arrived, not as fearing the severity of St. Theodore the archbishop, but bowing to his authority. And farther, while long absent abroad, he endured not only with temper, but, I may say, with magnanimity, the substitution of another abbat, without his knowledge, by the monks of Wearmouth; and on his return, admitted him to equal honour with himself, in rank and power. Moreover, when stricken so severely with the palsy that he could move none of his limbs, he appointed a third abbat, because the other, of whom we have spoken, was not less affected by the same disease. And when the disorder, increasing, was just about to seize his vitals, he bade adieu to his companion, who was brought into his presence, with an inclination of the head only; nor was he better able to return the salutation, for he was hastening to a still nearer exit, and actually died before Benedict. . . .

Here my abilities fail, here my eloquence falls short: ignorant which to praise most, the number of Bede's writings, or the gravity of his style. No doubt he had imbibed a large portion of heavenly wisdom, to be able to compose so many volumes within the limits of so short a life. Nay, they even report, that he went to Rome for the purpose either of personally asserting that his writings were consistent with the doctrines of the church; or of correcting them by apostolical authority, should they be found repugnant thereto. That he went to Rome I do not however affirm for fact: but I have no doubt in declaring that he was invited thither, as the following epistle will certify; as well as that the see of Rome so highly esteemed him as greatly to desire his presence. . . .

So extensive was his fame then, that even the majesty of Rome itself solicited his assistance in solving abstruse questions, nor did Gallic conceit ever find in this Angle any thing justly to blame. All the western world yielded the palm to his faith and authority; for indeed he was of sound faith, and of artless, yet pleasing eloquence: in all elucidations of the holy scriptures, discussing those points from which the reader might imbibe the love of God, and of his neighbour, rather than those which might charm by their wit, or polish a rugged style. Moreover the irrefragable truth of that sentence, which the majesty of divine wisdom proclaimed to the world, forbids any one to doubt the sanctity of his life, "Wisdom will not enter the malevolent soul, nor dwell in the person of the sinful"; which indeed is said not of earthly wisdom, which is infused promiscuously into the hearts of men, and in which, even the wicked, who continue their crimes until their last day, seem often to excel, according to the divine expression, "The sons of this world are in their generation wiser than the children of light"; but it rather describes that wisdom which needs not the assistance of learning, and which dismisses from its cogitations those things which are void of understanding, that is to say, of the understanding of acting and speaking properly. Hence Seneca in his book, "De Causis," appositely relates that Cato, defining the duty of an orator, said, "An orator is a good man, skilled in speaking." This ecclesiastical orator, then, used to purify his knowledge, that so he might, as far as possible, unveil the meaning of mystic writings. How indeed could that man be enslaved to vice who gave his whole soul and spirit to elucidate the scriptures? For, as he confesses in his third book on Samuel, if his expositions were productive of no advantage to his readers, yet were they of considerable importance to himself, inasmuch as, while fully intent upon them, he escaped the vanity and empty imaginations of the times. Purified from vice, therefore, he entered within the inner veil, divulging in pure diction the sentiments of his mind.

But the unspotted sanctity and holy purity of his heart were chiefly conspicuous on the approach of death. Although for seven weeks successively, from the indisposition of his stomach, he nauseated all food, and was troubled with such a difficulty of breathing that his disorder confined him to his bed, yet he by no means abandoned his literary avocations. During whole days he endeavoured to mitigate the pressure of his disorder and to lose the recollection of it by constant lectures to his pupils, and by examining and solving abstruse questions, in addition to his usual task of psalmody. Moreover the gospel of St. John, which from its difficulty exercises the talents of its readers even to the present day, was translated by him into the English language, and accommodated to those who did not understand Latin. Occasionally, also, would he admonish his disciples, saying, "Learn, my children, while I am with you, for I know not how long I shall continue; and although my Maker should very shortly take me hence, and my spirit should return to him that sent and granted it to come into this life, yet have I lived long, God hath rightly appointed my portion of days, I desire to be dissolved and to be with Christ."

Often too when the balance was poised between hope and fear, he would remark "It is a fearful thing to fall into the hands of the living God. I have not passed my life among you in such manner as to be ashamed to live, neither do I fear to die, because we have a kind Master"; thus borrowing the expression of St. Ambrose when dying. Happy man! who could speak with so quiet a conscience as neither being ashamed to live, nor afraid to die; on the one hand not fearing the judgment of men, on the other waiting with composure the hidden will of God. Often, when urged by extremity of pain, he comforted himself with these remarks, "The furnace tries the gold, and the fire of temptation the just man: the sufferings of this present time are not worthy to be compared to the future glory which shall be revealed in us." Tears and a difficulty of breathing accompanied his words. At night, when there were none to be instructed or to note down his remarks, he passed the whole season in giving thanks and singing psalms, fulfilling the saying of that very wise man, "that he was never less alone than when alone." If at any time a short and disturbed sleep stole upon his eye-lids, he immediately shook it off, and showed that his affections were always intent on God, by exclaiming "Lift me up, O Lord, that the proud calumniate me not. Do with thy servant according to thy mercy." These and similar expressions which his shattered memory suggested, flowed spontaneously from his lips whenever the pain of his agonizing disorder became mitigated. But on the Tuesday before our Lord's ascension his disease rapidly increased, and there appeared a small swelling in his feet, the sure and certain indication of approaching death. Then the congregation being called together, he was anointed and received the sacrament. Kissing them all, and requesting from each that they would bear him in remembrance, he gave a small present, which he had privately reserved, to some with whom he had been in closer bonds of friendship. On Ascension day, when his soul, tired of the frail occupation of the body, panted to be free, lying down on a hair-cloth near the oratory, where he used to pray, with sense unimpaired and joyful countenance, he invited the grace of the Holy Spirit, saying, "O King of glory, Lord of virtue, who ascendedst this day triumphant into the heavens, leave us not destitute, but send upon us the promise of the Father, the Spirit of truth." This prayer ended, he breathed his last, and immediately the senses of all were pervaded by an odour such as neither cinnamon nor balm could give, but coming, as it were, from paradise, and fraught with all the joyous exhalations of spring. At that time he was buried in the same monastery, but at present, report asserts that he lies at Durham with St. Cuthbert.

With this man was buried almost all knowledge of history down to our times, inasmuch as there has been no Englishman either emulous of his pursuits, or a follower of his graces, who could continue the thread of his discourse, now broken short. Some few indeed, "whom the mild Jesus loved," though well skilled in literature, have yet observed an ungracious silence throughout their lives; others, scarcely tasting of the stream, have fostered a criminal indolence. Thus to the slothful succeeded others more slothful still, and the warmth of science for a long time decreased throughout the island. The verses of his epitaph will afford sufficient specimen of this indolence; they are indeed contemptible, and unworthy the tomb of so great a man:

> Presbyter hic Beda, requiescit carne sepultus;
> Dona, Christe, animam in coelis gaudere per aevum:
> Daque illi sophiae debriari fonte, cui jam
> Suspiravit ovans, intento semper amore.

Can this disgrace be extenuated by any excuse, that there was not to be found even in that monastery, where during his lifetime the school of all learning had flourished, a single person who could write his epitaph, except in this mean and paltry style? But enough of this: I will return to my subject.

Ceolwulf thinking it beneath the dignity of a Christian to be immersed in earthly things, abdicated the throne after a reign of eight years, and assumed the monastic habit at Lindisfarne, in which place how meritoriously he lived, is amply testified by his being honourably interred near St. Cuthbert, and by many miracles vouchsafed from on high.

He had made provision against the state's being endangered, by placing his cousin, Eadbert, on the throne, which he filled for twenty years with singular moderation and virtue. Eadbert had a brother of the same name, archbishop of York, who, by his own prudence and the power of the king, restored that see to its original state. For, as is well known to any one conversant in the history of the Angles, Paulinus, the first prelate of the church of York, had been forcibly driven away, and died at Rochester, where he left that honourable distinction of the pall which he had received from pope Honorius. After him, many prelates of this august city, satisfied with the name of a simple bishopric, aspired to nothing higher: but when Eadbert was seated on the throne, a man of loftier spirit, and one who thought, that, "as it is over-reaching to require what is not our due, so is it ignoble to neglect our right," he reclaimed the pall by frequent appeals to the pope. This personage, if I may be allowed the expression, was the depository and receptacle of every liberal art; and founded a most noble library at York. For this I cite Alcuin, as competent witness; who was sent from the kings of England to the emperor Charles the Great, to treat of peace, and being hospitably entertained by him, observes, in a letter to Eanbald, third in succession from Eadbert, "Praise and glory be to God, who hath preserved my days in full prosperity, that I should rejoice in the exaltation of my dearest son, who laboured in my stead, in the church where I had been brought up and educated, and presided over the treasures of wisdom, to which my beloved master, archbishop Egbert, left me heir." Thus too to Charles Augustus: "Give me the more polished volumes of scholastic learning, such as I used to have in my own country, through the laudable and ardent industry of my master, archbishop Egbert. And, if it please your wisdom, I will send some of our youths, who may obtain thence whatever is necessary, and bring back into France the flowers of Britain; that the garden of Paradise may not be confined to York, but that some of its scions may be transplanted to Tours."

This is the same Alcuin, who, as I have said, was sent into France to treat of peace, and during his abode with Charles, captivated either by the pleasantness of the country or the kindness of the king, settled there; and being held in high estimation, he taught the king, during his leisure from the cares of state, a thorough knowledge of logic, rhetoric, and astronomy. Alcuin was, of all the Angles, of whom I have read, next to St. Aldhelm and Bede, certainly the most learned, and has given proof of his talents in a variety of compositions. He lies buried in France, at the church of St. Paul, of Cormaric, which monastery Charles the Great built at his suggestion: on which account, even at the present day, the subsistence of four monks is distributed in alms, for the soul of our Alcuin, in that church.

But since I am arrived at that point where the mention of Charles the Great naturally presents itself, I shall subjoin a true statement of the descent of the kings of France, of which antiquity has said much: nor shall I depart widely from my design; because to be unacquainted with their race, I hold as a defect in information; seeing that they are our near neighbours, and to them the Christian world chiefly looks up: and, perhaps, to glance over this compendium may give pleasure to many who have not leisure to wade through voluminous works.

The Franks were so called, by a Greek appellative, from the ferocity of their manners, when, by order of the emperor Valentinian the First, they ejected the Alani, who had retreated to the Maeotian marshes. It is scarcely possible to believe how much this people, few and mean at first, became increased by a ten years' exemption from taxes: such, before the war, being the condition on which they engaged in it. Thus augmenting wonderfully by the acquisition of freedom, and first seizing the greatest part of Germany, and next the whole of Gaul, they compelled the inhabitants to list under their banners. Hence the Lotharingi and Allamanni, and other nations beyond the Rhine, who are subject to the emperor of Germany, will have themselves more properly to be called Franks; and those whom we suppose Franks, they call by an ancient appellative Galwalae, that is to say, Gauls. To this opinion I assent; knowing that Charles the Great, whom none can deny to have been king of the Franks, always used the same vernacular language with the Franks on the other side of the Rhine. Any one who shall read the life of Charles will readily admit

the truth of my assertion. In the year then of the Incarnate Word 425 the
Franks were governed by Faramund, their first king. The grandson of
Faramund was Meroveus, from whom all the succeeding kings of the
Franks, to the time of Pepin, were called Merovingians. In like manner
the sons of the kings of the Angles took patronymical appellations from
their fathers. For instance; Eadgaring the son of Edgar; Eadmunding the
son of Edmund, and the rest in like manner; commonly, however, they
are called ethelings. The native language of the Franks, therefore, partakes of that of the Angles, by reason of both nations originating from
Germany. The Merovingians reigned successfully and powerfully till the
year of our Lord's incarnation, 687. At that period Pepin, son of Ansegise,
was made mayor of the palace among the Franks, on the other side of the
Rhine. Seizing opportunities for veiling his ambitious views, he completely subjugated his master Theodoric, the dregs as it were of the Merovingians, and to lessen the obloquy excited by the transaction, he indulged him with the empty title of king, while himself managed every
thing, at home and abroad, according to his own pleasure. The genealogy
of this Pepin, both to and from him, is thus traced: Ausbert, the senator,
on Blithilde, the daughter of Lothaire, the father of Dagobert, begot Arnold: Arnold begot St. Arnulph, bishop of Metz: Arnulph begot Flodulph,
Walcthise, Anschise: Flodulph begot duke Martin, whom Ebroin slew:
Walcthise begot the most holy Wandregesil the abbat: duke Anschise
begot Ansegise: Ansegise begot Pepin. The son of Pepin was Carolus
Tudites, whom they also call Martel, because he beat down the tyrants
who were raising up in every part of France, and nobly defeated the
Saracens, at that time infesting Gaul. Following the practice of his father, whilst he was himself satisfied with the title of earl, he kept the
kings in a state of pupilage. He left two sons, Pepin and Caroloman.
Caroloman, from some unknown cause, relinquishing the world, took his
religious vows at Mount Cassin. Pepin was crowned king of the Franks,
and patrician of the Romans, in the church of St. Denys, by pope Stephen,
the successor of Zachary. For the Constantinopolitan emperors, already
much degenerated from their ancient valour, giving no assistance either
to Italy or the church of Rome, which had long groaned under the tyranny of the Lombards, this pope bewailed the injuries to which they were
exposed from them to the ruler of the Franks; wherefore Pepin passing
the Alps, reduced Desiderius, king of the Lombards, to such difficulties,
that he restored what he had plundered to the church of Rome, and gave
surety by oath that he would not attempt to resume it. Pepin returning
to France after some years, died, leaving his surviving children, Charles
and Caroloman, his heirs. In two years Caroloman departed this life.
Charles obtaining the name of "Great" from his exploits, enlarged the
kingdom to twice the limits which it possessed in his father's time, and

being contented for more than thirty years with the simple title of king, abstained from the appellation of emperor, though repeatedly invited to assume it by pope Adrian. But when, after the death of this pontiff, his relations maimed the holy Leo, his successors in the church of St. Peter, so as to cut out his tongue, and put out his eyes, Charles hastily proceeded to Rome to settle the state of the church. Justly punishing these abandoned wretches, he stayed there the whole winter, and restored the pontiff, now speaking plainly and seeing clearly, by the miraculous interposition of God, to his customary power. At that time the Roman people, with the privity of the pontiff, on the day of our Lord's nativity, unexpectedly hailed him with the title of Augustus; which title, though, from its being unusual, he reluctantly admitted, yet afterwards he defended with proper spirit against the Constantinopolitan emperors, and left it, as hereditary, to his son Louis. His descendants reigned in that country, which is now properly called France, till the time of Hugh, surnamed Capet, from whom is descended the present Louis. From the same stock came the sovereigns of Germany and Italy, till the year of our Lord 912, when Conrad, king of the Teutonians, seized that empire. The grandson of this personage was Otho the Great, equal in every estimable quality to any of the emperors who preceded him. Thus admirable for his valour and goodness, he left the empire hereditary to his posterity; for the present Henry, son-in-law of Henry, king of England, derives his lineage from his blood.

To return to my narrative: Alcuin, though promoted by Charles the Great to the monastery of St. Martin in France, was not unmindful of his countrymen, but exerted himself to retain the emperor in amity with them, and stimulated them to virtue by frequent epistles. I shall here subjoin many of his observations, from which it will appear clearly how soon after the death of Bede the love of learning declined even in his own monastery: and how quickly after the decease of Eadbert the kingdom of the Northumbrians came to ruin, through the prevalence of degenerate manners.

He says thus to the monks of Wearmouth, among whom Bede had both lived and died, obliquely accusing them of having done the very thing which he begs them not to do, "Let the youths be accustomed to attend the praises of our heavenly King, not to dig up the burrows of foxes, or pursue the winding mazes of hares; let them now learn the Holy Scriptures, that, when grown up, they may be able to instruct others. Remember, the most noble teacher of our times, Bede, the priest, what thirst for learning he had in his youth, what praise he now has among men, and what a far greater reward of glory with God." Again, to those of York he says, "The Searcher of my heart is witness that it was not for lust of gold that I came to France or continued there, but for the necessities of the church." And thus to Offa, king of the Mercians, "I was prepared to come to you with the presents of king Charles and to return to my country, but it seemed more advisable to me, for the peace of my nation, to remain abroad, not knowing what I could have done among those persons, with whom no one can be secure, or able to proceed in any laudable pursuit. Behold every holy place is laid desolate by Pagans, the altars are polluted by perjury, the monasteries dishonoured by adultery, the earth itself stained with the blood of rulers and of princes." Again, to king Ethelred, third in the sovereignty after Eadbert, "Behold the church of St. Cuthbert is sprinkled with the blood of God's priests, despoiled of all its ornaments, and the holiest spot in Britain given up to Pagan nations to be plundered; and where, after the departure of St. Paulinus from York, the Christian religion first took its rise in our own nation, there misery and calamity took their rise also. What portends that shower of blood which in the time of Lent, in the city of York, the capital of the whole kingdom, in the church of St. Peter, the chief of the apostles, we saw tremendously falling on the northern side of the building from the summit of the roof, though the weather was fair? Must not blood be expected to come upon the land from the northern regions?" Again, to Osbert, prince of the Mercians, "Our kingdom of the Northumbrians has almost perished through internal dissensions and perjury." So also to Athelard, archbishop of Canterbury, "I speak this on account of the scourge which has lately fallen on that part of our island which has been inhabited by our forefathers for nearly three hundred and forty years. It is recorded in the writings of Gildas, the wisest of the Britons, that those very Britons ruined their country through the avarice and rapine of their princes, the iniquity and injustice of their judges, their bishops' neglect of preaching, the luxury and abandoned manners of the people. Let us be cautious that such vices become not prevalent in our times, in order that the divine favour may preserve our country to us in that happy prosperity for the future which it has hitherto in its most merciful kindness vouchsafed us."

It has been made evident, I think, what disgrace and what destruction the neglect of learning and the immoral manners of degenerate men brought upon England! These remarks obtain this place in my history merely for the purpose of cautioning my readers. . . .

After Ethelred no one durst ascend the throne; each dreading the fate of his predecessor, and preferring a life of safety in inglorious ease, to a tottering reign in anxious suspense: for most of the Northumbrian kings had ended their reigns by a death which was now become almost habitual. Thus being without a sovereign for thirty-three years, that province became an object of plunder and contempt to its neighbours. For when the Danes, who, as I have before related from the words of Alcuin, laid waste the holy places, on their return home represented to their countrymen the fruitfulness of the island, and the indolence of its inhabitants; these barbarians came over hastily, in great numbers, and obtained forcible possession of that part of the country, till the time we are speaking of: indeed they had a king of their own for many years, though he was subordinate to the authority of the king of the West Saxons. However, after the lapse of these thirty-three years, king Egbert obtained the sovereignty of this province, as well as of the others, in the year of our Lord's incarnation 827, and the twenty-eighth of his reign. And since we have reached his times, mindful of our engagement, we shall speak briefly of the kingdom of the Mercians; and this, as well because we admire brevity in relation, as that there is no great abundance of materials. . . .

Wulfhere died at the end of nineteen years, and his brother Ethelred ascended the throne; more famed for his pious disposition than his skill in war. Moreover he was satisfied with displaying his valour in a single but illustrious expedition into Kent, and passed the remainder of his life in quiet, except that attacking Egfrid, king of the Northumbrians, who had passed beyond the limits of his kingdom, he admonished him to return home, by the murder of his brother Elfwin. He atoned however for this slaughter, after due deliberation, at the instance of St. Theodore, the archbishop, by giving Egfrid a large sum of money. Subsequently to this, in the thirtieth year of his reign, he took the cowl, and became a monk at Bardney, of which monastery he was ultimately promoted to be abbat. This is the same person who was contemporary with Ina, king of the West Saxons, and confirmed by his authority also the privilege which St. Aldhelm brought from Rome. His wife was Ostritha, sister of Egfrid, king of the Northumbrians, by whom she had issue a son named Ceolred.

He appointed Kenred, the son of his brother Wulfhere his successor, who, equally celebrated for piety to God and uprightness towards his subjects, ran his mortal race with great purity of manners, and proceeding to Rome in the fifth year of his reign, passed the remainder of his life there in the offices of religion; chiefly instigated to this by the melancholy departure of a soldier, who, as Bede relates, disdaining to confess his crimes when in health, saw, manifestly, when at the point of death, those very demons coming to punish him to whose vicious allurements he had surrendered his soul.

After him reigned Ceolred, the son of Ethelred his uncle, as conspicuous for his valour against Ina, as pitiable for an early death; for not filling the throne more than eight years, he was buried at Lichfield, leaving Ethelbald, the grandnephew of Penda by his brother Alwy, his heir. This king, enjoying the sovereignty in profound and long-coninued peace, that is, for the space of forty-one years, was ultimately killed by his subjects, and thus met with a reverse of fortune. Bernred, the author of his death,

left nothing worthy of record, except that afterwards, being himself put
to death by Offa, he received the just reward of his treachery. To this
Ethelbald, Boniface, archbishop of Mentz, an Angle by nation, who was
subsequently crowned with martyrdom, sent an epistle, part of which I
shall transcribe, that it may appear how freely he asserts those very vices
to have already gained ground among the Angles of which Alcuin in
after times was apprehensive. It will also be a strong proof, by the remarkable deaths of certain kings, how severely God punishes those guilty
persons for whom his long-suspended anger mercifully waits.

*To Ethelbald, my dearest lord, and to be preferred to all other kings of the
Angles, in the love of Christ, Boniface the archbishop, legate to Germany from
the church of Rome, wisheth perpetual health in Christ.* We confess before God
that when we hear of your prosperity, your faith, and good works, we rejoice;
and if at any time we hear of any adversity befallen you, either in the chance
of war or the jeopardy of your soul, we are afflicted. We have heard that, devoted
in almsgiving, you prohibit theft and rapine, are a lover of peace, a defender of
widows, and of the poor; and for this we give God thanks. Your contempt for
lawful matrimony, were it for chastity's sake, would be laudable; but since you
wallow in luxury and even in adultery with nuns, it is disgraceful and damna-
ble; it dims the brightness of your glory before God and man, and transforms
you into an idolater, because you have polluted the temple of God. Wherefore,
my beloved son, repent, and remember how dishonourable it is, that you, who,
by the grant of God, are sovereign over many nations, should yourself be the
slave of lust to his disservice. Moreover, we have heard that almost all the nobles
of the Mercian kingdom, following your example, desert their lawful wives and
live in guilty intercourse with adultresses and nuns. Let the custom of a foreign
country teach you how far distant this is from rectitude. For in old Saxony,
where there is no knowledge of Christ, if a virgin in her father's house, or a
married woman under the protection of her husband, should be guilty of adultery, they burn her, strangled by her own hand, and hang up her seducer over
the grave where she is buried; or else, cutting off her garments to the waist,
modest matrons whip her and pierce her with knives, and fresh tormentors
punish her in the same manner as she goes from town to town, till they destroy
her. Again the Winedi, the basest of nations, have this custom—the wife, on the
death of her husband, casts herself on the same funeral pile to be consumed
with him. If then the gentiles, who know not God, have so zealous a regard for
chastity, how much more ought you to possess, my beloved son, who are both
a Christian and a king? Spare therefore your own soul, spare a multitude of
people, perishing by your example, for whose souls you must account. Give heed
to this too, if the nation of the Angles, (and we are reproached in France and
in Italy and by the very pagans for it,) despising lawful matrimony, give free
indulgence to adultery, a race ignoble and despising God must necessarily proceed from such a mixture, which will destroy the country by their abandoned
manners, as was the case with the Burgundians, Provençals, and Spaniards,
whom the Saracens harassed for many years on account of their past transgres-

sions. Moreover, it has been told us, that you take away from the churches and monasteries many of their privileges, and excite, by your example, your nobility to do the like. But recollect, I entreat you, what terrible vengeance God hath inflicted upon former kings, guilty of the crime we lay to your charge. For Ceolred, your predecessor, the debaucher of nuns, the infringer of ecclesiastical privileges, was seized, while splendidly regaling with his nobles, by a malignant spirit, who snatched away his soul without confession and without communion, while in converse with the devil and despising the law of God. He drove Osred also, king of the Deirans and Bernicians, who was guilty of the same crimes, to such excess that he lost his kingdom and perished in early manhood by an ignominious death. Charles also, governor of the Franks, the subverter of many monasteries and the appropriator of ecclesiastical revenues to his own use, perished by excruciating pain and a fearful death.

And afterwards,

Wherefore, my beloved son, we entreat with paternal and fervent prayers that you would not despise the counsel of your fathers, who, for the love of God, anxiously appeal to your highness. For nothing is more salutary to a good king than the willing correction of such crimes when they are pointed out to him; since Solomon says "Whoso loveth instruction, loveth wisdom." Wherefore, my dearest son, showing you good counsel, we call you to witness, and entreat you by the living God, and his Son Jesus Christ, and by the Holy Spirit, that you would recollect how fleeting is the present life, how short and momentary is the delight of the filthy flesh, and how ignominious for a person of transitory existence to leave a bad example to posterity. Begin therefore to regulate your life by better habits, and correct the past errors of your youth, that you may have praise before men here, and be blest with eternal glory hereafter We wish your Highness health and proficiency in virtue.

I have inserted in my narrative portions of this epistle, to give sufficient knowledge of these circumstances, partly in the words of the author and partly in my own, shortening the sentences as seemed proper, for which I shall easily be be excused, because there was need of brevity for the sake of those who were eager to resume the thread of the history. Moreover, Boniface transmitted an epistle of like import to archbishop Cuthbert, adding that he should remonstrate with the clergy and nuns on the fineness and vanity of their dress. Besides, that he might not wonder at his interfering in that in which he had no apparent concern, that is to say, how or with what manners the nation of the Angles conducted itself, he gave him to understand, that he had bound himself by oath to pope Gregory the Third, not to conceal the conduct of the nations near him from the knowledge of the apostolical see; wherefore, if mild measures failed of success, he should take care to act in such manner, that vices of this kind should not be kept secret from the pope. Indeed, on account of the fine texture of the clerical vestments, Alcuin obliquely glances at

Athelard the archbishop, Cuthbert's successor, reminding him that, when he should come to Rome to visit the emperor Charles the Great, the grandson of Charles of whom Boniface was speaking above, he should not bring the clergy or monks dressed in party-coloured or gaudy garments, for the clergy amongst the Franks dressed only in ecclesiastical habits.

Nor could the letters of so great a man, which he was accustomed to send from watchful regard to his legation and pure love of his country, be without effect. For both Cuthbert, the archbishop, and king Ethelbald summoned a council for the purpose of retrenching the superfluities which he had stigmatised. The acts of this synod, veiled in a multiplicity of words, I shall forbear to add, as I think they will better accord with another part of my work, when I come to the succession of the bishops: but as I am now on the subject of kingly affairs, I shall subjoin a charter of Ethelbald's, as a proof of his devotion, because it took place in the same council.

It often happens, through the uncertain change of times, that those things which have been confirmed by the testimony and advice of many faithful persons, have been made of none effect by the contumacy of very many, or by the artifices of deceit, without any regard to justice, unless they have been committed to eternal memory by the authority of writing and the testimony of charters. Wherefore I Ethelbald, king of the Mercians, out of love to heaven and regard for my own soul, have felt the necessity of considering how I may, by good works, set it free from every tie of sin. For since the Omnipotent God, through the greatness of his clemency, without any previous merit on my part, hath bestowed on me the sceptre of government, therefore I willingly repay him out of that which he hath given. On this account I grant, so long as I live, that all monasteries and churches of my kingdom shall be exempted from public taxes, works, and impositions, except the building of forts and bridges, from which none can be released. And moreover the servants of God shall have perfect liberty in the produce of their woods and lands, and the right of fishing, nor shall they bring presents either to king or princes except voluntarily, but they shall serve God without molestation.

Lullus succeeded Boniface, an Englishman by birth also; of whose sanctity mention is made in the life of St. Goar, and these verses, which I remember to have heard from my earliest childhood, bear witness:

> Lullus, than whom no holier prelate lives,
> By God's assistance healing medicine gives,
> Cures each disorder by his powerful hand,
> And with his glory overspreads the land.

However, to return to my history, Offa, descended from Penda in the fifth degree, succeeded Ethelbald.

Otto of Freising

13

Otto of Freising has been called "the first philosopher of history." With Saint Augustine in mind, we may find such an ascription arguable but it is clear that Otto was by birth, position, training, and ability more than adequately prepared to write philosophical history. Born c. 1113 into one of the most prominent German princely families, he was a grandson of Emperor Henry IV of Germany and closely related to three other emperors. As a younger son he was destined for high ecclesiastical office. We know that he studied for some time in Paris and that in 1133 he joined the Cistercian Order and entered the monastery of Morimund in France. By 1137, he was abbot of the monastery but in that same year he was named Bishop of Freising in Bavaria. In that post he pursued an active career, involved in secular as well as ecclesiastical matters. He traveled to Rome in 1145 and two years later he joined the Second Crusade, accompanying his half-brother, the Emperor Conrad III, and his nephew, Frederick Barbarossa. The Crusade was a military disaster but Otto did manage to reach Jerusalem in 1148. The last decade of his life he spent in Germany, active as ever but plagued by ill health. In 1158 he traveled to his favorite monastery, at Morimund, where he died peacefully, in the midst of the monks of his order.

Otto's literary legacy comprises two works: *The Deeds of Emperor Frederick I* (1156–1158), written to celebrate the accomplishments of that powerful ruler; and his *Chronicle* or *History of the Two Cities* (1143–1147). It is the latter work which established Otto's reputation as a historian. In the *Chronicle* Otto set out to trace the course of history from the Creation down to 1146. He brought to his task great intellectual ability and a strong philosophical orientation. He had pursued a rigorous scholarly career while a student at Paris, participating in the Aristotelian renaissance then under way and absorbing the lessons to be learned from studies of Roman and Canon law. In writing his *Chronicle,* he drew upon the works of Tacitus, Varro, Eusebius, Josephus, and, as he takes care to inform us, a great many other Christian and pagan historians. His organizing philosophical principles however came from two sources: "In this work I follow most of all those illustrious lights of the Church, Augustine and Orosius, and have planned to draw from their fountains what is pertinent to my theme and my purpose." Otto, then, writes of the Two Cities and their experiences since the Creation within the Augustinian tradition. Living in an age when the Catholic world was in turmoil over the struggles between pope and emperor, Otto, faithful brother of the emperor, faithful servant of the pope, was distressed by what seemed to him the rending of Christ's seamless robe. He feared it was a time when both State and Church "were passing from perfection to overthrow." Looking to history, he found it a record of wretchedness, sorrow and perfidy. What saved him from utter pessimism was his Christian belief that the historical process was a working out of God's plan. He looked from "the visible to the invisible" city and drew comfort from his faith that God would preserve what He had created. Thus he could contemplate with equanimity the demise of empires and the death of kings, beholding as he did the "King of Kings, in His incomparable and unfading grace and glory."

Yet, Otto's Chronicle is not entirely an apology based on philosophical and theological principles. In his use of Christian and classical historians, his reliance on documentary evidence, his critical weighing of the meaning of events and the motives of men, Otto attempted to rise above the medieval chronicle tradition and to write a history. He was biased in his approach to history but critical in the writing of it. Unlike medieval chroniclers, he does not accept and copy into his work all that his authorities tell him. He indicates where his sources are weak or contradictory; he manifests skepticism concerning some legends and notes the incredible bases of others. He was in active combat, as it were, against the demands of his Providential view of historical movement. What he seeks is to give a clear description of the unfolding of history as the evidence, illuminated by his philosophy, dictates, "that the truth may be held in esteem, inasmuch as it is better to fall into the hands of men than to lose the function of a historian by covering up a loathsome sight by colors which conceal the truth." Augustinian in his philosophy of history, Otto was yet enough of an empirical historian to perceive, however dimly, the fact of development of Church and State as it had occurred in western Europe down to his time. History and his own circumstances led him away from Saint Augustine's philosophy. He saw between the Two Cities not a great gulf fixed but rather a state of tension which both bound and separated them and which made doubly difficult the fulfillment of Christ's enjoinder: "Render unto Caesar what is Caesar's, and unto God what is God's." It is this perception, elaborated in a work of historiographic art, that earned him his fame as the greatest of the German medieval historians.

The selections here include Otto's discussion of the "Two Swords" thesis and his account of Constantine's conversion and his "donation" of imperial power to the Roman pope.

Selected Bibliography

Charles C. Mierow includes a lengthy and informative introduction to his translation of Otto of Freising's *The Two Cities* eds. Austin P. Evans and Charles Knapp, (1928). Mierow is particularly perceptive in his section on "Otto's Philosophy of History" (pp. 61–72) in which he stresses Otto's debt to Augustinian principles of philosophical history. Mierow is thus in agreement with Theodor E. Mommsen, "Orosius and Augustine," in E. F. Rice, Jr., ed., *Theodor E. Mommsen, Medieval and Renaissance Studies* (1959), who concludes that Otto was one of the few medieval historians who correctly saw the difference between Augustine and Orosius. Walther Lammers has edited an excellent collection of articles in the *Wege der Forschung* series, vol. 21, *Geschichtsdenken und Geschichtsbild im Mittelalter* (1961). Most of the articles included are pertinent to Otto's time and circumstances and three of them especially so: Eberhard F. Otto, "Otto von Freising und Friedrich Barbarossa"; Johannes Spörl, "Die *Civitas Dei* im Geschichtsdenken Ottos von Freising"; and Josef Koch, "Die Grundlagen der Geschichtsphilosophie Ottos von Freising." All of these are rich in bibliographic material, all are penetrating in their analyses. Spörl and Koch are particularly persuasive in their discussions of how Otto took his Augustinian heritage and necessarily transformed and transcended it in his life's mission in a world so different from that of Augustine. Friedrich Heer, *The Medieval World* (English translation, 1963), includes interesting material on Otto and much material, with Heer's very personal interpretations, on the late Middle Ages.

THE TWO CITIES

The Prologue of the Fourth Book

I think there is now no wise man who does not consider the works of God —no wise man who, having considered them, does not stand amazed and is not led through the visible to the invisible. For the Lord had wished His City, though foreordained before the foundation of the world, to lie hid until the appointed time and made ready to exalt it at the proper time. Therefore at the time of its humiliation He graciously consoled it, by foretelling through His prophet that time of exaltation: "Stretch forth thy tents," He said, "and strengthen the curtains of thy habitations. Lengthen thy cords." And again: "Whereas thou hast been forsaken, I will make thee a joy of many generations." When therefore the Lord willed to exalt His Church, which had been exhausted by many trials and persecutions, He chose, in preference to all others, a personage through whom He might the more readily accomplish this exaltation. Accordingly He commissioned the emperor of the Romans, to whom the whole world at that time paid honor, to effect it; and gave him not only faith whereby, departing from the darkness of error, he might come to know the true light, but also love whereby he might exalt His city with many honors and enrich it with many treasures and possessions. And that you may know that all this was brought to pass not by chance, at haphazard, but through the profound and righteous judgments of God, behold a man who but yesterday was skulking in hiding and fleeing from every man (of even the lowest condition) become speedily of so great authority that he rules kings, judges kings; behold him held in so great veneration by the world that the lords of the earth come to bow before him and worship the soles of his feet as he sits upon the throne.

But here a serious question arises and a great argument regarding the justification of kingship and of priesthood. For some under color of religion, others out of regard for secular dignity—since by such dignity the authority of the kingship is seen to have been diminished—claim that this temporal glory and honor are not permissible to priests of Christ, to whom the glory of the heavenly kingdom is promised, and they point out

From *The Two Cities,* translated by Charles Christopher Mierow, edited by Austin P. Evans and Charles Knapp (New York, Columbia University Press, 1928). Reprinted by permission of the publisher. Pp. 271–283, 288–290, 322–324, 513–514.

many arguments in support of this contention. Two roles, they say, have
been established by God in the Church: the priestly and the kingly. Of
these the priest ought to administer the sacraments of Christ and to
render ecclesiastical judgments with the sword of the spirit. The other
bears a material sword, for the exercise of secular judgments against the
enemies of the Church, by defending the poor and the churches of God
from the assaults of evil men, and by punishing the wicked. These are
the two swords which we read about in the story of the passion of the
Lord. But Peter is found to have used only one. Therefore, as spiritual
gifts also pertain to the spiritual sword—that is tithes, first fruits, obla-
tions of the faithful and other things of this sort—so all earthly dignities,
dukedoms, counties and matters of that kind belong to the material
sword. These things God has desired to exist in his Church in orderly
fashion, not confusedly, that is, not together in one person but separately
in the two I have mentioned. Accordingly, just as it is not permissible for
the person who bears the material sword to deal with those things that
are spiritual, so it is not fitting that the other should usurp those powers
which are not properly his. Men adduce many passages of Scripture to
establish what I have just said. In fact they adduce the example of our
Lord himself and of the saints, as for instance the well-known gospel
command: "Render unto Caesar the things that are Caesar's, and unto
God the things that are God's." And even as the Lord declared this in His
words, so He showed it forth in His deeds, on that occasion when, recognizing the principle "to whom tribute, tribute"—He paid the tribute for
Himself and for Peter. Paul too, understanding that honor must be paid
to whom honor is due, and believing that all authority is of God—Paul,
I say, when brought to trial appealed not to Peter (who then presided over
the Roman See) but to Nero, a most vile and impious man who by God's
will had been appointed king over the whole world. This much regarding
the honoring of kings. But that every possession is of the grace of kings
men prove from Augustine, who says: "By what right do you possess
villas? divine or human? By divine: 'The earth is the Lord's and the
fulness thereof.' By human, that is from kings: this is why we say 'This
land is mine, this estate is mine.' Likewise if you say, 'What have I to do
with a king?' 'Tell me, what have you to do with possessions?' " To all this
the reply is made that the Lord wished those powers which are called
royal to honor His Church with earthly dignity. For the explanation that
we have made above indicates that this was done by God's ordering.
Finally, it is not to be believed that Christ permitted His Church, His
bride, His body, to which He is believed to have given His life's breath
as an earnest, to be deceived by the spirit of error; upon it, as I have said,
He had bestowed the spirit of truth. Besides, men of established sanctity
are found who are believed to have had kingly honors, to have won the

kingdom of God in addition to those kingly honors. By these arguments, therefore, and by others which it would take too long to recount, it is shown that Constantine properly bestowed royal powers upon the Church, and that the Church legitimately accepted them. For when we inquire of kings by what sanction they have their powers, they are accustomed to reply, "By the ordination of God and election by the people." If, therefore, God did not act unrighteously in ordaining that the aforesaid honor should be conferred upon kings, how much more surely is He not to be called unrighteous for ordaining this also, that the honor should be transferred from that role to the ecclesiastical authority? Finally, in addition to the fact that He Himself had ordained it, He wished that in this latter case, as in the former, election by the people (and furthermore, in this specific instance, the nomination of a successor) should be in harmony with His own will, then we must believe that neither did He Himself arrange matters unjustly, nor did the emperor wrongfully designate a successor, nor did the Church receive these honors illegitimately.

But you say that, to the ecclesiastical role, powers were given which it is neither seemly nor expedient for it to have by reason of the sanctity of its office. In answer to this I confess I know no argument in which to take refuge save that we know that those holy men of apostolic faith and merit —Sylvester, Gregory, Ulric, Boniface, Lambert, Gothard and many others —had these prerogatives. For, to speak as I think myself, I admit that I am absolutely ignorant whether the exaltation of His Church which is so clearly visible today pleases God more than its former humiliation pleased Him. Indeed, that former state seems to have been better, this present condition more fortunate. However I agree with the holy Roman Church, which, I doubt not, was built upon a firm rock, and I believe that what she believes must be believed and that what she possesses can legitimately be possessed. For that she can be deceived by no error can be proved by this: "And the gates of hell shall not prevail against it." Moreover, that her faith is to abide forever we may know from what was said to Peter: "I made supplication for thee, Peter, that thy faith fail not." But that every least point of controversy may be solved by its own authority and example is again implicitly intimated by what is said to Peter: "Put out into the deep, and let down your nets for a draught." Let what has been said concerning the righteousness of the priesthood and of the kingship suffice. But if anyone wishes to reason about it more subtly and profoundly, he will by no means submit to having the matter prejudged by me.

Here Begins the Fourth Book

Now in the three hundred and eleventh year from the incarnation of the Lord, Constantine, the thirty-fourth in line from Augustus, succeeded his father on the throne, the more pious heir of a pious father. Meanwhile the praetorian guard chose Maxentius, the son of Herculeus, as Augustus. Caesar Severus was sent against him by Augustus Galerius but was driven in flight to Ravenna and killed there. When Maximian Herculeus heard that Constantine had been proclaimed emperor in the Gauls, laying aside the garb of a private citizen he planned to trap Constantine through treachery. But when he had come into the Gauls for this purpose he was betrayed by his daughter, Constantine's wife, forced to flee and killed at Marseilles. When Severus had been killed Galerius made Licinius emperor. After he had cruelly carried on a persecution of the Christians for ten years, Galerius was smitten with a divine punishment by the Lord and paid the penalty. For his vital organs decomposed within him and he reached so horrible a state that he belched forth worms. When he had been despaired of by physicians and realized that his was the vengeance of heaven he ceased from his persecution; but finding the violence of his malady beyond endurance he died.

When Constantine had been appointed emperor in the Gauls by his father, as I have said above, Maximin and Licinius aspired to the throne. They practiced cruelty and lust without measure upon those of our faith. Besides, Maxentius oppressed the citizens of Rome with many afflictions. Finally, among other deeds of his this tale is told of him, that he ordered the wives of the senators and the chief nobles to be promiscuously carried off to satisfy his lust; the senators themselves being overwhelmed with terror, submitted in silence, groaning. The senators too, or if you will those who appeared to be rather prominent in the senate house, he contrived to have proscribed, trumping up false charges against them. To these crimes he added the infamous chicanery of the art of magic, putting to death pregnant women and examining their viscera and making predictions of what was to happen through incantations composed by diabolic art. And so while the emperor Constantine, who was a religious man and by this time a supporter of the Christian faith, was preparing war against this most impious tyrant, he was troubled in many ways and frequently raised his eyes to heaven. By night, as he was buried in sleep, he saw the sign of the cross gleaming with fiery radiance in the eastern sky. When he inquired what it meant, he heard angels saying to him, "Constantine ΘΟΥΘΩ ΝΥΚΑ," which is to say, "In this sign thou shalt conquer." In the morning when he awoke he summoned to him the soldiers who were Christian and, learning from them with regard to what he had seen that it was the sign of the Christian faith, happy now and carefree about the vision he fortified his brow with the sign of the cross and promised that he would be a Christian if success should be his portion. Now this most serene prince was sorely distressed because he could not overcome the tyrant without much shedding of the blood of the citizens. Therefore the Lord, being minded to reward the devotion of the

emperor as well as to come to the rescue of His afflicted Church, destroyed the tyrant in marvellous wise, without danger either to the emperor or to the Roman people. The tyrant had assembled ships in the
manner of a mousetrap near the Mulvian bridge that he might take his
enemy at unawares as he came up in ignorance of the trap. Augustus was
in fact already approaching, already the pennons were flying at close
quarters, and lo! the tyrant was himself by God's will swept by a fiendish
spirit into the devices which he had prepared for his enemy—even as it
is written, "He is fallen into the ditch which he made"—and unaccom-
panied by any associate, alone, according to the desire of the emperor,
without danger to either army he perished. When Constantine, having
won the longed-for victory, had entered the city he was received with
great rejoicing by the citizens. But when, according to custom, a triumph
was being prepared for him, he declared that this victory must be attributed not to him but to Christ. The cross, through whose might the
enemy had been conquered, he had put in the place of a triumph and
caused it to be worshipped.

Upon the death of Melchiades, Sylvester had succeeded. According to
traditional practice of the Romans, Constantine was baptized by him in
the Church which is called St. John's. The cause of his conversion is as
stated above. Accordingly what we read in the Life of Saint Sylvester
about his leprosy and his conversion is seen to be apocryphal. However,
the Tripartite History states that he was baptized in Nicomedia toward
the end of his life.

When Constantine became a Christian he restored peace to the
churches. In fact, even Licinius gave his assent to this policy. Therefore
both emperors by passing decrees ordained that Christ, Who had freed
the State from the tyrant, must be worshipped as God; and after entering
upon this policy they wrote about it to Maximinus, who held authority
over the East. When he learned of it Maximinus ordained by an edict that
the Christians should no longer suffer persecution for their faith. He
even gave this as a reason: "The more they seem to be held in check, the
more they grow." Therefore he affirmed that no one should be forced to
worship the [pagan] gods unless he be drawn thereto by his own inclination. Although Maximinus was doing this out of fear of the Augusti, he
pretended that he was doing it of his own authority. For though he was
the most self-willed of men, he desired not only to be placed on an equality with the most moderate princes but even to be preferred to them.
After the lapse of a short interval Licinius broke the treaty and prepared
to take the offensive. And so after harrying many cities and provinces he
finally, relying on the aid of demons and responding to their promptings,
went forth to war and ventured on a battle. But when he saw his army
routed in that battle he took off the imperial insignia and, mingling in

the throng of camp followers, fled from the fight, disgraced as he deserved to be. Then, returning to his own country, he at first indeed put to
death his priests on the ground that they had deceived him. But when he
saw himself smitten by God with the most fearful maladies, and realized
that a very terrible death was drawing near, moved by penitence (though
too late) he confessed the God of the Christians. . . .

Who would not wonder at this change wrought by the right hand of the
Most High, whereby a most godless man, who had proscribed our people
in tablets of brass, meant to endure as it were forever, wrote so suddenly
in their behalf against his will, when touched by the hand of God. Presently Maximinus, being afflicted by the most bitter ravages of disease,
which began with the loss of his eyes, put an end to his life. Licinius, who
had previously afforded Constantine generous assistance respecting the
City of God, now driven to madness by the instigation of demons, drove
the Christians out from the palace and strained all his energies to persecute them. Constantine moved his fighting forces against him, defeated
him—first in Pannonia, afterwards at Cybalae—and finally, when he was
venturing frequent battles on land and on sea, compelled him to surrender. Fearing what had been done by Maximian Herculeus he stripped
him of his rank and put him to death. His sons, Constantine and Crispus,
and the sons of his sister by the aforesaid Licinius—namely Constantius
and Licinius—he made Caesars. Of these he afterwards killed Crispus
and Licinius, from what motive I know not.

Therefore, when his associates had reached the end of their reign, and
in consequence Constantine was now ruling alone and held the sole
power over the empire, the longed-for peace was restored in full to the
long afflicted Church, even as it is written: "I have seen the wicked in
great power, and exalted, and I passed by, and, lo, he was not." Since
wicked men and persecutors had been removed from the earth and the
righteous had been set free from distress, therefore, as though a cloud
had been dissipated, a joyful day began to gleam forth upon the City of
God all over the world. You might have seen the peoples that had been
in hiding rush forth now from all sides to join other peoples and unite
with them, unified into one body as members of a single organism. You
might have seen also, now that sorrow was turned to joy, festivals and
dedications of churches in every city, stronghold and village attended by
the greatest rejoicing of our people. For the Christian emperor, out of his
devotion to his faith, wished with all his heart that these things should
be done. Then for the first time edicts were promulgated that churches
should be built; then for the first time the Catholics were permitted to
enrich their churches with their estates. And, as the history of the Romans has it, his Most Serene Highness not only granted his consent to
these things but also, setting an example to others, so greatly exalted the

Roman Church that he handed over the imperial insignia to Saint Sylvester, pope of that city, and withdrew to Byzantium and there established the seat of his realm. This is why the Church of Rome claims that
the Western realms are under its jurisdiction, on the ground that they
had been transferred to it by Constantine, and in evidence thereof does
not hesitate to exact tribute to this day—except from the two kingdoms
of the Franks. But the advocates of empire affirm that Constantine did not
hand over his kingdom in this way to the Roman pontiffs, but out of
reverence for the Lord accepted them as fathers—thinking of them as
priests of the most high God—and consented that he and his successors
should be blessed by them and sustained by the protection of their prayers. And to prove this they adduce the fact that Constantine himself,
when he divided the kingdom among his sons, handed over the West to
one, the East to the other; and thus Rome with the West fell by lot to
Theodosius and to others in succession, not merely to heretics but also to
religious princes. They say that never would so devout a ruler have left
to his sons what he had previously handed over to the Church, nor would
so Catholic an emperor as Theodosius have appropriated what was not
his, if it belonged to the Church. To settle definitely all these matters is
not the purpose of the present work.

But it is pleasing to contemplate in how marvelous a way—a way past
all expression—the City of Christ, making its gradual progress among the
citizens of the world, grew to such heights. For to go rather far back,
when the first man had been created and had fallen from the delights of
paradise, a merciful God left him a guide for learning the truth in this
vale of tears. Because the sons of men were constantly led away therefrom (though some few continued in the knowledge of the truth yet the
majority went astray) God preserved his own people but destroyed the
rest by the waters of the Flood. Then when the human race was propagated anew from those thus preserved, gradually the knowledge of the
truth was [again] blotted out in them and error began to increase to such
an extent that at about the time of Abraham, the tenth in line from Noah,
you would find few citizens of Jerusalem save himself and his wife. From
him also you will find citizens of both cities descended, and from his son
Isaac the two peoples whom I have mentioned. But by Jacob (who is
known also as Israel), the third generation, you will find that there were
begotten twelve princes of the people of God, which was called after him
Israel. This people went down into Egypt and, after it had wandered long
among the citizens of the world and in that very pilgrimage had grown
into a great people, was led back by signs and wonders to the land of its
fathers, receiving on the way the Law as a provision, so to say, for its
journey, and there it received many temporal blessings. Yet although, as
time went on, it had very powerful kings; it never held sole sway over its

realm. But when the Lord wished His city to spread abroad and to be extended from that people to all nations, He permitted the realm to be weakened under pressure of the people's sins, and the people itself to be led into captivity. But among the nations which He was to summon to faith in himself, He established the sovereignty of the Romans to rule over the rest. When this had reached its fullest development and the pinnacle of power, He willed that His Son Christ should appear in the flesh. When, as the Gospel says, He had come unto His own and was not received by them that were His—nay was even despitefully entreated by them and nailed to a cross—by a righteous judgment the chosen were taken out from that people and the rest were blinded; and when, though reconciliation was offered them, they did not return to their senses, they were miserably scattered into captivity among all nations. So then the Lord, transferring His city from that people to the Gentiles, willed that they should first be humbled, despised and afflicted by many misfortunes —even as it is written, "He scourgeth every son whom He receiveth." But because scourgings, when they exceed due measure, break the spirit rather than heal it (as medicines taken to excess), at the proper time, as I have said before, He exalted His forsaken and humbled Church. That it might therefore become more tranquil with respect to the promised heavenly kingdom, He bestowed upon it the greatest temporal power possessed by any realm. And thus as I have said the City of God, increasing gradually, reached its pinnacle and undivided authority. And observe that before His incarnation His city was not honored to the full, but that afterwards, when He had risen to the skies with the body He had assumed and had, so to say, accepted His throne, [then] according to the parable He exalted His kingdom, which is the Church, to the highest dignity—than which there is nothing loftier on earth—that hereby He might reveal Himself to the citizens of the world as not only the God of heaven but also the Lord of the earth, and that through the prosperity of this land of our sojourn He might teach His citizens that the delights of their own country were eagerly to be sought.

Nor ought it perplex you that we said above that sorrows and changes in our estate were the way to our country, whereas now we affirm that prosperity constitutes that way. For while the variety and prosperity of the way draw the fool the more to self love, on the other hand both of these withdraw the wise man through that contemplation of which we have spoken, and kindle his love for the heavenly country. This is why, I think, the wise man, in the book which is called Ecclesiastes (that is to say, the Preacher), alike when the misfortunes and when the successes of our mortal lot are portrayed, preaches about both in such a way as to show more clearly than light that he is induced by the consideration of either state to despise the world and to love the heavenly country. Hence

when he has spoken at sufficient length regarding each topic, he termi-
nates the argument with that conclusion to which all things tend: "Let
us hear the conclusion of the whole matter," he says. "Fear God, and keep
his commandments; for this is the whole duty of man." And that you may
know that one and the same thing draws the fool to the abyss of sin and
inspires the wise with a desire for the heavenly life, hear the prophet:
"For thou, Jehovah, hast made me glad through thy works," he says, "and
I will triumph in the works of thy hands." And he adds: "A brutish man
shall not know this, nor shall a fool understand." It is as though he were
to say, "Thy work, which is not apprehended by a fool, why or for what
it is made, and draws him beyond all measure to a destructive love of self,
inflames *me* to know Thee, who, being Thyself most fair and sweet, hast
made that work fair and pleasing."

So then the City of Christ is seen to have received already, at the
present time, practically all that was promised it—all, indeed, except
immortality. Then, that through those things which you see fulfilled
already you may know that all the other things also which are promised
must indubitably be fulfilled, mark that the cross of Christ, His shame,
His punishment—and the very mention of crucifixion was once abhor-
rent to the whole world—has now attained to so great glory that the cross
is now worshipped by kings and has become to almost all men the object
of love and veneration. Note that kings now glory in having their insignia
adorned with that whereby, previously, punishment was meted out to
sinners and to men utterly debauched. If therefore God has so honored
His punishment, how will He honor His body, His saints, His likeness?
Therefore the seasons of prosperity and of present peace are to the minds
of the wise an evidence of future blessedness. But let us now return to the
sequence of history.

Constantine, as I have said, transferred the seat of empire to Byzantium and, having enriched it by the treasures of almost all other cities,
called it after his own name Constantinople. Hereafter, for this reason,
it was known as The Royal City or New Rome. Having obtained a patriar-
chal see it won a place next to that held by the Church of Rome itself,
the place which the church of Alexandria had previously held. From this
time on we find the sovereignty of the Romans transferred to the Greeks.
On account of the one-time exalted position of the City, sovereignty remained with it in name, though in fact power went to the Greeks. The
situation, then, was like that of Babylon. Note that as the kingdom of
Christ expands the worldly kingdom is constantly diminishing.

So when the City of Christ was prospering in many ways and had peace
without from its foes, the devil, the enemy of the human race, sought to
assail it from within. After Peter had been crowned with martyrdom in
the time of persecution, Achillas had undertaken the direction of the

Alexandrine patriarchate; when he died with the church at peace, Alexander ruled that church. In his time the presbyter Arius, the vilest of all men, devised his most impious heresy regarding the inequality of the persons of the Trinity. To answer him that very famous Council of Nicaea was assembled, and there Arius with his adherents was condemned and the Catholic faith was strengthened in the presence of the emperor. . . .

In the three hundred and sixty-fourth year from the incarnation of the Lord, upon the death of Constantius, Julian, the thirty-sixth in line from Augustus, assumed imperial power. He at first, as though censuring the deeds of his predecessor, ordered the bishops to be recalled from exile, but afterwards he set out to persecute the Church of God—by craft, however, rather than by violence. Then, as though swayed by religious scruples, he decreed that Christians must be excluded from the games, must be kept from taking the oath of military service, and finally that they must be stripped of every earthly possession, inasmuch as their own law declares, "So therefore whosoever he be of you that renounceth not all that he hath, he cannot be my disciple." He ordered the temples of the heathen to be opened; the imperial prerogatives—such as cooks, eunuchs, barbers, a public race course for horses and mules—he dispensed with, as a philosopher; he devoted himself to study, staying awake by night and writing, and by day reading in the senate what he had written. In consequence he esteemed the philosophers above all other men; he alone of the emperors since Julius Caesar cultivated the study of philosophy. But in his writings he assailed not only the emperors who preceded him but also the Christians. Hence Socrates, in the Tripartite History, speaks thus of him: "In that he expelled the cooks and the barbers he acted the part of a philosopher but not of an emperor; but to belittle and to abuse was in keeping neither with a philosopher nor with an emperor."

At that time lived very famous citizens of the City of God, certain bishops, Meletius of Antioch, Maris of Chalcedon, Basil of Caesarea and Gregory of Nazianzus. Of these Maris alone, who was advanced in age and of feeble health and failing vision, resisted Julian to his face once while he was sacrificing to Fortune in the Royal City, and was not afraid to call him impious and godless and an apostate, as Sozomen relates in the Tripartite History. When Julian, posing as a man of philosophic calm, had reproached him for nothing save his blindness, saying, "Nor is your Galilean god able to cure you," he is said to have replied, "I thank my God for blindness, because this has been done to keep me from seeing you stripped of your piety." Basil and Gregory, being removed from the life of philosophers and hermits to the highest priesthood, not only resisted this tyrant and the heretic Valens by their priestly authority, but also left for the Church of God very useful and profound writings as memorials.

Julian, desiring, as I have said, in consequence of the subtlety of his intellect to follow the philosophers, was raised out of himself into such folly that, following the example of Pythagoras, he said that the spirit of Alexander rested in him and he was preparing—in imitation of him—to make the whole world subject to himself. While to achieve this purpose he was moving his army against the Persians, he was enticed into an ambush by a certain man. And there, when the soldiers were losing their strength because of the barrenness of the place, he was struck by a missile hurled at random and died in the thirty-first year of his age, one year and eight months from the time at which he had become emperor, and in the seventh year from the time when he had been ordained Caesar.

It is related of him that when he saw the spear coming toward him he realized that this was the act of divine vengeance; yet he was not moved to repentance but only rendered the more obstinate, and that he cried with blasphemous lips, "Thou hast conquered, O Galilean." For this was the name he had been wont to use of Christ. Thus then did the Lord fully free His City from a most impious tyrant who had devoted the blood of the Christians to his own gods. We read in the Life of Saint Basil that it was in consequence of the prayers of this holy man Basil (for Julian had then determined that on his return he would utterly destroy Caesarea in Cappadocia, over which Basil presided) that this weapon had been sent from heaven by the blessed martyr Mercurius; by way of proof it is declared that a spearhead, which lay near the tomb of the martyr, was found to be bloody in the morning. . . .

In the three hundred and seventy-eighth year from the incarnation of the Lord, Valens, the thirty-ninth in line from Augustus, ruled in the East; Gratian and Valentinian, the sons of Valentinian, governed in the West. Valens—deceived, as I said above, by the trickery of the Arians— then made a law that monks should be forced into military service. Hence many soldiers of Christ in Egypt were crowned with martyrdom for refusing to be the soldiers of an earthly king. Meanwhile he sought to discover by necromantic arts who was to reign after him. Because four letters Θ. E. D. A. were revealed to him he caused all those men to be put to death who, he learned, had these letters at the beginning of their names. In harmony with this plan he ordered the death of Count Theodosius, the father of the Theodosius who afterwards became emperor; although Theodosius, when sent by Valens against Firmus, had destroyed not only Firmus himself but also the tribes of the Moors that he had stirred to rebellion. Theodosius, first receiving the sacrament of baptism at Carthage, voluntarily bared his neck to the executioner.

Meanwhile Gratian, relying upon the aid of Christ, routed more than thirty thousand of the Alemanni at Strassbourg, a town of Gaul, with small loss to the Roman troops.

At about the same time a controversy which arose in the kingdom of the Goths between Fritigern and Athalarich compelled Fritigern, because he had the weaker case, to ask for the aid of the Romans. When he had come to Valens he received soldiers from him and drove Athalarich in flight. Accordingly, desiring to repay the emperor for his kindness, he embraced his pernicious dogma and in consequence the Goths became Arians. Ulfila, the bishop of the Goths, then invented a Gothic alphabet, and when he had translated the Holy Scriptures into Gothic and begun to preach in the kingdom of Athalarich, the latter, because he was a pagan, inflicted punishment upon many of the Goths whom the Arians hold in reverence as martyrs.

Not long afterwards, when the Goths were now at peace among themselves, the Huns—a horrible race (for they derive their origin, as Jordanes relates, from evil spirits and harlots)—guided by a deer, made their way out of the swamps of Lake Maeotis and so greatly terrified the Goths (a very valiant race) together with Hermanric, their king, that the aforesaid king—who had previously conquered many nations—died in the one hundred and tenth year of his life, as much from dread of this race as from a wound treacherously inflicted upon him by a certain soldier. Jordanes records that Hermanric was king of the Ostrogoths. The aforesaid writer, who was himself a Goth, relates that the Goths had two kingdoms, the one that of the Visigoths, the other that of the Ostrogoths.

After the death of Hermanric the Goths, broken in spirit, again sent to Valens and asked him for a place to dwell in. Valens permitted them to settle among the Thracians. When, because of the hatred and envy of their neighbors, they were suffering there from an unbelievably severe famine, they were treacherously invited by a certain leader to a banquet. But they first guarded themselves against the trap by slaying those who had invited them, and afterwards, scattering everywhere, devastated the whole country with fire and sword. Valens, moving his army from Antioch against them, was moved by a late repentance and ordered the orthodox Catholic bishops to be recalled from exile. Yet on account of his oath he himself did not abjure his own heresy. A battle was fought in Thrace. When the Roman army was put to flight the emperor, wounded by an arrow, fled and wished to hide in the shelter of a certain little hut. The Goths, pursuing him, burned him and the hut together in the fifteenth year of his reign and the fourth year after his brother's death. This is believed to have happened through a righteous judgment of God; he who had consumed the Goths with the fire of faithlessness when they were seeking the true faith was himself burned by them with actual fire and lacked even ordinary burial.

In the three hundred and eighty-third year from the incarnation of the Lord, Gratian, the fortieth in line from Augustus, obtained with his brother Valentinian the imperial power. He had previously held it in company with Valens. Desiring to aid the state, Gratian made Theodosius, a Spaniard by race (a brave and God-fearing soldier) Emperor of the East, investing him with the purple at Sirmium.

In his time a second synod, of one hundred and fifty bishops, was assembled in the Royal City under Pope Damasus to oppose Macedonius and Sabellius. The former was maintaining that the Holy Spirit has been created by the Son, the other was asserting that the Holy Spirit was indistinguishable from the Father; indeed he asserted that the Father was the Son too. When these heresies had been condemned and anathematized together with the Arian heresy, the orthodox Catholic faith was strengthened.

Now Theodosius conquered the Gothic tribes not only by valor but also by wisdom. Entering upon a truce with Athalarich their king he invited him to visit him in Constantinople. When Athalarich had come to that city he brought his last day to a close. But the tribes of the Goths, noting the courage and the gentleness of the emperor, subjected themselves to the sway of the Romans. Theodosius chose Arcadius, his son, as his associate in the imperial government. Meanwhile Maximus, seizing the rule in Britain by making himself tyrant, killed Gratian in Gaul in the sixth year of his reign after the death of Valens and expelled his brother Valentinian from Italy. Valentinian fled to Theodosius and was received by him like a son.

In the three hundred and eighty-eighth year from the incarnation of the Lord, after Gratian was slain, Theodosius, the forty-first in line from Augustus, obtained the sole rule of the Roman empire.

During these days the City of Christ began to have full joy and perfect peace, since troubles from abroad and from within the state were ended. There flourished at that time men of renown influential because of their characters, their manner of life and their wisdom: Martin bishop of Tours, Ambrose ecclesiastical head of Milan, Severinus prelate of Cologne and Jerome the presbyter. We find that Augustine too as catechumen was baptized by Ambrose at that time.

Accordingly, this most Christian prince, trusting in God more than in man, moved his army against Maximus to avenge the dead and restore the exile. He attacked Maximus in the territory of Aquileia and put him to death. Seeing this Count Andragathius, who had been his supporter, drowned himself. When the victory was won Theodosius came to Rome with his little son Honorius. After setting the state in good order there and leaving to Valentinian the government of the West, he returned to Constantinople. Valentinian, while he was on his way back, was (so some say) hanged by treachery of Arbogast and Eugenius. Eugenius was made emperor by Arbogast. But others claim that out of grief by his own hands he brought death on himself in this way.

The Prologue of the Fifth Book

As part of the fundamentals, like the alphabet and the rules of the art of grammar, children are usually told that the younger they are so much the more observant they are. This I think is not inaptly said, since we are on the one hand trained by the writings and institutions of our ancestors, who devoted themselves to wisdom before us, and by the passage of time and the resultant experience in life, yes, trained the more quickly the more advanced the age of the world is in which we are set; on the other hand, after mastering for ourselves the things that were discovered before us, we can devise new things with the same inspiration as those of old. The prophet foresaw that, in the old age of the world (for the reasons which I have mentioned), wisdom must be multiplied; and so he said: "Many shall run to and fro, and knowledge shall be increased." That is why, though our ancestors were men renowned for wisdom and of notable ability, the causes of many things lay hidden from them which have begun to be revealed to us through the lapse of time and the course of events. And so all now see to what the Roman Empire came—that Empire which, because of its pre-eminence, was thought by the pagans to be eternal and even by our people to be almost divine.

As I said above, all human power or wisdom, originating in the East, began to reach its limits in the West. Regarding human power—how it passed from the Babylonians to the Medes and the Persians and from them to the Macedonians, and after that to the Romans and then again to the Greeks under the Roman name—I think enough has been said. How it was transferred from the Greeks to the Franks, who dwell in the West, remains to be told in the present book. That wisdom was found first in the East (that is, in Babylonia) and was carried thence into Egypt, because Abraham went down to Egypt in a time of famine, Josephus makes clear in the first book of his *Antiquities,* speaking as follows concerning Abraham: "He bestowed on them a knowledge of arithmetic and himself delivered over to them also all the lore of astronomy. For before Abraham the Egyptians were absolutely ignorant of these things." That wisdom passed from Egypt to the Greeks in the time of the philosophers the same author indicates in these words: "For these are known to have been implanted by the Chaldeans in Egypt, whence also they are said to have made their way to the Greeks." Thus far Josephus. From the

Greeks it appears to have been carried to the Romans, under the Scipios, Cato and Tullius, and especially in the times of the Caesars, when a group of poets sang songs of many kinds and afterwards to the extreme West—that is, to the Gauls and the Spains—very recently, in the days of those illustrious scholars Barengar, Manegold and Anselm. Men divinely inspired were able to foresee and as it were to have a vision of these things. But we are in position not merely to believe but also actually to see the things which were predicted, since we behold the world (which, they predicted, was to be despised for its changeableness) already failing and, so to speak, drawing the last breath of extremest old age.

Furthermore, enough has been said above, I think, regarding the two cities: how one made progress, first by remaining hidden in the other until the coming of Christ, after that by advancing gradually to the time of Constantine. But after Constantine, when troubles from without had finally ceased, it began to be grievously troubled at the instigation of the devil by internal strife even to the time of the Elder Theodosius; Arius was the author of this and the lords of the world, the Augusti, were his coadjutors. But from that time on, since not only all the people but also the emperors (except a few) were orthodox Catholics, I seem to myself to have composed a history not of two cities but virtually of one only, which I call the Church. For although the elect and the reprobate are in one household, yet I cannot call these cities two as I did above; I must call them properly but one—composite, however, as the grain is mixed with the chaff. Wherefore in the books that follow let us pursue the course of history which we have begun. Since not only emperors of the Romans but also other kings (kings of renowned realms) became Christians, inasmuch as the sound of the word of God went out into all the earth and unto the ends of the world, the City of Earth was laid to rest and destined to be utterly exterminated in the end; hence our history is a history of the City of Christ, but that city, so long as it is in the land of sojourn, is "like unto a net, that was cast into the sea," containing the good and the bad. However, the faithless city of unbelieving Jews and Gentiles still remains, but, since nobler kingdoms have been won by our people, while these unbelieving Jews and Gentiles are insignificant not only in the sight of God but even in that of the world, hardly anything done by these unbelievers is found to be worthy of record or to be handed on to posterity. . . .

Let it suffice to have said this much, in accordance with the capacity of our understanding, concerning the end of the City of Christ. Herein, to use the words of Dionysius, "Taking thought of the limitations of our powers of speech, we have passed over certain matters, at the same time also honoring with silence the mystery which is above our powers." For "it is the glory of kings to conceal a matter," and so he who divulges mysteries disparages majesty. I am, of course, aware that great things ought to be spoken of in such a way that there shall always remain something to be investigated with care, lest if the whole matter be unfolded promiscuously it may appear of little value. Accordingly, though we devotedly offer to your love these matters which have been set forth, in however rude a style—not out of our own wisdom but in accordance with the teachings of the Scriptures—we do not bestow them upon those who are unwilling to receive or who scornfully reject them. For, as I have said above of Augustine, some matters are set down in his writings not as assertions but only on the basis of opinion and investigation, and the decision of final judgment has been left to those who are wiser. It will be our task to supplement what has been said insufficiently, to correct what has been said imperfectly, to prune away the superfluous and as, laden with sins, I struggle in this wide sea of the world, to aid me by the solace of your prayers.

Matthew Paris

c. 1200—c. 1273

14

Matthew was probably born in France and educated in Paris (whence his surname). We know little else. He became a monk and joined St. Alban's Abbey in England. There, he seems to have confined his scholarly attention to the study of history. He wrote, or compiled, a long *Chronicle* or, as it is now known, an *English History from the Year 1235 to 1273*. To this work he added a number of biographies and an abridgment of all his historical works. Since his major chronicle breaks off at 1273, our assumption is that he died soon after that year.

Matthew's *English History* is indeed a chronicle. Matthew opens his work at the year 1235, the year at which Roger of Wendower's chronicle, *The Flowers of History,* ended, and then moves on, year by year of Our Lord, king by English king, until the pen falls from his hand sometime in 1273. He gives us a chronological record of events, telling us of reigning kings, new taxes imposed, royal marriages, international squabbles, papal politics, and clerical concerns. He includes, helter-skelter, reports of prodigies, storms, miracles, tournaments, famines, and, even, terrible noises. Running through his *Chronicle* are reports of the chronic persecution of the Jews in medieval England. Matthew uncritically accepts all stories concerning the alleged wickedness of the Jews and recounts with approval the punishments inflicted upon them.

Credulous, uncritical, naïve, and biased in his approach to historical events and personalities, Matthew epitomizes the defects of the medieval chronicler, and it is for this reason that he is of historiographic interest. With his simple philosophy of history, his view of God's Providence actively guiding the affairs of men, Matthew is representative of most of what passed as historical writing throughout the Middle Ages. He is apparently ignorant of the great classical writers and unversed in the best of the Christian authorities. So atrophied is Matthew's analytical and conceptual sense that wars, social upheavals, international rivalries, Church-State conflicts, natural catastrophes all interpreted as in some way related to God's plan of history. Matthew contributes to historical knowledge only, it seems, in spite of himself. By his inclusion of letters and documents, usually in the form of digressions, he preserved for posterity records of his time whose true significance he usually mistook. By his unselfconscious and rather crude style of writing, he demonstrates the extent to which both pagan and Christian literary and historical arts had declined in western Europe. He affords us insight into an unhistorical world which, with all its intensely lived experiences and great political and intellectual developments, remains an enigma unfolding in the hands of God.

Selected Bibliography

J. A. Giles has translated Matthew's *English History* for the Bohn Antiquarian Library in 3 volumes (1852–1854). In a short preface he sums up the scanty knowledge we have of Matthew and at the end of Vol. III he has appended over one hundred pages of "Additamenta," documents compiled by Matthew as a supplement to his *History.* Maurice Powicke surveys Matthew's world, and draws upon his *History,* in *The Thirteenth Century* (second edition, 1952). James Gairdner includes Matthew among the *Early Chroniclers of Europe: England* (n.d.), pp. 243–257. His discussion of Matthew is enthusiastic and rather uncritical and should be balanced by V. H. Galbraith's more measured analysis in *Roger Wendover and Matthew Paris* (1944).

ENGLISH HISTORY FROM THE YEAR
1235 TO 1273

A brief description of the whole year of 1247.

This year throughout was very abundant in corn, but barren of fruit; was productive of injury to England, of tyranny to Wales; was hostile to the Holy Land, a turbulent despoiler of the Church; a source of bloodshed to Italy, and warlike and hostile to the empire and the Roman court, and especially so the kingdom of Germany; generated hatred in the hearts of prelates and several others against the pope, because he forcibly despoiled their patrons, and suspended them from the collation of benefices, a circumstance hitherto unheard of, and adverse to the king, because he tolerated such proceedings.

How the king kept Christmas at Winchester.

Anno Domini 1248, the thirty-second year of the reign of King Henry the Third, the said king was at Winchester at Christmas, at which place he observed the festivities of that season in the company of a great many of his nobles. On the morrow of Christmas-day he breakfasted with William, bishop of that city.

How the earl of Leicester and many other nobles assumed the cross.

About this same time, the earl of Leicester took the sign of the holy cross, in order that he might be absolved from his sins and gain admission to heaven; from reflecting within himself, he was in great alarm concerning the marriage he had contracted with his wife, who had formerly, in the presence of St. Edmund, archbishop of Canterbury, made a vow of chastity. The countess too, influenced, it is believed, by the same spirit, as soon as she saw her husband bearing the sign of the cross, flew with all speed to assume it also. Many knights and others of their household too received the same holy symbol, to obtain the reward of eternal salvation. Besides these, many of the nobles did the same, purpos-

---

From *English History,* translated by J. A. Giles (Bohn Antiquarian Library, 1852–1854). Vol. II, pp. 251–257, 263–270, 273–278, 280–282, 286–287.

ing to set out on their journey in company with the most Christian king of the French, whom the Lord had deigned miraculously to recall from the gates of death, or rather from death itself; which seemed to have been done not without purpose, for it was stated as though prognostically or in a prophetic spirit, and was everywhere asserted as a fact that the Lord had restored the said king to life that he might forcibly rescue his inheritance from the hands of the enemies of the cross.

The bishop of Bangor flees to the abbat of St. Alban's.

About this same time, Richard, bishop of Bangor, came to the abbat of St. Alban's, begging that abbat to open the bosom of compassion to him in his poverty, and that he might dwell with him until his bishopric, which was ruined by war, should be restored in some slight degree, in order that he and his clerks might recover breath after their troubles and oppressions which had surrounded them, in the same way as the bishop of Hereford, who remained there and was honourably supported for about twenty years.

The dangerous illness of Richard Seward.

About the same time, Richard Seward, a distinguished knight, of whom much mention has been previously made in this book, was seized by an incurable palsy, and took to his bed in a hopeless state, trusting that, by God's favour, he might, during his protracted illness, be cleansed from his former sins and fly to the life eternal.

The arrival in England of Beatrice, countess of Provence.

In this year too, Beatrice, the widow of Raymond, late count of Provence, came into England, accompanied by Thomas of Savoy, formerly count of Flanders, as if to visit her friends and relatives; but that the true reason of their coming may be explained to those who wish to know it, in order that she and the said Thomas, being thirsty, might resort to the same spring, and might, from the king's abundant riches and from his prodigality, fill their empty and gaping saddle-bags at their departure.

The death of Robert, bishop of Bath.

About the same time, that is about the feast of St. Hilary, Robert, bishop of Bath, went the way of all flesh; whereupon the king, according to custom, laid his greedy hands upon the property of his bishopric, to carry off whatever he could scrape together from it.

The French king re-assumes the cross.

At this time, the king of the French, who it was well known had assumed the cross, was severely blamed and reproached by his nobles
because he would not, in accordance with their advice, redeem or alter
his vow in any way whatever. Amongst others, the Lady Blanche, his
mother, and the bishop of Paris, who were aware of his imbecility, became more urgent, and persevered diligently with their arguments; the
bishop saying to him, "My lord, recollect, when you assumed the cross,
you made the vow suddenly and unadvisedly,—you were ill, and, to speak
the truth, were deprived of your senses; your blood was carried to your
brain, and you were not of sound mind, wherefore the words you then
uttered were devoid of the weight of truth and influence. His holiness the
pope will benignly grant us a dispensation, when he knows the necessi-
tous condition of the kingdom and the weak state of your bodily health.
In one quarter we have to fear the power of the schismatical Frederick;
in another the wiles of the wealthy king of England; here the treacherous
deceit of the Poitevins, although only lately conquered; there the cavil-
lings of the Albigenses are a matter of suspicion. Germany is in a disturbed state, Italy is restless, the means of access to the Holy Land are
difficult, and scarcely is there any place therein to receive you, and behind you you leave the inexorable hatred and implacable enmity of the
pope and the emperor Frederick. For whom do you leave us desolate?"
His mother also more effectually pressed him with her solicitations, for,
said she, "My dearest son, hear and give heed to the counsels of your
discreet friends, and do not strive against your own prudence; remember
what a virtue it is, and how pleasing it is to God, to obey and to comply
with the wishes of your mother. Remain in your kingdom, and the Holy
Land will suffer no detriment therefrom. A much larger army will be
sent there than if you went there in person. God is not calumnious or
cavilling. You, my son, are sufficiently excused by the loss of your reason,
the dulling of all your senses which came on you in your illness, or even
by death itself or estrangement of mind." To these arguments the king,
in no slight degree disturbed, replied: "You plead that the loss of my
senses was the cause of my assuming the cross, therefore, according to
your desire and advice, I lay aside the cross,—I resign it to you"; then,
raising his hand to his shoulder, he tore away the cross therefrom, saying, "My lord bishop, here is the cross which I have assumed; I voluntarily resign it to you." On this, all who sat around were seized with
unspeakable joy, when on a sudden the king, with an altered countenance and tone, said: "My friends, now I am not devoid of reason or sense;
I am not powerless or infirm; therefore I now require my cross to be

restored to me. For He who is ignorant of nothing knows that nothing eatable shall enter my mouth till I again bear the sign of the cross." Those seated round, on seeing this, declared that the finger of the Lord was in this proceeding, and that the Divine power had effected this from heaven, and no one dared to raise any further dispute on the aforesaid matters. We have fully and expressly stated all things, that every one may be made aware of the constancy of the most Christian king of the French in continuing in the service of Christ.

Of the general parliament held at London.

About the beginning of the year, in the octaves of the Purification, the nobles of all England were convoked to London, to confer with the king on the affairs of the kingdom, which was now greatly disturbed, impoverished, and injured. In accordance with this summons, therefore, there came thither nine bishops and nine earls, besides a great number of barons, knights, and other nobles, and also of abbats, priors, and clerks. Amongst them were the archbishop of York, and the bishops of Winchester, Lincoln, Norwich, Worcester, Chichester, Ely, Rochester, and Carlisle; Earl Richard, the earls of Gloucester, Leicester, Winchester, and Hereford; Roger Bigod earl marshal, the earl of Oxford, and besides them the earl of Lincoln, Earl Ferrers, Earl Warrenne, and P. of Savoy, earl of Richmond. The prelates who were not present at this great assembly were Boniface, archbishop of Canterbury, who was fighting for the pope on the continent, the bishop of Durham, who was ill at a distance, and the bishop of Bath, who had lately died. The king then explained to them his purpose, which indeed was not a secret to the community in general, and asked pecuniary aid from them; whereupon he was severely rebuked and reproached, in that he was not ashamed to demand such assistance at that time, especially because on the last exaction of a similar kind, to which the nobles of England were with difficulty induced to give their consent, he gave his charter that he would not again make such an exaction. He was also most severely blamed (and no wonder) for the indiscreet way in which he summoned foreigners into the kingdom, and for lavishly and indiscreetly scattering the property of the kingdom amongst them, and also for marrying the nobles of the kingdom to ignoble foreigners; thus despising and putting aside his native and natural subjects, and without asking the consent of both parties, which is necessary to the completion of a marriage. He was also blamed, and not without reason, because he seized by force on whatever he used in the way of meat and drink—especially wine, and even clothes—against the will of those who sold those things, and were the true owners; wherefore the native dealers withdrew and hid themselves, as also did foreigners, who would otherwise bring their goods for sale to that country; thus a stop was put to trade, by which different nations are mutually enriched and strengthened, and thus we are defamed and impoverished, because they obtain nothing but lawsuits and anger from the king; and by this, he the said king incurs awful maledictions from numberless people, to the peril and disgrace of himself and the whole kingdom. From these traders, moreover, he, in order that he may bestow alms indiscreetly, and may make immoderate illuminations, forcibly seizes wax, silk, stuffs, and other things, without making any terms of pacification; thus bringing scandal on himself, his kingdom, and all who inhabit it, and not without giving serious offence to God, who holds rapine in abhorrence when connected with an offering. In all these proceedings he tyrannizes and oppresses to such a degree that even on the sea-coast he does not allow the herrings and other fish to be disposed of at the will of the poor fishermen, nor do they dare to appear in the places adjoining the sea-coast, or in the cities, for fear of being robbed; so that they consider it safer to trust themselves to the stormy billows, and to seek the further shore. The miserable traders also are so cruelly oppressed and annoyed by the royal agents, that punishment is added to loss; and injury is heaped upon injury, both as regards their own persons, and as regards their carriages and their horses already jaded. The king was, moreover, reprehended, in that he, contrary to the first and chief oath which he made at his coronation, impoverished even to their ruin the bishoprics and abbacies, as well as the vacant wardships founded by the noble and holy fathers, which he for a long time detains in his own hands, of which he ought to be the protector and defender; and therefore they are said to be in his hands, that is, under his protection. Another complaint also was made against him by each and every one, and which was no slight one; and this was, that, unlike his noble predecessors, he never appointed either a justiciary, a chancellor, or treasurer, in consonance with the advice of the kingdom in general, as he ought and was expedient, but only such persons as obeyed his pleasure in everything, provided that it was advantageous to himself, and who did not seek the advancement of the common weal, but only their own especial benefit by collecting money and obtaining wardships and revenues for themselves.

The king endeavours to appease the community of England by promises.

The king, at hearing these complaints, was confused and ashamed of himself, as he knew that all the charges were true. He therefore promised most faithfully that he would willingly amend these matters, hoping by this humiliation, although only feigned, more easily to bend the hearts of all to accede to his demand. To this, however, the community, who had been often ensnared by such promises, replied, "This will be seen plainly enough, and within a short time; we will still wait patiently, and as the king shall conduct and bear himself towards us, so we will obey him in all matters." Everything then was put off, and referred to consideration until the fortnight of the Nativity of St. John the Baptist. The king, in the mean time, either of his own accord, or at the instigation of his courtiers, who did not wish their power to be weakened, became obdurate and more exasperated against his subjects, and took but very little trouble to make any amends to them for the above-mentioned excesses, as he had promised to do. . . .

About this time, the English coin was so intolerably debased by money-clippers and forgers, that neither natives nor foreigners could look upon it with other than angry eyes and disturbed feelings. For it was clipped round almost to the inner part of the ring, and the border which bore the letters was either entirely destroyed or enormously defaced. Proclamation was therefore made by herald in the king's name in all cities, boroughs, and markets, that no penny should be taken which was not of legitimate weight and circumference, nor be received in any way, either in buying, selling, or exchange, and that all trangressors of this order would be punished. Great diligence was used to discover the aforesaid false dealers, that, if found guilty of the crime, they might meet with condign punishment, according to the decision of a court. A careful inquisition, therefore, was made, and there were found to be guilty of this crime certain Jews and notorious Caursins, and also some Flemish wool-merchants. The French king also ordered all persons guilty of this crime who were found in his kingdom to be suspended on gibbets and exposed to the winds.

The death of Walter Mauclerc and two other of the Preacher brethren.

In the same year, about the feast of the apostles Simon and Jude, Walter Mauclerc, formerly bishop of Carlisle, commendably terminated his mortal career, and, throwing off the burden of worldly cares and riches, went the way of all flesh. In the same year also there departed from this world to the Lord two brothers of the same order, who were, as it is believed, unsurpassed, indeed unequalled, whilst living, in theology and other sciences: these were the brothers Robert Bacon and Richard de Fishakele, who had for many years lectured in that same faculty, and were distinguished in preaching the word of the Lord to the people.

Of the marriages of Frederick and his son Conrad.

In this year, Frederick, in order to strengthen his cause in the contest he had engaged in against the pope, entered into a confederacy with certain chiefs, and married a lady rich in money, of pleasing appearance, and illustrious birth: his son, also influenced by a similar intention, espoused the daughter of the duke of Bavaria. On learning this, the archbishop of Cologne and those who held by the party of the newly-elected king of Germany, more than usually urged the necessity of William, the said elect, being fully and solemnly crowned at Aix-la-Chapelle; but, owing to the opposition of the said Frederick and his son Conrad, he was precluded from all access to that city. The archbishop of Cologne, therefore, and the legate, in conjunction with innumerable prelates and nobles who favoured the cause of the Church (the greatest part of whom had received the sign of the cross at the hands of the Preachers and Minorites), most vigorously besieged the said city of Aix-la-Chapelle, where frequent conflicts, attended with various success, ensued between the two parties and many fell on both sides. The siege continued, attended with great bloodshed and loss on both sides, and the number of the besiegers daily increased, as a river which is increased by the torrents; yet the confidence of the besieged was kept up by letters which were frequently sent by Frederick and his son Conrad, exhorting them not to lose courage, for that their release, as they declared, was at hand

Of a tournament held at Newbury.

On Ash-Wednesday, a grand tournament was held at Newbury amongst the knights of England, to try their knightly prowess and strength; and as the king was favourable to it, it began and ended well. At this tournament, William de Valence, the king's uterine brother, a novice, conducted himself with great daring, in order to acquire a famous name in chivalry; but being of tender age, and not able to sustain the force of the hardy and marshalled knights, he was thrown to the ground, whereby he suffered considerable losses, and was well batoned, in order that he might receive his apprentisage in knighthood.

Of the trouble and vexation of the people, owing to the changing of the money.

In the course of this year the people were so troubled by divers precepts of the king concerning the receiving of money, proclaimed by the voice of a herald throughout the cities of England, that they would rather a measure of corn had cost more than twenty shillings; for exchange was carried on but in few cities; and when they got there, they received a certain weight of new money for a certain weight of old, and were obliged to pay thirteen pence on every pound for the smith's work, or moneying, which was commonly called whitening. The form of this money differed from the old, insomuch that a double cross traversed the border where the letters were marked; but in other respects, namely, as to weight, chief impression, and the lettered characters, it remained as before. The people were therefore reduced to great straits, and suffered no slight injury, inasmuch as twenty shillings could scarcely be obtained from the money-changer's table for thirty, without a trouble and expense of several days' duration and tedious expectation. As a great increase of profit accrued to the king by these matters, his brother, Earl Richard, to whom he was deeply indebted, came to him, like another Jacob and a subtle supplanter, and said to him, "My king and brother, pay me the debts you owe me." And as he perseveringly continued to press his demand, the king replied: "My only brother by the same parents, you see my necessities on all sides. The very small portion of territory which remains to me on the continent is exposed to peril and injury. Gascony is protected by the shield of Bordeaux alone; to liberate which province I find it necessary to expend a no small sum of money." The earl, however, with an insolently loud voice, demanded satisfaction for his debt out of the profits arising from the money coinage; and as he unceasingly reiterated his demands with importunity, he obtained a promise that he should receive the profits arising from the coinage, which, according to the exchangers, would continue for seven years, and the profits themselves would amount to twenty thousand pounds, a third portion of the proceeds only being reserved to the king; and thus he was freed from his debt to the earl. The earl, having obtained this, procured preceptory letters from the king, that no coin which had been clipped should be passed in England—indeed, that all clipped money should be bored through; and if any exchanger should be anywhere discovered giving two pence for one, or three for two, that he should be taken and severely punished, both in his property and person, as being an offender against the king, and a transgressor of the royal precept. The form of this brief, which was sent to the sheriffs, may be found fully given in the book of Additamenta.

An eclipse of the moon.

On the feast of June in this year, just after sunset, the moon underwent an almost total eclipse.

Of the proceedings of the grand parliament held at London.

In the month of June, as the fortnight of the feast of St. John the Baptist drew near, all the nobility of England assembled in London, firmly believing, from the positive promises of the king, that he would amend his faults, and, by the grace conferred on him from above, would incline his ear to wiser counsels. On the assembling, therefore, of all the chief men of England, the following graceless reply to their former complaints flowed from the king's mouth: "All you, the chief men of England, have endeavoured to bend your lord and king to your will, little courteous as it is, and to impose on him a very servile condition; whilst whatever any one chooses is insolently denied him, but every one is allowed to adopt what and whose plans he chooses. Again, every father of a family is allowed to appoint any one soever to this or that office in his house, or to suspend or even to depose them; but this liberty, forsooth, you rashly presume to deny to your king, especially as servants ought not to judge and bind their master to their conditions, nor ought vassals their prince, but those who are considered as inferiors ought rather to be ruled and governed at the will and pleasure of their lord. For the servant is not above his lord, nor is the pupil above his master; and your king, therefore, would be no longer so, but would be, as it were, a slave, if he were thus to incline to your will. Wherefore he will not dismiss either the chancellor, justiciary, or treasurer, as you propose arranging it, nor will we appoint others in their stead." In the same manner, also, a cavilling reply was given to other matters beneficial to the king himself. "But he asks pecuniary aid from you, to recover his rights on the continent, which also concerns you." The nobles, on hearing these words, thought it as clear as the light that they had emanated from his present advisers, whose power would be weakened and extinguished if the advice of the community of barons were listened to. However, seeing that they were answered and opposed by craft and cunning, they all, influenced, as it were by one spirit, plainly replied that they would on no account again uselessly impoverish themselves, that foreigners might revel in their pride on their property, and the enemies of the king as well as the kingdom be strengthened, as was lately the case in Poitou, and also in Gascony, whither he had precipitately and indiscreetly hurried, contrary to their advice and wish, whereby he had met with adversity. And we truly believe, for it so appears from the king's greediness and state of need, that he was secretly made and detained a prisoner, but, on quietly paying a fine, pledging his faith, and giving his oath and charters, he was cautiously set at liberty and dismissed when thus deprived of his honour, and money, and territory, and was allowed to depart ingloriously amidst all kinds of insult. The council therefore broke up in anger, and all of them were thus deceived in the hopes which they had long conceived from this parliament, and after all their trouble and expenses to no purpose, gained nothing but derision and frivolous answers to their complaints.

How the king of England sold his treasure.

When the king saw this result to his proceedings, he burst out into violent anger, and said to his counsellors: "It is by you that the affections of my nobles are estranged from me; here I am about to lose Gascony; I have been deprived of Poitou; and, being destitute of money, what am I to do?" After holding a pusillanimous council, therefore, it was determined, without any prudence, that all the vessels, utensils, and jewels of the royal treasury should be sold by weight, without regard to the gold or silver, or to the laborious artificial work, although the work excelled the material, in order that money might be obtained by these means. The royal councillors, moreover, added the following consolatory speech, and to sooth the king, insinuated to him, "That, as all rivers flow back to the sea, so everything which was now sold will at some time return to you in remunerative gifts; therefore, let not our lord the king be disturbed." After the sale of the above-mentioned treasure, the king inquired where and to whom they were sold, and on the reply being given, "At London," he said, "I know, I know that if the treasure of Octavian were for sale, the city of London would purchase and suck it all up; for these ill-bred Londoners, who call themselves barons, possess abundance even to a surfeit: that city is an inexhaustible well." He then immediately conceived a design, on the slightest opportunity arising, to despoil them of their property; of which subsequent events have fully proved his fulfilment, and the following narrative will fully relate.

How the French king set out on his expedition to Jerusalem.

As the equinoctial season proved favourable, with pleasant weather, and autumn furnished an abundance of corn and wine, the French king, having obtained special license at St. Denis and other holy places in his kingdom, and having made a vow, set out on his journey to Jerusalem. Passing through Lyons, where the pope was residing, he humbly and devoutly paid his respects to him, and earnestly begged of him, saving the honour of the Church in all matters, to condescend to accept the humiliation of Frederick, who demanded his pardon, and to grant him the favour of a reconciliation, and to open the bosom of his paternal affection to him, a penitent; "At least," said he, "that the passage may be safer to me on my pilgrimage." As, however, he saw the pope assuming a look of refusal, he went away in sorrow, saying: "I am afraid that, when I am gone, hostile treachery will be planned against the French kingdom, owing to your inexorable severity. It will lie at your door, if the progress of the affairs of the Holy Land is impeded. However, I will guard France as the pupil of my eye, because on the condition of that kingdom depends your prosperity, as well as that of all Christendom." To this the pope replied: "I, as long as I live, will stand by France against this schismatic Frederick, whom the Church has condemned and hurled by a general council from the imperial dignity; and indeed I will act the same against the king of England, our vassal, if he presumes to kick against the kingdom of France, or the rights pertaining to it; as I also will against all the enemies of the said kingdom." The king, somewhat soothed by these words, then replied: "As you make such promises, I intrust the reins of government of my kingdom of France to you"; and it was forthwith arranged that a special messenger should be sent to the king of England to forbid him from attacking or in any way harassing any of the dependencies of the French kingdom; and for this purpose, Masters Albert and Paul were sent especially, who came to the king at Windsor, on the feast of the Exaltation of the Holy Cross, to deliver their message to him; but this circumstance was kept a secret, in order that the king might more easily exact money for the purpose of reclaiming and recovering his rights by force of arms. The French king, then, having made a long and deliberate confession to the pope, and obtained from him a remission of his sins, took leave of his holiness, and departed, with his blessing, from Lyons, directing his course with his army towards Marseilles. When he was drawing near the city of Avignon, the inhabitants of that city, not choosing to endure the insults of the haughty French, who called them Albigenses, traitors, and poisoners, made an attack on them in the narrow passes well known to themselves; and, their hatred and anger being roused by their long-standing enmities, pillaged some of the French army, and put to death those who opposed them. On this, some of the French nobles suggested to the king that he should lay siege to the city, if for no other purpose, at least to take just and vigorous vengeance for the murder of his father, who was poisoned there, or if he proceeded on his journey, that he should allow them to do it under his favour. The king with difficulty restrained their fury, and said to them: "I go from France, not to avenge my own injuries, or those of my father, or mother, but those of my Lord Jesus Christ." This most Christian monarch then proceeded immediately on his journey, and suffered much greater losses at Marseilles; so much so, that the French nobles were much provoked, and, had they not been restrained by the discreet and holy moderation of the king, would, in their anger, have vigorously besieged Marseilles. The king, however, said: "The time for our passage is close at hand; God forbid that Satan should prevail; for he is grieving on that account, and is seeking to interpose some obstacles to impede it." Having with difficulty appeased their disturbed feelings, the king, on the morrow of St. Bartholomew, took with him some picked soldiers, leaving more than a thousand crossbowmen behind him, and a great many more knights and retainers. These returned in great shame and anger, and with difficulty restrained themselves from joining the king of England, and from voluntarily stirring up war against the king of France; but, on weighing future perils in the scale of reason and prudence, they returned peaceably to the pope, and offered to enter his service, to fight for him, at his command, against any one soever. Being, however, circumvented by the pope's arguments, and those of his court, who knew that they had abundance of money, they laid aside the symbols of the cross, resigned their travelling supplies to the pope to obtain remission from their pilgrimage, and, with their pockets emptied, that they might travel more lightly, they returned to their homes with only a very small portion of their property remaining, wherewith to support themselves on their journey. The French king in the mean time put to sea, and with spreading sails directed his course with a fair wind towards Cyprus, which abounded in all luxuries, in order to pass the winter there in peace, and recover breath. . . .

Of an unusual inundation of the sea.

On the 24th of November in this year; the sea overflowed its bounds to a great distance, and caused irreparable injury to those dwelling near the coast; for when the moon, according to the computation of the calendar, was in its fourth quarter, the tide flowed with swollen waters without any subtle ebb or decrease. This is believed to have occurred in consequence of the strong wind which blew from the sea; but as it had often happened that the wind blew in strong from the sea, and yet the sea itself did not rise in such a way, even old persons were astonished at this new and unusual occurrence.

Of a dreadful earthquake in Savoy.

In this year an awful earthquake occurred in Savoy, in the valleys of Maurienne, by which five villages were overwhelmed, with their cowsheds, sheepcots, and mills; and the mountains and rocks in the neighbourhood were torn away from the places where they had stood since the creation, and were swallowed up in some of their own caverns. It is not known whether this destruction of mountains occurred, and the earthquake vented its fury on the said villages, by a miracle or naturally;

but, inasmuch as it destroyed about nine thousand men, and animals without number, it seems to have been caused by a miracle rather than the common course of events. It was said that the severity of divine punishment justly vented its fury on the abodes of the inhabitants of those parts, because they so shamelessly and indiscriminately practised the disgraceful trade of usury, and were so contaminated with the stain of avarice, that, in order to cover their wickedness with an appearance of virtue, they did not hesitate to call themselves money-merchants. They had no horror of simony, and fearlessly and without mercy engaged in theft and pillage. Traders or scholars compelled to go to the Roman court, who passed their way or dwelt with them when on their journey, they never failed to cut the throats of or to poison; not being aware that the more tardy the Divine vengeance is, the more severely it is said to exercise its fury, as witness the blessed Gregory, who says, "Divine rigour proceeds to punishment with a slow step, but it afterwards makes up for its tardiness by its severity."

How the prior of Thetford was stabbed by one of his monks.

In order that what is written in the Gospel may be fulfilled it is necessary, that is to say inevitable, "that scandal should woe to the world, proceed from scandal": in the month of December in this year, the prior of Thetford, a Savoyard by birth, and a monk of Clugny, who declared himself to be a relation or kinsman of the queen, and had assumed airs of pride from that circumstance, invited his brothers, Bernard a knight, and Guiscard, a beastly clerk, to come to his house at Thetford. There he remained, according to custom, the whole night till cock-crow, indulging in immoderate eating and drinking with them, and forgetting his matin devotions; seldom did he trouble himself to be present at mass, even at the little masses; seldom did he appear at canonical hours; but in the morning, being surfeited with food, he vomited forth his nightly potations. If the cry of the hungering poor sounded in his ears, this was a minor care in his breast, and whenever Bernard, one of his said brothers, went away, Guiscard, the other, whose belly was like a bladder in frosty weather, and whose body would load a waggon, stayed longer with him, and swallowed up all the food of the monks in the Charybdis of his belly, and afterwards, when well gorged, despised and loaded them with insults. Whilst the said prior then was thus entertaining his brothers, who had borne the toil and heat of the day, in a manner unbecoming to him, and was disgracefully wasting the substance of his little church, transgressing, as was stated, the bounds of all moderation in his gluttony, a dispute and strife arose between him and one of his monks, a Welshman by birth. This monk, whom he, the prior, had some little time before summoned from Clugny, he was now endeavouring to send back thither against his will, not out of charity, but from hatred, although the said monk opposed the proceeding and excused himself on reasonable grounds. But when the prior with a loud voice swore horribly that the said monk should proceed on a pilgrimage with the scrip and wallet, this demoniac monk, inflamed with violent anger, or rather with madness, drew a knife and plunged it into the prior's belly, without the least hesitation at perpetrating such a crime within the precincts of the church. The wounded prior, with the very death-rattle in his throat, endeavoured to call the monks to his aid by his cries, or, at any rate, to arouse them; but he was unable to do so, owing to the stoppage of the arteries; whereon the said monk again rushed upon him, and with heavy blows, three or four times repeated, buried the knife up to the handle in his lifeless body; and thus this wretch, to the enormous injury and disgrace of the monastic order, sent the wretched prior to hell, beneath the anger of an offended God. These circumstances I have related fully, that those who read may be warned and chastened, and prevented from perpetrating such crimes, lest they be hurled by an angry God into a similar ruin. The author of this crime was seized by persons who came to the spot, and, being well secured, was committed to prison. When the circumstance came to the knowledge of the king, worried by the continual complaints of the queen, he ordered the murderer to be chained, and, after being deprived of his eyes, to be thrown into the lowest dungeon in the castle of Norwich, notwithstanding the principle for which St. Thomas the Martyr combated in defence of a certain priest who had committed homicide, shedding even his blood and his brains, that a clerk, and especially a priest, could not be condemned before a lay tribunal, or hanged after his orders had been taken from him; a principle for which he suffered martyrdom; that God does not punish twice for the same offence; that He puts a limit upon the punishment of the wicked, and rewards far beyond a man's deserts; and that a single fault is sufficiently and reasonably atoned for by a single punishment. These occurrences having been mentioned by an enemy of the monks, as an opprobrium to religious men, a certain person, a friend to them and a lover and special advocate of religion, said in reply, "Amongst the angels the Lord found a rebel; amongst the seven deacons, a deviator from the right path; and amongst the apostles, a traitor: God forbid that the sin of one or of a few should redound to the disgrace of such a numerous community." This moderation is taught by the heathen poet, who says:

> Parcite paucorum diffundere crimen in omnes.
> [Let not the crime of some redound on all.]

Of a quarrel and battle between the monks of Selby and John Francis.

In the same year, a quarrel having arisen between the monks of Selby and John Francis, a clerk of the king's, as to the collection of hay and corn, one monk was slain, and several others were wounded and beaten. And in order that scandal might not come singly, in this same year, in the priory at Canterbury, one monk mortally wounded another.

Of the miserable death of the prior of Benethly.

In the same unfortunate month a prior of the canons of a small church near the monastery of St. Alban's happened to be inspecting a heap of wheat, which we commonly call a rick, and reckoning the value of it, when the rick, being improperly built, suddenly tottered and fell upon him; and before the sheafs which were heaped upon him could be dispersed, this prior, a simple-minded man of small substance, died of suffocation. Others who were by, the servants and companions of the prior, escaped; as only smaller masses had fallen upon them, but did not overwhelm them.

Of the severe punishment of an adulterer.

The following circumstance I think ought not to be passed over, although it may appear ridiculous. In this same unlucky month, in order that it might not be said that scandal rose against religious men only, disgrace and irreparable loss was brought on certain members of the order of knighthood. For a certain knight of Norfolk, named Godfrey de Millers, of noble birth and distinguished in knightly deeds, being shamefully led astray, secretly entered the lodgings of John the Briton, a knight, for the purpose of lying with his daughter, but was seized by some persons concealed, with the connivance of the harlot herself, who was afraid of being thought a married man's mistress, violently thrown to the ground, and severely beaten and wounded. After this he was suspended to a beam, with his legs stretched apart, and, when thus exposed to the will of his enemies, he was disgracefully mutilated to such a degree that he would have preferred decapitation, and, thus wounded and mutilated, was ejected, half-dead, from the house. A complaint of this proceeding having reached the king, the authors of this great cruelty were seized, and John the Briton being found guilty of it, he was disinherited and banished for ever. The adulteress, however, could not be found, as she secreted herself in inaccessible places, and thus, with some trouble, escaped the plots which were laid against her life. All who were present at the perpetration of this deed of enormous cruelty, were dispersed in exile, homeless fugitives; and thus this inhuman and merciless crime involved many nobles in a lamentable calamity. About the same time, too, a certain handsome clerk, the rector of a rich church, who surpassed all the knights living round him in giving repeated entertainments and acts of hospitality, was involved in a similar misfortune. However, the king, touched with compassion and deeply grieved, ordered it to be proclaimed as a law by herald, that no one should presume to mutilate another for adultery except in the case of his wife. . . .

Of the oppressions daily practised on the English by the Roman court.

In the same year, the oppressions devised in manifold ways, which flowed forth from the Roman court on wretched England, were daily increased and multiplied. Besides the oppression and unusual slavery, owing to the suspension of prelates from the collation of benefices until the Roman avarice was satisfied, and against which their petty king in his pusillanimity did not cry out, detestable swarms of new oppressions daily shot forth; and although we cannot mention all the injuries (for it is difficult, indeed impossible, to do so), we have thought proper to insert some of them in this work, that those who read of them may grieve, and grieving, may complain to God, and at some future time may be released from them by his favour, and that all may clearly see the pitiable misery of England, which was deprived of its rulers and defenders. The abbat of Abingdon had received a mandate from the pope to make immediate provision for a certain Roman; but this Roman, not choosing to accept any church except a rich one, quietly waited, concealing his intentions, till some noble and rich church should be vacant. The first which became so was the church of St. Helen, in the town of Abingdon, which was reckoned to be worth a hundred marks, and supplied with every advantage, as being in a borough which was subject to the said monastery. The said Roman, who had been so long quiet, at once demanded this church, and urgently pressed his demand that it should be given to him on the authority of the Apostolic See. On the day on which the church became vacant, the abbat received a most urgent order from the king, intermingled with threats, entreaties, and promises, that he should give that church to his, the king's, uterine brother Ethelmar, although the latter now held such an abundance of churches and revenues that we should not wonder if he himself did not know their number and value. The abbat, therefore, being in a state of perplexity, and as if crushed between two revolving millstones, consulted the brethren of his convent, and two revolving millstones, consulted the brethren of his convent, and some discreet and faithful friends in the matter, who replied, "It is clearly a case of hardship both ways; but if the king is willing to protect you from the pope's violence, we think it will be more endurable to give the church to this brother of his, as he is our prince and patron, than to this Roman, who would always be sedulously plotting against you, an indefatigable persecutor, and, as it were, a thorn in your eye." This determination was therefore signified to the king in due time, who at once promised the said abbat his certain protection, together with indemnity from loss, and the abbat accordingly, relying on these deceitful words, gave the church to the said Ethelmar at the king's entreaty. The aforesaid Roman, then, in great anger, immediately went to the pope with a heavy complaint, and related to him the particulars of the affair, with additions of his own to provoke the pope's anger. His Holiness then cited the said abbat to appear before him, to answer to the charge of disobedience, and the latter being destitute of all consolation and assistance from the king, although it was often asked for, although an old and infirm man, went, in great sorrow, fear, and bitterness of heart, to the Roman court, where, after much suffering and no slight expense, he was made to give satisfaction to the evil Roman, according to the decision of the pope, by paying him fifty marks annually from his chamber, to the great injury of his church. . . .

Of an earthquake in England.

In the same year, on the day of our Lord's Advent, which was the fourth day before Christmas, an earthquake occurred in England, by which (as was told to the writer of this work by the bishop of Bath, in whose diocese it occurred) the walls of buildings were burst asunder, the stones were torn from their places, and gaps appeared in the ruined walls. The vaulted roof which had been placed on the top of the church of Wells by the great efforts of the builder, a mass of great size and weight, was hurled from its place doing much damage, and fell on the church, making a dreadful noise in its fall from such a height, so as to strike great terror into all who heard it. During this earthquake a remarkable occurrence happened: the tops of chimneys, parapets, and pillars were thrown from their places, but the bases and foundations of them were not at all disturbed, although the reverse ought naturally to have happened. This earthquake was the third which had occurred within three years on this side the Alps: one in Savoy, and two in England; a circumstance unheard of since the beginning of the world, and therefore the more terrible.

The conclusion of the year.

This year passed, temperate and calm, filling the barns with abundance of corn, and making the presses flow with wine; so much so, that a measure of corn fell in price to two shillings, and a cask of choice wine was freely sold for two marks; the orchard fruit was very abundant in some places, but scanty in others; but the gourd-worms entirely destroyed everything green where the disease made its way into the shrubs. The events of the year proved hostile to the Holy Land, inimical to Italy, deadly to Germany, adverse to England, and destructive to France; and, to sum up much in a few words, consumptive of money in almost every country of Christendom: by many indications it gave tokens of the end of the world approaching, as we read, "Nation shall rise against nation, and there shall be earthquakes in places," and other similar prophecies. To the Roman court it was a source of disgrace, pestiferous, and injurious, and evidently threatening the divine anger. The temperature of winter was entirely changed to that of spring, so that neither snow or frost covered the face of the earth for two days together; trees might be seen shooting in February, and the birds singing and sporting as if it were April.

John Froissart

1337—c. 1404

15

John Froissart was born in Valenciennes, France, in 1337, the year of the outbreak of the Hundred Years' War between France and England. We know nothing of his family beyond the possibility that his father was a skilled craftsman attached to the court of the Count of Hainault. Froissart himself indicates that from early youth he loved hunting, music, dancing, and women, tastes to be indulged only within wealthy, that is, aristocratic circles. The enjoyment of such pastimes was apparently no bar to his becoming a priest, and, in time, canon and treasurer of the collegiate church of Chimay. It was no doubt a positive experience to him in his other roles of historian and poet. He wrote love poems and romances in the French fashion of that age of chivalry, that age of sublimated aggression and routine violence, and his intense and passionate outpouring reappeared in his historical works. He traveled widely in France and, attached as he was to the neutral court of Hainault, in England as well. He moved easily in the cosmopolitan French culture of the ruling families of his time. While in England, he was made secretary to Queen Philippa (1361) and he apparently remained in that position until the death of his patroness in 1369. In the next three decades Froissart found patrons in both France and England and he was able to travel to Spain and Portugal where he gathered much material for his chronicles. He returned to England late in the century and was well received by Richard II to whom he presented a copy of his history. He died sometime after 1404.

Froissart's *Chronicles of England, France, Spain, and the Adjoining Countries* is a monumental work in size and significance. It covers the period from 1326 to 1400 in western Europe, with asides on events in the rest of the known world. Froissart chose as his central theme the wars between England and France. In a phrase that recalls Herodotus he writes: "That the honorable enterprises, noble adventures, and deeds of arms . . . may be properly related, and held in perpetual remembrance—to the end that brave men taking example from them may be encouraged in their well-doing, I sit down to record

410

a history deserving great praise." Froissart, however, was not interested in analyzing the causes or issues of the war. He was interested rather in describing the kings, princes, and knights—his heroes—at war, at tournament, and at love. What he discourses about are not the institutions or economics of his time but the living out of an aristocratic, knightly, warrior credo. He is interested not in philosophy but in noble actions and important events—and in the realm of events the death of a king or the birth of a prince is to him much more momentous than a widespread peasant revolt. He wrote, as he tells us, "for people of reason and understanding," that is, for the warrior aristocrats among whom he found his patrons. He knew his audience, and thus he wrote, and rewrote with embellishments, more of a brilliant entertainment than a history.

But, regardless of his audience, it appears that Froissart would have found it most difficult to rise from romantic narrative to history. He manifests a credulous and superstitious nature which precluded an analytical or objective approach to either human or natural phenomena. He uncritically records accounts of miracles, prophecies, and magical occurrences. Although he did make an effort to find corroboration for some of his facts he is usually woefully deficient on matters beyond his immediate ken. He cannot tender an unbiased opinion of Germans, Englishmen, Spaniards, or Italians; only Frenchmen evoke in him sympathetic understanding. "Superficial description of outward circumstances," J. Huizinga has written, "this is all we get from writers like Froissart."

And yet, Froissart's *Chronicles* both contain history and further our understanding of history. Froissart imparts to us a sense of the life and values of the declining Middle Ages. His historiographic principle was derived from the conception of chivalry and if this principle leads to inferior historiography it nevertheless allows us to understand how Froissart and his contemporaries visualized their world, a world of violence and confusion in which notions of historical and social development were absent. In Froissart, a superstitious but thoroughly secular man, even the idea of Providence is muted. More dominant in his history is the pagan idea of Fortune ruling the destinies of men. Froissart may thus be seen as a chronicler-*engagé,* active in the affairs he writes of, unselfconsciously expounding the principles of his aristocratic contemporaries, a reflection of his historical times more than a writer of history. "Froissart was our Herodotus," wrote Macaulay (among many others), meaning that with our chronicler the beginning of modern historiography may be dated. The shift of emphasis from Providence to Fortune in Froissart's most mundane (but hardly prosaic) work foretells the move of Western man and his historiography from the Middle Ages to the Renaissance.

Selected Bibliography

William Ker Paton has a helpful introduction to his edition of Lord Berners' translation of *The Chronicle of Froissart* (6 vols., 1901). The Thomas Jones translation (from which we take our selections), *Chronicles of England, France, Spain,* in the New York edition of 1874, contains the translator's "Life of the Author, An Essay on His Works, and a Criticism on His History," all interesting, all still valuable today. J. Huizinga, *The Waning of the Middle Ages* (1956, a translation of the 1924 original) offers a splendid account of the medieval background to Froissart, along with some telling criticisms of his *Chronicles.* Auguste Molinier, *Les sources de l'histoire de France* (1901–1905), Vol. IV, has an informative entry on Froissart, accompanied by a helpful but out of date bibliography. John Jolliffe has translated and edited *Froissart's Chronicles* (1967). It is a convenient introduction to Froissart and it includes a fine, annotated bibliography.

CHRONICLES

Preface

That the honourable enterprises, noble adventures, and deeds of arms, performed in the wars between England and France, may be properly related, and held in perpetual remembrance—to the end that brave men taking example from them may be encouraged in their well-doing, I sit down to record a history deserving great praise; but, before I begin, I request of the Saviour of the world, who from nothing created all things, that he will have the goodness to inspire me with sense and sound understanding to persevere in such manner, that all those who shall read may derive pleasure and instruction from my work, and that I may fall into their good graces.

It is said, and with truth, that all towns are built of many different stones, and that all large rivers are formed from many springs; so are sciences compiled by many learned persons, and what one is ignorant of is known to another: not but that every thing is known sooner or later. Now, to come to the matter in hand, I will first beg the grace of God and the benign Virgin Mary, from whom all comfort and success proceed; and then I will lay my foundation on the true Chronicles formerly written by that reverend, wise, and discreet man, John le Bel, canon of St. Lambert's, at Liege; who bestowed great care and diligence on them, and continued them, as faithfully as he could, to his death, though not without much pain and expense: but these he minded not, being rich and powerful. He was also a man of courteous manners, generous, and a privy counsellor, well beloved by sir John de Hainault; who is spoken of in these books, and not without reason, for he was the chief of many noble enterprises, and nearly related to several kings; and by his means the above-mentioned John le Bel could see as through a perspective the many gallant actions recorded in the following sheets.

The true reason of my undertaking this book was for my amusement, to which I have ever been inclined, and for which I have frequented the company of many noblemen and gentlemen, as well in France as in England and Scotland, and in other countries, from whose acquaintance

From *Froissart's Chronicles,* translated by Thomas Jones (London, Routledge & Kegan Paul Ltd.). Reprinted by permission of the publisher. Pp. 1–4, 160–161, 163–166, 477–480, 652–657.

I have always requested accounts of battles and adventures, especially since the mighty battle of Poictiers, where the noble king John of France was taken prisoner; for before that time I was young in years and understanding: however, on quitting school, I boldly undertook to write and relate the wars above mentioned—which compilation, such as it was, I carried to England, and presented to my lady Philippa of Hainault, queen of England, who most graciously received it from me, to my great profit. And perhaps as this book is neither so exactly now so well written as such feats of arms require—for such deeds demand that each actor who therein performs his part nobly should have due praise—in order to acquit myself to all, as in justice is due, I have undertaken this present work on the ground before mentioned, at the prayer and request of my dear lord and master, sir Robert de Namur, knight, lord of Beaufort, to whom I owe all love and obedience, and God give me grace to do always according to his pleasure.

Chapter I.—Of the bravest knights of this present book.

To encourage all valorous hearts, and to show them honourable examples, I, John Froissart, will begin to relate, after the documents and papers of master John le Bel, formerly canon of St. Lambert's, at Liege, as followeth: That whereas various noble personages have frequently spoken of the wars between France and England, without knowing any thing of the matter, or being able to assign the proper reasons for them; I, having perceived the right foundation of the matter, shall neither add nor omit, forget, corrupt, nor abridge my history: but the rather will enlarge it, that I may be able to point out and speak of each adventure from the nativity of the noble king Edward of England, who so potently reigned, and who was engaged in so many battles and perilous adventures, and other feats of arms and great prowess, from the year of grace 1326, when he was crowned in England.

Although he, and also those who were with him in his battles and fortunate rencounters, or with his army when he was not there in person, which you shall hear as we go on, ought to be accounted right valiant; yet as of these there is a multitude some should be esteemed supereminent. Such as the gallant king himself before named; the prince of Wales, his son; the duke of Lancaster; sir Reginald lord Cobham; sir Walter Manny of Hainault, knight; sir John Chandos; sir Fulke Harley; and many others who are recorded in this book for their worth and prowess: for in all the battles by sea or land, in which they were engaged, their valour was so distinguished that they should be esteemed heroes of highest renown— but without disparagement to those with whom they served. In France also was found good chivalry, strong of limb and stout of heart, and in great abundance; for the kingdom of France was never brought so low as to want men ever ready for the combat. Such was king Philip of Valois, a bold and hardy knight, and his son, king John; also John, king of Bohemia, and Charles, count of Alençon, his son; the count of Foix; the chevaliers de Santré, d'Arnaud d'Angle, de Beauveau, father and son, and many others that I cannot at at present name; but they shall all be mentioned in due time and place: for, to say the truth, we must allow sufficient bravery and ability to all who were engaged in such cruel and desperate battles, and discharged their duty, by standing their ground till the discomfiture.

Chapter cxxv.—The king of France pursues the king of England, in the country of Beauvais.

I wish now to return to king Philip, whom we left at St. Denis with his army, which was increasing every day. He marched off with it, and pushed forward until he came to Coppigny les Guises, which is three leagues distant from Amiens, where he halted. The king of England, who was still at Airaines, was much embarrassed how to cross the Somme which was wide and deep, as all the bridges had been broken down, and their situation were well guarded by men at arms. The two marshals, at the request of the king, followed the course of the river, in order if possible to find a passage for the army: they had with them a thousand men at arms and two thousand archers. They passed by Lompré, and came to Pont de Remy, which they found defended by numbers of knights, squires, and people of the country. The English dismounted, and attacked the French from the very dawn of the morning until near ten o'clock: but the bridge was so well fortified and guarded that they could not gain anything; so they departed, and went to a large town called Fontaines-sur-Somme, which they completely plundered and burnt, as it was quite open. They next came to another town, called Long, in Ponthieu; but they could not gain the bridge, so well was it guarded. They then rode on to Pecquigny, but found the town, castle, and bridge, so well garrisoned that it was impossible to pass. In this manner had the king of France ordered all the bridges and fords of the river Somme to be guarded, to prevent the king of England from crossing it with his army; for he was resolved to force them to fight when he should see the most favourable opportunity, or else to starve them.

The two marshals, having thus in vain followed the course of the Somme, returned to the king of England, and related to him that they were unable to find a passage anywhere. That same evening, the king of France took up his quarters at Amiens, with upwards of one hundred thousand men. The king of England was very pensive: he ordered mass before sunrise, and his trumpets to sound for decamping. All sorts of people followed the marshals' banners, according to the orders the king had issued the preceding day; and they marched through the country of Vimeu, drawing near to the good town of Abbeville. In their march, they came to a town where a great number of the country people had assembled, trusting to some small fortifications which were thrown up there; but the English conquered the town, as soon as they came to it, and all that were within. Many of the townsmen and those from the adjoining country were slain or taken prisoners. The king lodged, that night, in the great hospital.

The king of France set out from Amiens, and came to Airaines about noon: the English king had quitted it about ten o'clock. The French found there provisions of all sorts; meat on the spits, bread and pastry in the ovens, wine in barrels, and even some tables ready spread, for the English had left it in very great haste. The king of France fixed his quarters there, to wait for his nobles and their retinue. The king of England was in the town of Oisemont. When his two marshals returned in the evening, after having overrun the country as far as the gates of Abbeville, and to St. Valery, where they had had a smart skirmish, the king of England summoned a council, and ordered many prisoners, whom his people had made in the districts of Ponthieu and Vimeu, to be brought before him.

The king, most courteously, asked, "if any of them knew a ford below Abbeville, where he and his army could pass without danger"; and added, "Whoever will show us such a ford shall have his liberty, and that of any twenty of his fellow-soldiers whom he may wish to select." There was among them a common fellow whose name was Gobin Agace, who answered the king, and said, "Sir, I promise you, under peril of my life, that I will conduct you to such a place, where you and your whole army may pass the river Somme without any risk. There are certain fordable places where you may pass twelve men abreast twice in the day, and not have water above your knees; but when the tide is in, the river is full and deep, and no one can cross it; when the tide is out, the river is so low that it may be passed, on horseback or on foot, without danger. The bottom of this ford is very hard, of gravel and white stones, over which all your carriages may safely pass, and from thence is called Blanchetaque. You must therefore set out early, so as to be at the ford before sun-rise." "Friend," replied the king, "if I find what thou hast just said to be true, I will give thee and all thy companions their liberty; and I will besides make thee a present of a hundred nobles." The king gave orders for every one to be ready to march at the first sound of his trumpet, and to proceed forward.

Chapter cxxvii.—The order of battle of the English at Crecy, who
were drawn up in three battalions on foot.

The king of England, as I have mentioned before, encamped this Friday in the plain: for he found the country abounding in provisions; but,
if they should have failed, he had plenty in the carriages which attended
on him. The army set about furbishing and repairing their armour; and
the king gave a supper that evening to the earls and barons of his army,
where they made good cheer. On their taking leave, the king remained
alone, with the lords of his bed-chamber: he retired into his oratory, and,
falling on his knees before the altar, prayed to God, that, if he should
combat his enemies on the morrow, he might come off with honour.
About midnight he went to his bed; and, rising early the next day, he and
the prince of Wales heard mass, and communicated. The greater part of
his army did the same, confessed, and made proper preparations. After
mass, the king ordered his men to arm themselves, and assemble on the
ground he had before fixed on. He had enclosed a large park near a wood,
on the rear of his army, in which he placed all his baggage-waggons and
horses; and this park had but one entrance: his men at arms and archers
remained on foot.

The king afterwards ordered, through his constable and his two marshals, that the army should be divided into three battalions. In the first,
he placed the young prince of Wales, and with him the earls of Warwick
and Oxford, sir Godfrey de Harcourt, the lord Reginald Cobham, lord
Thomas Holland, lord Stafford, lord Mauley, the lord Delaware, sir John
Chandos, lord Bartholomew Burgherst, lord Robert Neville, lord Thomas
Clifford, the lord Bourchier, the lord Latimer, and many other knights
and squires whom I cannot name. There might be, in this first division,
about eight hundred men at arms, two thousand archers, and a thousand
Welshmen. They advanced in regular order to their ground, each lord
under his banner and pennon, and in the centre of his men. In the second
battalion were the earl of Northampton, the earl of Arundel, the lords
Roos, Willoughby, Basset, Saint Albans, sir Lewis Tufton, lord Multon,
the lord Lascels, and many others; amounting, in the whole, to about
eight hundred men at arms, and twelve hundred archers. The third battalion was commanded by the king, and was composed of about seven
hundred men at arms, and two thousand archers.

The king then mounted a small palfrey, having a white wand in his
hand, and attended by his two marshals on each side of him: he rode a
foot's pace through all the ranks, encouraging and entreating the army,
that they would guard his honour and defend his right. He spoke this so
sweetly, and with such a cheerful countenance, that all who had been

dispirited were directly comforted by seeing and hearing him. When he had thus visited all the battalions, it was near ten o'clock: he retired to his own division, and ordered them all to eat heartily, and drink a glass after. They ate and drank at their ease; and, having packed up pots, barrels, etc., in the carts, they returned to their battalions, according to the marshal's orders, and seated themselves on the ground, placing their helmets and bows before them, that they might be the fresher when their enemies should arrive.

Chapter cxxviii.—The order of the French army at Crecy.

That same Saturday, the king of France rose betimes, and heard mass in the monastery of St. Peter's in Abbeville, where he was lodged: having ordered his army to do the same, he left that town after sun-rise. When he had marched about two leagues from Abbeville, and was approaching the enemy, he was advised to form his army in order of battle, and to let those on foot march forward, that they might not be trampled on by the horses. The king, upon this, sent off four knights, the lord Moyne of Bastleberg, the lord of Noyers, the lord of Beaujeu, and the lord of Aubigny, who rode so near to the English that they could clearly distinguish their position. The English plainly perceived they were come to reconnoitre them: however, they took no notice of it, but suffered them to return unmolested. When the king of France saw them coming back, he halted his army; and the knights pushing through the crowds, came near the king, who said to them, "My lords, what news?" They looked at each other, without opening their mouths: for neither chose to speak first. At last, the king addressed himself to the lord Moyne, who was attached to the king of Bohemia, and had performed very many gallant deeds, so that he was esteemed one of the most valiant knights in Christendom. The lord Moyne said, "Sir, I will speak, since it pleases you to order me, but under the correction of my companions. We have advanced far enough to reconnoitre your enemies. Know, then, that they are drawn up in these battalions, and are waiting for you. I would advise, for my part, (submitting, however, is better counsel,) that you halt your army here, and quarter them for the night; for before the rear shall come up, and the army be properly drawn out, it will be very late, your men will be tired and in disorder, whilst they will find your enemies fresh and properly arrayed. On the morrow, you may draw up your army more at your ease, and may reconnoitre at leisure on what part it will be most advantageous to begin the attack; for, be assured they will wait for you." The king commanded that it should so be done: and the two marshals rode, one towards the front, and the other to the rear, crying out, "Halt banners, in the name of God and St. Denis." Those that were in the front halted; but those behind said they would not halt, until they were as forward as the front. When the front perceived the rear pressing on, they pushed forward; and neither the king nor the marshals could stop them, but they marched on without any order until they came in sight of their enemies. As soon as the foremost rank saw them, they fell back at once, in great disorder, which alarmed those in the rear, who thought they had been fighting. There was then space and room enough for them to have passed forward, had they been willing so to do: some did so, but others remained shy. All the roads between Abbeville and Crecy were covered with common people, who when they were come within three leagues of their enemies, drew their swords, bawling out, "Kill, kill"; and with them were many great lords that were eager to make show of their courage. There is no man, unless he had been present, that can imagine, or describe truly, the confusion of that day; especially the bad management and disorder of the French, whose troops were out of number. What I know, and shall relate in this book, I have learnt chiefly from the English, who had well observed the confusion they were in, and from those attached to sir John of Hainault, who was always near the person of the king of France.

Chapter cxxix.—The battle of Crecy, between the kings of France and of England.

The English, who were drawn up in three divisions, and seated on the ground, on seeing their enemies advance, rose undauntedly up, and fell into their ranks. That of the prince was the first to do so, whose archers were formed in the manner of a portcullis, or harrow, and the men at arms in the rear. The earls of Northampton and Arundel, who commanded the second division, had posted themselves in good order on his wing, to assist and succour the prince, if necessary.

You must know, that these kings, earls, barons and lords of France, did not advance in any regular order, but one after the other, or any way most pleasing to themselves. As soon as the king of France came in sight of the English, his blood began to boil, and he cried out to his marshals, "Order the Genoese forward, and begin the battle, in the name of God and St. Denis." There were about fifteen thousand Genoese cross-bowmen; but they were quite fatigued, having marched on foot that day six leagues, completely armed, and with their cross-bows. They told the constable, they were not in a fit condition to do any great things that day in battle. The earl of Alençon, hearing this, said, "This is what one gets by employing such scoundrels, who fall off when there is any need for them." During this time a heavy rain fell, accompanied by thunder and a very terrible eclipse of the sun; and before this rain a great flight of crows hovered in the air over all those battalions making a loud noise. Shortly afterwards it cleared up, and the sun shone very bright; but the Frenchmen had it in their faces, and the English in their backs. When the Genoese were somewhat in order, and approached the English, they set up a loud shout, in order to frighten them; but they remained quite still, and did not seem to attend to it. They then set up a second shout, and advanced a little forward: but the English never moved. They hooted a third time, advancing with their cross-bows presented, and began to shoot. The English archers then advanced one step forward, and shot their arrows with such force and quickness, that it seemed as if it snowed. When the Genoese felt these arrows, which pierced their arms, heads, and through their armour, some of them cut the strings of their cross-bows, others flung them on the ground, and all turned about and re-treated quite discomfited. The French had a large body of men at arms on horseback, richly dressed to support the Genoese. The king of France, seeing them thus fall back, cried out, "Kill me those scoundrels; for they stop up our road, without any reason." You would then have seen the above-mentioned men at arms lay about them, killing all they could of these runaways.

The English continued shooting as vigorously and quickly as before; some of their arrows fell among the horsemen, who were sumptuously equipped, and, killing and wounding many, made them caper and fall among the Genoese, so that they were in such confusion they could never rally again. In the English army there were Cornish and Welshmen on foot, who had armed themselves with large knives: some advancing through the ranks of the men at arms and archers, who made way for them, came upon the French when they were in this danger, and, falling upon earls, barons, knights, and squires, slew many, at which the king of England was afterwards much exasperated. The valiant king of Bohemia was slain there. He was called Charles of Luxembourg; for he was the son of the gallant king and emperor, Henry of Luxembourg: having heard the order of the battle, he inquired where his son, the lord Charles, was: his attendants answered, that they did not know, but be-lieved he was fighting. The king said to them: "Gentlemen, you are all my people, my friends and brethren at arms this day; therefore, as I am blind, I request of you to lead me so far into the engagement that I may strike one stroke with my sword." The knights replied, they would di-rectly lead him forward; and in order that they might not lose him in the crowd, they fastened all the reins of their horses together, and put the king at their head, that he might gratify his wish, and advanced towards the enemy. The lord Charles of Bohemia, who already signed his name as king of Germany, and bore the arms, had come in good order to the engagement; but when he perceived that it was likely to turn out against the French, he departed, and I do not well know what road he took. The king, his father, had rode in among the enemy, and made good use of his sword; for he and his companions had fought most gallantly. They had advanced so far that they were all slain; and on the morrow they were found on the ground, with their horses all tied together.

The earl of Alençon advanced in regular order upon the English, to fight with them; as did the earl of Flanders, in another part. These two lords, with their detachments coasting, as it were, the archers, came to the prince's battalion, where they fought valiantly for a length of time. The king of France was eager to march to the place where he saw their banners displayed, but there was a hedge of archers before him. He had that day made a present of a handsome black horse to sir John of Hainault, who had mounted on it a knight of his, called sir John de Fusselles, that bore his banner: which horse ran off with him, and forced his way through the English army, and, when about to return, stumbled and fell into a ditch and severely wounded him: he would have been dead, if his page had not followed him round the battalions, and found him unable to rise: he had not, however, any other hindrance than from his horse; for the English did not quit the ranks that day to make prisoners. The page alighted, and raised him up; but he did not return the way he came, as he would have found it difficult from the crowd. This battle, which was fought on the Saturday between la Broyes and Crecy, was very murderous and cruel; and many gallant deeds of arms were performed that were never known. Towards evening, many knights and squires of the French had lost their masters: they wandered up and down the plain, attacking the English in small parties: they were soon destroyed; for the English had determined that day to give no quarter, or hear of ransom from any one.

Chapter cxxx.—The English on the morrow again defeat the French.

When, on this Saturday night, the English heard no more hooting or shouting, nor any more crying out to particular lords or their banners, they looked upon the field as their own, and their enemies as beaten. They made great fires, and lighted torches because of the obscurity of the night. King Edward then came down from his post, who all that day had not put on his helmet, and, with his whole battalion, advanced to the prince of Wales, whom he embraced in his arms and kissed, and said, "Sweet son, God give you good perseverance: you are my son, for most loyally have you acquitted yourself this day: you are worthy to be a sovereign." The prince bowed down very low, and humbled himself, giving all honour to the king his father. The English, during the night, made frequent thanksgivings to the Lord, for the happy issue of the day, and without rioting; for the king had forbidden all riot or noise. On the Sunday morning, there was so great a fog that one could scarcely see the distance of half an acre. The king ordered a detachment from the army, under the command of the two marshals, consisting of about five hundred lances and two thousand archers, to make an excursion, and see if there were any bodies of French collected together. The quota of troops, from Rouen and Beauvais, had, this Sunday morning, left Abbeville and St. Ricquier in Ponthieu, to join the French army, and were ignorant of the defeat of the preceding evening: they met this detachment, and, thinking they must be French, hastened to join them.

As soon as the English found who they were, they fell upon them; and there was a sharp engagement; but the French soon turned their backs, and fled in great disorder. There were slain in this flight in the open fields, under hedges and bushes, upwards of seven thousand; and had it been clear weather, not one soul would have escaped.

A little time afterwards, this same party fell in with the archbishop of Rouen and the great prior of France, who were also ignorant of the discomfiture of the French; for they had been informed that the king was not to fight before Sunday. Here began a fresh battle: for those two lords were well attended by good men at arms: however, they could not withstand the English, but were almost all slain, with the two chiefs who commanded them; very few escaping. In the course of the morning, the English found many Frenchmen who had lost their road on the Saturday, and had lain in the open fields, not knowing what was become of the king, or their own leaders. The English put to the sword all they met: and it has been assured to me for fact, that of foot soldiers, sent from the cities, towns and municipalities, there were slain, this Sunday morning, four times as many as in the battle of the Saturday.

Chapter lxxiii.—The populace of England rebel against the nobility.

While these conferences were going forward, there happened in England great commotions among the lower ranks of the people, by which England was near ruined without resource. Never was a country in such jeopardy as this was at that period, and all through the too great comfort of the commonalty. Rebellion was stirred up, as it was formerly done in France by the Jacques Bons-hommes, who did much evil, and sore troubled the kingdom of France. It is marvellous from what a trifle this pestilence raged in England. In order that it may serve as an example to mankind, I will speak of all that was done, from the information I had at the time on the subject.

It is customary in England, as well as in several other countries, for the nobility to have great privileges over the commonalty, whom they keep in bondage; that is to say, they are bound by law and custom to plough the lands of gentlemen, to harvest the grain, to carry it home to the barn, to thrash and winnow it: they are also bound to harvest the hay and carry it home. All these services they are obliged to perform for their lords, and many more in England than in other countries. The prelates and gentlemen are thus served. In the counties of Kent, Essex, Sussex and Bedford, these services are more oppressive than in all the rest of the kingdom.

The evil-disposed in these districts began to rise, saying, they were too severely oppressed; that at the beginning of the world there were no slaves, and that no one ought to be treated as such, unless he had committed treason against his lord, as Lucifer had done against God; but they had done no such thing, for they were neither angels nor spirits, but men formed after the same likeness with their lords, who treated them as beasts. This they would not longer bear, but had determined to be free, and if they laboured or did any other works for their lords, they would be paid for it.

A crazy priest in the county of Kent, called John Ball, who, for his absurd preaching, had been thrice confined in the prison of the archbishop of Canterbury, was greatly instrumental in inflaming them with those ideas. He was accustomed, every Sunday after mass, as the people were coming out of the church, to preach to them in the market place and assemble a crowd around him; to whom he would say,—"My good friends, things cannot go on well in England, nor ever will until every thing shall be in common; when there shall neither be vassal nor lord, and all distinctions levelled; when the lords shall be no more masters than ourselves. How ill have they used us! and for what reason do they thus hold us in bondage? Are we not all descended from the same parents, Adam and Eve? and what can they show, or what reasons give, why they should be more the masters than ourselves? except, perhaps, in making us labour and work, for them to spend. They are clothed in velvets and rich stuffs ornamented with ermine and other furs, while we are forced to wear poor cloth. They have wines, spices, and fine bread, when we have only rye and the refuse of the straw; and, if we drink, it must be water. They have handsome seats and manors, when we must brave the wind and rain in our labours in the field; but it is from our labour they have wherewith to support their pomp. We are called slaves; and, if we do not perform our services, we are beaten, and we have not any sovereign to whom we can complain, or who wishes to hear us and do us justice. Let us go to the king, who is young, and remonstrate with him on our servitude, telling him we must have it otherwise, or that we shall find a remedy for it ourselves. If we wait on him in a body, all those who come under the appellation of slaves, or are held in bondage, will follow us, in the hopes of being free. When the king shall see us, we shall obtain a favourable answer, or we must then seek ourselves to amend our condition."

With such words as these did John Ball harangue the people, at his village, every Sunday after mass, for which he was much beloved by them. Some who wished no good declared it was very true, and murmuring to each other, as they were going to the fields, on the road from one village to another, or at their different houses, said, "John Ball preaches such and such things, and he speaks truth."

The archbishop of Canterbury, on being informed of this, had John Ball arrested, and imprisoned for two or three months by way of punishment; but it would have been better if he had been confined during his life, or had been put to death, than to have been suffered thus to act. The archbishop set him at liberty, for he could not for conscience sake have put him to death. The moment John Ball was out of prison, he returned to his former errors. Numbers in the city of London having heard of his preaching, being envious of the rich men and nobility, began to say among themselves, that the kingdom was too badly governed, and the nobility had seized on all the gold and silver coin. These wicked Londoners, therefore, began to assemble and to rebel: they sent to tell those in the adjoining counties, they might come boldly to London, and bring their companions with them, for they would find the town open to them, and the commonalty in the same way of thinking; that they would press the king so much, there should no longer be a slave in England.

These promises stirred up those in the counties of Kent, Essex, Sussex and Bedford, and the adjoining country, so that they marched towards London; and, when they arrived near, they were upwards of sixty thousand. They had a leader called Wat Tyler, and with him were Jack Straw and John Ball: these three were their commanders, but the principal was Wat Tyler. This Wat had been a tiler of houses, a bad man, and a great enemy to the nobility. When these wicked people first began to rise, all London, except their friends, were very much frightened. The mayor and rich citizens assembled in council, on hearing they were coming to London, and debated whether they should shut the gates and refuse to admit them; but, having well considered, they determined not to do so, as they should run a risk of having the suburbs burnt.

The gates were therefore thrown open, when they entered in troops of one or two hundred, by twenties or thirties, according to the populousness of the towns they came from; and as they came into London they lodged themselves. But it is a truth, that full two-thirds of these people knew not what they wanted, nor what they sought for: they followed one another like sheep, or like to the shepherds of old, who said they were going to conquer the Holy Land, and afterwards accomplished nothing. In such manner did these poor fellows and vassals come to London from distances of a hundred and sixty leagues, but the greater part from those counties I have mentioned, and on their arrival they demanded to see the king. The gentlemen of the country, the knights and squires, began to be alarmed when they saw the people thus rise; and, if they were frightened, they had sufficient reason, for less causes create fear. They began to collect together as well as they could.

The same day that these wicked men of Kent were on their road towards London, the princess of Wales, mother to the king, was returning from a pilgrimage to Canterbury. She ran great risks from them; for these scoundrels attacked her car, and caused much confusion, which greatly frightened the good lady, lest they should do some violence to her or to her ladies. God, however, preserved her from this, and she came in one day from Canterbury to London, without venturing to make any stop by the way. Her son Richard was this day in the Tower of London: thither the princess came, and found the king attended by the earl of Salisbury, the archbishop of Canterbury, sir Robert de Namur, the lord de Gommegines, and several more, who had kept near his person from suspicions of his subjects who were thus assembling, without knowing what they wanted. This rebellion was well known to be in agitation in the king's palace, before it broke out and the country people had left their homes; to which the king applied no remedy, to the great astonishment of every one. In order that gentlemen and others may take example, and correct wicked rebels, I will most amply detail how this business was conducted.

Chapter lxxiv.—The populace of England commit many cruelties on those in official situations.—They send a knight as ambassador to the king.

On Monday preceding the feast of the Holy Sacrament, in the year 1381, did these people sally forth from their homes, to come to London to remonstrate with the king, that all might be made free, for they would not there should be any slaves in England. At Canterbury, they met John Ball (who thought he should find there the Archbishop, but he was at London), Wat Tyler and Jack Straw. On their entrance into Canterbury, they were much feasted by every one, for the inhabitants were of their way of thinking; and, having held a council, they resolved to march to London, and also to send emissaries across the Thames to Essex, Suffolk, Bedford, and other counties, to press the people to march to London on that side, and thus, as it were, to surround it, which the king would not be able to prevent. It was their intention that all the different parties should be collected together on the feast of the Holy Sacrament, or on the following day.

Those who had come to Canterbury entered the church of St. Thomas, and did much damage: they pillaged the apartments of the archbishop, saying as they were carrying off different articles,—"This chancellor of England has had this piece of furniture very cheap: he must now give us an account of the revenues of England, and of the large sums he has levied since the coronation of the king." After they had defrauded the abbey of St. Vincent, they set off in the morning, and all the populace of Canterbury with them, taking the road towards Rochester. They collected the people from the villages to the right and left, and marched along like a tempest, destroying every house of an attorney or king's proctor, or that belonged to the archbishop, sparing none.

On their arrival at Rochester, they were much feasted, for the people were waiting for them, being of their party. They advanced to the castle, and seizing a knight called sir John de Newtoun, who was constable of it and captain of the town, they told him that he must accompany them as their commander in chief, and do whatever they should wish. The knight endeavoured to excuse himself, and offered good reasons for it, if they had been listened to; but they said to him, "Sir John, if you will not act as we shall order, you are a dead man." The knight seeing this outrageous mob ready to kill him, complied with their request, and very unwillingly put himself at their head. They had acted in a similar manner in the other counties of England, in Essex, Suffolk, Cambridge, Bedford, Stafford, Warwick and Lincoln, where they forced great lords and knights, such as the lord Manley, a great baron, sir Stephen Hales, and sir Thomas Cossington, to lead and march with them. Now, observe how fortunately matters turned out, for had they succeeded in their intentions they would have destroyed the whole nobility of England: after this success, the people of other nations would have rebelled, taking example from those of Ghent and Flanders, who were in actual rebellion against their lord. In the same year the Parisians acted a similar part, arming themselves with leaden maces. They were upwards of twenty thousand, as I shall relate when I come to that part of my history; but I will first go on with this rebellion in England.

When those who had lodged at Rochester had done all they wanted, they departed, and, crossing the river, came to Dartford, but always following their plan of destroying the houses of lawyers or proctors on the right and left of their road. In their way, they cut off several men's heads, and continued their march to Blackheath, where they fixed their quarters: they said they were armed for the king and commons of England. When the citizens of London found they were quartered so near them, they closed the gates of London-bridge: guards were placed there by orders of sir William Walworth, mayor of London, and several rich citizens who were not of their party; but there were in the city more than thirty thousand who favoured them.

Those who were at Blackheath had information of this: they sent, therefore, their knight to speak with the king, and to tell him, that what they were doing was for his service, for the kingdom had been for several years wretchedly governed, to the great dishonour of the realm and the oppression of the lower ranks of the people, by his uncles, by the clergy, and in particular by the archbishop of Canterbury, his chancellor, from whom they would have an account of his ministry. The knight dared not say nor do any thing to the contrary, but, advancing to the Thames opposite the Tower, he took boat and crossed over. While the king and those with him in the Tower were in great suspense, and anxious to receive some intelligence, the knight came on shore: way was made for him, and he was conducted to the king, who was in an apartment with the princess his mother. There were also with the king his two maternal brothers, the earl of Kent and sir John Holland, the earls of Salisbury, Warwick, Suffolk, the archbishop of Canterbury, the great prior of the Templars in England, sir Robert de Namur, the lord de Vertain, the lord de Gommegines, sir Henry de Sausselles, the mayor of London and several of the principal citizens.

Sir John Newtoun, who was well known to them all, for he was one of the king's officers, cast himself on his knees and said,—"My much redoubted lord, do not be displeased with me for the message I am about to deliver to you; for, my dear lord, through force I am come hither." "By no means, sir John, tell us what you are charged with: we hold you excused." "My very redoubted lord, the commons of your realm send me to you to entreat you would come and speak with them on Blackheath. They wish to have no one but yourself; and you need not fear for your person, for they will not do you the least harm: they always have respected and will respect you as their king; but they will tell you many things, which, they say, it is necessary you should hear; with which, however, they have not empowered me to acquaint you. But, dear lord, have the goodness to give me such an answer as may satisfy them, and that they may be convinced I have really been in your presence; for they have my children as hostages for my return, whom they will assuredly put to death, if I do not go back."

The king replied, "You shall speedily have an answer." Upon this, he called a council to consider what was to be done. The king was advised to say, that if on Thursday they would come down to the river Thames, he would without fail speak with them. Sir John Newtoun, on receiving this answer, was well satisfied therewith, and, taking leave of the king and barons, departed: having entered his boat, he recrossed the Thames, and returned to Blackheath, where he had left upwards of sixty thousand men. He told them from the king, that if they would send on the morrow morning their leaders to the Thames, the king would come and hear

what they had to say. This answer gave great pleasure, and they were
contented with it: they passed the night as well as they could; but you
must know that one-fourth of them fasted for want of provision, as they
had not brought any with them, at which they were much vexed, as may
be supposed. . . .

*Chapter xxiii.—A grand tournament is holden at London.—The king
of England gives splendid entertainments during the siege of the
town of Africa by the christians.—The Count d'Ostrevant receives the
Order of the Garter, which displeases the king of France.*

News of the splendid feasts and entertainments made for Queen Isa-
bella's public entry into Paris was carried to many countries, and very
justly, for they were most honourably conducted. The king of England
and his three uncles had received the fullest information of them: for
some of his knights had been present, who had reported all that had
passed with the utmost fidelity. In imitation of this, the king of England
ordered grand tournaments and feasts to be holden in the city of London,
where sixty knights should be accompanied by sixty noble ladies, richly
ornamented and dressed. The sixty knights were to tilt for two days; that
is to say, on the Sunday after Michaelmas-day, and the Monday following
in the year of grace 1390. The sixty knights were to set out at two o'clock
in the afternoon from the Tower of London, with their ladies, and parade
through the streets, down Cheapside, to a large square called Smithfield.
There the knights were to wait on the Sunday the arrival of any foreign
knights who might be desirous of tilting; and this feast of the Sunday was
called the challengers. The same ceremonies were to take place on the
Monday, and the sixty knights to be prepared for tilting courteously with
blunted lances against all comers. The prize for the best knight of the
opponents was to be a rich crown of gold, that for the tenants of the lists
a very rich golden clasp: they were to be given to the most gallant tilter,
according to the judgment of the ladies, who would be present with the
queen of England and the great barons, as spectators.

On the Tuesday, the tournaments were to be continued by squires,
against others of the same rank who wished to oppose them. The prize
for the opponents was a courser saddled and bridled, and for the tenants
of the lists a falcon. The manner of holding this feast being settled,
heralds were sent to proclaim it throughout England, Scotland, Hainault,
Germany, Flanders, and France. It was ordered by the council to what
parts each herald was to go; and, having time beforehand, they published
it in most countries.

Many knights and squires from foreign lands made preparations to
attend it: some to see the manners of the English, others to take part in

the tournaments. On the feast being made known in Hainault, sir William de Hainault count d'Ostrevant, who was at that time young and gallant, and fond of tilting, determined, in his own mind, to be present and to honour and make acquaintance with his cousin, king Richard, and his uncles whom he had never seen. He therefore engaged many knights and squires to accompany him; in particular the lord de Gomegines, because he was well known in England, having lived there some time. Sir William resolved, while his preparations were making, to visit his father, the count of Hainault, Holland, and Zealand, to speak with him on the subject, and to take leave of him before he went to England. He therefore set out from Quesnoy, in Hainault, and continued his journey to the Hague, a good town in Holland, where his father then resided. During the visit, he told his father his intentions to partake of the great feast in England, to see his cousins and other English lords whom he was desirous of knowing. "William," replied the count, "my good son, you have nothing to do in England: you are now connected by marriage with the blood royal of France, and your sister is the wife of the eldest son of our cousin the duke of Burgundy: you have no occasion, therefore, to seek other connections." "My lord," answered sir William, "I do not wish to go to England to form any alliance, but merely to tilt and enjoy this feast, which has been publicly proclaimed everywhere, and visit my cousins, whom I have never seen. Should I not go thither, after the particular invitation I have had, for a purpose messenger brought it me, my refusal will be considered as the effect of pride and presumption. I feel myself bound therefore in honour to go, and I beg, father, that you will not refuse me your consent." "William," replied the count, "you are your own master; act as you please; but I should think, for the sake of peace, it were better you did not go."

The count d'Ostrevant, perceiving this subject was disagreeable to his father, turned the conversation to other matters; but his resolution was fixed, and his purveyances were continued to be made and forwarded to Calais. His herald, Gomegines, was sent to England to inform the king and his uncles, that he would come honourably attended to his feast. They were much pleased at this intelligence, and presented the herald with great gifts, which were very acceptable, for he became blind towards the end of his days. I know not if he had angered God, that he was afflicted with such a punishment; but this herald, when in power, had behaved with so much insolence, that he was little pitied in his distress. The count d'Ostrevant took leave of his father, and, on his departure from the Hague, returned to his lady at Quesnoy. Many noble knights were busy in preparations for this feast that had been so pompously proclaimed.

The count Waleran de Saint Pol, who had married the half-sister to king Richard, assembled a handsome body of knights and squires, and with them made for Calais, where passage-vessels were waiting to convey to Dover the lords and knights going to this tournament. From Dover they continued their journey to London, where their servants had previously secured their lodgings.

The count d'Ostrevant set out from Hainault with a numerous attendance of knights and squires, and travelled through Artois to Calais, where he met the count de St. Pol. When the wind was favourable, and their attendants embarked, they crossed the channel; but it was told me, and I believe it, that the count de St. Pol arrived first at London, where he found the king and his brother-in-law, sir John Holland, who with many other nobles, made him a hearty welcome, and enquired the news in France. The count d'Ostrevant having crossed the sea, stopped at Canterbury, and on the Friday morning, without breaking his fast, paid his devotions at the shrine of Thomas à Becket, making at the same time a very rich offering at that altar. He remained that whole day at Canterbury, and on the following went to Rochester. On account of his numerous train, he travelled but a short day's journey, to spare his horses that carried the baggage. After mass he left Rochester and dined at Dartford, whence he continued his journey to London, for it was on this Sunday the tournaments were to begin.

This Sunday, according to proclamation, being the next to Michaelmas-day, was the beginning of the tiltings, and called the feast of the challengers. About three o'clock, there paraded out from the Tower of London, which is situated in the square of St. Catherine, on the banks of the Thames, sixty barded coursers ornamented for the tournament, on each was mounted a squire of honour that advanced only at a foot's pace; then came sixty ladies of rank, mounted on palfreys most elegantly and richly dressed, following each other, every one leading a knight with a silver chain completely armed for tilting; and in this procession they moved on through the streets of London, attended by numbers of minstrels and trumpets, to Smithfield. The queen of England and her ladies and damsels were already arrived and placed in chambers handsomely decorated. The king was with the queen. When the ladies who led the knights arrived in the square, their servants were ready to assist them to dismount from their palfreys, and to conduct them to the apartments prepared for them. The knights remained until their squires of honour had dismounted and brought them their coursers, which having mounted, they had their helmets laced on, and prepared themselves in all points for the tilt.

The count de Saint Pol with his companions now advanced, handsomely armed for the occasion, and the tournament began. Every foreign knight who pleased tilted, or had time for so doing, before the evening set in. The tiltings were well and long continued until night forced them to break off. The lords and ladies then retired where they had made appointments. The queen was lodged in the bishop of London's palace near St. Paul's church, where the banquet was held.

Towards evening, the count d'Ostrevant arrived, and was kindly received by king Richard and his lords. The prize for the opponents was adjudged to the count de St. Pol, as the best knight at this tournament, and that for the tenants to the earl of Huntingdon. The dancings were at the queen's residence, in the presence of the king, his uncles and the barons of England. The ladies and damsels continued their amusements, before and after supper, until it was time to retire, when all went to their lodgings, except such as were attached to the king or queen, who, during the tournament, lived at the palace of the bishop of London.

You would have seen on the ensuing morning, Monday, squires and varlets busily employed, in different parts of London, furbishing and making ready armour and horses for their masters who were to engage in the justs. In the afternoon, king Richard entered Smithfield magnificently accompanied by dukes, lords, and knights, for he was chief of the tenants of the lists. The queen took her station as on the preceding day, with her ladies, in the apartments that had been prepared for her. The count d'Ostrevant came next, with a large company of knights and squires fully armed for tilting; then the count de Saint Pol and the knights from France.

The tournament now began, and every one exerted himself to the utmost to excel; many were unhorsed, and more lost their helmets. The justing continued with great courage and perseverance until night put an end to it. The company now retired to their lodgings or their homes; and, when the hour for supper was near, the lords and ladies attended it, which was splendid and well served. The prize for the opponents at the tournament was adjudged, by the ladies, lords, and heralds, to the count d'Ostrevant, who far eclipsed all who had tilted that day; that for the tenants was given to a gallant knight of England called sir Hugh Spenser.

On the morrow, Tuesday, the tournament was renewed by the squires, who tilted in the presence of the king, queen, and all the nobles, until night, when all retired as on the preceding day. The supper was as magnificent as before at the palace of the bishop, where the king and queen lodged; and the dancing lasted until day-break, when the company broke up. The tournament was continued on the Wednesday by all knights and squires indiscriminately, who were inclined to just; it lasted until night, and the supper and dances were as the preceding day. . . .

As we have dwelt too long on these matters, we will return to the barons and knights of France, who were besieging the strong town of Africa against the Saracens.

72 73 74 75 10 9 8 7 6 5 4 3 2 1